The Uses of Sociology

Sociology and Society

This book is part of a series produced in association with The Open University. The complete list of books in the series is as follows:

Understanding Everyday Life, edited by Tony Bennett and Diane Watson

Social Differences and Divisions, edited by Peter Braham and Linda Janes

Social Change, edited by Tim Jordan and Steve Pile

The Uses of Sociology, edited by Peter Hamilton and Kenneth Thompson

The books form part of the Open University course DD201 *Sociology and Society*. Details of this and other Open University courses can be obtained from the Course Information and Advice Centre, PO Box 724, The Open University, Milton Keynes MK7 6ZS, United Kingdom: tel. +44 (0)1908 653231, e-mail ces-gen@open.ac.uk

For availability of other course components, contact Open University Worldwide Ltd, The Open University, Walton Hall, Milton Keynes MK7 6AA, United Kingdom: tel. +44 (0)1908 858785; fax +44 (0)1908 858787; e-mail ouwenq@open.ac.uk; website http://www.ouw.co.uk

The Uses of Sociology

edited by Peter Hamilton and Kenneth Thompson

The Open University

Blackwell
Publishing

First published 2002 by Blackwell; written and produced by The Open University

Blackwell Publishers

108 Cowley Road
Oxford OX4 1JF
UK

238 Main Street
Cambridge, Massachusetts 02142
USA

Index compiled by Isobel McLean

Edited, designed and typeset by The Open University

Printed and bound in the United Kingdom by the Alden Group, Oxford

British Library Cataloguing in Publication Data

A catalogue record for this book is available from The British Library.

Library of Congress Cataloguing in Publication Data

A catalogue record for this book has been requested.

ISBN   0 631 23313 X (hbk)
        0 631 23314 8 (pbk)

1.1

Contents

The Open University Course Team

Hedley Bashforth, Tutor Panel Member and Author
Melanie Bayley, Editor
Tony Bennett, Joint Course Chair, Author and Book Editor
Peter Braham, Author and Book Editor
Lene Connolly, Print Buying Controller
Margaret Dickens, Print Buying Co-ordinator
Richard Doak, Tutor Panel Member and Author
Molly Freeman, Course Secretary
Richard Golden, Production and Presentation Administrator
Peter Hamilton, Author and Book Editor
Ramaswami Harindranath, Media Author
Celia Hart, Picture Researcher
Sue Hemmings, Author
David Hesmondhalgh, Media Author
Karen Ho, Course Secretary
Rich Hoyle, Graphic Designer
Jonathan Hunt, Co-publishing Advisor
Denise Janes, Course Secretary
Linda Janes, Author and Book Editor
Yvonne Jewkes, Tutor Panel Member and Author
Tim Jordan, Author and Book Editor
Hugh Mackay, Author
Liz McFall, Author
Margaret McManus, Copyrights Co-ordinator
Gerry Mooney, Author
Karim Murji, Author
Janet Parr, Tutor Panel Member and Author
Steve Pile, Author and Book Editor
Winifred Power, Editor
Peter Redman, Author
Roger Rees, Course Manager
Halimeh Sharifat, Course Manager Assistant
Norma Sherratt, Author
Elizabeth B. Silva, Author
Kenneth Thompson, Joint Course Chair, Author and Book Editor
Diane Watson, Author and Book Editor
Emma Wheeler, Production and Presentation Administrator
Kathryn Woodward, Author

Consultant Authors

Mitchell Dean, Macquarie University
Celia Lury, Goldsmiths College
Jim McGuigan, Loughborough University
Mike Savage, University of Manchester
Merl Storr, University of East London
Bryan S. Turner, University of Cambridge

External Assessor

Rosemary Pringle, University of Southampton

Preface to the series

Sociology and Society is a series of four books designed as an introduction to the sociological study of modern society. The books form the core study materials for The Open University course *Sociology and Society* (DD201), which aims to provide an attractive and up-to-date introduction to the key concerns and debates of contemporary sociology. They also take account of the ways in which sociology has been shaped by dialogue with adjacent disciplines and intellectual movements, such as cultural studies and women's studies.

The first book in the series is *Understanding Everyday Life*, whose aim is to 'defamiliarize' our relations to everyday life by showing how the perspectives of sociology, cultural studies and feminism can throw new light on, and prompt a reflexive attention to, varied aspects of day-to-day social life that are usually taken for granted. The book is designed as a means of illustrating and debating different aspects of everyday life in a number of key sites – the home, the street, the pub, the neighbourhood and community – and in various social activities, such as work and consumption, and teenage romance.

The second book, *Social Differences and Divisions*, in addition to looking at class, which sociologists have treated as one of the central forms of social stratification, also explores social differences and divisions based on gender, 'race' and ethnicity. The book then examines the concepts of citizenship and social justice – concepts that both reflect and influence the perception of social divisions. Finally, the book contains case studies of two key sectors – education and housing – which highlight significant divisions and inequalities; it also looks at the social policies that have been designed to address them.

Social Change, the third book, shows how, from sociology's early concerns with the transition to industrial and democratic social forms to recent debates over the rise of information, networked or global societies, sociology has been centrally concerned with the nature and meaning of social change. However, the book seeks to frame these debates through an explicit examination of the spaces and times of social change. Social transformations are exemplified and questioned by looking at the ways in which societies organize space–time relations. The topics and examples include: urbanism and the rhythms of city life, colonialism and post-colonialism, the alleged transition from industrial to information society, new media and time–space reconfiguration, intimacy and the public sphere, and the regulation of the self. Finally, it examines new perspectives on how sociology itself is implicated in social change.

The last book in the series, *The Uses of Sociology*, discusses the various ways in which sociology is practised and the consequences of sociological activity for public affairs. It explores the main debates in sociology concerning its social purposes. Comparing and contrasting different sociological traditions in sociological thought, it examines a variety of their engagements with 'the social'.

The relevance of sociological knowledge is considered in relation to government, the public sphere (including the media), economic life, social movements, 'race' and ethnicity. The book also considers related questions, such as whether sociology is a science or a cultural endeavour, and whether sociological research and analysis can be detached and unbiased. Finally, it considers different views of what Max Weber called the 'vocation' of sociology, and asks whether sociologists have taken the role of prophets – criticizing present social arrangements and envisaging possible future developments.

Although edited volumes, each of the chapters has been specially commissioned for the series in order to provide a coherent and up-to-the minute introduction to sociology. Each chapter is accompanied by a set of extracts from key, previously published, readings that are relevant to the chapter topic. At the end of each book there is also a set of 'generic' readings selected for their broader relevance to the overall themes of the book. Together these supply a wider view of the subject, with samples of historically important writing as well as of current approaches. Throughout the chapters, key terms and names are highlighted. These can be further studied by consulting a sociological dictionary, such as *The Blackwell Dictionary of Sociology* or *The Penguin Dictionary of Sociology*. The overall approach taken is interactive, and we hope general readers will use the activities and the questions based on the readings in order to engage actively with the texts.

Peter Hamilton
Kenneth Thompson
on behalf of The Open University Course Team

The uses of sociology: introduction

Peter Hamilton and Kenneth Thompson

Of what use is sociology? This is a question that has drawn a variety of responses, from people outside the discipline as well as from sociologists themselves. The eighteenth century saw European thinkers of the Enlightenment developing most of the ideas about society, the economy and human psychology that would later form the central elements of the new 'social' sciences which emerged during the course of the nineteenth century. But these ideas were also part of a 'science of progress', a fundamental belief that the application of rational processes of scientific explanation would yield answers to the hitherto intractable problems of society. These led directly to the radical ideas underpinning the American and French revolutions, and nourished the emergence of most modern conceptions of democracy and justice. It is not surprising, then, that sociology has long been associated with progressive political change.

In the nineteenth century, encouraged by advances in sciences and technology, some thinkers believed there could be a rational explanation for everything and that scientific study could lead to solutions to all social problems. For Auguste Comte (1798–1857), who gave sociology its name, the discipline was envisaged as standing at the pinnacle of the sciences and as a means of establishing laws of social functioning and development. On such a basis, he believed it would be possible to predict future trends of development and thereby enlightened leaders would be able to steer society by utilizing those currents. His successor in French sociology, Emile Durkheim (1858–1917), held similar views, but sought to establish sociology as a respectable academic discipline by advocating that sociologists should distance their studies from political engagement – a view shared by his German contemporary Max Weber. In the nineteenth century, Karl Marx (1818–83), who had a major influence on sociological thinking (although he was often as much an object of criticism as of inspiration), advocated a much closer engagement with radical social movements. In the 1960s and 1970s, sociology seemed to be constantly portrayed by the media as identifying with radical movements or marginal social groups. Today, an accurate image of sociology would have to take account of the manifold uses to which it has been put in social administration, business, and even in the mass media, where its ideas and methods are employed widely and influence the thinking of all of us.

It sometimes seems as if sociology is so adaptable that it can be put to a multitude of uses. This may be because – by contrast with the natural sciences

– it does not possess a clear-cut experimental methodology, an incremental process by which such knowledge can accumulate as invariant laws – such as Newton's First Law of Motion – or through which evidence of social processes can be subjected to unequivocal tests. In the nineteenth century it seemed to offer the social scientific equivalent of the theory of evolution in the natural sciences and its support for statistical data collection and analysis was welcomed by governments. But there was another side to sociology that led some of those writing within this disciplinary framework – both radicals and conservatives – to be more critical and pessimistic about social progress and modernity. This tendency was strengthened by the tragedy of the First World War and the later economic slump that only ended with the Second World War. In post-war America, and subsequently in Britain and Europe, it expanded as an academic discipline and began to supply a steady stream of graduates for the burgeoning occupations servicing the welfare state or managing people in industry. It became recognized that sociological study had much to offer in terms of increasing understanding of social relations in institutions and of what has been described as the 'human side of enterprise'. However, despite its usefulness to government and business, sociology has also maintained a critical edge. This may show itself in radical critiques of widely accepted beliefs and practices in contemporary mainstream society. (The impact of feminism on sociological analyses of major institutions is a prominent example.) At other times it can take the form of sociologists engaging closely with 'unrespectable' movements or marginal groups and attempting to see the world from their perspective, which may raise controversial questions.

Does close engagement with the object of study threaten the academic and scientific integrity of sociology, or should it be seen as an advantage? This is a question that has concerned sociologists and occasionally has excited public criticism and debate – either because sociology has seemed too detached from concrete social problems or too involved with them. John Urry's 1995 article 'Sociology as a parasite' (Reading G in the generic readings at the end of this volume) offers a good way into such debates.

The British sociologist, Laurie Taylor, who has enjoyed a successful career in the media, recently regaled readers of *The Independent* newspaper with his recollection of sociologists who tried to get involved with the people they were studying in the 1970s:

> Back in the Seventies, it was difficult to find a sociologist working in the area of deviance who was not involved in participant observation. Academics could be found hanging out on street corners with youth gangs, sitting in squats with drug-users and standing on terraces with hooligans. A former colleague of mine remembers stepping off a late-night train at Waterloo and suddenly hearing a familiar voice issue from what looked like a bundle of old rags on a bench. 'Goodnight, Mary,' said the voice. The bundle was an old friend from the University of Essex, pursuing research on vagrants.
>
> (*The Independent*, 8 June 2001)

The article had a serious point to make. Taylor was reviewing a new sociological study by Simon Winlow, *Badfellas: Crime, Tradition and New Masculinities* (2001), in which the sociological researcher had become a bouncer, standing on the door of a club, in order to study how that burgeoning occupation provided ways of asserting masculinity for working-class men who had been deprived of

The academic who got a kick out of sociology

BACK IN the Seventies, it was difficult to find a sociologist working in the area of deviance who was not involved in participant observation. Academics could be found hanging out on street corners with youth gangs, sitting in with drug-users and standing with hooligans. A former members stepping Waterloo and miliar voice bundle ...ays of asserting virility sought out ...that allowed them to

FRIDAY BOOK

Badfellas:
crime, tradition and
new masculinities
by Simon Winlow
(Berg, £14.99)

went right ahead and obtained a job on the door of a club. It wasn't long be-

first just as the man with his back to the bar catches a punch squarely on the nose and another flush on the mouth. He stops swinging and although he doesn't go down he seems defeated. I grab the victor from behind, swear at him and drag him to the door. Dom [another bouncer] joins me, swears at him, grabs him by the collar and yanks him so hard I lose my grip and he falls to the floor. While he is down another customer kicks him in the ribs."

Episodes like this...

other times he is perilously close to being drawn into the protection rackets that form a valuable financial sideline for many doormen.

It's difficult to drag oneself away from the stories that Winlow has to tell about his life as a bouncer. He is so good at upsetting the stereotypical media images of northern gangsters, so adept at capturing the ambience of urban nightlife and the excitement and intrigue surrounding extreme violence, that one fi...

Figure 1 'The academic who got a kick out of sociology', The Independent, 8 June 2001

traditional occupational ways of asserting virility. The problem for the researcher arose when, having gone in incognito, he faced the dilemma of whether to intervene when 'his new mates look as though they are only moments away from kicking an antagonist to death' or should he keep his mouth shut for fear of jeopardizing his research? Laurie Taylor concludes that this is just one of the dilemmas faced by the ethnographer who gets closely involved with those he or she is studying, when they may have different values and ideas. Can it also raise the question of whether sociology is exploitative of its subjects?

The problem arises in a different form when researchers appear to be too closely engaged with their subject-matter and are accused of lacking 'scientific detachment'. This has been a frequent problem for sociologists of religion as well as sociologists of social or political movements. In France, where sociology has enjoyed relatively high esteem since Durkheim's time, the national press take seriously the scientific standing of sociology. On 18 April 2001, the most authoritative French newspaper, *Le Monde*, published a front-page article under the title 'Sociology under a bad star'. In the article, two sociologists fulminated, in the name of sociological rigour, against the damage that might be done to the reputation of the discipline by the award of a university doctorate to a media astrologer, who had successfully submitted a sociological thesis on astrology. Not only was this considered a sufficiently important issue for *Le Monde* to concern its readers with, but it was responded to by the rival newspaper, *Libération* (19 April 2001). The sociologist writing the full-page article in *Libération* pointed out that, although it was permissible to raise the question of whether scientific distance had been respected in such a thesis, it had to be recognized that there had been some excellent theses on the sociology of religion by Catholic priests. However, his concern was that the professional and scientific status of sociology might be endangered by debating this issue in the media. He concluded, echoing Comte, that sociology ('and French sociology remains one of the best') has a considerable richness that might be jeopardized as 'an instrument for organizing the present and imagining the future'. He himself was a sociologist working in an urban studies institute and directly involved with local organizations and professionals; consequently, he feared that negative publicity might mean sociology would be seen as less useful.

Clearly, there are important issues that need to be addressed about the uses of sociology and sociologists' engagement with their subject-matter. It is not

JEUDI 19 AVRIL 2001

Rebonds

*En donnant le titre de docteur à une astrologue médiatique, le monde
universitaire se ridiculise et laisse la porte ouverte aux pseudo-sciences.*

La sociologie, l'antithèse de Teissier

par ALAIN BOURDIN

La thèse de sociologie soutenue à l'université René-Descartes par l'astrologue Elizabeth Teissier n'est pas passée inaperçue, et provoque des réactions diverses. En première page d'un quotidien, les Prs Beaudelot et Establet s'indignent au nom de la rigueur sociologique («La ~~~~~~~ une m~~ ~~~~~~ mercie '

L'on vient d'offrir à ceux que nous gênons un argument massif pour nous ridiculiser ou justifier l'appel aux pseudo-sociologues.
La sociologie – et la sociologie française reste l'une des ~~~~~~~

giner l'avenir. Cette aventure dérisoire caricature un enjeu majeur: la reconquête de la sociologie par la société ●

Alain Bourdin *est professeur à l'Institut français d'urbanisme-université de Paris-VIII, laboratoire de théories des mutations urbaines, CNRS. ~~~ ~~~~~ paru: «La Question locale», PUF, «La politique éclatée», 2000.*

Figure 2 'La sociologie, l'antithèse de Teissier', Libération, 19 April 2001

only the sociological study of religious or pseudo-scientific movements that raises questions. As you will see in the chapters that follow, issues arise when sociology enters into other areas, such as government and policing, the media, the organization and management of economic life, social movements engaged in direct action, 'race' and 'racism'. It is not simply a question of whether sociology as a discipline can maintain its academic integrity if it becomes involved in such areas; we will also consider questions about the values implicit in such studies and the ethical problems raised by research.

Many sociologists have shared the vision that sociology provides a scientific basis for social intervention and political action. Some have believed that, in order for sociology to establish its academic and scientific credentials, it is necessary to adopt a detached and 'value-free' stance. Whether this is a feasible approach is a moot point, but it has to be recognized as a common one. Other sociologists have seen their endeavours as closer to the humanities than the sciences: in their view, sociological descriptions and analyses of social actions and relations are bound to draw on the imaginative and descriptive faculties of the arts, rather than imitating the methods of natural science. In terms of methods, this may incline such sociologists to give preference to ethnographic and qualitative methods over quantitative methods. Of course, this does not mean that one method is inevitably more value free than another.

Not everyone can be a sociological researcher or interact directly with sociological research. Indeed, as a whole, professional sociologists are relatively few in number in Britain and Europe, compared with the 13,000 members of the American Sociological Association (20 per cent of whom work for government, business or non-profit organizations). Nevertheless, many students in Britain do study some sociology, either on its own or in courses ranging from media studies to social policy, and do go on to use its ideas and methods in a variety of institutions, as well as in their everyday lives. But numbers are not the only sign of influence and it is certainly the case that a kind of reformist empirical sociological research has performed administrative and intelligence functions for governments in Britain since the nineteenth century. In the leading academic centre for sociological research during most of the twentieth century, The London

School of Economics, the discipline was split between two departments – sociology and social administration – and most of the most famous names were associated with the latter department (for instance, R.H. Tawney, Clement Attlee, Richard Titmuss, Peter Townsend, David Donnison, Brian Abel-Smith and T.H. Marshall). It is only recently, in the figure of the director of the LSE, Anthony Giddens, that a theoretically minded sociologist has risen to national prominence and provided New Labour with ideas about the 'Third Way' (discussed by Tony Bennett in Chapter 2).

Perhaps more significant than these specific engagements by professional sociologists in politics and social administration is the broader influence of sociological ideas on the ways in which people now reflect on their social actions and institutions. In a sense, we are all sociologists now, even those who simply use sociological ideas in their everyday lives, without necessarily realizing that they are thinking sociologically. It is this permeating effect of 'reflexive' sociological thinking that has the greatest practical consequence for society. As Giddens puts it:

> The practical impact of social sciences is both profound and inescapable. Modern societies, together with the organisations that compose and straddle them, are like learning machines, imbibing information in order to regularise their mastery of themselves ... Only societies reflexively capable of modifying their institutions in the face of accelerated social change will be able to confront the future with any confidence. Sociology is the prime medium of such reflexivity.
>
> (Giddens, 1990/1979, p.21)

In one sense, therefore, sociologists' knowledge cannot be wholly neutral and detached because it is used by people to interpret and reshape the very social phenomena that the sociologists have studied. Consequently, unlike the early sociologists, many contemporary sociologists tend not to see themselves as discovering laws and as legislators of the truth. They have been described as more like 'interpreters' than 'legislators':

> I am rather inclined to see sociology today as an eddy on a fast-moving river, an eddy which retains its shape but which changes its content all the time ... sociology is a constant interpretation of, or commentary on, experience ... and this commentary is sent back into society itself.
>
> (Bauman, 1992, p.213)

In the chapters that follow we will be exploring some of the different styles and forms of sociological engagement with important areas of social life.

In Chapter 1, *'The practice of sociology: mapping the field'*, Peter Hamilton focuses particularly on three broad types that represent different modes of sociological engagement with the social. He refers to these as the 'rational-scientific', the 'political', and the 'expressionistic'. The rational-scientific approach is typical of sociologists who believe it is important for sociology to model itself on the natural sciences in certain respects. This may take various forms: it may involve developing very abstract theories that can be tested and validated by reference to empirical (preferably statistical) data; it may also refer to the insistence on maintaining a neutral, value-free, stance towards the subject-matter.

The political approach is represented by sociologists who do not accept the idea of taking up a position of value neutrality towards their subject-matter, but rather believe sociologists should be politically engaged with it. They may wish to use sociology to criticize existing institutions and to promote radical change, and perhaps even join a social movement with this aim in mind. Or, if they are of a conservative disposition, they may be critical of contemporary trends and use their sociology to advocate a return to traditional values and ways of doing things. In between those advocating radical change and those wanting a return to tradition there are the 'gradualist reformers' or 'ameliorists', whose sociology is directed to diagnosing inefficiencies and suggesting improvements in institutions.

Expressionistic sociology is conceived of as being more like an art form than as either a science or a programme for political change. Descriptive and interpretative of social action and symbolic meanings, there is a particular emphasis on understanding the meaning people give to their actions. This may involve practising an imaginative empathy towards others' beliefs and actions, even though we may disagree with them, which raises many problems, but, as we shall see, it can also lead to penetrating insights.

It would be mistaken to think that these three different modes of engagement between sociology and society are always mutually exclusive, or that individual sociologists can be neatly pigeon-holed or labelled in that way. Sociology, like life itself, is more messy and complicated than that. But the typology does help in thinking about the dilemmas that arise.

Tony Bennett's Chapter 2, *'Sociology and government'*, takes up the question of the relationship of sociology to government. In some ways, sociology has a long history of involvement with government and social administration in Britain, beginning with the collection of social statistics in the nineteenth century and continuing in the development of the welfare state. Bennett uses the concept of 'governmentality', taken from the work of the French philosopher, Michel Foucault, to examine how sociology has contributed to the development of these modern 'technologies of government'. He also discusses how the particular theory of community developed by the most prominent contemporary British sociologist, Anthony Giddens, provided an intellectual framework and agenda for New Labour during its first period in office (1997–2001) under the label of the Third Way. Although seemingly absent from the political ideas underpinning Labour's second term from 2001, the emphasis in the Third Way was on avoiding the opposing dangers of too much individualism or too much state intervention by strengthening the sphere of 'civil society' that lies between the individual and the state.

Another way in which sociology has engaged with the problem of the relationship of the individual to society is by envisaging an ideal 'public sphere', in which there would be the maximum opportunities for rational communication and debate, and then examining the actual operations of the media and other institutions to see how far this exists. It is the idea of the public sphere (developed by the German social theorist, Jürgen Habermas) and the problems it faces that Jim McGuigan examines in Chapter 3, *'The public sphere'*. He begins by considering the controversy about the Millennium Dome in Greenwich and asks whether the public debate had any impact on policy, or whether it was a manifestation of a 'pseudo' or 'phantom' public sphere. He then goes on to examine analyses of the role of the mass media and particular genres, such as television talk shows, and new media in the form of the internet. Finally, he considers the efforts of various movements and groups to gain public attention for their views by staging spectacular protests, as in the case of the Zapatistas in Mexico.

One of the areas of social life with which sociology has had an ambivalent and controversial relationship is that of economic life. Liz McFall shows in Chapter 4 (*'Tools for commerce? Sociology and economic life'*) that sociological studies of economic life have ranged from radical critiques to prescriptions offering increasing efficiency. Marx and his followers mounted powerful critiques of the capitalist economy, emphasizing the exploitative nature of the relations of production whereas sociologists influenced by the ideas of Weber adopted a more reformist approach, criticizing some of the ways in which markets and bureaucracies operated, but regarding them as an inevitable part of the modern economy. Sociological ideas and prescriptions, however, have also been widely adopted in business and many sociologists have been employed as researchers or consultants by businesses, especially in areas such as human resource management and culture change programmes aimed at the development of a more flexible and enterprising workforce.

Liz McFall – who draws on a variety of sources in sociology, anthropology and feminism – maintains that most of these approaches have taken too narrow a view of economic life. She argues that they have tended to view economic life as a separate 'thing in itself', equating it with the sphere of production and work, as opposed to that of consumption and leisure. Furthermore, rather than viewing the relationship of sociology and economic life in terms of detached study or of economic organizations' use of sociology, she suggests they are better understood as caught up in a pattern of mutual dependence and interaction.

The investigation of social movements and their relationships with sociology, which is broached by Jim McGuigan in Chapter 3, is taken further by Merl Storr in Chapter 5, *'Sociology and social movements: theories, analyses and ethical dilemmas'*. She begins by reviewing the different definitions and theories of social movements. The two main theories are illustrated by showing how they can be applied to the analysis of two recent examples of social movements – the Gay Liberation Front and Reclaim the Streets. She then shows how both resource mobilization theory and the new social movement theory embody certain attitudes towards social movements and contain assumptions about the relationship between activists and sociologists. One takes an 'outsider' perspective and the other adopts an 'insider' perspective. In the latter case, the methodology has an explicitly ethical orientation in which researchers and activists are required to form a relationship that promises mutual benefit and equality. There is also a dilemma about whether and how sociologists should distinguish between 'good' movements and 'bad' movements. This raises the question: what is the sociology of social movements actually for? The various theories may also differ in the answers they give to this question. They are not just theories, but also different ways of doing sociology. One important social movement of the recent past – feminism – has also been influential within sociology in precisely this sense. Feminist sociologists have in some cases put forward the idea that sociology can be a vital weapon in ensuring that the social changes it aimed at could be instituted. But feminist thinking could not proceed, many argued, unless it could sweep away the epistemological bases of 'masculinist thinking'. Contemporary feminist theory has tackled the most intractable questions of the nature of knowledge itself – arguing that its very construction is often 'masculinist'.

In Chapter 6, *'Sociology unbound'*, Karim Murji examines the issues raised when sociological ideas cross over into debates in the public sphere and become, to some extent, part of everyday language. In the case of the concept of 'institutional racism', the term was first used by black activists in the late 1960s, but was subsequently taken up by sociologists to explain how patterns of discrimination and oppression were reproduced by institutions even though the individuals involved were acting without racist intent. It came to new public prominence when it was used as a central criticism of the police in the Macpherson report concerning the failures to solve the racist murder of the black teenager Stephen Lawrence in London in 1993. When sociologists presented different reactions to the Macpherson report's analysis of institutional racism, some responses got more attention than others, partly depending on whether they chimed with the prevailing views in the media. Murji shows how different types of sociological analysis of this issue exhibited different forms of engagement – some advocating maintaining a distance, others taking an explicitly moral approach. He also questions whether sociological conceptions of 'society' itself have been over influenced by western perspectives and the practices of colonialism.

Finally, in Chapter 7, *'Understanding the past and predicting the future: sociologists as prophets'*, Kenneth Thompson shows how sociology has always sought to understand the present age by comparing it with the past and then making predictions about future trends. He asks if the classic tradition in sociology, with its focus on the problems of modernity as viewed from a particular standpoint, needs to be radically revised or even discarded. A central question in Chapter 7 is: what are the challenges facing sociology today? And is sociology sufficiently adaptable to be useful in helping people to understand the present and prepare for the future?

The generic readings for this volume cover a number of central issues about the role of sociology as a mode of public discourse on society.

In Reading A,[*] 'The positive philosophy', from Auguste Comte, we find one of the earliest arguments for the need for sociology within the modern world. Comte developed the influential notion that science is a 'positive' form of knowledge and that all sciences evolved through three phases. Emerging from primitive and theological thought, through the use of metaphysical ideas, they eventually reach a point where they achieve the status of 'positive philosophy', considering 'all phenomena as subject to invariant natural laws. The exact discovery of these laws and their reduction to the least possible number constitutes the goal of all of our efforts' (Comte, 1830, p.8). Ultimately, Comte suggested, all sciences will become 'positive' and unify into a single natural system. A central component of positivism, as it develops from Comte into a way of thinking that many writers have described as the 'philosophy' of nineteenth-century science, is sociology.

[*] The Readings referred to in this Introduction represent different views on the uses of sociology. As such, they raise issues which span the concerns of the different chapters rather than being limited to any single chapter. For this reason, these readings are located at the end of the book, arranged in the order indicated here. This Introduction provides a context and setting within which they should be read.

Comte's view of sociology contrasts strongly with that of the American sociologist, Robert Nisbet, who, in 'Sociology as an art form' (Reading B), offers a compelling case to support the 'expressive' argument for sociology's relevance. One of the most interesting arguments about the political role of sociology was offered by the American sociologist and activist, C. Wright Mills (1916–62). A major critic of what he saw as the conservative bias of functionalist sociology, Mills made a strong case for the committed, politically liberal nature of sociology in his famous book, *The Sociological Imagination*, first published in 1959. Reading C, 'The sociological imagination', introduces some of his arguments.

One of the central figures in recent sociological thinking about post-modernity and the ethical construction of social thought has been the Polish intellectual Zygmunt Bauman. Despite his honourable war record fighting to liberate Poland from German occupation, Bauman suffered from anti-semitic persecution by the communist authorities in Poland, and migrated to the West in the 1960s. His writing on the Holocaust and on the uses of social thought have been highly influential, and in Reading D, 'Legislators and interpreters' (taken from his 1987 book of the same name), Bauman contrasts two of the important modes in which sociology has attempted to influence 'practice' – the first a key aspect of modernity and its concern with social engineering; the second a feature of post-modernity and its fascination with culture and meaning.

The writings of Michel Foucault have played a highly influential part in contemporary thought about power and government, and in particular the role of the social sciences in this process. His term 'governmentality' encapsulates this new paradigm of sociological thought, and is discussed in his essay, Reading E, 'Govermentality'. The focus is no longer on 'society' but on 'populations' and the ways in which they are regulated. Feminism has been a key aspect of late twentieth-century social thought in the West. Its social programme included the notion that sociology could be a vital weapon in ensuring that the social changes it aimed at could be instituted. Its role in rejuvenating social thought about gender is well summarized in Anne Witz's essay on 'The feminist challenge' (Reading F).

Finally, in Reading G, 'Sociology as a parasite: some vices and virtues', John Urry explores the question of whether sociology is useful by examining the advantages and disadvantages of its essentially parasitical nature. In his essay, Urry attempts to deconstruct some central ideas and theories of sociology in order to demonstrate that most of its key concepts originated in other disciplines and social movements. His argument supports the contention that sociology is a form of discourse, rather than a science, but that this can be turned to advantage and might even be seen as its distinctive strength.

References

Bauman, Z. (1989) *Modernity and the Holocaust*, Ithaca, NY, Cornell University Press.

Bauman, Z. (1992) *Intimations of Postmodernity*, London, Routledge.

Comte, A. (1830) *Cours de Philosphie Positive*, Paris, Bachelier.

Giddens, A. (1990) *The Consequences of Modernity*, Cambridge/Oxford, Polity Press in association with Basil Blackwell.

Giddens, A. (1990) *Central Problems in Social Theory: Action, Structure and Contradiction in Social Analysis,* Berkeley, CA, University of California Press. (First published in 1979.)

Urry, J. (1995) 'Sociology as a parasite: some vices and virtues' in Urry, J. *Consuming Places,* Routledge, London and New York.

Winlow, S. (2001) *Badfellas: Crime, Tradition and New Masculinities,* Oxford, Berg.

The practice of sociology: mapping the field

Peter Hamilton

Contents

1 Introduction

In 1913, not long before the Great War that would bring to an end the 'long nineteenth century' of Victorian progress, a prophetic lecture was announced. It was to be given at a time when sociology was in its infancy. Yet the 'science of society' was slowly gaining recognition in the new universities and colleges that had emerged from the fascination with training and education that seemed to promise so much for the future: the models were American and German, in the main. As the leading industrial powers of the era (though Britain still believed it too was in the forefront), they had done the most to ground science and technology within institutions of the higher learning. Economic growth and military prowess, or so it appeared, would both benefit from the creation of a trained elite of scientists, engineers and administrators who could run the country under the watchful eye of those who held the reins of power. Britain was developing its own versions of the colleges, polytechnics and institutes of higher education, and it was in this context that the eminent economist and social historian R.H. Tawney gave an inaugural lecture at the London School of Economics. He was deeply interested in developing the new field of sociology, and had recently been appointed to a post as Director of the Ratan Tata Foundation, established for the study of poverty. Discussing the prospects of such a discipline for helping to resolve social problems, Tawney also made it clear that he 'should be very sorry to be thought to suppose that the future welfare of mankind depended principally upon the multiplication of sociologists' (Tawney, 1978/1913, p.111).

Since Tawney's time, the number of sociologists has multiplied many thousands of times. It is possible to argue that the rise of sociology as a profession coincides with the rise of socially progressive political institutions and the spread of democracy, and with the generalization of various forms of national welfare state. But as one recent commentator has suggested, 'it is arguable whether the growing numbers of sociologists have made any contribution to the welfare of others, least of all the poor, in whose name such multiplication was justified in the first place' (Hogan, 1998, p.151). On the other hand, it might be argued that, although sociology cannot be expected to have a direct effect on welfare, it can help to develop a consciousness of inequalities and their causes.

At the outset of a new and optimistic social science, the promise that greater knowledge of social problems might help to alleviate them seems, on the face of it, reasonable. After all, greater knowledge of human physiology has palpably increased medicine's ability to treat disease and the other ills which afflict the human body. At the beginning of the twentieth century, the typical life expectancy of a male child born in Great Britain was 48.5 years, while for a female it was 52.4 years. By 2000, these figures had become 75.5 and 80.3 (ONS, 2001, Figure 1.6). To get a better image of what these changes mean, we shall consider an example.

ACTIVITY 1

Look at Figure 1.1. What conclusions might you draw about the reasons for changes in life expectancy?

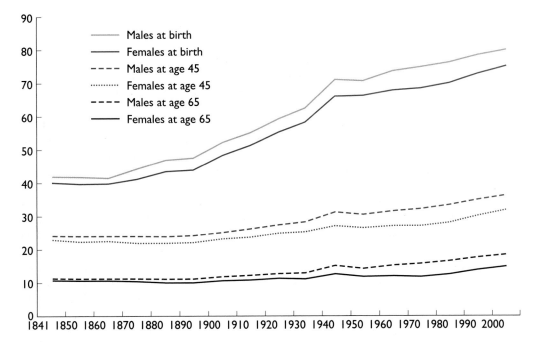

Figure 1.1 *Life expectancy in England and Wales, 1841–2000*
Source: Office of National Surveys, 2001, *Population Trends*, no.101

These are, of course, extremely gross measures of the population's life expectancy, and tell us very little indeed about the social distribution of life expectancy, as opposed to its most basic gender distribution – men have a shorter life expectancy than women. But in very simple terms they do make it clear that, in the period since the first decade of Queen Victoria's reign, people live longer with each decade that passes. We know that in the nineteenth century shorter life expectancy was closely associated with poverty: this was manifested in health, diet, work and living conditions. In the crudest sense, people died younger, the poorer they were.

By the end of the twentieth century, life expectancy has all but doubled compared with 1840. If we think about why this might have happened, a large part of the answer must relate to important changes in the health, diet and living conditions of the vast mass of the population. But compare the figures for life expectancy at birth, and life expectancy at age 65. What do they tell us? They seem to indicate that the biggest changes in life expectancy are those for babies and children: so it is in the early years of life that the largest contributions of better medical care, better diet, better hygiene, better living conditions, have had most effect. In the broadest sense, these improvements are not accidental: they have come about through the application of various forms of scientific or technological knowledge to pressing issues of human society. If we go back to Tawney's time, when social research into the conditions of the poor was still in its infancy, we can begin to understand why there may have been a certain *optimism* about the ability of a discipline such as sociology to be of practical use to society. It seemed to follow then, that by the application of a form of scientific or technological knowledge – sociology – to the most pressing of society's problems, that it too could make an impact on them.

AIMS
The aims of this chapter are:
1   To provide a simple 'mapping' of the broad traditions in terms of which sociology and sociologists have approached the questions of its 'uses'.
2   To provide some resources for identifying key themes of sociological debate about use and practice.
3   To introduce the main intellectual threads through which the encounter between the intellectual activity of sociology and its wider social and political context has been maintained.
4   To discuss three 'ideal-type' traditions – 'rational-scientific', 'political', and literary or 'expressionistic'.

2 Sociology and social action

From its origins in Enlightenment thought during the eighteenth century, the ways in which sociology relates to society and social action have been a key concern of the discipline. This chapter identifies some of the key themes of sociological debate about its uses – its 'practice' – and discusses the main intellectual threads through which the encounter between the intellectual activity of sociology and its wider social and political context has been maintained.

Attempts to classify various intellectual traditions within sociology have been made since the early days of the discipline's existence, but in most cases they do not concentrate on the relationship of theories and methodologies to their practical uses – or the absence of such uses. So in discussing them I am offering a model for looking at the complex history of sociology, one which takes account of how its ideas have been seen as relating to action. This is as important for understanding its present as its past. As a model it tries to simplify complexity. Other models may well be possible: I happen to think that this one has been devised sufficiently comprehensively so that it encompasses most of the ways in which the pursuit of sociology by sociologists has been directed towards making their work relevant and useful – or not.

What is clear about the relationship between the discipline and its practical role – its 'uses' – is that the key debates have concerned the very nature of sociology itself, and have influenced its theories and subject matter from the very beginning until the present day. We might even say that sociology has been very much defined by what sociologists *thought* it could be used for. And this is mainly because sociology has had to advocate its utility, rather than being a necessary instrumental form of knowledge or technique serving an established profession.

I think there are three general ways of approaching this issue. Firstly, is sociology a way of knowing something more profound about human affairs? Secondly, is it an indispensable guide to socially transformative action? Or, thirdly, is it a way of writing about society, of imagining what is distinctive about the social domain?

The argument I advance in this chapter is that there have in consequence appeared three very broad traditions of sociology, and that each of them has been characterized by one of these 'modes of engagement' with the social. If we were to argue that sociology *should* be 'useful' in a particular fashion – i.e. that by knowing more about how society works we can thereby invent a method of 'improving' social processes – then we would focus on the tradition that I would term 'rational-scientific', though it might as easily be called utilitarian ('useful') or even 'positivist' (creating positive knowledge). And, by extension, sociology might also be seen as useful to those wanting to change society for *political* reasons, who see it as the servant of a particular model of how society 'ought' to be organized. The point is that those working in such traditions *believe* that sociology might have such uses. They act according to those beliefs and construct a career accordingly.

Yet, either as students following sociology or as sociologists in academic life, we are not forced to take the view that sociology is an *inherently* practical or useful discipline. Perhaps sociology is really of no *practical* use at all. It may, of course, be no more than an intellectual pursuit, a way of talking and thinking about an invented symbolic domain we call 'society'. Some contemporary sociologists certainly take this view. For example, both Goffman and Baudrillard, as we shall see later, represent a 'literary' – or what I term an *expressionistic* – strand within sociology. This is a mode that has become more obvious in the 'post-modern' world, where much greater attention to the symbolic – signs, metaphors, representations and so on – has become more 'normal' in sociological writing. Sociological work of this type can be seen as having many affinities to literature, to work in the media industries, and as a form of 'commentary' about social life. This is not to suggest it is uncritical or politically unaware, more that it considers the practice of rational-scientific and political traditions to have been surpassed, no longer appropriate to modern (or rather post-modern) life.

2.1 The three traditions

The present image of sociology to many in the non-academic world tends to emphasize the often 'radical' position taken by its practitioners in therecent past – one in which various forms of Marxism were dominant. This is due in part to the political critique developed by radical and left-wing sociologists in the 1960s and 1970s. However, it is important to bear in mind that sociology is not inherently wedded to one political tradition rather than another, and nor is it an intellectual discipline which has been organizationally yoked to any particular profession outside of the university realm. The broad range of its concerns – which cover the economic, cultural and political dimensions of society – do not lead to any particular occupation apart from that of sociologist: a role most associated with education, and to some extent with organizations designed to provide statistical information about the population to charities, state bodies or international agencies. Very few jobs with the title 'sociologist' are advertised outside of the academic world. Nonetheless, as Tony Bennett notes in Chapter 2 on sociology and government, 'in the late 1990s and into the early 2000s sociology entered into a close relationship with government through its association with the agendas of the Third Way as represented, in Britain, by New Labour.'

It may, however, be misleading to assume that politics and government are the same thing – indeed Bennett explores the idea that the sphere of government itself has been greatly expanded, to replace much of what had passed for politics before. Even the use of 'rational-scientific' methodologies to document social injustice may fall prey to the insidious spread of what is now termed 'governmentality'. As an example, a recent study has shown that 'the social survey method was pioneered as throwing light on social problems', but even social surveys have become administrative in character. The Report of the Rayner Review (GBPCO, 1981) emphasized that the work of OPCS in Britain 'stems from governmental policies rather than being concerned with social conditions [and] statistics [may] become "cognitive commitments" taking their subject matters out of politics and putting it into the nexus of intra-governmental interactions … the production of statistics transforms social problems into problems of resource allocation …' (Thomas, 1996). This illustrates how one important mode in which sociology has been linked to social action is 'political' in the widest sense.

Although I have distinguished the 'rational-scientific' mode from the 'political', it should be clear that to be 'rational-scientific' is not to be *apolitical* in the sense of being wholly separate from political practice. But those working in this tradition would tend to see sociology as an intellectual practice designed to elicit objective information about social processes and structures, and to make it available as information open to scrutiny and debate. Political values or policy matters may well be the source of the problems studied by those working in the 'rational-scientific' mode. The destination of the information produced may also be part of the manifesto programme of a political party. But most crucially, those working in this way would argue that they are able to follow a position first elaborated by Max Weber, whose sociological theories aimed at a 'rational-scientific' ideal. Weber offered a model which separates intellectual from political interests.

'Political' traditions stress the intimate interconnectedness of political values with sociological theory: traditions from Marxism to feminism (but also some conservative traditions) can be identified here. The arguments of this position tend to identify political with scientific knowledge, in the sense that they connect political interests with epistemology, saying in effect that ideas themselves have political sources and effects, and thus that it is impossible to keep science and politics separate. Sociological knowledge is inherently political because it deals with the organization of society. Only by testing this knowledge via intervention in the real world of social action can its validity be assessed. It must offer a theory of action or practice which contributes to the reorganization or emancipation of society.

Finally, there is a growing domain of cultural and theoretical sociology (especially but not exclusively contemporary work) which is relatively uninterested in political issues in the broader sense, though it may have moral and philosophical concerns. It tends to be *expressionistic* in its formulations, relying on much that is literary or artistic to generate examples and debate.

When the US sociologist Erving Goffman (1972) wrote about 'role-playing' behaviour and describes what he called the 'tie-signs' that couples use to signal their relationships to each other in public, it soon becomes clear what he was *not* doing. He was not offering a way of scientifically plotting the dynamics of couple relationships. Nor was he interested in creating knowledge about these relationships so that they can be changed or 'improved' in some way according to a political theory – of whatever colour.

Goffman's 'research' involved a close and detailed observation of what went on in public places. He then thought about its dynamics, and about the 'little theatre' in which it took place, the public stage. Yet Goffman's books and articles are not at first sight literary works – although he seems to have written about social behaviour because the rich variety of human behaviour interested him, much in the same way as it might intrigue a novelist. Close attention to social attitudes and values can help a novelist produce wonderful stories, and offer insight into ways of life that are historically or culturally distant from the reader. In *Talking Heads*, Alan Bennett's monologues written for television, for instance, similar insights about character, about the little dramas of everyday life, appear and seem every bit as telling in their analysis of social behaviour as the best sociology. Goffman's work appeals to literary writers and Alan Bennett is in fact a great fan of his work, and has written an interesting essay about his approach (Bennett, 1994). But this is not its only appeal: many sociologists have also been inspired by his work, and have taken its ideas into both rational-scientific and political traditions. Its role has been to entertain, interest, and inspire. But clearly, then, we can't place Goffman easily within the rational-scientific or political traditions – even if his work seems to be an important part of the sociological 'canon'.

Although Goffman's work is distinctive and unique, we might also identify other sociological writers who work in a similar way. In the late nineteenth century, the German sociologist Georg Simmel produced much of his work in the form of aphoristic essays, offering small 'snapshots' of life to which he would bring some sociological insight. A far more recent example would be the French sociologist Jean Baudrillard, whose work is perhaps as far from the 'rational-scientific' as could be imagined – one of his books, *L'Amérique*, takes the form of a highly impressionistic account of US culture, as epitomized by Las Vegas (Baudrillard, 1989). Indeed, so 'literary' or personal seems Baudrillard's writing that many of his erstwhile sociological colleagues (he taught sociology for many years at the University of Nanterre near Paris) now regard him as no longer contributing to the discipline. Yet Baudrillard is one of the most widely read authors on contemporary culture, and his work is taught in sociology courses across the world.

Baudrillard and Goffman have made a significant impact through developing such a form of sociological writing. Expressionist sociology tends to reject universalism, and is often relativistic and allusive. The original writings of Michel Foucault, for instance, also took this form, although their translation into the technical language of sociology has often located them within the 'political' mode. Yet Foucault himself made frequent reference to the fact that he wanted to explore power without reference to politics and political thought. As he wrote, 'techniques of government have become the only political issue, the only real space for political struggle and contestation' (Foucault, 1991, p.103). Indeed, the particular form of Foucault's writing is a good example of why it may be difficult to read off broader and generalist political meta-narratives from some micro-structural and a good deal of 'post-modernist' sociology. Much writing on themes such as ethnicity, multi-culturalism and difference (and indeed some of the impetus behind cultural studies itself) displays such characteristics.

These three positions or traditions of sociological thought are strong *modes* to which individual sociologists are drawn. They are reflected in differing forms of research, writing and intellectual dissemination. But most of these have taken place within some aspect or another of the 'public sector' – the world of the university, the education system, government and administration. To confine our consideration of the relationship of sociology to social action to the 'public sphere' considered in that way would, however, be potentially misleading. Although there may be few jobs with the title 'sociology' advertised in the private sector, there are nonetheless many ways in which sociology as a form of knowledge and a practice may be evident. This is particularly clear in marketing and sales organizations using various forms of market research. As Elizabeth McFall shows in Chapter 4, ideas generated within the 'academic' world of sociology are applied in commercial organizations. As she points out, one view of this has been that 'the practices, activities, techniques and tools that make up the "real world" of the economy exist quite independently from those of "ivory tower" academics – the belief that clever people with no common sense or practical experience theorize and teach, while "those who can, do".' This is inherently problematic for it does not deal with the ways in which interchanges between the academic and the commercial worlds operate.

The idea that sociology and commercial practice are mutually incompatible forms of activity may have been one of the results of a particular 'political' tradition of sociological research. Indeed sociologists have for some time seen themselves as inhabiting a different social and cultural universe to that of the manager or the entrepreneur, for instance. On the one hand this stemmed from a patrician disdain for 'trade', which characterized the university world in general, but another and more influential source was probably the much-vaunted 'critical' stance of sociology vis-à-vis the status quo. This was a feature of the largely Marxist-influenced research on class, status and the work environment from the 1960s to the 1980s (see Braverman's *Labor and Monopoly Capital* (1974), Beynon's *Working for Ford* (1976), Willis's *Learning to Labour* (1977)). Capitalism in general and capitalist managers in particular were seen as exploitative of the working class as a whole, but in particular of production-line employees (especially in the motor industry). Many sociologists actively identified themselves with labour unions and working-class activist politics, not just in the UK, but throughout Europe and the USA. Yet, as McFall shows, sociology's impact on wider society now seems to be increasingly transacted through its incorporation in the design and management of commercial, capitalist organizations, a situation that many radical sociologists would have considered unacceptable in the 1970s. And in the form of the neo-liberal 'Third Way', it may even become part of government itself, as an integral element of the management and control of a capitalist society.

SUMMARY OF SECTION 2

In section 2 we have:

1　Explored the idea that there are differing traditions of sociological practice.

2　Outlined three traditions: *rational-scientific, political* and *expressionistic.*

3　Shown that sociologists writing in the rational-scientific tradition see the main use of sociology as the production of better, useful (or positive) knowledge.

4　Discussed how sociologists from the political tradition view the main use of sociology as a guide to social change.

5　Illustrated that sociologists coming from the expressionist tradition see the main use of sociology as a way of representing the meanings of the social dimension.

We will now turn to look in greater detail at each of the three traditions, and at examples of work made in each mode.

3　The rational-scientific tradition

The French sociologist Pierre Bourdieu acted the role of the engaged and politicized intellectual, and his ideas have informed political debate in France, and played a vital role in giving sociology a new and important role within contemporary French society. Yet at the same time, he was always committed to the idea that sociology is a social *science*. This involves objectifying social relations, practices and ideas, so that they can be objectively and consensually discussed and made available to anyone capable of understanding the terminology in use and the theoretical system in which they operate (Robbins, 2000, p.15). The sociologist, Bourdieu maintained, must objectify the 'primary experience' of the social in order to analyse it with scientific objectivity.

In that sense Bourdieu took over an important tradition in sociology, from his predecessor Emile Durkheim, who had sought to establish sociology as a new science in the late nineteenth century by 'treating social facts as things'. Understanding that sociology is concerned with the political – or that its conclusions might have political consequences – does not mean that it cannot be practised via rational-scientific techniques, and produce objective knowledge. In placing his work within this tradition, Bourdieu aligned himself with a long tradition in sociology which examines the relationship between facts and values. Sociology is inevitably concerned with what people believe, with the values that underpin their social behaviour. Sociologists, too, have values and beliefs about the social world, and may even have political aspirations for how it ought to be organized. But in studying society and culture, is it possible for sociologists to separate their values and beliefs from the conclusions they draw from their work? This problem is known as the fact-value dilemma, and it seems to be inherent to the type of knowledge created by the social sciences, but not the natural sciences. For if we look closely at the natural sciences, it is clear that values and beliefs are not a part of the **hypothetico-deductive** knowledge

hypothetico-deductive model

Figure 1.2 Emile Durkheim   **Figure 1.3** Francis Galton

that we call scientific laws. Although Newton was a devout Christian who believed he was revealing the work of a divine creator in his scientific experiments, his first law of motion remains forever demonstrable in its predictions, and it does not matter whether the person testing it believes in God, or anything else for that matter. In the same way, attempting to analyse gravitational attraction from a Conservative or Communist perspective would make no sense at all. But at the same time, this does not stop objective scientific knowledge becoming linked to non-scientific ideologies and beliefs, or being used for political ends that we might define as oppressive. A key example can be found in the uses of the scientific theories of genetics.

Social Darwinism

Spencer, Herbert

The natural selection theories of Charles Darwin made such an impression on his fellow scientist and cousin, Francis Galton, that after publication of *On the Origin of Species* (1859) Galton shifted his attentions from geography and meteorology to heredity and 'the very biological foundations of human society'. In the process he developed one of the most influential theories in what is called '**Social Darwinism**' (the application of Darwinian evolution and natural selection theories to human society) – that biological inheritance is more important than environment in determining character and intelligence, known as 'hereditarianism'. Galton's ideas were to be more fully developed as part of a systematic theory of society by **Herbert Spencer**, who opposed state intervention in social planning on the basis that it interfered with the 'survival of the fittest' as an evolutionary principle leading to social progress. Galton's indefatigable efforts to apply his cousin's biological ideas to understanding the social issues of his day is of some relevance to debates about the rational-scientific tradition within sociology.

Galton's work was highly respected in sociology and anthropology:

Galton ... turned his insatiable desire for numbers and measurements increasingly towards domestic 'problems' of inheritance and anthropometry informed by Darwinism. He suffered a succession of 'maladies prejudicial to mental effort', culminating in a breakdown in 1866; amongst other disappointments, it was in this period that it became apparent that his own marriage was likely to prove infertile; he became ever more fascinated by the question of evolution and inheritance at large, urging Britain's transformation from 'a mob of slaves, clinging together, incapable of self-government and begging to be led' ... into a new race of 'vigorous self-reliant men' .... In Galton's work, deeply troubling questions about the nation's level of social and political maturity, and specifically about the effects of a changing and widening electoral constituency after 1867, were deflected onto the problem of the racial body and mind; politics was dissolved into mathematics and biology.

(Pick, 1989, p.197)

In order to support his ideas, Galton surveyed and measured people in an attempt to establish 'types', and from 1865 was employing photography and cranial measurement. In 1877, his work on the British Association for the Advancement of Science's Racial Committee led him into a more detailed examination of the 'degenerate mental type', and particularly that of the criminal. He obtained some photographs of prisoners and began work on devising a new system of physiognomic record which would show the common features of three types of criminal: violent criminals, felons, and sexual offenders (see Figure 1.4).

Galton's interest in mathematics and statistics had led him to experiments which would offer an 'averaging' of physical characteristics in a single image, so that the 'normal' distribution would be observable in the same way as a graph indicated how a population's characteristics were related to their statistical mean, via a bell-shape curve. His system involved the rephotographing of portraits of criminals on the same plate, so that a composite image would be created, and that this 'photographic mean' would offer an image of the 'type'. He noted that these types meshed nearly perfectly with the 'different physiognomic classes'. Yet the resulting images, he found, seemed more attractive than any of the individual portraits: 'The special villainous irregularities in the latter have disappeared, and the common humanity that underlies them has prevailed. They represent, not the criminal, but the man who is liable to fall into crime' (see Figure 1.4).

Thus, photographic portraits of individuals might be employed alongside other forms of measurement such as those derived from 'Life History Albums' designed to be compiled for each child: together they could be used to gauge what was, for Galton, the 'condition of the race', and become part of the methodology he employed to support his theory of **eugenics**, 'the science which deals with all influences that improve the inborn qualities of a race' (Galton, 1904). His major concern was with the inheritance of natural characteristics, and the consequences of the imbalances which existed between the rates of reproduction of the various strata of Victorian society. Galton believed that the 'residuum' (that portion of the working class which, through mental and physical weakness could fulfil no useful function) represented a biological problem for modern society, that it constituted a reservoir of disease and deficiency that threatened the 'hereditary complexion of the nation' (Green, 1984, p.9). The basic proposition of eugenics was that this residuum should be separated out

eugenics

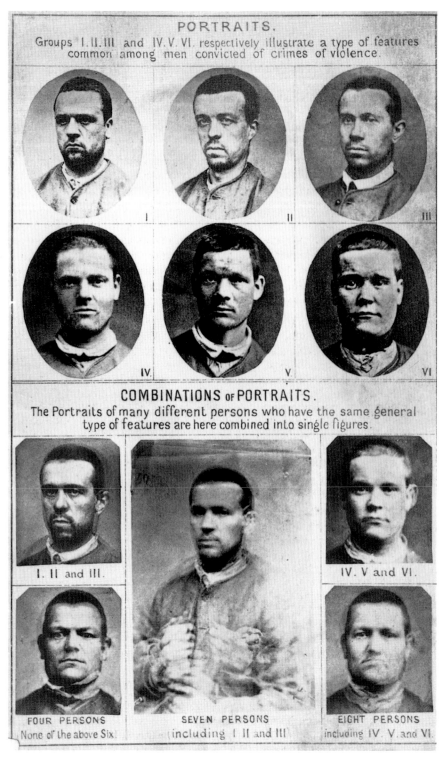

Figure 1.4 An example of Galton's technique of composite photography to create an 'ideal type'. He thought you could then use it to assess an indivdual by how close he came to this type: in this example, of men likely to commit violent crimes

from the rest of society, cared for in special institutions, but above all prevented from procreating, and thus from degenerating the race. Eugenics was also influential in the birth-control movement associated with the feminist writer Marie Stopes, who in 1921 founded the Society for Constructive Birth Control. She observed that many women died of self-induced abortions or raised large families in poverty. Influenced by an American socialist writer, Margaret Sanger, Stopes adopted many of her ideas in favour of birth-control and abortion, especially Sanger's main theme that 'no woman can call herself free who doesn't own and control her own body.' Such ideas would eventually become part of the apparatus of racism, and key elements in the Nazi theories of racial purity although Galton himself was not directly involved.

The rational-scientific techniques developed by Galton could thus be applied to ends which would now seem to us to be highly ethically suspect. Yet the same methods yielded much of great value to science, including the technique of fingerprinting. Galton's contributions to statistics and to psychology are still considered highly relevant today. Yet on certain matters – for instance, the question of eugenics – when Galton applied his scientific findings to questions of social organization, the gap between facts and values became a gulf.

Those sociologists most clearly linked with the 'rational-scientific' tradition also tend to stress the importance of thinking of sociology as fundamentally akin to the natural sciences in its mode of operating. A highly influential figure in this tradition has been the American sociologist, **Robert Merton**. As Jeffrey Alexander has pointed out in his discussion of Merton's work:

Merton, Robert K.

> In an influential argument first formulated more than fifty years ago, Robert Merton railed against what he called the merging of the history and systematics of sociological theory (Merton, 1967/1949). His model for systematic theorizing was the natural sciences, which consisted almost entirely of codified empirical knowledge and precise, empirically-referenced covering laws. Scientific theory is systematic, then, because it can be tested through experimental procedures that compare fact with speculation. This is what allows steady accumulation of true knowledge. Insofar as there is such a condition for the steady growth of knowledge, Merton suggested, there is absolutely no need for classical texts. 'Canons', consisting of widely referenced classical texts, exist only in fields where progress is impossible, fields like painting, literature, and music. In the humanities, Merton writes, 'each classical work – each poem, drama, novel, essay, or history – tends to remain a part of the direct experience of succeeding generations.' In a real science, by contrast, the 'commemoration of the great contributors of the past is substantially reserved to the *history* of the discipline' – it does not enter into what is considered the contemporary practice of the discipline. In Merton's idealized and positivist world, in other words, interpretation and critical discourse about sociological classics would remain, but they would constitute a discipline called the history of sociology, not sociology, in either its theoretical or empirical forms.

> Merton was confident that sociology was, in principle, scientific rather than humanistic, despite what he viewed as the confusions in the practice of social scientists of his day. He invoked Max Weber's confident assertion that 'in science, each of us knows that what he has accomplished will be antiquated in ten, twenty, fifty years' and Weber's insistence that 'every scientific [contribution] asks to be "surpassed" and outdated.' Merton urged sociologists not to confuse arguments about the classics – critical discourse – with sociological arguments about reality. Such arguments were, in fact, history or philosophy, not sociology.

To confuse these, Merton warned, was to succumb to 'intellectually degenerate tendencies.' It would be degenerate because it would reveal an anti-rational idealization of 'illustrious ancestors' and a mindless commitment to dogmatic 'exegesis' of sacred texts. Merton condemns such practices because they engage in 'erudition' rather than 'originality.' At all costs, sociologists should avoid 'commentary', 'critical summaries' and 'critical synopses'. Instead, they should treat earlier texts in a utilitarian way, mining them for 'previously unretrieved information' which can be 'usefully employed as new points of departure' for research programs.

(Alexander, 2001, p.xvi)

If it is worthwhile to attempt to create objective sociological knowledge, then the 'fact-value dilemma' in sociology must be faced: and it includes, as Merton argued, being very careful not to cling onto earlier 'canonical' theories or literatures for nostalgic reasons or because they seem to offer 'authority' for certain propositions – such as the American philosopher A.N. Whitehead's aphorism that 'a science that hesitates to forget its founders is dead'. Yet much of sociology seems still to devote its attentions to revisiting the canons. Perhaps one of the reasons is that, even in the context of the rational-scientific tradition, certain formulations still retain instructive power. For the fact-value dilemma often plays a more important role in the social sciences than it does within the natural sciences, except of course as in the example above of social Darwinism when scientific principles are used to underpin a suspect social or political theory.

One of the most interesting analyses of this problem was offered by the German sociologist Max Weber in a famous essay titled 'Science as a vocation'. Weber gave this as a public lecture at Munich University in 1918, at the end of the Great War, and at a time when he was an advisor to the German delegation to the Versailles conference on Germany and the consequences of its defeat.

READING 1.1

Now read Reading 1.1 which is an extract from Weber's essay, 'Science as a vocation'. After reading it, consider the following questions:

1   Does Weber account for the differences between facts and values in the social sciences?

2   How is it possible for sociology to be *free* of political 'presuppositions'?

3   What influence do values have on objectivity, according to Weber?

It will be clear that Weber thought it was impossible for sociology and the other 'cultural sciences' to work with other than morally loaded concepts. 'All knowledge of cultural reality … is always knowledge from particular points of view' (Weber, 1918/1949, p.81). What counts as a social fact depends greatly on the interpretational or moral goggles that the sociologist is wearing. Unlike Emile Durkheim, Weber did not think it possible to 'empty one's mind' of preconceptions. This does, however, pose some quite serious problems for Weber's belief that it would be possible to create a 'value-free' sociology or cultural science. For if all social constructs and concepts are inevitably coloured by the values and beliefs of the sociologist, how could the resulting knowledge not be 'saturated with the observer's own values and preconceptions' (Parkin, 1982, p.32)? Weber's answer would have been that he is in fact making quite modest claims about what he means by being value-neutral in sociology. He readily recognizes that the keystone of his methodological position, the **'ideal type'**, is a concept quite explicitly formulated to reflect 'a one-sided interpretation of reality':

ideal type

> For Weber, on the other hand, since the eradication of all preconceptions was not humanly possible, the social construction of facts was extremely problematic. Because social facts only existed by virtue of the concepts employed to define and organize them, we could in effect bring new facts into being and dispose of others simply by altering our conceptual frame of reference. Entities like social classes, for example, could be abolished at a single conceptual stroke. Now you see them, now you don't.
>
> Weber's insistence that all theoretical constructs are shot through with biases of one kind or another is not easy to reconcile with the explanatory claims he makes on behalf of ideal-types. Since it is possible to construct quite different ideal-types of the same phenomenon, there is an initial problem of how to decide between them. On what grounds could we conclude that one carried greater explanatory weight than another? The natural temptation would be to say that the matter could be settled by exposing them to the test of the factual world and comparing their performance. But since for Weber such a factual world does not exist independently of the constructs through which we view it, a straightforward comparison is not really possible. Each ideal-type would simply feed upon those social facts of its own making.
>
> (Parkin, 1982, p.33)

By value-neutrality, Weber seems to have intended little more than that the sociologists should not openly proclaim their personal views on matters of social fact. They might well be able to point out the social consequences of poverty, such as poor health or high crime rates for instance, but they should not, as sociologists, then use those social facts to advocate either that poverty should be eradicated or that the poor should be more rigidly controlled by the police.

Issues of power and authority are the domain in which the 'rational-scientific' tradition might appear to offer most scope for creating value-neutral sociological knowledge. The most complete example is to be found in the work of the social philosopher Jürgen Habermas, whose writings on technical rationality, communication and the public sphere are dependent upon the possibility of free, rational, discourse. Later in this book both Tony Bennett and Jim McGuigan discuss Habermas's concept of the public sphere in greater detail, but here I want to introduce the debate around this conception by relating it to the strong rational-scientific tradition which begins in sociology with Max Weber, but is rooted in the ideas about rationality and its application to social institutions in the eighteenth century, with the work of a key thinker of the Enlightenment, Immanuel Kant.

***Figure 1.5** Jürgen Habermas*

'With Kant, the modern age is inaugurated', says Habermas (1987, p.260), who cites the importance of Kant's attempt to develop a universal rational foundation for democratic institutions. Habermas agrees with Kant as to the need to develop such a foundation for democracy and its institutions, but he points out that Kant failed to achieve his goal. Habermas argues that a democratic, communicative rationality can bring a 'value-free' method of relating sociological (and other) knowledges to bear on the problems of modern society. Habermas suggests that it is through an undistorted, rational discourse that a 'better argument' will win the day, and ensure thereby the victory of validity, truth and justice.

Although Habermas sees communicative rationality as being threatened by actual modern society, he nevertheless argues that the core of communicative rationality, 'the unconstrained, unifying, consensus-bringing force of argumentative speech' is a 'central experience' in the life of a human being. According to Habermas, this central experience is inherent in human social life: 'Communicative reason is directly implicated in social life processes insofar as acts of mutual understanding take on the role of a mechanism for co-ordinating action' (1987, p.316).

In a recent discussion of Habermas's attempt to construct a 'rational-scientific' approach to the problem of making sociological knowledge practical, yet without biasing it in terms of any given political values, the Scandinavian sociologist Bengt Flyvbjerg has offered 'a corrective to Habermas's thinking'. Flyvbjerg's 'corrective' seeks to bridge Habermas's 'formulation of the thinking' on precisely these weak points and to introduce an element of what he calls *phronesis* into critical theory. *Phronesis* is a term originally coined by the ancient Greek philosopher Aristotle, which has been translated mainly as 'prudence or practical wisdom' (Flyvbjerg, 2001, p.2). He uses this notion to argue that the social sciences are potentially 'phronetic' in their strongest role, in that they offer guidance on the solution of social issues and problems, because they cannot really measure up to what the natural sciences do best: that is construct 'episteme', Aristotle's term for the creation of analytical, scientific knowledge – or what we would call *rational-scientific* sociology. Phronesis is a resolution of the tension between 'episteme' and what Aristotle called 'techne' or technical knowledge, or what we might call 'know-how':

> At present, social science is locked in a fight it cannot hope to win, because it has accepted terms that are self-defeating. We will see that in their role as phronesis, the social sciences are strongest where the natural sciences are weakest: just as the social sciences have not contributed much to explanatory and predictive theory, neither have the natural sciences contributed to the reflexive analysis and discussion of values and interests, which is the prerequisite for an enlightened political, economic, and cultural development in any society, and which is at the core of phronesis. This should also be the core of social science …
>
> (Flyvbjerg, 2001, p.3)

The 'phronetic' approach then seeks to reconcile the benefits of rational-scientific approaches with the demands raised by specific values and interests. It does not require a commitment to a specific set of values or political ideas as a prerequisite of action-oriented or 'practical' sociology. But it does demand that the sociologist must be entirely aware of, and especially attentive to, the political dynamics and power interests of the social context in which his or her work will be employed. Thus it does not require that the sociologist have any fundamental commitment to the interests of those who form his or her subject matter. Indeed those very interests would themselves form part of the data which would be taken into account, and subjected to rational-scientific criteria as to their validity and significance in explaining the situation.

We have examined some of the key problems involved in developing the rational-scientific tradition, particularly in terms of its engagement with the idea of 'value-freedom', and we will now turn to look in more detail at the *political tradition* in sociology.

SUMMARY OF SECTION 3

In section 3, we have examined some of the key problems involved in developing the rational-scientific tradition, particularly in terms of its engagement with the idea of 'value-freedom'. I have discussed:

1   The fact–value dilemma: if facts and values are not separated, the result will be one-sided knowledge that is not objective, truthful or free from bias.

2   The notion that 'society' has an objective, independent existence and the main purpose of sociology is to find out the truth about it.

3   The model for sociology, which is that of the natural sciences, such as physics.

4   The belief that sociologists should keep their values out of their research.

4   Weber's argument that values influence how sociologists define the focus of their theories or research, but thereafter should be kept out.

5   Habermas's focus (like Weber's) on the rise of technical or instrumental rationality, and his suggestion that it should be displaced by communicative rationality which promotes argument and discourse as the path to truth and justice.

---

4   The political tradition

In Chapter 5 Merl Storr discusses 'sociology's relationship with groups and individuals whose politics take place not just *outside*, but often *against*, the institutions of liberal democracy' (section 1; emphasis in original). Storr makes clear that how sociologists make sense of this kind of politics, how activists make sense of sociology, and in whose interests should they (we) attempt to do so, are all central issues within the sociological perspective.

As Storr explains matters, one of the major problems involved in sociology is precisely its (apparent) embeddedness in social issues of the day. This is a two-way street. Activists of any persuasion can (and do) use the social knowledge created by sociology. Similarly, a sociologist may decide to get involved in some form of political or other action, perhaps with the aim of both advancing political goals and at the same time studying the action itself. Certain consequences might follow, which include a whole range of ethical questions about whether the activism itself can be made 'public' through research (if knowledge is power, should the activist organization be opened to scrutiny? How will the sociological knowledge be used? Do the participants need to be consulted before reference is made to them?). As Storr suggests, 'These questions about the relationship between sociology and activism have profound implications for the *practice* of sociology' (Ch. 5, section 1; emphasis in original).

These questions have been present within the discipline since the nineteenth century. Weber and Habermas take one view: sociology can offer certain 'practical hints about the feasibility of realizing certain values, but it cannot tell us whether or not we are right to pursue those ideals whatever the cost' (Outhwaite, 1996, pp.98–9). By contrast, those who would accept the 'political tradition' will tend to see that sociology and sociologists cannot avoid making value judgements in their work, and that its dissemination and use, as well as the reasons for its construction in the first place, are irretrievably founded in a political process. The role of sociology, then, becomes one of emancipation and change: social knowledge is politically charged or, as Michel Foucault put it, 'power is always present'. A variant of this position has recently been argued by Alexander:

> There is a relativity at the heart of the sociological enterprise, one that represents an irrefutable dimension of the human sciences more generally. The relativity comes about because sociology is a human science rather than a science of nature. Max Weber understood the implications of this fateful distinction, but Marx, Durkheim, and Parsons did not. Yet, this fundamental fact explains the very distinctiveness of our discipline and our science, whatever that term may actually mean. It explains why Marx, Durkheim, Weber, and Parsons are still living classics, and why, at the same time, none among them could ever succeed in shaping the past, present, or future of sociology in their own image. Sociological practitioners can never be as certain of their knowledge as natural scientists, and even when they feel certain, they aim to use their knowledge not only for explaining the world but also for changing it, that is, for moral purposes.
>
> (Alexander, 2001, p.xv)

Perhaps the most significant impetus to the political tradition has come from Karl Marx's idea of 'praxis', or the notion that the only way of knowing the world is via the 'dialectical' interplay of action in and upon it, through which we come to know the world as we change it. This idea, originating with Hegel, underpins Marxist thought generally, and it has long figured as a key pole of the debate within sociology about values and action.

Historically, the era when this idea about praxis infused sociological thinking most fully was the 1960s and 1970s – precisely the moment when mass university education was emerging in the West – and particularly in the United States, France and Germany as the baby-boom population of those born just after the Second World War began to enter higher education. Sociology was a popular 'new' discipline which was rapidly established in universities and colleges, and which appeared to offer some insight into contemporary conditions, and to be in tune with the social aspirations of this large social group. The Vietnam War, feminism, the student revolutions of 1968, racism, civil rights, apartheid in South Africa, emergent environmentalism, gay liberation, and the Cold War all loomed large as contemporary social issues, about which the new discipline might be

Figure 1.6 *The Soviet invasion of Czechoslovakia, 1968*

expected to contribute some insights and also to offer solutions. 'Traditional' sociology seemed immured within a rational-scientific tradition which operated with a fact–value distinction that appeared out of tune with contemporary needs for political action, and appeared to have few answers to these issues.

It is against such a backdrop that the popularity of various forms of Marxism and 'critical theory' at this time might be seen. The centrality of praxis-based approaches to the political tradition is a result of the idea that sociology is a component of society's reflection upon itself: in other words, that acting upon the social world to change it might be done in order to know something about its underlying mechanisms. As a result, sociology becomes an inherently 'reflexive' discipline which has a duty to link its intellectual processes to questions of social change.

A classic and still influential formulation of this argument was made by Alvin Gouldner in a book written at the end of the 1960s, *The Coming Crisis of Western Sociology* (1971) that appeared to presage a fundamental break with the non-reflexive sociologies he associated with conservative traditions in social thought. One of these was the then dominant paradigm of US sociology – **functionalism** – which he identified as emerging from the work of **Talcott Parsons**. But Gouldner also directed strong critical attention to the 'state Marxism' of the Communist bloc, as another form of conservative theory about society. A little earlier, Gouldner had outlined some of the reasons why he was developing a radical movement away from 'rational-scientific' sociology in his attack on value-freedom as a 'myth' (1962).

functionalism, Parsons, Talcott

READING 1.2

Now read extracts from Alvin W. Gouldner's (1962) 'Anti-minotaur: the myth of a value-free sociology' in Reading 1.2. As you read this article, keep in mind the following questions:

1   What does Gouldner think are the reasons for Weber upholding the value-free doctrine?

2   What does Gouldner claim are the disadvantages of trying to remain value-free?

3   Why have many sociologists adopted a value-free stance?

4   Why does Gouldner think that value-free sociology is a myth?

5   How does he deal with the problem of value neutrality?

Gouldner's arguments about value-free sociology became highly influential through the latter part of the 1960s and the early 1970s, when they were associated with a general move towards more radical conceptions of sociology's role in social change. As the reading indicates, however, these ideas were not wholly induced by the incorporation of Marxism as a mainstream component of the sociology of that era, but also reflected libertarian and anarchist principles. Their net effect was to make it essential for sociologists to consider the role of their discipline in the organization of society, and to make them think about the implications of their work for public morality.

The sentiments expressed by Gouldner in *The Coming Crisis of Western Sociology* and presaged by his critique of 'value-free' sociology seem to have influenced a large swathe of sociology in the period after his book was written, but for reasons perhaps not always linked to his own work. It might have seemed that what he was concerned with was a more general issue within the discipline, that those who took up sociology were doing so precisely because they saw it as a means of effecting social change.

Nowhere is this clearer, perhaps, than in the feminist movement. The emergence of a feminist sociology in the 1970s appears as part of a wider set of changes in social, philosophical, political and psychological ideas about gender roles and sexuality more generally. Central to feminism's social programme was the notion that sociology could be a vital weapon in ensuring that the social changes it aimed at could be instituted. But feminist thinking could not proceed, many argued, unless it could sweep away the **epistemological** bases of 'masculinist thinking'. As Terry Lovell has argued,

epistemology

> The challenge of contemporary feminist theory has necessarily taken it into the heart of the most intractable questions of the nature of knowledge itself. The first move which has had to be made within each discipline has been to **deconstruct** what has passed for knowledge so as to expose its masculinist perspective and associated exclusions. The second has often quickly followed the first, that of advancing either strong claims for 'women's knowledge' or perhaps more cautious affirmations of the possibilities of 'feminist standpoint epistemology'.

deconstruction

(Lovell, 1996, p.335)

READING 1.3

Now turn to Reading 1.3 which is an extract from Terry Lovell's article on 'Feminist social theory'. This explores this idea of a theory of knowledge from a feminist standpoint. After reading this extract, consider the following questions:

1   How does Lovell explain the emergence of new epistemological ideas linked to feminism?

2   Is feminism a 'special case' or simply another example of the ways in which the 'political tradition' in sociology has come to the fore as a major theme of the discipline?

As Lovell makes clear, the feminist approach within social theory is resolutely devoted to challenging the truth-claims of masculinist epistemologies, and in that sense it provides a neat picture of one of the major consequences of much thinking about the political tradition in sociology. Inevitably, as a consequence of the ways in which social or political aspirations are considered to be central elements of the sociological enterprise itself, this has raised debate as to whether the methodology of knowledge creation itself is seen as subservient to these aspirations. One radical solution to this dilemma has been to see all knowledge creation itself as socially *relative* or contextual, contingent upon the viewpoint or social position of the thinker. This is essentially the position taken by Michel Foucault and also many post-modernist thinkers, who have increasingly seen the activity of writing about society as a form of knowledge creation in its own right – one that can have important consequences for analysing and reconstructing social phenomena. For instance, multiple critical theories, Marxist, neo-Marxist and feminist models now circulate within the discourses of qualitative research. Kincheloe and McLaren (2000) trace the history of critical research (and Marxist theory), from the Frankfurt School, through more recent versions associated with such terms as *post-structural, post-modern, feminist, critical pedagogy* and *cultural studies.* Critical theorists seek to produce practical, pragmatic knowledge that is judged by its degree of historical situatedness, and its ability to produce praxis (action).

We have looked at the 'political tradition' within sociology as one which insists upon the need for the sociologist to recognize the socially embedded nature of their work, and the consequent impossibility of the sort of 'value-freedom' that is so much a concern of the *rational-scientific* tradition.

Because the typical issues tackled by such uses of sociology are so closely linked to the perceived need to effect one form of social change or another – compare the examples of feminism and anti-globalization movements – it may be appropriate to describe them as 'relativist', in the sense that they present the researcher with entirely specific or 'relative' forms of knowledge creation. Feminist theory, as pointed out earlier, has been primarily concerned with 'challenging the truth-claims of masculinist epistemologies'. Although political theories and positions may be thought of as forms of 'relativism' because of their particularism and bias in favour of specific interests, they often contain the assumption that the specificity of their approach, and particularly their attention to the need to 'open up' hitherto concealed or repressed areas of knowledge, will lead to a more inclusive epistemology in which the particular interests they promote receive wider attention.

But there is another 'relativist' tradition that we should now turn to examine. It is less frequently 'political' in scope. It has placed even greater emphasis on meaning and on the style in which sociological thought is expressed. The next section will turn to look at the relativist, 'expressionist tradition' that has been present for some time in sociology, but which now finds greater relevance in what some have termed 'post-modernity'.

SUMMARY OF SECTION 4

To summarize, the key points from the political tradition are the ideas that:

1   Value-freedom is a myth and that sociology always involves value judgements (as Gouldner argued).

2   Sociology is fundamentally different to the natural sciences because 'society' – the object of sociological study – is fundamentally different to nature.

3   Marxism, critical theory and feminism have developed as a reaction to the dominance of the rational-scientific tradition.

4   Political approaches may seek to invent new methods and new 'particularistic' or 'relativist' epistemologies that challenge rational-scientific 'truth claims'.

---

5 The expressionist tradition

Sociology and literature are often thought to be uneasy bedfellows. Yet some of the most interesting and well-known sociological writing has become famous because it offers narrative thrust and imaginative characterization. A number of community studies fall into this category: Whyte's *Street Corner Society* (1943) (discussed by **Hamilton, 2002**[1]; Wylie's *Village in the Vaucluse* (1957); Young and Willmott and Young's *Family and Kinship in East London* (1957) (discussed by **Jordan, 2002a**) are iconic examples. There are a number of more recent works which have entered this select canon.

One of the most interesting writers on sociological matters has been Erving Goffman, whose work was referred to earlier. Alvin Gouldner, for instance, called him 'the William Blake of sociology' (Gouldner, 1962). Goffman's 'dramaturgical' approach to the 'play-acting' involved in social situations is at its most intriguing when he discusses the simple processes of social interaction that we might see anywhere, at any time. A classic is his analysis of 'couple tie-signs' – the symbolic markers, such as hand-holding, that couples use to signal to the rest of the world that they are just that:

Having begun to learn about the meaning of hand-holding by looking at those who do it and those who don't, we can go forward. Given the people who do it, we can ask when it is they do it, and when it is they don't (when they might).

First, not doing it. There is a rule in formal etiquette that it is improper for couples to walk down the fashionable shopping streets of a city holding hands. There is another rule that married couples at social parties are supposed to

---

[1] A reference in bold type indicates a chapter in a book, or a book, in the *Sociology and Society* series.

'mix' that is, to lay aside their excluding relationship temporarily so that they can be active simply in their capacity as members of the party. A corollary of this rule is that they are not supposed to hold hands. (They may hold hands on the way to the party and back from the party but not during the party.) It is also the case that although college students can walk on the campus holding hands – in fact that seems to be one of the special places for this sort of activity – they ought not to listen to lectures thusly encumbered. Furthermore, in some social establishments holding hands even outdoors is forbidden. In industrial schools for persons with a court charge, handholding may be prohibited within the gates, as it may be to nurse–physician pairs on the hospital grounds. In these latter cases, of course, whether for penal or professional reasons, the members must be so strictly disciplined that even when walking between buildings, a high orientation to the purposes of the establishment must be maintained. (As may be expected, other self – involving side – involvements such as smoking may also be prohibited.) It appears, then, that when much of an individual's orientation and involvement is necessary, hand-holding may have to be forborne along with other acts through which the mutual involvement of the closely related might be thrust upon the public at large.

The significance of this discipline will be emphasized if we look at situations where hand-holding seems to be approved and even idealized. In our pictorial world of advertising and movies – if not in the real world – vacationing couples are featured walking down crooked little streets in foreign places holding hands. At issue here is the fact that tourists often feel they do not owe the business streets of foreign societies the deference these places often demand from locals; tourists can therefore withdraw, just as they can wear informal clothing. Further, the very foreignness of the place suggests a slight exposure, if not fear, and, for the woman at least, holding the hand of the one she is paired with is a pictured source of support. Magazine couples are also featured holding hands while walking barefooted (shoes in other hand) on the seashore. Here, obviously, the absence of civil society allows a greater withdrawal than might otherwise be tolerated, an undisguised mooning as it were, and the very empty reaches of the ocean might cause an anomic flutter nicely checked by the confirmation of a held hand.

(Goffman, 1972, pp.228–9)

Now it soon becomes obvious that while he may be particularly interested in understanding the dynamics of social behaviour, Goffman is not really interested in treating such behaviour as if it were something that can be analysed in a 'rational-scientific' manner. Nor does he wish to use this insight for political purposes. He is most interested in exploring the form of social expression that 'tie-signs' appear to denote. And his technique for examining them involves him in the use of entirely 'qualitative' methods: judgement, insight, empathy, and alertness to the implicit and fluid rules governing social behaviour. All of this is typical of what I term the 'expressionist' tradition within sociology. And although it has some obvious affinities with it, my use of the term 'expressionist' sociology should not be confused with the 'interpretative' sociology of Max Weber, which placed great emphasis on what he termed **'Verstehen'**   **Verstehen** (interpretative understanding). At first sight they seem quite close. But Weber was working within the rational-scientific tradition, using an approach which aimed at delivering general insights into the dynamics of society and history, and concerned with developing sociology as a 'cultural science'. Perhaps he would have recognized the work of those working in the present 'expressionist' tradition, with its emphasis on the performance of the written text (or even oral

Figure 1.7 *Street festival, Limoux, France (1987): the expressionist tradition would include visual sociology amongst its approaches*

performance, another aspect of this emergent tradition), but he might well have concluded that it had other objectives, more concerned with humanistic expression than with scientific explanation.

One index of the ways in which 'expressionistic sociology' has become more evident can be gauged from the fact that so-called 'qualitative' methods are increasingly prevalent within sociology, in contrast to the quantitative techniques employed in various forms of survey research that involve counting of some sort. What are termed **ethnographic** approaches have become widely used. Ethnographers immerse themselves in a society to collect descriptive data via fieldwork concerning the culture of its members from the perspective of the meanings members of that society attach to their social world; they then render the collected data intelligible and significant to fellow academics and other readers.

ethnography

The ethnographer is part insider, since s/he is a participant in the social world that is the object of investigation; and part outsider, since, although prior frameworks are to be eschewed in favour of contaminating the field of observation as little as possible, the results of the fieldwork must be transmitted to professional (and other) audiences and thereby interpreted in the context of frameworks that bestow credibility on the fieldwork. This last point means that the fieldwork must be written and indeed it is significant in this context that the term 'ethnography' is frequently employed to refer to the written account that is the product of ethnographic research. As one writer has put it: 'ethnography is something you may do, study, use, read or write' (Bryman, 2001, p.x).

Much of ethnography, then, deals with meanings and symbolic processes: it is often used to attempt to interpret non-Western cultures, or to understand the behaviour of 'sub-cultural' groups within, say, Western societies (and this is why it is a mode of expression also widely used by anthropologists). This has long raised pertinent issues about how (and whether) meanings can be 'universalized' through the interpretative process. Increasingly, this process has been seen as essentially a question of how the work is *written*. Indeed its 'universalization' would often be taken as problematic, and many practitioners of this approach would see themselves as producing highly 'relative' and specific accounts, rather than material which would form part of a wider understanding of social processes. The creative process of writing thus becomes the object of the game.

Figure 1.8 Jacques Derrida

The importance of writing as a mode of expression in the social sciences has also become a central issue within post-modernist social thought. The French philosopher Jacques Derrida expressed this most clearly in his argument that 'there is nothing beyond the text' ('*Il n'y a pas de hors-texte*'): in other words that all thinking about society and – by extension – modernity is inextricably connected to how these ideas have been constructed within books, articles and other literary forms (Derrida, 1978).

Derrida's contention has become a central element of the post-modernist contention that we have reached a point where there are no longer any 'grand narratives' to guide thinking about the development and evolution of human society. Within such a context, the idea that an activity such as sociology could exist, within either the rational-scientific or the political tradition, itself becomes untenable – a grand narrative in its own right.

This reading is quite difficult, but it will provide you with a good idea of the terminology and quality of the ideas at play within the post-modern, expressionist mode: for example, the use of terms such as 'intertextuality' – the notion that all texts refer to each other, and that there is nothing else but 'the text' as an authority on social knowledge. Similarly, as Smart (1996) makes clear, the ideas of the semiotician, **Ferdinand de Saussure**, which are concerned with the symbolic dimensions of language, are central to this approach.

Saussure, Ferdinand de

READING 1.4

Now turn to Reading 1.4, 'Post-modern social theory' by Barry Smart. When reading this short extract from Smart's article, the following questions are relevant:

1 What does Derrida mean by 'text'?

2 What does Derrida mean by 'there is nothing beyond the text'?

More recently, some sociologists such as John Urry have even begun to question whether the concept of society – for so long thought to be the lynchpin of a discipline which aimed to call itself sociology – has any real or shared meaning. It may be that Mrs Thatcher's famous dictum that 'there is no such thing as society' has more to it than the ideological assertions of a politician (Urry, 1995, 2000). Urry's argument is with older modes of sociological thought, and proceeds from the idea that new forms of communication, and the globalization that follows from them, have set up new fluidities that cannot be captured any longer by the notion of society as previously constituted in sociological thought. His surprising agreement with Margaret Thatcher's contention that there is 'no such thing as society' might be considered evidence that sociology is becoming more conservative, but in fact his purpose is rather different. It is to suggest that recent social change has so corroded the shell of the 'unitary' society that it becomes difficult to discern as a sociological entity at all.

The emergence of a new 'paradigm' of post-modern social theory has also raised questions about what sociology is 'for'. Urry previously suggested (1995) that sociology is in essence 'parasitical' – largely because it trades on the insights of other disciplines for most of its characterizing ideas. But worse than that, it cannot easily be differentiated from common-sense notions of what the social actually consists of (Urry, 1995, p.42). And more worryingly still, progress in sociology does not seem to involve greater empirical insight – knowing 'more' about society, in the same way that progress in physics or chemistry means knowing more about the material world – but merely theoretical innovation, the replacement of one set of theories (or discourses) about the social by another (*ibid.*, p.41).

We are left, then, with some interesting issues. For if sociology cannot be shown to have any powerful status as either a rational-scientific discipline or as a method for directing various forms of social engineering, either from the top down through the state or from the bottom up through radical social movements, then what is the activity of sociology directed towards? The post-modernist answer, very much like the ethnographic answer, is that it is nothing more than a part of culture itself, or in other words an attempt to impose some form of meaning on the flux of human affairs, the interactions between individuals. Hence the importance of 'expression': how and in what style something is written can indicate what 'meaning' it has within a wider 'discourse'. In Barry Smart's discussion of the implications of such ideas, we can see the major components of the post-modernist version of the 'expressionist' tradition.

The general idea of post-modernism – that there is no longer any point in attempting to discern social processes or even any general trajectory of development – has some interesting consequences for sociological thinking. Perhaps the most famous example of this was Jean Baudrillard's famous argument that the 'Gulf war did not take place' (Baudrillard, 1993). (For a more detailed discussion on this, see **Jordan, 2002b**.) Basing his argument on the idea that the mediatization of war had removed it almost entirely from the direct experience of the (western) populations who were implicated in the war, Baudrillard suggested in an extraordinarily shocking form of *writing* that the whole event had not, in any real sense, taken place at all. It had been a sort of virtual event, staged for the media. Baudrillard's chosen mode of publishing his work – articles in newspapers, books, lectures, photographs, exhibitions and interviews – thus present the 'expressionist tradition' at its clearest, and seem to support Derrida's idea that there is 'nothing beyond the text'.

SUMMARY OF SECTION 5

In section 5, I have shown how the expressionist tradition:

1   Concentrates on the meaning of social experience, rather than emphasizing scientific knowledge or political utility.

2   Can be seen as more in tune with 'post-modern' society, though as an approach it is quite old.

3   Emphasizes relativity, but also suggests that sociology is an attempt to impose some form of meaning on the flux of human affairs.

4   Argues that sociology is essentially 'parasitical'.

5   Stresses the literary or rhetorical construction of sociological work.

6 Conclusion

The aim of this chapter has been to tease out the limits of thinking about sociological practice, and its conclusion is to suggest that the question about whether sociology has any practical value really depends upon the point from which you ask it. The conventional line in a book of this type is to argue that sociology does have a practical purpose, even that it leads to certain careers. While those outcomes should not be discounted – after all, many sociologists and educationalists would agree that sociology has real-world uses, and that there is some point therefore in following a course of study devoted to it – it seems to me that the arguments about its utility and value are not cut and dried.

In this chapter, I have reviewed what I have identified as the three main positions taken by sociologists (no matter of what theoretical persuasion, though these do have some impact on which 'node' they are likely to gravitate towards). If they take the 'rational-scientific' route, they are likely to think that sociology can be practised as a form of fact-finding, as the pursuit of greater knowledge about the dynamics of a very wide range of social institutions and behaviour. If they take the 'political' route, they are likely to hold the view that sociology is inherently concerned with how to change society in some form, and that the sociologist cannot but be involved in that process – for good or ill. Finally, I have argued that another, more 'expressionist' position exists that sees sociology as concerned with writing, illustrating or performing around the 'social', but without pretensions to offer scientific knowledge or to claims of political significance. This latter type of sociology is no less valid, but it is an essentially cultural form, and thus would need to be compared with those disciplines in the humanities which can aim to create insights about cultural objects, even if they do not suggest that they have the status of scientific knowledge. It is my further contention that these three positions really exhaust the range of possible perspectives about sociology and that they define the field around which questions about sociology's uses or practical value have to be considered. But, as with so much of what is offered in the sociological literature, it is up to you, the reader, to decide on whether my contentions are sustainable.

References

Alexander, J. (2001) 'Introduction', *Mainstream and Critical Social Theory*, London, Sage.

Baudrillard, J. (1989) *L'Amérique*, Paris, Editions Du Seuil.

Baudrillard, J. (1993) *The Gulf War Did Not Take Place* (trans. P. Patton), Bloomington, IN, Indiana University Press.

Bennett, A. (1994) 'Cold sweat', reprinted in Bennett, A., *Writing Home*, London, Faber & Faber.

Beynon, H. (1976) *Working for Ford*, Harmondsworth, Penguin Books.

Braverman, H.N. (1974) *Labor and Monopoly Capital*, London, Monthly Review Press.

Bryman, A. (2001) 'Introduction' in *Ethnography*, London, Sage.

Darwin, C. (1926) *On the Origin of Species* , London, Dent.

Derrida, J. (1974) *Of Grammatology*, Baltimore, John Hopkins University Press. First published in 1967 as ''Linguistics and grammatology'.

Derrida, J. (1978) *Writing and Difference*, London, Routledge.

Flyvbjerg, B. (2001) *Making Social Science Matter*, Cambridge, Cambridge University Press.

Foucault, M. (1991) 'Governmentality' in Burchell, G., Gordon, C. and Miller, P. (eds) *The Foucault Effect*, London, Harvester Wheatsheaf, pp.87–104.

Galton, F. (1904) 'Eugenics: its definition, scope, and aims', *The American Journal of Sociology*, vol.x, no.1, July.

Goffman, E. (1972) *Interaction Ritual: Essays on Face to Face Behaviour*, Harmondsworth, Penguin Books.

Gouldner, A.W. (1962) 'Anti-minotaur: the myth of a value-free sociology', *Social Problems*, no.9, pp.199–213.

Gouldner, A. (1971) *The Coming Crisis of Western Sociology*, London, Heinemann.

GBPCO (Great Britain Privy Council Office) (1981) *Government Statistical Services (Report of the Rayner Review)*, Cmnd 8236, London, HMSO.

Green, P. (1984) 'Veins of resemblance: photography and eugenics', *The Oxford Art Journal*, vol.7, no.2, pp.3–16.

Habermas, J. (1987) *The Philosophical Discourse of Modernity*, Cambridge, MA, MIT Press.

Hamilton, P. (2002) 'The street and everyday life' in Bennett, T. and Watson, D. (eds) *Understanding Everyday Life*, Oxford, Blackwell/The Open University. (Book 1 in this series.)

Hogan, T. (1998) 'Dead Indians, flawed consumers and snowballs in hell: on Zygmunt Bauman's New Poor', *Arena Journal*, no.10, pp.151–8.

Jordan, T. (2002a) 'Community and everyday life' in Bennett, T. and Watson, D. op. cit..

Jordan, T. (2002b) 'Totalities and multiplicities' in Jordan, T. and Pile, S. (eds) *Social Change*, Oxford, Blackwell/The Open University. (Book 3 in this series.)

Kincheloe, J. and McLaren, P. (2000) 'Rethinking critical theory and qualitative research', Denzin, N. and Lincoln, Y.S. (eds) *Handbook of Qualitative Research*, Thousand Oaks, London and New Delhi, Sage, pp.279–314.

Lovell, T. (1996) 'Feminist social theory' in Turner, B.S. (ed.) *op. cit.*, pp.335–7.

Merton, R.K. (1949) 'On the history and systematics of sociological theory', reprinted in Merton, R.K. (1967) *On Theoretical Sociology*, New York, The Free Press.

Office of National Statistics (2001) *Population Trends*, London, The Stationery Office.

Outhwaite, W. (1996) *Positivism and Sociology*, London, Allen & Unwin.

Parkin, F. (1982) *Max Weber*, London and Chichester, Tavistock and Ellis Horwood.

Pick, D. (1989) *Faces of Degeneration*, Cambridge, Cambridge University Press.

Robbins, D. (2000) *Bourdieu and Culture*, London, Sage.

Smart, B. (1996) 'Post-modern social theory' in Turner, B.S. (ed.) *op. cit.,* pp.401–04.

Tawney, R.H. (1978) *History and Society*, Harmondsworth, Penguin Books. First published in 1913.

Thomas, R. (1996) Statistics as organizational products', *Sociological Research Online*, vol.1, no.3, http://www.socresonline.org.uk/socresonline/1/3/5.html

Turner, B.S. (ed.) (1996) *The Blackwell Companion to Social Theory*, Oxford, Blackwell.

Urry, J. (1995) 'Sociology as a parasite – some vices and virtues' in Urry, J., *Consuming Places*, London, Routledge, pp.33–45.

Urry, J. (2000) *Sociology Beyond Societies*, London, Routledge.

Weber, M. (1918/1949) 'Science as a vocation' in Weber, M., *From Max Weber: Essays in Sociology* (trans. and ed. H.H. Gerth and C.Wright Mills), London, Routledge, pp.143–8.

Whyte, W.F. (1995) *Street Corner Society: The Social Structure of an Italian Slum*, Chicago, IL, Chicago University Press Midway Reprint. First published in 1943.

Willis, P. (1977) *Learning to Labour: How Working-Class Kids Get Working-Class Jobs*, Westmead, Saxon House.

Wylie, L. (1957) *Village in the Vaucluse*, London, Oxford University Press.

Young, M. and Willmott, P. (1957) *Family and Kinship in East London*, Harmondsworth, Penguin Books.

Readings

 ## Max Weber, 'Science as a vocation' (1918)

… [W]hat is the meaning of science as a vocation, now after all these former illusions, the 'way to true being', the 'way to true art', the 'way to true nature', the 'way to true God', the 'way to true happiness', have been dispelled? Tolstoi has given the simplest answer, with the words: 'Science is meaningless because it gives no answer to our question, the only question important for us: "What shall we do and how shall we live?"' That science does not give an answer to this is indisputable. The only question that remains is the sense in which science gives 'no' answer, and whether or not science might yet be of some use to the one who puts the question correctly.

Today one usually speaks of science as 'free from presuppositions.' Is there such a thing? It depends upon what one understands thereby. All scientific work presupposes that the rules of logic and method are valid; these are the general foundations of our orientation in the world; and, at least for our special question, these presuppositions are the least problematic aspect of science. Science further presupposes that what is yielded by scientific work is important in the sense that it is 'worth being known.' In this, obviously, are contained all our problems. For this presupposition cannot be proved by scientific means. It can only be *interpreted* with reference to its ultimate meaning, which we must reject or accept according to our ultimate position towards life.

Furthermore, the nature of the relationship of scientific work and its presuppositions varies widely according to their structure. The natural sciences, for instance, physics, chemistry, and astronomy, presuppose as self-evident that it is worth while to know the ultimate laws of cosmic events as far as science can construe them. This is the case not only because with such knowledge one can attain technical results but for its own sake, if the quest for such knowledge is to be a 'vocation.' Yet this presupposition can by no means be proved. And still less can it be proved that the existence of the world which these sciences describe is worth while, that it has any 'meaning', or that it makes sense to live in such a world. Science does not ask for the answers to such questions.

Consider modern medicine, a practical technology which is highly developed scientifically. The general 'presupposition' of the medical enterprise is stated trivially in the assertion that medical science has the task of maintaining life as such and of diminishing suffering as such to the greatest possible degree. Yet this is problematical. By his means the medical man preserves the life of the mortally ill man, even if the patient implores us to relieve him of life, even if his relatives, to whom his life is worthless and to whom the costs of maintaining his worthless life grow unbearable, grant his redemption from suffering. Perhaps a poor lunatic is involved, whose relatives, whether they admit it or not, wish and must wish for his death. Yet the presuppositions of medicine, and the penal code, prevent the physician from relinquishing his therapeutic efforts. Whether life is worth while living and when – this question is not asked by medicine. Natural science gives us an answer to the question of what we must do if we wish to master life technically. It leaves quite aside, or assumes for its purposes, whether we should and do wish to master life technically and whether it ultimately makes sense to do so.

Consider a discipline such as aesthetics. The fact that there are works of art is given for aesthetics. It seeks to find out under what conditions this fact exists, but it does not raise the question whether or not the realm of art is perhaps a realm of diabolical grandeur, a realm of this world, and therefore, in its core, hostile to God and, in its innermost and aristocratic spirit, hostile to the brotherhood of man. Hence, aesthetics does not ask whether there *should* be works of art.

Consider jurisprudence. It establishes what is valid according to the rules of juristic thought, which is partly bound by logically compelling and partly by conventionally given schemata. Juridical thought holds when certain legal rules and certain methods of interpretations are recognized as binding. Whether there should be law and whether one should establish just these rules – such questions jurisprudence does not answer.

It can only state: If one wishes this result, according to the norms of our legal thought, this legal rule is the appropriate means of attaining it.

Consider the historical and cultural sciences. They teach us how to understand and interpret political, artistic, literary, and social phenomena in terms of their origins. But they give us no answer to the question, whether the existence of these cultural phenomena have been and are *worth while*. And they do not answer the further question, whether it is worth the effort required to know them. They presuppose that there is an interest in partaking, through this procedure, of the community of 'civilized men'. But they cannot prove 'scientifically' that this is the case; and that they presuppose this interest by no means proves that it goes without saying. In fact it is not at all self-evident.

Finally, let us consider the disciplines close to me: sociology, history, economics, political science, and those types of cultural philosophy that make it their task to interpret these sciences. It is said, and I agree, that politics is out of place in the lecture-room. It does not belong there on the part of the students. If, for instance, in the lecture-room of my former colleague Dietrich Schäfer in Berlin, pacifist students were to surround his desk and make an uproar, I should deplore it just as much as I should deplore the uproar which anti-pacifist students are said to have made against Professor Förster, whose views in many ways are as remote as could be from mine. Neither does politics, however, belong in the lecture-room on the part of the docents, and when the docent is scientifically concerned with politics, it belongs there least of all.

To take a practical political stand is one thing, and to analyze political structures and party positions is another. When speaking in a political meeting about democracy, one does not hide one's personal standpoint; indeed, to come out clearly and take a stand is one's damned duty. The words one uses in such a meeting are not means of scientific analysis but means of canvassing votes and winning over others. They are not plowshares to loosen the soil of contemplative thought; they are swords against the enemies: such words are weapons. It would be an outrage, however, to use words in this fashion in a lecture or in the lecture-room. If, for instance, 'democracy' is under discussion, one considers its various forms, analyzes them in the way they function, determines what results for the conditions of life the one form has as compared with the other. Then one confronts the forms of democracy with non-democratic forms of political order and endeavors to come to a position where the student may find the point from which, in terms of his ultimate ideals, he can take a stand. But the true teacher will beware of imposing from the platform any political position upon the student, whether it is expressed or

suggested. 'To let the facts speak for themselves' is the most unfair way of putting over a political position to the student.

Why should we abstain from doing this? I state in advance that some highly esteemed colleagues are of the opinion that it is not possible to carry through this self-restraint and that, even if it were possible, it would be a whim to avoid declaring oneself. Now one cannot demonstrate scientifically what the duty of an academic teacher is. One can only demand of the teacher that he have the intellectual integrity to see that it is one thing to state facts, to determine mathematical or logical relations or the internal structure of cultural values, while it is another thing to answer questions of the *value* of culture and its individual contents and the question of how one should act in the cultural community and in political associations. These are quite heterogeneous problems. If he asks further why he should not deal with both types of problems in the lecture-room, the answer is: because the prophet and the demagogue do not belong on the academic platform.

To the prophet and the demagogue, it is said: 'Go your ways out into the streets and speak openly to the world', that is, speak where criticism is possible. In the lecture-room we stand opposite our audience, and it has to remain silent. I deem it irresponsible to exploit the circumstance that for the sake of their career the students have to attend a teacher's course while there is nobody present to oppose him with criticism. The task of the teacher is to serve the students with his knowledge and scientific experience and not to imprint upon them his personal political views. It is certainly possible that the individual teacher will not entirely succeed in eliminating his personal sympathies. He is then exposed to the sharpest criticism in the forum of his own conscience. And this deficiency does not prove anything; other errors are also possible, for instance, erroneous statements of fact, and yet they prove nothing against the duty of searching for the truth. I also reject this in the very interest of science. I am ready to prove from the works of our historians that whenever the man of science introduces his personal value judgement, a full understanding of the facts *ceases*. But this goes beyond tonight's topic and would require lengthy elucidation.

I ask only: How should a devout Catholic, on the one hand, and a Freemason, on the other, in a course on the forms of church and state or on religious history ever be brought to evaluate these subjects alike?

This is out of the question. And yet the academic teacher must desire and must demand of himself to serve the one as well as the other by his knowledge and methods. Now you will rightly say that the devout Catholic will never accept the view of the factors operative in bringing about Christianity which a teacher who is free of his dogmatic presuppositions presents to him. Certainly! The difference, however, lies in the following: Science 'free from presuppositions', in the sense of a rejection of religious bonds, does not know of the 'miracle' and the 'revelation'. If it did, science would be unfaithful to its own 'presuppositions'. The believer knows both, miracle and revelation. And science 'free from presuppositions' expects from him no less – and no more – than acknowledgement that if the process can be explained without those supernatural interventions, which an empirical explanation has to eliminate as causal factors, the process has to be explained the way science attempts to do. And the believer can do this without being disloyal to his faith.

But has the contribution of science no meaning at all for a man who does not care to know facts as such and to whom only the practical standpoint matters? Perhaps science nevertheless contributes something.

The primary task of a useful teacher is to teach his students to recognize 'inconvenient' facts – I mean facts that are inconvenient for their party opinions. And for every party opinion there are facts that are extremely inconvenient, for my own opinion no less than for others. I believe the teacher accomplishes more than a mere intellectual task if he compels his audience to accustom itself to the existence of such facts. I would be so immodest as even to apply the expression 'moral achievement'. though perhaps this may sound too grandiose for something that should go without saying.

Thus far I have spoken only of practical reasons for avoiding the imposition of a personal point of view. But these are not the only reasons. The impossibility of 'scientifically' pleading for practical and interested stands – except in discussing the means for a firmly given and presupposed end – rests upon reasons that lie far deeper.

'Scientific' pleading is meaningless in principle because the various value spheres of the world stand in irreconcilable conflict with each other. The elder Mill, whose philosophy I will not praise otherwise, was on this point right when he said: If one proceeds from pure experience, one arrives at polytheism. This is shallow in formulation and sounds paradoxical, and yet there is truth in it. If anything, we realize again today that something can be sacred not only in spite of its not being beautiful, but rather because and in so far as it is not beautiful. You will find this documented in the fifty-third chapter of the book of Isaiah and in the twenty-first Psalm. And, since Nietzsche, we realize that something can be beautiful, not only in spite of the aspect in which it is not good, but rather in that very aspect. ... It is commonplace to observe that something may be true although it is not beautiful and not holy and not good. Indeed it may be true in precisely those aspects. But all these are only the most elementary cases of the struggle that the gods of the various orders and values are engaged in. I do not know how one might wish to decide 'scientifically' the value of French and German culture; for here, too, different gods struggle with one another, now and for all times to come.

Source: Weber, 1970/1918, pp.143–8

1.2 Alvin W. Gouldner, 'Anti-minotaur: the myth of a value-free sociology' (1961)

Presidential address delivered at the annual meetings of the Society for the Study of Social Problems, 28 August 1961.

This is an account of a myth created by and about a magnificent minotaur named Max – Max Weber, to be exact; his myth was that social science should and could be value-free. The lair of this minotaur, although reached only by a labrynthian logic and visited only by a few who never return, is still regarded by many sociologists as a holy place. In particular, as sociologists grow older they seem impelled to make a pilgrimage to it and to pay their respects to the

problem of the relations between values and social science.

  ...

[T]he myth of a value-free sociology has been a conquering one. Today, all the powers of sociology, from Parsons to Lundberg, have entered into a tacit alliance to bind us to the dogma that 'Thou shalt not commit a value judgement', especially as sociologists. Where is the introductory textbook, where the lecture course on principles, that does not affirm or imply this rule?

  ...

I do not here wish to enter into an examination of

the *logical* arguments involved, not because I regard them as incontrovertible but because I find them less interesting to me as a sociologist. Instead what I will do is to view the belief in a value-free sociology in the same manner that sociologists examine any element in the ideology of any group. This means that we will look upon the sociologist just as we would any other occupation, be it the taxi-cab driver, the nurse, the coal miner, or the physician. In short, I will look at the belief in a value-free sociology as part of the ideology of a working group and from the standpoint of the sociology of occupations.

...

That we are in the presence of a group myth, rather than a carefully formulated and well validated belief appropriate to scientists, may be discerned if we ask, just what is it that is believed by those holding sociology to be a value-free discipline? Does the belief in a value-free sociology mean that, in point of fact, sociology is a discipline actually free of values and that it successfully excludes all non-scientific assumptions in selecting, studying, and reporting on a problem? Or does it mean that sociology *should* do so. Clearly, the first is untrue and I know of no one who even holds it possible for sociologists to exclude completely their non-scientific beliefs from their scientific work; and if this is so, on what grounds can this impossible task [be] held to be morally incumbent on sociologists?

Does the belief in a value-free sociology mean that sociologists cannot, do not, or should not make value judgements concerning things outside their sphere of technical competence? But what has technical competence to do with the making of value judgements? If technical competence does provide a warrant for making value judgements then there is nothing to prohibit sociologists from making them within the area of their expertise. If, on the contrary, technical competence provides no warrant for making value judgements then, at least sociologists are as *free* to do so as anyone else; then their value judgements are at least as good as anyone else's, say, a twelve year old child's. And, by the way, if technical competence provides no warrant for making value judgements, then what does?

Does the belief in a value-free sociology mean that sociologists are or should be indifferent to the moral implications of their work? Does it mean that sociologists can and should make value judgements so long as they are careful to point out that these are different from 'merely' factual statements? Does it mean that sociologists cannot logically deduce values from facts? Does it mean that sociologists do not or should not have or express *feelings* for or against some of the things they study? Does it mean that sociologists

may and should inform laymen about techniques useful in realizing their own ends, if they are asked to do so, but that if they are not asked to do so they are to say nothing? Does it mean that sociologists should never take the initiative in asserting that some beliefs that laymen hold, such as the belief in the inherent inferiority of certain races, are false even when known to be contradicted by the facts of their discipline? Does it mean that social scientists should never speak out, or speak out only when invited, about the probable outcomes of a public course of action concerning which they are professionally knowledgeable? Does it mean that social scientists should never express values in their roles as teachers or in their roles as researchers, or in both? Does the belief in a value-free sociology mean that sociologists, either as teachers or researchers, have a right to covertly and unwittingly express their values but have no right to do so overtly and deliberately?

I fear that there are many sociologists today who, in conceiving social science to be value-free, mean widely different things, that many hold these beliefs dogmatically without having examined seriously the grounds upon which they are credible, and that some few affirm a value-free sociology ritualistically without having any clear idea what it might mean. Weber's own views on the relation between values and social science, and some current today are scarcely identical. While Weber saw grave hazards in the sociologist's expression of value judgements, he also held that these might be voiced if caution was exercised to distinguish them from statements of fact. If Weber insisted on the need to maintain scientific objectivity, he also warned that this was altogether different from moral indifference.

...

The needs which the value-free conception of social science serves are both personal and institutional. Briefly, my contention will be that, among the main institutional forces facilitating the survival and spread of the value-free myth, was its usefulness in maintaining both the cohesion and the autonomy of the modern university, in general, and the newer social science disciplines, in particular. There is little difficulty, at any rate, in demonstrating that these were among the motives originally inducing Max Weber to formulate the conception of a value-free sociology.

...

When Weber condemned the lecture hall as a forum for value-affirmation he had in mind most particularly the expression of *political* values. The point of Weber's polemic is not directed against all values with equal sharpness. It was not the expression of aesthetic or even religious values that Weber sees as most objectionable in the University, but, primarily, those of politics. His promotion of the value-free doctrine may, then, be seen not so much as an effort to amoralize as to depoliticize the University and to remove it from the political struggle. The political conflicts then echoing in the German university did not entail comparatively trivial differences, such as those now between Democrats and Republicans in the United States. Weber's proposal of the value-free doctrine was, in part, an effort to establish a *modus vivendi* among academicians whose political commitments were often intensely felt and in violent opposition.

Under these historical conditions, the value-free doctrine was a proposal for an academic truce. It said, in effect, if we all keep quiet about our political views then we may all be able to get on with our work. But if the value-free principle was suitable in Weber's Germany because it served to restrain political passions, is it equally useful in America today where, not only is there pitiable little difference in politics but men often have no politics at all. ...

...

In a *realpolitik* vein, Weber acknowledges that the most basic national questions cannot ordinarily be discussed with full freedom in government universities. Since the discussion there cannot be completely free and all-sided, he apparently concludes that it is fitting there should be no discussion at all, rather than risk partisanship. But this is too pious by far. Even Socrates never insisted that all views must be at hand before the dialogue could begin. Here again one might as reasonably argue to the contrary, holding that one limitation of freedom is no excuse for another. Granting the reality of efforts to inhibit unpopular views in the University, it seems odd to prescribe self-suppression as a way of avoiding external suppression. Suicide does not seem a reasonable way to avoid being murdered. It appears, however, that Weber was so intent on safeguarding the autonomy of the university and the autonomy of politics that he was willing to pay almost any price to do so, even if this led the university to detach itself from one of the basic intellectual traditions of the west – the dialectical exploration of the fundamental purposes of human life.

Insofar as the value-free doctrine is a mode of ensuring professional autonomy, note that it does not, as such, entail an interest peculiar to the social sciences. In this regard, as a substantial body of research in the sociology of occupations indicates, social scientists are kin to plumbers, house painters, or librarians. For most if not all occupations seek to elude control by outsiders and manifest a drive to maintain exclusive control over their practitioners.

Without doubt the value-free principle did enhance the autonomy of sociology; it was one way in which our discipline pried itself loose – in some modest measure – from the clutch of its society, in Europe freer from political party influence, in the United States freer of ministerial influence. In both places, the value-free doctrine gave sociology a larger area of autonomy in which it could steadily pursue basic problems rather than journalistically react to passing events, and allowed it more freedom to pursue questions uninteresting either to the respectable or to the rebellious. It made sociology freer – as Comte had wanted it to be – to pursue all its own theoretical implications. In other words, the value-free principle did, I think, contribute to the intellectual growth and emancipation of our enterprise.

...

The value-free doctrine thus had a paradoxical potentiality: it might enable men to make *better* value judgements rather than *none*. It could encourage a habit of mind that might help men in discriminating between their punitive drives and their ethical sentiments. Moralistic reflexes suspended, it was now more possible to sift conscience with the rod of reason and to cultivate moral judgements that expressed a man's total character as an adult person; he need not now live quite so much by his past parental programming but in terms of his more mature present.

The value-free doctrine could have meant an opportunity for a more authentic morality. It could and sometimes did aid men in transcending the morality of their 'tribe'. to open themselves to the diverse moralities of unfamiliar groups, and to see themselves and others from the standpoint of a wider range of sgnificant cultures. But the value-free doctrine also had other, less fortunate, results as well.

Doubtless there were some who did use the opportunity thus presented; but there were, also, many who used the value-free postulate as an excuse for pursuing their private impulses to the neglect of their public responsibilities and who, far from becoming more morally sensitive, became morally jaded. Insofar as the value-free doctrine failed to realize its potentialities it did so because its deepest impulses were – as we shall note later – dualistic; it invited men to stress the separation and not the mutual connectedness of facts and values: it had the vice of its virtues. In short, the conception of a value-free sociology has had *diverse* consequences, not all of them useful or flattering to the social sciences.

On the negative side, it may be noted that the value-free doctrine is useful both to those who want to escape *from* the world and to those who want to escape *into* it. It is useful to those young, or not so young men, who live off sociology rather than for it, and who think of sociology as a way of getting ahead in the world by providing them with neutral techniques that may be sold on the open market to any buyer. The belief that it is not the business of a sociologist to make value-judgements is taken, by some, to mean that the market on which they can vend their skills is unlimited. From such a standpoint, there is no reason why one cannot sell his knowledge to spread a disease just as freely as he can to fight it. Indeed, some sociologists have had no hesitation about doing market research designed to sell more cigarettes, although well aware of the implications of recent cancer research. In brief, the value-free doctrine of social science was sometimes used to justify the sale of one's talents to the highest bidder and is, far from new, a contemporary version of the most ancient sophistry.

In still other cases, the image of a value-free sociology is the armor of the alienated sociologist's self. Although C. Wright Mills may be right in saying this is the Age of Sociology, not a few sociologists and Mills included, feel estranged and isolated from their society. They feel impotent to contribute usefully to the solution of its deepening problems and, even when they can, they fear that the terms of such an involvement require them to submit to a commercial debasement or a narrow partisanship, rather than contributing to a truly public interest.

...

Self-doubt finds its anodyne in the image of a value-free sociology because this transforms their alienation into an intellectual principle; it evokes the soothing illusion, among some sociologists, that their exclusion from the larger society is a self-imposed duty rather than an externally imposed constraint.

Once committed to the premise of a value-free sociology, such sociologists are bound to a policy which can only alienate them further from the surrounding world. Social science can never be fully accepted in a society, or by a part of it, without paying its way; this means it must manifest both its relevance and concern for the contemporary human predicament. Unless the value-relevances of sociological inquiry are made plainly evident, unless there are at least some bridges between it and larger human hopes and purposes, it must inevitably be scorned by laymen as pretentious word-mongering. But the manner in which some sociologists conceive the value-free doctrine disposes them to ignore current human problems and to huddle together like old men seeking mutual warmth. ...The issue, however, is not whether we know enough; the real questions are whether we have the courage to say and use what we do know and whether anyone knows more.

...

One latent meaning, then, of the image of a value-free sociology is this: 'Thou shalt not commit a critical or negative value-judgement – especially of one's own society.' Like a neurotic symptom this aspect of the value-free image is rooted in a conflict; it grows out of an effort to compromise between conflicting drives: On the one side, it reflects a conflict between the desire to criticize social institutions, which since Socrates has been the legacy of intellectuals, and the fear of reprisals if one does criticize – which is also a very old and human concern. On the other side, this aspect of the value-free image reflects a conflict between the fear of being critical and the fear of being regarded an unmanly or lacking in integrity, if uncritical.

The doctrine of a value-free sociology resolves these conflicts by making it seem that those who refrain from social criticism are acting solely on behalf of a higher professional good rather than their private interests. In refraining from social criticism, both the timorous and the venal may now claim the protection of a high professional principle and, in so doing, can continue to hold themselves in decent regard....

Should social scientists affirm or critically explore values they would of necessity come up against powerful institutions who deem the statement or protection of public values as part of their special business. Should social scientists seem to compete in this business, they can run afoul of powerful forces and can, realistically, anticipate efforts at external curbs and controls. In saying this, however, we have to be careful lest we needlessly exacerbate academic timorousness. Actually, my own first-hand impressions of many situations where sociologists serve as consultants indicate that, once their clients come to know them, they are often quite prepared to have sociologists suggest (not dictate) policy and to have them express their own values. Nor does this always derive from the expectation that sociologists will see things their way and share their values. Indeed, it is precisely the expected difference in perspectives that is occasionally desired in seeking consultation. I find it difficult not to sympathize with businessmen who jeer at sociologists when they suddenly become more devoted to business values than the businessmen themselves.

Clearly all this does not mean that people will tolerate disagreement on basic values with social scientists more equably than they will with anyone else. Surely there is no reason why the principles governing social interaction should be miraculously suspended just because one of the parties to a social relation is a social scientist. The dangers of public resentment are real but they are only normal. They are not inconsistent with the possibility that laymen may be perfectly ready to allow social scientists as much (or as little) freedom of value expression as they would anyone else. And what more could any social scientist want?

The value-free image of social science is not consciously held for expedience's sake; it is not contrived deliberately as a hedge against public displeasure. It could not function as a face-saving device if it were. What seems more likely is that it entails something in the nature of a tacit bargain: in return for a measure of autonomy and social support, many social scientists have surrendered their critical impulses. This was not usually a callous 'sell-out' but a slow process of mutual accommodation; both parties suddenly found themselves betrothed without a formal ceremony.

Nor am I saying that the critical posture is dead in American sociology; it is just badly sagging. ...By no means have all sociologists rejected the legacy of the intellectual, namely, the right to be critical of tradition. This ancient heritage still remains embedded in the underground culture of sociology; and it comprises the enshadowed part of the occupational selves of many sociologists even if not publicly acknowledged.

...

... The dominant drift in American sociology is toward professionalization, the growth of technical specialists, toward the diffusion of the value-free outlook to the point where it becomes less of an intellectual doctrine and more of a blanketing mood. American sociology is in the process of accommodating itself.

... Weber's doctrine of a value-free sociology ... creates a gulf between science and values. ... The core of Weber's outlook rested on a dualism between, on the one hand, reason or rationality, especially as embodied in bureaucracy and science, and, on the other hand, more elemental emotional forces, partly encompassed in his notion of Charisma. He regards each of these forces as inimical to the other. He himself is ambivalent to each of them, viewing each as both dangerous and necessary.

On the one side, Weber is deeply concerned to protect the citadel of modern reason, the University, and fiercely opposes the professorial 'cult of personality' which was the academic expression of the charismatic claim. This in turn disposes him to project an image of the university which is essentially bureaucratic, as a faceless group of specialists, each sovereign in his own cell and all sworn to foresake their individuality. Nonetheless he also hates bureacracy precisely because it submerges individuality and dehumanizes men and is thus led to deny that he intended to bureaucratize the university in pleading for the doctrine of a value-free social science. (Yet while this was doubtless not his *intention*, his two-pronged polemic against the cult of academic personality and in favour of the value-free doctrine does seem to drive him toward such a bureaucratic conception of the University.)

If Weber is concerned to protect even the bureaucratic dwelling-places of rationality, he also seeks to confine bureaucracy and to circumscribe the area of its influence. In particular, he wishes to protect the highest reaches of statecraft from degenerating into a lifeless routine; he seeks to preserve politics as a realm in which there can be an expression of personal will, of serious moral commitment, a realm where greatness was possible to those who dared, persevered and suffered, a realm so powerful that it could overturn the institutional order or preserve it. He wants to safeguard high politics as an arena of human autonomy, of pure value choices, at its finest.

Yet Weber also fears for the safety of rationality in the modern world. He knows that there are powerful forces abroad which continue to threaten rationality, that there are still untamed things in men which he, more than most, had had to face. Not unlike Freud, Weber was both afraid of and drawn to these unbridled forces, the passionate Dionysian part of men. While he believed that they were being slowly subdued by an onmarching rationalization, he continued to fear that they could yet erupt and cleave modern institutional life. Although fearing these irrational forces, he also felt their disappearance from the modern world to be a 'disenchantment'. for he believed that they contained springs of vitality and power indispensable to human existence.

Weber is a man caught between two electrodes and torn by the current passing between them; he fears both but is unable to let go of either. He attempts to solve this dilemma by a strategy of segregation, seeking the exclusion of charismatic irrationality from certain modern *institutions*, such as the university, but admitting it into and, indeed, exalting its manifestations in the inward personal life of individuals. He wanted certain of the role structures of modern society to be rational; but he also wanted the role-players to be passionate and wilful. He wanted the play to be written by a classicist and to be acted by romanticists. Unusual man, he wanted the best of both worlds. Yet whatever the judgement of his intellect, his sentiments are not poised midway between them, but tend toward one of the two sides.

This becomes clear when we ask, if science cannot be the basis of value judgements, what then, according to Weber, was to be their basis? To answer this, we must go beyond his formal doctrine of a value-free sociology, to Weber's own personal profession of belief. Weber certainly did not hold that personal values should derive from the existent culture, or from ancient tradition, nor again from formal ethical systems which he felt to be empty and lifeless. Unless men were to become inhuman robots, life, he insisted, must be guided by consciously made decisions. If men are to have dignity, they must choose their own fate.

To Weber as a man, only those values are authentic which stem from conscious decision, from a consultation of the inner conscience and a wilful commitment to its dictates. From his *personal* standpoint, it is not really true that all values are equally worthy. Those consciously held by men are more worthy than those which are merely traditional and unthinkingly repeated. Those values that men feel deeply about and passionately long to realize are better than those which are merely intellectually appealing and do not engage their entire being.

In short, Weber, too, was seeking a solution to the competing claims of reason and faith. His solution takes the form of attempting to guard the autonomy of both spheres but, most especially I believe, the domain of conscience and faith. He wants a way in which reason and faith can cohabit platonically but not as full partners. The two orders are separate but unequal. For in Weber, reason only consults conscience and perhaps even cross-examines it. But conscience has the last word, and passion and will the last deed. Here Weber stands as half-Lutheran, half-Nietzschian.

If Weber thrusts powerfully at traditionalism, nonetheless his main campaign here is waged against science and reason and is aimed at confining their influence. To Weber, even reason must submit when conscience declares, Here I stand; I can do no other! Weber saw as authentic only those values that rest on the charismatic core of the self and on its claims to intuitive certainty. Weber, too, was a seeker after certainty, the certainty that is more apt to come from the arrogance of individual conscience. For while

much may be truly said of the arrogance of reason, reason always seeks reasons and is ready to sit down and talk about them.

…

The problem of a value-free sociology has its most poignant implications for the social scientist in his role as educator. If sociologists ought not express their personal values in the academic setting, how then are students to be safeguarded against the unwitting influence of these values which shape the sociologist's selection of problems, his preferences for certain hypotheses or conceptual schemes, and his neglect of others. For these are unavoidable and, in this sense, there is and can be no value-free sociology. The only choice is between an expression of one's values, as open and honest as it can be, this side of the psychoanalytical couch, and a vain ritual of moral neutrality which, because it invites men to ignore the vulnerability of reason to bias, leaves it at the mercy of irrationality.

…

I have suggested that, at its deepest roots, the myth of a value-free sociology was Weber's way of trying to adjudicate the tensions between two vital Western traditions: between reason and faith, between knowledge and feeling, between classicism and romanticism, between the head and the heart. Like Freud, Weber never really believed in an enduring peace or in a final resolution of this conflict. What he did was to seek a truce through the segregation of the contenders, by allowing each to dominate in different spheres of life. … many of his would-be followers today tend to … [a] conception of themselves as narrow technicians who reject responsibility for the cultural and moral consequences of their work. It is precisely because of the deeply dualistic implications of the current doctrine of a value-free sociology that I felt its most appropriate symbol to be the man-beast, the cleft creature, the Minotaur.

Source: Gouldner, 1962, pp.199–213

 # Terry Lovell, 'Feminist social theory: situated knowledges?' (1996)

The challenge of contemporary feminist theory has necessarily taken it into the heart of the most intractable questions of the nature of knowledge itself. The first move which has had to be made within each discipline has been to deconstruct what has passed for knowledge so as to expose its masculinist

perspective and associated exclusions. The second has often quickly followed the first, that of advancing either strong claims for 'women's knowledge', or perhaps more cautious affirmations of the possibilities of 'feminist standpoint epistemology.'

Feminists have not addressed these difficult issues

in a vacuum. There has been a longstanding crisis in the status and credentials of what passes for knowledge, especially within the social sciences, that dates back at least to the last decades of the nineteenth century. Two limit positions may be identified. The first is an unreconstructed objectivism still prevalent within the most prestigious of the natural sciences. The second is that of disavowing epistemological claims.

In this second category many of the contemporary postmodernists and poststructuralists are to be found, including Richard Rorty, who advances a pragmatic theory of knowledge. He offers 'an anti-representationalist account of the relation between natural science and the rest of culture ... one which does not view knowledge as a matter of getting reality right, but rather as a matter of acquiring habits of action for coping with reality' (1991, p.1).

I must remain skeptical, struck, for example, by the double standard so often in evidence. Rorty's critique of his opponents, the scientific and philosophical realists, is not based on pragmatic criteria ('Is it good for us to believe this?' (1991, p.22)) but on the traditional exposure of intellectual error. He simply does not arraign at the bar of pragmatism theories which might presumably be wrong, but useful, and indeed it is hard to see how he could. Rosi Braidotti echoes Gilles Deleuze in presenting ideas as 'projectiles launched into time' that can be neither true nor false (Braidotti, 1991, p.125). We may only ask their effects. Unfortunately our answers, in turn, must be no more than further projectiles. If the truth of an assertion is unknowable, so too must be the truth of assertions about its effects.

The task of most feminist epistemology has been to attempt to construct an approach that on the one hand enables the deconstruction of natural and social sciences for their accounts of 'women' and 'the feminine', while yet avoiding cutting the epistemological ground from under feminism's own feet. A number of feminists have attempted to construct what they have termed 'feminist standpoint epistemology' to steer a course between objectivism and epistemological denial.

Feminist standpoint epistemology, as developed by Nancy Hartsock (1983), Sandra Harding (1986; 1987), Donna Haraway (1991), and others, is rooted in Marxism (although Liz Stanley (Stanley and Wise, 1993) advances claims for another genealogy, which traces radical feminist standpoints back to Dorothy Smith and phenomenology (Smith, 1987; Stanley, 1990)).

It is my intention here to do no more than to trace the manner in which feminist standpoint theory has

attempted to address the critique from diversity. For although the term most often used is 'feminist standpoint' there is an elision in much of this writing between 'feminist' and 'women', a gap which is papered over by the assumption that to be a feminist is precisely 'to take the standpoint of women'. But the critique from diversity instantly forces us to ask 'which women?' Women do not all share the same interests; indeed sometimes their interests may be directly opposed.

Donna Haraway has offered us the concept of 'situated knowledges' as a way forward. Her own intellectual trajectory, like that of Harding, has taken her away from her starting point into a stance that is more postmodernist than socialist-feminist (in spite of the title) in the essay 'A Cyborg Manifesto: Science, Technology, and Socialist-Feminism in the Late Twentieth Century.' She was surely one feminist that Susan Bordo had in mind in her criticism of postmodernist feminism and 'gender-scepticism' (Bordo, 1990), and the essay on 'situated knowledges' may be read as Haraway's response to this criticism. Bordo accused postmodernism of substituting for 'the view from nowhere' of traditional objectivist science an equally imaginary 'view from everywhere'. Haraway insists that all knowledge is produced from somewhere – all knowledge is 'situated'. She offers the vision of 'a joining of partial views and halting voices into a collective subject position that promises a vision of the means of on-going finite embodiment, of living within limits and contradictions, i.e., of views from somewhere' (1991, p.196). This position, or one like it, is becoming the dominant view within contemporary feminism. Attractive though it is, a number of difficulties remain.

The idea of 'standpoints' within Marxist-feminist epistemology was one which was tenable only so long as a limited number of standpoints might in principle be specified. It depended in other words on the belief that the terrain which gives us our 'standpoint' might be mapped, to enable bearings to be taken. The structure that mapped the Marxian 'social formation' was that of the (contradictory) 'social forces and relations of production'. Marxist feminists added 'gender'; black feminists 'race'. However, within postmodernist worlds, the terrain within which we are situated is itself shifting. It is a landscape with constantly changing features. How may we situate ourselves and our knowledges in such landscapes? What counts as a 'situation' from which knowledge may be produced? Do we share our 'situation' with others? Can we even be said to do so 'partially' in the light of the arguments mounted by Spelman and others? What is to stop the slide from 'standpoints' to familiar individualistic liberal pluralism, which is where much postmodernist thought has ended? Even postmodernists continue, *de facto,* to take soundings in terms of 'race', class, gender, and ethnicity. Does this not suggest that, after all, these *are* the major *structuring* dimensions of the contemporary world. Does this discredit 'poststructuralism?'

It is my belief that we are still at the early stages in the development of feminist social, political, and philosophical theory, but that we have at least reached a juncture in which we are perhaps rather better tooled for the task of the historical analysis of gender in society and culture. And finally, it is by substantive, historically specific but theoretically informed *analysis* rather than pure theory alone that the feminist project will be advanced. On this perhaps Marxist, postmodernist, and radical feminisms may be agreed.

References

Bordo, S. (1990) 'Feminism, postmodernism, and gender-scepticism' in Nicholson, L.J. (ed.) *Feminism/Postmodernism*, New York and London, Routledge.

Braidotti, R. (1991) *Patterns of Dissonance* (trans. E. Gould), Oxford, Polity Press.

Haraway, D.J. (1991) *Symians, Cyborgs, and Women*, London, Free Association Books.

Harding, S. (1986) *The Science Question in Feminism*, Milton Keynes, Open University Press.

Harding, S. (1987) *Feminism and Methodology*, Bloomington and Indianapolis, IN, Indiana University Press.

Hartsock, N. (1983) 'The feminist standpoint: developing the ground for a specifically feminist historical materialism' in Harding, S. and Hintikka, M. (eds) *Discovering Reality*, Dordrecht, Reidel.

Rorty, R. (1991) *Objectivity, Relativism and Truth*, Cambridge, Cambridge University Press.

Smith, D. (1987) *The Everyday World as Problematic*, Boston, MA, North Eastern University Press.

Stanley, L. (1990) *Feminist Praxis: Research, Theory and Epistemology in Feminist Sociology*, London, Routledge.

Stanley, L. and Wise, S. (1993) *Breaking Out*, London, Routledge.

Source: Lovell, 1996, pp.335–7

1.4 Barry Smart, 'Post-modern social theory' (1996)

… Derrida's view is that Western thought is characterized by a 'metaphysics of presence'… But this is unrealizable, for reason is necessarily burdened with language and cannot achieve pure, self-authenticating truth. There is no possibility of an unmediated access to reality, for the logic of analysis is itself constituted through various spatial and visual metaphors. Reason then cannot dispel the opacity of intertextuality, and this is one of the ways in which Derrida's much celebrated, derided, and misunderstood observation that *'Il n'y a pas de hors-texte'* (1967, p.227) has been read. But such an interpretation does not exhaust the meaning of this disputed phrase; indeed it constitutes, at best, a limited reading.

The comment that there is nothing outside the text has licensed all manner of wild responses, particularly from critics eager to consign Derrida's philosophy to a metaphysical dustbin. But if we are to do something more than simply lend our voice to the chorus of derision which has greeted the idea that there is 'nothing beyond the text' it is necessary to abstain from premature judgement and to give careful consideration to Derrida's notion of *text.* When this is done it becomes clear that the notion of text and the associated practices of deconstruction are not confined to books, discourses, and conceptual and semantic contents alone. Rather, the concept of text is recast and extended 'almost without limit' to encompass not only systems of thought but also the social and political institutions with which they are articulated, that is, why 'there is nothing *"beyond* the text"' (Derrida, 1986, p.167). Furthermore, clarification of the notion of text makes possible a recognition of the political character of deconstructive practice. As Derrida remarks, 'because it is never concerned only with signified content, deconstruction should not be separated from this political-institutional problematic and should seek a new investigation of responsibility, an investigation which questions the codes inherited from ethics and politics' (1984, p.42).[1] In short, deconstruction is necessarily political … (Derrida, 1978).

… [I]t is with the deconstruction of metaphysics that Derrida's work is generally identified …

… Derrida portrays Western metaphysics as based upon a series of metaphorical binary oppositions in which one element is accorded a privileged status, the most pertinent to his argument being the writing/ speech opposition intrinsic to the metaphysics of presence or 'logocentrism' [word-focused thought]. Deconstruction works to unravel Western metaphysics by challenging the primacy accorded to speech and promoting the claims of *writing* as effectively the precondition of language. In short, Derrida takes issue with the idea that speech is closer to 'psychic inferiority (that itself reflects things in the world by means of natural resemblance)' (Kamuf, 1991, p.30) and that writing is merely mirroring speech, is simply phonetic transcription. After identifying a series of metaphors which serve to privilege speech and to draw attention away from the signifying system through which it is constituted and sustained, Derrida proceeds to develop a more radical sense of writing to refer to the element of undecidability intrinsic to communication, 'to the endless displacement of meaning which both governs language and places it for ever beyond the reach of a stable, self-authenticating language' (Norris, 1982, p.29). As with the notion of text, Derrida produces a new concept of *writing,* one which is 'not limited to the paper which you cover with your graphism' [handwriting] (1986, p.167).

At issue here is the model of phonetic writing and the Saussurean exclusion of writing from the field of linguistics. Given, as Derrida demonstrates, that there is 'no purely phonetic writing ... then the entire phonologist or logocentrist logic becomes problematical' (1982, pp.25–6). It is in this context of working to overturn and displace the privileging of the phonic (temporal) over the graphic (spatial) that Derrida argues that a simple inversion of the dissymmetry which privileges writing still leaves us within the binary opposition speech/writing and, in consequence, is no less problematic. It is in acknowledgement of the play of differences and 'economy of traces' which are intrinsic to all processes of signification that Derrida introduces the concept of writing as *différance*. No conceptual element signifies by itself, 'an element functions and signifies, takes on or conveys meaning, only by referring to another past or future element in an economy of traces' (p.29). Hence the idea that it is through difference, that is, the 'systematic play of differences', that the process of signification is possible.

In sum the position taken by Derrida is that 'the medium of the great metaphysical, scientific, technical, and economic adventure of the West [phonetic writing], is limited in time and space' (1978, p.10), indeed is drawing to a close. Taking issue with the logocentricity of Western metaphysics, Derrida, identifies the (re-)entry of language as the moment at which Western metaphysics begins to unravel, the moment when it became necessary to recognize that no fixed, permanent centre or fundamental ground is available. Indeed, more than that, that there never was a centre or foundation which could provide the reassurance of certitude. ...

...

Whilst both Foucault and Derrida have been increasingly closely identified with postmodern social and philosophical thought there is no sustained address of the postmodern in their respective works, and to that extent perhaps they constitute less significant figures than Lyotard and Baudrillard, both of whom have sought to elaborate, albeit in different ways, on the question of the postmodern. Because his report on transformations in the condition of knowledge has had such an impact upon contemporary debates the figure of Lyotard is frequently equated with the notion of the postmodern. However, Baudrillard's claims to postmodern status are no less significant, particularly if the frame of reference is broadened beyond the confines of the academy to embrace contemporary culture, communications, and the proverbial signs in the streets.

Note

1   The text is a translation of the French original: 'parce qu'elle n'a jamais concerné seulement des contenus de sens, la déconstruction devrait ne pas être séparable de cette problématique politico-institutionnelle et réquérir un questionnement nouveau sur la responsabilité. un questionnement qui ne se fie plus nécessairement aux codes hérités du politique ou de l'ethique.'

References

Derrida J. (1967) *De la Grammatologie*, Paris, Editions de Minuit.

Derrida, J. (1978) *Writing and Difference*, London, Routledge.

Derrida, J. (1982) *Positions*, Chicago, IL, University of Chicago Press.

Derrida, J. (1984) 'MOCHLOS ou le conflit des facultés', *Philosophie*, vol.2, pp.21–53.

Derrida, J. (1986) Open letter to Anne McClintock and Rob Nixon, *Critical Inquiry*, 13, pp.155–70.

Kamuf, P. (ed.) (1991) *A Derrida Reader: Between the Blinds*, London, Harvester-Wheatsheaf.

Norris, C. (1982) *Deconstruction: Theory and Practice*, London, Methuen.

Source: Smart, 1996, pp.401–04

Sociology and government

Tony Bennett

Contents

1 Introduction

On the face of it, sociology and government make strange bedfellows. Sociology, in the UK at least, is usually seen as a generalist discipline rather than a strongly vocational one, and it is not the most obvious choice – compared with law, say – for those seeking a career in government. It has also, especially since the 1960s, been seen – and has seen itself – as a radical discipline with strong attachments to social movements, with the result that it has often adopted a critical stance in relation to government. Rather than providing a cadre of intellectuals who have sought to work within government, it has produced social critics who have been more likely to call government to account for its shortcomings in tackling difficult social problems. This is true, for example, of

Habermas, Jürgen

sociologists working in the tradition represented by **Jürgen Habermas**, as you will see from Jim McGuigan's discussion in the next chapter. For them, sociology's most important responsibility is to contribute to the development of a public sphere that will call the bureaucratic mechanisms of government to task, to the extent that these mechanisms fall short of the demands generated by a general human interest in emancipation.

third way politics

Yet in the late 1990s and early 2000s some schools of sociology entered into a close relationship with government through an association with the agendas of **third way politics**, as represented in the UK by New Labour. The significance of this association has been noted by several commentators. For Alan Finlayson, New Labour's distinctiveness lies in the fact that it formulates its political ideas 'on the basis of a "sociological" claim about the novel condition of contemporary society; a belief that the world has been transformed, while our political ideas have not kept up the pace' (Finlayson, 1999, p.271). For Angela McRobbie, the Third Way is 'a sociology of government' and, as such, represents 'the first time that the once-ridiculed discipline of sociology has gained such recognition' (McRobbie, 2000, p.98). And for Martin Albrow, the Third Way is to be welcomed by sociologists for 'its rehabilitation of society as a focus for policy concern' (Albrow, 2001, p.10).

Giddens, Anthony

Albrow goes on to suggest that 'British sociologists must take satisfaction in the influence that **Anthony Giddens** has enjoyed as the world spokesman for the Third Way' (2001, p.10), and in doing so he highlights another important aspect of this phenomenon: the fact that these new symbiotic relations between sociology and government have become publicly visible in distinctive ways through the high profile of Anthony Giddens and his close relationship with Tony Blair. As the author of *The Third Way: The Renewal of Social Democracy* (1998) and its sequel *The Third Way and its Critics* (2000), Anthony Giddens – Director of the London School of Economics and Political Science, and previously Professor of Sociology at the University of Cambridge – has enjoyed a public prominence unrivalled by any contemporary British intellectual and without parallel in the history of British sociology (see Peter Hamilton's and Ken Thompson's discussion of this in the Introduction to this volume). Featured regularly in the weekend colour supplements, and honoured by the BBC in being invited to give the prestigious Reith Lectures for 1999 (his topic was globalization), he has been seen as 'Tony Blair's guru' – as a part of his inner circle, enjoying access to the highest echelons of government as a matter of course. (Giddens was part of Blair's entourage when Blair flew to Washington to meet President Clinton in 1999.) For David Walker, writing in *The Guardian*, Giddens was 'the brain behind Tony Blair's "third way"' (Walker, 1999, p.17), while for Anne Karpf, also in *The Guardian*, he was 'globalisation in one person' (Karpf, 1999, p.9). Similarly, in the *Sunday Times*, Frederick Mount, while complaining of the 'eerie vacuousness' and 'utter staleness' of Giddens's Reith Lectures, grudgingly acknowledged that Giddens was 'perhaps our first home-grown global guru' (Mount, 1999).

If we look at the matter a little more closely, however, the picture becomes more complicated. For some, Martin Albrow included, sociology's influence in developing the agendas of the Third Way does not make up for the fact that, in his estimation, British sociology has had little impact on the bureaucratic machineries of government, as represented by the various Whitehall departments in which the details of government policies are developed and monitored. For others, the links between Giddens (and the tendencies in sociology he represents), the Third Way and New Labour are politically problematic. This is especially true for those sociologists who were associated with the New Times analysis that was developed in *Marxism Today* in the 1980s. The most influential representative of this analysis was **Stuart Hall**. It developed initially as a critique of Thatcherism and argued the need for new political ideas to be developed in response to rapid changes in society. Its influence in this respect was significant: it played a major role in revising the language, strategies and priorities of the Old Left and contributed to the development of New Labour. Blair, for example, was a regular reader of *Marxism Today* and was featured in its 'Back page' questionnaire in July 1990 (see Figure 2.1). In the end, however, the New Times analysis was to prove less influential with the Labour leadership than that of the Third Way. With strong attachments to the emergence of **new social movements** and a continuing commitment to a view of society as inherently conflict-ridden, New Times proved to be less adept in developing a language and forms of analysis that could interface with those of New Labour as it made the transition into office. If the work of Anthony Giddens and other theorists of the Third Way proved more successful in this respect, then this has been at the price, so their New Times critics have argued, of offering an anodyne analysis of society that masks its key contradictions. In a special issue of *Marxism Today*, revived solely for the purpose of reviewing New Labour's first year in office, Stuart Hall criticized the Third Way for behaving 'as if there are no longer any conflicting interests which cannot be reconciled' (Hall, 1998, p.10). In response, this attracted the criticism that the New Times analysis had itself fallen behind the times in failing to keep up with new social tendencies that made inherently conflictual models of society outmoded (see Mulgan, 1998).

Nor are these the only voices raised in criticism of the rapprochement between the concerns of sociology and the politics of New Labour that Anthony Giddens most publicly represents. Far from it: Angela McRobbie (2000), while welcoming aspects of this rapprochement, takes both Giddens and New Labour to task for their failure to accord sufficient attention to the needs and circumstances of women. Nikolas Rose castigates Giddens's conception of the Third Way for what he sees as its utter lack of political inventiveness (Rose, 1999b). My interest here, however, is not with the rights and wrongs of the different sides in these debates about the relative merits of New Times or the Third Way. It is rather in what the very existence of such debates tells us about one aspect of the uses of sociology. For we can see, in the claims and counter-

Hall, Stuart

new social movements (NSMs)

BACK PAGE

Tony Blair

What newspapers/magazines do you take? *Daily Mirror, The Financial Times, The Guardian, The Independent, Marxism Today* and *The Economist.*

What foreign languages do you speak? French.

What is your favourite tv programme? *Fawlty Towers.*

When do you listen to music? In the car.

When was the last time you prayed? Yesterday.

What was your first thought this morning? Kathryn's nappy needs changing.

What is the most common colour in your wardrobe? Dark blue.

What is your favourite meeting place? The Fox and Hounds, Trimdon village, for its atmosphere.

What is your favourite piece of architecture? Durham Cathedral and Holly Street Estate, Hackney, London.

Who do you reveal your secrets to? Depends on the secret, but usually to Cherie.

What makes you feel secure? Love.

What do you blame your parents for? Thinking that sending me to public school would be a good career move?

When did you last visit your parents? Last month.

How do you envy your children's lifestyle? Getting up early in the morning and apparently enjoying it.

You're driving through a hot, desolate expanse. What's playing on the stereo? Tom Petty: *Runnin' Down A Dream.*

What is your city of the 90s? Any capital of Eastern Europe, I hope.

Tony Blair was born in Edinburgh in 1953. He studied law at St John's College, Oxford, where he shunned student politics to play lead guitar in a band called *Ugly Rumours*. After university he joined the Labour Party, though his father carries the Tory Party card. For seven years he practised as a barrister and then entered parliament in 1983 as MP for Sedgefield. In 1988, he was elected to the shadow cabinet and today he is Labour's chief spokesperson on employment. He is married to barrister Cherie Booth and they have three young children

Where do you wish you were living? County Durham

Where is your favourite holiday destination? The west coast of Scotland.

How has your diet changed in the past 10 years? Less fat, more balance.

What physical exercise do you do? Tennis and walking

Under what circumstances would you use private medicine? If my kids were ever at risk and it was the only way I could help them

At what age do you want to stop working? When I die.

Do you really need your car? No.

Do you own shares? No

What is your favourite advertisement? Hamlet cigars.

What are you doing for the environment? The usual things: lead-free car, etc. But more importantly, making it connect with my politics.

What part of your life would you take into another life? Childhood.

Who is your hero? I don't have a hero, but the person who most influenced me was Peter Thompson, the principal of St Mark's College, Adelaide.

What do you no longer believe in? Certainty.

What would you die for? That's not something you can answer until the choice is real.

What current campaign do you most support? Campaigns for the Third World.

What do you now own that you had never dreamed of owning? A British car with a Japanese engine

What is the greatest amount of money you've spent on an item of clothing? Two hundred pounds on a suit.

What hi-tech device scares you? Any.

How much time do you spend each day on the phone? Too much.

What were you doing when Mandela was freed? Watching it on tv.

In one word, how has the Rushdie affair left you thinking? Depressed

Complete this sentence: If I was dictator for a day... I'd make sure my political monument was more than a gesture

How do you personally hope to change by the end of the millennium? To have a sense of achievement ●

Figure 2.1 *Blair before Blairism*

Source: *Marxism Today*, July 1990, p.48

claims of these different schools of sociological thought, an interest – and, in Giddens's case, some degree of success – in making sociological ideas practical in terms of the influence they exert on the intellectual frameworks within which government policies are developed. This is an important aspect of the relationships between sociology and government. At the same time, however, the perspective that it offers on those relationships is a limited one, restricted to the extent to which sociological ideas can capture the thinking of the political and administrative elites which – if elected – are able to determine the directions of state policy.

ACTIVITY I

Why is this a limited perspective? Draw on your studies in earlier parts of the course to suggest how a broader perspective on the relations between sociology and government might be developed.

The chief limitation of this perspective is that it restricts what is understood by 'government' to the activities of the **state**. While this is a long-standing concept **state** of government in western social and political thought, it has recently been challenged by the literature that developed in the wake of the writings of **Michel** **Foucault, Michel** **Foucault** on the subject of 'governmentality'. The effect of this literature has been to expand the concept of government to include the activities of a whole range of agents and authorities that *do not* form part of the state. Here, for example, is how Mitchell Dean defines this expanded concept of government:

> Government is any more or less calculated and rational activity, undertaken by a multiplicity of authorities and agencies, employing a variety of techniques and forms of knowledge, that seeks to shape conduct by working through our desires, aspirations, interests and beliefs, for definite but shifting ends and with a diverse set of relatively unpredictable consequences, effects and outcomes.
>
> (Dean, 1999, p.11)

You might think this too broad a definition, and it certainly runs the risk of being so all-encompassing that there is little that would *not* count as government. Leaving this difficulty aside for the moment, however, the aspects of the definition I want to note are those that see 'techniques and forms of knowledge' as central to the ways in which government works. This, too, reflects the influence of Foucault, who argued for a break with the concern, evident in earlier theories of the state, with examining how **ideologies** legitimate state power, in favour **ideology** of a broader inquiry into the ways in which different forms of knowledge are tangled up in the exercise of the varied forms of power that make up different fields of government (see **Dean, 2002**). And in arguing this, Foucault also urged the need to consider knowledge in its technical aspects – that is, knowledge in the form of the varied practical techniques for knowing that characterize different disciplines – rather than as just a set of abstract ideas.

It is, then, from these two perspectives – the broader understanding of government that is involved in the concept of governmentality, and the stress this concept places on the importance of knowledge – that I want to look at the relations between sociology and government in this chapter. I shall do so, moreover, with a view to looking at how sociology is translated into a range of technical forms in its application in different fields of government. This will involve a consideration of the respects in which both statistics and communities can be examined as parts of *technologies of government* which depend on the kinds of social knowledge and understanding produced by sociologists. Rather than pursue these matters abstractly, however, I shall take the agendas of the Third Way as a point of entry that will help to highlight their practical and current significance.

AIMS

In summary, the aims of this chapter are:

1   To examine the relations between sociology and government from the perspective of the concept of governmentality.

2   To consider how distinctive kinds of sociological knowledge, techniques and expertise function in the context of different fields of government.

3   To examine the role of sociology in the development of statistics as a modern technology of governing.

4   To consider the role assigned to sociology, in providing ways of knowing about and organizing communities, in contemporary strategies of government.

---

2 Social agendas of the Third Way

It is difficult, writing as I am just a few months after George W. Bush's election as President of the USA, to know whether to use the past or present tense in writing about the Third Way. For it is already clear that its use as a common currency for a shared transatlantic understanding of a new centrist political programme and philosophy is no longer viable. Whether this will sound the death knell for the Third Way in the UK remains to be seen, although the term was notably not a key part of the Labour Party's campaign in the 2001 General Election. I shall, however, use the present tense, but do so knowing that while the social and political perspectives that are currently 'branded' as the Third Way are unlikely to go away in the near future, the terms in which they are 'sold' politically may well change significantly.

What, then, given this qualification, are the main principles of the Third Way? Like all third ways, this question can be answered only by identifying the contending extremes to which the Third Way presents itself as an alternative. For as a political brand the Third Way is and has been, above all else, an attempt to redraw the political map, to redefine where the political right, left and centre are, and to do so in a way that allows the Third Way to emerge not as a middle way but as a new centrist political programme that can, at the same time, claim to be radical. The Third Way, in other words, does not simply place itself between the left and right of the existing political spectrum. Rather, it seeks to *redefine* the very space of politics, to declare the traditional divisions of left and right outmoded, and to place itself at the centre of a new way of mapping both political space (the left–right spectrum) and time (the division, for example, between Old and New Labour). And – as we have already seen – what drives this political programme is its responsiveness to social change. As Anthony Giddens puts it:

I shall take it 'third way' refers to a framework of thinking and policy-making that seeks to adapt social democracy to a world which has changed fundamentally over the past two or three decades. It is a third way in the sense that it is an attempt to transcend both old-style social democracy and neoliberalism.

(Giddens, 1998, p.26)

To understand what the Third Way is, then, we need to look first at what it is not – classical, old-style social democracy (Old Labour, for example) or neoliberalism (the radical free-market agendas of the Reagan and Thatcher administrations). Giddens provides the following summaries for each of these programmes.

Classical social democracy (the 'old left')

Pervasive state involvement in social and economic life

State dominates over civil society

Collectivism

Keynesian demand management, plus corporatism

Confined role for markets: the mixed or social economy

Full employment

Strong egalitarianism

Comprehensive welfare state, protecting citizens 'from cradle to grave'

Linear modernization

Low ecological consciousness

Internationalism

Belongs to bipolar world

(Giddens, 1998, p.7)

Thatcherism, or neoliberalism (the 'new right')

Minimal government

Autonomous civil society

Market fundamentalism

Moral authoritarianism, plus strong economic individualism

Labour market clears like any other

Acceptance of inequality

Traditional nationalism

Welfare state as safety net

Linear modernization

Low ecological consciousness

Reality theory of international order

Belongs to bipolar world

(Giddens, 1998, p.8)

Surprisingly, Giddens does not provide a matching boxed summary of the principles of the Third Way. However, in his book *The Third Way and its Critics* (Giddens, 2000), he does provide a useful summary of its main guiding principles.

READING 2.1

You should now read 'Third way politics' by Anthony Giddens which is Reading 2.1 at the end of the chapter. When you have done so, look again at his summaries of classical social democracy and neoliberalism. How is Giddens able to present the Third Way as something that goes beyond these two political programmes?

It is important, I think, that Giddens portrays classical social democracy and neoliberalism as diametrically opposed on some issues (the relations between the state and civil society, for example) while sharing common ground on others (both support linear modernization and have a low ecological consciousness). This allows him to depict the Third Way as something that transcends these political programmes in two overlapping but nonetheless significantly different ways. In the first, the Third Way comes to the rescue in proposing a better balance between the polarized and unacceptable extremes represented by old-style social democracy and neoliberalism. Rather than advocating too much or too little state power, allowing too much or too little influence to the operation of markets, or granting communities too much or too little power, the Third Way gets it 'just right' (a little like Baby Bear in the Goldilocks tale). In the second strategy, however, the Third Way emerges not as a sensible alternative to polarized extremes but as something that *goes beyond* both old-style social democracy and neoliberalism in respect of the ground they share: their low ecological consciousness, for example.

Having looked at some of the guiding principles of the Third Way and at how they inform its attempt to redraw the political map, I now want to look more closely at how these arguments inform the distinctive social agenda of the Third Way. I shall focus for this purpose on two agendas: the Third Way's commitment to the renewal of **civil society**, especially the role of **community**; and its definition of questions of social inequality as ones concerned with relations of social inclusion and social exclusion.

civil society,
community

READING 2.2

You should now read 'The question of civil society' by Anthony Giddens (Reading 2.2). As you do so, keep im mind the following questions:

1   How does Giddens contrast the attitudes of the Third Way, the 'old left' and the 'new right' to the importance of an active civil society?

2   What role does he attribute to community and the voluntary sector in the promotion of an active civil society?

3   How does he see the relations between government and community?

4   What role does sociological research play in this account of the relations between government, community and civil society?

The concept of community appears in a new light here. Within sociology, the concept has often formed part of a system of contrasts that places community on one side of a divide and government on the other. Community is what people make for themselves; it emerges out of the forms of social interaction that are associated with what **Alfred Schutz** and Jürgen Habermas called the **life-world**

Schutz, Alfred
life-world

– that is, the daily round of personal social relations, rather than those social relations associated with the more anonymous and bureaucratized structures of government and business. Yet Giddens suggests a different perspective (and, as we shall see later, is by no means alone in doing so). For he implies that communities cannot simply sustain themselves; they cannot survive solely as a result of the social dynamics arising out of the life-world. On the contrary, the activity of government is needed to bolster communities against the trends that threaten to sweep them away or weaken them. And, in its turn, government has an interest in promoting the spread of effective communities and the strength of people's attachment to them as a means of renewing civil society and thereby achieving greater social solidarity and cohesion.

Although Giddens does not mention them in the reading, these arguments owe a good deal to the influence of two American sociologists – Amaiti Etzioni and Robert Putnam – who, in slightly different analyses appearing at roughly the same time, argued the need for a renewal of the USA's civil society. This was to be accomplished, in the case of Etzioni (1996), by a renewal of community and, in the case of Putnam (1995), by replenishing the USA's depleted stock of 'social capital'. This, as Putnam defines it, comprises the reserves that can be drawn on to promote an active involvement in civil society and, as such, is measured by the extent to which people participate in a whole range of voluntary civic and community organizations and activities. These range from membership of a political party or religious community through to neighbourhood associations and sports clubs (Putnam's most famous measure of US civic decline is that Americans now tend to go bowling alone, rather than in clubs and teams). The sociological studies Giddens cites, while not necessarily explicitly indebted to Putnam, are concerned with measuring the degrees of 'social capital' that governments can draw on (and which they need to strengthen) to promote an active civil society.

What emerges from this reading is a sense of community, not as the vis-à-vis of government but, on the contrary, and to use a term I shall define more fully later, as a *technology of government*. Community, and voluntary and associational life more generally: these, in Giddens's conception, are the things that government needs to nurture in order to form a strong and active civil society. And it is clear that sociology has a central role to play in this technology of government, in providing the research that can help in assessing whether the existing forms of community and associational life constitute an adequate stock of 'social capital'.

READING 2.3

Now turn to 'Inclusion and exclusion' by Anthony Giddens (Reading 2.3). When you have read it, consider the following questions:

1   What are the two main types of exclusion that Giddens is concerned with? And how does he envisage that they might be addressed?

2   Why is overcoming social exclusion not the same thing as overcoming social inequality?

3   What connections are there between the struggle against social exclusion and the promotion of an active civil society?

For Giddens, exclusion can take place just as much at the top of society as at the bottom. At the top, it is a matter of economic and social elites voluntarily excluding themselves from the social mainstream. At the bottom, exclusion is largely involuntary, the result of a lack of opportunity associated with poverty. It is clear, however, that it is not inequality as such that Giddens identifies as the problem (although he does note that social exclusion at both ends of the social scale is likely to be greatest in societies where the inequalities are greatest). Nor does he object to inequalities on the grounds of social justice (see **Braham, 2002**). The problem is rather that poverty, in giving rise to involuntary forms of social exclusion, may be a threat to the overall cohesion and integration of society itself. The voluntary exclusion of the corporate rich, professional and moneyed middle classes poses the same threat – hence the need for a 'civic liberalism' which, like the promotion of an active civil society, will help pull all social and income groups together into some shared sense of an integrating and unifying national community.

There are, it is important to add, other accounts of social exclusion. Ruth Levitas suggests that three different discourses of social exclusion – she calls them RED, MUD and SID – have been evident in the political and policy debates that have accompanied the rise of New Labour. She proposes RED as an abbreviation for a redistributionist approach to social exclusion, representing a continuing commitment to principles of social equity and relying mainly on social policies to combat poverty in all its forms. MUD – or the moral underclass discourse – sees social exclusion as largely a result of a moral failure on the part of an underclass, and sees the moral reform of this delinquent underclass as the key to their inclusion in the mainstream of society. And SID is a social integrationist discourse which views unemployment and economic inactivity as the most damaging forms of social exclusion, which are to be overcome through inclusion in paid work and, thence, the social mainstream (Levitas, 1998, pp.7–8). Giddens's version adds a fourth discourse to this list – we might call it CID, or a civic integrationist discourse, which sees involvement in an active civil society and civic community as the main route to social inclusion.

Putting these differences to one side, however, Levitas suggests that the shift from a political and policy vocabulary organized in terms of inequality to one organized in terms of social inclusion and exclusion represents not only the declining influence of socialist conceptions but also what she calls 'the new Durkheimian hegemony' (Levitas, 1998, p.178). She is referring here to the influence of **Emile Durkheim** on current social and political thought. Here is how she puts the matter:

Durkheim, Emile

> Durkheim was trying to negotiate a route between free market capitalism and state socialism, both deemed unacceptable. Adamantly opposed to Spencer's view that social cohesion could arise from the pursuit of self-interest, he was trying to avoid the Scylla and Charybdis of a 'conflict of unfettered egoisms', and 'despotic socialism'. This was, in a sense, a third way – which rejected the alternatives as being based in forms of utilitarian economism, and as neglecting the necessary moral dimension in social life. Durkheim stressed the importance of intermediate groups between the individual and the state, bastions against the excesses of the market and the potential excesses of a hypertrophied state. He was not concerned to limit the range of activities of the state, which necessarily become more extensive as the division of labour and the complexity of society develop. The state has a key role in articulating the moral content of

the *conscience collective*, establishing the conditions for individualism, and sustaining a 'sentiment of common solidarity' … For Durkheim, democratic government depends on the degree of communication between state and society, which is facilitated by the increasing reach of the state into society. Intermediate associations are crucial to this communication, and play a dual role. They 'are essential if the state is not to oppress the individual: they are also necessary if the state is to be sufficiently free of the individual … They liberate the two conflicting forces, whilst linking them together at the same time'.

(Levitas, 1998, pp.180–1)

ACTIVITY 2

Take another look at the three readings by Giddens and make a brief checklist of those aspects of the discussions that strike you as similar to these aspects of Durkheim's position.

My point in making these connections between Giddens and Durkheim is not to undertake an academic exercise in the history of ideas. There are many other ways of reading and interpreting Durkheim's work and of assessing its relevance to the twenty-first century. These are not relevant to my point here, however, which is to underscore the role that sociological ideas play as parts of what I have called *technologies of government*. For we can see how, in Giddens's writings on the Third Way, the legacy of Durkheim is at work, not just in outlining a political philosophy but also in devising particular ways of acting on and in social relationships to bring about particular results – an increase in social capital, for example. And these ways of acting on society depend on particular kinds of sociological expertise – the sociologist's knowledge of how communities are formed and maintained, for example, and the use of particular kinds of sociological and statistical investigation to monitor and assess the stock of social capital, or whether social exclusion is rising or falling. These are issues that I shall return to in section 4 when I come to place the relations between sociology, statistics and the practices of government in a longer historical perspective. And in section 5 I shall look more closely at the relationships between community and government in the Third Way. First, though, it is necessary to explain what I mean by *technologies of government*, to provide a context for these concerns. And this means taking a closer look at the concept of governmentality.

SUMMARY OF SECTION 2

In this section we have:

1　Reviewed how, in the work of Giddens, the Third Way aims to redraw the political map in order to present itself as transcending the political options of old-style social democracy and neoliberalism.

2　Looked more closely at what this involves in Giddens's approach to the renewal of civil society and the overcoming of social exclusion.

3　Considered the respects in which these aspects of the Third Way represent a 'new Durkheimian hegemony'.

4　Introduced the concept of *technologies of government* with respect to the use of community and sociological statistics in the processes of government.

3 The perspective of governmentality

The concept of governmentality – so called because it defines government in terms of a certain type of attitude or mentality – has enjoyed considerable influence since it was first introduced by Michel Foucault in 1978. Its principal effect has been to dispute the centrality that had previously been enjoyed by accounts of the state in co-ordinating debates about the relations between the organization of society and the distribution of political power. In doing so, it has proposed new ways of thinking about how the activity of governing is organized, where it takes place and how it is related to society. Mitchell Dean, in summarizing the effect of the perspective of governmentality in these regards, asserts that its main consequence has been to substitute what he calls an *analytics of government* for a *theory of the state* (Dean, 1999). In the latter, attention is typically focused on the relationships between the organization and distribution of power in society and control over the state. A famous example is the contention in *The Manifesto of the Communist Party* that the state was 'but a committee for managing the common affairs of the whole bourgeoisie' (Marx and Engels, 1969, p.44), a formulation in which the state is interpreted as the means through which the economic power of the dominant class is translated into political form. In such accounts, the role of ideas – of ideology – is to legitimate the particular ways in which economic power is translated into political power in particular forms of the state. Marx and Engels again provide a famous example in their contention that 'in an age and in a country where royal power, aristocracy, and bourgeoisie are contending for mastery and where, therefore, mastery is shared, the doctrine of the separation of powers proves to be the dominant idea and is expressed as an "eternal law"' (Marx and Engels, 1965, p.61).

How, then, does an *analytics of government* differ from a *theory of the state*? To answer this question fully would take a chapter – indeed, a book – in itself. I therefore want to focus on two related points that have already emerged in the previous sections: the stress that the perspective of governmentality places on the role of ideas and knowledge as central to the actual mechanisms of government; and the respects in which – when translated into particular technical forms – knowledge becomes a part of particular *technologies of government*. I shall pursue these points, first, by commenting on the passage in which Foucault first introduced the concept of governmentality, and then by looking at how two influential commentators on Foucault's work – Nikolas Rose and Peter Miller – have interpreted and expanded on Foucault's initial formulations.

In saying that he would like to undertake a history of 'governmentality', Foucault indicated that he meant three things by the word.

1 The ensemble formed by the institutions, procedures, analyses and reflections, the calculations and tactics that allow the exercise of this very specific albeit very complex form of power, which has as its target population, as its principal form of knowledge political economy, and as its essential technical means apparatuses of security.

2 The tendency which, over a long period and throughout the West, has steadily led towards the pre-eminence over all other forms (sovereignty, discipline, etc) of this type of power which may be termed government,

resulting, on the one hand, in the formation of a whole series of specific governmental apparatuses, and, on the other, in the development of a whole complex of *savoirs* [or 'knowledges'].

3   The process, or rather the result of the process, through which the state of justice of the Middle Ages, transformed into the administrative state during the fifteenth and sixteenth centuries, gradually becomes 'governmentalised'.

(Foucault, 1991, pp.102–3)

These are complicated arguments, so let's unpack them one by one.

The *first argument* is that governmentality as a new way of thinking about the scope and purpose of government first became evident in the late eighteenth and early nineteenth centuries, with the emergence of the view that governing was an activity that should concern itself with maintaining and improving the conditions of life (physical, economic, social, cultural and moral) of the whole population. As such, this new 'mentality' of governing was closely associated with the emergence of **political economy** as a new science which aimed to provide a knowledge of the relations between population, territory and wealth (of the consequences, for example, that a declining population might have for the wealth of the nation). It could then guide governmental action to organize a mutually productive relationship between these three entities (say, policies to increase the population should it threaten to fall below the level judged optimum for the balanced growth of the national wealth). The translation of this knowledge into effective means of governing, however, requires the invention of new technical instruments – what Foucault calls the 'apparatuses of security'. What he has in mind here are the new measures that were developed in the course of the nineteenth century to provide for security against the many risks associated with the ups and downs of economic cycles – for example, the forms of mutual support and social insurance that emerged from the early history of friendly and provident societies, and which later became a part of state-provided forms of social security.

political economy

The *second argument* is that this governmental form of power has tended to become more important than the two other types of power that characterized earlier periods of western history: the sovereign power associated with earlier, absolutist regimes, and the forms of power associated with the development of enclosed institutions (prisons, asylums, schools) for the disciplining and training of bodies and minds. Foucault stresses, however, that this does not mean that these earlier forms of power disappear entirely. Rather, they continue to exist alongside governmental forms of power in a subordinate position, in the sense that their role and function are determined by the broader context supplied by governmental power. The growth of these new kinds of governmental power, Foucault argues, is also tied up with the multiplication of new knowledges (or, as Foucault calls them in the passage cited above, *savoirs*). These knowledges include sociology and psychology, for example, and political economy – and there are new apparatuses through which these knowledges are put into practical effect. The relationship between sociology and the development of social policies directed at families, or between psychology, the asylum and the management of those classified as insane, are all relevant in this context.

The *third argument* is that these new governmental forms of power gradually transform the state, displacing the purely legal and administrative forms of power that had been the dominant characteristics of the state in the medieval and early modern periods. An important aspect of this argument is the contention that governmental forms of power usually emerge first in developments outside the state, as the result of programmes developed by a wide range of non-state agencies – the social insurance and mutuality provisions of friendly societies, for example. It is only later – in being subject to the influence of these new developments – that the state becomes governmentalized when, as was the case in early twentieth-century Britain, the state itself assumes a degree of responsibility for the provision of social insurance. It is on the basis of this argument that Foucault warns against thinking of the state as having an essential and unified function of the kind imputed to it in Marxist thought, with the corollary that all key political issues come to hinge on one question: which class controls the state? In place of this view, Foucault argues that the state must be seen as a loose assemblage of different forms of governmentality, each with its distinctive knowledges, experts, programmes and technical apparatuses, rather than as a coherent programme with a logic derived from the interests of a social class. This in turn means that different regions of government give rise to different political issues, which have to be engaged with on their own terms, rather than all political issues forming a sub-set of one big political issue – the conflict between labour and capital, for example.

These are still fairly general arguments. I therefore now want to look more closely at the implications of the perspective of governmentality for the mechanisms of government. I shall do so by considering selected passages from Nikolas Rose and Peter Miller's application of the perspective of governmentality to the analysis of (a) the political rationalities of government, (b) programmes of government, (c) technologies of government and (d) the necessary failure of government.

ACTIVITY 3

As you read through the passages that follow, try to identify examples of what Rose and Miller have in mind.

(a) The political rationalities of government

They elaborate upon the fitting powers and duties for authorities. They address the proper distribution of tasks and actions between authorities of different types – political, spiritual, military, pedagogic, familial. They consider the ideals or principles to which government should be directed – freedom, justice, equality, mutual responsibility, citizenship, common sense, economic efficiency, prosperity, growth, fairness, rationality and the like.

Second, political rationalities have what one might term an *epistemological* character. That is to say, they are articulated in relation to some conception of the nature of the objects governed – society, the nation, the population, the economy. In particular, they embody some account of the persons over whom government is to be exercised …

Third, political rationalities are articulated in a distinctive *idiom*. The language that constitutes political discourse is more than rhetoric. It should be seen, rather, as a kind of intellectual machinery or apparatus for rendering reality thinkable in such a way that it is amenable to political deliberations.

(Rose and Miller, 1992, pp.178–9)

Conservatism, socialism, fascism, liberalism, feminism – these all count as political rationalities for Rose and Miller. It is, of course, more usual to refer to these as political philosophies or ideologies. What is gained by calling them political rationalities? Rose and Miller argue that the focus that this label brings to bear includes not just the moral and evaluative aspects of different schools of political thought but also the ways in which – by functioning as intellectual machineries for rendering reality 'thinkable' in particular ways – they make the social and political world 'actionable' in particular ways. Thus liberalism does not merely assert that individuals have a right to a certain freedom and autonomy of action; it marks off a line between the state and civil society – the realm of freedom and autonomy that the state must respect. In doing this, liberalism calls on the state to cultivate and promote the development of civil society, just as it calls on individuals to become active in their own self-government in order to preclude the need for state intervention in the affairs of civil society. In this way, liberal government makes the freedom and autonomy of individuals, and the responsibility placed on individuals to be self-governing, a distinctive component of its political rationality. In communism, by contrast, it is the individual's subordination to the collective cause that provides the basic rationality of government.

(b) Programmes of government

Government is a *problematising* activity: it poses the obligations of rulers in terms of the problems they seek to address. The ideals of government are intrinsically linked to the problems around which it circulates, the failings it seeks to rectify, the ills it seeks to cure. Indeed, the history of government might well be written as a history of problematisations, in which politicians, intellectuals, philosophers, medics, military men, feminists and philanthropists have measured the real against the ideal and found it wanting ...

The programmatic is the realm of designs put forward by philosophers, political economists, physiocrats, and philanthropists, government reports, committees of inquiry, White Papers, proposals and counterproposals by organisations of business, labour, finance, charities and professionals, that seek to configure specific locales and relations in ways thought desirable.

(Rose and Miller, 1992, p.181)

The programmatic aspect of government is a critical nodal point in the relay of governmental activity. It is the point at which political rationalities get translated into historically specific sets of diagnoses of current ills, proposed remedies and courses of action. The Third Way is a good example of a programme of government in this sense. It is important to note, however, that Rose and Miller deliberately propose a broad definition of the programmatic aspect of government, encompassing the activities of all kinds of social reformers and campaigners – philanthropists, feminists, medical professionals – as well as politicians. We can see an example of this today, as advances in the life sciences, especially genetics, have resulted in a whole range of medically initiated programmes of government aimed at changing how we view and manage our bodies. Those viewed as being genetically at risk have to manage their personal and working lives differently, for example, just as they are treated differently in employment and insurance regulations (Novas and Rose, 2000).

(c) **Technologies of government**

> Government is a domain of strategies, techniques and procedures through which different forces seek to render programmes operable, and by means of which a multitude of connections are established between the aspirations of authorities and the activities of individuals and groups. These heterogeneous mechanisms we term *technologies of government* ... We need to study the humble and mundane mechanisms by which authorities seek to instantiate government: techniques of notation, computation and calculation; procedures of examination and assessment; the invention of devices such as surveys and presentational forms such as tables; the standardisation of systems for training and the inculcation of habits; the inauguration of professional specialisms and vocabularies; building designs and architectural forms – the list is heterogeneous and in principle unlimited.
>
> (Rose and Miller, 1992, p.183)

Government, in this conception, emerges as a broadly based activity, and one that is to be looked for as much in the operation of the mundane techniques and procedures that form part of our daily lives as in the edicts of the state. Indeed, the latter – alongside the programmes of government that might be developed by, for example, social movements – need the mediation of technologies of government in order to be translated into practical effect. Think of league tables for universities, reporting on their performance in research and teaching, or of comparative performance indicators detailing the lengths of waiting lists in regional health authorities: these are both examples of the technological means through which programmes aimed at improving service in higher education and the NHS are put into effect. Or, to take the example of genetics again, think of the ways in which new developments in genetics are translated into new forms of counselling through which those assessed as genetically at risk are urged to take responsibility for both the health of their own bodies and the risks of transmitting disease to their partners or children (Novas and Rose, 2000).

(d) **The necessary failure of government**

> Government is a congenitally failing operation ... Things, persons or events always appear to escape those bodies of knowledge that inform governmental programmes, refusing to respond according to the programmatic logic that seeks to govern them. Technologies produce unexpected problems, are utilised for their own ends by those who are supposed to merely operate them, are hampered by under-funding, professional rivalries, and the impossibility of producing the technical conditions that would make them work – reliable statistics, efficient communication systems, clear lines of command, properly designed buildings, well framed regulations or whatever ... We do not live in a governed world so much as a world traversed by the 'will to govern', fuelled by the constant registration of 'failure', the discrepancy between ambition and outcome, and the constant injunction to do better next time.
>
> (Rose and Miller, 1992, pp.190–1)

This passage helps to underscore an important aspect of Foucault's discussion of governmentality. He remarks that 'techniques of government have become the only political issue, the only real space for political struggle and contestation' (Foucault, 1991, p.103). While this contention raises some general issues that I

shall return to in my conclusion, the point to note here is the extent to which –
far from resulting in a totally administered society, as some critics have implied
– the perspective of governmentality gives us a means of accounting for the
veritable explosion of politics in modern societies. For it is the very activity of
government that generates political issues. The clashes between the programmes
of different authorities; the contradictory ways in which different programmes
seek to enlist us as active agents in support of their objectives; the controversies
generated by technologies of government such as performance indicators –
these are just some of the manifold ways in which the perspective of
governmentality accounts for the constant generation of political issues through
the practice of government.

ACTIVITY 4

To make the perspective of governmentality more concrete, make a list of the
different ways in which, in the course of an average week, you might be called on to
discharge responsibilities related to your role as a citizen, parent, employee, resident,
patient, sexual subject, student or consumer. Try to identify, in each case, what is
expected of you and the means that are available for putting it into effect.

Writing at the time of the 2001 General Election, I am conscious of the appeals
that have been made to my responsibility as a citizen to vote (I did!) and, given
the low rate of voter turnout for that election, the subsequent complaint that
too many citizens were ducking this responsibility. As an employee, I am
constantly being urged to do better – to improve my teaching and my research
– to satisfy the auditing requirements that are currently placed on universities
through the Teaching Quality Assessment and Research Assessment Exercise
processes. As a resident, I am constantly invited by the local council to take part
in campaigns to keep the streets tidy or to join the neighbourhood watch
programme. In the area of sexual relations, I'm aware of both the legal and the
cultural forces working to curb sexual harassment, both at work and in leisure
situations. I am also constantly aware, as a consumer, of the variety of forces –
from pro-organic food movements through anti-GM crop campaigns to the
animal welfare aspects of vegetarianism – attempting to bring ethical
considerations to bear on what I eat and drink. And I'm aware, too, of the wide
range of pressures – from keep-fit clubs through to weight watchers' associations
– seeking to persuade me to exercise more and eat less in the belief that, by
acquiring a healthier body, I will be a happier person.

What about you?

SUMMARY OF SECTION 3

In this section we have:

1   Reviewed the history and defining features of the perspective of
    governmentality.

2   Distinguished the concerns of an *analytics of government* from those of a
    theory of the state.

3   Reviewed some of the key concepts associated with the perspective of
    governmentality.

4 Governing by numbers: risk, social insurance and social management

I now want, in this and the next section, to return to the suggestion I made in discussing the Third Way that statistics and community can be regarded as *technologies of government* which have been developed as part of the practical history of sociology. I do so in order to see what light the perspective of governmentality can throw on these uses of sociology, and vice versa. I look first at statistics.

<hr>

READING 2.4

You should now read 'How should we do the history of statistics?' by Ian Hacking (Reading 2.4). Hacking claims in this reading that the development of statistics (a) 'has helped determine the form of laws about society and the character of social facts', (b) 'has engendered concepts and classifications within the human sciences' and (c) 'has created ... a great bureaucratic machinery'. What arguments does he develop to substantiate these claims?

<hr>

I was struck by Hacking's contention that, but for the power of statistics, neither you nor I would exist, given the overwhelming likelihood that our nineteenth-century forebears would not have lived to puberty. This is a graphic illustration of his argument that statistics may be malevolent or benign, depending on the nature of the governmental programmes and rationalities that regulate their use. But we can also see from Hacking's discussion the role that statistics, understood as a technology of government, have played in making society thinkable in certain ways. The view of what can count as a social fact today is certainly broader than that proposed by Emile Durkheim, but it is still true that the ability to demonstrate law-like regularities of behaviour on the part of those occupying similar social positions remains a powerful aspect of the uses of

life-chances

sociology. It is, for example, still important in assessing the different **life-chances** that are associated with different class positions (see **Savage, 2002**). But we can also see how the frameworks in which statistical data are collected are productive ones, in the sense that, by making certain kinds of social division statistically visible in particular ways, they can generate unforeseen consequences. Hacking thus suggests that the emergence of Marx's class analysis and the subsequent development of class politics can be understood, at least in part, as something generated by the categories used in the Census. The use of racially or ethnically derived principles of classification for the collection of statistical data has had similar consequences, often contributing significantly to a racialization of social divisions (see **Murji, 2002**).

It is, however, the final aspect of Hacking's discussion that I want to focus on here. You may have noticed that Hacking's arguments echo Foucault's interest in the relations between governmentality, in its concern with population, and the development of what Foucault called 'apparatuses of security'. This is evident in Hacking's reference to Daniel Defert's work on the part played by social insurance in providing a technology of government (*technologie assurentiel*) that contributed to the development of a stable social order. It is worth following this issue a little further in view of the light that changes in the social management of risk can throw on the ways in which 'governing by numbers' can give rise to sharply contrasting consequences when interpreted in the light of different political programmes and rationalities. I shall focus for this purpose on the different assumptions underlying the actuarial calculations of insurance companies – that is, the techniques they use to calculate risk – in different historical circumstances.

At the start of the essay to which Hacking refers, Defert suggests that the emergence in mid–nineteenth-century France of a 'state of affairs in which financial compensation for an industrial accident is automatic, unquestioned and guaranteed by a system of insurance may seem like a people's victory' (Defert, 1991, p.211). He does so, however, only to go on to note that the development of industrial accident insurance and, subsequently, of more general programmes of social insurance was not initially supported by the French workers' movement:

> For the history of insurance in industrial society begins with the invention of a technique for managing a population and creating funds for compensation damages, an emerging technology of risk which was originally devised by financiers, before later becoming a paradigm of social solutions to all cases of non-labour: first that of industrial accidents, then sickness and old age, and finally unemployment.
>
> (Defert, 1991, p.211)

Defert's interest is in how this new technology of insurance – which depended on the use of sociological categories to make actuarial calculations of the risks (of accident, sickness and so on) associated with particular occupations, ages, regions and so on – was able to provide 'bourgeois solutions to proletarian problems' (Defert, 1991, p.212). For in doing so, he argues, it was responsible for bringing about a significant transformation in the management of industrial capitalist societies, reducing the scope and possibility for class conflict by dismantling the forms of solidarity and capacity for political action that had been developed in association with earlier forms of mutual support developed from within the working classes. Insurance, as he puts it, demutualized the working classes by dismantling the social relations on which early forms of mutual support (such as savings banks) had depended and cultivating new ones – and new habits – in their place. A selection from the list of points Defert offers at the end of his essay summarizing these aspects of the effect of the new technology of insurance makes the point:

1   Unlike workers' mutualism, insurance does not link its associated participants horizontally with one other, but links each client individually and serially to a central management. Its entire juridical framework consists in the contract between the individual client and the company manager.

2   The insurance company's reserves are not at the disposal of the insured. (This was one of the *raisons d'être* of the savings bank.) For the labourer to work regularly, he has to be induced not to consume the whole of his pay ... But in order for the inculcation of the savings habit not to provide the worker with the means of forming a strike fund, the worker must be deprived of free disposal of these savings. Insurance funds were tied by contract to the purpose of providing precisely specified forms of indemnity, their level fixed in advance by a scale of compensation.

3 ...

4   Only the client's subscription ensures the provident cover: it therefore implies regular work, ordered time, disciplined consumption, individual responsibility. The system dispenses with the need for the benevolence of the wealthy or the participation of the state.

(Defert, 1991, p.231)

The last phrase is a telling one since, of course, in France as in the UK the state was later to become significantly involved in the provision of social insurance of various kinds. This is an interesting example of what Foucault calls the 'governmentalization of the state'. A solution to a particular problem (compensating workers for industrial accidents), initially developed by private financiers, provided a model for the later development of state-run programmes of generalized social insurance – that is, for the social welfare state. Once developed, however, technologies of insurance can be redeployed and put to work in different ways, managing social relationships and regulating behaviour differently and to different effect. This has been true in the UK since Margaret Thatcher's radical revolution which, in seeking to roll back the welfare state, sought to make individuals responsible for themselves in new ways. Pat O'Malley argues that an important aspect of this process has been 'the partial transformation of socialised actuarialism into privatised actuarialism (prudentialism)' (O'Malley, 1996, p.199), as technologies of insurance have been redesigned to accord better with the agendas of neoliberalism.

READING 2.5

'Risk and responsibility' by Pat O'Malley is reproduced here as Reading 2.5. When you have read it, try to answer the following questions:

1   Why does privatized actuarialism make risk management an 'everyday practice of the self'? How does this manifest itself?

2   What attributes distinguish prudentialism as a technology of government?

O'Malley's discussion highlights an important aspect of the perspective of governmentality that we have yet to consider: namely, that government is an activity which always enlists those over whom it is exercised as active accomplices in their own governance. Another way of putting this is to say that particular technologies of government always work through particular technologies of the self. These, as Foucault defines them, 'permit individuals to effect by their own means or with the help of others a certain number of operations on their own bodies and souls, thoughts, conduct, and way of being, so as to transform themselves in order to attain a certain state of happiness, purity, wisdom, perfection, or immortality' (Foucault, 1988, p.18). Or, one might add, to save, invest and generally regulate their daily lives so as to behave prudentially or, in a countervailing everyday practice, to mortgage the present against the future by acting in accordance with new regimes of credit (see **Lury, 2002**). Precisely how such technologies of the self work, or are meant to work, however, varies according to how the persons they address are conceived: as isolated individuals, as members of families, as citizens or – the concern of the next section – as members of communities.

SUMMARY OF SECTION 4

In this section we have:

1   Considered the role that statistics have played in the development of modern forms of insurance.

2   Investigated the notion of the 'governmentalization of the state' with reference to the history of insurance, and shown how technologies of insurance can be applied in the context of different governmental programmes.

3   Examined the relationship between technologies of government and technologies of the self.

5 Communalizing the citizen

In registering the force and pertinence of contemporary neoliberal critiques of the welfare state, Anthony Giddens accepts that many of them have some degree of validity. The welfare state is, he says, undemocratic in depending too heavily on the top-down distribution of welfare benefits and, at the same time, too intrusive in not giving enough space to personal liberty. He suggests, however, that these criticisms present better reasons for reconstructing the welfare state than they do for dismantling it. In continuing to develop this idea, he suggests that we must go beyond the welfare state to develop a *social investment state* that will aim to build a 'positive welfare society' (Giddens, 1998, p.117). This is a view of the Third Way that has its critics (see Figure 2.2). It means that the state should aim to alter the balance between the forms of welfare support it provides directly and those that emerge out of 'the third sector' – that is, out of those community-based organizations and associations Giddens calls on governments to develop and promote in order to generate the active civil society that is the precondition for social inclusion.

Figure 2.2 *The Third Way and its critics*

Source: Steve Bell, *If* cartoon, *The Guardian*, 25 May 2001

This takes us back to the issues discussed in section 2. It was suggested that the political programme of the Third Way depended in part on the emergence of community as a technology of government. What does it mean to say this? How can community serve as a technology of government? In the history of sociological thought, it has usually served to describe a particular kind of social relationship – close and intimate, as distinct from the more abstract and anonymous forms of relationship found in urban and industrial societies. And how can it serve as a technology of government when community is usually written and spoken of – by sociologists and in everyday life – as something that has been lost? The answer is that such analyses usually bemoan the disappearance of community in order to call for its reinvention. The lack of community is regretted, but only so that it can be called into being again, in order to serve as a means of restoring some kind of moral order to society: taking care of the elderly, restoring law and order and so on. In short, community is constantly invoked in order that it might be reinvented to function as a technology of government with, as we shall see, seemingly no limits to what it might be expected to accomplish.

These are the issues that Nikolas Rose addresses in the next reading. This traces the influence that the revival of an interest in community on the part of US sociologists has had on the agendas of the Third Way. It is important to note in reading Rose's account that he has been critical of many aspects of New Labour and of Giddens's advocacy of the Third Way (see Rose, 1999b), and this shows in a number of places in his discussion. The issues for you to focus on, however, are not the more immediately polemical aspects of his argument but the more general aspects of his interpretation of community from the perspective of governmentality.

READING 2.6

Turn now to 'Community' by Nikolas Rose (Reading 2.6). When you have done so, consider the following questions:

1   How, according to Rose, does the community of the third sector, the third space, and the third way of governing differ from earlier uses of the language of community?

2   What does Rose mean when he says that community 'becomes governmental when it becomes technical'? And how is community given a technical form?

3   In what distinctive ways does this new technology of community call on individuals and involve them in new tasks of self-governance? How do these tasks differ from and call into question the ways in which individuals were addressed as citizens in earlier universalistic and uniform forms of social citizenship?

4   How does this new version of community involve a new game of power?

Perhaps the first thing to say is that if you found this a difficult reading you're not alone! It is, therefore, worth reviewing some of its main arguments. The main point to focus on is Rose's argument that 'community' has meant different things at different points in time, and has been called on for different purposes at different moments in the history of sociology, depending on how its role in relation to contemporary social problems has been defined. In the case of the community discourse of the 'third way of governing', 'community' refers primarily to 'a moral field binding persons into durable relations'. As such, appeals to community within the context of neoliberal conceptions of government are part and parcel of a programme aimed at reducing reliance on state-run institutions and catering for social citizens by cultivating new forms of affective support that will operate only within the confines of particular communities. This new understanding of community is given a technical form through the development of new groups of experts (Community Development Officers, for example) and new ways of sociologically knowing and measuring the strength of community (Putnam's notion of social capital, for example) which can help determine what measures might be needed to strengthen communities and their ability to regulate the lives of their members. As a consequence, this strategy of governing addresses and involves us in new ways by appealing to us, and inviting us to see ourselves, less and less as citizens with common bonds, rights, duties and obligations and more and more as the members of differentiated communities with bonds, rights, duties and obligations specific to those communities. The resulting 'community–civility' game of power involves a new kind of 'ethico-politics' through which questions of consumption, lifestyle and identity come to be increasingly important to the development of new forms of self-government.

SUMMARY OF SECTION 5

In this section we have:

1   Reviewed the role played by appeals to community in the context of neoliberal programmes of government.

2   Examined how community functions as a technology of government and investigated the distinctive kinds of self-governance that this involves.

3   Placed these concerns in the context of the shifting meanings of 'community' within the history of sociological thought.

6 Conclusion

I started by suggesting that sociology and government might seem strange bedfellows. But you might now be thinking that, on the contrary, sociology and government have been fairly promiscuous in their relations with one another. In following the implications of the expanded concept of government associated with the perspective of governmentality, we have been able to show that sociology plays a significant role in many of the programmes and technologies of government that are involved in directing and regulating our behaviour in modern societies. If sociology is implicated in the mechanisms of insurance and the workings of community as a means of shaping and regulating identities, it has also – as Liz McFall shows in Chapter 4 – played a significant role in the management and regulation of economic life. But the same can be said of many other disciplines. Psychology, economics and medicine can be studied in the same way in terms of the roles they have played in developing distinctive programmes and technologies of government through which we are both governed and govern ourselves. Think, for example, of the role of psychology in the development of the many varied forms of counselling that are used in many different circumstances – from marriage counselling to grief counselling – to help us govern ourselves. Or of the role of economics in the complex forms of accounting that are central to the government of economic life in a complicated modern economy.

However, rather than multiplying examples that make the same point, I want to conclude by drawing your attention to two more general issues associated with the perspective of governmentality. The first is the understanding of the relations between knowledge and power that informs this perspective. I argued earlier, you might remember, that the perspective of governmentality differs from theories of the state in being concerned with the role that 'techniques and forms of knowledge' play in the processes of government, rather than with the role played by ideologies in legitimating the exercise of power by the state. This aspect of the perspective of governmentality builds on Foucault's earlier criticisms of the theory of ideology as functioning, first, in a manner external to power and, second, by means of falsehood. For in Marxist theories of ideology, Foucault argues, power is held to arise from the economy and be exercised through a class's control of the state and is only then, as a secondary process, legitimated by means of specific ideologies that achieve this end by, in one way or another, pulling the wool over the eyes of those who fall under their influence. As Foucault puts it, the concept of ideology 'always stands in virtual opposition to something else which is supposed to count as truth' (Foucault, 1970, p.118).

The perspective of governmentality differs from such theories of ideology in two main ways. First, it displaces any notion of an absolute distinction between truth and falsehood with a relative one. What this means is most simply illustrated by Foucault's preparedness to speak of *knowledges* in the plural. What counts as knowledge, for Foucault, is what is taken to be true – what functions as truth – in any particular context. What matters, then, is to examine how particular systems of knowledge operate – not abstractly, as sets of ideas, but in the ways in which, as integral and functioning parts of technologies of government, they are tangled up in particular forms of power and its exercise. This, then, is the second difference: from the point of view of the perspective of governmentality, specific knowledges – like sociology – are examined to identify the role they play in *making up* certain kinds of power, rather than to show how they legitimate power relations that have already been formed somewhere else, in the economy for example. Knowledge and power are, for Foucault, like Tweedledum and Tweedledee: you can't have one without the other.

The second issue I want to comment on concerns the implications of the perspective of governmentality for the way in which the social distribution of power is conceptualized. It is helpful here, again, to recall a point made earlier when, in discussing Nikolas Rose and Peter Miller's contention that government is 'a congenitally failing operation', I quoted Foucault to the effect that 'techniques of government have become the only political issue, the only real space for political struggle and contestation' (Foucault, 1991, p.103). When considered closely, this offers an alternative to – and a critique of – the strong tendency for theories of the state to offer a polarized view of the distribution of power with all of it on one side (the state), so that accounting for opposition or contestation becomes a problem that can be addressed only by locating pockets of potential resistance in various outsider or marginal groups. This is true, for example, of Michel de Certeau's distinction between *strategies* and *tactics*, in which strategies are the means by which the behaviour of others, those with powers direct, while tactics refers to the ways of resisting power developed by those who lack it (see de Certeau, 1984, pp.35–9).

There are, of course, other traditions within sociology of which this is not true – or at least not to the same degree. Max Weber's theory of **bureaucracy**, for example, is concerned with how particular forms of power are embedded in routine administrative procedures. There is, however, a strong tendency for sociological ways of thinking about power to pose the issue in terms of a bipolar (but unequal) contest between forms of power that are imposed 'from above' and resisted 'from below'. Within the perspective of governmentality, by contrast, power is more fluid and dispersed, so that resistance, opposition and contestation can be accounted for as being generated by a wide range of miscellaneous factors – by the clashes and contradictions between the governmental programmes of different authorities; by the different ways in which different programmes seek to enlist us as active agents in support of their objectives; or by breakdowns or imperfections in the functioning of technologies of government. In this perspective, resistance, opposition and contestation are routine events located within, and generated by, practices of government and the contradictions between them. They are not exceptional events that have to be accounted for by locating a source that is capable of generating opposition because it is located outside of, and is therefore uncontaminated by, power. From the perspective of governmentality, the concern to offer a general theoretical account of resistance or opposition, which has occupied the attention of much of critical sociology and cultural studies, is no longer a meaningful one. In its place, there emerges the task of accounting for particular forms of resistance, opposition and contestation as these emerge from particular constellations of competing rationalities, programmes and technologies of government.

Nikolas Rose touches on these matters when he remarks that the perspective of governmentality tends to generate complexity. It does so, he argues, by requiring us 'to jettison the division between a logic that structures ... "from above" according to protocols that are not our own, and a more or less spontaneous anti-logic "from below" that expresses our own needs, desires, aspirations' (Rose, 1999a, p.277). By looking empirically at how different knowledges are in play in different areas of government – in the government of health, welfare, childhood, the family, education – and at the issues, problems and tensions these generate, attention is focused instead on the manifold different ways in which power is exercised and the equally manifold ways in which it is disputed and contested.

bureaucracy

References

Albrow, M. (2001) 'Sociology after the Third Way, in the UK and USA', *Network* (the newsletter of the British Sociological Association), no.78, January, pp.10–12.

Braham, P. (2002) 'Social justice' in Braham, P. and Janes, L. (eds) *op. cit.*.

Braham, P. and Janes, L. (eds) (2002) *Social Differences and Divisions*, Oxford, Blackwell/The Open University. (Book 2 in this series.)

Burchell, G., Gordon, C. and Miller, P. (eds) (1991) *The Foucault Effect: Studies in Governmentality*, London, Harvester/Wheatsheaf,

Dean, M. (1999) *Governmentality: Power and Rule in Modern Society*, London, Sage.

Dean, M. (2002) 'The regulation of the self' in Jordan, T. and Pile, S. (eds) *Social Change*, Oxford, Blackwell/The Open University. (Book 3 in this series.)

de Certeau, M. (1984) *The Practice of Everyday Life* (trans. S.F. Randell), Berkeley and Los Angeles, CA, University of California Press.

Defert, D. (1991) '"Popular life" and insurance technology' in Burchell, G., Gordon, C. and Miller, P. (eds) *op. cit.*, pp.211–34.

Etzioni, A. (1996) *The New Golden Rule: Community and Morality in a Democratic Society*, New York, Basic Books.

Finlayson, A. (1999) 'Third Way theory', *Political Quarterly*, vol.70, no.3, pp.271–9.

Foucault, M. (1970) *Power/Knowledge: Selected Interviews and Other Writings 1972– 1977*, New York, Pantheon Books.

Foucault, M. (1988) 'Technologies of the self' in Martin, L.H., Gutman, H. and Hutton, P.H. (eds) *Technologies of the Self: A Seminar with Michel Foucault*, London, Tavistock Publications, pp.16–49.

Foucault, M. (1991) 'Governmentality' in Burchell, G., Gordon, C. and Miller, P. (eds) *op. cit.*, pp.87–103 (originally given as a lecture at the College de France in 1978).

Giddens, A. (1998) *The Third Way: The Renewal of Social Democracy*, Cambridge, Polity Press.

Giddens, A. (2000) *The Third Way and its Critics*, Cambridge, Polity Press.

Hacking, I. (1991) 'How should we do the history of statistics?' in Burchell, G., Gordon, C. and Miller, P. (eds) *op. cit.*, pp.181–4.

Hall, S. (1998) 'The great moving nowhere show', *Marxism Today*, November/December, pp.9–14.

Karpf, A. (1999) 'A talent to annoy: Anne Karpf meets Anthony Giddens, the bestselling author who invented Tony Blair's "third way"', *The Guardian*, 11 March, p.9.

Levitas, R. (1998) *The Inclusive Society? Social Exclusion and New Labour*, London, Macmillan.

Lury, C. (2002) 'Everyday life and the economy' in Bennett, T. and Watson, D. (eds) *Understanding Everyday Life*, Oxford, Blackwell/The Open University. (Book 1 in this series.)

Marx, K. and Engels, F. (1965) *The German Ideology*, London, Lawrence and Wishart.

Marx, K. and Engels, F. (1969) *The Manifesto of the Communist Party*, Moscow, Progress Publishers.

McRobbie, A. (2000) 'Feminism and the Third Way', *Feminist Review*, no.64, pp.97–112.

Mount, F. (1999) 'Talking rubbish in the name of Reith', *Sunday Times*, 9 May.

Mulgan, G. (1998) 'Whinge and a prayer', *Marxism Today*, November/December, pp.15–16.

Murji, K. (2002) 'Race, power and knowledge' in Braham, P. and Janes, L. (eds) *op. cit.*.

Novas, C. and Rose, N. (2000) 'Genetic risk and the birth of the somatic individual', *Economy and Society*, vol.29, no.4, pp.485–513.

O'Malley, P. (1996) 'Risk and responsibility' in Barry, A., Osborne, T. and Rose, N. (eds) *Foucault and Political Reason: Liberalism, Neo-liberalism and Rationalities of Government*, London, UCL Press, pp.199–200.

Putnam, R. (1995) 'Bowling alone: America's declining social capital', *Journal of Democracy*, vol.6, no.1, pp.65–78.

Rose, N. (1999a) *Powers of Freedom: Reframing Political Thought*, Cambridge, Cambridge University Press.

Rose, N. (1999b) 'Inventiveness in politics', *Economy and Society*, vol.28, no.3, pp.467–493.

Rose, N. and Miller, P. (1992) 'Political power beyond the state: problematics of government', *British Journal of Sociology*, vol.43, no.2, pp.173–205.

Savage, M. (2002) 'Social exclusion and class analysis' in Braham, P. and Janes, L. (eds) *op. cit.*.

Walker, D. (1999) 'Anthony Giddens: sixties' man of the world', *The Guardian*, 23 March, p.17.

Readings

 2.1 Anthony Giddens, 'Third way politics' (2000)

The fundamentals of third way politics, as I would see them, can now be briefly stated. The third way:

(1) Accepts the logic of '1989 and after' – that while left and right still count for a good deal in contemporary politics, there are many issues and problems that this opposition no longer helps illuminate. The attention which the third way gives to the political centre stems from this fact. This emphasis is wholly compatible with the claim that third way politics should involve radical policies.

(2) Argues that the three key areas of power – government, the economy, and the communities of civil society – all need to be constrained in the interests of social solidarity and social justice. A democratic order, as well as an effective market economy, depends upon a flourishing civil society. Civil society, in turn, needs to be limited by the other two.

The sociologist Claus Offe (1998) points to six fallacies that a sophisticated political theory must avoid – each of which we have, or should have, learned a lot about through the experience of the past few decades. The state can become too large and overextended – the neoliberals were right about this. But where the state is too confined, or loses its legitimacy, major social problems develop too. The same applies to markets. A society that allows the market to infiltrate too far into other institutions will experience a failure of public life. One that finds insufficient space for markets, however, will not be able to generate economic prosperity. Similarly, where the communities in civil society become too strong, democracy as well as economic development can be threatened. Yet if the civic order is too weak, effective government and economic growth are put at risk.

(3) Proposes to construct a new social contract, based on the theorem 'no rights without responsibilities'. Those who profit from social goods should both use them responsibly, and give something back to the wider social community in return. Seen as a feature of citizenship, 'no rights without responsibilities' has to apply to politicians as well as citizens, to the rich as well as the poor, to business corporations as much as the private individual. Left-of-centre governments should be prepared to act upon it in all these areas.

(4) In the economic sphere, looks to develop a wide-ranging supply-side policy, which seeks to reconcile economic growth mechanisms with structural reform of the welfare state. In the new information economy, human (and social) capital becomes central to economic success. The cultivation of these forms of capital demands extensive social investment – in education, communications and infrastructure. The principle 'wherever possible invest in human capital' applies equally to the welfare state – which needs to be reconstructed as a 'social investment state'.

The creation of a 'new mixed economy' depends on a balance of regulation and deregulation, nationally and transnationally. The old left attributes many of the world's problems to the activities of business corporations. Corporate power certainly needs to be controlled by government and by international legislation. Yet when no one knows of any viable alternative to a market economy, demonizing the corporations makes no sense. Economic policy should not treat ecological considerations as peripheral. Ecological modernization is consistent with economic growth, and can sometimes be one of its motive forces.

(5) Seeks to foster a diversified society based upon egalitarian principles. Social diversity is not compatible with a strongly defined egalitarianism of outcome. Third way politics looks instead to maximize equality of opportunity. However, this

has to preserve a concern with limiting inequality of outcome too. The chief reason is that equality of opportunity can generate inequalities of wealth and income – that then hamper opportunities for subsequent generations.

Inequality can no longer, if it ever could, be countered only by income transfers from the more to the less affluent. Some forms of welfare provision, for example, designed in some part to reduce poverty, have had the effect of creating or perpetuating it. Moreover, the old 'project of exclusion' which drove social democracy – admitting the working class to full social, political and economic citizenship – has lapsed. Social democrats today need to combat newer forms of exclusion – at the bottom and at the top. At the bottom, 5% or so of the population risks becoming detached from the wider society – some, such as those imprisoned in decaying tower blocks, are casualties of the welfare state. At the top, an equivalent proportion, consisting mostly of affluent managers and professionals, may threaten to opt out of the wider society, into 'ghettos of the privileged'.

(6) Takes globalization seriously. Many authors and politicians, while recognizing the significance of globalization, concentrate only upon policies on a national plane. We must respond to global change on a local, national and world-wide level.

Third way social democrats should look to transform existing global institutions and support the creation of new ones. The left in the past has always been internationalist. Socialists used to champion international solidarity and were the leaders in promoting the economic development of poorer countries – even if the strategies they endorsed were largely failures. Today, ironically, the old left has become isolationist, sometimes opposing almost every aspect of the global economy (Amsden and Hikino, 1999). The intensifying of globalization, however – which in any case goes well beyond the economic marketplace alone – offers many benefits, which it should be the aim of third way politics to maximize.

In the rest of the book I shall try to develop each of the above points in greater detail, beginning with problems of state, government and economic policy.

References

Amsden, A.H. and Hikino, T. (1999) 'The left and globalisation', *Dissent*, vol.46, no.2, Spring, pp.7–9.

Offe, C. (1998) 'The present historical transformation and some basic design options for societal institutions', paper presented at the seminar on 'Society and the Reform of the State', São Paulo (26–29 March).

Source: Giddens, 2000, pp.50–4

2.2 Anthony Giddens, 'The question of civil society' (1998)

The fostering of an active civil society is a basic part of the politics of the third way. In contrast to the old left, which tended to be dismissive of worries about civic decline, the new politics accepts that such anxieties are genuine. Civic decline is real and visible in many sectors of contemporary societies, not just an invention of conservative politicians. It is seen in the weakening sense of solidarity in some local communities and urban neighbourhoods, high levels of crime, and the break-up of marriages and families.

The right tends to deny that economic deprivation is associated with these problems. But it is just as wrong to reduce civic decline to economics, as the old left often did, as to deny the influence of poverty and underprivilege. We can't blame the erosion of civility on the welfare state, or suppose that it can be reversed by leaving civil society to its own devices. Government can and must play a major part in renewing civic culture.

> **The renewal of civil society**
> Government and civil society in partnership
> Community renewal through harnessing local initiative
> Involvement of the third sector
> Protection of the local public sphere
> Community-based crime prevention
> The democratic family

State and civil society should act in partnership, each to facilitate, but also to act as a control upon, the other. The theme of community is fundamental to the new politics, but not just as an abstract slogan. The advance of globalization makes a community focus both necessary and possible, because of the downward pressure it exerts. 'Community' doesn't imply trying to recapture lost forms of local solidarity; it refers to practical means of furthering the social and material refurbishment of neighbourhoods, towns and larger local areas. There are no permanent boundaries between government and civil society. Depending on context, government needs sometimes to be drawn further into the civil arena, sometimes to retreat. Where government withdraws from direct involvement, its resources might still be necessary to support activities that local groups take over or introduce – above all in poorer areas. Yet it is particularly in poorer communities that the fostering of local initiative and involvement can generate the highest return.

Diminished trust in politicians and other authority figures is sometimes taken to indicate general social apathy. As mentioned, it does not – perhaps the opposite. An increasingly reflexive society is also one marked by high levels of self-organization. Research in the US, the UK and elsewhere tends to indicate a burgeoning civil sphere, at least in some areas and contexts. Some older forms of civil association and civic engagement are losing their purchase, but other sorts of communal energy are replacing them. The point is to harness these to wider social ends in ways that benefit local communities as well as the society as a whole.

Robert Wuthnow has studied the development of the small-group movement in the US. By small groups, he means small numbers of people who meet together in a regular way to develop their common interests. On the basis of extensive research, he concludes that 40 per cent of Americans – some 75 million – belong to at least one small group that meets regularly. In such groups a feeling of community is generated, but not only in the old sense of being part of a local area. Rather, people with similar concerns get together to pursue a 'journey through life':

> Small groups are doing a better job than many of their critics would like to think. The communities they create are seldom frail. People feel cared for. They help one another … The attachments that develop among the members of small groups demonstrate clearly that we are not a society of rugged individualists who wish to go it entirely alone but, rather, that … even amidst the dislocating tendencies of our society, we are capable of banding together in bonds of mutual support.
>
> (Wuthnow, 1994)

Many of the groups originated in the 1960s, and reflect ideas about group process that became widespread then. Some quite explicitly aim for the sorts of value

Inglehart calls post-materialist. Therapeutic models have influenced most such groups, no matter what their specific fields of concern are. Self-help groups are particularly prominent. As with all groups and communities, small groups obviously have their limitations and problems, but they do give evidence of rich civic life.

In his study of the UK in the post-1950 period, Peter Hall shows that activity in the third sector – voluntary work – has expanded over the past forty years. More traditional groups have declined, but they have been more than made up for by new ones, particularly self-help and environmental groups. A major change is the increased participation of women. Charitable groups have shown a considerable increase – there were over 160,000 registered charitable groups in Britain in 1991. Nearly 20 per cent of the population engages in some form of voluntary work during the course of the average year, and about 10 per cent do so on a weekly basis. Hall found that younger people are involved in voluntary work now at least as frequently as was the case in earlier generations.

Significantly, however, most of the increase in civic activity has happened among the more affluent strata. People from poorer backgrounds are more likely to centre their informal social contacts upon close kin. Much smaller proportions of people in the more affluent groups suffer from a complete absence of social support than do those in the poorer strata (Hall, 1997).

One of the prime concerns of government involvement should be to help repair the civil order among such groups. The integrated working-class community is a persistent image, but now largely belongs to the past. Civic involvement is least developed in areas and neighbourhoods marginalized by the sweep of economic and social change. The renewal of deprived local communities presumes the encouragement of economic enterprise as a means of generating a broader civic recovery. The lessons of 1960s social engineering have by now been learned everywhere. Recent studies indicate that with appropriate external support, local initiative can reverse even strongly embedded processes of decline (Power, 1997).

References

Hall, P. (1997) 'Social capital in Britain', mimeo, Center for European Studies, Cambridge, MA, Harvard University.

Power, A. (1997) *Estates on the Edge*, London, Macmillan.

Wuthnow, R. (1994) *Sharing the Journey*, New York, Free Press.

Source: Giddens, 1998, pp.78–82

2.3 Anthony Giddens, 'Inclusion and exclusion' (1998)

Exclusion is not about gradations of inequality, but about mechanisms that act to detach groups of people from the social mainstream. At the top, voluntary exclusion is driven by a diversity of factors. Having the economic means to pull out of the wider society is the necessary condition for, but never the whole explanation as to why, groups choose to do so.

> **The inclusive society**
> Equality as inclusion
> Limited meritocracy
> Renewal of public space (civic liberalism)
> 'Beyond the work society'
> Positive welfare
> The social investment state

Exclusion at the top is not only just as threatening for public space, or common solidarity, as exclusion at the bottom; it is causally linked to it. That the two go together is easily seen from the more extreme examples that have developed in some countries, such as Brazil or South Africa. Limiting the voluntary exclusion of the elites is central to creating a more inclusive society at the bottom.

Many suggest the accumulation of privilege at the top is unstoppable. Income inequalities seem to be rising across a wide front. In the US, for example, 60 per cent of income gains over the period from 1980 to 1990 went to the top 1 per cent of the population, while the real income of the poorest 25 per cent has remained static more or less for thirty years. The UK shows similar trends in less extreme form. The gap between the highest-paid and lowest-paid workers is greater than it has been for at least fifty years. While the large majority of the working population are better off in real terms than twenty years ago, the poorest 10 per cent have seen their real incomes decline.

Yet it does not follow that such trends are set to continue or worsen. Technological innovation is imponderable, and it is possible that at some point the tendency towards greater inequality might shift the other way. These trends are in any case more complicated than appears at first sight. As measured by some of the most exhaustive studies, income inequality has gone down rather than up in some developed countries over the past thirty years. Of course, we don't know exactly how reliable income data are – attempts to measure the secondary economy are guesswork. That economy may increase

inequality, but it is more likely to act the other way, because informal economic activities, barter and unofficial cash transactions are normally more common among poorer groups. Finally, those countries having lengthy periods of neoliberal government have shown higher increases in economic inequality than others, with the US, New Zealand and the UK leading the way.

Writing in relation to the US, the political journalist Mickey Kaus has suggested a distinction between 'economic liberalism' and 'civic liberalism'…. The gap between rich and poor will keep growing and no one can stop it. The public realm, however, can be rebuilt through 'civic liberalism'. Kaus is surely right to argue that the emptying of public space can be reversed, and that tackling social exclusion at the top isn't only an economic issue. Yet economic inequalities are certainly not irrelevant to exclusionary mechanisms and we don't have to give up on reducing them.

In the context of Europe, one key element is sustaining levels of welfare spending. The welfare state might stand in need of radical reform, but welfare systems do and should influence resource distribution. Other strategies can also be contemplated, some of them capable of wide application, such as employee stock ownership schemes, the redistributive implications of which might be substantial. A basic influence upon the distribution of income is growing sexual equality. Here income inequality is decreasing, not increasing, contradicting again the simple statement that society is becoming more unequal. Changes in the family affect structures of inequality. Thus in the UK in 1994–5, half of those in the top 20 per cent of incomes were either single full-time workers or couples both working full-time. The new patterns of inequality are not just given. They can be influenced by government policies, such as ones that support the involvement of single parents in the labour force.

'Civic liberalism' – the recapturing of public space – nonetheless must be a basic part of an inclusive society at the top. How can this liberalism be renewed or sustained? The successful cultivation of the cosmopolitan nation is one way. People who feel themselves members of a national community are likely to acknowledge a commitment to others within it. The development of a responsible business ethos is also relevant. In terms of social solidarity, the most important groups are not only the new corporate rich but also the members of the professional and moneyed middle class, since they are closest to the dividing lines which threaten to pull away from public space. Improving the quality of public education, sustaining a well-resourced health service, promoting safe public amenities, and controlling levels of crime are all relevant. It is for these reasons that reform of the welfare state should not reduce it to a safety net.

Only a welfare system that benefits most of the population will generate a common morality of citizenship. Where 'welfare' assumes only a negative connotation, and is targeted largely at the poor, as has tended to happen in the US, the results are divisive.

Source: Giddens, 1998, pp.104–8

2.4 Ian Hacking, 'How should we do the history of statistics?'[1] (1991)

1 Statistics and the human sciences

Statistics is not a human science, but its influence on those sciences has been immense. I do not have in mind the fact that it is a tool of the sociologists, for it is used in many other fields as well – agriculture, meteorology, and sometimes even physics. I am concerned with something more fundamental than methodology. Statistics has helped determine the form of laws about society and the character of social facts. It has engendered concepts and classifications within the human sciences. Moreover the collection of statistics has created, at the least, a great bureaucratic machinery. It may think of itself as providing only information, but it is itself part of the technology of power in a modern state.

1.1 The form of laws

Different schools of sociology assign different roles to statistics. In the early 1830s August Comte wanted to give the name of 'social mechanics' or 'social physics' to his new science. But at about the same time the Belgian astronomer Adolphe Quetelet took the very same name for a new statistical science of mankind. Comte always resisted this, and coined the name 'sociology' just to get away from probabilities.[2] But Quetelet was a great propagandist. He organized the world statistical congresses and was even instrumental in starting the statistical section of the British Association in 1833. He became the grand old man of a new 'science'. Today we see that Quetelet triumphed over Comte: an enormously influential body of modern sociological thought takes for granted that social laws will be cast in a statistical form.

1.2 The character of statistical facts

It was long thought to be possible that statistical laws are epiphenomena deriving from non-statistical facts at the level of individuals. By the 1890s, Durkheim had the opposite idea, urging that social laws act from above on individuals, with the same inexorable power as the law of gravity. This opinion had philosophical roots. Durkheim was well versed in the debates about emergent laws in science, laws that come into being at a certain stage of evolution. Durkheim's innovation was to found his argument on the sheer regularity and stability of quantitative social facts about statistics and crime. One name for statistics, especially in France, had been 'moral science': the science of deviancy, of criminals, court convictions, suicides, prostitution, divorce. There had been an earlier practice, also called 'moral science'. That was an a priori science of good reason, founded upon Lockeist theory of ideas. It was institutionalized as the second class of the Academy, and was abolished by Napoleon in 1803. The second class was re-established in 1834, but by then 'moral science' meant something completely different.[3] It was above all the science that studied, empirically and en masse, immoral behaviour. By the time that Durkheim wrote, moral science had flourished for 60 years. The great founder of modern numerical psychology, William Wundt, could say even by 1862 that statisticians had demonstrated that there are laws of love just as for all other human phenomena. In 1891, even before Durkheim's *Suicide*, Walter F. Willcox published his doctoral thesis *The Divorce Problem* noting that divorce and suicide rates are correlated social indicators. During his enormously long career, Willcox (1861–1964) was to play almost as dominant a role in American statistical sociology and the census as Quetelet had once done. From the time of Quetelet to that of Willcox social facts simply became facts that are statistical in character.

1.3 Concepts and classifications

Many of the modern categories by which we think about people and their activities were put in place by an attempt to collect numerical data. The idea of recidivism, for example, appears when the quantitative study of crimes began in the 1820s. Thanks to medical statistics a canonical list of causes of death was established during the nineteenth century. It is perpetuated to this day. The classification demanded by the World Health Organization is based on that devised for the (England and Wales) Registrar General's office, run by William Farr. In most parts of the world it has long been illegal to die of anything except causes on the official list – although the list of causes is regularly revised. It is illegal, for example, to die of old age.[4] As for the censuses: Article 1, §2 of the American constitution decrees that there shall be a census every ten years. At first that was only to determine the boundaries of electoral districts, and only four questions were asked. In 1870, 156 questions were asked; in 1880, the number was 13,010. More important, perhaps, were the changing categories. New kinds of people came to be counted, and the categories of the census, and of other bureaucracies such as the Factory Inspectorate in England and Wales, created (or so I would urge) the official form of the class structure of industrial societies. … In addition to new kinds of people, there are also statistical meta-concepts of which the most notable is 'normalcy'. It is no accident that Durkheim conceived that he was providing a general theory to distinguish normal from pathological states of society. In the same final decade of the nineteenth century, Karl Pearson, a founding father of biometrics, eugenics and Anglo-American statistical theory, called the Gaussian distribution the normal curve.

1.4 Bureaucratic power

It is a well-known thesis of Michel Foucault that a new kind of power emerges in the nineteenth century. In one form it is a strategic development of medicine and law. More generally he sees it as part of what he calls biopolitics. There is a certain preoccupation with bodies. The disciplines of the body that he describes in his work on the prison and on sexuality form 'an entire micro-power concerned with the body', and match up with 'comprehensive measures, statistical assessments and interventions' which are aimed at the body politic, the social body. One need not subscribe fully to this model to see that statistics of populations and of deviancy form an integral part of the industrial state. Such a politics is directly involved in capital formation through social assurance; there is what Daniel Defert calls a *technologie assurentiel* which has to do with providing a stable social order.[5] He notes that of the two chief French funds for industrial assurance, one provided the capital for home investments while the other gave us Indo-China.

It is certainly not true that most applications of the new statistical knowledge were evil. One may suspect the ideology of the great Victorian social reformers and still grant that their great fight for sanitation, backed by statistical enquiries, was the most important single amelioration of the epoch. Without it most of you would not exist, for your great-great…-grandparents would never have lived to puberty. Statistical data do have a certain superficial neutrality between ideologies. No one used the facts collected by the factory inspectors more vigorously than Marx. Yet even Marx did not perceive how statistical bureaucracy would change the state. It is a glib but true generalization that proletarian revolutions have never occurred in any state whose assurantial technology was working properly. Conversely, wherever after any even partial industrialization it has failed, a revolution, either to left or to right, has occurred.

Notes

1 A colloquium with the general title, 'Comment et pourquoi faire l'histoire des sciences humaines?' was held at Nanterre, Université de Paris X, 30 May–1 June 1980. This is the translation of one of the numerous papers invited for discussion. It was intended to provide enough factual background to address some of the methodological questions suggested by the title of the conference. …

2 The most convenient source of references for work by Quetelet, and his relationship to Comte, is still Lottin (1912).

3 This distinction between the two kinds of moral science, with special emphasis on enlightenment 'moral science', is well described in Daston (1979).

4 I owe this observation to Anne Fagot's remarkable draft dissertation of 1978. An English translation is in preparation for Reidel.

5 No theoretical exposition of this idea is yet available (Defert *et al.*, 1977; Ajtony *et al.*, 1979).

References

Atjony, A., Callens, S., Defert, D., Ewald, F. and Maillet, G. (1979) *Assurance-Prevonance-Sécurité: Formation Historique des Techniqes de Gestion Sociale dans les Sociétés Industrielles*, Paris, Ministere du Travail et de la Participation.

Daston, L. (1979) 'The reasonable calculus: classical probability theory 1650–1840', doctoral thesis, Cambridge, MA, Harvard University.

Defert, D., Donzelot, J. Ewald, F., Maillet, G. and Mevel, C. (1977) *Socialization du Risque et Pouvoir dans L'enterprise*, Paris, Ministère du Travail.

Fagot, A. (1978) 'L'explication causale de la mort', draft dissertation.

Lottin, J. (1912) *Quetelet, Statisticien et Sociologue*, Paris, Louvain.

Willcox, W.F. (1891) 'The divorce problem: a study in statistics', *Studies in History and Economics and Public Law*, vol.1, pp.1–74.

Source: Hacking, 1991, pp.181–4

2.5 Pat O'Malley, 'Risk and responsibility' (1996)

Prudentialism

The past decade or more, has witnessed the partial transformation of socialized actuarialism into privatized actuarialism (prudentialism) as an effect of political interventions promoting the increased play of market forces. More specifically, this has involved three integrally related changes: the retraction of socialized risk-based techniques from managing the risks confronting the populace; their progressive replacement through the extension of privatized risk-based techniques; and the articulation of this process with the strategic deployment of sovereign remedies and disciplinary interventions that facilitate, underline and enforce moves towards government through individual responsibility.

While these processes have been outlined above in relation to crime control, they have become characteristic of many other areas of government. In the field of health, for example, the provision of publicly provided or subsidized medical treatment is downscaled, the scale and range of services provided by the State is narrowed, qualifying conditions for access to such services are made more rigorous and may also be allowed to become less attractive (e.g. long waiting lists for surgery). Reliance on publicly provided medicine is deterred, for example, by increasing the contributory payments, or by implying that it is immoral for the middle class to rely on public medicine, regardless of salary-indexing of contributions. This is paralleled by promotion of private health insurance and provision of private medical services, as both State and private sector voices stress the moral and rational basis for preferring private sector treatment. The rational and responsible self-interest of the medical consumers is thus relied upon to remove them from dependence on the public health services, *per medium* of a material and moral manipulation of the service environment.[1] At the same time, all manner of regimes and routines are promoted with respect to the care of the body. Whether commercially provided (weight-loss programmes, fitness centres) or State-funded (public endorsement of low fat diets, anti-smoking campaigns), a disciplinary regime of the body has been promoted, founded on the assumption that subjects of risk will opt to participate in a self-imposed programme of health and fitness.

Across this spectrum of developments, two closely related images recur – those of the responsible (moral) and of the rational (calculating) individual. The rational individual will wish to become responsible for the self, for (albeit via some neo-liberal manipulation of the environment) this will produce the most palatable, pleasurable and effective mode of provision for security against risk. Equally, the responsible individual will take rational steps to avoid and to insure against risk, in order to be independent rather than a burden on others. Guided by actuarial data on risks (e.g. on smoking and lung cancer; bowel cancer and diet, etc.) and on the delivery of relevant services and expertise (e.g. relative costs and benefits of public and private medicine), the rational and responsible individual will take prudent risk-managing measures. Within such prudential strategies, then, calculative self-interest is articulated with actuarialism to generate risk management as an everyday practice of the self. This is backed up by a moral responsibility, or duty to the self – or as Greco (1993) has termed it, a 'duty to be well':

Each individual acquires a personal preventative capacity *vis-à-vis* the event of his or her illness … If the regulation of lifestyle, the modification of risky behaviour and the transformation of unhealthy attitudes prove impossible through sheer strength of will, this constitutes at least in part *a failure of the self to take care of itself* – a form of irrationality, or simply a lack of skilfulness.

(Greco, 1993, p.361)

…

Contemporary liberal approaches to government adopt a rather different view. In the first place, as is argued by Aharoni, risk by no means is to be understood as indicative of an imperfectly governed world. Rather, risk is a source or condition of opportunity, an avenue for enterprise and the creation of wealth, and thus an unavoidable and invaluable part of a progressive environment. Without risk, wealth would not be created, innovation would be stultified, individuals would lose a spur to action and a crucial condition for generating responsibility. In this vision, the efforts of social engineers to eliminate risk have been a major contributor to the malaises of contemporary society. This is not to say that *all* risks are so conceived. Clearly, neo-liberalism would regard many *specific* risks as ones that can and should be prevented or minimized. But this is quite different to the social engineering vision of a society of universal security, 'no-risk society', in which risk as such, ideally, should be eliminated. For neo-liberalism it is always necessary to ask 'Which risk?' before deciding whether a constricting or a sustaining response is required.

For this reason the management of risk becomes the responsibility of neo-liberal governance only with considerable circumspection. On the one hand, this is because, as argued throughout, individuals should take responsibility for the management of risks, as part of their rational and responsible existence. On the other hand, it is because the definition of many risks as significant or insignificant, ideally, must also be devolved to the individual. To the extent that neo-liberal subjects confront risks, unmediated by interference from the State and social engineers (although, of course, provided with advice and information by such experts as police and the medical profession), then they will be moved to act on their own behalf. Those risks that will receive their attention will be the ones they identify as significant problems. The risk-management techniques they support – through personal advocacy and effort, or by purchase

in the market place – will be the ones they define as the best available. And we can be sure of the efficiency of this process, because the success of the measures taken will be assessed in terms of the cost-benefit calculus of individuals who put their own resources and their own security on the line.[2] Prudentialism thus embodies a key technique for dealing with one of the central problematics of liberal governmentalities – defining the minimal parameters of State activity consistent with an ordered, prosperous and peaceful nation.

Notes

1 The obvious, if partial exception here is the (unrealized) proposal for a public health programme under the Clinton regime from 1993. However, it will readily be recognized that in that context, the process of downscaling public medicine and the promotion of private sector responsibility had been implemented considerably earlier. Clinton's reforms relate specifically to another generation of *political* problems. Such changes underline a general point in this chapter that politics is far more important than is implied by a focus on allegedly 'given' effects of social technologies, and indeed, that the effects themselves are a matter of political negotiation rather than automatic consequence.

2 It may be argued that many important risks in everyday life could not be left to such a process. Crime control would be one of these, especially with reference to police. But as has been seen already, there is considerable scope for increasing the role of prudential strategies here. Beyond the forms discussed in this chapter, it should be considered that, to the extent that the provision of expertise shifts towards the 'customer' or to 'partnership' models, so the determination of police priorities and practices in crime risk management is determined by the individuals who make up the 'local community'. These people direct police activities, and personally bear the costs and benefits of their preferred risk-management strategies. As Britain currently is witnessing, even a regime investing heavily in the politics of law and order is quite capable of subjecting the police to such neo-liberal practices (McLaughlin and Muncie, 1993).

References

Greco, M. (1993) 'Psychosomatic subjects and the "duty to be well": personal agency within medical rationality', *Economy and Society*, vol.22, no.3, pp.357–72.

McLaughlin, E. and Muncie, J. (1993) 'The silent revolution: market-based criminal justice in England', *Socio-Legal Bulletin*, vol.8, pp.5–12.

Source: O'Malley, 1996, pp.199–200, 204–5

2.6 Nikolas Rose, 'Community' (1999)

Policy debates in the 1990s also appealed to this third space as a solution to problems of government. Since perhaps the mid-1960s, the community was proclaimed to be the appropriate locus for crime control, punishment, psychiatric services, social welfare and much more: community care, community correction, community architecture, community policing, community safety … As is now well known, whatever images of spontaneity of care it conjured up, this community was actually a diagram for the reorganization of publicly provided, bureaucratically organized and professionally staffed services. In the political programmes of Clinton and Blair, references to community have a different resonance: they are infused with notions of voluntarism, of charitable works, of self-organized care, of unpaid service to one's fellows. The space appealed to here has been made increasingly real and given its own name: the third sector (e.g. Van Til, 1988; Drucker, 1995). In 1995, a widely discussed book by Jeremy Rifkin gave a boost to these arguments. He suggested that the problem of structural underemployment generated by technological advances in the labour process could be overcome by creating millions of new jobs in the 'third sector' between market and government. This would empower all those voluntary and not-for-profit organizations, through which many people already devote their time to their neighbourhoods and communities: volunteers who assist the elderly and handicapped, refurbish apartments, work in hospitals and clinics, deliver meals to the poor, act as volunteer firefighters, assist in day-care centres, work for advocacy organizations and participate in local theatre groups, choirs and orchestras. '[T]he commercial and public sectors are no longer capable of securing some of the fundamental needs of the people, the public has little choice but to begin looking out for itself, once again, by re-establishing viable communities as a buffer against both the impersonal forces of the global market and increasingly weak and incompetent central governing authorities' (Rifkin, 1995, p.238). But, whilst, for Rifkin, the third sector was distinct from both the market and government, its revitalization was nonetheless a key element in government. Like the political objectification of civil society in the early phase of liberalism, this third sector was 'a fertile ground for experimentation in the development of political technologies of government': it was a space in which one could observe the hybridization of political power and other non-political forms of authority in a variety of attempts to enframe and instrumentalize the forces of individuals and groups in the name of the public good (Burchell, 1991, p.141).

Of course, communitarianism is one of the traditional themes of constitutional thought: liberal political discourse always tempered the ideal of individual liberties and rights with claims made in the interests of communities. The idea that communities could take upon themselves responsibility for governing themselves would not have been foreign to many philanthropists and reformers in eighteenth-century Britain, nor to many who tried to define a federal politics for the United States based on the idea of self-rule (Tully, 1995; Hindess, 1996a)[1]. The theme of loss of community, and the need to remake community or substitute something for its benefits, emerges with remarkable regularity in critical reflections on the state of the nation from the nineteenth century onwards. From the familiar nineteenth-century tales of the loss of tradition and the rise of individualism in the shift from *Gemeinschaft* to *Gesellschaft*, through the analyses of the damaging effects of metropolitan life in the 1920s and 1930s, to the community studies of the 1950s, sociologists, moralists, politicians and pamphleteers rehearse similar themes. But this similarity is a little misleading. The community appealed to is different in different cases: differently spatialized and differently temporized. When social and political theorists in the late nineteenth and early twentieth centuries claimed that there had been a shift from community to society, they located this within a metaphysics of history: community was that set of moral bonds among individuals fragmented by the division of labour and capitalist production, to be re-assembled in a 'social' form through a politics of solidarism and social right. The community of 'community studies' in the UK in the period after the Second World War was associated with the apparent anomie created by the disturbance of 'settled' working-class urban communities. This was community as the 'traditional' order of neighbourhood – a localized space of habitation – eroded by the bureaucratic incompetence of well-intentioned but patronizing planners, the bonds of mutuality destroyed by the very welfare regime that sought to support them. The community of welfare reformers of the 1960s and 1970s was different again: it was a network of professional institutions and services for social citizens that was spread across the territory of their everyday lives.

The community of the third sector, the third space, the third way of governing is not primarily a geographical space, a social space, a sociological space or a space of services, although it may attach itself to any or all such spatializations. It is a moral field binding persons into durable relations. It is a space of *emotional relationships* through which *individual identities* are constructed through their bonds to *micro-cultures* of values and meanings. 'Community', says Etzioni (1997), 'is defined by two characteristics: first, a web of affect-laden relationships among a group of individuals, relationships that often criss-cross and reinforce one another … and second, a measure of commitment to a set of shared values, norms, and meanings, and a shared history and identity – in short, to a particular culture' (p.127). And it is through the political objectification and instrumentalization of *this* community and its 'culture' that government is to be re-invented.

…

Whilst the term 'community' has long been salient in political thought, it becomes governmental when it is made technical. By the 1960s, community was already being invoked by sociologists as a possible antidote to the loneliness and isolation of the individual generated by 'mass society'. In social politics, this idea of community as lost authenticity and common belonging was initially deployed as part of the language of critique and opposition directed against remote bureaucracy. Community activists were to identify not with a welfare system that they saw as degrading, policing and controlling, but with those who were the subjects of that system – the inhabitants of the housing estates, projects and ghettos. More or less simultaneously, the language of community was utilized by authorities such as police to comprehend the problems they encountered in dealing with difficult zones – 'the West Indian community', the criminal community. Community here was a point of penetration of a kind of ethnographic sociology into the vocabularies and classifications of authorities. Reciprocally, sociology itself intensified its investigations of collective life in terms of community: it anatomized the bonds of culture and the ties of locality that were thought to be essential conditions for the moral order of society and for individual and familial well-being. Within a rather short period, what began as a language of resistance and critique was transformed, no doubt for the best of motives, into an expert discourse and a professional vocation – community is now something to be programmed by Community Development Programmes, developed by Community Development Officers, policed by Community Police,

guarded by Community Safety Programmes and rendered knowable by sociologists pursuing 'community studies'. Communities became zones to be investigated, mapped, classified, documented, interpreted, their vectors explained to enlightened professionals-to-be in countless college courses and to be taken into account in numberless encounters between professionals and their clients, whose individual conduct is now to be made intelligible in terms of the beliefs and values of 'their community'.

No doubt a whole range of other local shifts in vocabulary in diverse sites contributed to the emergence of community as a valorized alternative, antidote or even cure to the ills that the social had not been able to address – or even to the ills of the social itself. In the 1980s, in the midst of this shift, sociologists were already seeking to diagnose what was occurring in terms of power. Most notable here was the suggestion that, at least as far as deviance was concerned, the space of community was being colonized by agents, institutions and practices of control.[2] This argument remains valuable and insightful. But I would frame it slightly differently. For what is happening here is not the colonization of a previous space of freedom by control practices; community is actually instituted in its contemporary form as a sector for government. And this is not a process of social control if this be understood in the sense of mechanisms to ensure that members of a society conform to expectations. Rather, in the institution of community, a sector is brought into existence whose vectors and forces can be mobilized, enrolled, deployed in novel programmes and techniques which encourage and harness active practices of self-management and identity construction, of personal ethics and collective allegiances. I term this *government through community.*

Political subjectivity

In part, what was involved here was a remaking of political subjectivity. Whilst the policies and programmes of the social accorded individuals personal responsibility for their conduct, this individual responsibility was always traversed by external determinations: the advantages or disadvantages conferred by family background, social class, life history, located within a wider array of social and economic forces such as changes in the labour market, booms, slumps, industrial cycles, the exigencies of urban environments, problems of housing supply. Of course, the extent to which such external determinants could or should mitigate personal responsibility was subject to continual dispute, as was the extent to which they could or should be compensated for in education, in the decisions of the criminal court and so forth. Nevertheless, this configuration of ethical vectors is reorganized under the sign of community. The subject is addressed as a moral individual with bonds of obligation and responsibilities for conduct that are assembled in a new way – the individual in his or her community is both self-responsible and subject to certain emotional bonds of affinity to a circumscribed 'network' of other individuals – unified by family ties, by locality, by moral commitment to environmental protection or animal welfare. Conduct is retrieved from a social order of determination into a new ethical perception of the individualized and autonomized actor, each of whom has unique, localized and specific ties to his or her particular family and to a particular moral community.

The regulative ideal of universal and uniform social citizenship is called into question by these new collectivizations of political subjectivity. The practices that assembled the social certainly entailed 'identification projects': programmes of mass schooling, of public housing, of public broadcasting, of social insurance and so forth had at their heart an image and a goal of the socially identified citizen, the person who, above all, understood him- or herself to be a member of a single integrated national society. The vocabulary of community also implicates a psychology of identification. To imagine oneself, or to imagine another, as a member of a community is to posit its actual or potential existence as a fulcrum of personal identity. Yet these lines of identification are configured differently. Community proposes a relation that appears less 'remote', more 'direct', one which occurs not in the 'artificial' political space of society, but in matrices of affinity that appear more natural. One's communities are nothing more – or less – than those networks of allegiance with which one identifies existentially, traditionally, emotionally or spontaneously, seemingly beyond and above any calculated assessment of self-interest.

Hence, like so many other similar loci of allegiance – class, civil society, ethnicity – arguments about community employ a Janus-faced logic (cf. Hindess, 1996b). Each assertion of community refers itself to something that already exists and has a claim on us – our common fate as gay men, as women of colour, as people with AIDS, as members of an ethnic group, as residents in a village or a suburb, as people with a disability. Yet our allegiance to each of these particular communities is something that we have to be made

aware of, requiring the work of educators, campaigns, activists, manipulators of symbols, narratives and identifications. Within such a style of thought, community is to be achieved, yet the achievement is nothing more than the birth-to-presence of a form of being which pre-exists.

This new relation between community, identity and political subjectivity is exemplified in debates over 'multi-culturalism' or the rights of indigenous peoples, and in political controversies over the implications of 'pluralism' – of ethnicity, religion, of sexuality, of ability and disability – and the recognition to be accorded to the 'rights' and 'values' of different communities.[3] The shift from the image of the 'melting pot' to that of the 'rainbow' illustrates the way that the politics of recognition stresses the existence and legitimacy of incommensurable – or at least distinct – domains of culture, values, mores. These are not unified across a nation but localized, fragmented, hybrid, multiple, overlapping, activated differently in different arenas and practices. The uniform social citizenship that was the objective of the citizen-forming and nation-building strategies of the nineteenth and twentieth centuries is challenged by a diversity of forms of identity and allegiance no longer deferential to such an image of national and territorialized civic culture. … [I]ndividuals no longer inhabit a single 'public sphere', nor is their citizenship conferred upon them through a singular relationship with the state. Rather, citizenship is multiplied and non-cumulative: it appears to inhere in and derive from active engagement with each of a number of specific zones of identity – lifestyle sectors, neighbourhoods, ethnic groups – some private, some corporate, some quasi-public. The political problem of citizenship is reposed: it is no longer a question of national character but of the way in which multiple identities receive equal recognition in a single constitutional form. We have moved from 'culture' to 'cultures'.

This multiplication of the forms of political subjectivity is linked to new practices of identity formation. These fuse the aim of manufacturers to sell products and increase market share with the identity experiments of consumers. They are mediated by highly developed techniques of market research and finely calibrated attempts to segment and target specific consumer markets. Advertising images and television programmes interpenetrate in the promulgation of images of lifestyle, narratives of identity choice and the highlighting of the ethical aspects of adopting one or other way of conducting one's life. Practices and styles of aestheticized life-choice that were previously the monopoly of cultural elites have been generalized in this new habitat of subjectification: that is to say, the belief that individuals can shape an autonomous identity for themselves through choices in taste, music, goods, styles and habitus (see Osborne, 1998). This embodies a shift away from emphasis upon morality – obedience to an externally imposed code of conduct and values in the name of the collective good – and towards ethics – the active and practical shaping by individuals of the daily practices of their own lives in the name of their own pleasures, contentments or fulfilments.

As Cindy Patten has suggested, within such a regime, the spaces of lifestyle and culture are no longer integrated in a total governmental field (Patten, 1995, p.226; cf. Hardt, 1995). They are spaces of territorial competition and ethical dispute. Within these spaces, it is possible for subjects to distance themselves from the cohesive discourses and strategies of the social state – schooling, public service broadcasting, municipal architecture and the like. They can now access a whole range of resources and techniques of subject formation in order to invent themselves, individually and collectively, as new kinds of political actors. This fragmentation of the social by the new technologies of images and identities, of lifestyles and choices, of consumption, marketing and the mass media has thus produced new collectivizations of 'habitus' outside the control of coherent discourses of civility or the technologies of political government. The commercialization of lifestyle formation thus allows the possibility of 'other subjectivities' – novel modes of individuality and allegiance and their public legitimation. The politics of conduct is faced with a new set of problems: governing subject formation in this new plural field. Our current 'wars of subjectivity' emerge here.

...

The community–civility game

Reading Bellah, Coleman, Putnam, Etzioni, Fukuyama and the others, I am reminded of Jeremy Bentham's preface to his *Panopticon*, and the list of benefits that were to be obtained from his 'inspection house':

> *Moral reformed – health preserved – industry invigorated – instruction diffused – public burthens lightened –* Economy seated, as it were, upon a rock – the Gordian knot of the Poor-Laws not cut, but untied – all by a simple idea in architecture!
>
> (Bentham, 1843, p.39, quoted in Foucault, 1977, p.207, italics in original)

Now perhaps, one would write:

> virtue regenerated – crime reduced – public safety enhanced – institutionalization banished – dependency transformed to activity – underclass included – democratic deficit overcome – idle set to work – political alienation reduced – responsive services assured – economy reinvigorated by seating it, as it were, within networks of trust and honour – the Gordian knot of State versus individual not cut but untied, all by a simple idea in politics: community.

Almost a quarter of a century ago, Michel Foucault notoriously took Bentham's inspection house as the model for a certain type of power which he termed 'discipline': a versatile and productive micro-physics of power 'comprising a whole set of instruments, techniques, procedures, levels of application, targets' (Foucault, 1977, p.215). The Panopticon was the diagram of a political technology, one that was individualizing, normalizing, based on perpetual surveillance, classification, a kind of uninterrupted and continuous judgement enabling the government of multiplicities, reducing the resistant powers of human bodies at the same time as it maximized their economic and social utility. Foucault argued that the forms of individual civility and docile citizenship set in place by the minute web of panoptic techniques and disciplinary norms was to be the real foundation of the formal political liberties of the abstract juridical subject of law and the rational economic individual of contract and exchange.

Suppose, then, that instead of considering all these debates about communities, associations, networks and the like as descriptions of states of affairs, we thought of them in terms of government. Could one say that these programmatics of communities, associations, and so forth are related to a new diagram of power? I am tempted to answer this in the affirmative. That is to say, I suggest that one can discern here the emergence of a new 'game of power'. We could call this the 'community–civility' game. It involves new conceptions of those who are to be governed, and of the proper relations between the governors and the governed. It puts new questions into play about the kinds of people we are, the kinds of problems we face, the kinds of relations of truth and power through which we are governed and through which we should govern ourselves.

I have suggested that this new game of power operates in a field one could term *ethico-politics*. Foucault, of course, identified the rise of *disciplinary power*, focusing upon maximizing the utility and docility of individuals, and *bio-power*, focusing upon maximizing the health and welfare of the population. Ethico-politics reworks the government of souls in the context of the increasing role that culture and consumption mechanisms play in the regulation of forms of life and identity and self-techniques. If discipline *individualizes and normalizes*, and bio-power *collectivizes and socializes,* ethico-politics concerns itself with the *self-techniques necessary for responsible self-government* and the *relations between one's obligations to oneself and one's obligations to others*. Ethico-politics has a particular salience at the close of the twentieth century. For it appears that somehow 'we' – the subjects of advanced liberal democracies – in the absence of any objective guarantees for politics or our values, have become obliged to think ethically. Hence it is likely to be on the terrain of ethics that our most important political disputes will have to be fought for the foreseeable future. If this is the case, it would be pointless to condemn this ethical mutation in our ways of thinking about politics. More usefully, we would need to find ways of evaluating the new technologies and the new authorities that seek to find a way of governing us, as free individuals, through ethics.

Notes

1   For England, see, for example, Andrew (1989).

2   This argument was made brilliantly by Cohen (1985). His argument is much more complex than this, and I cannot do it justice here. But I think it remains true to say that he envisions control as a dispersal of the techniques of disciplinary individualization and normalization across the territory of everyday life and that he understands these disciplinary techniques as essentially negative and constraining in their intentions and effects.

3   The best discussions of these issues are to be found in Tully (1995), Connolly (1995), especially Chapter 6, and Shapiro (1997).

References

Andrew, D. (1989) *Philanthropy and Police: London Charity in the Eighteenth Century,* Princeton, NJ, Princeton University Press.

Bentham, J. (1843) *Works* (ed. J. Bowring), vol.IV, London, Tait.

Burchell, G. (1991) '"Peculiar interests": governing the system of natural liberty' in Burchell, G., Gordon, C. and Miller, P. (eds) *The Foucault Effect: Studies in Governmentality*, Hemel Hempstead, Harvester Wheatsheaf, pp.119–50.

Cohen, S. (1985) *Visions of Social Control*, Cambridge, Polity Press.

Connolly, W. (1995) *The Ethos of Pluralization*, Minneapolis, MN, University of Minnesota Press.

Drucker, P. (1995) 'Really reinventing government', *Atlantic Monthly*, vol.275, no.2, pp.49–61.

Etzioni, A. (1997) *The New Golden Rule: Community and Morality in a Democratic Society,* London, Profile.

Foucault, M. (1977) *Discipline and Punish: The Birth of the Prison*, (trans. A. Sheridan), London, Allen Lane.

Hardt, M. (1995) 'The withering of civil society', *Social Text*, vol.14, pp.27–44.

Hindess, B. (1996a) 'Multiculturalism and citizenship', unpublished manuscript.

Hindess, B. (1996b) 'Liberalism, socialism and democracy: variations on a governmental theme' in Barry, A., Osborne, T. and Rose, N. (eds) *Foucault and Political Reason*, London, UCL Press, pp.65–80.

Osborne, T. (1998) *Aspects of Enlightenment: Social Theory and the Ethics of Truth*, London, UCL Press.

Patten, C. (1995) 'Refiguring social space' in Nicholson, L. and Seidman, S. (eds) *Social Postmodernism: Beyond Identity Politics,* Cambridge, Cambridge University Press, pp.216–49.

Rifkin, J. (1995) *The End of Work: The Decline of the Global Labor Force and the Dawn of the Post-Market Era*, New York, Tarcher/Putnam.

Shapiro, M. (ed.) (1997) 'Bowling blind: post-liberal civil society and the worlds of neo-Toquevillean social theory', *Theory and Event*, vol.1, no.1 at http://128.220.50.88/journals/theory-&event/v001/1.shapiro.html.

Tully, J. (1995) *Strange Multiplicity: Constitutionalism in an Age of Diversity*, Cambridge, Cambridge University Press.

Van Til, J. (1988) *Mapping the Third Sector: Volunteerism in a Changing Social Economy*, New York, The Foundation Center.

Source: Rose, 1999b, pp.170–3,175–9,187–8

3

The public sphere

Jim McGuigan

Contents

Readings

1 Introduction

The public sphere is a social phenomenon just as elementary as action, actor, association, or collectivity ... The public sphere cannot be conceived as an institution and certainly not as an organization. It is not even a framework of norms ... The public sphere can best be described as a network for communicating information and points of view (i.e. opinions expressing affirmative or negative attitudes); the streams of communication are, in process, filtered in such a way that they coalesce into bundles of topically specific *public* opinions.

(Habermas, 1996/1992, p.360)

In the UK, during the year 2000, the exposition in the Millennium Dome at Greenwich was an object of immense public controversy. It cost £628 million of National Lottery money to build, stock and run for a year. In addition nearly £200 million of 'taxpayers' money' was used to buy and reclaim the site of a former gasworks on a south-eastern peninsula of the Thames. Around £150 million was also contributed by corporate sponsors. The Dome attracted only just over half of its projected visitor number of 12 million. That may have been, at least partly, due to its damnation in the media, dubbed, for instance, by Polly Toynbee in both *The Guardian* and *The Daily Mail* as a 'disaster'. The Dome was also defended in some quarters. According to MORI polling, visitors to the Dome generally liked it. Yet, people who had never been there would tell you exactly what was wrong with the Dome. It was the biggest issue in the news media in 2000, if only because of the sheer volume of column inches and broadcast time devoted to it. It took a lorry drivers' protest against the price of petrol, which threatened to bring the UK's economy to a standstill, to topple the Dome's latest troubles from lead story in the news media on 12 September 2000. However, the Dome was still the second story in broadcast news bulletins that day.

The slogan for the soap opera *EastEnders*, 'Everybody's talking about it', applied even more aptly to the Dome in the millennium year. It was a constant topic of everyday conversation as well as attracting media coverage. People had strong opinions about the Dome and were not reluctant to state them. This may be taken to illustrate what is meant by the **public sphere** – the space for **public sphere** free and open debate in a democratic society which is supposed to have policy consequence. Such debate is meant to be critical and rational so that the better argument may prevail. However, there was a great deal of irrationality surrounding the Dome, including its funding and disposal, and a great strength of feeling for and against it was expressed around the country. Did the public debate on the Dome have a rational impact upon policy or was this just the manifestation of a 'pseudo' or 'phantom' public sphere in which there is a great deal of distracted talk but no consequential action?

Figure 3.1 *A homeless man selling* The Big Issue *magazine in a shopping centre*

ACTIVITY 1

1   What 'big issue' has grabbed your attention most recently?

2   Did you feel able to participate in the debate on the issue?

3   From where did you get your information?

4   What channels of expression were open to you?

It is worth considering the extent to which sociology helps us understand public controversy over issues that really matter to people in their everyday lives. Does sociology have a political role to play or is it just a detached and neutral 'science'? The sociological problem of the public sphere emerges from a long-standing tradition of **critical theory**. As Craig Calhoun (1995) argues, critical social theory seeks to go beyond what he calls 'descriptive social science' by taking up a position on controversial matters; by questioning inequality, oppression and exclusion; and by imagining a better society. A key exponent of critical social theory today is **Jürgen Habermas**, the leading figure in descent from the neo-Marxist **Frankfurt School** of **Theodor Adorno** and **Herbert Marcuse**. This school originally established itself as a radical wing of sociology in the 1920s and 1930s. In terms of Peter Hamilton's distinction between *rational-scientific*,

critical theory

Habermas, Jürgen,
Frankfurt School,
Adorno,
Theodor W.,
Marcuse, Herbert

political and *expressive* orientations in sociology (see Chapter 1 in this volume), critical theory is a notable example of the political orientation, although it displays rational-scientific and expressive aspects too.

Habermas himself is famous for stressing the fundamental role of **communication** in everyday social life and in politics in the broadest sense. Habermas is not only a major social theorist. He is also a public intellectual who regularly comments upon current issues in the German press concerning, for instance, multiculturalism and the constitutional status of the European Union. Like his Frankfurt School precursors, Habermas is not so much concerned with the **instrumental rationality** (the use of the technically most efficient and rational means to reach a desired end or purpose) and immediate use of sociology in government (see Tony Bennett, Chapter 2 in this volume, on Giddens and third way politics), but rather with keeping open a questioning public discourse on issues – such as the damaging effects of global capitalism and neo-liberal economics – in terms of critical rationality and in the interests of emancipatory politics.

Habermas and his ideas, it must be said, are often caricatured and, in effect, represented by his detractors – in my view, mistakenly – as unrealistic. Part of the purpose of this chapter is to rescue Habermas from such misrepresentation whilst demonstrating why the public sphere is an important concept in a politically critical sociology.

communication

instrumental rationality

Figure 3.2 *Jürgen Habermas, theorist of the public sphere*

The aims of this chapter are:

1 To introduce Jürgen Habermas's concept of the public sphere as a classic example of critical social theory.

2 To compare contrasting perspectives on the media and the public sphere, one pessimistic and the other optimistic.

3 To discuss new and old media in relation to the public sphere and popular protest.

4 To consider how Habermas's latterly revised 'sluice-gate model' of the public sphere might aid the understanding of the role and impact of the anti-capitalist movement.

2 The rise and fall of the bourgeois public sphere

In 1962 the young Jürgen Habermas – who was to become the most eminent German social theorist of his generation – published *The Structural Transformation of the Public Sphere*, subtitled 'an inquiry into a category of bourgeois society'. Although this classic study served as the key point of departure for much subsequent sociological theorizing and research on the public sphere, it was not published in English translation until 1989. When *The Structural Transformation of the Public Sphere* was published in English, a wide-ranging set of criticisms and developments of Habermas's original thesis were presented at a conference in the USA (Calhoun, 1992). Habermas (1992) himself responded positively to arguments made at the conference and outlined revisions to his thinking on the public sphere since the German publication of his book 27 years earlier.

Before considering alternative perspectives on the public sphere and Habermas's later revision of the concept, it is necessary to grasp the fundamentals of his original thesis. As Habermas was to say, 'my first aim had been to derive the ideal type of the bourgeois public sphere from the historical context of British, French and German developments in the eighteenth and early nineteenth centuries' (1992, p.422). The Weberian construction of an **ideal type** – for instance, **Max Weber**'s own **bureaucracy** or Habermas's public sphere – involves the abstraction of salient characteristics from a set of historical cases. These are then used as an analytical tool for studying how such a phenomenon works in general, as well as in particular empirical instances.

ideal type, Weber, Max, bureaucracy

2.1 The rise of the bourgeois public sphere

Habermas identified the emergence of the public sphere in eighteenth-century Great Britain, France and the German regions. The emergent public sphere marked out a social space for argument and debate between the private life of **civil society** and the public life of the **state**. It afforded the opportunity for critical discussion amongst acknowledged equals to take place. Critical discussion

civil society, state

occurred in, for instance, the coffee houses of London and the salons of Paris. Richard Sennett has commented specifically upon the social conventions of the typical London coffee house, where there was:

> a cardinal rule: in order for information to be as full as possible, distinctions of rank were temporarily suspended; anyone sitting in the coffeehouse had the right to talk to anyone else, to enter any conversation, whether he knew the other people or not, whether he was bidden to speak or not. It was bad form even to touch on the social origins of other persons when talking to them in the coffeehouse, because the free flow of talk might then be impeded.
>
> (Sennett, 1986/1977, p.81)

Figure 3.3 *Gentlemen in discussion in an eighteenth-century London coffee house*

Similarly to Habermas's own account of the eighteenth-century public sphere, Sennett describes an idealized social situation. This is a good deal rosier than the actual culture of London coffee houses where commercial interests, sheer prejudice and downright snobbery were, no doubt, prominent. Nevertheless, this idealization plays an important function in the self-understanding of emergent democracy. Ideally, participants in the eighteenth-century public sphere would debate the issues of the day. Differences of opinion were expressed but a consensus amongst participants might be arrived at by the force of the better argument, thereby crystallizing a 'public opinion'. The issues in dispute could be of a diffuse nature, generally to do with life, art and letters: this was 'the literary public sphere', in Habermas's term. Other issues in dispute could be more directly to do with current matters of state, such as taxation and warfare – that is, 'the political public sphere'. Public sphere debate not only occurred in face-to-face conversation but was also mediated and represented by publications, ranging from novels, plays and poetry to newspapers. For example, in London coffee houses, gentlemen would read *The Spectator* and *The Times*, discuss the issues reported upon and contribute to their further elaboration through talk and writing, including articles and letters.

The public sphere is not only an ideal type, a heuristic device of Weberian methodology; it also signifies a utopian ideal, which is an official ideology, of how debate should be conducted over issues of culture and politics that is supposed to have policy consequence in an egalitarian democracy. Sceptics argue that it was never really like that and never will be. While they may be right on historical grounds, sceptics miss the critical function of the public sphere ideal as a measure of actually existing democracy, particularly drawing attention to how the reality of public deliberation and democratic process falls short of official claims. It was ever thus.

The original public sphere was *bourgeois*, narrowly restricted in class terms to the agents and intermediaries of capitalism, gentlemen of property and their allies – industrialists, merchants, bankers, landed gentry, lawyers and journalists – with a stake in wresting power from the feudal aristocracy. In America and France, this fomented violent revolution, leading to the constitution of the United States and the French Republic. The emancipation of the British bourgeoisie was somewhat less dramatic. In 1832, all 'men of property' – the chattering class of the public sphere – obtained the vote for electing parliamentary representatives, thus ensuring their rights, crucially, to trade and communicate freely. The working class, peasants and women were still, in effect, excluded from the rights and privileges of **citizenship**.

citizenship

The official rhetoric of equal and universal participation in the public sphere was difficult, to say the least, to reconcile with the manifest realities of social inequality and political exclusion. However, logically and politically it was impossible, in the longer run, for the 'included' to stop the 'excluded' from campaigning for – and eventually obtaining – the formal rights of citizenship, legal inclusion in the culture and practice of liberal democracy. This happened most notably in Britain with the Chartist, Labour and suffragette movements.

Marx, Karl

Karl Marx, as a journalist in the 1840s and 1850s, 'treated the public sphere ironically' (Habermas, 1989b/1962, p.123). Marx regarded it as an ideological construct that masked the real foundations of bourgeois democracy under the cover of 'freedom' and 'equality'. The public sphere for Marx was not, though, just a sham. Marx operated in the official public sphere, mainly at a distance once he became notorious for his association with revolutionary agitation. As European correspondent for *The New York Daily Tribune* he published more than 350 articles on critical topics (some with the help of Friedrich Engels). He also, of course, engaged in what Habermas named 'the plebeian public sphere' of radical politics.

Habermas was criticized for neglecting the plebeian public sphere (Negt and Kluge, 1993/1972), although he did register and name it. More recently, Habermas (1992) acknowledged E.P. Thompson's (1963) research for *The Making of the English Working Class*, which was published the year after his book on the public sphere. Thompson traced a radical intellectual tradition and culture in Britain – inspired by the American and French Revolutions – and functioning through reading groups, corresponding societies and publications that were harried and criminalized by the British state in the late eighteenth and early nineteenth centuries. This unofficial public sphere, represented by popular newspapers such as *The Poor Man's Guardian*, had a powerful impact on the bourgeois public sphere, not only in opposition but also as a source of progressive ideas. These were, to a considerable extent, incorporated and realized after much bitter struggle throughout the nineteenth century and into the twentieth century, resulting in suffrage reform and trade union recognition. Marx, like the protagonists of the plebeian public sphere, took the official claims of the bourgeois public sphere very seriously indeed. The principles of rational-critical debate, universal equality and justice had to be seen as potentially realizable in practice, not only in order to expose the contradictions of liberal democracy but also because, for Marx, they were held to be the philosophical grounds for a general emancipation of humanity and would be essential to a socialist democracy (Williams, 1983).

2.2 The fall of the bourgeois public sphere

For the young Habermas, however, it had all gone horribly wrong by the middle of the twentieth century. From about the 1870s, according to Habermas, the bourgeois public sphere went into decline. The press became increasingly commercialized with the expansion of advertising. In Britain, for instance, the radical press had been legalized but was eventually replaced mid-century by the sensationalism of *The News of the World* and, by the end of the century, the petit-bourgeois preoccupations of *The Daily Mail*. There was also the rise of public relations in the United States, spreading to Europe in the early twentieth century. As we shall see in the next section, the idea took hold that 'public opinion' had to be 'manufactured' rather than freely formed and expressed.

Generally speaking, Habermas argued that the public sphere had been 're-feudalized': by this he meant that a small elite held more or less unquestioned power while the broad mass of the population were comparatively powerless and largely unresponsive to politics. This had two aspects: first, in the conduct of public life; second, in the conduct of private life. In public life, capitalist power grew in alliance with the state, commodifying and administering everything; and, while the social-welfare state improved the living conditions of the general public, it did so at the cost of effectively restricting popular participation in politics. To quote Habermas:

> Today the conversation is administered. Professional dialogues from the podium, panel discussions, and round table shows – the rational debate of private people becomes one of the production of numbers of the stars in radio and television, a salable package ready for the box office; it assumes commodity form even at 'conferences' where anyone can 'participate'. Discussion, now a 'business', becomes formalized; the presentation of positions and counterpositions is bound to certain prearranged rules of the game; consensus about the subject matter is made largely superfluous by that concerning form. What can be posed as a problem is defined as a question of etiquette; conflicts, once fought out in public polemics, are demoted to the level of personal incompatibilities. Critical debate arranged in this manner certainly fulfils important social-psychological functions, especially that of a tranquilising substitute for action; however, it increasingly loses its publicist function.

> (Habermas, 1989b/1962, p.164)

According to Habermas, this formal rather than substantive public sphere is a 'pseudo' public sphere. If that is the case, then it is hardly surprising to find many 'apathetic' people who are turned off public debate and, indeed, politics itself. Such a view is similar to the one expressed later by Jean Baudrillard (1988), the 'post-modern' sociologist, who argued that 'the masses' quite rightly view 'public debate' with indifference and even contempt. Political argument and rational deliberation are merely simulated by media personalities and image-conscious politicians who appear on the television day in and day out.

consumer
culture,
commodification

The young Habermas argued that this separation of the public sphere from the people was clinched by the twentieth century's development of **consumer culture** and the **commodification of** entertainment, much of which is focused upon the intimate sphere of family and home. People become increasingly concerned with their own private lives, their consumption and mass-mediated pleasures rather than with the great public issues of the day. Such a critical attitude towards consumption and modern media reiterated a long-standing intellectual disdain for the **popular culture** of cinema, television, chart music and pulp fiction. Yet, nevertheless, Habermas was right **empirically** to stress the trend towards **privatization** of cultural consumption under late-modern conditions. However, this is a more complex and contradictory phenomenon than was suggested by the young Habermas. Raymond Williams (1974), for instance, characterized television-viewing as a form of *mobile privatization*. Television may confine people's attention to the home, the intimate sphere, the realm of privacy, but it also affords public access to a world of images and information to an extent that was previously unimaginable.

popular culture,
empirical,
privatization

Now, it is useful to check back on the main points of Habermas's thesis as a prelude to examining pessimistic and optimistic perspectives on the contemporary public sphere. In 1964 Habermas published an encyclopedia article which summarized his general argument.

READING 3.1

Now read Jürgen Habermas's 'The public sphere: an encyclopedia article' which is reproduced as Reading 3.1. This will help to reinforce your understanding of the points already made in this section.

Here are some questions that should help you to negotiate what is a condensed piece of writing:

1   How does Habermas define 'the public sphere'?

2   What was 'bourgeois' about the emergent public sphere in the eighteenth century?

3   What is the liberal model of citizenship rights?

4   What was the role of the press in the early public sphere?

5   How was the bourgeois public sphere eventually undermined?

6   Is it possible to revive the public sphere under present conditions?

COMMENT

The young Habermas's largely pessimistic conclusions concerning the rise and fall of the bourgeois public sphere were in line, at the time, with a great deal of critical sociology on the 'manipulative' power of 'mass communications'. He was later to revise his views on the present-day public sphere in a more optimistic direction (see section 6 of this chapter). The original thesis was criticized on several counts (Thompson, 1993). Habermas's neglect of the plebeian public sphere has already been mentioned. This and other criticisms – such as limited attention to gender inequality – are slightly disingenuous since Habermas was well aware of the exclusionary character of the *bourgeois* public sphere as a gentlemen's club. More problematic was Habermas's sweepingly negative attitude to the electronic media of radio and television. There are schools of social-scientific research and **cultural studies**, however, that evince a much more positive view of contemporary media. In the next two sections alternative pessimistic and optimistic perspectives will be illustrated, the former by Herman and Chomsky's propaganda model of the US news media, and the latter by Livingstone and Lunt's research concerning television audience-participation talk-shows. They both represent viewpoints within a politically oriented social science, albeit very different from one another.

cultural studies

■ ■ ■

SUMMARY OF SECTION 2

This section has:

1 introduced the public sphere as a key concept of critical social theory;

2 outlined how the young Habermas told a tragic story about the rise and fall of the bourgeois public sphere between the eighteenth and twentieth centuries in Europe;

3 indicated that the public sphere is a contested concept which has been revised and used in various ways, as we shall see in subsequent sections.

3 Manufacturing consent

A fundamental democratic belief is that citizens should be well informed and directly engaged in opinion formation which has political consequence. This may have been experienced in the *agora* of ancient Athens, the market-place of ideas where aristocratic men met with one another and debated what should be done. It may also have seemed like that amongst members of the political class of bourgeois men in London and Paris from the eighteenth century until the advent of mass democracy several decades later. But, is such an assumption realistic under conditions of universal suffrage in large-scale, complex and highly mediated societies? Are mass-democratic societies today likely to generate spontaneous public opinions based upon reliable knowledge of the facts that are communicated by the press and broadcasting?

3.1 Lippmann on public relations

The questions above are of the kind posed by the US journalist, Walter Lippmann in his hugely influential book, *Public Opinion*, published in 1922. Lippmann was one of the first to argue that the relationship between the news media and the social world is not simply that of a transparent window or a reflecting mirror. Inevitably, journalism involves selection from an enormous range of potential topics and representation from a slant or angle on the topic.

public opinion

Moreover, Lippmann firmly believed that people do not form opinions spontaneously when left to their own devices. **Public opinion** is mediated by social institutions and systems of communication, for instance the news media. In a modern mass-mediated democracy, public opinion is in effect 'manufactured' by professional intermediaries – or 'opinion leaders' – in business, politics, journalism and public relations. To name this process, Lippmann coined the term, 'the manufacture of consent', and spelt out its significance:

> Within the life of the generation now in control of affairs, persuasion has become a self-conscious art, a regular organ of popular government. None of us begins to understand the consequences, but it is no daring prophecy to say that knowledge of how to create consent will alter every political calculation and modify every political premise. Under the impact of propaganda, not necessarily in the sinister meaning of the word alone, the old constants of our thinking have become variables. It is no longer possible, for example, to believe in the original dogma of democracy; that the knowledge needed for the management of human affairs comes up spontaneously from the human heart. Where we act on that theory we expose ourselves to self-deception, and forms of persuasion we cannot verify. It has been demonstrated that we cannot rely on intuition, conscience, or the actions of casual opinion if we are to deal with the world beyond our reach.
>
> (Lippmann, 1997/1922, p.158)

Lippmann's argument on the mediated construction of opinion was the grandest and most eloquent theoretical exposition of the practice now commonly known as 'spin doctoring'. It gave a substantial, or perhaps spurious, intellectual legitimacy (depending on your point of view) to the growth of professions dedicated to 'manufacturing consent', the communication and information managers. Lippmann's position, developed in the 1920s, was quite subtle and philosophically sophisticated, drawing as it did on Plato's parable of the Cave where spectators can only see the shadows on the interior wall of things passing behind them in the world outside. This is a normal state of affairs where knowledge is concerned, according to Lippmann. In communications, then, meaningful sense of the world has to be made and appropriate opinions formed. For Lippmann, this is pragmatic and realistic: persuasion is necessary and even propaganda is not inherently 'sinister'; others, however, have disagreed – for instance, Edward Herman and Noam Chomsky, to whom we now turn.

3.2 Herman and Chomsky's propaganda model

The manipulation and, indeed, 'manufacture' of loyal public opinion was a key defining feature of both Nazi Germany and the Soviet Union in the twentieth century – undemocratic and totalitarian states that used techniques of 'thought control' to keep their populations in order. By contrast, it is often claimed that democracy's superiority over totalitarianism resides in freedom of thought and the public contest of opinions. Lippmann believed this 'original dogma of democracy' to be naive and argued that the manufacture of consent in a democracy was essential and, also, benign. Herman and Chomsky adopted Lippmann's phrase for the title of their book, *Manufacturing Consent: The Political Economy of the Mass Media* (1988). Differing from Lippmann, however, they regard the manufacture of consent as malign. Herman and Chomsky claim that the news media in the USA routinely distort what is going on in the world, present a partial view and thereby misinform the public. To explain how this works, Herman constructed what he and Chomsky call 'a propaganda model' of the US news media.

Herman and Chomsky's propaganda model has been challenged as a simplistic conspiracy theory of media manipulation by, for instance, Karl Meyer of *The New York Times:* 'If one takes literally the various theories that Professor Chomsky puts out one would feel that there is a tacit conspiracy between the establishment press and the government in Washington to focus on certain things and ignore certain things' (quoted in Achbor, 1994, p.111).

Figure 3.4 *Noam Chomsky, described by the* New York Times *as 'arguably the most important intellectual alive' for his scientific research on language, but not for his critique of the US news media*

Meyer was struck particularly by Chomsky's critique of the lack of coverage of Indonesia's annexation of East Timor and the genocide of its population in the 1970s. There had been a great deal of coverage of the communist Pol Pot's genocidal regime in Cambodia around the same time. Why should such similar atrocities be treated so differently? Did this differential media treatment reflect US corporate, governmental and military interests abroad? Meyer raised the issue with the international editor of *The New York Times*, who replied, 'there are dozens of atrocities around the world that we don't cover' (quoted by Achbor, 1994, p.108). While agreeing with his colleague's argument that there are always practical limits to news coverage, Meyer himself sought to rectify the situation regarding East Timor, thus seeking to demonstrate the liberal fairness of the mainstream media.

Nevertheless, from the critical perspective of Herman and Chomsky some limited coverage of East Timor was merely a legitimation of liberal journalism in a specific case rather than a genuine rectification of the overwhelming structural imbalance in the selection and framing of news topics generally. The analytical issue at stake, for **media sociology**, is whether or not Herman and Chomsky's propaganda model is, as defenders of mainstream journalism say, paranoid conspiracy theory. Were Herman and Chomsky claiming that representatives of US government and big business conspire directly with agenda-setting media, such as *The New York Times*, and instruct them on what to cover and what not to cover?

sociology of the mass media

Chomsky himself insisted in several interviews that the propaganda model is not a conspiracy theory but, rather, an institutional analysis of the routine operations of US news media (Achbor, 1994). In the Preface to *Manufacturing Consent*, Herman and Chomsky state their position succinctly:

> Institutional critiques such as we present in this book are commonly dismissed by establishment commentators as 'conspiracy theories', but this is merely an evasion. We do not use any kind of 'conspiracy' hypothesis to explain mass

media performance. In fact, our treatment is much closer to a 'free market' analysis, with the results largely an outcome of the workings of market forces. Most biased choices in the media arise from the preselection of right-thinking people, internalized preconceptions, and the adaptation of personnel to the constraints of ownership, organization, market, and political power. Censorship is largely self-censorship, by reporters and commentators who adjust to the realities of source and media organizational requirements, and by people at higher levels within media organizations who are chosen to implement, and have usually internalized, the constraints imposed by proprietary and other market and governmental centers of power.

(Herman and Chomsky, 1988, p.xii)

Let us now consider the propaganda model in some detail. While censorship and disinformation are salient features of authoritarian rule in state-dominated and blatantly unfree societies, it is much harder to understand why something similar happens 'where the media are private and formal censorship is absent'. Herman and Chomsky's five filters of the propaganda model provide a straightforward account of why this might be so.

First, there is 'the size, concentrated ownership, owner wealth and profit orientation of the dominant mass media firms' (Herman and Chomsky, 1988, p.2). Free exchange of information is not the main concern of the media businesses which dominate the market. In fact, a free market in communications media does not really exist. It is in the interests of the leading players in the media to seek profit and represent their own and other capitalist interests, according to Herman and Chomsky.

Second, 'advertising ... [is] the primary income source of the mass media'. In consequence, advertiser interests are put before those of the public. Media products that do not attract sufficient advertising revenue or disrupt the ideological universe of the advertisers and their clients are at a disadvantage even where viable readerships and audiences for such products exist.

Third, there is 'the reliance of the media on information provided by government, business, and "experts" funded and approved by these primary sources and agents of power'. Such powerful agents employ legions of information and communication managers, public relations experts, dedicated to getting their point of view across to various publics through the news media in particular.

Fourth, there is '"flak" as a means of disciplining the media'. When news media occasionally transgress implicit boundaries and break tacit agreements, they are attacked for misrepresentation and irresponsibility by political and corporate leaders. This is especially so in times of war when an adherence to 'objective' reporting is likely to be met with accusations of insufficient patriotism and disloyalty.

Fifth, Herman and Chomsky cite 'anticommunism' as a 'national religion and control mechanism'. This was still a key filter in 1988, the year Herman and Chomsky published their *Manufacturing Consent*, a year before the fall of the Berlin Wall.

In the USA, anti-communism was indeed a national religion, a crusade against the epitome of political evil in the world, accentuated during successive Cold Wars with the Soviet Union. Dissent from conventional wisdom and received opinion, virtually no matter what actual views were expressed, was likely to be denounced as 'commy'. The slur of communism really mattered when it still represented a serious and threatening alternative to the capitalist economic and liberal-democratic system. Anti-communism legitimized disinformation concerning the military-industrial complex in the USA, support for oppressive regimes, the Vietnam War in the 1960s and innumerable US-sponsored covert actions across the globe and particularly in South America. The collapse of European communism and the dramatic intellectual eclipse of Marxism-Leninism created a vacuum for scaremongering, but only up to a point. This vacuum was rapidly occupied by Islamic fundamentalism as the declared enemy of 'the West' and by the demon of Iraq, Saddam Hussein, in particular. The Gulf War in 1991 and subsequent actions to protect oil interests and to police ethnic conflicts in the Balkans, were publicly legitimized by an ostensible western humanism, and routinely justified by the US news media, led in recent years by CNN.

As with Lippmann's 'manufacture of consent', Chomsky (1989) also adopts the theologian Rheinhold Niebuhr's formulation that most people need 'necessary illusions' inculcated into them by elites. Chomsky turns this around and argues that, given the true facts of a situation, people are usually able to figure out what they mean and make rational judgements for themselves. Unfortunately, instead of that happening, the mainstream news media distort the truth, 'manufacture consent' and disseminate 'necessary illusions', according to Chomsky. Furthermore, he is inclined to suggest that entertainment media distract the general public from attending to serious issues. This includes, for instance, 'Joe Sixpack's' addiction to televised sport (Achbor, 1994).

Although Chomsky and Herman's critique of the US news media is well substantiated in many cases, their position is somewhat one-dimensional and deeply pessimistic. Ordinary people, it can be argued, are treated by Herman and Chomsky as media 'dopes', manipulated in their opinions and drugged by trivial entertainment. In addition to the institutional critique of how news media work, Herman and Chomsky's practical method for producing evidence in support of their claims concerning distorted journalism is **content analysis**,   **content analysis** that is, a means of counting column inches and broadcast time devoted or not devoted, as the case may be, to particular themes and issues. They do not back up their claims concerning the effects of news distortion on public opinion with audience and readership research. Moreover, while Herman and Chomsky hold out some faith in alternative media and the historical example of European public service broadcasting, they underestimate aspects of the public sphere that are facilitated by mainstream and commercial media.

SUMMARY OF SECTION 3

This section has:

1 outlined Walter Lippman's classic argument for the legitimate manipulation of public opinion in a mass democracy;

2 discussed Herman and Chomsky's forceful critique of the US news media's manufacture of consent;

3 identified some problems with the propaganda model from the point of view of audience research.

4 Talk television

On a Monday morning recently, I tried to follow three broadcast discussion programmes simultaneously, one on radio and two on television. This involved listening to the radio whilst flicking between television channels. I also used audio and video cassettes to record the programmes for subsequent analysis. The programmes were *Start the Week* on BBC Radio 4 (9–9.45 a.m.), *Kilroy* on BBC1 Television (9–10 a.m.) and ITV's *Trisha* (9.25–10.30 a.m.). *Start the Week* differed from the other two programmes, not only in being on radio rather than television but also because its participants were all 'expert' intellectuals, academics and writers with specialist knowledge. The discussion was chaired by Jeremy Paxman, best known as anchor and relentless interviewer for BBC2's heavyweight *Newsnight*. Of the four guests, three were promoting their recently published books. The fourth talked about her forthcoming inaugural lecture as a professor at the London School of Economics. Topics under discussion were the protectiveness of parents, Polish genocide of Jews in a village during the Second World War, gambling, law and responsibility. These various topics were loosely tied together by the overarching themes of risk and the ethics of personal conduct. For instance, the sociologist Frank Furedi was talking about his book, *Paranoid Parenting: Abandon Your Anxieties and be a Good Parent*, in which he argues that modern-day parents are over-protective of their children. He was interrogated ferociously by the dogged Paxman. The link to Al Alvarez's book, *Poker*, was to do with risk-taking and risk aversion in gambling and everyday life. The debate over why Polish villagers had turned murderously on their Jewish neighbours was connected to questions of criminal responsibility outlined by Professor Nicola Lacey which, in turn, could be related to another kind of responsibility, that of parents towards their children.

BBC1's *Kilroy* – hosted by the former Labour MP, Robert Kilroy-Silk – posed the question, 'Can money buy you happiness?' Guest interviewees, including a woman who had inherited £1 million and another who had made several million pounds in business, answered the question in the negative or tended to be defensive about their wealth. They sat amongst audience members, some of whom said that relatively modest amounts of windfall cash would change their lives for the better. Frequent reference was made to the game show *Who Wants to be a Millionaire?* and the National Lottery. Kilroy wandered around questioning participants in a sometimes mildly challenging but usually supportive manner. *Kilroy* is an audience-participation talk-show made by a public service corporation. It takes itself seriously in a way that was pioneered in the USA by programmes such as *The Oprah Winfrey Show* since the early 1980s and *Donahue* before that.

Figure 3.5 *Television talk-show presenter, Trisha*

The black Australian presenter of *Trisha* hosted a succession of young heterosexual and apparently working-class couples who were suspicious of their partners' loyalty or dissatisfied with them in some respect. A question was posed at the beginning – 'Is my pregnant girlfriend cheating?' – and this was followed by linked questions to the general theme throughout the programme. Typically, just one of the couple would come out on stage while the other one stayed in the wings unaware of what was being said. The partner on stage voiced his or her misgivings and was questioned by Trisha and members of the studio audience. The second partner would then join the first partner on stage for a discussion of their problems with Trisha and the audience. In this programme – made by an English regional company for national networking on 'Independent', that is, 'commercial' TV – personal revelations were made public in a similar but less sensational manner than in *The Jerry Springer Show.*

Both television audience-participation shows gave voice to 'ordinary people', either as selected individuals telling their own stories or as members of the studio audience commenting upon these stories. On the other hand, the radio programme was exclusively a discussion between professional intellectuals who are highly articulate in a conventional sense. *Start the Week* may be considered a latter-day example of Habermas's literary public sphere mediated by broadcasting. Where, then, do the **populist** television audience-participation shows – *Kilroy* and *Trisha* – stand in relation to the public sphere? **populism**

4.1 Audience-participation talk-shows

Contrary to the pessimistic view of mainstream media and the public sphere represented by Herman and Chomsky, here we may have evidence for greater optimism concerning the opportunities for democratic debate in contemporary society. Audience-participation talk-shows tend, however, to be regarded as 'cheap and trashy'. They exploit ordinary people's troubles in the name of entertainment. In the *Trisha* programme some of the partners were reduced to tears. On *The Jerry Springer Show* fighting frequently breaks out. *The Rikki Lake Show* provokes high tension as well. Nevertheless, on these programmes, ordinary people do get to speak in public through a mass medium. The audience-participation talk-show is a popular **genre** with a characteristic format that **genre** addresses issues of concern to members of the viewing public. Moreover, it is conventional, in sociology and cultural studies today, to assume that TV-viewers and consumers in general are not simply passive recipients of messages and commodities but that they are actively engaged in making meaning for themselves.

Sonia Livingstone and Peter Lunt studied audience-participation talk-shows from the point of view of the public sphere. In their book, *Talk on Television: Audience Participation and Public Debate*, they pose the following questions: 'Is this a new form of public space or forum, part of a media public sphere? Or is this a travesty of real public debate with no "real" consequence?' (Livingstone and Lunt, 1994, p.1).

Livingstone and Lunt had access to 500 diary respondents from BBC/BRB audience research. They conducted 16 in-depth interviews with programme participants and viewers. An episode of *Kilroy*, from May 1989, on doctor–patient relations, was shown to 12 focus groups and their discussions were recorded. Thus, Livingstone and Lunt were able to **triangulate** different sources of data, **triangulation** quantitative and qualitative, for analysis. They were primarily concerned with how ordinary people talk in and about audience-participation programmes so were, in effect, conducting **conversational analysis**. **conversational analysis**

Although Livingstone and Lunt found much to value in their study of audience-participation talk-shows, they are wary of simply adopting an optimistic position against the pessimistic position on the mediated public sphere: 'We suggest that pessimistic answers tend to underestimate the complex and contradictory or fragmented nature of contemporary mass media which opens the way for some escape from institutional control, while more optimistic positions often set too high ideals for the public sphere' (Livingstone and Lunt, 1994, p.10). Here, they take issue with Habermas.

4.2 Communicative action

Freud, Sigmund

In the 1970s Habermas (1984/1976) formulated the notion of an 'ideal speech situation', modelled upon **Freudian** psychotherapy – 'the talking cure' – where the aim is to solve psychological problems through conversation rather than medication. Thus might 'undistorted communication' be achieved by talking truthfully with one another. Furthermore, Habermas (1987/1981) argued that an orientation to mutual understanding is actually a constitutive feature of mundane social interaction. We habitually try to make sense together in the everyday '**life-world**'. Routine forms of what Habermas calls 'communicative action' run counter to the means–end instrumental and strategic actions which characterize the systemic processes of the economy and the state where money and power predominate. From a more optimistic and latter-day Habermasian perspective, therefore, audience-participation talk-shows could be construed as a space for communicative action, articulating life-world concerns in a socially therapeutic manner, though this stance is not necessarily that taken by Habermas himself.

life-world

This view of communicative action is roughly the conclusion reached by Livingstone and Lunt but, in their estimation, actual outcomes never tie up the loose ends of difference that might be imagined by a Habermasian ideal speech situation. Conversation in talk-shows rarely, if ever, achieves a consensual resolution, an agreed 'public opinion'. The reality is much more messy than that. Typically, there is a concatenation of different voices. Discussion usually results, at best, in negotiated understanding and compromise rather than mutual agreement. In the case of the *Kilroy* show on doctor–patient relations, the experts – the doctors – were confronted with popular criticism of their profession's aloofness. Ordinary people were facilitated by the host to complain about this caring profession's apparent lack of care for patients. These doctors defended themselves against such accusation but they may have learnt something. The programme created a space for lay opinion to challenge expertise, for private sentiments to be expressed in public, for, in the psychologist Carol Gilligan's (1993/1982) phrase, 'a different voice' to be heard.

femininity, masculinity, discourse

According to Livingstone and Lunt, the audience-participation talk-show is a space for an 'oppositional public sphere', as they put it. Furthermore, it is a space for **feminine discourse** in contrast to the **masculine discourse** of the official public sphere and unqualified Habermasian theory. Sonia Livingstone expanded upon this argument in a journal article.

Now read 'Watching talk: gender and engagement in the viewing of audience discussion programmes' by Sonia Livingstone, which is Reading 3.2 at the end of the chapter. When you have done so, consider the following questions and note down your answers.

1   What does feminism have to do with the audience-participation talk-show?

2   Is there a 'traditional gender assumption' in broadcasting and especially day-time broadcasting?

3   How does feminine discourse oppose 'patriarchal conceptions of rationality'?

4   What were the similarities and differences between men's and women's viewing of the episode of *Kilroy* on doctor–patient relations?

5   How is an 'ethic of care' articulated in women's talk about audience-participation shows?

6   Are audience-participation talk-shows really a space for an 'oppositional public sphere'?

1   Livingstone remarks, 'The intervention of feminism in the public sphere debate has, by raising the issues of diverse, marginalized and excluded voices and of competing interests, proved central to analysis of the public sphere' (1994, p.430). If the audience-participation talk-show is a significant space of public sphere debate, giving voice to the 'diverse, marginalized and excluded', including women, then, it is evidently of interest to feminists.

2   Whether or not there is a 'traditional gender assumption' throughout the media, it is certainly the case that daytime broadcasting has traditionally addressed 'the ordinary housewife' in her domestic space. And, undoubtedly, the great majority of broadcasters have been men. This may be changing with more women working in broadcasting – and not confined to 'women's programmes' – and with more men at home during the day watching television.

3   Livingstone defines 'patriarchal conceptions of rationality (abstract and logical rather than narrative, conversational, emotional and particular)' (1994, p.430). This is the basis for regarding the audience-participation talk-show as a gendered genre, as, in some sense, feminine and perhaps even feminist. Men participate in these programmes and they watch them but the discursive rules of such talk-shows privilege anecdotal story-telling, conversation and emotion instead of tightly logical exposition of argument.

4   Both men and women watch audience-participation talk-shows but their specific modes of engagement tend to differ. According to Livingstone, 'Compared with men, women were more likely to consider that the genre offers a sphere in which they can participate, feeling involved and that issues are relevant to their own lives ...' (1994, p.435). Women, in Livingstone and Lunt's research, were interested in the process and men interested in the product.

5   In Gilligan's (1993/1982) research, women were found generally to be more empathetically concerned with the feelings of others than with the exercise of

abstract moral principles, which more typically characterizes 'masculine' morality. For Livingstone, this is borne out by research on women's responses to, and engagment with, shows like Kilroy. That is the meaning of an 'ethic of care'.

6   In her concluding paragraphs, Livingstone makes a large claim for the audience-participation talk-show as a site for 'the oppositional or negotiated conception of the public sphere' and suggests that this is 'compatible with feminist theory', where the voices of the excluded, including women, are valued (1994, pp.444–5).

■   ■   ■

There has been a wide-ranging debate over recent years about the public significance of mass-popular forms such as the television audience-participation talk-show. Several commentators have argued that the binary oppositions which have bedevilled media and cultural analysis should be dispensed with or, at least, thoroughly reconsidered. From this point of view, 'serious' news and current affairs programmes may be less important sites for the public sphere than 'popular' shows that, arguably, encourage learning and debate through entertainment. Nevertheless, there are still differences of opinion amongst sociologists, media and cultural analysts. As Graham Murdock points out: 'Some commentators see talk-shows' hospitality to previously neglected issues and voices as a welcome extension of democratic debate. Others accuse them of following the tabloid press in trivializing social issues, replacing rational deliberation with emotive expression, and elevating sensation over the search for feasible solutions' (Murdock, 2000, p.202).

What is at stake is not just a difference of opinion amongst academic commentators. Surveying the situation in European broadcasting, Murdock notes the impact of the US shows and formats and, also, the resistance mounted by a public service tradition in Europe that is little known in the USA. To use **Mills, C. Wright** **C. Wright Mills**' (1970/1959) famous distinction in sociology there is undoubtedly a discernible trend away from a focus upon 'public issues' in the direction of a preoccupation with 'personal troubles'. Mills urged sociologists to study the connections between public issues of social structure and personal troubles of milieu. Both are important: making sense of their interrelatedness is at the heart of 'the sociological imagination'. This is a political as well as a sociological matter.

Livingstone (1994) claims that the audience-participation talk-show is a site of the 'oppositional' public sphere. Her main reason for arguing thus is that talk-shows enable the articulation of a feminine sensibility which is marginalized by the masculine rationality and discursive procedures of the official public sphere. That may have been more so at one time than it is now. Emotive communication and its associated personalization of politics are hardly marginal today. These are not exclusively feminine traits in any case. Furthermore, feminism itself has, in a sense, become popularized and indeed normalized in countries such as the UK and the USA, though this does not mean that the actual position of women has improved as much as talk about it might suggest. All things considered, to dub such a mainstream television genre – the audience-participation talk-show – 'oppositional' suggests a peculiarly limited sense of opposition in the mediated public sphere.

SUMMARY OF SECTION 4

This section has:

1   discussed the television audience-participation talk-show as a site for public discussion;

2   looked at Livingstone and Lunt's research which qualifies the Habermasian public sphere from a populist and feminist perpective;

3   questioned the claim that audience-participation talk-shows are vehicles of an 'oppositional' public sphere.

5   New and old media

Pessimism about capitalist news media in manufacturing consent, on the one hand, and optimism about popular participation in television talk-shows, on the other, are the thesis and antithesis of a broken dialectic in media sociology. According to the pessimistic view, general publics are misinformed, manipulated in their opinions by distorted news and distracted from attention to serious issues by endlessly trivial and pacifying entertainment. In contrast, according to the optimistic view, publics are far from passive in their media consumption. They choose what to consume and they make sense of it for themselves. A medium like television must, in any event, address popular concerns and desires in order to attract large audiences. The apparently degraded genre of the audience-participation talk-show is a perfect example of the active role of audiences, both in the studio and at home.

Whether or not such shows have ever represented a genuine public sphere, to ignore the discernible trend towards increasingly sensational displays of personal troubles for purposes of entertainment, and the shift away from reasoned argument to emotive expression, would be an abrogation of critical responsibility in media sociology. While emotional identification in popular culture is a legitimate object of study so, too, is the framing of public knowledge and debate in the media. Critics typically argue that the frames are often limited and distorting.

5.1   The politics of new media

In critical thought and oppositional practice, there is a long-standing tendency to depict mainstream 'old' media as corrupted and to vest hope in 'new' media as alternative means of communication. So, for instance, the comparatively recent advent of a 'new' medium – the internet – turns a relatively new medium, television, into an 'old' medium. To make such a sharp distinction between 'new' and 'old' media is problematical since they are interconnected in various ways. Moreover, there is a drive towards technological convergence that is facilitated by digitalization.

Furthermore, throughout the history of emergent media the dominant trend is not one of new media simply usurping and replacing old media. Theatre was not obliterated by cinema. In its turn, television undermined the popularity of cinema-going but did not destroy the cinema as a significant medium. We live in a complexly mediated world with many different yet interconnecting means of communication – and, hence, diverse possibilities for creating public spheres, oppositional as well as official and mainstream.

New technologies are integrated into mainstream professional media production and business communications. Simpler and cheaper versions of equipment are marketed as production tools for amateur use in leisure time. The on-line desktop PC in the home, for instance, provides access to information on the Web and various software applications, encompassing publishing as well as games. However, there has usually been a gulf between 'professional' standard equipment and equipment for 'amateur' use: professionals jealously guard their special terrain from the incursions of amateurs. Nevertheless, a grey area exists where cheaper media technologies are used not only for leisure but for counter-cultural and oppositional purposes. Local protesters and campaigning groups, for instance, make videos and distribute them through alternative networks, including satellite and cable distribution (Dowmunt, 1993). The general aim of such media practice is to circumvent mainstream news and cultural agendas by fostering what Nancy Fraser (1992) calls 'subaltern counterpublics'. Alternative print media, facilitated by photo-litho instead of hot metal, were especially important, from the 1960s onwards, in mediating, for instance, the entry of feminism from marginal politics into the mainstream of social life.

Since the mid-1990s computer-mediated communications (CMCs) or information and communication technologies (ICTs) have been the focus for much optimism. Easy access to networking through the internet and the World Wide Web (WWW) is especially extolled as the means for much more democratic, horizontal communications than is possible in the vertical, top-down communications characteristic of 'old' media. This is perhaps surprising considering the origins of the internet and its main lines of development. It was originally constructed by US federal government in 1969 and paid for out of the defence budget. For many years, the major use of this public sector facility was not so much military but academic. University researchers used it to collaborate and share their findings with one another. The huge expansion of the internet was largely determined by business usages, deregulation and privatization of telecommunications and the potential profitability of consumer services such as on-line shopping (Schiller, 1999). Digital networking facilitated greater efficiency and speed in corporate communications. And, by the turn of the century, there was enormous speculation and much investment (very soon imperilled) in the hyped-up 'new economy' of ICTs and their seemingly infinite applications.

Alternative modes of cultural communication and community-building in 'cyberspace' also became features of internet use, as Howard Rheingold (1994) documented in *The Virtual Community: Surfing the Internet*. He saw this as a manifestation of Habermas's public sphere. In modern societies, place-based community is elusive. The internet created the conditions for strangers to meet across cyberspace, where the inhibitions of face-to-face communication don't apply. Discussion between digitalized versions of the self in internet chat, argued Rheingold, is undistorted by extraneous power and authority. This kind of communication is only regulated by enabling rules of 'netiquette'. The virtual communities of the internet were not just of therapeutic value, according to Rheingold; they invoked new practices of citizenship.

The impact of ICT development on economic, social, political and cultural life generally is transformative on a global scale, according to Manuel Castells, author of the trilogy, *The Information Age* (1996, 1997, 1998). In the second volume of the trilogy, he argues:

> The information technology revolution, and the restructuring of capitalism, have induced a new form of society, the network society. It is characterized by the globalization of strategically decisive economic activities. By the networking form of organization. By flexibility and instability of work, and the individualization of labor. By a culture of real virtuality constructed by a pervasive, interconnected and diverse media system. And, by the material foundations of life, space and time, as expressions of dominant activities and controlling elites.
>
> (Castells, 1997, p.1)

Social organization itself starts to mirror the complex interconnectedness of information technology systems, networked computers and satellite distribution around the Earth, claims Castells. The **network** society is characterized by fast, extensive and interweaving communications. In such a world, politics is inevitably mediated politics for both dominant and oppositional forces. **network/social network**

Mainstream and official politics are now very much marked by rapid publicity and counter-publicity in the media's thirst for scandal. Castells says: *'I contend that scandal politics is the weapon of choice for struggle and competition in informational politics'* (1997, p.337; his italics). So, for instance, President Clinton's dalliance with Monica Lewinsky became more important in the news media than his policies and this nearly ended his Presidency. The obsession with scandal could be taken to confirm the pessimistic conclusions of the younger Habermas. Reports of scandal, often with little concern for corruption in the traditional sense, are also largely consistent with Herman and Chomsky's propaganda model insofar as they may function as distractions from 'serious' issues. Nonetheless, scandal generates much popular talk. When it comes to scandal, people really do seem to be debating something 'political'. It is exactly this kind of 'personalization', 'distraction' or 'trivialization' of politics that is challenged by campaigning groups, non-governmental organizations (NGOs) and **social movements** that seek to communicate their alternative and oppositional perspectives through both new and old media. **social movements**

5.2 The Zapatistas and informational politics

Castells argues that **globalization** – which is so much facilitated by ICTs – provokes resistance that is sometimes reactionary and occasionally progressive. His major example of progressive resistance and mediated politics is the Zapatista movement in Mexico. At the inauguration of the North American Free Trade Agreement (NAFTA) on 1 January 1994, 3000 men and women of the *Ejercito Zapatista de Liberacion National* (EZLN) took over a mountain town in Chiapos Mexico in protest at the effects of joining NAFTA. The economic liberalization policy of the governing *Partido Revolucionario Institucional* (PRI) had ended protection against corn imports and of the coffee price. In preparation for entering NAFTA, the law on communal occupation of land was also repealed, **globalization** thus undermining the fragile peasant economy of Chiapas in the interests of 'globalization'.

The visible leaders of the revolt were urban intellectuals wearing ski masks. It later transpired that their spokesperson, the pipe-smoking Subcommandante Marcos, was a graduate in sociology and communications. The followers were a peasantry of Mayan Indians, although Marcos himself always claimed to be supporting their struggle rather than leading it: hence his chosen title, *sub*commandante. The Zapatistas derived their inspiration from the memory of the agrarian revolutionary of the 1910s, Emiliano Zapata.

Figure 3.6 *Subcommandante Marcos embracing Zapata's daughter, Anna Maria*

The Chiapas revolt lasted just twelve days, during which time several dozen peasants, many of them without real weapons, were killed by the military. On 12 January, the Mexican President ordered a cease-fire in response to widespread expressions of public sympathy for the peasant insurgents, whereupon they retreated into the forest. The insurgents remained there peaceably – though not altogether safely in spite of national and international support for them – until March 2001. Then they marched upon Mexico City to great popular acclaim – the 'Zapatour' – for negotiations with the new President, Vicente Fox, whose party had succeeded the seventy-year rule of the PRI. It has even been suggested that the Zapatistas had brought down the corrupt PRI since their cause was so evidently just, and they had been so difficult for the government to counter.

Castells' interest in the Zapatista insurgency is that it represented, for him, a new kind of 'informational politics'. It was never a realistic military force like the Cuban revolutionaries of 1959 but, in some ways, a 'virtual' movement. Marcos mobilized support around the world and broke into the mainstream global media through his ironic and poetic communiqués on the Web. For instance:

> There is nothing to fight for any longer. Socialism is dead. Long life to conformism, to reform, to modernity, to capitalism and all kind of cruel etceteras. Let's be reasonable. That nothing happens in the city, or in the countryside, that everything continues the same. Socialism is dead. Long life to capital. Radio, press and television repeat it. Some socialists, now reasonably repentant, also repeat the same.

(quoted by Castells, 1997, p.77)

Castells stresses the distinctly informational, symbolic and 'virtual' politics of the Zapatistas in relation to the regional role of *La Neta* in non-governmental action – ironically facilitated by a grant from the Ford Foundation – without, however, underplaying the life-threatening risks of insurgency. Of course, the Zapatistas were no match militarily for the Mexican army. Still, a symbolic game was being played with real political consequence. The Zapatista insurgency was not a post-modern re-run of Woody Allen's old movie, *Bananas*, as cynical observers might suggest. It is important to appreciate that the extent to which the Zapatistas were successful in getting their message across was not only to do with mobilizing support through the 'new' medium of the internet, but also with capturing the attention of the 'old' media of national and international press and broadcasting.

SUMMARY OF SECTION 5

This section has:

1   looked at how oppositional politics is drawn to the use of new media because old media are held to be in the control of dominant interests;

2   considered the Zapatista movement as an example of what Castells calls 'informational politics';

3   stressed the interconnectedness of new and old media for both mainstream politics and oppositional movements.

---

6 The sluice-gate model of the public sphere and the anti-capitalist movement

In this final section, we shall consider the later Habermas's revisions of his public sphere concept – the formulation of a 'sluice-gate model' of the public sphere – with regard to recent manifestations of opposition to systemic forces, as represented by the anti-capitalist movement.

6.1 The cultural public sphere

Responding to his critics at the North Carolina conference on the theory of the public sphere in 1989, Habermas said:

> I must confess ... that only after reading Mikhail Bakhtin's great book *Rabelais and his World* have my eyes become really opened to the *inner* dynamics of a plebeian culture. This culture of the common people apparently was by no means only a backdrop, that is, a passive echo of the dominant culture; it was also the periodically recurring violent revolt of a counterproject to the hierarchical world of domination with its official celebrations and everyday disciplines. Only a stereoscopic view of this sort reveals how a mechanism of exclusion that locks out and represses at the same time calls forth countereffects that cannot be neutralized. If we apply the same perspective to the bourgeois public sphere, the exclusion of women from this world dominated by men now looks different than it appeared to me at the time.
>
> (Habermas, 1992, p.427)

The implication of this statement is to bring back consideration of *affective*, that is, aesthetic and emotional, communications into public sphere theory, which was present in Habermas's original distinction between the literary and political public spheres but subsequently neglected. Media research has tended to concentrate on news events in the manifestly political public sphere rather than the more diffuse politics of a literary public sphere where the conduct of life and the purposes of art are focal topics of concern. The literary public sphere must now, of course, be broadened to include the various channels of art and popular culture in the *cultural public sphere*, defined as the articulation of politics, public and personal, as a contested terrain through affective – aesthetic and emotional – modes of communication (McGuigan, 1996, 1998a, 1998b, 2000). This idea of a cultural public sphere problematizes an exclusively – or excessively – cognitive notion of the public sphere in an austere sociology of news media, as in Herman and Chomsky's work. It also encompasses Livingstone and Lunt's defence of audience-participation talk-shows and much else besides. Moreover, it is extremely relevant to studying the carnivalesque forms and styles of anti-capitalist protest.

Mikhail Bakhtin (1968) identified the typical features of carnival in medieval Europe as 'ritual spectacle', 'comic verbal composition' and 'various genres of billingsgate' (i.e., foul language). Carnival is utopian, jolly and caring. It involves what Bakhtin called 'a characteristic logic, the peculiar logic of the "inside out" (*à l'envers*), of the "turnabout", of a continual shifting from top to bottom, from front to rear, of humorous parodies and travesties, humiliations, profanations,

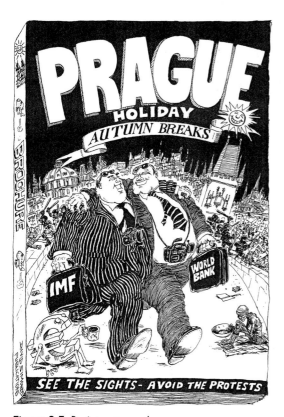

comic crownings, and uncrownings' (Bakhtin, 1968, p.11). Seen from this perspective, the antics of the protesters in, for instance, the City of London (J18 – June 1999), against the World Trade Organisation (WTO) in Seattle (N30 – November–December 1999) and at Prague (S28 – September 2000) were indeed carnivalesque. As a student of mine who participated in the Prague protest said to me: 'It's difficult for a copper to hit you when you're dressed up as a pink fairy.'

Here, however, we need to make some distinctions concerning the functions and varied traditions of carnival and cultural politics, as Murdock (2000) has suggested. The power of carnival, it has often been argued, is limited by its ephemerality. It is an occasional and, therefore, transient safety valve for discontent. Moreover, carnival is symbolic and ritualistic, not practical. Such criticism of the political force of carnival may not apply to the anti-capitalist movement since this displays considerable resilience and mature development, most notably in establishing the anti-Davos of the World Social Forum in opposition to the World Economic Forum in January 2001. Moreover, anti-capitalism clearly has roots in anarchism, libertarian socialism and in the

Figure 3.7 *Business as usual*   counter-culture of the 1960s. These movements found renewed expression towards the end of the twentieth century in various waves of 'DIY' cultural politics, such as roads protests and illicit partying to reclaim public space, 'senseless acts of beauty' (see Chapter 5 in this volume – Merl Storr on social movements). On the other hand, the audience-participation talk-shows, as Murdock (2000) points out, owe much of their origin to the travelling freak-shows of American huckster culture, rather than to subversive carnival and historical forms of popular protest. In this sense, the anti-capitalist movement, 'reclaiming the streets', more evidently represents an oppositional public sphere than do audience-participation talk-shows on mainstream television.

Figure 3.8
The tabloid response to anti-capitalist protest (front page of The Mirror, *2 May 2000, after a demonstration in Whitehall and at the Cenotaph)*

6.2 The sluice-gate model

The second statement of the later Habermas, which is especially relevant here, comes from the chapter on the public sphere in his book, *Between Facts and Norms*:

> The communicative structures of the public sphere are linked with the private life spheres in a way that gives the civil-social periphery, in contrast to the political center, the advantage of greater sensitivity in detecting and identifying new problem situations. The great issues of the last decades give evidence for this. Consider, for example, the spiraling nuclear-arms race; consider the risks involved in the peaceful use of atomic energy or in other large-scale technological projects and scientific experimentation, such as genetic engineering; consider the ecological threats involved in an overstrained environment (acid rain, water pollution, species extinction, etc.); consider the

dramatically progressing impoverishment of the Third World and problems of the world economic order; or consider such issues as feminism, increasing immigration, and the associated problems of multiculturalism. Hardly any of these topics were *initially* brought up by exponents of the state apparatus, large organizations, or functional systems. Instead, they were broached by intellectuals, concerned citizens, radical professionals, self-proclaimed 'advocates', and the like. Moving in from the outermost periphery, such issues force their way into newspapers and interested associations, clubs, professional organizations, academies, and universities. They find forums, citizen initiatives, and other platforms before they catalyze the growth of social movements and new subcultures. The latter can in turn dramatize contributions, presenting them so effectively that the mass media take up the matter. Only through their controversial presentation in the media do such topics reach the larger public and subsequently gain a place on the 'public agenda'. Sometimes the support of sensational actions, mass protests, and incessant campaigning is required before an issue can make its way via the surprising election of marginal candidates or radical parties, expanded platforms of 'established' parties, important court decisions, and so on, into the core political system and there receive formal consideration.

(Habermas, 1996/1992, p.381)

This sluice-gate model of the public sphere (Carleheden and Gabriels, 1996) incorporates many of the critiques of and creative developments around the theory of the public sphere that have been made since the original publication of *The Structural Transformation of the Public Sphere* in 1962. It recognizes the multiplicity of public spheres on the margins, subordinate, unofficial and oppositional – Habermas's 'periphery'. This is where critical issues are generated, not at the dominant 'core' of politics and corporate business though it may take 'sensational actions, mass protest, and incessant campaigning' to force the issues onto the agendas of official public spheres, national and international.

This is a complex and processual model of the public sphere. Its operations, in practice, are greatly facilitated by the recent development of ICTs and networking logic but they are not simply determined by technology. Oppositional forces use comparatively cheap media technologies to communicate alternative perspectives on the effects of 'globalization', as the catch-all object of discontent, that derive from actual experience and the struggle for survival. The 'battle for Seattle' in November and December 1999 – in which a loose coalition of anti-capitalists prevented the Third Ministerial Conference of the World Trade Organisation (WTO) from agreeing further neo-liberal measures on worldwide trade – may be taken to illustrate the articulation of different voices in the global public sphere.

The N30 gathering in Seattle of diverse environmental, labour and political campaign groups, representing various subordinate interests, was co-ordinated by the Direct Action Network. Anti-capitalist websites around the world were linked up in preparation for 'a festival of resistance' to disrupt the WTO summit. In Seattle itself, the Independent Media Centre (IMC) collected and distributed alternative sources of news and analysis of events around the WTO protest that contested mainstream coverage and, to an extent, came to inform it (Deep Dish, 2000). As John Downey and Natalie Fenton comment:

The IMC was inspired by the video web-stream that documented the J18 (June 18 1999) Carnival Against Capitalism in the City of London. An ad hoc group of media activists saw the possibility of providing alternative coverage of the N30 demonstrations in Seattle. IMC bought the web-server but relied upon free software for the operating system, the web-server and databases, thus benefiting from the shareware history of the Internet and W3 [World Wide Web]. A small computer service company, encoding.com, donated web server space and bandwidth. Additional funding came from donations and selling videos. The budget for the N30 coverage was in the region of $75000. IMC provided two locations, video-editing facilities, networked computers, faxes and telephones for around 400 volunteers. The web-site received 1.5 million hits from individual users by the end of the week, largely a consequence of the site being linked to the front page of Yahoo News and OneWorld. Video of the demonstrations was also picked up by organisations such as Reuters, CNN, and the BBC. N30 and the establishment of the IMC presented the opportunity for a number of alternative media groups to join forces including Free Speech TV, Paper Tiger TV, Deep Dish, and Adbusters.

(Downey and Fenton, 2001, pp.21–2)

On-line alternative news and video footage mediate the anti-capitalist movement's oppositional public sphere and challenge the official public sphere's dominant media frameworks. The obscure deliberations of the WTO in Seattle were highlighted and the questionable impact of 'free trade' policies – especially regarding barely subsistence wages and diabolical working conditions in poorer parts of the world – became a matter of widespread public awareness and debate.

6.3 Anti-capitalism

It is important to appreciate that the relation of the anti-capitalist movement to oppositional and official public spheres is not only about getting an alternative message across during intermittent occasions of spectacular contestation such as the WTO summit and protest in Seattle towards the end of 1999; it also involves campaigning NGOs such as Greenpeace and an in-depth critique of western consumer culture's dependence on global networks of exploitation and mystification. The construction of apolitical or, more accurately, politically indifferent consumerist **identity** is called into question by the journalist Naomi Klein in her celebrated book, *No Logo* (2000a), which is frequently cited as the 'manifesto' of the anti-capitalist movement. *No Logo* is, however, less a simplifying manifesto statement than a remarkable and complex work of critical sociology. Klein fixes particularly upon the pivotal role of 'branding' corporations, such as Nike, in the culture and economy of the contemporary social world.

identity

READING 3.3

The *No Logo* thesis is summarized by Naomi Klein herself in a *New Statesman* article and reprinted here as Reading 3.3, 'The tyranny of the brands' (2000b). You should read this succinct version of Klein's *No Logo* argument now while considering the following questions:

1   Why and how was the World Trade Organisation's meeting in Seattle disrupted in November–December 1999?

2   What is 'branding' and how has its function changed in recent years?

3   What is the 'weightless' business organization?

4   How do brand-led corporations locate the actual production of commodities?

5   What are the implications of branding culture for employment in rich and poor countries?

6   What are 'free-trade zones' and how do they function?

7   What is the impact of branding culture on public space?

8   What is 'culture jamming'? Does it work?

COMMENT

Klein's focus on brand-led and multinational corporations makes connections across apparently disparate phenomena of culture and economy. For instance, the appeal of the logo and its connotations, such as Nike's 'swoosh' symbol and 'just do it' ideology – which is seemingly of greater value to many consumers than product utility – is linked to the extreme exploitation of child and predominantly female labour in sweatshop conditions in poor countries where such goods are made. Branding corporations have largely divested themselves of responsibility for material production, concentrating instead on symbolic production, design, advertising and marketing. These corporations are 'weightless', informational businesses, neither owning nor operating the actual means of production. Branding corporations deal in signs and symbols. To attack the brand, then, is not only to subvert its meanings but to illuminate the hidden and complex infrastructure upon which it is founded. Moreover, Klein identifies a 'brand boomerang' effect. Brands are vulnerable to cultural contestation since symbolism is their game, as the 'No Sweat' campaign against Nike and others in the USA demonstrated (Ross, 1997). A feature of such campaigns, but not necessarily the most important, is 'culture jamming', such as Dadaistic resignification of advertising hoardings and circulating 'subvertisements' on the internet.

Figure 3.9 *International 'Buy Nothing Day'*
(http://www.adbusters.org/campaigns/bnd; accessed March 2002)

According to Klein, public space is increasingly privatized and commercial speech and imagery have come to dominate the cultural landscape. The anti-capitalist movement, then, is battling for hearts and minds as much as campaigning against global economic policies and transnational capital. This is, of necessity, a cultural and mediated politics, an intervention in the public sphere. It is marginal and easily dismissed as insignificant or misrepresented as wholly irrational and violent, as at President George W. Bush's April 2001 Summit of the Americas in Quebec City which sought to extend the NAFTA protocols from North America to South America whilst still excluding Cuba.

SUMMARY OF SECTION 6

This section has:

1   considered aesthetic and emotional aspects of popular protest, exemplified by the anti-capitalist movement, in relation to the concept of the cultural public sphere;

2   shown how Habermas's latterly revised sluice-gate model of the public sphere helps to explain how anti-capitalist protest forces issues onto mainstream agendas that would otherwise be ignored;

3   indicated that the anti-capitalist movement is not just about spectacular and occasionally violent demonstration but manifests, amongst other things, deep disquiet about and dissent from the exploitative networks of the western consumer culture that is represented by brand-led corporations.

7 Conclusion

Reading this chapter, it has no doubt become manifestly evident to you that the public sphere is an extremely malleable concept in that it is used in many different and, perhaps, confusing ways. Habermas's original thesis was about the historical formation and fate of a liberal-democratic culture of the modern nation-state that was dominated by bourgeois men in the first instance. The recently mediated politics of the anti-capitalist movement is oppositional rather than mainstream, operating in local contexts but with a global reach. There are dominant and official public spheres; there are subordinate and unofficial public spheres.

We have also considered optimistic and pessimistic views of the public sphere. From an optimistic point of view, even television audience-participation talk-shows facilitate actively egalitarian and feminine-inflected public debate. Pessimists, however, believe that mainstream media news and entertainment are distorting and have a pacifying effect. That is why oppositional forces seek to use new media, such as the internet, to circumvent the restrictions of 'old' media like television. However, in practice, old and new media are interconnected technically and politically.

The anti-capitalist movement's use of alternative and new media, for instance, must be seen in relation to its controversial appearance in the official public sphere of older media where television is of central importance. That is how the sluice-gate model of the public sphere works. Critical issues are generated outside dominant networks of meaning and power, putting issues onto official public sphere agendas that would not otherwise be there. In this respect, those who dismiss the campaigns that come under the broad umbrella of the anti-capitalist movement for unlawfulness, irrationality and simple-mindedness, thereby justifying increasingly repressive policing of public protest, as at Genoa in Summer 2001, have little historical sense of how progressive change has occurred through the desperate actions of oppositional movements, public debate and the incorporation of 'unrealistic' demands. Still, the question has to be posed: is the anti-capitalist movement an actual threat to global capitalism coming from the life-world or, alternatively, is it likely to be its unacknowledged and poetic means of system rectification?

References

Achbor, M. (ed.) (1994) *Manufacturing Consent: Noam Chomsky and the Media*, Montreal, Black Rose Books.

Alvarez, A. (2001) *Poker: Bets, Bluffs and Bad Beats*, London, Bloomsbury.

Bakhtin, M. (1968) *Rabelais and his World*, Cambridge, MA, Massachusetts Institute of Technology.

Baudrillard, J. (1988) *Selected Writings*, Cambridge, Polity Press.

Calhoun, C. (ed.) (1992) *Habermas and the Public Sphere*, Cambridge, MA, Massachusetts Institute of Technology.

Calhoun, C. (1995) *Critical Social Theory*, Oxford, Basil Blackwell.

Carleheden, M. and Gabriels, R. (1996) 'An interview with Jürgen Habermas', *Theory, Culture and Society*, vol.13, no.3, pp.1–17.

Castells, M. (1996) *The Rise of the Network Society* (*The Information Age*, Vol. I), Malden, MA, Basil Blackwell.

Castells, M. (1997) *The Power of Identity* (*The Information Age*, Vol. II), Malden, MA, Basil Blackwell.

Castells, M. (1998) *End of Millennium* (*The Information Age*, Vol. III), Malden, MA, Basil Blackwell.

Chomsky, N. (1989) *Necessary Illusions: Thought Control in Democratic Societies*, London, Pluto Press.

Deep Dish (2000) *Showdown in Seattle: Five Days that Shook the WTO*, New York, Deep Dish Television.

Dowmunt, T. (ed.) (1993) *Channels of Resistance: Global Television and Local Empowerment*, London, British Film Institute.

Downey, J. and Fenton, N. (2001) 'Constructing a counter public sphere: the N30 demonstrations and the World Wide Web', Media, Communication and Cultural Studies Association Conference, Stanford Hall, Leicestershire, January, pp.1–27.

Fraser, N. (1992) 'Rethinking the public sphere: a contribution to the critique of actually exisiting democracy' in Calhoun, C. (ed.) *op. cit.*, pp.109–42.

Furedi, F. (2001) *Paranoid Parenting: Abandon Your Anxieties and be a Good Parent*, London, Allen Lane The Penguin Press.

Gilligan, C. (1993) *In a Different Voice: Psychological Theory and Women's Development*, Cambridge, MA, Harvard University Press. First published in 1982.

Habermas, J. (1984) *Communication and The Evolution of Society*, Cambridge, Polity Press. First published in 1976.

Habermas, J. (1987) *The Theory of Communicative Action, Volume Two: The Critique of Functionalist Reason*, Cambridge, Polity Press. First published in 1981.

Habermas, J. (1989a) 'The public sphere: an encyclopedia article' in Bronner, S.E. and Kellner, D.M. (eds) *Critical Theory and Society: A Reader*, New York, Routledge. Article first published in 1964.

Habermas, J. (1989b) *The Structural Transformation of the Public Sphere: An Inquiry into a Category of Bourgeois Society*, Cambridge, Polity Press. First published in 1962.

Habermas, J. (1992) 'Further reflections on the public sphere' in Calhoun, C. (ed.) *op. cit.*, pp.421–61.

Habermas, J. (1996) *Between Facts and Norms: Contribution to a Discourse Theory of Law and Democracy*, Cambridge, Polity Press. First published in 1992.

Herman, E.S. and Chomsky, N. (1988) *Manufacturing Consent: The Political Economy of the Mass Media*, New York, Pantheon Books.

Klein, N. (2000a) *No Logo: Taking Aim at the Brand Bullies*, London, Flamingo.

Klein, N. (2000b) 'The tyranny of the brands', *New Statesman*, 24 January, pp.25–8.

Lippmann, W. (1997) *Public Opinion*, New York, The Free Press. First published in 1922.

Livingstone, S. (1994) 'Watching talk: gender and engagement in the viewing of audience discussion programmes', *Media, Culture and Society*, issue 16, pp.429–47.

Livingstone, S. and Lunt, P. (1994) *Talk on Television: Audience Participation and Public Debate*, London, Routledge.

McGuigan, J. (1996) *Culture and the Public Sphere*, London, Routledge.

McGuigan, J. (1998a) 'What price the public sphere?' in Thussu, D.K. (ed.) *Electronic Empires: Global Media and Local Resistance*, London, Arnold, pp.91–107.

McGuigan, J. (1998b) 'National government and the cultural public sphere', *Media International Australia incorporating Culture and Policy*, no.81, pp.68–83.

McGuigan, J. (2000) 'British identity and "the people's princess"', *Sociological Review*, vol.48, no.1, pp.1–18.

Mills, C. Wright (1970) *The Sociological Imagination*, Harmondsworth, Penguin Books. First published in 1959.

Murdock, G. (2000) 'Talk shows: democratic debates and tabloid tales' in Wieten, J., Murdock, G. and Dahlgren, P. (eds) *Television Across Europe: A Comparative Introduction*, London, Sage, pp.198–220.

Negt, O. and Kluge, A. (1993) *Public Sphere and Experience: Toward an Analysis of the Bourgeois and Proletarian Public Sphere*, Minneapolis, MN, University of Minnesota Press. First published in 1972.

Rheingold, H. (1994) *The Virtual Community: Surfing the Internet*, London, Secker & Warburg.

Ross, A. (ed.) (1997) *No Sweat: Fashion, Free Trade, and the Rights of Garment Workers*, New York, Verso.

Schiller, D. (1999) *Digital Capitalism: Networking the Global Market System*, Cambridge, MA, Massachusetts Institute of Technology.

Sennett, R. (1986) *The Fall of Public Man*, London, Faber & Faber. First published in 1977.

Thompson, E.P. (1963) *The Making of the English Working Class*, London, Victor Gollancz.

Thompson, J.B. (1993) 'The theory of the public sphere', *Theory, Culture and Society,* vol.10, no.3, pp.173–89.

Williams, R. (1974) *Television: Technology and Cultural Form*, London, Fontana.

Williams, R. (1983) 'Culture' in McLellan, D. (ed.) *Marx: The First 100 Years*, London, Fontana, pp.15–55.

Readings

3.1 Jürgen Habermas, 'The public sphere: an encyclopedia article' (1964)

The concept

By 'the public sphere' we mean first of all a realm of our social life in which something approaching public opinion can be formed. Access is guaranteed to all citizens. A portion of the public sphere comes into being in every conversation in which private individuals assemble to form a public body.[1] They then behave neither like business or professional people transacting private affairs, nor like members of a constitutional order subject to the legal constraints of a state bureaucracy. Citizens behave as a public body when they confer in an unrestricted fashion – that is, with the guarantee of freedom of assembly and association and the freedom to express and publish their opinions – about matters of general interest. In a large public body, this kind of communication requires specific means for transmitting information and influencing those who receive it. Today, newspapers and magazines, radio and television are the media of the sphere. We speak of the political public sphere in contrast, for instance, to the literary one, when public discussion deals with objects connected to the activity of the state. Although state authority is, so to speak, the executor of the political public sphere, it is not a part of it.[2] To be sure, state authority is usually considered 'public' authority, but it derives its task of caring for the well-being of all citizens primarily from this aspect of the public sphere. Only when the exercise of political control is effectively subordinated to the democratic demand that information be accessible to the public, does the political public sphere win an institutionalized influence over the government through the instrument of law-making bodies. The expression *public opinion* refers to the tasks of criticism and control which a public body of citizens informally – and, in periodic elections, formally as well – practises vis-à-vis the ruling structure organized in the form of a state. Regulations demanding that certain proceedings be public [*Publizitätsvorschriften*] – for example, those providing for open court hearings – are also related to this function of public

opinion. The public sphere as a sphere which mediates between society and state, in which the public organizes itself as the bearer of public opinion, accords with the principle of the public sphere[3] – that principle of public information which once had to be fought for against the arcane policies of monarchies and which since that time has made possible the democratic control of state activities.

It is no coincidence that these concepts of the public sphere and public opinion arose for the first time only in the eighteenth century. They acquire their specific meaning from a concrete historical situation. It was at that time that the distinction of 'opinion' from 'opinion publique' and 'public opinion' came about. Though mere opinions (cultural assumptions, normative attitudes, collective prejudices and values) seem to persist unchanged in their natural form as a kind of sediment of history, public opinion can by definition come into existence only when a reasoning public is presupposed. Public discussions about the exercise of political power which are both critical in intent and institutionally guaranteed have not always existed – they grew out of a specific phase of bourgeois constitutional society and could enter into the order of the bourgeois state only as a result of a particular constellation of interests.

History

There is no indication that European society of the high Middle Ages possessed a public sphere as a unique realm distinct from the private sphere. Nevertheless, it was not coincidental that during that period symbols of sovereignty, for instance, the princely seal, were deemed 'public'. At that time there existed a public representation of power. The status of the feudal lord, at whatever level of the feudal pyramid, made it unnecessary to employ the categories 'public' and 'private'. The holder of the position represented it publicly; he showed himself, presented himself as the embodiment of an ever-present 'higher' power. The concept of this representation has been maintained up to the most recent constitutional history. Regardless of the degree to which it has loosened itself from the old base, the authority of political power today still demands a representation at the highest level by a head of state. Such elements, however, derive from a prebourgeois social structure. Representation in the sense of a bourgeois public sphere,[4] for instance, the representation of the nation or of particular mandates, has nothing to do with the medieval representative public sphere – a public sphere directly linked to the concrete existence of a ruler. As long as the prince and the estates of the realm still 'are' the land, instead of merely functioning as deputies for it, they are able to 'represent'; they represent their power 'before' the people, instead of for the people.

The feudal authorities (Church, princes and nobility), to which the representative public sphere was first linked, disintegrated during a long process of polarization. By the end of the eighteenth century they had broken apart into private elements on the one hand, and into public elements on the other. The position of the Church changed with the Reformation: the link to divine authority which the Church represented, that is, religion, became a private matter. So-called religious freedom came to insure what was historically the first area of private autonomy. The Church itself continued its existence as one public and legal body among others. The corresponding polarization within princely authority was visibly manifested in the separation of the public budget from the private household expenses of a ruler. The institutions of public authority, along with the bureaucracy and the military, and in part also with the legal institutions, asserted their independence from the privatized sphere of the princely court. Finally, the feudal estates were transformed as well: the nobility became the organs of public authority, parliament, and the legal institutions; while those occupied in trades and professions, insofar as they had already established urban corporations and territorial organizations, developed into a sphere of bourgeois society which would stand apart from the state as a genuine area of private autonomy.

The representative public sphere yielded to that new sphere of 'public authority' which came into being with national and territorial states. Continuous state activity (permanent administration, standing army) now corresponded to the permanence of the relationships which with the stock exchange and the press had developed within the exchange of commodities and information. Public authority consolidated into a concrete opposition for those who were merely subject to it and who at first found only a negative definition of themselves within it. These were the 'private individuals' who were excluded from public authority because they held no office. 'Public' no longer referred to the 'representative' court of a prince endowed with authority, but rather to an institution regulated according to competence, to an apparatus endowed with a monopoly on the legal exertion of authority. Private individuals subsumed in the state at whom public authority was directed now made up the public body.

Society, now a private realm occupying a position in opposition to the state, stood on the one hand as if in clear contrast to the state. On the other hand, that society had become a concern of public interest to the degree that the production of life in the wake of the developing market economy had grown beyond the bounds of private domestic authority. *The bourgeois public sphere* could be understood as the sphere of private individuals assembled into a public body, which almost immediately laid claim to the officially regulated 'intellectual newspapers' for use against the public authority itself. In those newspapers, and in moralistic and critical journals, they debated that public authority on the general rules of social intercourse in their fundamentally privatized yet publicly relevant sphere of labor and commodity exchange.

The liberal model of the public sphere

The medium of this debate – public discussion – was unique and without historical precedent. Hitherto the estates had negotiated agreements with their princes, settling their claims to power from case to case. This development took a different course in England, where the parliament limited royal power, than it did on the Continent, where the monarchies mediatized the estates. The Third Estate then broke with this form of power arrangement, since it could no longer establish itself as a ruling group. A division of power by means of the delineation of the rights of the nobility was no longer possible within an exchange economy – private authority over capitalist property is, after all, unpolitical. Bourgeois individuals are private individuals. As such, they do not 'rule'. Their claims to power vis-à-vis public authority were thus directed not against the concentration of power, which was to be 'shared'. Instead, their ideas infiltrated the very principle on which the existing power is based. To the principle of existing power, the bourgeois public opposed the principle of supervision – that very principle which demands that proceedings be made public [*Publizität*]. The principle of supervision is thus a means of transforming the nature of power, not merely one basis of legitimation exchanged for another.

In the first modern constitutions, the catalogue of fundamental rights were a perfect image of the liberal model of the public sphere: they guaranteed the society as a sphere of private autonomy and the restriction of public authority to a few functions. Between these two spheres, the constitutions further insured the existence of a realm of private individuals assembled into a public body who as citizens transmit the needs of bourgeois society to the state, in order, ideally, to transform political into 'rational' authority within the medium of this public sphere. The general interest, which was the measure of such rationality, was then guaranteed, according to the pre-suppositions of a society of free commodity exchange, when the activities of private individuals in the marketplace were freed from social compulsion and from political pressure in the public sphere.

At the same time, daily political newspapers assumed an important role. In the second half of the eighteenth century, literary journalism created serious competition for the earlier news sheets, which were mere compilations of notices. Karl Bücher characterized this great development as follows: 'Newspapers changed from mere institutions for the publication of news into bearers and leaders of public opinion – weapons of party politics. This transformed the newspaper business. A new element emerged between the gathering and publication of news: the editorial staff. But for the newspaper publisher it meant that he changed from a vendor of recent news to a dealer in public opinion.' The publishers insured the newspapers a commercial basis, yet without commercializing them as such. The press remained an institution of the public itself, effective in the manner of a mediator and intensifier of public discussion, no longer a mere organ for the spreading of news but not yet the medium of a consumer culture.

This type of journalism can be observed above all during periods of revolution, when newspapers of the smallest political groups and organizations spring up – for instance, in Paris in 1789. Even in Paris of 1848 every half-way eminent politician organized his club, every other his journal: 450 clubs and over 200 journals were established there between February and May alone. Until the permanent legalization of a politically functional public sphere, the appearance of a political newspaper meant joining the struggle for freedom and public opinion, and thus for the public sphere as a principle. Only with the establishment of the bourgeois constitutional state was the intellectual press relieved of the pressure of its convictions. Since then it has been able to abandon its polemical position and take advantage of the earning possibilities of a commercial undertaking.

In England, France, and the United States, the transformation from a journalism of conviction to one of commerce began in the 1830s at approximately the same time. In the transition from the literary journalism of private individuals to the public services of the mass media, the public sphere was transformed by the influx of private interests, which received special prominence in the mass media.

The public sphere in the social welfare state mass democracy

Although the liberal model of the public sphere is still instructive today with respect to the normative claim that information be accessible to the public,[5] it cannot be applied to the actual conditions of an industrially advanced mass democracy organized in the form of the social welfare state. In part, the liberal model had always included ideological components, but it is also in part true that the social preconditions, to which the ideological elements could at one time at least be linked, had been fundamentally transformed. The very forms in which the public sphere manifested itself, to which supporters of the liberal model could appeal for evidence, began to change with the Chartist movement in England and the February revolution in France. Because of the diffusion of press and propaganda, the public body expanded beyond the bounds of the bourgeoisie. The public body lost not only its social exclusivity; it lost in addition the coherence created by bourgeois social institutions and a relatively high standard of education. Conflicts hitherto restricted to the private sphere now intrude into the public sphere. Group needs which can expect no satisfaction from a self-regulating market now tend toward a regulation by the state. The public sphere, which must now mediate these demands, becomes a field for the competition of interests, competitions which assume the form of violent conflict. Laws which obviously have come about under the 'pressure of the street' can scarcely still be understood as arising from the consensus of private individuals engaged in public discussion. They correspond in a more or less unconcealed manner to the compromise of conflicting private interests. Social organizations which deal with the state act in the political public sphere, whether through the agency of political parties or directly in connection with the public administration. With the interweaving of the public and private realms, not only do the political authorities assume certain functions in the sphere of commodity exchange and social labour, but, conversely, social powers now assume political functions. This leads to a kind of 'refeudalization' of the public sphere. Large organizations strive for political compromises with the state and with one another, excluding the public sphere whenever possible. But at the same time the large organizations must assure themselves of at least plebiscitary support from the mass of the population through an apparent display of openness [*demonstrative Publizität*].[6]

The political public sphere of the social welfare state is characterized by a peculiar weakening of its critical functions. At one time the process of making proceedings public [*Publizität*] was intended to subject persons or affairs to public reason, and to make political decisions subject to appeal before the court of public opinion. But often enough today the process of making public simply serves the arcane policies of special interests; in the form of 'publicity' it wins public prestige for people or affairs, thus making them worthy of acclamation in a climate of nonpublic opinion. The very words 'public relations work' [*Öffentlichkeitsarbeit*] betray the fact that a public sphere must first be arduously constructed case by case, a public sphere which earlier grew out of the social structure. Even the central relationship of the public, the parties, and the parliament is affected by this change in function.

Yet this trend towards the weakening of the public sphere as a principle is opposed by the extension of fundamental rights in the social welfare state. The demand that information be accessible to the public is extended from organs of the state to all organizations dealing with the state. To the degree that this is realized, a public body of organized private individuals would take the place of the now-defunct public body of private individuals who relate individually to each other. Only these organized individuals could participate effectively in the process of public communication; only they could use the channels of the public sphere which exist within parties and associations and the process of making proceedings public [*Publizität*] which was established to facilitate the dealings of organizations with the state. Political compromises would have to be legitimized through this process of public communication. The idea of the public sphere, preserved in the social welfare state mass democracy, an idea which calls for a rationalization of power through the medium of public discussion among private individuals, threatens to disintegrate with the structural transformation of the public sphere itself. It could only be realized today, on an altered basis, as a rational reorganization of social and political power under the mutual control of rival organizations committed to the public sphere in their internal structure as well as in their relations with the state and each other.

Notes

1 Habermas's concept of the public sphere is not to be equated with that of 'the public', i.e., of the individuals who assemble. His concept is directed at the institution, which to be sure only assumes concrete form through the participation of people. It cannot, however, be characterized simply as a crowd. (This and the following notes by Peter Hohendahl.)

2 The state and the public sphere do not overlap, as one might suppose from casual language use. Rather, they confront one another as opponents. Habermas designates that sphere as public which antiquity understood to be private, i.e., the sphere of nongovernmental opinion making.

3 The principle of the public sphere could still be distinguished from an institution which is demonstrable in social history. Habermas thus would mean a model of norms and modes of behaviour by means of which the very functioning of public opinion can be guaranteed for the first time. These norms and modes of behaviour include: (a) general accessibility, (b) elimination of all privileges, and (c) discovery of general norms and rational legitimations.

4 The expression *represent* is used in a very specific sense in the following section, namely, to 'present oneself'. The important thing to understand is that the medieval public sphere, if it even deserves this designation, is tied to the *personal*. The feudal lord and estates create the public sphere by means of their very presence.

5 Here it should be understood that Habermas considers the principle behind the bourgeois public sphere, but not its historical form, as indispensable.

6 One must distinguish between Habermas's concept of 'making proceedings public' [*Publizität*] and the 'public sphere' [*Öffentlichkeit*]. The term *Publizität* describes the degree of public effect generated by a public act. Thus, a situation can arise in which the form of public opinion making is maintained, while the substance of the public sphere has long ago been undermined.

Source: Habermas, 1989a/1964, in Bronner and Kellner, 1989, pp.136–42

3.2 Sonia Livingstone, 'Watching talk: gender and engagement in the viewing of audience discussion programmes' (1994)

I felt really good because I'd spoken because in the past I've actually spoken to friends about it and they hadn't been in difficult situations and so they couldn't quite relate and strangely enough the audience was really really sympathetic and I felt more empathy with them than I had with friends who hadn't been through it. It felt really like the audience was on your side so it was actually a really nice feeling, you felt like you were being supported.

(Woman participant in a studio discussion)

What is the significance of conversations held in public places? How can diverse, even conflicting, publics meet to resolve their arguments? Is open access programming a democratic opening up of elite broadcasting practices or just a new form of cheap entertainment? A nexus of these and similar questions is currently being addressed by debates across different disciplines concerned with the public sphere and the mass media. In this article, I present an audience-based analysis of one particular public place for conversation and argument, in order to examine how these broader questions relate to, and may be informed by, consideration of concrete examples from audience research.

Specifically, I shall focus on the relations between gender and genre in audience responses to audience discussion programmes. The double use of 'audience' is not accidental here, for when audiences at home watch (and talk about) audiences in the television studio (who talk about everyday life outside the studio), our traditional categories of media analysis are challenged. Text (or author) and audience, public and private, expert and ordinary person, information and entertainment, critical and normative, subject and object – all are problematized by a genre in which ordinary people are invited to participate in a television studio debate about topical issues. A focus on gender further complicates these categories, for television genres are gendered (and, typically, research has focused on either news/current affairs or soap/romance (Corner, 1991)), as are television audiences (e.g. Fiske, 1987). According to the traditional gender assumptions, in the mass media male producers and experts disseminate information to 'the ordinary housewife', while more broadly the public sphere follows masculine rules of discourse and women are relegated to the private sphere of domesticity and gossip.

While social and political theorists debate the fate, or future, of the public sphere – in which rational, disinterested discussion to resolve public matters may be held, free from intervention by commerce or state (Habermas, 1989), media scholars are concerned to understand the specific role of the mass media in undermining, or providing potential for, the public sphere (Garnham, 1990), whether this is understood as Habermasian or radical (Curran, 1991; Fraser, 1990; Mann, 1990). In relation to audiences, one might ask what role individuals, as citizens and viewers, can play in a public sphere when public spaces are transformed, or indeed created, by the mass media?

The intervention of feminism in the public sphere debate has, by raising the issues of diverse, marginalized and excluded voices and of competing interests, proved central to analysis of the public sphere (Fraser, 1989; Phillips, 1991). This has resulted in a challenge both to the implied unity of 'the public', for people participate in multiple, overlapping publics, and also to the implicit claims to neutrality in analyses of 'rational' and 'moral' discourse (Benhabib, 1992; Fraser, 1990). However we conceptualize the public sphere, a heavy burden is placed on 'rational' dialogue. Having said this, the forms of discourse valued by the public sphere, which have traditionally valorized patriarchal conceptions of rationality (abstract and logical rather than narrative, conversational, emotional and particular) can be challenged. Habermas's bourgeois public sphere aims for a social consensus in favour of the public good, to be achieved through disinterested, rational, critical discussion among the public. In contrast, alternative conceptions of a plural, radical or oppositional public sphere, influenced by feminist theory, aim for a negotiated compromise among diverse, interested publics through a discussion which attempts to *facilitate* the representation of the less powerful and *regulate* the discourse of the more powerful.

Curiously, despite theoretical work which connects the public sphere to both feminist theory and to the mass media it is the case that, as McLaughlin (1993, p.600) notes, 'feminist work on the Habermasian public sphere gives the media scant attention'. It implicitly adopts a simple and outdated transmission model of the media, and ignores the ways in which the media now play an inextricable and constitutive role in modern public life. Yet the mass media have a particular role to play in relation to the feminist critique of the public sphere, for significantly they bring political issues and political processes into domestic spaces.

Consequently, the issues raised by feminist re-analysis of the public sphere are crucial for our understanding of the present-day media (and vice versa), inviting us especially to look anew at the linking of gender and genre in terms of actual, everyday practices. In genres from the news to the talk show to the soap opera, we must question the media regulation of public access, participation, discourse and interest. In the context of the present paper, one might argue that television debates and discussions among ordinary people may contribute towards the potential for a plural, radical or oppositional public sphere which gives a more central role to women and women's voices, and in the process, reformulates more general conceptions of the role of the media in public discourse (Livingstone and Lunt, 1994). Although empirical exploration of audience reception has not been without its critics (e.g. Seaman, 1992), media researchers (should) now hesitate to infer meanings and influences without recourse to this in some form. Here too, feminist media theory has been central in showing a way forward for analysing specific audience interpretations of texts (Ang, 1985), for showing the often surprising responses of actual audiences (Radway, 1984) and for challenging the unity of 'television' by identifying the complex relations between gender and genre (Curti, 1988).

Talk on television: the case of the audience discussion programme

The television studio is focal for the media public sphere, for, as 'the studio is the institutional discursive space of radio and television' (Scannell, 1991, p.2), it is a public space where, in the audience discussion programme, ordinary people meet together with experts of various kinds to discuss a social, political or personal issue. Often audience discussion programmes deal with 'trivial' issues in a light-hearted manner (although feminism leads us to rethink supposedly trivial chat). Often, however, the topics are serious, and the political, personal and moral dimensions of these topics may be addressed, albeit chaotically, within the terms of the debate. In current programmes such as *Donahue* (ITV), *Oprah Winfrey* (Channel 4), *Kilroy* (BBC) and *The Time, The Place* (ITV), the discussions are fairly free-flowing and often

heated. While clearly the host manages the discussion tightly, the programmes are nonetheless unique in allowing ordinary people to question and answer, challenge and support, tell personal stories and make political arguments.

In the space of any one programme, transmitted live or *as live*, any or most of the studio audience (of between twenty-five and a hundred people) may have had their say, a say not always scripted in advance and not entirely controllable by the host. Access to the programmes may be restricted insofar as those who make 'bad television' may be excluded, but those who disagree with the consensus or make an idiosyncratic argument or speak for a marginalized group are *not* excluded. Everyone must talk in ordinary, personal, narrative discourse – a constraint which causes the so-called experts considerable difficulties (Livingstone and Lunt, 1992, 1994) but which actually favours the contribution of ordinary people.

Carpignano *et al.* (1990) argue that a contemporary unease about public debate and public opinion may be seen in this genre, and, indeed, that the audience discussion programme might be seen as a form of (oppositional) public sphere. In these programmes:

> The crisis of the bourgeois public sphere is fully visible and displayed in front of our eyes. The crisis of representational democracy is the crisis of the traditional institutions of the public sphere, the party, the union etc., and most importantly the present mass refusal of politics. If we think about the reconstitution of a public sphere in terms of the revitalisation of old political organizations … then the embryonic discursive practices of a talk show might appear interesting, but ultimately insignificant … but if we conceive of politics today as … consolidated in the circulation of discursive practices rather than formal organisations, then a commonplace that formulates and propagates common senses and metaphors that govern our lives might be at the crossroads of a reconceptualization of collective practices.
>
> (Carpignano *et al.*, 1990, p.54)

Similarly, Masciarotte (1991, p.90) analyses *Oprah Winfrey* in terms of the feminist debate over women's voices and empowerment, claiming that 'talk shows afford women the political gesture of overcoming their alienation through talking about their particular experience as women in society'. …

…

Analysing the audience of audience discussion programmes

...

Compared with men, women are more likely to consider that the genre offers a sphere in which they can participate, feeling involved and that the issues are relevant to their own lives. They are more likely than men to believe that the genre provides a fair and valuable debate within this sphere, and hence to disagree that the debates are too chaotic and biased. Men are more likely to consider experts more worth hearing than the laity while women especially emphasize the importance of giving a say to ordinary people. Also, women in particular consider that the debates are of *social* value, while men were more likely to consider them pointless in that they reached no clear conclusion and were considered to have little influence.

...

Positioning the self within audience discussions

By analysing reception of this relatively ambiguous, fluid genre, the ways in which viewers actively position themselves more generally in relation to television texts can be seen. In order to explore further how men and women position themselves in relation to what are, often, highly moral issues, let us focus in on reception of a specific programme. First, however, we must examine the relation between the public sphere and morality, as morality itself is also highly gendered.

Gilligan (1993) has counterposed an ethical orientation of care and responsibility to that of justice and rights, arguing that, instead of being woolly and inconsistent, as it appeared when judged against traditional, formal moral reasoning, women's moral judgement tends to be more contextual, being immersed in the details of relationships and narratives. Women, she argued, more readily empathize with the particular other, while men intellectualize to an inappropriate extent, denying the complex claims of interpersonal situational details. Benhabib (1992) suggests that the formal, philosophical, non-feminist definitions of the moral domain, of which men's judgements are a reflection, lead to a privatization of women's experience, excluding it from public view. The moral self, on this social contract view, is disembedded and disembodied, making moral decisions for humanity rather than for individuals, from the viewpoint of the 'generalized other' whose sociohistorical (and gendered) particularity is hidden behind a 'veil of ignorance'. While retaining an overarching framework of universalist principles, Benhabib reinstates (women's) 'everyday, interactional morality' into ethical theory, arguing that 'neither the concreteness nor the otherness of the "concrete other" can be known in the absence of the *voice* of the other' (Benhabib, 1992, p.168).

When women viewers appear more tolerant of the lay arguments, the lack of conclusiveness or the emotional nature of the audience discussion programme, it is not that women fail to use higher, abstract principles to judge a debate but that their judgements are more concrete, contextual and relational. As in that other women's genre, the soap opera, the stories told of personal/political experience in the audience discussion programme express women's involvement in the lives of others, following the narratives, speculating about the relationships and drawing analogies with their own lives. The personal narratives in the programmes serve to *embed* the arguments, to ground the concrete individuality of the participants, to move away from their general humanity to their distinctive, often competing, individual claims. The fascination is that of the blow-by-blow account of relationships through which, Gilligan (1993) suggests, women negotiate their connectedness to each other and hence generate a contextualized, relational sense of self. Audience discussion programmes resist the restriction of such concerns to the private domain and publicize the heartfelt conversations of situated individuals.

In specifying the requirements of the public sphere, Habermas, like Kohlberg, the target of Gilligan's critique, draws on the neo-Kantian tradition which separates the personal from the moral, arguing that issues such as love, sex and divorce concern evaluative decisions over the good life rather than moral decisions over the just distribution of scarce resources, as are evident in issues such as poverty, equal opportunities or education. He argues that 'the concrete ethical life of a naively habituated lifeworld is characterized by the fusion of moral and evaluative issues. Only in a rationalized lifeworld do moral issues become independent of issues of the good life' (Habermas, quoted in Benhabib, 1992, p.182). One might then argue that, at best, audience discussion programmes are a mixed genre, dealing on occasion with the moral although most programmes concern the good life. More pessimistically, one might argue that this genre displays precisely a fusion of moral and evaluative issues, and hence cannot offer space for proper public sphere activities.

However, the appropriate response, I would argue, is not to attempt to deify this or any other media genre as a Habermasian rationalized lifeworld, but rather to challenge the *possibility of undoing* such a fusion of the evaluative and the moral and, particularly, to challenge the possibility of finding a public place in which citizens can meet together to address moral issues, as thus defined, *independent* of issues of the good life.

...

... I want to examine the responses of actual viewers, from the focus group discussions, to one programme in which the dominant and the different voice clashed in public. This was an argument between doctors (mainly male) and patients (mainly female), including an acrimonious exchange between a male doctor and a female patient, in an episode of *Kilroy* (16 May 1989) examining the problems of doctor–patient communication.

As I noted earlier, while men more often express dissatisfaction with the form or rules of the discussion, women are more likely to take the perspective of the concrete other:

> *Man:* I don't think it really is a form of debate, because there's no drawing together of conclusion or one side of an argument and then the other side of an argument.

> *Woman:* I could identify with some of the problems that those people were putting forward.

Women seem more tolerant of the absence of formal debating rules because, to them, it is more important to hear from diverse voices, however expressed. In the quotation below, a woman empathizes with the studio audience in order precisely to understand why it appears that women are disrupting the orderly debate format:

> *Woman:* I think it was a bit heated. Most of the people who complained were the women, I noted, I don't know why that was. Maybe they are more sensitive when they go to the doctor whereas the man who goes to the doctor just goes, just to get it over and done with, and isn't going for that communication, whereas the women need the communication more.

Similarly, there were a number of often quite lengthy attempts by women, but rarely if at all by men, to understand and empathize with the position being expressed, albeit unclearly, by the women – as patients – in the studio:

> *Woman:* What was that woman complaining about? It wasn't clear, she

started off by saying that she had had a bad relationship with her doctor, and it had now sorted itself out, it was entirely clear why, I think that it was partly because she thought the implication was that she felt always that she had been hurried, and not given a long time to say what was wrong with her. In fact when she said that they had got onto decent terms, and she had written and said that she wanted to come down and ask the following questions, she had in fact made quite a breakthrough herself without realizing it. If she had given the person half a chance, to set aside some time. Because he had had time in his own time to read the letter, which of course was a much more satisfactory way of doing it, as it turned out from what she had to do.

Using the dominant voice of principles and instrumentality, a man then implies that women have unreasonable expectations, while men are direct and efficient at communication:

> *Man:* I don't think that men have such high expectations, when you walk through that door, you know you state your case, I've been kicked in the balls, or whatever, you know you can go straight to the point, there is no high expectations about things.

...

It is not coincidental that the oppositional or negotiated conception of the public sphere is more compatible with feminist theory and that women, more than men, are engaged with these kinds of participatory media discussions and debates. Maybe not surprisingly, given their relative exclusion from the expert professions, women viewers especially appreciate the opportunity to hear the voices and experiences of ordinary people talking about issues relevant to their everyday lives and, as they see it, to political concerns more broadly. In accordance with the negotiated public sphere, women valued hearing from diverse publics on these programmes even though the orderly achievement of a consensual conclusion was often lacking. In accordance with Gilligan's analysis of voice, women were more likely to understand the genre in terms of communicative relations among a set of people, including themselves, which require regulation to ensure fair and diverse representation, and which are embedded in the everyday lives of all participants. Conversely, in line with Gilligan's analysis of the dominant voice, which draws more on the principled morality discussed by Kohlberg, Habermas and others, men were more likely to be concerned about the formal constitutions of the genre, its conformity to rules of argumentation and its abstract goals.

Both the viewers' gender and whether they are a programme fan affect their understanding of the genre and this in turn affects the position they negotiate in relation to public discussions, with consequences for their critical response, their participation and involvement, and their motivations for viewing. It is not simply that women are fans and men are not, nor is that men who watch necessarily adopt a 'feminine reading' or a 'different voice' (although women who do not watch sound very like men who do not watch, judging the genre harshly on its perceived failure to offer a classic, Habermasian debate). Nonetheless, the resonances between the viewers' everyday experiences and their gendered readings of the genre mean that a more positive construction of the genre is relatively more available to women, who consequently become viewers, than to men.

References

Ang, I. (1985) *Watching* Dallas*: Soap Operas and the Melodramatic Imagination*, New York, Methuen.

Benhabib, S. (1992) *Situating the Self: Gender, Community and Postmodernism in Contemporary Ethics*, Cambridge, Polity Press.

Carpignano, P., Andersen, R., Aronowitz, S. and Difazio, W. (1990) '"Chatter" in the age of electronic reproduction: talk television and the "public mind"', *Social Text*, pp.25–6,33–55.

Corner, J. (1991) 'Meaning, genre and context: the problematics of "public knowledge" in the new audience studies' in Curran, J. and Gurevitch, M. (eds) *Mass Media and Society*, London, Methuen.

Curran, J. (1991) 'Rethinking the media as a public sphere' in Dahlgren, P. and Sparks, C. (eds) *Communication and Citizenship: Journalism and the Public Sphere in the New Media Age*, London, Routledge.

Curti, L. (1988) 'Genre and gender', *Cultural Studies*, vol.12, no.2, pp.152–67.

Fiske, J. (1987) *Television Culture*, London, Methuen.

Fraser, N. (1989) 'What's critical about critical theory? The case of Habermas and Gender' in Fraser, N., *Unruly Practices: Power, Discourse and Gender in Contemporary Social Theory*, Minneapolis, MN, University of Minnesota Press.

Fraser N. (1990) 'Rethinking the public sphere: a contribution to the critique of actually existing democracy', *Social Text*, pp.25–6,56–80.

Garnham, N. (1990) 'The media and the public sphere' in Garnham, N., *Capitalism and Communication: Global Culture and the Economics of Information*, London, Sage.

Gilligan, C. (1993) 'Preface' to *In a Different Voice: Psychological Theory and Women's Development* (2nd edn), Cambridge, MA, Harvard University Press.

Habermas, J. (1989) *The Structural Transformation of the Public Sphere: An Inquiry into a Category of Bourgeois Society* (trans. T. Burger and F. Lawrence), Cambridge, MA, MIT Press.

Livingstone, S.M. and Lunt, P.K. (1992) 'Expert and lay participation in television debates: an analysis of audience discussion programmes', *European Journal of Communication*, vol.7, no.1, pp.9–35.

Livingstone, S.M. and Lunt, P.K. (1994) *Talk on Television: Audience Participation and Public Debate*, London, Routledge.

McLaughlin, L. (1993) 'Feminism, the public sphere, media and democracy', *Media, Culture and Society*, vol.15, pp.599–620.

Mann, P. (1990) 'Unifying discourse: city college as a post-modern public sphere', *Social Text*, pp.25–6,81–102.

Masciarotte, G.-J. (1991) 'C'mon girl: Oprah Winfrey and the discourse of feminine talk', *Genders*, vol.11, pp.81–110.

Phillips, A. (1991) *Engendering Democracy*, Cambridge, Polity Press.

Radway, J. (1984) *Reading the Romance: Women, Patriarchy and Popular Literature*, Chapel Hill, NC, University of North Carolina Press.

Scannell, P. (1991) 'Introduction: the relevance of talk' in Scannell, P. (ed.) *Broadcast Talk*, London, Sage.

Seaman, W.R. (1992) 'Active audience theory: pointless populism', *Media, Culture and Society*, vol.14, pp.301–11.

Source: Livingstone, 1994, pp.429–33,435,437–8,440–41, 444–5

3.3 Naomi Klein, 'The tyranny of the brands' (2000)

What are we to make of the extraordinary scenes in Seattle that brought the 20th century to a close? A *New York Times* reporter observed that this vibrant mass movement opposed to unregulated globalisation had materialised 'seemingly overnight'. On television, the reliable experts who explain everything couldn't sort out whether the protesters were right-wing nationalists or Marxist globalists. Even the American left seemed surprised to learn that, contrary to previous reports, it did, in fact, still exist.

Despite the seemingly unconnected causes that converged in Seattle that week, there was a common target: the multinational corporation in general and McDonald's, The Gap, Microsoft and Starbucks in particular. And what has given the movement against them a new energy and a new urgency is a profound shift in corporate priorities. That shift centres on the idea of corporate branding and the quest to build the most powerful brand image. It will, I believe, be one of the issues that shapes the first decade of the 21st century.

Branding seems like a fairly innocuous idea. It is slapping a logo on a product and saying it's the best. And when brands first emerged, that was all it was. At the start of the industrial revolution, the market was flooded with nearly identical mass-produced products. Along came Aunt Jemima and Quaker Oats with their happy comforting logos to say: our mass-produced product is of the highest quality.

But the role of branding has been changing, particularly in the past fifteen years: rather than serving as a guarantee of value on a product, the brand itself has increasingly become the product, a free-standing idea pasted on to innumerable surfaces. The actual product bearing the brand-name has become a medium, like radio or a billboard, to transmit the real message. The message is: It's Nike. It's Disney. It's Microsoft. It's Diesel. It's Caterpillar. The late graphic designer, Tibor Kalman, said that a brand used to be a mark of quality; now, it is 'a stylistic badge of courage'.

This shift in the role of the brand is related to a new corporate consensus, which emerged in the late 1980s. It held that corporations were too bloated: they were oversized, they owned too much, they employed too many people, they were weighed down with too many things. Where once the primary concern of every corporation was the production of goods, now production itself – running one's own

factories, being responsible for tens of thousands of full-time, permanent employees – began to seem like a clunky liability.

The Nikes and Microsofts, and later the Tommy Hilfigers and Intels, made the bold claim that production was only an incidental part of their operations. What these companies produced primarily were not things, they said, but ideas and images for their brands, and their real work lay not in manufacturing, but in building up their brands. Savvy ad agencies began to think of themselves as brand factories, hammering out what is of true value: the idea, the lifestyle, the attitude. Out of this heady time, we learnt that Nike was about 'Sport', not shoes; Microsoft about 'Communications', not software; Starbucks about 'Community', not coffee; Virgin about a 'Fun-loving Attitude', not an airline, a record label, a cola, a bridal gown line, a train – or any of the other brand extensions the company has launched. My favourite is Diesel, whose chief executive says he has 'created a movement', not a line of clothes.

The formula for these brand-driven companies is pretty much the same: get rid of your unionised factories in the west and buy your products from Asian or Central American contractors and sub-contractors. Then take the money you save and spend it on branding – on advertising, superstores, sponsorships. Based on the overwhelming success of this formula, virtue in the corporate world has become a sort of race towards weightlessness: the companies which own the least, keep the fewest employees on the payroll and produce the coolest ideas (as opposed to products) win the race.

I have come to think of such companies as transcendent brands because their goal is to escape almost all that is earthbound and to become pure idea, like a spirit ascending. This is a goal that is available not only to companies, but also to people. We have human brands as well as company brands and they, too, are cutting ties with what might be broadly described as 'doing things'. Bill Gates has quit as chief executive of Microsoft so that he can tend to his true mission: being Bill Gates. Michael Jordan has stopped playing basketball and has become a pure brand-identity machine. And not only does he now have his own 'Jordan' superstores, he is the first celebrity endorser to get other celebrities endorsing his label. Michael Jordan is no longer an athlete, he is an attitude.

It wasn't until the Internet stock explosion that the extent of this shift became apparent. It marks the complete triumph of branding: the ascent of companies, most of which have yet to make a profit, that exist almost purely as ideas of themselves, leaving no real-world trace at all. What they are selling to Wall Street is unadulterated brand.

This shift to branding explains many of the most fundamental economic and cultural shifts of the past decade. Power, for a brand-driven company, is attained not by collecting assets per se, but by projecting one's brand idea on to as many surfaces of the culture as possible: the wall of a college, a billboard the size of a sky-scraper, an ad campaign that waxes philosophic about the humane future of our global village. Where a previous generation of corporate giants used drills, hammers and cranes to build their empires, these companies need an endless parade of new ideas for brand extensions, continuously rejuvenated imagery for marketing and, most of all, fresh new spaces to disseminate their brand's idea of itself.

In this way, these corporate phantoms become real. If we think of a brand-driven company as an ever-expanding balloon, then public space, new political ideas and avant-garde imagery are the gases that inflate it: it needs to consume cultural space in order to stave off its own deflation. This is a major change. Marketing, in the classic sense, is about association: beautiful girl drinks soda, uses shampoo, drives car: soda/shampoo/car become associated with our aspiration to be beautiful like her.

Branding mania has changed all that: association is no longer good enough. The goal now is for the brands to animate their marketing identities, to become real-world, living manifestations of their myths. Brands are about 'meaning', not product attributes. So companies provide their consumers with opportunities not merely to shop but to experience fully the meaning of their brand. The brand-name superstore, for instance, stands as a full expression of the brand's lifestyle in miniature. Many of these stores are so palatial, so interactive, so hi-tech that they lose money hand over fist. But that doesn't mean they aren't working. Their real goal, since they are never the company's only source of sales, is to act as a 3D manifestation of the brand, so grand that their rather mundane products will carry that grandeur with them like a homing device.

But this is only the beginning. Nike, which used just to sponsor athletes, has taken to buying sporting events outright. Disney, which through its movies and theme parks has sold a bygone version of small-town America, now owns and operates its very own small town, Celebration, Florida.

In these branded creations, we see the building blocks of a fully privatised social and cultural infrastructure. These companies are stretching the fabric of their brands in so many directions that they are transformed into tent-like enclosures large enough to house any number of core activities, from shopping to entertainment to holidays. This is the true meaning of a lifestyle brand: living your life inside a brand. Brand-based companies are no longer satisfied with having a fling with their consumers, they want to move in together.

These companies are forever on the prowl for new and creative ways to build and strengthen their brand images. This thirsty quest for meaning and virgin space takes its toll on public institutions such as schools, where, in North America, corporate interests are transforming education, seeking not only to advertise in cafeterias and washrooms but to make brands the uncritical subjects of study. Maths textbooks urge students to calculate the circumference of an Oreo cookie, Channel One broadcasts Burger King ads into 12,000 US schools and a student from Georgia was suspended last year for wearing a Pepsi T-shirt on his school's official 'Coke Day'.

Another effect is to restrict choice. Brands, at the core, are selfish creatures, driven by the need to eliminate competitors and create self-enclosed branded systems. So Reebok, once it lands a deal to sponsor campus athletics, wants to exclude not only competing brands but also, as was the case at the University of Wisconsin, all disparaging remarks made about Reebok by officials of the university. Such 'non-disparagement' clauses are standard in campus sponsorship deals. Disney, after it bought ABC, decided that it would rather *ABC News* no longer covered Disney's scandals, and focused instead on promoting its movies in various feats of 'synergy'. We can look forward to more of the same, no doubt, from this month's merger of AOL and Time Warner.

There is another, more tangible, effect of this shift from products to brands: the devaluation of production itself. The belief that economic success lies in branding – production is a distant second – is changing the face of global employment. Building a superbrand is extraordinarily costly. A brand needs constant managing, tending, replenishing, stretching. The necessity for lavish spending on marketing creates intense resistance to investment in production facilities and labour. Companies that were traditionally satisfied with a 100 per cent mark-up from the cost of factory production to the retail price have spent the decade scouring the globe for factories that can make their products so inexpensively that the mark-up is closer to 400 per cent.

That's where the developing world's 'free-trade zones' (free, that is, of taxes and wage or other labour regulations) come in. In Indonesia, China, Mexico, Vietnam, the Philippines and elsewhere, the export-processing zones (as these areas are also called) are emerging as leading producers of garments, toys, shoes, electronics and cars. There are almost 1,000 zones around the world, spread through 70 countries and employing approximately 27 million workers.

Inside the gates of the zones, workers assemble the finished products of our branded world: Nike running shoes, Gap pyjamas, IBM computer screens, Old Navy jeans, or VW Bugs. Yet the zones appear to be the only places left on earth where the superbrands actually keep a low profile. Indeed, they are positively demure. Their names and logos aren't splashed on the facades of the factories. In fact, where a particular branded product is made is often kept secret. And unlike in the brand-segregated superstores, competing labels are often produced side by side in the same factories; glued by the same workers, stitched and soldered on the same machines.

Regardless of where the zones are located, the hours will be long – 14-hour days in Sri Lanka, 12 in Indonesia, 16 in southern China, 12 in the Philippines. The workers are mostly young women; the management military-style; the wages, sub-subsistence; the work, low-skill and tedious. The factories are owned by contractors or subcontractors from Korea, Taiwan or Hong Kong; the contractors meet orders for companies based in the US, Britain, Japan, Germany and Canada.

These pockets of pure industry are cloaked in a haze of transience: the contracts come and go with little notice (in Guatemala the factories are called 'swallows' because they might take flight at any time); the workers are predominantly migrants, far from home with little connection to the place in which they find themselves; the work itself is short-term, often not renewed. Many factory workers in the Philippines are hired through an employment agency inside the zone walls which collects their cheques and takes a cut – a temp agency for factory workers, in other words.

We tend to think that globalisation moves jobs from one country to another. But in a brand-based economy, the value of the work itself moves to a drastically degraded rung of the corporate hierarchy. What is being abandoned in the relentless quest to reduce the costs of production is the Fordist principle: that labour not only creates products but, by paying workers a decent wage, creates the consumer market for that product and others like it. In Indonesia, the young women factory workers making Nike shoes and Gap jeans live a notch above famine victims and landless peasants. And though it may seem indecent to compare them with the relatively privileged retail workers in the western shopping malls, the same pattern is at work. In developed countries, too, jobs are increasingly temporary, part-time, contract-based. Just as factory jobs that once supported families in the west have been reconfigured in the developing world as jobs for teenagers, so have the brand-name clothing companies and restaurant chains – Wal-Mart, Starbucks, The Gap – pioneered the idea that fast-food and retail-sector jobs are disposable and unfit for adults.

And so we are left with an odd duality: brands have never been more omnipresent in our lives, nor have they ever generated as much wealth. All around us we see these new branded creations replacing our cultural institutions and our public spaces. And yet, at the same time, these same companies are oddly absent from our lives in the most immediate of ways: as steady employers. Multinationals that once identified strongly with their role as engines of job growth – and used it as leverage to extract all kinds of government support – now prefer to identify themselves as engines of 'economic growth'.

The extent of this shift cannot be overstated. Among the total number of working-age adults in the USA, Canada and the UK, those with full-time, permanent jobs working for someone other than themselves are in the minority. Temps, part-timers, the unemployed and those who have opted out of the labour force entirely – some because they don't want to work but many more because they have given up looking for jobs – now make up more than half of the working-age population.

We know that this formula reaps record profits in the short term. It may, however, prove to be a strategic miscalculation. When corporations are perceived as functioning vehicles of wealth distribution – trickling down jobs and tax revenue – they get deep civic loyalty in return. In exchange for steady pay cheques and stable communities, citizens attach themselves to the priorities and fortunes of the local corporate sector and don't ask too many questions about, say, water pollution. In other words, dependable job creation served as a kind of corporate suit of armour, shielding companies from the wrath that might otherwise have been directed their way. Only now, without realising it, brand-driven multinationals have gradually been shedding that armour: first came their inability to respect public space, next came their betrayal of the central promise of the information age – the promise of increased choice – and, finally, they severed the bond between employer and employee.

They may be big, they may be rich, but suddenly there is nothing to protect them from public rage.

And that is the true significance of Seattle. All around us we are witnessing the early expressions of this anger, of the first, often crudely constructed lines of defence against the rule of the brands. We have, for example, the growth of 'culture-jamming' which adapts a corporation's own advertising to send a message starkly at odds with the one that was intended. So, for example, Apple Computers' 'Think Different' campaign acquires a photograph of Stalin with the slogan 'Think Really Different'. The process forces the company to foot the bill for its own subversion, either literally, because the company is the one that bought the billboard being altered, or figuratively, because whenever anyone messes with a logo, they are tapping into the vast resources spent to make that logo meaningful.

I've never been thoroughly convinced by the powers of culture-jamming: in a war fought strictly with images, surely the one with the most images will win? But the principles of culture-jamming – using the power of brand-names against themselves in a kind of brand boomerang – are being imported to much more direct and immediate political struggles. People are beginning to fight the big global economic battles by focusing on one or two brand-name corporations and turning them into large-scale political metaphors. They are having more luck with this strategy than they had with decades of fighting these battles on a policy level with governments.

Think of the campaigns that trace the journeys of brand-name goods back to their unbranded points of origin: Nike sneakers back to the sweatshops of Vietnam; Starbucks lattes back to the sun-scorched coffee fields of Guatemala and now East Timor; and virtually every ingredient of a McDonald's hamburger dissected into its bio-engineered beginnings.

There is a clear difference between these campaigns and the corporate boycotts of the past, whether against Nestlé for its baby formula, or against Union Carbide for its infamous toxic accident in Bhopal, India. In those cases, activists had targeted a specific corporation engaged in an anomalously harmful practice. Today's anti-corporate campaigns simply piggyback on the high profile of their brand-name targets as a tactical means of highlighting difficult, even arcane issues. The companies being targeted – Disney, Mattel, The Gap and so on – may not always be the worst offenders, but they do tend to be the ones who flash their logos in bright lights on the global marquee. It may seem unfair to single such companies out for their 'success', as some have argued, but it is precisely this success which is becoming an odd sort of liability.

Take McDonald's. In opening more than 23,000 outlets worldwide, the company has done more than spread the gospel of fast, uniform food. It has also, inadvertently, become equated in the public imagination with the 'McJob', 'McDonaldisation' and 'McWorld'. So when activists build a movement around McDonald's, as they did around the McLibel Trial, they are not really going after a fast-food chain, but harnessing the branding might behind the chain as a way to crack open a discussion on the otherwise impenetrable global economy: about labour, the environment and cultural imperialism.

Many superbrands are feeling the backlash. With typical understatement, Shell Oil's chief executive, Mark Moody, states: 'Previously, if you went to your golf club or church and said, "I work for Shell", you'd get a warm glow. In some parts of the world, that has changed a bit.' That change flowed directly from the anti-corporate campaign launched against Shell after the hanging of the Nigerian author and activist Ken Saro-Wiwa, who was fighting to get Shell to clean up the environmental devastation left behind when it pumped oil out of the Niger Delta. Had the campaigners focused on the dictatorship alone, the death of the activist could well have been yet another anonymous atrocity in Africa. But because they dared to name names – to name Shell as the economic interest behind the violence – it became an instantly globalised campaign, with protests at petrol stations around the world. The brand was the campaign's best asset. Something similar happened in the campaign against the brutal regime in Burma; almost all the major brand-name companies have now pulled out. The campaign against Monsanto – which has abandoned its plans for 'terminator' seeds, genetically altered so as to yield only one crop – worked because the pressure was put on the heavily branded supermarkets and packaged food companies.

At the heart of this shift in focus is the recognition that corporations are much more than purveyors of the products we all want; they are also the most powerful political forces of our time, the driving forces behind bodies such as the World Trade Organisation. By now, we've all heard the statistics: how corporations such as Shell and Wal-Mart bask in budgets bigger than the gross domestic products of most nations: how, of the top 100 economies 51 are multinationals and only 49 are countries. So, although the media often describe campaigns like the one against Nike as 'consumer boycotts', that tells only part of the story. It is more accurate to describe them as political campaigns that use consumer goods as readily accessible targets, as public-relations levers and as popular education tools.

I doubt this current surge of anti-corporate activism would have been possible without the mania for branding. Branding, as we have seen, has taken a fairly straightforward relationship between buyer and seller and – through the quest to turn brands into media providers, art producers, town squares and social philosophers – transformed it into something much more intimate. But the more successful this project is, the more vulnerable these companies become to the brand boomerang. If brands are indeed intimately entangled with our culture and identity, then, when they do wrong, their crimes are not easily dismissed as another corporation trying to make a buck. Instead, many of the people who inhabit these branded worlds feel complicit in their wrongs, both guilty and connected. And this connection is a volatile one, akin to the relationship of fan and celebrity: emotionally intense but shallow enough to turn on a dime.

Branding as I have stated, is a balloon economy: it inflates with astonishing rapidity but it is full of hot air. It shouldn't be surprising that this formula has bred armies of pin-wielding critics, anxious to pop the corporate balloon and watch it fall to the ground.

Behind the protests outside Nike Town, behind the pie in Bill Gates's face, behind the shattering of a McDonald's window in Paris, behind the protests in Seattle, there is something too visceral for most conventional measures to track – a bad mood rising. And the corporate hijacking of political power is as responsible for this mood as the brands' cultural looting of public and mental spaces.

All around the world, activists are making liberal use of the tool that has so thoroughly captured the imagination of the corporate world: branding. Brand image, the source of so much corporate wealth, is also, it turns out, the corporate Achilles' heel.

Source: Klein, 2000b, pp.25–8

Tools for commerce?
Sociology and economic life

Liz McFall

Contents

1 Introduction

> Clever people in universities study advertising the way biologists study insects. ... [F]rom work like this, they produce theories of how advertising works. Advertising agencies coexist with these theories, generally by ignoring them. Most advertising people – especially creatives – go through life without ever meeting a single academic thinker. When was the last time you saw a Senior Research Fellow chilling at the Groucho or dancing on a table at a Grosvenor House awards do?
>
> (Broadbent, 1998)

Leaving aside the question of whether academics are, as Broadbent implies, temperamentally unsuited to 'chilling', the aim in this chapter is to explore the relationship between academic sociology and the broader area of 'economic life'. Broadbent's comments appear in the advertising trade journal *Campaign* in an article about the relationship between the academic study and the practice of advertising. His analysis is light-hearted but, nevertheless, it invokes some widely accepted ideas about the essential divide between study on the one hand and practice on the other. According to such ideas, the practices, activities, techniques and tools that make up the 'real world' of the economy exist quite independently from those of 'ivory tower' academics. Clever people with no common sense or practical experience theorize and teach, while 'those who can, do'. This chapter aims to show that this is a simplified account of the division between academic work – in sociology in particular – and economic life and it overlooks the significance of the many forms of exchange of information, knowledge, tools and techniques between the domains.

economic
sociology

There are three relatively distinct but overlapping perspectives on the relationship between the academic discipline of sociology and **economic life**. The first of these concerns the classical sociological heritage of studies of the economy. Here, accounting for the relationship between the economy and social life is understood to be one of the key objectives of sociology. Indeed the early development of sociology as a discipline has been attributed to the economic changes associated with the processes of industrialization in the nineteenth and early twentieth centuries. It was during this period that some of the most influential sociological accounts of the nature and consequences of particular economic systems were formulated by theorists like **Karl Marx** and **Max Weber**.

Marx, Karl
Weber, Max

Section 2 will provide a brief overview of these explanations and their subsequent development in more recent sociological work. Underlying these very different explanations, this chapter argues, is an approach that regards the economy as a self-evident 'thing'. In this view the economy objectively exists in the 'real' world and the task of sociology and the other social sciences is to describe and analyse its operation.

These sociological and social scientific observations of the economy have, in some respects, contributed to the development of the second perspective on the relationship between sociology and the economy. Sociology emerges as a source of knowledge that can be used to counteract some of the deleterious effects associated with the large-scale economic processes of industrialization and the increasing division of labour. Sociology and the social sciences can be employed to restructure and reform the workplace to the mutual advantage of worker satisfaction and company profitability. A number of schools of thought seeking to apply sociological and socio-psychological forms of knowledge to such ends

appeared throughout the twentieth century and these will be reviewed in section 3. The argument here will be that throughout such approaches as Human Relations and Organizational Psycho-technology, the underlying ethos is to apply **'objective'**   objectivity
knowledges drawn from the social sciences to economic practice.

There is considerable overlap between these two perspectives. What starts as academic theory often filters through to commercial practice, while knowledge borne out of commercial practice often becomes the subject of academic study. Study of both these perspectives begins to reveal the extent of the interplay between sociology and the 'economy'. However, there are some problems with the ways in which the economy and economic life have been conceptualized in both these perspectives. Foremost amongst these are the notion of the economy as an objective 'thing in itself' and the equation of economic life with the sphere of production and work rather than consumption and leisure. These conceptions have been the subject of criticism from a variety of different sources in sociology, anthropology and feminist critique. Accordingly, in section 4 the case will be put forward for a broader conception of economic life as embracing not only production and work but also consumption and leisure.

This will help to prepare the way for a discussion in section 5 of the third and final perspective on the relationship between sociology and economic life. In this section it will be suggested that this relationship is not best viewed in terms of sociology's detached study of the economy nor in terms of the economy's use of sociological knowledge; rather it might be better understood as one in which sociological study and economic life are simultaneous and interdependent. What this means is that the two should be understood as caught up in a pattern of mutual dependence where practices carried out in one domain interact, in some way, with practices in the other. This involves rethinking the classical model of the economy as a sort of global balancing mechanism in which an *invisible hand* acts to bring the forces of supply and demand into equilibrium; instead, attention will be drawn to the ways in which the *visible hands* of retail managers, marketing consultants, sociologists and cultural theorists pattern everyday economic life.

Before proceeding further it is worth noting that the sociology of economic life is a vast field and the approach here is not to attempt a systematic overview. Rather the intention is to consider some influential schools of thought and work towards a conception of economic life that is sensitive to everyday economic experiences. For this reason the focus throughout the chapter will be primarily at the micro level of work and consumption activities, not at the level of markets and economic processes on a grander scale.

AIMS

The aims of this chapter are:

1   To consider the heritage of sociological studies of the economy.

2   To consider how sociological forms of knowledge have been used for economic or commercial purposes.

3   To review 'economic life' as a sociological concept embracing both production and consumption.

4   To introduce the idea of a mutually constitutive relation between sociology and economic life.

2 Classic sociological studies of work and the economy

Sacked M&S European staff bring protest to London
by Matthew Beard

Marks & Spencer staff from Barcelona to Bruges rose at dawn yesterday to travel in a convoy of coaches across Europe and through the Channel Tunnel via Eurostar to march in London. An international band of about 3,000 shop workers marched through the wet and windy streets of the capital in a noisy protest at Marks & Spencer's decision to shut up shop in continental Europe. Union activists from France, Germany, Belgium and Spain united for a day to voice their anger at the "brutal" manner in which the retailer – a once-loved feature of European city centres – has shed 4,400 jobs after deciding to close its 39 stores in Europe in an attempt to halt its decline. Led by a Scottish pipe band from the GMB general workers union, the demonstrators marched down Baker Street but found a dozen police outside Michael House and management refusing to discuss calls for thorough consultation if, as likely, the Belgian chief

Protests at the announcement of the planned closure of Marks & Spencer in Paris

executive, Luc Vandevelde, persists with closure plans. There was a brief scuffle as police seized a Belgian protester letting off firecrackers, but his comrades failed to respond to his incitement to break through the line of police. Instead the protesters, who produced an ear-splitting combination of whistles and drums, grew increasingly frustrated that their act of international solidarity had been met with a wall of silence. Ridah Bouhlel, 24, who led a group of 18 workers from M&S's doomed store in Nice, said he was impressed with the turn-out but not by the store's management. Mr Bouhlel, a shop steward and shelf-filler, said: "Despite the weather we are in high spirits and united, but it is disappointing that the people from head office have gone into hiding." The store's continental staff are angry that they received no advance warning before redundancies, affecting all of Europe, the US and Hong Kong, were announced in March. The ailing retailer says £100m was lost in three years in continental Europe. The company has been praised by City analysts for "radical" redundancy measures. But the staff's treatment has been condemned by other governments and branded "extremely brutal" by the French economic minister, Laurent Fabius. A French court recently ordered a suspension of the process. In April, unions staged a protest outside the flagship store in Boulevard Haussmann in Paris. M&S's withdrawal from Europe was also met with disbelief from shoppers abroad and there have been reports of panic-buying of favourite lines, such as chicken tikka masala and baked beans.

Source: *The Independent,* 17 May 2001

Why do you think the Marks & Spencer closure programme provoked such an angry response?

My guess is that the threat of redundancy and the associated losses of money, security and a certain lifestyle were probably amongst your first thoughts. But perhaps there were other factors – the lack of consultation or even the loss of the store itself? Different sociological accounts of the economy would explain the closure programme and the reaction to it in quite different ways. The two sociological positions on the economy – Marxist and Weberian – that you are about to be introduced to would certainly emphasize quite different aspects both of the causes of the closure and the reaction to it. This is because Marx and Weber had quite distinctive theories of how the economy worked and quite different political reasons for studying it. Marx advanced a radical critique of economic processes while Weber adopted a more reformist attitude. For Marx, only a complete dismantling of the economy could overcome its exploitative nature, while, for Weber, the project for change was articulated in terms of a more moderate programme of social and economic reform. As you read through section 2 bear in mind your responses to Activity 1 and consider whether the different theories would explain all or only some aspects of the Marks & Spencer case study.

2.1 Karl Marx: work, alienation and class conflict

The economic structure of a society, for Marx, was defined by the sum total of the relations of production. These relations of production determine class position: in capitalist societies, the bourgeoisie own the means of production while the proletariat own only their labour power (see **Savage, 2002**). This pattern of ownership is directly related to the exploitative nature of the production process because it forces the labour of the proletariat to function like a commodity. As Marx's theory of surplus value outlines, labour is a special sort of commodity as only labour has the capacity to generate *new* value by transforming raw materials into commodities for sale in the market place. However, the price paid to the worker for this labour is never equal to the *surplus value* it generates for the owners of capital. As Marx expresses it:

> … capital … pumps a certain quantity of surplus labour out of the direct producer, the worker, surplus labour for which no equivalent is returned and which always remain essentially forced labour, no matter how much it may seem to be the result of a freely concluded contract. This surplus labour is represented by a surplus value, and this surplus value is embodied in a surplus product. Surplus labour generally, in the sense of a quantity of labour beyond that required to satisfy existing needs there must always be. But in the capitalist system … it has an antagonistic form and is complemented by the complete idleness of a section of society.
>
> (Marx in Bottomore and Rubel, 1956, p.156)

It is important to note here that labour is 'forced' regardless of how fair and free the contract of employment may appear to the worker. The reason for this apparent contradiction lies in Marx's conception of labour as definitive of a human 'species being'. For Marx, the key distinction of the human species is our capacity to produce creatively beyond the means of our immediate subsistence. Where other animal species 'produce' only to meet immediate physical needs, 'man' [*sic*] produces material objects in excess of those needs. The development of human consciousness is intrinsically linked to this process of creative production. In this respect, labour, for Marx, is the *constitutive activity* of man – it is through labour that 'man really proves himself to be a species being' (Marx in Gaukroger, 1986, p.303). Labour, then, is fundamental to the full realization of human potential. The problem that arises under capitalism is that this realization is prevented through what Marx understood as the **alienation** of the labour process.

alienation

Alienation is really the key to Marx's account of work under capitalism but it is a difficult concept and one that he used in a variety of different ways. Two main aspects of alienation are of particular significance: alienation from the product and alienation from the act of production itself. The first form of alienation emanates from the nature of human production:

> The object which labour produces – labour's product – confronts it as *something alien*, as a power independent of the producer. The product of labour is labour which has been embodied in an object, which has become material: it is the objectification of labour.
>
> (Marx in Gaukroger, 1986, p.303)

This objectification of the product occurs in all human production but it is only under capitalism that it becomes alienation. This is because the owners of the means of production – the bourgeoisie – are in a position to appropriate products created by others and offer them for sale on the market as commodities. It is the surplus value generated by this process and retained by the bourgeoisie that enables them to be 'idle' at the expense of the workers. This is a central factor in Marx's characterization of the labour process as essentially exploitative.

The second form of alienation, from the process of production, occurs because of the lack of satisfaction or meaning to be derived from work under capitalism. Work, in these economic conditions, is external to the worker and does not allow him to realize his true nature or 'species being':

> He does not fulfil himself in his work but denies himself, has a feeling of misery, not of well-being, does not develop freely a physical and mental energy, but is physically exhausted and mentally debased. … His work is not voluntary but imposed, *forced labour*. It is not the satisfaction of a need, but only a means for satisfying other needs. Its alien character is clearly shown by the fact that as soon as there is no physical or other compulsion it is avoided like the plague. Finally, the alienated character of work for the worker appears in the fact that it is not his work but work for someone else …
>
> (Marx in Bottomore and Rubel, 1956, pp.169–70)

It is because these facets of alienation are inherent to the capitalist process of production that labour is essentially forced irrespective of individuals' subjective experiences of it. Individual workers are caught up in an antagonistic and conflictual relation with their employers even where their immediate experience is of a consenting and free agreement. For Marx, 'the capitalist is merely capital personified' as the capitalist process transcends the experience of individuals (Marx in Bottomore and Rubel, 1956, p.156). The objective condition of alienation here takes precedence over the subjective experience of individual workers because their very position in the capitalist system of production prevents them from perceiving their own situations clearly (du Gay, 1996).

Marx's views about alienation and the inherently conflictual nature of work proved enormously influential throughout twentieth-century sociology. One of the most significant attempts to apply his formulation can be found in Braverman's *Labour and Monopoly Capital* (1974). Braverman aimed to establish: first, that capital was bound to extract surplus value from labour by bringing it under its own control; second, that the growth in the significance of management as a category emanated from this need for control; and, finally, that the systematic subdivision of labour was particular to the capitalist mode of production (Thompson, 1984). In linking these three factors, Braverman was able to construct a logical account of some of the main developments in the organization of work in the twentieth century.

For Braverman, the development of management and the increasing division of labour were key dynamics in the progress of monopoly capitalism. His account lighted, in particular, on the practices of **scientific management** associated with one of the earliest management theorists, Frederick Taylor. Taylor believed that management was largely ignorant of the details of the production process and that this ignorance left it vulnerable to employees' attempts to restrict output due to their fears of underpayment. The solution to this advocated by Taylor was to extend the division of labour so that each task was broken down into its smallest units and measured. Workers could then be scientifically matched to tasks to maximize productivity and management could 'control each step of the labour process and its execution' (Braverman, 1974, p.119). Braverman saw the result of these new managerial techniques as the systematic de-skilling and dehumanizing of labour, grounded in the separation of the conceptual from the practical dimensions of work.

scientific management

Braverman's work has met with a variety of different criticisms. He has been accused of overestimating the influence of scientific management, and of understating the difficulties of demonstrating overall reductions in skill levels across a range of different and changing jobs. Underlying both these criticisms is Braverman's objectivist view of the labour process (du Gay, 1996). For Braverman, the subjective experiences of workers were of far less significance than the alienating and exploitative structure of the capitalist mode of production.

The Marxist theorist, Burawoy (1979), challenged this approach and attempted to reinstate workers' everyday experiences in his analysis of the labour process. Burawoy argued that workers' consent to be managed was secured by their involvement in the shop-floor 'game' of making the bonus. This 'game-playing' deflected attention from conflicts with management and helped counteract the boredom of the work. The manufacture of 'consent' in this way enabled management to continue to extract an increasing amount of surplus value from labour whilst simultaneously concealing the exploitative nature of the process. Although Burawoy pays greater attention to workers' subjective experiences than did either Marx or Braverman, his approach is still not without its problems. For example, du Gay (1996) argues that Burawoy's theory relies upon a fundamental split between people's identities in and outside of work.

Burawoy's workers seem to construct their workplace identities independently of their pre-existing social attributes, such as 'race', gender, age or disability. This, according to du Gay, stems from the primacy Burawoy attaches to the category of labour. As in Marx, individuals are ultimately to be understood as the bearers of economic categories: workers' identities as labour therefore have primacy over their ethnicity, gender or individual personalities. In this way Burawoy's account of the subjective experience of workers ultimately falls back on the Marxist notion of alienation as an objective process.

> That workers 'play the game' is deemed to have less to do with anything else – such as the maintenance of their identity as particular sorts of male persons … than their desire to compensate for a thwarted human essence.
>
> (du Gay, 1996, p.18)

In conclusion, the view that work under capitalism necessarily involves antagonism and conflict between the two classes is foundational to the Marxist account. Wages, as Baldamus explained, are costs to the employer while effort is cost to the employee and therefore the interests of the two are 'diametrically opposed' (cited in du Gay, 1996, p.52). This essential conflict and antagonism, as should be clear by now, exists regardless of any individual's actual experience of work.

SUMMARY OF SECTION 2.1

1   The economic structure of society is constituted by the sum total of the relations of production.

2   Marx's theory of surplus value regards workers as essentially 'forced' labour.

3   Labour is the constitutive activity of man [sic] but under capitalism the process is characterized by alienation.

4   Alienation from the product and the act of production is an objective process that transcends individual experience.

5   Marxist theorists have continued to emphasize the interests of labour and capital as inherently and objectively opposed.

2.2 Max Weber: market distribution and the bureaucratic rationalization of work

A quite different approach to the nature of economic organization and work in industrialized societies can be found in the writings of Max Weber. Where Marx emphasized the determinative nature of the mode of economic organization, Weber rejected such a 'totalizing' explanation (see **Jordan, 2002**). He stressed instead that all collective human phenomena have to be understood in terms of their individual constituents. For Weber, all social collectivities, including work organizations, should be understood, not as structures in their own right, but as the sum of individual members' thoughts and actions. Accordingly, Weber advocated an 'interpretative method' in which the subjective views and experiences of individuals would provide the key to explaining social action.

A sense of this interpretative focus on individual circumstances can be garnered from his discussion of class. Weber regarded class as deriving not from the mode of production but from an individual's situation in the market derived from access to property, skills and education (see **Savage, 2002**). Class, however, was not the only source of division in society; also of significance were status and command. In certain circumstances, Weber, believed that status and command could be more pressing sources of division and inequality than class. For Weber there was no inevitability to class-based conflict; different historical circumstances had to be considered and explained in their own terms. In this respect Weber rejected the objectivist basis of Marxist theory and specifically the notion 'that the individual may be in error concerning his interests but that the class is infallible about its interests' (Weber, 1948, p.185).

As an alternative to Marx's totalizing, objectivist explanation Weber posited the **'ideal type'** (see **Jordan, 2002**). The 'ideal type' was an explanatory device **ideal type** intended to signal the most important characteristics or traits of a given phenomenon. Ideal types were meant neither as a normative description of what should be, nor as an empirical description of what is, rather they were meant to assist in the measurement and comparison of existing forms. Perhaps the most significant ideal type that Weber identified was the bureaucratic form of organization. Weber saw **bureaucracies** as indelibly associated with the **bureaucracy,** broader process of **rationalization**. Weber used the term rationalization to refer **rationalization** to a shift away from dependence on magical, metaphysical forms of explanation and towards known, formalized and most importantly, calculable rules. This reliance on rules was epitomized in the 'legal-rational' form of the bureaucracy. In the ideal-type bureaucracy, decisions are made through the application of explicit rules and procedures, and responsibilities are allocated clearly throughout the organizational hierarchy. Bureaucracy, for Weber, was the key mechanism for the control of workers and managers as both were subject to clear and mutually agreed sets of rules and procedures.

The account of working life implied by the model of bureaucracy is in sharp contrast to that offered by Marx. As we have seen, Marx viewed the working relation as essentially forced. In contrast, in the bureaucracy, both workers and management share a commitment to the legitimacy of organizational rule. Bureaucracies are characterized by a number of elements including:

> … an abstract, legal code of conduct; individual spheres of competence structured within a hierarchy of offices; the non-ownership of offices; selection and promotion through qualifications and proven ability; fixed salaries, and a pension and security of tenure for all office holders.
>
> (Grint, 1991, p.109)

Weber regarded the bureaucracy as a structure that met the requirement for a **'legal-rational'** form of administration rather than a more universal standard **legal-rational** of efficiency. Nevertheless, Weber's model has had a profound influence on **authority** thinking about management and the organization of work. The formal organizational style of the bureaucracy became the standard on which many firms modelled themselves and, as we shall see in section 3, it continues to be of major significance despite challenges from more humanistic styles of management. Yet, in spite of this dominance, the bureaucracy has been subjected to enduring criticism based on its red tape, inefficiency and the dehumanizing effects of relying on rules and procedures (cf. du Gay, 2000). A number of empirical studies have highlighted that the existence of rules does not determine the manner of their execution and have questioned exactly whose needs are met by the principle of rationality (see Grint, 1991).

While Weber emphasized the legal-rational basis of authority in bureaucratic work organizations, like Marx, he was also aware of the importance of economic need if industrial control was to work efficiently. The distinction was that, for Weber, economic need did not have an objective or universal primacy over other possible sources of motivation at work such as prestige or power. In particular Weber regarded the experience of work as being influenced by the meanings and interpretations that individual workers brought to it. More recent neo-Weberian sociology has sought to explore how workers have negotiated their market situations and the significance of economic factors to their motivation.

One of the most important of these studies is *The Affluent Worker* project (Goldthorpe *et al.*, 1968, 1969). This, partly as a counterbalance to the objectivism of contemporary Marxist analyses, focused directly on the subjective experiences of Luton factory workers, and aimed to explore the idea that the British working classes in the post-Second World War period were becoming increasingly middle-class or ***embourgeoised***. According to Goldthorpe *et al.*, the Luton workers did not have a conflictual 'them' and 'us' attitude to work but neither did they identify with the firm. They drew little satisfaction from their work and rarely had any involvement with collective or community institutions; instead most of their leisure activities took place within the nuclear family. The Luton workers were thus described as 'privatized workers' for whom 'class divisions are seen mainly in terms of differences in income and material possessions' and who display an 'instrumental orientation' to work (Lockwood in du Gay, 1996, p.20).

embourgeoise-
ment

This notion of 'orientations to work' referred to the meanings workers attached to their work and the ways in which this influenced how they felt and acted in the workplace. The researchers rejected the embourgeoisement thesis arguing that the 'typically privatized, family centred and consumption-based lifestyle of the affluent worker conditioned worker's orientations rather than an aspirant desire to become part of the middle class' (du Gay, 1996, p.22). In this respect the Luton workers' attitudes to work seemed primarily driven by the desire to consume rather than to be class mobile, as in the embourgeoisement thesis, or class-conscious, as in the Marxist account. This lack of identification with work coupled with the preoccupation with consumption, Goldthorpe *et al.* acknowledged, could be interpreted as evidence of the alienating nature of work under capitalism. Perhaps workers used the 'cheap fun' of consumption to compensate for the lack of true satisfaction in work. Yet while the researchers conceded that the Marxist account of alienation seemed to provide a fair description of the Luton workers, they rejected it entirely as an explanation. The orientations of the workers, they argued, did not originate from the workplace but existed prior to their involvement with it:

> Rather than an overriding concern with consumption standards reflecting alienation in work, it could be claimed that precisely such a concern constituted the motivation for these men to take, and to retain, work of a particularly unrewarding and stressful kind which offered high pay in compensation for its inherent deprivations.

(Goldthorpe *et al.* in du Gay, 1996, p.24)

Despite the apparently increased attention to worker subjectivity represented by the notion of 'orientations to work', the Goldthorpe *et al.* study has met with criticism because of the way in which these orientations are regarded as the outcome of social structures. Instrumental orientations, for instance, are regarded as an outcome of the affluent worker's place within the broader work community rather than an outcome of individual biography or personality (du Gay, 1996). Workers' identities therefore appear stable and unchanging and the role of workers' ongoing thoughts, feelings and experiences in renegotiating their responses to work is left unaccounted for.

ACTIVITY 2

Can you think of any instances when your attitude to work altered significantly as a result of some event or change in your circumstances?

The examples that came to my mind included pregnancy, stress-related illness, a partner's promotion or redundancy or even the outcome of studying an Open University course. In different ways, these factors all might lead to a reappraisal of 'orientations' towards, and meanings associated with, work. In neglecting the role of such factors *The Affluent Worker* researchers never quite delivered on the project of inserting the subjective experiences of workers into a sociological account of work and the economy. In the final part of this section some possible reasons why this is the case will be reviewed.

SUMMARY OF SECTION 2.2

1 Weber regards all forms of social and economic organization as the sum of individual members' thoughts and actions.

2 The ideal type is posited as a tool to aid the interpretation of social phenomena.

3 The ideal-type bureaucracy embodies the shift towards legal-rational forms of organization.

4 Relations between workers and management in the bureaucracy are based on mutual consent.

5 Economic factors are not the only source of motivation at work; also significant are individuals' meanings and attitudes.

6 Neo-Weberian approaches to work have not been entirely successful in their attempt to reinstate the subjective meanings and experience of workers into a sociological analysis of work.

2.3 Discussion: the economy as a 'thing' in itself

By this point you may be beginning to ask questions about the sort of economy and the sorts of work with which these theorists were concerned. Marx made it explicit that, for him, the economic was about 'the relations of production' while for Weber it was about the negotiation of market situations. In both cases the economic seems to revolve around production and work. Further, both Marx and Weber seem to have had particular sorts of work in mind. Marx was interested primarily in what he described as 'productive labour': this was the sort of labour from which surplus value could be extracted and he generally equated it with manufacturing wage labour. The form of work Marx theorized most explicitly was paid, and based in the manufacturing industry. Similarly, the Weberian account is also underscored by a very specific conception of work. The formulation of market situation reveals Weber's concern with the way in which the rewards associated with different occupations were negotiated on the market. His adoption of the bureaucracy as the ideal type might also seem to privilege work carried out in such organizations over more arbitrary and less formalized types of work.

You might reasonably object that these formulations neglect a number of different forms of work. For Marx, work in management, administration or the caring professions would be regarded as unproductive. While for both Marx and Weber unpaid work in the voluntary sector or in the home would have no economic status. The crucial point to note here is that both theoretical traditions share a rather narrow conception of the 'economic' as the realm of paid production. In classical sociology the economy appears as an object to be studied, as a stable, self-evident 'thing'. This involves an understanding of the economy as something which really, objectively exists in the world. It could be argued that it is this investment in an objectivist account of the economy that has hampered sociological attempts to develop greater sensitivity to the subjective experiences of workers.

ACTIVITY 3

Cast your mind back to the Marks & Spencer case study at the start of the chapter. How would these protests be explained from a Marxist and from a Weberian perspective? Are there any aspects of these protests that would be difficult to explain in these terms?

You could argue that a Marxist account would regard the protest as the inevitable outcome of the inherently opposed interests of workers and capitalists. From a Weberian perspective the closure programme might be interpreted as the result of an insufficiently rationalized production process, while workers' responses to it could be seen as a reaction to the detrimental effects of the job losses on their market situations and associated life-chances. Both of these accounts offer quite reasonable explanations of some aspects of the protest. There are, however, two aspects that neither Marxist nor Weberian theory would have much to say about. First, as we have seen, both these theoretical perspectives have traditionally been concerned with particular sorts of work, predominantly that carried out by male, industrial full-time workers (Pateman, 1989). The typically female, part-time workforce characteristic of many branches of the retail sector did not figure, in any substantive way, in the development of these theoretical perspectives. Second, consider the following newspaper report of the initial protest in Paris:

> Paris has seen many odd demonstrations, but the protest outside Marks & Spencer's flagship store on the Boulevard Haussman yesterday was one of the strangest and most moving. Activists from the revolutionary left, carrying battle-worn red flags, stood shoulder to shoulder with old ladies who like 'classic' British clothes and shop employees wearing M&S shopping bags as T-shirts or hats. All were united, briefly, in demanding the suspension of the company's decision to close all 18 French stores and the 20 others on the continent by the end of the year.
>
> (Lichfield and Shepard, *The Independent*, 7 April 2001)

It is clear from this that the protest was not only about the job losses or the manner of their execution. The protest was also about the loss of the stores themselves. The media reported 'panic buying' of M&S favourites. These responses to the loss of a source of particular consumer goods would fall outside of the remit of much economic sociology due to its focus on production. However, you may well question whether these consumption processes are not in themselves economic transactions and therefore relevant. Moreover, the split between producer and consumer in this instance is far from clear or stable. One of the 'perks' that retail organizations, including Marks & Spencer, routinely offer their workforce is discounts on their own produce and the chance to buy perishable goods at substantial reductions at the end of the day's trading. Might some of the workers be concerned about the loss of this as well as of direct earnings? This raises the question of the workers' subjective experiences of their work: to what extent might the protest be motivated by people's feelings about the loss of this *particular* store or these *particular* jobs? As we have seen, these subjective experiences of work have been largely left out of sociological accounts of the economy.

The question of how work and the economic are defined will be considered more closely in section 4, but for the moment you might like to bear in mind the tension between the conceptualization of the economy as an objective 'thing', and its interrelation with the human activities of work and production. Before moving on to the next section it is worth noting that this 'objectification' of the economy was certainly not something that either Marx or Weber intended. Indeed at the time of writing both Marx and Weber explicitly positioned themselves against conventional, narrow definitions of the economy. What is interesting is that this objectification arguably occurs *in spite* of their efforts, through focusing on some economic processes and not others.

In the next section attention will shift to another perspective on the relation between sociology and economic life, that concerning how the economic domain of commerce has reacted to some of the insights derived from sociology.

3 Commercial uses of sociological knowledge

The aim in this section is to review the relationship between sociology and economic life from the opposite direction. Here the focus will be on how sociological forms of knowledge have been put to use in the economy. There have been a number of different attempts to apply sociology and the social sciences to restructure and reform the workplace to the mutual advantage of worker satisfaction and company profitability. In many of these attempts the objective has been to develop new techniques and processes to transform workers' subjective experience of the workplace and these approaches are of primary concern in this section.

There is some overlap between sociology that seeks to study the operation of the economy and sociology that has been applied in order to improve its operation. As the discussion in section 2 highlighted, the model of bureaucracy had a major impact on the ways in which economic organizations were structured throughout the twentieth century. Weber's work on bureaucracy was multi-faceted and sought to provide an ideal-type analysis and a critique of some of its effects. It was not his aim to provide a blueprint description upon which large organizations could model themselves but, nevertheless, his work has been widely appropriated in this way. The emphasis on the establishment of a clear and formalized hierarchy in which the principles of order, authority and responsibility can be instilled has had a huge impact upon management theory. Around the same time that Weber was writing, Frederick Taylor's proposals were also coming to the fore. As described in section 2.1, Taylor advocated the establishment of a 'science' of management based on the minute analysis and measurement of different work tasks. Although quite distinct in approach and focus – Weber concentrated on delineating the responsibilities of the manager while Taylor addressed the tasks of the worker – both shared an enthusiasm for a formalized approach to economic organization. This 'formalization' involved a dehumanization of work. As Weber commented, organizations 'develop more perfectly the more bureaucracy is dehumanized' (1948, p.215). Moreover Weber, although critical of some of its effects, believed Taylor's methods would contribute to the 'rational conditioning … of work performances' (1948, p.261).

Unsurprisingly both these approaches have met with criticism over the years. The idea that dehumanizing and de-skilling work processes would produce widespread rationalization has been far from universally accepted and many have balked at the human costs in terms of monotony, boredom and the suppression of creativity at work. In addition, both approaches have been regarded as symptomatic of the need of management, in capitalist modes of economic organization, to exert increasing control over the workplace. Rose (1999), however, has argued that these managerial approaches should not be understood simply as a function of the inexorable drive of capitalism, but as part of a broader series of programmes in which new techniques and forms of knowledge were applied in an attempt to improve national efficiency. Taylorism, Rose argues, shared with other programmes:

> ... a belief in the improvement of individuals through the application of expertise. ... [I]t did this by constructing norms and standards that accorded a visibility to previously obscure and unimportant aspects of the activities of persons, and by calibrating and governing these minutiae of existence in accordance with these norms ...
>
> (Rose, 1999, p.59)

Despite its associations with a dehumanized and mechanized approach to work, Taylorism, conversely, also involved a greater attention to individual differences than hitherto. Taylor believed that individuals could be scientifically matched in terms of their weight, strength and other characteristics to the jobs that best suited them; it was only through such matching that optimal efficiency could be achieved. This attention to the management of the organization and individuals in the interests of a more efficient system of production is not restricted to Taylorism and bureaucracy but can be found in many subsequent attempts to apply social scientific forms of knowledge to the practice of management.

Taylor's concerns with 'fitting the job to the man and the man to the job', for instance, also preoccupied the occupational psychologist Charles Myers. Where Taylor had been concerned primarily with the physical specifications of work and the worker, Myers was concerned with the psychological. Different sorts of work, he believed, exacted different psychological demands and people should be matched to work in terms of their 'particular psychological make-up and idiosyncrasies' (Rose, 1999, p.68). Myers rejected Taylor's mechanistic approach to workers and he argued that industry had to take into consideration the 'complex subjective life' of workers. This was to be achieved by managing the 'mental atmosphere of the work' through management style and the satisfaction of worker interests (*ibid.*, p.69).

The emphasis on 'mental hygiene' as the key to industrial efficiency was complemented by the development in the US around the same time of what became known as the **Human Relations** school of management. Human Relations is associated with the work of Elton Mayo. Mayo's initial concern had been with the effects of work-breaks, light and environmental conditions on productivity. He put these factors to the test in a now famous series of investigations at the Hawthorne Electric Works in the 1920s. During the course of this research, the researchers uncovered increases in productivity that bore no obvious relation to variations in the environmental conditions (Grint, 1991). The explanation advanced by the researchers for this unanticipated outcome was that it derived from improvements in the overall human relations of the enterprise. Mayo argued that the research team's presence in the works had produced a greater sense of group identity and co-operation amongst the workforce. For Mayo, this demonstrated the material significance to the firm's long-term efficiency of a workforce with a commitment to the organization as a collective enterprise:

Human Relations

> Productivity, efficiency and contentment were now to be understood in terms of the attitudes of the workers to their work, their feelings of control over their pace of work and environment, their sense of cohesion within their small working group, their beliefs about the concern and understanding that the bosses had for their individual worth and personal problems.
>
> (Rose, 1999, p.71)

The Hawthorne investigations involved some 20,000 'non-directed interviews'. In the course of these interviews the researchers became increasingly conscious of the subjective, emotional significance to the worker of particular events in the workplace. From these data the researchers developed a view of the factory as a social organization in which conflict arose not as a result of the objectively alienating nature of the work, as in the Marxist account, nor as an outcome of individual maladjustment, as in Myers' mental hygiene approach. Rather, conflict here was construed as a result of the different values of different groups in the organization. Management's concern with cost and efficiency, for example, might frequently be at odds with workers' attachment to established ways of doing things (Rose, 1999). The Human Relations approach advocated that study of the values and practices of different groups would promote organizational harmony and therefore efficiency:

> The task of management was to manage the enterprise and change within it in light of a knowledge of the values and sentiments of the workforce, and to act upon these so as to make them operate for rather than against the interests of the firm.

(Rose, 1999, p.72)

Chicago School

This emphasis on the social and psychological dynamics of the workplace continued to structure thinking about organizational efficiency in the post-Second World War period. The ideas rehearsed in the mental hygiene movement and in Human Relations were combined with insights from the developing disciplines of social psychology and **Chicago School** sociology to reinforce the emphasis on the primacy of social relationships and the informal work group (Rose, 1999). Non-profit organizations such as the Tavistock Institute for Human Relations and Kurt Lewin's Research Centre for Group Dynamics were formed and acted as a conduit between academic research and commercial practice. Nevertheless, by the 1950s, there was growing dissatisfaction in a number of quarters with this approach to organization and management. Critics from a managerialist perspective complained that attention to the social relations of the workplace had failed to produce the anticipated increases in productivity, while critics adopting the perspective of the workforce complained that 'tinkering' with human relations failed to address the real, social and economic conflicts of interest that existed between workers and management. Yet, as Rose (1999) has argued, to dismiss the Human Relations approach as naïve in its preoccupation with the emotional over the material life of the enterprise overlooks the extent to which it represented a new way of structuring the meaning and reality of work. Moreover, it would be a mistake to regard the Human Relations approach as obsolete since its influence on the thinking and practice of management can still be traced.

READING 4.1

Read Box 4.2 and also Reading 4.1 by Yvonne Roberts at the end of this chapter. As you read, try to answer the following questions:

1   Of the approaches to management you have encountered in this chapter, which one do you feel is closest to the style adopted by Happy Computers?

2   What particular elements of their approach influenced your choice?

BOX 4.2: HAPPY COMPUTERS CASE STUDY

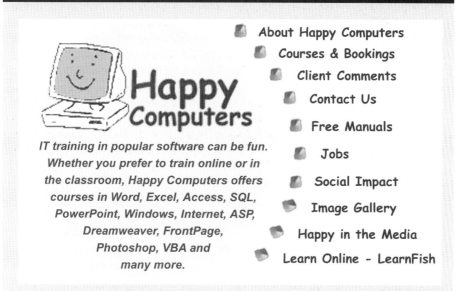

IT training in popular software can be fun. Whether you prefer to train online or in the classroom, Happy Computers offers courses in Word, Excel, Access, SQL, PowerPoint, Windows, Internet, ASP, Dreamweaver, FrontPage, Photoshop, VBA and many more.

- About Happy Computers
- Courses & Bookings
- Client Comments
- Contact Us
- Free Manuals
- Jobs
- Social Impact
- Image Gallery
- Happy in the Media
- Learn Online - LearnFish

Our Mission Statement

Our business is that of empowering people to reach their full potential in their work. Happy Computers' mission is to provide the highest quality training in the UK, creating standards which others follow.

To this end we will actively develop new training approaches, and other ways to help people learn, to enable all students to overcome easily any obstacles and be able to learn quickly and enjoyably.

Empower our People

People are our greatest asset at Happy Computers. We have a responsibility for their training and for their personal growth while they are working with us. We will always look for ways to enable people to push back their personal limits and to reach their full potential.

If we treat our people excellently then we will receive excellent work in return.

Excellence in Everything We Do

We must strive to ensure that everything we do, we do excellently. We always look to provide the best possible service. This means that, however satisfied our customers, we must never be complacent. We must always ask how things could be better.

If we cannot provide a truly excellent service, then Happy Computers should not be providing that service at all.

The Customer

The customer is the whole reason for our existence and their needs must come before our convenience. We must listen carefully to all our customers and strive to find out (and to find new ways to find out) what they need and how we can help them.

If we cannot serve our customers better than our competitors (or at the same level for a lower price) then we should not be providing that particular service.

Innovation – Go Make Mistakes!

We must look for innovation in everything we do at Happy Computers – and particularly in the training process. Most people have lost much of their inherent capacity and eagerness to learn. A core element of Happy Computers' mission is to find new ways to enable people to regain that capacity and that eagerness.

Experimenting and innovation are crucial in this process. We must try out new ways of doing things and celebrate the mistakes we make along the way.

Have Fun!

We are in the business of empowering people and helping them to learn new skills. That is a challenging, but potentially very enjoyable experience. We must take delight in the process, including the obstacles and blockages which appear to get in the way.

Relax and have fun.

Source: http://www.happy.co.uk (accessed March 2001)

It struck me that Happy Computers' emphasis on organizational flexibility, teamwork and developing a contented workforce is very reminiscent of the Human Relations approach. If you looked closely, however, you may also have detected some other elements. The firm is clearly concerned with profitability and sees the management of 'work-life issues' as a way of achieving profitability. There is also a concern with success and an implication that financial reward is associated with performance. 'Working here isn't an easy ride, you have to be seen to succeed' and 'Salaries are an open book' suggest a slightly different emphasis to that of the Human Relations school. As you read the remainder of the section, consider whether 'Organizational Psycho-technology' and other, more recent management approaches may also have influenced the firm.

By the late 1950s the emphasis began to shift away from the human relations of the enterprise, and earlier concerns with the rationality of the production process began to resurface. Human relations, according to this new trend in management thought, were secondary to the concerns of earlier theorists, like Weber and Taylor, with establishing a clear relation between pay and production and the explicit lines of authority and responsibility within the organization. This did not signal the end of the influence of socio-psychology on management thought but it did signal a change in approach. It was in this context that the 'organizational psycho-technology' style developed. As Douglas McGregor, one of the key theorists associated with this approach, commented:

> It has become clear that many of the initial, strategic interpretations accompanying the 'human relations approach' were … naïve … We have now discovered that there is no answer in the simple removal of control – that abdication is not a workable alternative to authoritarianism.
>
> (McGregor in Pugh, 1984, p.325)

The solution advocated by theorists like McGregor involved a reassertion of the role of the formal structure of the enterprise and of financial incentive in producing motivation amongst the workforce. The mainstay of their approach, however, lay in a reformulation of the underlying nature of work. Rather than being characterized as something that workers had to be induced to do through some combination of coercion, financial or social reward, the psycho-technologists argued that, under the right conditions, work would be enjoyed and sought out for its own rewards. Once individuals' immediate physical and security needs had been met, they would seek satisfaction, responsibility and self-expression in the workplace. The challenge for management was to design work in such a way that individuals could meet these needs and reach their full potential. This was not the way in which managers, according to McGregor, were accustomed to working. Most managers, he argued, operated what he termed a 'Theory X' approach in which workers were understood as inherently lazy, irresponsible and in need of coercion and direction at work (Pugh, 1984). As an alternative he advocated the adoption of a 'Theory Y' approach in which work was regarded as a natural human activity:

> The average human does not inherently dislike work. … External control and the threat of punishment are not the only means for bringing about effort towards organizational objectives. Man [*sic*] will exercise self-direction and self-control in the service of objectives to which he is committed … the satisfaction of ego and self-actualization needs, can be direct products of effort towards organisational objectives.
>
> (McGregor, in Pugh, 1984, p.326)

Another theorist, Frederick Herzberg, argued along similar lines that individuals had to achieve satisfaction in their work. Herzberg made a distinction between two factors necessary to achieve satisfaction in work – 'hygiene' and 'motivators' (Grint, 1991). 'Hygiene' concerned physical factors such as salary, security and working conditions, whereas 'motivators' concerned the type of work and the feelings of satisfaction, achievement and recognition that could be derived from it. While hygiene factors were essential for satisfaction to occur, true motivation could only be achieved if the design of the work itself permitted it. These concerns also surfaced in the work of Chris Argyris. Argyris shared the view that work should meet individuals' psychological needs for satisfaction and recognition, but he argued that these needs were likely to be thwarted by formal bureaucratic structures based on clear demarcations of authority and responsibility. Such structures, Argyris argued, involved a child-like view of the worker as the subject of discipline and control, and this attitude prevented individuals from achieving their potential as mature, adult workers.

These concerns with the design of work and the issue of job satisfaction have continued to filter through a range of new management initiatives. Organizational Psycho-technology fed into programmes like the Quality of Working Life Movement in the 1970s, and its influence can also be traced through a range of new management theories which began to appear in the 1980s. These more recent trends in management thinking have been collectively labelled 'culture change programmes' and refer to the importance to organizational performance of developing internal work cultures based on 'excellence', 'enterprise' or 'empowerment'. These ideas are the product of a new generation of 'gurus' such as Tom Peters, Robert Waterman and Rosabeth Kanter who have argued that the rapid pace of technological change at the end of the twentieth century requires flexible and innovative organization structures. This new theory of management was based on the idea that organizations had to strive for excellence through fostering flexibility, creativity, initiative, collaboration and informality among its employees:

At root it was based on a different image of the person. People were not that rational, they were self-centred, they liked to think of themselves as winners or losers. While the old paradigm berated people for failure, the new constantly reinforced people for success.

(Rose, 1999, p.115)

ACTIVITY 4

Think back now to Reading 4.1 about Happy Computers. Does the firm's approach seem to be influenced by any other management styles?

It seems to me that Happy Computers' emphasis on the 'celebration' of mistakes as a chance to learn is very reminiscent of the new excellence discourse. Interestingly, the firm's website, (http://www.happy.co.uk/) lists Robert Waterman's *The Frontiers of Excellence* (1994) as 'one of the books that have given us ideas' and offers an immediate link to the Amazon online bookstore to enable browsers to buy the book. This provides a very neat illustration of how the worker is presented in the excellence discourse. The worker here is not simply a producer but is simultaneously a consumer, in search of meaning, personal enrichment, achievement and recognition at work (du Gay, 1996; Rose, 1999). The ethos of Happy Computers reflects this concern with work as something more than production in the narrow sense, and as something that involves the production of the worker as a particular sort of person.

What is crucial to take away from this discussion is that the ideas and theories of sociologists, psychologists and other social scientists about how the economy and its organizations work do not simply stay in academic institutions. They travel outwards and are applied to the conduct and practice of work in what is often characterized as the 'real world'. It could be argued that these schools of thought are simply theories and rhetoric and that they reveal little about how work is actually conducted and managed in real organizations. It is undoubtedly the case that for every Happy Computers that actively aims to apply the ideas of management gurus, there are many other businesses run with no systematic adherence to any management theory. But what is going on here is not simply academic or business rhetoric. These approaches to management involve the construction and use of specific sorts of knowledge, tools and practices. Employee surveys and interviews, organizational charts, time and motion studies, audits, career development appraisals and performance-related pay are all examples of techniques that have, at various times, been in widespread use as part of the application or 'instrumentalization' of specific management approaches. In this way academic knowledge can have material effects on the everyday experience of economic life.

Section 2 argued that there is an underlying tendency in sociological studies to treat the economy as an objective 'thing' in itself; this section has shown that there seems to be a parallel tendency for economic organizations to treat sociology as an objective source of knowledge. What can be gleaned from considering both these perspectives, however, is that the relation between sociology and economic life is not one-way. Sociology both studies and is studied by the economy. In section 5 it will be suggested that combining these perspectives to allow for a two-way exchange between sociology and the economy still does not really capture the nature of the relation. What is going on here is more than simply an exchange of ideas and theories. Rather the relation between sociology and economy seems to produce material effects in both domains. Before trying to explain in more detail what this means section 4 will prepare the ground by looking more closely at the terms 'economy' and 'economic life'.

SUMMARY OF SECTION 3

1 Both Weber's and Taylor's ideas regarding the rationalization of work processes have had a huge influence on organization and management practices.

2 The Human Relations approach advocated greater attention to the social group as a way of engineering a harmonious and efficient enterprise.

3 Organizational Psycho-technology approaches integrated rationalist and Human Relations ideas to produce an emphasis on redesigning jobs to allow satisfaction and creativity to flourish.

4 These concerns have continued to flourish in a new generation of management philosophies aimed at securing organizational culture change.

5 All these different approaches to management have involved the integration of social science knowledges and have had material effects on economic practices.

4 So what is economic life?

> It should be obvious that there is nothing like an economy out there unless and until men construct such an object.
>
> (Dumont, 1977, p.24)

The aim in this section is to develop an understanding of the 'economy', not as an objective 'thing' but as an intellectual concept or 'construct'. This may seem an odd or unlikely argument. Of course, there is such a thing as an 'economy' out there. It is the economy that the Chancellor of the Exchequer presides over; it is the economy that 'booms' or 'slumps'; it is the economy that represents the whole of production, consumption and exchange in a society. The economy, then, involves actual practices and outcomes that really take place. The argument here, nevertheless, is to suggest that we need to look more closely at our commonsense understanding of the economy to develop an awareness of the processes involved in its construction. It is through examining these processes that a sense of the historical bias towards particular sorts of production in the formulation of the 'economy' can be detected. The underlying goal here is to move away from this productionist bias towards an understanding of 'economic life' as encompassing both production and consumption activities.

The economy in classical economics is very closely related to the concept of the **market**. The market is generally defined in economics as a co-ordination device for the exchange of goods. Buyers and sellers are brought together in the market in order to negotiate an exchange. The needs of buyers and sellers are antagonistic, in that the former seeks to buy at the lowest possible price whilst the latter seeks to sell at the highest. Thus the price finally negotiated

market

between both parties represents a compromise. Individual buyers and sellers here are economic creatures, *homo economicus*, who make rational decisions to gain the highest possible degree of satisfaction, or utility, in market transactions. At the macro level, this rational behaviour produces the forces of supply and demand. The market acts as an 'invisible hand' to bring these forces of supply and demand into equilibrium by negotiating a price at which exchange can take place. At a basic level the economy has been understood as the sum total of all markets and transactions.

However, this understanding of the term 'economy' is of relatively recent origin. Buck-Morss (1995) points out that, prior to the eighteenth century, the term economy meant simply domestic accounts and could be applied to both household and national budgets. The 'discovery' of the economy in its contemporary sense, she argues, arose as a result of the increasing centrality of processes of trade and exchange in the everyday life of communities:

> The proposition that the exchange of goods, rather than denoting the edge of community, is capable of functioning as the fundament of collective life necessitated the discovery that within the polity such a thing as an 'economy' exists. This discovery can be traced to a particular historical site: Europe (specifically England and France) during the eighteenth century Enlightenment.
>
> (Buck-Morss, 1995, p.439)

The economy, however, was not 'discovered' as an object with a real existence in the world; rather it was brought into being as a result of specific human processes. Buck-Morss argues that in order for the economy to be 'seen' and understood as an object it had, first, to go through a process of representational mapping. This involved an abstraction whereby specific aspects of the economy are seen as if from the outside. The first techniques used to represent the economy in this way borrowed from those of navigational mapping. Figure 4.1 is an example of an early visual representation of the economy. This chart – by the French economist, François Quesnay – aimed to provide an 'economic picture' of society through tracing the interdependence of the three sectors of the economy – farmers, landowners and artisans – in their exchange of goods and labour (Buck-Morss, 1995). The remarkable thing about this chart, and others like it, is that it marked the beginning of a new form of representation. Unlike the navigational maps that inspired them, these charts did not attempt to provide a *direct* representation or analogy of the physical world. Instead they placed different quantities, abstracted from a range of different contexts, in relation to each other. As a result of being quantified, measured and mapped in this way, these different quantities were given a new status as economic phenomena.

From their first appearance, these techniques for measuring and representing the newly discovered economy have been particularly concerned with the category of production. Where medieval 'economics' had primarily referred to the circulation of money, the tendency since the eighteenth century has been to refer to production as the key economic category. Quesnay's theory was probably the first to consider the economy in this way. In his account, the most important form of labour in the economy was agricultural because only agricultural labour could be seen to *generate* rather than simply *circulate* wealth. For Quesnay, this was because the use of the powers of nature enabled agriculture to produce an output greater than its inputs. The resulting surplus qualified agriculture as the only truly productive form of labour.

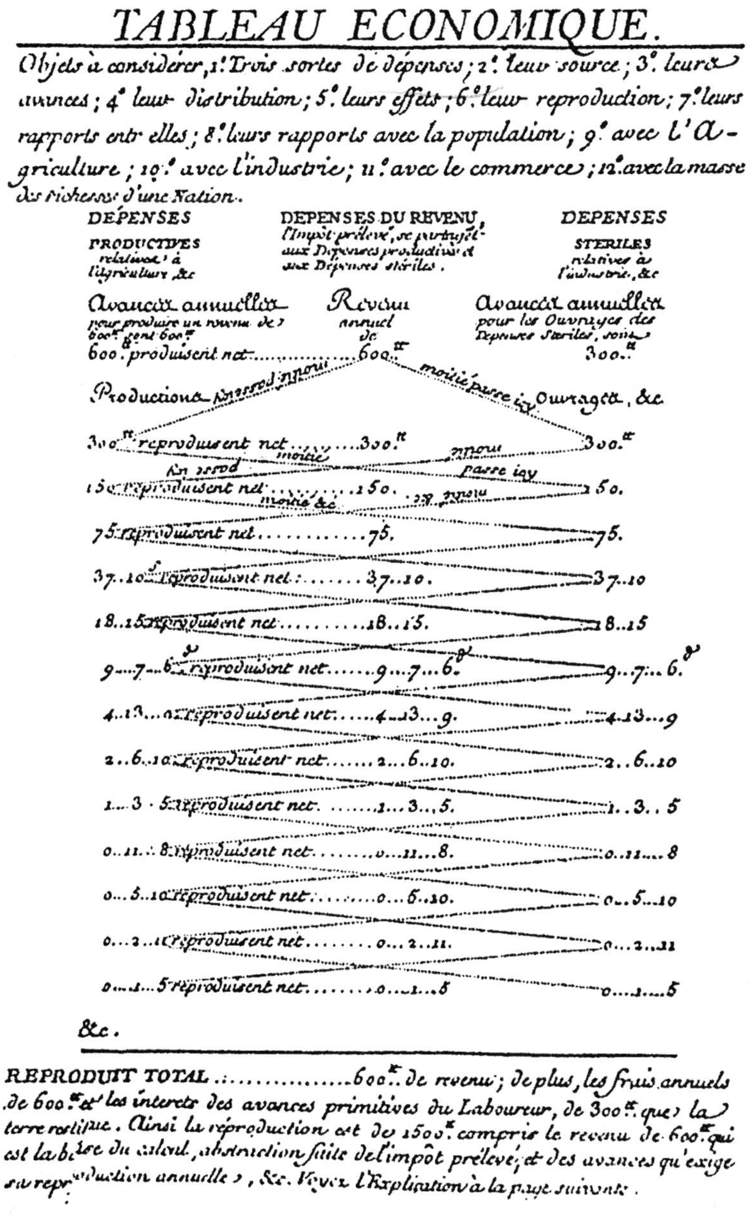

TABLEAU ECONOMIQUE.

Objets à considérer, 1.º Trois sortes de dépenses; 2.º leur source; 3.º leurs avances; 4.º leur distribution; 5.º leurs effets; 6.º leur reproduction; 7.º leurs rapports entr' elles; 8.º leurs rapports avec la population; 9.º avec l'Agriculture; 10.º avec l'industrie; 11.º avec le commerce; 12.º avec la masse des richesses d'une Nation.

DEPENSES PRODUCTIVES	DEPENSES DU REVENU	DEPENSES STERILES

Figure 4.1 'Tableau Economique', from François Quesnay, The Economical Table, 1766

This notion of 'productive labour' has continued to be a key economic and sociological concept. By the mid-nineteenth century Marx credited Quesnay with the discovery that surplus value originated in the sphere of production. Marx differed from Quesnay, however, in that, for him, the key form of productive labour – labour from which surplus value could be extracted – was manufacturing wage labour. This is a view that has been shared by subsequent generations of economists who have continued to argue that, as the only productive form of labour, manufacturing labour is the key to economic growth.

This position is not universal, though. Economists working in different theoretical traditions have taken a variety of positions on the question of productive labour. Adam Smith, the founder of modern neo-classical economics, understood productive labour as that which is employed in the service of capital. In his assessment, if the value generated when a product is offered for sale exceeds the value of the inputs to the production process then the labour employed can be understood as productive. Productive labour, in this view, is labour that produces commodities for sale. This view has had a profound influence on UK economic policy in the last two decades. The notion that productive labour yields a marketed output lies at the heart of many major policy initiatives such as privatization and deregulation. According to this variant of economic theory, it is not the type of labour, whether agricultural or manufacturing, that defines its productivity but the eventual use to which it is put.

ACTIVITY 5

Can you think of any sorts of labour that would not be considered as productive by any of these definitions?

There are many possible examples. Many forms of education, government and healthcare occupations produce no physical product and are not offered for sale on the open market. One of the largest categories of labour that would be excluded by these definitions is that performed in the home. The care of children, elderly and disabled people, the activities of food preparation, cleaning and general household maintenance when carried out in the home would all be classed as unproductive. Yet the same sorts of activity when carried out in restaurants or private nurseries or nursing-homes might well qualify. Women undertake the bulk of labour in the home and remain the largest category in many public sphere occupations like teaching and nursing (see **Hemmings et al., 2002**). It is no accident that economics has revolved around the concept of *homo economicus* or 'economic man'. The category of economic man refers to 'man' as an individual who makes free, rational choices to maximize his satisfaction. But this category, feminist economists have argued, is an abstraction that ignores the role of 'women's work':

> Yet humans do not simply spring out of the earth. Humans are born of women, nurtured and cared for as dependent children, socialized into family and community groups, and are dependent on nourishment and shelter to sustain their lives. These aspects of human life, whose neglect [in economics] is often justified by the argument that they are unimportant or intellectually uninteresting or merely 'natural' are, not just coincidentally, the areas of life thought of as 'women's work'.
>
> (Nelson, 1996, p.31)

'Women's work' has thus traditionally been regarded as irrelevant to, or outside of, the remit of, the disciplines of economics and economic sociology. This may seem in some ways reasonable or natural: economics is the study of the economy and should, therefore, only include activities that contribute to the economy. The problem is that although the association of economy with the realm of paid production is so well-established that it seems inevitable, the logic for restricting the economic in this way is far from clear. As feminists have argued, the domain of public paid production depends entirely on labour in the unpaid, private domain to sustain and reproduce it. Moreover women's work is not the only category of activity that is frequently neglected in studies of the economy. Also omitted is the entire field of economically significant consumption activities. It is probably no coincidence that consumption has itself traditionally been considered a female domain.

READING 4.2

Now turn to Reading 4.2, 'Taking Marx to Sainsbury's' by Daniel Miller. While you are reading it, bear the following question in mind:

- What does Miller think Marx would learn from considering consumption?

According to Miller (1995) there are at least three lessons that Marx could have learnt from considering consumption more closely. First, Miller sees Marx's theory in *Das Kapital* as an abstract and universal, economistic vision. One of the primary benefits Miller argues Marx could have gained from going shopping with his wife would have been a reminder of how complex and diverse human behaviour is. This, Miller argues, might have saved Marx from the 'law-like model building' of 'pseudo-scientific economics' and allowed him to produce a theory more sensitive to the subjective experiences of individuals. Second, the sheer size, range and variety of products available at a contemporary Sainsbury's, Miller suggests, might have made Marx replace manufacturing with retail as the 'cutting-edge of capitalism'. Finally, if Marx had taken a closer, more anthropological look at consumption activities, he might have seen that these activities were not simply determined by capitalism. Shoppers, in Miller's view, are not passive dupes, soullessly buying whatever is on the shelves. Rather they shop creatively, selecting and appropriating goods as a sort of negation of the anonymous forces of commodity capitalism.

Miller's argument overall is that consumption should be understood not as a passive compensation for the alienating effects of work under capitalism but as an active, creative process. In contrast to the emphasis in much sociological theory, here consumption is neither secondary to, nor dictated by, capitalism but is of primary economic significance. The argument that consumption should be understood as an economic category has gained ground in recent years. While the development of cultural studies increased academic attention to the *cultural* significance of consumption activities, until recently little attention has been paid within sociology to their *economic* significance.

This productionist orientation in the sociology of economic life is something of a paradox because production would make little sense as an economic activity without consumption as its counterpart. Rose (1999), for instance, points out that the main economic image that people are routinely confronted with in the media addresses their role not as producers but as consumers. We are urged to shape our lives and make them meaningful through making consumption choices from the selections of products and services offered to us in advertising, retailing and the media. As sociologists such as Goldthorpe *et al.* (1969) have conceded, production activities occupy a secondary position to consumption as a life interest. As described in section 2, sociologists have offered different explanations for this. For some Marxists, consumption acts as a cheap compensation for alienation at work, while for neo-Weberians such as Goldthorpe *et al.* (1969) it is to be understood as the motivation for work itself. Whichever view is preferred, the closeness of the interrelation between production and consumption is hard to avoid. As Marx himself acknowledged:

> Each is directly its own counterpart. … Production furthers consumption by creating material for the latter which otherwise would lack its object. But consumption in its turn furthers production, by providing for the products the individual for whom they are products. The product receives its last finishing touches in consumption. A railroad on which no one rides, which is consequently not used up, not consumed, is only a potential railroad.
>
> (Marx, 1980/1857–8, p.24)

But it is not just that production and consumption are mutually interdependent in this way. It is also that the activities of consumption and production engaged in by individuals share considerable common ground. The contemporary emphasis on lifestyle choices, personal development and self-fulfilment has equal resonance in both consumption and production activities. Consumption and production, in this sense, involve very closely related types of activity:

> The 'employee', just as much as the 'sovereign consumer', is represented as an individual in search of meaning and fulfilment, one looking to 'add value' in every sphere of existence. Paid work and consumption are just different playing grounds for the same activity; that is, different terrains upon which the enterprising self seeks to master, better and fulfil itself.
>
> (du Gay, 1996, p.65)

ACTIVITY 6

Think back to the Happy Computers example once more. Are there any ways in which consumption and production activities seem linked in this company?

Happy Computers provides some good illustrations of the interconnections between production and consumption. The firm offers IT skills training in a direct attempt to 'add value' and enhance the career prospects of those looking for work. It also offers its workers and its customers the chance to, quite literally, 'buy into' its managerial ethos through purchasing books that have influenced the company. In addition the firm maintains a commitment to the 'personal growth' of both employees and customers. In many crucial respects, Happy Computers offers both workers and customers a similar set of activities and experiences. For both groups, the 'consumption' of particular meanings, values and skills are central to the 'production' of IT skills training.

READING 4.3

Now read Reading 4.3, 'The changing sites of sound: music retailing and the composition of consumers' by Paul du Gay and Keith Negus. As you read it, think about the ways in which production and consumption are linked.

Du Gay and Negus argue that the example of music retailing provides evidence that production and consumption are best not considered as separate spheres. Instead, they suggest that the two are caught up in 'unstable relations of imbrication'. What this means is that the two spheres are so closely related that they are overlapping. The precise form of these overlaps may alter over time but the basic dependence of the one sphere on the other will remain constant. This is what the authors mean when they refer to production and consumption as 'mutually constitutive' – specific forms of production depend for their existence upon specific forms of consumption and vice versa. The design of music stores to cater for the distinctive tastes of different identity groups of consumers or niche markets is just one example of this sort of link.

The aim throughout this section has been to rethink the definition of the categories of 'economy' and 'economic life'. In particular the section set out to challenge the notion of the economy as an objective 'thing' that exists alongside other things in the physical world; rather, it suggested, the economy is constructed as a result of very specific sets of human activities. The economy was 'discovered' in eighteenth-century Europe when exchange and commercial activity began to increase in importance in the everyday life of communities. This 'discovery' involved specific sorts of activity – economic categories had to be defined, measured, compared and visually represented in order for a shared sense of 'economy' as the domain of production and exchange to develop. These activities, tools and techniques were, then, centrally caught up or 'imbricated' in the making of the economy in its contemporary sense.

These processes, however, should not be seen as an attempt to represent the economy directly. Rather, the representation of the economy involved a deep level of abstraction wherein specific categories (for example, profit or productivity) were defined, measured and set against other categories. This inevitably involved privileging the economic significance of certain categories over others. In this way certain categories and types of production – historically those undertaken by men – have come to assume a vital role as measures of economic productivity, growth and stability.

Counter to this tendency of male focus, it was proposed that forms of production carried out in the main by women, as well as consumption activities, had equal claims for inclusion as categories of economic life. The economic logic of production would, after all, collapse without consumption as its counterpart. Furthermore, at the level of individual, subjective experience, the activities of consumption and production share a preoccupation with the goal of achieving personal meaning and satisfaction. In the final section the underlying logic of this argument will be applied in a review of the relationship between sociology and economic life.

SUMMARY OF SECTION 4

1 The economy does not exist independently of human efforts to construct it.

2 Constructing the economy involves the use of specific sorts of tools and techniques to measure and represent its elements.

3 These tools have tended to privilege certain sorts of production at the expense of other production and consumption activities.

4 Economic life might be better understood as involving both production and consumption as the categories are mutually interdependent.

5 Sociology and economic life: a mutually performative relation?

The aim in this final section is to suggest that sociology, rather than operating as an objective study of the economy or as a source of knowledge to increase the effectiveness of commercial organizations, can be understood as more intricately connected to the economy. This involves an understanding of sociology and economic life as interdependent categories caught up in a 'mutually performative' relation. This awkward term is intended to signal the tendency for practices in each domain to have material consequences in the other. The section begins with a discussion of how both sociology and economic life are made up of, or constituted by, specific tools, techniques and devices. In contrast to the economy ruled exclusively by the 'invisible hand' of market forces, it will be argued that practitioners in sociology and in economic life act as *visible hands*. This term is used to highlight the ways in which practitioners' knowledges and activities have material effects in the domain of economic life. In an attempt to make this clearer, the section features examples, from the fields of market and advertising research, in which sociological knowledges and practices are interchanged with commercial, economic ones. The important point throughout is that this exchange has very real, material effects in both domains. It is through such exchanges that specific ideas and practices which define 'economic life' and what it means to be an economic subject at a given time and place are constructed.

As described in section 4, the classical notion of the economy as a stable, self-evident 'thing' has been problematized by recent work that has sought to highlight the dependence of 'the economy' on historically specific practices for measuring, analysing and representing particular economic categories. In a similar vein Granovetter (1992) argued that the economy is not a sealed-off domain of rational action but is always embedded in a given social structure: actions, according to Granovetter, are never purely economic but are always socially situated. Underlying this argument is the view that any given economic act will also feature other dimensions. An individual attending a job interview or selling a house, for example, will usually be motivated by a number of social and personal factors in addition to their economic goals. Granovetter argued that the same logic applied to any economic actor, whether a small firm or a government agency: the motivation behind any given economic act would always be multiple.

What this highlights is that economic practices are not pure, rational and scientific. Rather they are informed and influenced by the specific social, cultural and personal contexts in which they occur. This argument has recently been given a further twist in work which proposes that the economy should be viewed as the outcome, not purely of the invisible hand of market forces, but of the interaction of these with visible hands that act to 'perform' the market. These visible hands are those of practitioners like managers, accountants, marketers and even social scientists whose specific working practices help to define the nature of the economy. The economy in this recent body of work is seen neither in classical academic terms as a 'thing in itself' nor in Granovetter's terms as an entirely social construction but as the outcome of mediation between economic calculations and social practices.

This formulation of the economy owes a great deal to work by theorists such as Callon (1998), Law (2000) and Thrift (2000). These theorists have proposed that the economy is shaped, or 'performed', through the activities and knowledges of commercial practitioners and academic social scientists. In Callon's (1998) analysis, the economy is the contingent outcome of a process in which economics and the economy move together in a mutual 'performance'. In this sense economics and other social sciences 'perform' the economy through shaping the ways in which institutions operate and calculate. The economy and the market are not natural, physical objects but constructions that emerge from the specific practices of economic actors on the one hand and external agents, including academics, managers and so on, on the other. The category of 'economic actor' here refers to those agents involved in a specific economic transaction – generally the sellers, buyers and any intermediaries. Callon draws a distinction between the economic actors involved in a specific transaction and other agents who, although outside the immediate transaction, also influence economies and markets:

> The market is no longer that cold, implacable and impersonal monster which imposes its laws and procedures while extending them ever further. It is a many-sided, diversified, evolving device which the social sciences as well as the actors themselves contribute to reconfigure.
>
> (Callon, 1998, p.51)

This may all seem rather vague and abstract. Yet if you cast your mind back to the discussion in section 3 you may be able to point to ways in which the specific practices and tools of management theorists and managers acted to shape the economic experiences of workers. All the management styles featured in that section, from bureaucracy through to the 'excellence' culture programme, required not only theories and ideas about how to manage but also specific tools and techniques. Bureaucracy, for instance, relied upon the organizational chart to clearly depict areas of authority and responsibility and the chain of command; Human Relations and Organizational Psycho-technology required tools through which the subjective experiences and needs of the workforce could be explored. Devices such as semi-structured interviews and questionnaires were formulated, their results tabulated through statistical techniques and presented to managers in the form of reports, tables and graphs. These processes and tools may seem mundane in themselves but their importance in structuring everyday experiences of economic life should not be underrated. Miller and Rose (1990, p.23), for instance, have argued that these 'intellectual technologies' have the capacity to link economic, political and personal values 'into a single theoretico-practical matrix'. It is this combination of theoretical and practical knowledges and techniques to shape economic life that is of crucial significance here.

This 'theoretico-practical matrix', moreover, is not only to be found in the domain of management. Theorists have pointed to the prominence of a similar relationship in domains as diverse as accounting, marketing, advertising and market research. Miller (1998) argues that even ostensibly neutral and objective techniques and tools such as those used in accountancy do not simply measure reality but effectively shape it through the very act of measurement. Accountancy tools, such as double-entry bookkeeping, he argues, are 'largely improvised and adapted to the tasks and materials at hand' (P. Miller, 1998, p.190). There is no general principle that defines what should and should not be measured; decisions about what categories should be measured are the subject of constant re-negotiation in professional accounting. Accountants, Miller points out, cannot perform calculations without tools and these tools shape the economic meaning of categories like human and material resources.

Cochoy (1998) has made analogous points about marketing and advertising practices. In his account, the conception of the consumer that informs the theory and practice of marketing is as much the consequence of marketing knowledge as it is the cause. This means that contemporary ideas about the consumer are as much a result of specific marketing practices as they are a result of objective knowledge about what influences consumers to buy specific products.

READING 4.4

Now turn to Reading 4.4 which is an extract from Miller and Rose's article 'Mobilising the consumer'. This is a difficult piece that uses many psychoanalytical concepts with which you may not be familiar. As you read, try not to dwell on the detail of their argument but focus instead on the ways in which the consumer is being described in accordance with a particular set of theoretical ideas.

It seems to me that the idea of the ice-cream consumer in Menzies and Trist's market research studies would be unthinkable without theoretical knowledge derived from psychoanalysis. Menzies and Trist's study was one of a series conducted in the 1950–'60s at the Tavistock Institute on a consultancy basis for large commercial clients such as Birds Eye Foods and Cadbury. In describing these studies Miller and Rose's goal is to throw light upon the ways in which contemporary ideas about the consumer are a result of an intricate technical process that combines both academic and commercial tools and knowledges. This process did not simply stamp the market research report but had material effects in shaping the style of advertising and other techniques calculated to 'mobilize' the consumer. The use of knowledges derived from the social sciences in advertising and market research, they argue, provides a way of exploring how consumers are 'mobilized' by 'forming connections between human passions, hopes and anxieties, and very specific features of goods enmeshed in particular consumption practices' (Miller and Rose, 1997, p.2).

As a specific marketing tool, psychoanalytically informed research can also contribute to a broader process of shaping or 'performing' the economy. This notion of 'performing the economy' flags the ways in which specific marketing tools and practices incorporate both 'hard' economic calculations and social scientific forms of knowledge. The function of marketing here is to invent 'special human and conceptual frames for market knowledge and practice' (Cochoy, 1998, p.194).

Psychoanalysis, however, is far from the only social science knowledge to have been applied to marketing. Box 4.3 features an extract from the website of the market research consultancy firm, Semiotic Solutions. **Semiotics** is an academic approach to the analysis of how meanings are constructed in society that has developed mainly within the disciplines of sociology and cultural studies. Semiotics has been primarily associated with the critical study of how meanings are circulated in order to produce the ideological effect of reproducing a given order in society (Barthes, 1973). For this reason the firm achieved brief notoriety in the academic community in the early 1990s as an example of the tendency for 'high critical theory' to be applied to 'low commercial practice' (Wernick, 1997, p.207):

semiotics

Semiotic Solutions is thus a phenomenon of the interface of academic and market research. It employs cultural theory, presented in its more scientistic and instrumental mode, to legitimate its knowledge, makes use of 'soft' social science methodologies and employs personnel who use Terry Eagleton's name as a guarantor of the expertise they employ.

(Lury and Warde, 1996, p.89)

BOX 4.3: SEMIOTIC SOLUTIONS CASE STUDY

Cultural Creativity

ALL SUCCESSFUL MARKETING works because it hits the right cultural button, creatively harnessing the power of culture – the greatest influence in all our lives and purchase decisions.

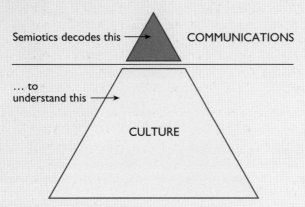

Code-breaking advertising such as Tango or Peperami; brands like Persil that seem to speak to consumers of their deepest values and beliefs; new product development that creates whole new markets (such as the cooking aid phenomenon); new segments of consumers (lads, post-feminists, kids) – all owe a large share of their success to cultural creativity.

Cultural creativity works the ultimate magic with consumers. And you can make it work for you with semiotics.

What makes semiotics different from other research approaches?

As an industry, market research lives or dies by its understanding of the consumer mindset.

Which is why, broadly speaking, most approaches take the methodological tack of addressing research questions to a consumer forum.

Focus groups, in-depth interviews, hall tests – they all set up 'the consumer' as the source of all marketing answers.

But consumers can only respond in certain anecdotal ways: recalling behaviour, expressing feelings and beliefs, pronouncing on products, ads, flavours, etc. Typically researchers interpret these responses in order to understand the drives behind them – sometimes on the basis of theory (predominantly psychology) but, more often, as inspired guesswork.

Semiotics is different. First, it looks at things through the other end of the marketing telescope – the cultural end.

Secondly, it bases the interpretation of what it sees firmly on the theory of consumers and culture.

Consumers are made not born

In semiotic theory, consumers are not independent spirits, articulating their own original opinions and making their own individual buying decisions.

By and large, consumers are products of the popular culture in which they live. They are constructed by the communications of that culture. As a result, they are not prime causes; they are cultural effects. So to find out what's really going on in the market place, the semiotician begins by looking beyond the consumer into the cultural context that surrounds and informs him.

THIS IS THE KEY DIFFERENCE between the semiotic approach and most other kinds of market research. Most market research starts with the customer. We first put the brand under the cultural microscope with a new desk-based methodological process called Semiotic analysis.

Source: http://www.semioticsolutions.com
(accessed March 2001)

What this illustrates once more is the existence of ongoing processes of exchange between the domains of academic and commercial practice. Of particular significance is that this exchange has material effects in the structuring or performation of particular aspects of economic life. Semiotic Solutions' research method helped to produce a very distinctive style of advertisement calculated not to tap into the hidden psychological desires and anxieties of consumers but to associate the product with desirable cultural meanings. The firm carried out research for the advertising campaign for the salami snack 'Peperami' which has been running since the early 1990s. One case history of this award-winning campaign remarked that this 'semiotic autopsy on *Peperami* revealed a truly schizophrenic personality. The brand had a unique ability to straddle both cultural meat values (power, masculinity, real food) and snack values (fun, unisexual, improper food) simultaneously' (Justin Kent, Account Planning Group Case History, www.semioticsolutions.com).

Semiotic Solutions' report on Peperami argued that the brand was a rule-breaker, a 'cultural rebel' and that the advertising had to tap into this 'radical' product identity. The important point to note here is that a very specific academic approach operated internally in this commercial production process and shaped the advertising produced. This is in sharp contrast to Broadbent's comments that staff in advertising agencies proceed with their work largely in ignorance of the work conducted in universities (quoted in the introduction). The Semiotics Solutions example reveals that not only is the economic domain formatted by knowledges that originated in universities but the relationship operates in reverse: economic conditions also act to format academic knowledges. The decision to commission a new advertising campaign was prompted in the first instance by the market conditions faced by the product. By the late 1980s Peperami sales were in steady decline fuelled by competition from supermarket own-brands and a listeria health scare in 1987 (Baker, 1995). The decision to use semiotic analysis emerged from the perceived need to do something ground-breaking to restructure the product identity in such difficult economic conditions.

Moreover, almost as soon as Semiotics Solutions began trading, academics gathered to debate the implications of this move (Hodgkinson, 1993; Lury and Warde, 1996; Wernick, 1997). While there is undoubtedly no routine, daily traffic between academia and advertising agencies, nonetheless their activities are indelibly shaped by a pool of knowledge, techniques and methods that is the property of neither but is the outcome of specific practices undertaken in both.

The aim in this section, and throughout the chapter as a whole, has been to develop an alternative understanding of the relationship between academic sociology and economic life. This has been informed by the belief that this relationship should not be considered in terms of sociology's study of the economy or in terms of the economy's use of sociology. Rather, sociology and economic life can be understood as involved in a relationship of mutual constitution in which each domain depends on the other for its form at any given time. In this respect it was suggested that specific practices, techniques and tools acted to construct or 'perform' the nature of sociology and economic life. Economic life, then, is not dictated by the invisible hand of the market but is shaped by the visible hands of a variety of different practitioners in both academia and commerce. One of the uses of sociology has undoubtedly been to provide 'tools' to inform commercial practice but this is only one aspect of an intricate and ongoing relation.

SUMMARY OF SECTION 6

1 Sociology and economic life are involved in a relationship of mutual performance.

2 Economic life is structured by the 'visible hands' of both academic and commercial practitioners.

3 Economic life can also shape sociological knowledge.

4 Intellectual technologies are combined with commercial practice to create a 'theoretico-practical matrix' that shapes the nature of economic life.

5 Examples of how invisible hands and the matrix of practical and theoretical tools, techniques and knowledges materially influence economic life can be found in management, accounting and market and advertising research.

References

Baker, C. (1995) *Advertising Works 8*, Henley on Thames, NTC Publications Ltd.

Baldamus, W. (1961) *Efficiency and Effort*, London, Tavistock.

Barthes, R. (1973) 'Myth today' in *Mythologies,* London, Paladin.

Bottomore, T.B. and Rubel, M. (1956) *Karl Marx: Selected Writings in Sociology and Social Philosophy*, London, Watts.

Braverman, H. (1974) *Labour and Monopoly Capital*, London, Monthly Review Press.

Broadbent, T. (1998) 'The new advertising thinkers', *Campaign*, 24 July.

Buck-Morss, S. (1995) 'Envisioning capital', *Critical Inquiry,* Winter, pp.434–67.

Burawoy, M. (1979) *Manufacturing Consent*, Chicago, IL, University of Chicago Press.

Callon, M. (ed.) (1998) *The Laws of the Market*, Oxford, Blackwell, pp.1–57.

Cochoy, F. (1998) 'Another discipline for the market economy: marketing as a performative knowledge and know-how for capitalism' in Callon, M. (ed.) *op. cit..*

du Gay, P. (1996) *Consumption and Identity at Work*, London, Sage.

du Gay, P. (2000) *In Praise of Bureaucracy*, London, Sage.

du Gay, P. and Negus, K. (1994) 'The changing sites of sound: music retailing and the composition of consumers', *Media, Culture and Society*, vol.16, pp.395–413.

Dumont, L. (1977) *From Mandeville to Marx*, Chicago, IL, University of Chicago Press.

Gaukroger, S. (1986) 'Romanticism and decommodification: Marx's conception of socialism', *Economy and Society*, vol.15, no.3, pp.287–333.

Goldthorpe, J.H., Lockwood, D., Bechhofer, F. and Platt, J. (1968) *The Affluent Worker: Industrial Attitudes and Behaviour*, Cambridge, Cambridge University Press.

Goldthorpe, J.H., Lockwood, D., Bechhofer, F. and Platt, J. (1969) *The Affluent Worker in the Class Structure*, Cambridge, Cambridge University Press.

Granovetter, M. (1992) 'Economic institutions as social constructions: a framework for analysis', *Acta Sociologica*, vol.35, pp.3–11.

Grint, K. (1991) *The Sociology of Work: An Introduction*, Cambridge, Polity Press.

Hemmings, S., Silva, E.B. and Thompson, K. (2002) 'Accounting for the everyday' in Bennett, T. and Watson, D. (eds) *Understanding Everyday Life*, Oxford, Blackwell/The Open University. (Book 1 in this series.)

Hodgkinson, T. (1993) 'The affluence of theory', *New Statesman & Society*, 12 March, pp.31–3.

Jordan, T. (2002) 'Totalities and multiplicities: thinking about social change' in Jordan, T. and Pile, S. (eds) *Social Change*, Oxford, Blackwell/The Open University. (Book 3 in this series.)

Law, J. (2000) 'Economics as interference', Paper given at the *Cultural Economy Workshop*, The Open University, 13–14 January.

Lichfield, J. and Shepard, K. (2001) 'Books of condolence as Paris mourns the end of M&S', *The Independent*, 7 April.

Lury, C. and Warde, A. (1996) 'Investments in the imaginary consumer: conjectures regarding power, knowledge and advertising' in Nava, M. *et al.* (eds) *op. cit..*

Marx, K. (1980) *Marx's Grundrisse* (ed. D. McLean), London, Paladin. First published in 1857–8.

Miller, D. (ed.) (1995) *Acknowledging Consumption*, London, Routledge.

Miller, D. (1998) 'Taking Marx to Sainsbury's', based on the Morgan Lectures 1998 (previously unpublished).

Miller, P. (1998) *The Margins of Accounting*, in Callon, M. (ed.) *op. cit..*

Miller, P. and Rose, N. (1990) 'Governing economic life', *Economy and Society*, vol.19, no.1, pp.1–31.

Miller, P. and Rose, N. (1997) 'Mobilising the consumer: assembling the subject of consumption', *Theory, Culture and Society*, vol.14, no.1, pp.1–36.

Nava, M., Blake, A., MacRury, I. and Richards, B. (eds) (1996) *Buy This Book: Studies in Advertising and Consumption*, London, Routledge.

Nelson, J. (1996) *Feminism, Objectivity and Economics,* London, Routledge.

Pateman, C. (1989) *The Disorder of Women*, Cambridge, Polity Press.

Pugh, D. S. (1984) *Organisation Theory: Selected Readings* (2nd edn), Harmondsworth, Penguin Books.

Roberts Y. (2001) 'Happy days', *The Guardian*, 16 January.

Rose, N. (1999) *Governing the Soul* (2nd edn), London, Routledge.

Savage, M. (2002) 'Social exclusion and class analysis' in Braham, P. and Janes, L. (eds) *Social Differences and Divisions*, **Oxford, Blackwell/The Open University. (Book 2 in this series.)**

Thompson, P. (1984) 'The labour process and deskilling' in Thompson, K. (ed.) *Work, Employment and Unemployment*, Milton Keynes, Open University Press.

Thrift, N. (2000) 'Virtual capitalism: the globalisation of reflexive business knowledge' in Carrier, J. and Miller, D. (eds) *Virtualism: A New Political Economy,* Oxford, Berg.

Waterman, R. (1994) *The Frontiers of Excellence,* London, Nicholas Brealey Publishing Ltd.

Weber, M. (1948) *From Max Weber: Essays in Sociology* (ed. Gerth, H.H. and Mills, C. Wright) London, Routledge and Kegan Paul.

Wernick, A. (1997) 'Resort to nostalgia: mountains, memories and myths of time' in Nava, M. *et al.* (eds) *op. cit.*.

Readings

 ## Yvonne Roberts, 'Happy days' (2001)

The future is bright, the future is orange – and yellow and red, with daisies on the loo seats, cartoons and a clutch of awards on the walls, a turnover of £2m and a commitment to work-life issues. 'Our view is that we can't afford not to operate like this,' says Cathy Callus, 39, training director of Happy Computers. 'It's all about getting the most out of our staff.'

The company, based in London, offers IT training. Set up by Henry Stewart in his back room a decade ago, it employed 20 people last year, now has 40 (a quarter male) and is still recruiting. Callus works four days a week; Stewart, 41, spends Thursday mornings in his children's school; another employee works only in term time.

Jane Roston, 38, joined four years ago. She has worked both a three-day and a four-day week, and during maternity leave she brought her daughter into the office once a month to keep up to date. 'It made the whole process seamless,' she says. 'Working here isn't an easy ride, you have to be seen to succeed, but the culture is wonderful because it's so human.'

Maternity leave is six weeks on full pay, six weeks on half; the job is held for nine months with additional unpaid leave granted for a further five years. Fathers are given five days' paid leave and up to four months' unpaid.

Salaries are an open book, staff choose their own job description and mistakes are 'celebrated' as a chance to learn from failure. Everyone is encouraged to join a union and to try another person's job to understand how the system works. 'We look for attitude and train for skill, so qualifications matter less,' Callus says. 'We believe in teamwork and positivity – if you are interested in status, there's no place for you here.' Each person spends a day a month on voluntary work and is given £75 a year to donate to charity.

It is said a major hurdle in the adoption of flexibility and a work-life agenda is that 97 per cent of Britain's companies employ under 20 staff. Stephen Alambritis heads the Federation of Small Businesses which represents 160,000 small companies, 40,000 run by women. He says the government may permit a clause that will allow a small business to opt out of, say, extending parental rights if it can be proved this may harm the company. He also warns that too many 'extras' attached to female employment might mean some bosses resist hiring women – a move he is at pains to condemn.

Happy Computers' experience, however, is that a modernised workplace boosts profits. Since staff stay, reduced recruitment costs have saved £40,000 in the past 12 months – and turnover is up 37%. 'Our approach isn't complicated,' Stewart explains. 'We believe people work best when they feel good about themselves.'

Source: Roberts, 2001; from http://www.guardian.co.uk/ Archive (accessed 31 January 2002)

 ## Daniel Miller, 'Taking Marx to Sainsbury's' (1998)

My title comes from the observations of one of my colleagues, Murray Last, that Marx was living in Kentish Town at the same time that Sainsbury's second shop, from where the chain began, had opened in the immediate vicinity. This was a period of change in Marx's life. Earlier on came both a more direct experience and observation of poverty and oppression and a more philosophical engagement with the problems of alienation. But while in Kentish Town Marx's emphasis moved to the library of the British Museum and the development of what became in *Das Kapital* a much more abstracted and economic vision – a universalising logic of the workings of capital. My speculation is not that Marx went shopping at Sainsbury's, but given that they lived in what were practically adjoining streets it is extremely likely that his wife did. My further contention, however, is that if Marx, rather than his wife, had actually spent more time involved in mundane consumption and provisioning this might just have helped prevent the retreat from the complexity of human diversity into law-like model building.

So my task today is to resurrect Marx from a fortunately not too distant Highgate cemetery (and I will spare you the obvious retail joke about Marx's grave being only a few yards from Spencer's), to take him to a contemporary Sainsbury's and consider the likely result. We might hope his radicalism would by now have included feminism, so he would not be too reluctant to undertake a spot of shopping. Still today's Sainsbury's would I suspect come as something of a shock. Marx saw a world run by manufacturing, whose primary concern was to find markets, that is to sell off the products of the industrial revolution. It was relations of production that were the motor force of history. I think Marx would not merely be awed by his first view of Sainsbury's but would realise that there has been a fundamental shift in the vanguard of history.

Today, it is said that, if the likes of Tesco's and Sainsbury's won't sell it, there is little point in making it. Modern retailers have become the cutting edge of capitalism. Their point of sale technology provides instant information on consumer demands, especially thanks to the new loyalty cards. Brand names, the great symbols of earlier capitalist firms are proving vulnerable to own-label retail products. Marx would confront over 8,000 label lines at Sainsbury's. It is competition between retailers that squeezes the profits of manufacturers, exerts increasing control over distributors and – thanks to new 'just-in-time' systems of stocking – virtually eliminates wholesalers.

That things have changed by no means implies that they have all changed for the better. The central question posed by Marx is no more clearly answered in today's Sainsbury's than in the capitalist firms of his day. As Marx examines the products on the supermarket shelves his first question might be about the relationship of these goods to their context of labour. But what could we tell him? Which products are made by affluent Norwegians who after work can pick up their children from a well-resourced crèche. Are those cut flowers from Kenya produced through huge quantities of pesticide destroying a tropical landscape, and is this sugar from cane still cut by peasants in lifelong debt to the plantation owners? The bitterness of exploitation still leaves no aftertaste.

Some geographers are now trying to trace back these lines of provisioning to their source. But Marx most likely would simply note with some sadness that, after all this time what he strove to reveal has at the point of shopping become ever more opaque. Anthropologists, by contrast, working in the developing world know only too well the connection between the way a supermarket chain can push down the price of coffee, and starvation in the producing area, or the link between hospitals for the disabled in the developing world, and a trade in landmines we seem so reluctant to relinquish. Taking Marx to Sainsbury's might astonish Marx, but there are many things that he would still have to teach us.

Actually while I am not suggesting Sainsbury's are expecting a visit from Marx in the near future, I am happy to note that last week it became the first major British store to introduce an ethical code of manufacture for its own-label brand.

The younger Marx was something of an anthropologist, concerned with larger questions of humanity's identity and the different ways society is constituted at particular historical periods. But this brings me to my principal reason for taking Marx shopping. As I have noted, by the time he was living in Kentish Town Marx was constructing something very different. In attempting to, as it were, beat political economy he was actually joining it, by putting the finishing touches to what became the foundations of Marxism. My emulation of Marx seeks to retain his earlier anthropological insights without following him into the kind of pseudo-scientific economics he went on to develop.

…

Marx had remarkably little to say about the implications of consumption in general, let alone shopping, for his analysis of the world. When in 1987 I published a book on consumption, its aim was not just to critique studies of consumption up to that time, but also to re-think where consumption might fit within the framework provided by the early Marx. It was of course also influenced by the perspicacity of anthropologists such as Pierre Bourdieu and also by Mary Douglas who while working at this same department of anthropology at UCL had argued for the potential contribution of anthropology to a critique of economics through the study of consumption.

I argued that the reason both academics and non-academics deluded themselves about consumption is precisely that they presume that such activities must reflect what they see as the spirit of the age. Consumption should be merely a reflection of materialism and hedonistic desire inculcated in us as commodity fantasy by those who wish to sell us goods. If we live under capitalism it is assumed that shopping should reflect capitalism. Academics, and in particular Marxists, thought they were emulating

Marx by creating a critique of consumption as a symbol of capitalism.

My argument was precisely the opposite. Sure, we all live within capitalism, but we experience the scale of modern commercial enterprise as also other modern institutions such as the state as a vast and often distant array of forces from which we feel alienated and often belittled. Faced with this sense of anonymity and irrelevance, we turn to consumption not to express these forces but to confront them, and use consumption to re-create for ourselves a sense of identity and particularity. We take the anonymous commodity and make it the highly specific possession or gift, giving these goods and thereby ourselves meaningfulness within that vastness. Consumption becomes an endless struggle to create through selection and appropriation – to create a self, a household, or a relationship of considerable specificity.

Consider the situation when you can start at one end of Oxford Street and despite seeing literally hundreds of examples of say wallpaper or skirts or whatever it is you are after, you can emerge at the other end of Oxford Street having decided that none of them is quite right. Well one was almost 'but they just don't make the right design I was after'. This is

quite bizarre, yet makes sense within an analytical framework, where such experiences are actually one of the main reasons for modern consumption, i.e. the affirmation not of some new subjectivity, but of a denied particularity, though this need not always be so individualistic, it being rather easier to buy one's way into the group that wears blue jeans for instance.

So far then from merely completing the forces of production and distribution, consumption acts to negate them. This is what creates the intense concern with morality and the making of social relations through shopping that we found in our recent study. It is equally true of the response to goods and services coming from the state, from the health service, or the local council, where again the specificity of the small social group is constructed through a sense of overcoming the anonymity and lack of care of huge institutions. Consumption has become the primary means by which society appropriates the economy or state and as it were renders them social. Commerce, of course, is only too happy to collude with and thereby profit from servicing these desires but the desire is not itself the creation of capitalist firms, rather it is a response to them.

Source: Miller, 1998; based on the Morgan Lectures 1998
(previously unpublished)

4.3　Paul du Gay and Keith Negus, 'The changing sites of sound: music retailing and the composition of consumers' (1994)

At a music business convention during September 1992, Maurice Oberstein, chairman of the British Phonographic Industry – the organization that represents the interests of British record companies, issued a blistering attack on music retailers. Referring to the increasing buying power of a few large chains, he declared that record companies would shortly need to 'take action against the inexorable pressure of retailers who control what we sell to the public'.[1] Employing rhetoric that is more commonly heard directed *at* record companies, he argued that the use of retail advertising was 'denigrating' music. Singling out Our Price, Oberstein argued that retailers were treating music as little more than baked beans, using it to promote their own corporate identity. The retailers immediately responded to this 'baked beans slur' by issuing a counter-argument that they were committed to providing a diversity of music. Simon Burke, managing director of Virgin Retail retorted that, far from the retailer's own corporate advertising dominating the music, the 'advertising said far too much about the

product and not enough about the shop'.[2]

That such exchanges should be occurring *within* the music industry rather than between artists and the corporations, is a significant development. It is an indication of an important series of tensions that are emerging as a result of changes in the relationship between 'production' and 'consumption' within the culture and entertainment industries. This paper focuses specifically on the changing character of music retailing in order to highlight the central place accorded to 'the consumer' within those industries. Through an analysis of contemporary developments in music retailing we trace the shift in power relations occurring within the industry; between those occupations and groups whose expertise is based upon the deployment of technologies and techniques of cultural and textual *production* (broadly speaking, the 'producers' and 'creators' of sounds, words and images), and those whose expertise is based upon knowledge of the *consumption* of cultural artefacts and services.

We argue that profound transformations in the distribution system have led to retailers exercising an increased influence within the music industry. Growing levels of concentration and centralization within music retailing, combined with the widespread deployment of EDP (Electronic Data Processing) technologies, have permitted the retail/distribution system and, increasingly, the whole production chain as well, to be arranged as an interconnected logistic package. Because the whole chain can now be organized as a single 'system', music retailers are able to enjoy a hitherto inconceivable degree of 'co-ordinated flexibility' in the face of market changes. This development has allowed music retailers to delineate, construct and monitor the 'consumer' of recorded music more intricately than ever before. The 'front-to-back visibility' accorded to music retailers by these changes has increased their influence on the formation of popular music and enhanced their ability to 'make up' the consumer.

In describing these developments, we also seek to critically interrogate recent conceptualizations of consumption within cultural studies (Chambers, 1985; Fiske, 1992; Willis, 1990). We argue that the representation of consumption as an inherently 'active', 'creative' or 'resistant' practice carries with it certain important interpretive costs. In particular, we suggest that from the quite plausible (if increasingly banal) premise that consumption practices cannot be derived from or reduced to a mirror of production – that consumers make meanings in reception and do not passively 'receive' and 'ingest' sent messages – these approaches appear to end up treating consumption 'as a quasi-autonomous reality diverging from another "reality" called "production" – which after Marxism we are supposed to know quite enough about for the time being' (Morris, 1988, p.21). While usefully highlighting the pleasures of and play of identities within contemporary cultures of consumption, this type of theorizing has tended to privilege consumption as a space in which audiences have the potential to engage in 'creative' activities of 'appropriation' which are entirely independent of processes of production.

In contrast to this position, we argue that such a division between 'production' and 'consumption' cannot be maintained. Rather than representing 'production' and 'consumption' as two fully constituted and mutually opposed objectivities we suggest that they should be conceptualized as inherently dislocated, or as Laclau (1990, p.24) puts it, as 'relational semi-identities' involved in 'unstable relations of imbrication'. Music retailing provides extensive evidence of the dislocated relationship.

Retailers now occupy an increasingly influential position within the production/consumption relations of popular music. Whereas in the past, the record corporations as 'producers' or 'manufacturers' tended to exert control over the retailers through 'forward integration' and control of the product, today it is 'backward integration' from the retailer which is shifting power relations within the industry. Through increased control over a range of processes and practices, including product design, product development and so forth (as our opening quotes indicate) retailers have begun to exert increasing control over their suppliers.

At the same time, and as a result of the same processes, retailers have also been able to exert more influence over consumers. Increased concentration and flexibilization within music retailing has allowed retailers to stay 'closer to the customer than ever before' (du Gay, 1992). The growing deployment of EPoS (Electronic Point of Sale) technologies, for example, has helped to provide retailers with increased information on consumers' tastes and dispositions thus allowing for more intricate marketing experiments and targeted promotions.

In putting this argument, we do not mean to suggest that music retailers are now replacing record companies in *determining* the behaviour of consumers nor do we imply that they are *determining* the manufacture of music-related products (Harker, 1980). Such an approach would sit uncomfortably with the notion of 'dislocation'.

The activities of retailers and consumers of recorded music are mutually constitutive. Following de Certeau (1984) we would suggest that, as consumers of recorded music, we have no 'proper' place of our own because we operate within a space delineated and monitored by music retailers.

In indicating the ways in which the acquisition of recorded music is shaped by the activities of retailers, we begin by highlighting the structural processes of concentration, centralization and flexibilization at work within the music retail sector over roughly the last three decades. In doing this we draw attention to the way that record shops have been reorganized as entertainment complexes.

...

Points of purchase: sites of sound

By focusing upon the store environment we depict various ways that music retailers attempt to regulate the conduct of consumers. We refer to this as a process of 'making up'. Ian Hacking (1986, p.234) (from whom we borrow the term) suggests that a partial framework for thinking through this regulatory activity would consist of two mutually constitutive vectors.

One is the vector of 'labelling from above' whereby a particular 'community of experts' – in this case retail managements and the other cultural intermediaries who service them – 'create a "reality"' – composed, for example, around musical taste formations, genre categories and their associated lifestyles. It is this created reality that some people are encouraged to make their own. Different from this, but equally important, is the vector of 'the actual behaviour of those so-labelled, which presses from below, creating a reality that every expert must face' (Hacking, 1986, p.234).

Although at first sight this framework appears to replicate some of the enduring dualisms associated with social science – those of object/subject, society/ individual – this is far from the case. As we argued earlier, these vectors should not be seen as two fully constituted objectives. Rather they should be viewed as mutually constitutive or 'dislocated'.

Clearly, the first vector does not 'determine' the second, for if it did so we would have nothing but a subject-less, automatic history. The fact that 'making up' is relational activity indicates that these two vectors are permanently dislocated, they are involved in 'unstable relations of imbrication'.

The design and layout of the store are major components of this process of 'making up'. The physical space in the major megastores (whether Virgin, Tower, HMV, Our Price, FNAC, etc.) has been organized in a very specific way.

First, a commercial-cultural geography is inscribed into the shop environment, visible in the way in which generic entertainment products are located throughout the store. The store provides the consumer with various guides, often a map of the shop, indicating the structure of the store and the various routes through it. Signs point to various sections – pathways to the pleasures of consumption. The store layout – the space and the routes through it – may give the impression of being just 'thrown together' but careful and continuous planning and surveillance is conducted to establish the store's 'narratives of consumption'. The aim is to 'lead the buyer through' various genres. As Kevin Sheehan, president of USA-based Hear Music retail outlets added to this explanation: 'The company, the catalogue and the store are all about developing a conversation between the musicians who make the music and the customer' (Reibman, 1992, p.58).

At the entrance to a megastore, the importance of high volume sales from contemporary blockbusters and the promotion of selected 'classics' from back catalogues immediately informs the initial shop arrangement. Research has revealed that most people look to the right when they walk into a record shop.

The right of the entrance has therefore been designated as the 'hot spot'. This is where the high turnover recordings and special promotions (often prioritized new releases) are placed (Martin, 1991).

The most noticeable cultural classification inside the store is the way in which music is divided into particular music genre/marketing categories and the way in which these are distributed between floors and into separate self-contained or semi-self-contained spaces, all tending to play different music. Since the late 1980s megastores have been building separate self-contained environments for different genres of music; most noticeably jazz, country and classical. The jazz section is often closely connected to or contains sections of reggae, Latin/salsa, and an international or world music section. Unobtrusive but effectively sound-proofed barriers, glass partitions or heavy sound-proof glass doors, mark out the space to the next section, often a country music/folk/blues section. Usually housed in a separate room is the classical section.

Slightly more chaotically organized, with racks closer together, punctuated by special promotions (and often quite removed from the jazz/country/ classical sections) are the general categories of rock/ pop/soul. Again, a separate room will act as a video store. Frequently lumped together are the ever smaller amounts of vinyl (mainly alternative and heavy rock, reggae, dance), cassettes, singles, books, comics, magazines, T-shirts and the increasingly important area devoted to computer games (which have gradually been receiving their own very distinctive and highly profitable section). These latter areas, being dominated by the younger record buyers, are often significantly removed from the musical genre categories purchased by the older demographic.

In some stores the classical consumer may leave and enter through a separate entrance and need not even walk through the contemporary rock/pop section. One of the most obvious reasons for these closed environments, as reported in the music trade press, is that research has suggested that 'the thirty-something Vivaldi CD buyer does not want to rub shoulders with the teenage Vanilla Ice single customer, and the feeling is probably mutual'.[3]

Clearly record buyers are members of more than one market segment. Are the clusters of genres linked and formed into routes in recognition of the particular dispositions and habits of related and overlapping consumer groups? There is a strong indication that this is so. A number of studies have highlighted the way in which fans and audiences use music to express very specific lifestyles and forms of identity and to communicate these to others (Lewis, 1991; Lull, 1987). Retailers are clearly deploying similar forms of knowledge. Through the increasing use of design, marketing and advertising, underpinned by the knowledges and 'techniques of subjectivity' (Rose, 1990), retailers collate and classify information concerning the taste divisions and distinctions adopted by different audience groups and the way in which music operates to mark out and map and communicate individual, social and cultural identities.

Record retailers have clearly put great effort and expense into the design of the store. Aisle width is calculated to ensure optimum customer flow. Observation of store 'traffic' suggests that there should be at least 4 feet between the displays to allow customers to form 'motorway-style lanes' – allowing browsers and quick purchasers to 'operate comfortably at different speeds' (Martin, 1991). Wolfgang Muncinski of Lift, a company involved in designing record store environments, has stressed that picking up a product without bending or stretching is 'crucial'.[4] Such an observation provides another indication of how 'knowledge' of the consumer is essential to the practice of music retailing (as well as acknowledging that the tactile/visual is part of the aesthetic of pop).

The consumption of popular music has always been associated with tactile and visual elements. This is very apparent in the store in terms of the way in which the packaging of the 'sound carrier' is part of the way in which appeals are made to consumers. During the 1960s, looking at album covers and sleeve designs became an integral part of the purchase of popular music, and the retail environment itself changed to accommodate the tactile experience of examining the sleeve before acquiring the music (as has continued with cassettes and CDs).

Not only looking, but listening is also important in entertainment retailing. Since the beginning of the decade, the large urban megastores have modified the audio-visual space within their stores, introducing 'listening posts' in the aisles between the display cases or placing headphones next to a CD, album or cassette. Personal, individualized, private listening has been (re)introduced into the retail environment – in contrast to the old space-taking booths that used to line one of the walls in the old record shops. Music still plays as customers browse through the store but a conscious decision has been made to play music more quietly. Aware of the importance of the 25–45-year-old demographic, the environment has been altered to try and accommodate a range of musical taste differences.[5] As one retailer remarked in the trade press: 'You can't afford to alienate anyone' (Martin, 1991, p.10).

These changes have come about as a direct result of market research. Surveys conducted during the late 1980s indicated that consumers found the shops 'noisy', 'boring', 'confusing', 'out of date' and 'intimidating'. So, the re-introduction of individual listening is partly a programmatic response to research that found that people were not entering shops because they were unattractive. However, it is also the result of increased uncertainties about what people can be encouraged to buy. It has become apparent, for example, that many more people are now purchasing music that they have not heard before entering the store (Martin, 1991). This is in turn related to the declining importance of record sales charts and the impending extinction of the single record (Hugill, 1992). At one time, there was a very clear correlation between record sales and the single and LP charts. When there were less printed publications and when rock and pop were barely covered by the quality press, radio was the main medium of musical knowledge. This is no longer the case, and there is something of a disjuncture between the 'national chart' and patterns of consumption.

The market has become more segmented, as the geography of the store indicates. It is increasingly difficult to select a sample that represents the sales of recordings in Britain. As the broadcast media proliferate, future years are likely to see a decline in the significance of the BBC's Radio One chart and televised perennial *Top of the Pops* and the development of a series of genre-based and airplay/broadcast charts. These are likely to be introduced for the benefit of broadcasters (who are increasingly following the USA and 'narrowcasting' and 'formatting' regional ILR radio stations), and for the use of retailers.

Many retailers compile and publicly display their own store charts in order to give customers a cognitive map of contemporary musical tastes and a simultaneous invitation to participate in the process of formation. Some retailers are also giving 'unknown' acts a higher chart position to 'boost their profile'. As Tower Records declared in a promotional supplement in the trade press: 'Tower is pledging to create the charts of the future, not just pandering to the charts of today'.[6]

As we indicated earlier, while concentration, centralization and flexibilization have led to dramatic decline in the number of independent record retailers, it has not led to any diminution in *competition* among those multiples now dominating the industry. Indeed, quite the contrary is true. The main reason for this appears to be that while large retail firms can dominate the supply side, they are faced by a multitude of purchasers whose loyalty depends on price, quality and so forth. Therefore the collusion between firms to be found in concentrated industries in manufacturing does not exist in retailing and even the largest firms continue to compete intensely with one another.

In these circumstances, it becomes important for retailers to find ways of differentiating themselves from one another. One of the most important sources of differentiation for music retailers concerns their 'brand' image or corporate identity – a point illustrated in 1992 when Our Price Marketing manager Neil Boote was renamed as Brand Marketing manager.

It is retailers' attempts to develop a particular corporate identity or branded image that has so infuriated the record companies. The latter are concerned that this activity is detracting from the uniqueness of the artistic products they are producing (which in turn conceals a greater anxiety about their declining influence over the *way* in which music is presented and sold). Whilst record companies claim that it is the music that is important, it is interesting to find retailers claiming this importance for the store. As HMV's Chairman Stuart McAllister has remarked: 'The brand names of stores such as HMV are important. Where you buy a record says as much about you as what you buy. There is far more credibility to buy in a specialist or an HMV than a non-specialist like Boots' (MBI, 1992, p.21).

Similarly, Trevor Abbott, MD of Virgin Group, has argued the 'Virgin's brand is of paramount importance and we're fanatically protective of it. Virgin retail has a strong association with Branson and his daredevil stunts, with the airline, and, although no longer part of the group, with a pioneering label' (MBI, 1992, p.22).

Another corporate identity-building tactic deployed by retailers is in-store appearances by stars. As HMV Marketing Director, David Terrill explained: 'In-store appearances are not designed to be sales enhancers. In fact, they frequently bring the store to a standstill ... for the store they're an opportunity to develop an image' (Smith, 1990, p.15).

The motivation for such events comes directly from the retailer, rather than representatives of the artist. It is the retailer who approaches the record company to arrange these appearances.

In recent years, staffing has also become a crucial means of differentiating one retail 'offer' from another. 'Customer care' and 'quality service' programmes have become important organizational technologies through which competitive distinction is attempted (du Gay, 1992). In addition to logistical developments music retailers have also been attempting to achieve greater levels of 'emotional proximity' through improvements in customer service. In each of the segmented areas of the store, retailers are now recruiting 'more mature staff with a wider knowledge'.[7] The quality of 'personal service'

provided by sales staff in-store is seen as an increasingly vital component of building the 'corporate identity', winning over consumers and achieving competitive advantage.

Through the medium of a variety of cultural technologies (such as Transactional Analysis and other interpersonal 'skills' techniques), sales staff in music retailing are being encouraged to develop particular predispositions and capacities which are aimed at enabling them to 'win over' the hearts and minds of customers.

Increasingly, these sales staff are trained to assemble and deploy aspects of their own experience and identity as consumers of popular music in their paid work under the rubric of providing 'quality service'. In attempting to 'make up' the consumer, music retailers are therefore also driven to 'make up' those charged with providing in-store 'emotional proximity': sales staff. In a further dislocation, interventions aimed at regulating the conduct of consumers have repercussions for the ways in which the conduct of sales staff in music retailing is regulated.

In response to market research conducted at the end of the 1980s, all megastores began reassessing their staff training. HMV claims to be leading the way forward in this area, with its 'First Moves' training scheme for sales assistants. To gain their City and Guilds certificate new staff are examined on safety, shop layout, displaying products and categorizing music. Trainees must also display a working knowledge of video and record companies (Martin, 1991). The interaction between staff and consumers has been recognized as vital to the future of the store. To quote Stuart McAllister, the Chairman and Chief Executive of HMV: 'We are responding to changing demographics ... We have specialist departments in store with specialist staff so that nobody feels intimidated about coming into the store' (MBI, 1992, p.21). Similarly, Our Price announced that it intended to develop a new 'common vision' among its staff. Boasting of 'millions of pounds' spent on research, Our Price indicated its intention to introduce new store layouts and displays, specific 'zones' within the store and special staff clothing. Perhaps most significant, they issued a 'manifesto' aimed at developing a shared approach to customer care by all the multiple's staff.[8] Our Price's accompanying 'vision and values programme' is aimed at 'empowering' store managers and counter staff (Scott, 1993). Such developments highlight the important position of retail staff – perhaps the most neglected 'cultural intermediaries' within the media and entertainment industry.

Concluding comments

In this essay we have offered a brief account of how the practice of music retailing contributes to an understanding of the ways in which the consumption of popular music is regulated.

In contrast to approaches that represent 'production' and 'consumption' as autonomous or simply read one off from the other, our analysis highlights their dislocated, contingent relationship.

By highlighting how music retailers attempt to 'make up' consumers we have indicated that two mutually constitutive processes are at work: *labelling from above* and *actual behaviour of those labelled*. Both processes involve 'real' consumers but the two are not reducible to one another. The first 'consumer' is something of a composite creation – though no less real for all that – being the product of several intersecting knowledges and techniques of information gathering and analysis deployed by retail managements. This 'ideal' consumer is inscribed within store layouts, genre charts, targeted promotions and 'customer care' programmes, for example. The second 'consumer' is also somewhat 'hybrid' but in a rather different way. Constituted through several interlocking histories and cultural experiences, none of which can be permanently unified, this 'consumer' follows a route through the retail environment that intersects with the composite creation but never achieves a total nor a final 'fit'. Neither consumer would exist without the other. They are mutually constitutive and cannot therefore be represented as either 'mirror images' or entirely independent of one another. For, as we have emphasized above, the routes of consumption lead directly into (and out of) the design offices, marketing departments, boardrooms and assembly plants of electronic, communication and media corporations. As these trajectories are increasingly monitored by retail corporations, the *un*predictable activities of the 'consumers' who move through the stores present a continual challenge to the constructed shadows that attempt to follow, and then to direct, their tracks.

Notes

1 'Obie slams retail giants', *Musicday* (Music Week Publication), 15 September 1992, p.1.

2 'Virgin Chief Burke dismisses Obie's baked beans slur', *Musicday* (Music Week Publication), 16 September 1992, p.1.

3 'Putting on the right style', *Music Business International*, June 1991, p.27.

4 'Room for a view', *Music Business International*, June 1991, p.27.

5 'Growing up with older customers', *Music Business International*, June 1991, p.25.

6 'Tower power', promotional supplement, *Music Week*, 5 December 1992.

7 'Putting on the right style', *Music Business International*, June 1991, p.27.

8 'Our Price revamp targets Woolies', *Music Week*, 15 May 1993, p.1.

References

Chambers, I. (1985) *Urban Rhythms*, Basingstoke, Macmillan.

de Certeau, M. (1984) *The Practice of Everyday Life*, London, University of California Press.

du Gay, P. (1992) '"Numbers and souls": retailing and the de-differentiation of economy and culture', *British Journal of Sociology*, vol.44, no.4.

Fiske, J. (1992) 'The cultural economy of fandom' in Lewis, L. (ed.) *The Adoring Audience: Fan Culture and Popular Media*, London, Routledge.

Hacking, I. (1986) 'Making up people' in Heller, T.C. *et al.* (eds) *Reconstructing Individualism*, Stanford, CA, University Press, pp.222–36.

Harker, D. (1980) *One for the Money: Politics and Popular Song*, London, Hutchinson.

Hugill, B. (1992) 'Top 40 on track for great jukebox in sky as single sales plummet', *The Observer*, 19 July, p.4.

Laclau, E. (1990) *New Reflections on the Revolution of Our Time*, London, Verso.

Lewis, G. (1991) 'Who do you love? The dimensions of musical taste' in Lull, J. (ed.) *Popular Music and Communication* (2nd edn), London, Sage.

Lull, J. (1987) 'Listeners' communicative use of popular music' in Lull, J. (ed.) *Popular Music and Communication*, London, Sage.

Martin M. (1991) 'The nineties' retail renaissance', *Music Week*, 20 April, pp.10–11.

MBI (1992) 'The power brokers on the shop floor', *Music Business International*, vol.2, no.11, pp.20–2.

Morris, M. (1988) 'Banality in cultural studies', *Discourse*, vol.10, pp.2–29.

Reibman, G. (1992) 'Hear music listens to retail call', *Billboard*, 19 September, p.58.

Rose, N. (1990) *Governing the Soul: The Shaping of the Private Self*, London, Routledge.

Scott, A. (1993) 'Our Price sharpens focus', *Music Week*, 29 May, p.6.

Smith, G. (1990) 'Stars in the stores', *The Independent*, 2 March, p.15.

Willis, P. (1990) *Common Culture: Symbolic Work at Play in the Everyday Cultures of the Young*, Milton Keynes, Open University Press.

Source: du Gay and Negus, 1994, pp.395–7,405–413

4.4 Peter Miller and Nikolas Rose, 'Mobilizing the consumer' (1997)

The pleasure of consumption

A mundane problem – how to increase ice cream sales in winter – can be taken as the starting point for the elaboration of a psychoanalytic notion of the consumer. This seems, at first sight, exactly the sort of endeavour attacked by the likes of Packard and Marcuse: the consumer industry, in an alliance with social scientists, was attempting to intrude on the sacrosanct domain of the private home and the psyche of the individual. Even in the privacy of the home, consumers were not to be free from the injunctions to consume according to certain patterns, to modify long-standing traditions to suit the revenue needs of corporations producing ever more standardized products, and to change the very nature of the individual to achieve such ends – in this case, to even out seasonal fluctuations in ice cream sales.

Isabel Menzies and Eric Trist sought to adapt the tools of psychoanalytic investigation that had already been developed at the Tavi [Tavistock Institute] for the study of the consumer – most notably the utilization of their newly discovered dynamics of 'the group' (Miller and Rose, 1994; see, for example, Menzies, 1960, pp.95–121). As far as ice cream was concerned, they began with the initial assumption that the 'ordinary private home was … the most likely market in which to realise a substantial increase in winter sales in the short term' (TIHR, 1950, p.1). The corollary of this was that the central objective was that of 'securing for ice cream an accepted and permanent place in the meal system of the family' (TIHR, 1950, p.1).

However, this initial assumption was quickly challenged once actual investigations were put into place. These used group discussions as technique of enquiry, a method broadly derived from the group work that had been pioneered at the Tavi by Wilfred Bion and which was to be used not just for therapeutic purposes but in such diverse settings as the investigations of poor industrial relations in a factory, group relations training courses, the education of general practitioners and marital therapists. The investigations of the psychodynamics of consumption was a further example of the versatility of the group for forcing into the open phenomena that would otherwise be almost invisible – in this case the unconscious meanings of goods. A group of potential consumers of ice cream – selected in a rather ad hoc

manner – were brought together and asked to discuss not this or that brand or product but ice cream in general; one investigator would sit with the group and prompt it along; another would take notes. Somewhat to the surprise of the investigators, the problem was not getting the group to start talking about the product, but getting them to stop – especially when the same technique was deployed later in the investigation of such things as motoring. And what was going on here, as the investigators perceived it, was a kind of free association which began from practical questions, of course, but which later took off into the underlying unconscious and preconscious dynamics of consumption.

As far as the consumption of ice cream in the home was concerned, there were technological problems to begin with: only 3 per cent of homes had refrigerators, and virtually none had home freezers. This meant that there was a kind of teasing quality to ice cream advertisements encouraging the consumption of ice cream at home, since there was no practical way of getting it. 'Why are they tempting and teasing us?' complained one consumer interviewed in the study (Menzies and Trist, published in a revised version in Menzies Lyth, 1989a, p.77). The idea of ice cream in the home became unreal, because the majority of consumers *saw no reality in it for themselves.*

There were also problems concerning the consumption of ice cream in the 'family meal system', a 'particularly central and emotionally charged feature in the culture of the home' (TIHR, 1950, p.2). For the housewife, having ice cream with meals in the home 'was sometimes experienced as rather an assault on the role of the housewife as provider of food: she had to do nothing to prepare it; gave nothing of herself' (Menzies Lyth, 1989a, p.76). Ice cream was a competitor to the custard the housewife made herself. The 'housewife's need to please her family by giving them what they wanted … was thus in conflict with her wish to sustain her feeding role' (Menzies Lyth, 1989a, p.76). Moreover, ice cream was a visible cost – 1s 6d or even 2 shillings, whereas custard *apparently* cost nothing, it was made from 'free' ingredients already available at home.

A way of understanding these tensions and conflicts was needed if manufacturers were to avoid the anger and hostility that consumers were held to feel, and the possibility that this might lead them to dismiss the idea of ice cream in the home. The psychoanalytic notion of 'pleasure foods' met this need. The concept of pleasure foods, a fusion of Kurt Lewin's field theory and psychoanalysis, 'brought together the environmental influences, the "field" and the internal situation through which the consumer responded to field forces' (Menzies Lyth, 1989a, p.72). Oral gratification, through the consumption of pleasure foods, was viewed as a way of alleviating current anxieties and depression, for such emotions were held to be derivatives of the infantile anxiety and depression connected with the loss of the breast. Compensation for the loss of the breast was sought in the consumption of substitute objects – the so-called pleasure foods. The need for pleasure foods appeared particularly acute in those situations that 'awaken again the residues of the earlier situations which to a greater or lesser extent exist in everyone' (Menzies Lyth, 1989a, p.72).

This was not to say the pleasure foods had no food value, but that their food value was viewed as secondary in relation to the pleasure they gave in eating. In a paper delivered to the Annual Conference of the Society for Psychosomatic Research in 1969, almost 20 years after the ice cream studies, Isabel Menzies drew more explicitly upon the work of Melanie Klein, to argue that the concept of the inner world, in particular the notion of the 'internal society', was what linked the psychological and the social (published as Menzies Lyth, 1989b). The internal society was 'composed of images, concepts, memories and fantasies about people, in a great complexity of roles, functions and relationships' (1989b, p.60). To become a significant influence on the individual, an external stimulus had to be taken in and experienced inside. This notion of the internal world and the internal society was 'a particularly significant influence in determining behaviour about food and eating' for 'in the earliest experiences that from the matrix of the internal society, feeding, the relationship with the mother and emotional experiences are inextricably linked' (Menzies Lyth, 1989b, p.61). The result of this early experience was that eating becomes and remains a significant social and emotional activity: 'people never eat alone or uninfluenced by others, since they always eat in the context of the internal society' (Menzies Lyth, 1989b, p.62).

Ice cream illustrated this point vividly, for it was, Menzies argued, 'the pleasure food *par excellence*' (Menzies Lyth, 1989a, p.73). The significance of ice cream stemmed 'from its symbolic closeness to the breast and the mother–child relationship' (Menzies Lyth, 1989a, p.69). The very term 'ice cream' established a 'link with the breast, but better than that, a breast that gives cream', a theme sustained 'in the little round blobs in which ice cream is served in dishes and in the cones or cornets in which it is sold from shops, kiosks or barrows'. This made one lick or suck the ice cream, while 'the more "sophisticated" children or childish adults bite off the narrow end off the cone and treat it as a nipple through which they suck down the ice cream' (Menzies Lyth, 1989a, pp.69–70). Ice cream has 'great power to act as a substitute for the breast, to wipe out anxieties and depression' (Menzies Lyth, 1989a, p.73). The physical sensation of eating ice cream, when 'optimally experienced', is so complete that it is capable of blotting out all other concerns. As for the child at the breast, there are no bad things left, and 'reality consists only of the good substance and the pleasure it gives' (Menzies Lyth, 1989a, p.73).

There are potential pitfalls in this experience of eating. The ice cream can be too cold, in which case pleasure becomes neuralgic pain, good turns to bad. Also, because of the 'consumer's infantile concrete attitude to ice cream' (Menzies Lyth, 1989a, p.75), because it is either in sight and in mind, or out of sight and out of mind, if the ice cream is not immediately available to satisfy the impulsive desire it is likely that this will touch off 'violent infantile hostility against the ice cream manufacturers' (Menzies Lyth, 1989a, p.70). The availability and condition of the ice cream supplied was thus crucial. Ice cream manufacturers were dealing with a dynamic that was much more complex than they had appreciated. They were, in effect, seeking to intervene in the mother–child relationship. For when the child is in a completely dependent position, food is love and security. In the mind of the child 'love is loving acts and good things, particularly the good breast' (Menzies Lyth, 1989a, p.70). Deprivation of the breast can lead to 'aggressive omnipotent phantasies which are followed by guilt, depression and anxiety. The breast and the good food it gives have complete and immediate power to assuage these feelings' (Menzies Lyth, 1989a, p.71). Ice cream eating was thus inextricably linked to deep-seated characteristics of human relations.

Even outside the home, the psychological significance of ice cream could not be ignored. Ice cream was already consumed in reasonably large quantities in the cinema, in hospitals and in midday restaurants and industrial canteens. In the cinema, the 'solitary gluttony' of eating ice cream could be hidden, but the 'need for perfection, the anger at being teased and tantalized' if it was not immediately available were ever-present potential problems (Menzies Lyth, 1989a, p.82). Because of the danger of arousing infantile reactions such as hostility and anger towards manufacturers, ice cream supplies in places such as cinemas should never run out, Menzies strongly recommended to the manufacturers. In institutions such as hospitals, where stress and anxiety are high for both staff and clients, ice cream could be particularly valuable, acting as a 'motherly' food, a 'sign that the hospital cared'. In midday restaurants and industrial canteens, pleasure foods act as compensation for having to eat away from home. This suggested that 'ice-cream consumption might be high in such places and could easily be stimulated' (Menzies Lyth, 1989a, p.85).

The concept of pleasure foods thus provided a novel interpretive grid for understanding the consumption of ice cream in a wide variety of settings. Clear recommendations followed from it. Manufacturers eager to build up winter trade in ice cream sales could be told that to increase sales in the home meant introducing more 'exotic' flavours, rather than restricting choice to vanilla (Menzies Lyth, 1989a, p.83). Also, there was 'considerable potential' for increasing sales to canteens and midday restaurants by means of a 'direct approach to the consumer and by sales efforts directed at gatekeepers' (Menzies Lyth, 1989a, p.86). A combined approach was called for in view of the possibility of arousing strong negative feelings on the part of the consumer if awakened desire is not met.

References

Menzies, I. (1960) 'Social systems as a defence against anxiety', *Human Relations*, vol.13, pp.95–121.

Menzies Lyth, I. (1989a) 'The development of the ice cream as a food', a revised version of a paper written with Eric Trist and originally entitled 'Changing the perspective on the psychological position of ice cream in society', published in Menzies Lyth, I. *The Dynamics of the Social: Selected Essays, Volume II*, London, Free Association Books.

Menzies Lyth, I. (1989b) 'Psychosocial aspects of eating', paper delivered to the 13th Annual Conference of the Society for Psychosomatic Research, London (1969). Reprinted as 'Introduction: psychosocial aspects of eating' in Menzies Lyth, I., *The Dynamics of the Social: Selected Essays, Volume II*, London, Free Association Books.

Miller, P. and Rose, N. (1994) 'On therapeutic authority: psychoanalytic expertise under advanced liberalism', *History of the Human Sciences*, vol.7, no.3, pp.29–64.

TIHR (1950) 'Changes in habits concerning the development of ice cream as a food', Document no.248 (September), Tavistock Institute of Human Relations.

Source: Miller and Rose, 1997, pp.7–11

5

Sociology and social movements: theories, analyses and ethical dilemmas

Merl Storr

Contents

1 Introduction

This chapter is about social movements and their relationships with sociology. So far in this book you have been thinking about the ways in which sociology is enmeshed in issues of power and government. Chapter 2 in particular explored sociology's relationship with 'governmentality' and public administration, and Chapter 3 explored sociology's engagement with the role of the public sphere in liberal democracies. In this chapter you will start to think about sociology's relationship with groups and individuals whose politics take place not just *outside*, but often *against*, the institutions of liberal democracy. How can sociologists make sense of this kind of politics? How, for that matter, can movement activists make sense of sociology? And in whose interests should they (we) attempt to do so?

Chapter 3's discussion of the public sphere mentioned some significant contemporary social movements – the Zapatista movement, and the 'carnivalesque' anti-capitalist movement (to which you will be returning later in this chapter). As these examples demonstrate, the term 'social movement' is generally used to refer to a form of politics which takes place outside of the institutions of parliament or government; it is sometimes also called 'extra-parliamentary' or 'street' politics. This form of politics is usually *oppositional* – in other words, social movements are usually articulated *against* something. Thus movements may be against particular laws or institutions, or against the political system as a whole; they may be against prevailing social or cultural 'norms' and structures. Even movements which aim to *preserve* existing social or political arrangements tend to be articulated against some *threat* to those arrangements, whether real or imagined: for example, an anti-feminist men's movement would fall into this category.

Contemporary social movements can take many forms: strikes, demonstrations, riots, street parties, armed uprisings, sit-ins, pickets, letter-writing campaigns and the throwing of custard pies at public figures are just some of them. Moreover, the diversity of social movements lies not just in their forms of action, but also in the causes they promote or defend. Some social movements come from the left of the political spectrum, such as anti-capitalist and socialist movements; some come from the right, such as neo-Nazis or the US militia movement; some movements cannot easily be situated within the traditional right–left spectrum at all, such as animal rights or 'deep ecology' movements. And some movements are at loggerheads with other movements, such as pro-choice and pro-life movements on the issue of abortion. The sociology of social movements, then, faces the daunting task of making sense of a great cacophony of political voices.

ACTIVITY 1

Go back to the three 'ideal types' of sociological thought – political traditions, rational-scientific approaches and the expressionist tradition – outlined in Chapter 1 of this book. Into which of these ideal types do you think the sociology of social movements is most likely to fall?

At first sight the obvious answer seems to be that the sociology of social movements will fall into the ideal type of *political traditions*. Such traditions stress the strong relationship between sociological theory and social action, and insist that all knowledge claims, including those of sociology itself, are inherently political. This tradition makes particular sense if we assume – not unreasonably – that most sociologists of social movements will tend to be fairly sympathetic towards, or at least benignly interested in, the movements they study.

However, the other two ideal types are by no means uncommon in the sociology of social movements. *Rational-scientific approaches* can be used, for example, to categorize social movements into different types, or to analyse the ways in which activists make political decisions. In fact one of the most influential strands in the sociology of social movements, resource mobilization theory (RMT), fits very much into the rational-scientific tradition. You will be examining RMT in section 3 of this chapter.

new social movements

The sociology of social movements also draws heavily on the *expressionist tradition*. This tradition can be found in approaches to **new social movements** which focus on the ways in which such movements re-imagine cultural meanings and values. In this sense the strand of sociology known as new social movement theory falls into the expressionist tradition: you will be examining new social movement theory in section 4. Some social movements themselves also draw on many of the key concepts explored by expressionist sociology. In particular, the concept of difference is central to many social movements which mobilize around the idea that certain groups or individuals (for instance, lesbians and gay men, 'homeless' people, disabled people) are marginalized or excluded by mainstream society. The expressionist tradition's interest in cultural and artistic matters is also relevant where social movements themselves use cultural and artistic forms of protest: as we will see in sections 3 and 4, groups such as the Gay Liberation Front and Reclaim the Streets deliberately use cultural forms such as street theatre, music, dance and visual arts as part of their activist repertoire.

This raises another crucial point about the relationship between sociology and social movements: the relationship is a two-way street. Sociologists do not just study different forms of activism; activists also draw on different forms of sociology. For example, the Reclaim the Streets London group's website includes links not just to other activist groups, but also to sociological texts and discussions (of, for example, Guy Debord, André Gorz, Murray Bookchin, situationism). This two-way relationship presents a particular set of *ethical* issues for sociologists of social movements. If I participate in, say, a demonstration, am I there as a sociologist or as an activist? What difference does this make to the risks I might take, or the decisions I might make, during the demonstration? Can I turn the words, ideas, attitudes and stories of my fellow activists into material for academic papers – and, if so, do I need to obtain written consent from every single person involved in the demonstration with me? These questions about the relationship between sociology and activism have profound implications for the *practice* of sociology. Another, perhaps even more difficult set of ethical questions arises when I reflect on my choices about the demonstrations I will and will not attend. I may be more than willing to participate in an anti-capitalist protest or a Lesbian and Gay Pride event, but I am by no means willing to march with neo-Nazi groups or to attend fascist demonstrations. But as a sociologist, shouldn't I be just as interested in neo-Nazi social movements as I am in gay or anti-capitalist social movements? Can – or indeed should – the sociology of social movements make value judgments to distinguish 'good' social movements from 'bad' ones? You will be considering some of these ethical dilemmas in section 5.

The aims of this chapter are:

1   To introduce you to some key aspects of the sociology of social movements.

2   To examine the concept of 'social movements'.

3   To explore two of the most influential theoretical approaches in the current sociology of social movements: resource mobilization theory and new social movement theory.

4   To introduce two specific activist groups as 'case studies' for the exploration of these theories: the Gay Liberation Front and Reclaim the Streets.

5   To consider some of the ethical issues involved in the practice of the sociology of social movements.

2 The concept of social movement

Before we can embark on our exploration of the sociology of **social movements**, we need to be a little clearer about what we mean by the term 'social movement'. So far I have been using terms like 'social movement', 'demonstration', 'activist group' and 'protest' fairly loosely, and you (I hope!) have generally known what I mean by these terms. But, of course, for the purposes of sociological analysis, we need to be clearer in our use of such terminology.

social movements

2.1 What is a social movement?

ACTIVITY 2

Take a few minutes to jot down your own definition of 'social movement'. Try to define it in a way which would distinguish it from terms such as 'demonstration', 'activist group' or 'protest'.

Activity 2 is more difficult than it might appear, especially when we try to distinguish 'social movement' from other terms. In fact, sociologists themselves have not always been very clear in their use of these terms. As Mario Diani complains:

> Even an implicit, 'empirical' agreement about the use of the term ['social movement'] is largely missing. In fact, social and political phenomena as heterogeneous as revolutions, religious sects, political organizations, single-issue campaigns are all, on occasion, defined as social movements. [...] This terminological ambiguity entails, however, a loss of specificity and theoretical clarity. This is reflected in that many valuable analyses of social movements pay hardly any attention to the concept itself. ... The question therefore rises, what does 'social movements' specifically refer to?
>
> (Diani, 1992, p.2)

Frustrated by this state of affairs, Diani provides his own definition of the term 'social movement' based on his reading and synthesis of a wide range of social movement studies.

READING 5.1

Now turn to Reading 5.1, Mario Diani's 'The concept of social movement' (1992). When you have finished reading, compare Diani's definition of 'social movement' with your own. Does Diani's definition include things that you haven't thought of? Does your definition include things that Diani hasn't thought of?

According to Diani, the key characteristics of a social movement as such are:

- It is an informal network of interactions between a number of activist groups, individuals or organizations.
- It is defined by a sense of collective identity among participants.
- It is engaged in political or cultural conflict over social change.

Diani is attempting to find a consensus among social movement theorists which he feels to be implicit in their work, despite their apparent differences and disagreements. By its very nature this is bound to be a thankless task – he is bringing together the work of sociologists who dispute one another's theories. Many of the sociologists whose work he cites will disagree with his final definition of 'social movement' – and you too may disagree with him and prefer your own definition. For the purposes of this chapter, though, I will be using Diani's definition to help guide our way through the debates. When you have finished this chapter, you may want to go back to your own definition and compare it again with Diani's: maybe your definition would lead to different questions (and different conclusions) about social movements than those discussed here.

Diani's definition is particularly useful for our purposes because it makes clear distinctions between social movements and other phenomena such as social movement organizations (SMOs), political parties, protest events (such as strikes or demonstrations) and coalitions. This makes it much easier for us to discuss the role and status of particular groups and organizations within social movements. For example, in section 3 we will be discussing the Gay Liberation Front (GLF); Diani's definition allows us to see the GLF as part of a network of groups, individuals and organizations involved in the lesbian and gay movement. Similarly, in section 4, we will be considering Reclaim the Streets as part of a network of groups, individuals and organizations involved in a larger social movement.

Now that we have established a working definition of social movements, we can turn to a substantive discussion of particular social movement theories.

SUMMARY OF SECTION 2

In this section we have seen that:

1   There has been little explicit agreement amongst sociologists on a definition of social movements as such.

2   Diani (1992) has argued that this lack of agreement damages social movement studies as a whole, and has put forward a definition of 'social movement' which attempts to synthesize elements from different theories.

3   According to Diani's definition: 'A social movement is a network of informal interactions between a plurality of individuals, groups and/or organizations, engaged in a political or cultural conflict, on the basis of a shared collective identity' (1992, p.13).

4   Diani distinguishes clearly between social movements as such and allied phenomena like protest events and social movement organizations (SMOs).

3 Resource mobilization theory

In this section we will examine resource mobilization theory, one of the most influential strands in contemporary social movement studies. Rather than examine this theory in a vacuum, we apply it to a real-life case study: this will give you an opportunity to think about the sociology of social movements as a *practice* as well as a set of theories. Our case study in this section will be the lesbian and gay movement, and we will focus on the Gay Liberation Front (GLF) as our test-bed for resource mobilization theory. Before embarking on our discussion of the GLF, however, we should first establish the basic claims of resource mobilization theory.

3.1 McCarthy and Zald's argument

Resource mobilization theory (RMT) is most closely associated with the work of John D. McCarthy and Mayer N. Zald, two sociologists working in the USA. Resource mobilization theory starts with a very simple question: why do people get involved in social movements? The obvious answer seems to be that people get involved in social movements because they want to bring about social change, and that they want to bring about social change because of their own experiences of disadvantage, oppression or deprivation. Thus, we might expect lesbians and gay men to join a movement for social change because they suffer homophobia, or black people to join an anti-racist movement because they suffer racism.

However, McCarthy and Zald (1987) suggest that this is an over-simplification. On the one hand, some people experience oppression without joining a social movement, and this may be a rational choice on their part. Not all lesbians and gay men actively participate in the lesbian and gay movement: why should I risk losing my job in the here and now by 'coming out' at work, in the hope that homophobia in general will end at some indefinite point in the future? On the other hand, some people who do not directly experience oppression are nevertheless sympathetic to, and even join, social movements. Some white people participate in anti-racist movements even though they themselves do not suffer racism; as we will see, some heterosexuals participated in the Gay Liberation Front. If this is the case, why do some people and not others join social movements? In other words, *how do social movements mobilize people to participate?*

READING 5.2

Now read Reading 5.2, 'Resource mobilization and social movements: a partial theory' by John D. McCarthy and Mayer N. Zald (1987/1977).

While you are reading, note down the main points of McCarthy and Zald's argument. Don't worry too much at this stage about whether you agree with their theory – just concentrate for now on understanding it.

The central insight of resource mobilization theory is actually very basic: social movements need resources. Suppose you and I are members of a social movement. If we want to call a meeting, we need to have somewhere to hold it.

If we want to publicize a protest action such as a demonstration, we need to be able to make leaflets, posters or fliers, and to reproduce large numbers of them, and to distribute them widely. If we want to book our meeting space or contact our printer, we are probably going to need a telephone – and some money to pay for it all. As well as these material resources, we are more likely to be successful if we can call on other, less tangible resources – an address book full of useful contacts, practical know-how in poster design or website construction, and even just the time and energy to devote to our activism. According to resource mobilization theory, the more of these resources we can mobilize, the more likely we are to be successful in our pursuit of social change.

The task of a social movement organization (SMO), therefore, according to resource mobilization theory, is to increase its pool of available resources. It does this by persuading people to become active members who will place some of their own resources at the disposal of the organization. In its search for greater resources, a social movement organization will not necessarily limit itself to those who stand to benefit directly from social change: thus some lesbian and gay organizations may try to secure the participation, and hence the resources, not just of lesbians, gay men and bisexuals, but also of sympathetic heterosexuals. And since there might be perfectly rational reasons for individual lesbians, gay men or bisexuals not to join the organization, it is no less irrational for heterosexuals to join than it is for anyone else.

As you can see, resource mobilization theory tends to assume that both social movement organizations and individuals operate on a rational basis and make rational choices. You may also have noticed that resource mobilization theory tends to discuss social movements as if they were companies in search of investors – indeed McCarthy and Zald elsewhere explicitly compare social movements with industries, and deliberately use terminology from economics to analyse social movements (see, for example, 1987, pp.21–2). These features of resource mobilization theory tend to produce strong reactions in readers, and you may already have formed an opinion of your own about them. But before we evaluate the strengths and weaknesses of resource mobilization theory, let's try to apply it to our first case study: the Gay Liberation Front.

3.2 Case study 1: the Gay Liberation Front

The origins of homosexual politics can be traced back as far as the 1860s. However, the wave of activism generally referred to as 'gay politics' is specifically rooted in the 1960s. Of course, it is impossible to pinpoint an exact date for the beginning of any social movement, but it has become conventional to date the beginning of gay politics from the Stonewall riots which took place in New York in June 1969. These riots, which lasted three days, were sparked when police raided a gay bar called the Stonewall Inn – such police raids were routine in gay bars at the time – and the gay clientele turned angrily on the police. That anger spilled over into subsequent meetings of existing homosexual rights groups; some members now decided that these groups were not radical or assertive enough, and broke away to form the Gay Liberation Front of New York. As news of the Stonewall riots and their aftermath spread, gays in London decided to set up their own Gay Liberation Front, which functioned from 1970 until 1974. GLF groups also appeared in other cities in the UK and elsewhere during the early 1970s. GLF was marked by an assertive, often angry style, an insistence on the importance of 'coming out' rather than hiding one's sexual identity, and a rejection of what it saw as the timid 'respectability' of existing homosexual rights groups like the Campaign for Homosexual Equality (Weeks, 1977).

London GLF engaged in more than three years of energetic and high-profile activity – including street theatre, hit-and-run protest actions called 'zaps', public demonstrations, political discussions, experiments in communal living, London's first ever Gay Pride march in 1972, and an amazing amount of dressing up. GLF's

Figure 5.1 *Dressing up at London's first Gay Pride event in 1972*

eventual demise was precipitated at a meeting in 1972 by a mass walk-out of women in protest at what they saw as sexism on the part of some of the men. Those who were left behind fell prey to infighting and exhaustion, and finally GLF imploded in 1974. However, its influence continues to this day:

> If you see GLF as a dandelion which grew, flowered and then degenerated into a fluffy but insubstantial head full of seeds which were then blown by several gusts into new areas of the meadow, it is easy to understand the way in which it is connected to a whole host of major lesbian and gay initiatives of the 1970s, 1980s and even 1990s.
>
> (Power, 1995, p.283)

After the collapse of the GLF, subsequent waves of lesbian and gay activism took on new challenges during the 1980s and 1990s. Lesbians and gay men joined together in the 1980s to protest at a range of Conservative policies, particularly the notorious Section 28 of the Local Government Act (1988) which prohibits the 'promotion' of homosexuality by local authorities; the disaster of HIV/AIDS in gay communities also became a focus of mobilization throughout the 1980s and 1990s. In the early 1990s a new wave of 'queer politics', advocated by groups such as Queer Nation, Lesbian Avengers and OutRage!, defined itself against what it saw as the timid 'respectability' of 1990s' gay politics – just as the GLF in its time had defined itself against 'homosexual' politics (Watney, 1994). Queer activists launched a series of high-profile protest actions: these included street theatre, 'zaps' and demonstrations of a kind which GLF would have recognized. The late 1990s also saw a vigorous and ultimately successful campaign to equalize the age of consent for sex between men – one of the GLF's original demands (see Box 5.1), and still the only one to have been achieved. All of this subsequent activity – including queer activism – included participants from the old GLF.

BOX 5.1: THE GAY LIBERATION FRONT DEMANDS …

- that all discrimination against gay people, male and female, by the law, by employers, and by society at large, should end
- that all people who feel attracted to a member of their own sex be taught that such feelings are perfectly normal
- that sex education in schools stop being exclusively heterosexual
- that psychiatrists stop treating homosexuality as though it were a problem or sickness, thereby giving gay people senseless guilt complexes
- that gay people be as legally free to contact other gay people through newspaper ads, on the streets and by any other means they may want, as are heterosexuals, and that police harassment should cease right now
- that employers should no longer be allowed to discriminate against anyone on account of their sexual preferences
- that the age of consent for gay males be reduced to the same as for straights
- that gay people be free to hold hands and kiss in public as are heterosexuals.

Source: Power, 1995, pp.23–4

So what can resource mobilization theory tell us about the GLF – and vice versa? I want you now to try to assess the strengths and weaknesses of resource mobilization theory by applying it to an analysis of the GLF.

READING 5.3

Now read Reading 5.3, 'Power to the people', which is taken from Lisa Power's (1995) oral history of the GLF. When you have done so, go back to your notes on McCarthy and Zald (Reading 5.2), and try to apply their argument to the GLF. In particular, you should think about the following questions:

■ What resources did the GLF mobilize?

■ Who participated in the GLF, and what resources did they have at their disposal?

It is clear even from this short extract that the GLF mobilized a huge pool of resources. The meeting spaces were at the London School of Economics (LSE); a bookshop provided GLF with its first postal address; meetings were publicized through leaflets which participants produced and distributed themselves; GLF went on to produce and distribute its own newspaper *Come Together*, which in turn was inspired by the US publication to which participants clearly also had access. In addition to these material resources, GLF made enormous demands on the time and energy of its participants. This was perhaps the richest resource of all – as one participant recalls elsewhere in Power's book, 'I had a meeting every night for the first eighteen months of GLF' (1995, p.76). In respect of its need for resources, then, the GLF fits in very well with McCarthy and Zald's analysis of social movements.

It is therefore not surprising that most of the GLF participants in this extract seem to have been people with considerable resources at their disposal. Many were students with access to LSE resources; some were academics; some worked in left-wing or counter-cultural bookshops, and had useful contacts and facilities there; some were working in less 'liberal' jobs, but many of these seem to have been fairly well-off – a dentist, a City manager. (Note, too, that GLF participants included some sympathetic heterosexuals, in line with McCarthy and Zald's argument that movement participation is based on rational choice rather than just personal experience of oppression.) Of course, this does not mean that everyone in the GLF was middle class and/or a student – indeed, Paul Theobald explicitly says that he was not – but it does seem, from this and other accounts, that middle-class people and students made up a very significant proportion of GLF participants.

This demonstrates one of the key strengths of RMT: its ability to explain the tendency of many social movements to be dominated by middle-class people and students. This tendency has often been noted by activists and sociologists alike. Activists in many recent social movements have struggled intensely over the middle-class character of their movement. **Linda Janes (2002)**, for example, notes the often conflicted status of class in feminist politics, as does Anne Phillips (1987); GLF participants also wrestled with issues of class and privilege within their ranks (Power, 1995). Sociologists' analyses of, for instance, the peace and ecological movements have also noted that activists are disproportionately middle-class, and are often young public sector professionals. Such observations have led to some lively debates about the role of class in the sociology of social movements (Pakulski,1995).

These debates about class and social movements also reveal one of the key weaknesses of RMT, which will lead us towards an alternative analysis of social movements in section 4. The problem with RMT's emphasis on resources is that it tends to reduce all sociological analysis of social movements to a form of economic analysis. RMT is not really interested in the aims of particular social movements, or the kinds of social change the movement wants to achieve, or the kinds of protest actions it uses to try to bring that change about; it is just interested in what resources the relevant social movement organizations can mobilize and how they try to increase those resources. In effect, resource mobilization theory sees all social movements as essentially middle-class, because it is middle-class people who have resources. This may or may not be a correct observation about social movements, but the problem is that resource mobilization theory can *only* see the movement's middle-class nature: there are many other important things about social movements which RMT cannot include in its analysis.

For example, although RMT may be able to produce a fairly convincing account of a social movement organization's attempts to garner resources, it has very little to say about the way in which participants then use those resources. Why do some social movements adopt particular protest 'styles' – such as digging tunnels, or holding street parties, or building communes – rather than others? Consider, for example, the propensity of many GLF participants – especially gay men – for wearing drag in public. Here is what one member of the GLF's Street Theatre group has to say:

> Street Theatre was formed there [in the Arts Lab in Camden]. I got very involved straight away. […] We had no regular place to meet so I opened up my office on Sunday afternoons, there were two big empty rooms upstairs. We planned our demos there. The first was quite simple. Howard Wakeling was a director and had a show on at the Aldwych. Somebody who worked at Berman's [the theatrical costumier] 'borrowed' the costumes from Fellini's *Satyricon*. We dressed up and walked down the Strand with banners to his show at the Aldwych, just a gentle stroll in costume. *(Stuart Feather)*
>
> (Power, 1995, pp.41–2)

Obviously this passage describes the mobilization of some formidable resources, and RMT might be able to produce a convincing analysis of that. But RMT cannot explain why Stuart Feather and his fellow activists wanted to dress up in costume in the first place. 'Radical drag' became increasingly important to many in the GLF, particularly among those who lived in the GLF communes from 1971 onwards, and it was deliberately used as a form of political action directed against heterosexual gender norms. Box 5.2 gives you a flavour of radical drag, and see Figures 5.2 and 5.3.

BOX 5.2

Drag was seen by many as politicizing in itself. The American activist Larry Mitchell asserted that, 'there is more to be learned from wearing a dress for a day, than there is from wearing a suit for life' (cited in Mieli, 1980, p.193). Some wore frocks to GLF dances, and some even to GLF meetings. The GLF's Street Theatre group believed that to wear drag on the underground or to the shops was an empowering act of confrontation. Gay men in bathing costumes picketed the trial of feminists charged with disrupting the Miss World contest, and in September 1971 drag played a central part in the GLF's most notorious zap. Operation Rupert: lesbians and gay men dressed as nuns released mice into the audience of the Christian rally, the Festival of Light, before climbing onto the stage and dancing the cancan in front of Cliff Richard and Malcolm Muggeridge.

A new kind of drag had evolved: Radical Drag. Its practitioners, the Rad Fems, were wary of straightforward female impersonation. 'We began to realise that there were ways of using drag', recalled GLF member Michael James, whose most famous creation was a half-man half-woman split right down the middle. 'It's a way of giving up the power of the male role. We were holding the mirror up to man, showing that we rejected what maleness stood for' (cited in Kirk and Heath, 1984, p.104). … They knew that there was a world of difference between how people reacted to men in frocks on a theatre stage, and how people reacted to them on the street. 'There are many questions we are just beginning to examine. Why is Danny La Rue a West End institution, when we get kicked out of our flats for wearing a skirt? Apparently it's alright if you're doing it for money, but perverted if you do it for personal satisfaction' (*Come Together*, 1972). Although they felt they themselves were engaged in a kind of performance, as 'radical drag was constant street theatre, to make ordinary people think about sex roles' (Kirk and Heath, 1984, p.102).

Source: Baker, 1994, pp.239–40

Clearly, radical drag meant a great deal more to activists than just a mobilization of resources. It was also intended to mean something to the GLF's opponents (such as the Festival of Light) and bystanders (such as the 'ordinary' people on the underground or in the shops). RMT cannot include this dimension of *meaning* in social movements – but, according to some sociologists of social movements, this dimension of meaning is perhaps the most significant dimension of all. We will turn to the analysis of meaning in social movements in the next section.

Figure 5.3 Michael James – 'a half-man half-woman split right down the middle'

Figure 5.2 Howard Wakeling in radical drag

SUMMARY OF SECTION 3

This section has introduced you to resource mobilization theory (RMT) and has tested some of the claims made by RMT by applying it to the Gay Liberation Front.

1   RMT's central insight is that social movements need resources.

2   RMT assumes that social movements and their participants operate on a rational basis and make rational choices.

3   RMT adopts terminology from economics to analyse the ways in which social movement organizations (SMOs) attempt to maximize their pool of available resources.

4   RMT therefore offers a coherent explanation for the middle-class character of many social movement participants.

5   However, in doing so, RMT also tends to reduce social movement analysis to a form of class analysis.

6   There are many important aspects of social movements for which RMT cannot so easily account. In particular, RMT can shed little light on the choices participants make about protest styles, or on the meanings attached to protest actions by people both inside and outside the movement.

4 New social movement theory

In this section we will be examining a second influential strand in the sociology of social movements, a form of analysis known (rather confusingly) as new social movement theory. Once again, rather than looking at this theory in the abstract, we will be testing it against a real-life social movement. Our case history in this section will be the London branch of the activist network Reclaim the Streets.

4.1 Why 'new social movements'?

As you will see, new social movement theory (NSM) differs from resource mobilization theory in many important respects; one is that NSM is centrally concerned with the question of meaning in social movements. Before turning to this question, however, I would like briefly to consider another important difference between new social movement theory and resource mobilization theory. This difference lies in the two theories' understandings of power and society, and it helps to explain why new social movement theory has such a confusing name. What is *new* in 'new social movement theory' is not the theory but the social movements; and the social movements are new because the form of society in which they occur is new.

As **Peter Hamilton (2002)** explains, some sociologists have recently argued that the fundamental basis of society is changing: that we are no longer living in an industrial age in the traditional sense, and that we are moving instead into a knowledge-based or informational form of society. According to this view, power

information society

in an **information society** is not simply a matter of ownership of the means of production, as Marxist analyses of industrial society previously claimed; it is now a matter of access to, control over, and distribution of *information*. New social movement theory adopts this view of society and argues that social movements are therefore engaged in struggles over information – and, indeed, that those struggles take place *by means of* information. This is why it is called '*new* social movement theory': it is a theory which situates contemporary social movements as participants in a *new* kind of society. Alberto Melucci writes:

> The contemporary shift towards symbolic and informational resources bears thus on our definition of power and inequality as well. Inequality cannot be measured solely in terms of distribution and control of economic resources [...]; analysis of structural imbalances in society should refer more to a differentiation of positions which allots to some a greater and specific control over master codes, over those powerful symbolic resources that frame the information. There are organizers of information directing its flow which are more powerful, more stable than others; they 'inform' a wider portion of the field, they are keys to other information. The access to these primary codes is not distributed randomly and it corresponds to a distribution of social positions and power.
>
> (Melucci, 1996, pp.178–9)

Now, RMT is certainly not based on any kind of Marxist or class analysis of industrial society (Melucci, 1989) – but its inspiration, as we have seen, is from traditional economics and industrial analysis. Thus RMT is, in Melucci's terms, an 'old' social movement theory – a social movement theory which does not take account of the fundamental changes taking place in society, or of the corresponding changes in the nature of social movements themselves.

4.2 Melucci's argument

As you have probably gathered by now, new social movement theory is most closely associated with the work of the Italian sociologist Alberto Melucci. Let's look at his argument in a little more detail.

READING 5.4

Now study Reading 5.4, 'The new social movements revisited: reflections on a sociological misunderstanding', by Alberto Melucci (1995). While you are reading, note down the main points of Melucci's argument. When you have finished, go through your notes on Melucci and compare them with your notes on McCarthy and Zald (Reading 5.2). Try to clarify in your own mind the main points of difference between the two theories before reading on.

Melucci begins by insisting that sociologists should not talk about social movements as if they were just 'there' in the world as pre-given entities. A social movement is not a thing, according to Melucci, but a process. This is an immediate difference between Melucci on the one hand and McCarthy and Zald on the other. McCarthy and Zald say things like 'Each SMO has a set of *target goals* … The SMOs must possess resources … An SMO may focus its attention upon adherents …' (Reading 5.2). Thus McCarthy and Zald describe social movement organizations as if they were characters with intentions, views and plans of their own. But, in Melucci's view, sociologists who talk about social movements as 'wanting X' or 'doing Y' are guilty of sloppy thinking: as he puts it, 'social movements … should not be viewed as *personages*, as living characters acting on the stage of history, but as socially constructed collective realities' (Melucci, 1995, p.110).

Having argued that social movements are complex constructions rather than pre-given entities, Melucci goes on to outline what he considers some of the key characteristics of the 'new' social movements in informational societies. These are:

- *The centrality of information resources.* Informational societies are organized around access to, control of and distribution of information. Activists in such societies are therefore centrally concerned with information, and specifically with the production and circulation of meaning in society.

- *The self-reflexive form of action.* Because new social movements are struggles about meanings, activists must also take account of the meanings generated by their own actions. Indeed, actions are primarily formulated and understood as acts of communication: the medium is the message, or rather, in this case, the protest action is the message – and so is the activist him or herself.

- *The planetary dimension.* As **Hugh Mackay (2002)** points out, new technologies in informational societies reconfigure our experiences of space and time. Social movement participants are therefore able to make links – both conceptually and practically – with global issues, global events, and global networks of communication. The role of the internet in organizing and communicating social movement activities is especially important.

■ *The specific relation between latency and visibility.* There are times when social movement activity is extremely visible – such as during the heyday of the Gay Liberation Front – and other times when such activity seems to wane or even disappear. Thus sociologists and historians of social movements sometimes talk of 'waves' of social movements – for example, it has become standard practice to divide feminism into the 'first' and 'second' (and, for some recent writers, a 'third') wave (*Feminist Review*, 2000). For Melucci, a wave of activism should not be understood as a new arrival of energy which subsequently disappears; sociologists should rather focus on the networks of individuals and communities which periodically become visible as 'waves' of activism.

cultural

Lastly, Melucci argues that the success or failure of a social movement is not just about its 'political' achievements in the conventional sense, but also about more subtle **cultural** results. Since new social movement activists operate at the level of *meaning*, the very fact that a protest action has taken place in itself can change old meanings or create new ones. In particular, a protest action which challenges power structures, even if it is 'unsuccessful' in conventional terms, can successfully reveal the existence of those structures, and make people newly aware of the power imbalances in society.

All of this may seem rather abstract and hard to grasp, so let's try to make it more concrete.

4.3 Case study 2: Reclaim the Streets

Reclaim the Streets groups can now be found in various parts of Australia, Europe and the USA, but in this chapter we will be focusing on London Reclaim the Streets – the first and probably still the most influential Reclaim the Streets group. Extensive media coverage of protest events in which Reclaim the Streets has participated has given the group an unusually high profile in the UK. Much of this media coverage has been extremely hostile, and the context in which most non-activists (including, perhaps, yourself) have learnt about Reclaim the Streets has thus been largely negative. The account of Reclaim the Streets given in this chapter may therefore be unfamiliar, and perhaps surprising.

Although Reclaim the Streets is now widely known as an anti-capitalist group, it began life as one of a range of anti-roads groups in the 1990s. That decade saw a new wave of direct action and protest events, as George McKay explains:

> The sheer popularity and widespread nature of street protest and direct action emanating from single-issue campaigns is in part a response to a lack of confidence in – or even a rejection of – parliamentary democracy, a result of approaching two decades of what [was] effectively one-party rule in Britain. Furthermore, it's possible that nineties direct action was kick-started by the nationwide uprising around the Poll Tax, from Scotland southwards, the Trafalgar Square riot of 1990, the tax's successful scrapping (or modification). Indeed, the radicalizing effect of the Poll Tax legislation was twofold. The Poll Tax both appealed to a wide constituency in terms of the campaign against it – that is to say, it mobilized massive numbers in opposition to it – and, ironically, it contributed to people's disillusionment with parliamentary politics by virtue of its perceived connection of tax paying and voting rights.
>
> (McKay, 1996, p.128)

Another key event in the 1990s was the passing of the Criminal Justice Act 1994. The provisions of this Act included an effective ban on the rave parties which had become an important feature of early 1990s' youth culture. This criminalization of rave culture resulted in the politicization of many ravers, a constituency which had previously been largely uninterested in politics as such (McKay, 1996; Huq, 1999). The campaign against the Criminal Justice Bill brought together a number of existing activist groups, networks and social movement organizations, and spawned new ones.

A significant voice in this new wave of protest was the burgeoning anti-roads movement, which had been active since the 1970s but gained a new lease of life in the 1990s (Field, 1999). The campaign against the M3 motorway bypass at Twyford Down, for example, brought together social movement organizations like the Friends of the Earth with New Age travellers, local residents, and newly forming activist groups such as the self-styled Dongas tribe (McKay, 1996). But the key moment in the history of Reclaim the Streets was the campaign against the building of the M11 link road in east London, and in particular the extended protest activity around a row of squats in Claremont Road E11 in 1994. The Claremont Road protestors were finally evicted in November 1994, and Reclaim the Streets arose from the ashes of Claremont Road. Box 5.3 gives you a flavour of Claremont Road before the eviction.

BOX 5.3

The idea of direct action as performance was seen at its most vibrant in the squatted row of terraces at Claremont Road, which gained much of its impetus from the artwork it produced. … This short street was squatted and blocked off to prevent any vehicles entering it; it was an effort to reclaim a safe public space. Armchairs on the road blurred the distinction of internal and external space … There were two cafés, an information centre and an exhibition area, the Art House. In the Art House coinage was painted onto the enamel of a sink: money going down the drain. The street itself was full of public art, a chessboard painted on to the road, hubcaps as pawns, traffic cones and broken hoovers as other pieces. Sculptures in the road were also barricades. A car was 'pedestrianized': chopped in two with each half placed on opposite sides of the road, painted and joined by the black and white strips of a pedestrian crossing. Another car sprouted plants, had RUST IN PEACE on its side. Walls were painted with bright slogans and murals, including a daisy chain the length of the terrace. Installations vied with rubbish for attention. Above the street there was strong netting, an aerial walkway from tree to roof. A scaffolding tower built on a roof reached up into the air, described by Claremont Road residents variously as a critical parody of the Canary Wharf tower, an update of Tatlin's unbuilt monument to the Russian Revolution, a NASA rocket launcher for other campaigns. It was also a landmark visible for miles and an effective obstruction to bailiffs when the eviction finally took place.

Source: McKay, 1996, pp.151–2

READING 5.5

Now read about 'The evolution of Reclaim the Streets' in Reading 5.5.

'The evolution of Reclaim the Streets' was published in 1997, and charts the development of Reclaim the Streets from anti-roads to anti-capitalist action. A key turning-point in this process was the alliance between Reclaim the Streets activists and sacked Liverpool dock-workers. On the anniversary of the lock-out of dock workers by the Mersey Docks and Harbour Company, Reclaim the Streets activists joined the dockers in a protest action they dubbed 'Reclaim the Future'. This event marked the intensification of Reclaim the Streets' commitment to anti-capitalist action.

Reclaim the Streets became the object of considerable media attention following the 'J18' protest event – a 'Global carnival against capital' – in June 1999. J18 saw a massive Reclaim the Streets street party in London as well as a number of similar protest events in other cities around the world. This was swiftly followed by 'N30' in November 1999: again, Reclaim the Streets and other activist groups held protest actions, the most high profile of which took place in Seattle where the World Trade Organization was holding meetings. Most of the media attention to both J18 and N30 focused on outbreaks of violence – events at Seattle turned particularly ugly, with curfews imposed and the National Guard called out. Nevertheless, Reclaim the Streets activists continued their many protest actions, such as the 'guerrilla gardening' in London in May 2000 during which activists planted trees in some unexpected places. The Reclaim the Streets website (www.reclaimthestreets.net) was and remains central to the organization of, and participation in, Reclaim the Streets protest events and other activities: it greatly facilitates the co-ordination of global protest events like J18 and N30, as well as linking Reclaim the Streets with other activist groups and networks worldwide.

(a)

(b)

Figure 5.4
(a) Poster for the first Reclaim the Streets street party, Camden Town, May 1995
(b) The Camden street party, May 1995

How can Melucci's new social movement theory (Reading 5.4) illuminate the activities of Reclaim the Streets – and how can Reclaim the Streets help us to think through Melucci's theory? Write some brief notes on this before you read on.

Now read Reading 5.6, 'A note on disorganization' (2000), and Reading 5.7, 'Street politics' (2000), which are both statements placed on the Reclaim the Streets website in response to media coverage of protest events.

When you have done so, go back and look again at Reading 5.5, 'The evolution of Reclaim the Streets'.

Now turn back to your notes on Melucci (Reading 5.4), and try to apply his argument to Reclaim the Streets. In particular, you should consider whether Reclaim the Streets embodies any of the characteristics of new social movements identified by Melucci: concern with information resources, self-reflexive forms of action, the planetary dimension, and the relationship between latency and visibility. You should also consider Melucci's claim that movement activity operates at the level of meaning, and thus cannot be judged by conventional measures of political success or failure.

For Melucci, as you will recall, social movements are to be understood as complex processes rather than whole or pre-given entities. Melucci would therefore argue that we cannot really grasp the significance of Reclaim the Streets by simply reading a few Reclaim the Streets statements – as the author of 'Street politics' points out, statements are produced by individuals (or groups of individuals), not by Reclaim the Streets as a whole. Nevertheless, even by examining these necessarily partial statements, I think we can see some of the ways in which Reclaim the Streets embodies characteristics of new social movements as outlined by Melucci.

First, Reclaim the Streets activism is clearly concerned with ownership, control and distribution of information. In a literal and rather prosaic sense this is illustrated by Reclaim the Streets' crucial use of the internet. More profoundly, Reclaim the Streets actions are (among other things) attempts to intervene in the flow of information about cars, roads and capitalism. For example, the author of 'The evolution of Reclaim the Streets' argues that the focus on cars and roads is '*symbolic*' and meant to '*highlight* the social, as well as the ecological, costs of the car system' (my italics) – in other words, to disseminate anti-capitalist information about the 'car system'. Meanwhile, the author of 'Street politics' blasts mainstream journalists and their 'day-to-day reality of producing a quick piece to keep the wages rolling in, increase the papers [*sic*] share of the market, keep the editor happy, massage their ego' – a clear attack, in other words, on corporate ownership of the media and information resources.

Second, Reclaim the Streets protest events are self-reflexive forms of action. At street parties or 'guerrilla gardening', the medium – or rather, the action – is the message. Indeed this is characteristic not just of Reclaim the Streets events but also more generally of direct action – the recent wave of which, since the 1990s, has become known as 'DiY culture' (McKay, 1998). At street parties, pedestrians actively seize (albeit temporary) control of space usually devoted to cars, while simultaneously sending a message about the tyranny of car culture and the possibilities for change. Guerrilla gardening both enacts and represents the greening of London. As the author of 'The evolution of Reclaim the Streets' puts it, 'Direct action is not just a tactic; it is an end in itself'.

Figure 5.5 *Gnomes go undercover at the RTS guerrilla gardening event in Parliament Square, May 2000*

The planetary dimension is also clearly present in Reclaim the Streets' activities. The targets of Reclaim the Streets' protests (global capitalism, car culture, environmental damage, global poverty) are clearly planetary in scale. Some of the protests themselves (such as J18 and N30) are likewise globally conceived; but even localized actions such as street parties and guerrilla gardening are intended as responses to global issues.

The relationship between latency and visibility is also present in 'The evolution of Reclaim the Streets', which describes the emergence of Reclaim the Streets from existing communities and networks of anti-roads protestors, travellers, squatters, hunt saboteurs and ravers. These networks and communities were already oppositional – 'laboratories in which other views of reality are created', in Melucci's expressionist phrase; through specific events, such as the Criminal Justice Act and Claremont Road, they gelled into the visible form of Reclaim the Streets.

All of these characteristics taken together strongly suggest that Reclaim the Streets does operate at the level of meaning in Melucci's sense. Events such as street parties take usually busy road junctions and turn them into pedestrian dancing zones; they can be seen as a challenge to the conventional meanings of roads and pavements, and as an attempt to offer alternative meanings, 'a reversal of cultural codes' which 'addresses forms of power hidden in the allegedly neutral rationality of administrative apparatuses' in Melucci's terms (1995, p. 114). Most people most of the time accept that the road is for cars, as if this were a neutral 'fact'; Reclaim the Streets street parties demonstrate that this regulation of urban space is not a fact, but an exercise of power.

But this emphasis on meaning brings us to a problem with Melucci's theory. Melucci deliberately refuses the conventional criteria of 'success' and 'failure' in his approach to social movements; he insists that the mere fact of a protest action is a kind of success, since it is in itself a challenge to existing power structures ('the very existence of direct action is the message sent to the society'). On one level this is a persuasive – and appealingly optimistic – view of protest actions like Reclaim the Streets' guerrilla gardening. On another level, though, it is not very helpful. The M3 bypass was built at Twyford Down, despite the protests; the squatters at Claremont Road were evicted; the M11 extension went ahead; the trees planted by the guerrilla gardeners were removed. We could argue that, in his focus on meanings, Melucci has unduly neglected more material concerns. Some movements win – women won the vote, the age of consent for gay men was equalized – and others fail.

For example, in the case of Twyford Down, it has been commonplace for activists to insist that, despite the fact that the bypass went ahead, the campaign against it was nevertheless a form of victory.

> Resistance to road building is not just about stopping a particular project. Every delay, every disruption, every extra one thousand pounds spent on police or security is a victory: money that is not available to be spent elsewhere. '*Double the cost of one road and you have prevented another being built*' is an opinion often expressed by activists. In such an unequal struggle, to resist is to win.
>
> (Field, 1999, p.74)

ACTIVITY 4

Spend a few moments thinking about this quotation from Field (1999). Do you agree that 'to resist is to win'?

I am broadly sympathetic to Melucci's argument, including his emphasis on the centrality of meaning and communication to new social movements. But I am not sure that I agree that 'to resist is to win'. Twyford Down is gone. And paradoxically, even that activist opinion – 'Double the cost of one road and you have prevented another being built' – seems to betray some unease on this point. If we were to discover that in fact *none* of these protests ever prevented *any* planned new roads from being built, would the protests themselves still be victories?

SUMMARY OF SECTION 4

This section has introduced you to new social movement theory (NSM) and has tested some of the claims made by NSM by applying it to Reclaim the Streets.

1   NSM treats social movements as complex and processual social constructs rather than as whole or unified entities.

2   NSM is so called because it situates 'new social movements' in the context of a shift from industrial to informational society.

3   NSM therefore analyses social movements' activities as struggles over information and meanings.

4   NSM also identifies key characteristics of new social movements – concern with information resources, self-reflexive forms of action, the planetary dimension, and the relationship between latency and visibility.

5   NSM is therefore able to offer persuasive analyses of certain social movements, particularly those whose activists participate in forms of direct action and 'DiY culture'.

6   However, NSM's refusal of conventional criteria for movement 'success' and 'failure' can be seen as a significant drawback.

5 Sociologists and/or activists?

So far in this chapter we have been considering resource mobilization theory and new social movement theory as two separate strands in the sociology of social movements. In this final section I want to think about them in a more integrated way. Are resource mobilization theory and new social movement theory rival explanations of the same phenomena? Or are they asking different questions, and explaining different aspects of social movements?

In some respects RMT and NSM are clearly rivals. Most obviously, NSM has a different view of contemporary society – as 'informational society' – which RMT does not seem to share. This means that the two theories start from different, perhaps incompatible, sociological premises.

In other respects, though, it seems that they are asking different questions about social movements. Resource mobilization theory can be seen as a theory about the 'how' of social movements on a *motivational and material* level. It tries to explain how social movements gain resources, and how some individuals rather than others are able and willing to join social movements. RMT is therefore actually quite preoccupied – if only implicitly – with the questions of success and failure which, as we saw in the last section, new social movement theory deliberately avoids. RMT suggests that social movements are more likely to be successful if they can call on a large pool of resources, probably from middle-class participants. New social movement theory, on the other hand, can be seen as a theory about the 'how' of social movements on a *symbolic and communicative* level, the level of meanings. It offers an analysis of the underlying rationale for new social movement activity – the struggle over information resources – and of the forms and tactics of protest activity appropriate to the informational society.

From this perspective, one might almost suggest that RMT and NSM are complementary rather than rival theories. Indeed, Mario Diani and Donatella della Porta have recently pursued this line and attempted to integrate them into a single theoretical framework (della Porta and Diani, 1999). I don't have space to explore that attempt here; if you are interested you might like to have a look at it for yourself. Instead I would like to focus in this section on the ways in which both RMT and NSM deal – or fail to deal – with some of the ethical issues involved in sociological research about social movements. In particular I am going to explore some questions about the relationship between activism and sociology. These questions will ultimately return us to the three 'ideal types' of sociology we considered in section 1, and in particular to the tension between the 'detached' attitude of rational-scientific sociology and the 'engaged' attitude of political sociology.

5.1 Ethical dilemmas 1: relationships with activists

'Sociologists, when they carry out research, enter into personal and moral relationships with those they study, be they individuals, households, social groups or corporate entities' (BSA, 1994, p.1) All research involving the participation of others necessarily includes an ethical dimension. In the case of social movement studies, this dimension can be particularly acute. Sociologists of social movements are faced not only with ethical responsibilities to the activists they study, but also with ethical questions about the activists' relationships with the movement, the movements' opponents, and wider society. For example, some activists routinely risk verbal abuse, physical harm, state surveillance, arrest or imprisonment as part of their movement activity. The involvement of a professional sociologist might increase that risk, or decrease it, in which case the effectiveness of the movement might also be compromised. Alternatively, the movement may actively seek to abuse, harm or just frighten opponents or bystanders, as is the case with some forms of direct action which threaten or use violence. Should a sociologist intervene to prevent the harm of others, or just observe the harm as it takes place? And to what extent, if any, should she allow her relationship with activists to put herself at risk?

The relationship between sociologist(s) and activist(s) is therefore a real and concrete issue. Both resource mobilization theory and new social movement theory are, by definition, *theories*, not research methodologies. Nevertheless, they do both embody certain attitudes towards social movements, and contain implicit assumptions about the relationship between activists and sociologists.

ACTIVITY 5

Based on your reading so far in this chapter, what kinds of attitudes do you think resource mobilization theorists would take to the social movements they study? What attitudes do you think new social movement theorists would take?

It seems to me that resource mobilization theory takes an 'outsider' perspective on social movements. Resource mobilization theory examines movements from an external vantage point and makes judgements about the success or failure of each social movement organization's attempts to mobilize resources. The 'outsider' perspective is visible in the language used by resource mobilization theory, which as we saw earlier is drawn from economics and compares social movements with companies and industries. I imagine that Reclaim the Streets activists, for example, would not be very pleased to hear their anti-capitalist activities discussed in such terminology; but for resource mobilization theorists the activists' displeasure would be irrelevant to the sociological analysis of their resources.

Resource mobilization theory, as we saw above, is basically uninterested in the *aims* or *content* of social movements – it is mainly interested in questions about resources and their mobilization. Little or no direct input is required from activists themselves; resource mobilization theorists can simply gather their data by reading social movement organizations' literature, for example. The task of a sociologist using resource mobilization theory, then, would just be to analyse the data according to resource mobilization theory. She would not necessarily need to participate in, or even particularly sympathize with, the movement in question. Indeed, in some cases, such as Reclaim the Streets, participation in the movement is positively unlikely, and might actually be a hindrance: a sociologist who treats social movements as if they were capitalist industries does not seem likely to be an anti-capitalist activist, or vice versa.

New social movement theory, on the other hand, takes a rather more 'insider' perspective on movement activities. Indeed, because NSM insists that movements should be understood as processes rather than entities, it actively requires some form of engagement between activists and sociologists: sociologists have to listen to, observe and engage with movement processes as they unfold. Sociologists using NSM therefore have to form ongoing relationships with activists, and these relationships cut both ways. Activists are unlikely just to turn up in sociology departments offering themselves as fodder for sociological analysis; there has to be something in it for them too.

In fact Melucci (1989) devised a distinctive research methodology for new social movement theorists and activists. This methodology has an explicitly ethical orientation, and aims to build an *equal* relationship between activists and researchers. Such research is very emphatically *not* about sociologists examining activists from the outside like specimens in a jar; it is about activists and researchers forming mutual relationships for mutual benefit. This is achieved through a form of contract:

> The relationship between researcher and actor [i.e. activist] can take the form of a *contractual relationship*. Both parties control specific resources. The researcher possesses 'know-how', consisting of a research hypothesis and techniques which cannot be verified or utilized without the participation of the actors. Meanwhile actors exercise control over action and its meanings, but they also require reflective knowledge to increase their potential for action: here they may value the researcher's analysis of their action. The relationship is thus one of interdependence, but not of coinciding or overlapping roles. […] The contract is therefore founded on a temporary convergence of two demands: the scientific objectives of the researcher; and the actors' need to respond to problems arising from their social practice. […] On this basis an exchange is possible which is neither authoritarian nor instrumental.
>
> (Melucci, 1989, p.240)

Melucci insists that sociologists should not try to 'recreate' real-life activist situations or protest events, but should acknowledge that 'the experimental situation' is 'contrived' rather than 'natural' (p.241). He also insists that the roles of sociologist and activist in such research must be clearly separated, so that each research participant is clear about his or her place in the research process. This critical distance between the sociologists and the activists is a necessary *ethical* component of the research: it preserves the 'transparency' of the research process, with all parties clear about their obligations to one another.

Sociologists who adopt Melucci's research methodology are therefore implicated in the groups they study in two ways. First, there is a self-reflexive recognition that the researcher's interactions with the activists are themselves part of the process under observation. 'The researcher … activates a process in which the actors (i.e. activists) play as significant a role as he or she does' (p.239). Although there is a critical distance between the sociologists and the activists, they are still, of course, interacting, and that interaction is an unavoidable part of the research itself. Second, and more important for our discussion, the end results of the research are available to the activists who took part; and the activists are only likely to participate in the first place if they think the end-results will prove useful to them. In other words, while it may not be the primary intention of the sociologist to *help* the activists, that will almost certainly be one of the outcomes. Choosing to conduct NSM research with a group of activists is also, in this sense, choosing to support that group of activists. But how is one to decide which groups to research – and hence to help – and which to avoid?

5.2 Ethical dilemmas 2: good movements and bad movements

This is the second of our ethical dilemmas: how can sociologists distinguish 'good' movements from 'bad' movements? For example, can or should sociologists distinguish between movements which seek to end inequality and movements which seek to increase it? Can sociologists make a substantive distinction between, say, feminism and white supremacism?

Resource mobilization theory's relative lack of interest in movement aims or content means that it cannot really make such a distinction. Indeed, resource mobilization theory as an 'outsider' perspective on social movements does not need to concern itself with such questions very urgently: resource mobilization theorists, as we have seen, do not particularly need to engage or sympathize with the movements they study. A white supremacist organization may make just as interesting or uninteresting an object of study as a feminist or gay one. Indeed, some prominent resource mobilization theorists have conducted studies not just of social movements but of what they call 'counter-movements', and of the relationship between them. For example, John D. McCarthy has made extensive comparisons between pro- and anti-abortion movements, and Zald (with his colleague Useem) has discussed white social movement organizations' opposition to black civil rights in the US in the 1950s (Zald and McCarthy, 1987). These discussions do not include any comment on the rights and wrongs of any of the movements in question: they are conducted as rationalist-scientific analyses of objectively observed social phenomena.

New social movement research, however, explicitly rejects the rationalist-scientific model: it insists that the presence of the researcher must be taken into account as a factor in the research process itself. Its 'insider' perspective on social movement activity, and its reciprocal relationship with the activists in question, make the question of ethics rather urgent. A researcher using NSM must, of necessity, be prepared to make ethical judgements about the activist groups with which she is and is not prepared to work.

Unfortunately, NSM is no better equipped to make such judgements than resource mobilization theory. NSM analyses the *processes* at work in new social movements and the ways in which such movements negotiate the informational society. It has no framework for evaluating the political aims or ethical values of such movements. There is no inherent reason why a new social movement researcher could not help, say, right-wing militia activists in the USA in 'increasing their potential for action' by forming a contractual research relationship with them in the manner Melucci describes. In fact NSM might have some quite illuminating things to say about the right-wing militia movement in the USA. It could help to make sense of many militia activists' obsessive concern with information resources – their belief, for example, in the 'New World Order' conspiracy to control the media, and their attempts to circulate their own alternative meanings through what one right-wing radio show calls 'Info Wars' (Ronson, 2001). Activists' core belief in the New World Order conspiracy certainly demonstrates a 'planetary dimension' to the movement – as does their extensive use of the internet. One could similarly argue that they exhibit 'self-reflexive forms of action' (arming themselves, which has both practical and symbolic significance) and 'the relationship between latency and visibility' (networks of individuals, groups and organizations moved to take visible action following, for example, the so-called Siege at Ruby Ridge and the notorious events at Waco). I am not really trying to produce a new social movement analysis of the militia movement, but simply to point out that such an analysis is perfectly possible. I do not know of any actual analyses of the militia movement which use NSM, and I do not intend to conduct one myself. One reason for this is that I am fundamentally opposed to the right-wing militia movement. But that opposition is not based on my knowledge of the sociology of social movements; it is based on personal conviction.

Is this really a problem? Should we expect the sociology of social movements to be able to make ethical judgements about the aims and values of the movements it studies? This question takes us back to the sociological traditions with which we started this chapter. Rational-scientific sociologists would probably argue that sociology should merely analyse without judging; that sociology should be 'detached' – neutral, objective and value-free. Sociologists working in the political tradition would strongly disagree; for them sociology, by its very nature, is not 'detached' but engaged with the world it studies. They would argue not only that sociology *should* not be neutral, but that it *cannot* be neutral: all knowledge claims are political, including those made by the sociology of social movements. Tim Jordan, for example, writes:

> If there are no principles outside of movements to appeal to, then how do we know which political movements might be considered liberatory? How do we judge exploitation and liberation? It might seem easy to reject neo-fascist social movements, but on what basis could this be done? Other movements, such as animal liberation, pose more complex problems. [...] The problem emerges of how to tell if any particular movement is a liberatory one.
>
> (Jordan, 1999, pp.148–9)

The ethical dilemma outlined here by Jordan is serious, and has several layers. Should the sociology of social movements be able to tell the 'good guys' from the 'bad guys'? If it should, then how is it to make that distinction? And if it should not – if it is just a neutral exercise intended neither to help nor to hinder the movements it studies – what is the sociology of social movements actually *for*?

SUMMARY OF SECTION 5

This section has considered some of the ethical dimensions of the sociology of social movements, and has compared the respective ethical standpoints of resource mobilization theory (RMT) and new social movement theory (NSM).

1   RMT tends to take an 'outsider' perspective on social movement. It does not require a reciprocal relationship between sociologists and activists, and is not concerned whether its findings are useful or even acceptable to the activists it studies.

2   NSM takes a more 'insider' perspective and insists that sociologists and activists should form equal, reciprocal and mutually beneficial relationships. NSM sociologists will only be able to enter such relationships if activists feel they have something to gain – that is, if the findings are likely to be useful to the activists in some way.

3   Neither RMT nor NSM offers any grounds on which sociologists can distinguish between 'good' and 'bad' social movements. For RMT this may not be a problem, since RMT regards itself as value-free. For NSM, however, this clearly *is* a problem, because any research will necessarily be of potential benefit to the activists who participate in the research project.

4   The inability of both theories to distinguish 'good' from 'bad' movements leaves us with three questions:

(a)   Should the sociology of social movements be able to make value judgements about the movements it studies?

(b)   If so, how is it to make those judgements?

(c)   If not, what is the sociology of social movements actually for?

6 Conclusion

We have covered a lot of ground in this chapter, and if you have completed all the reading and activities you may feel that you have worked very hard! You have: considered a detailed sociological definition of social movements; explored two key strands in the sociology of social movements, and tested their theoretical claims against some real-life social movements; examined some of the ethical questions which arise when sociologists attempt to conduct research on or with activist groups; and contemplated some rather profound questions about ethics, values, the political or apolitical nature of knowledge claims, and the purpose of the sociology of social movements as such.

As well as all the details of the theories, case histories and ethical questions we have pursued, though, there is one thing which I would like you to take away from this chapter as a whole. RMT and NSM are not *just* different theories; they also embody different ways of *doing* sociology. Perhaps by now you have formed a preference for one approach over the other; I am quite sure that my own preferences have been apparent in my accounts of them in this chapter, no matter how hard I have tried to be 'neutral' about them. Whatever your view – and even if you have not yet formed a view on these difficult questions – remember that our preferences as sociologists are not just a matter of what we think. They are also about what we *do*.

References

Baker, R. (1994) *Drag: A History of Female Impersonation in the Performing Arts*, London, Cassell.

BSA (1994) *British Sociological Association Statement of Ethical Practice*, Durham, British Sociological Association.

della Porta, D. and Diani, M. (1999) *Social Movements: An Introduction*, Oxford, Blackwell.

Diani, M. (1992) 'The concept of social movement', *Sociological Review*, vol.40, no.1, pp.1–25.

Feminist Review (ed.) (2000) 'Feminism 2000: one step beyond?', *Feminist Review*, no.64, pp.1–2.

Field, P. (1999) 'The anti-roads movement: the struggle of memory against forgetting' in Jordan, T. and Lent, A. (eds) *op. cit.*.

Hamilton, P. (2002) 'From industrial to information society' in Jordan, T. and Pile, S. (eds) *op. cit.*.

Huq, R. (1999) 'The right to rave: opposition to the Criminal Justice and Public Order Act 1994' in Jordan, T. and Lent, A. (eds) *op. cit.*.

Janes, L. (2002) 'Understanding gender divisions: feminist persepctives' in Braham, P. and Janes, L. (eds) *Social Differences and Divisions*, Oxford, Blackwell/The Open University. (Book 2 in this series.)

Jordan, T. (1999) 'Too many universals: beyond traditional definitions of exploitation' in Jordan, T. and Lent, A. (eds) *op. cit.*.

Jordan, T. and Lent, A. (eds) (1999) *Storming the Millennium: The New Politics of Change*, London, Lawrence and Wishart.

Jordan, T. and Pile, S. (eds) (2002) *Social Change*, Oxford, Blackwell/The Open University. (Book 3 in this series.)

Kirk, K. and Heath, E. (1984) *Men in Frocks*, London, GMP Publishers.

Maheu, L. (ed.) (1995) *Social Movements and Social Classes: The Future of Collective Action*, London, Sage.

McCarthy, J.D. and Zald, M.N. (1987) 'Resource mobilization and social movements: a partial theory' in Zald, M.N. and McCarthy, J.D. (eds) *op. cit.*. First published in 1977.

McKay, G. (1996) *Senseless Acts of Beauty: Cultures of Resistance Since the Sixties*, London, Verso.

McKay, G. (ed.) (1998) *DiY Culture: Party and Protest in Nineties Britain*, London, Verso.

Mackay, H. (2002) 'New media and time–space configuration' in Jordan, T. and Pile, S. (eds) *op. cit.*.

Melucci, A. (1989) *Nomads of the Present: Social Movements and Individual Needs in Contemporary Society*, London, Hutchinson Radius.

Melucci, A. (1995) 'The new social movements revisited: reflections on a sociological misunderstanding' in Maheu, L. (ed.) *op. cit.*.

Melucci, A. (1996) *Challenging Codes: Collective Action in the Information Age*, Cambridge, Cambridge University Press.

Mieli, M. (1980) *Homosexuality and Liberation*, London, GMP Publishers.

Pakulski, J. (1995) 'Social movements and class: the decline of the Marxist paradigm' in Maheu, L. (ed.) *op. cit.*.

Phillips, A. (1987) *Divided Loyalties: Dilemmas of Sex and Class*, London, Virago.

Power, L. (1995) *No Bath But Plenty of Bubbles: An Oral History of the Gay Liberation Front 1970–73*, London, Cassell.

Reclaim the Streets (1997) 'The evolution of Reclaim the Streets', www.gn.apc.org/rts/evol.htm (downloaded 9 April 2001; accessed 15 December 2001).

Reclaim the Streets (2000) 'On disorganization', www.gn.apc.org/rts/disorg.htm (downloaded 9 April 2001; accessed 15 December 2001).

Reclaim the Streets (2000) 'Street politics', www.gn.apc.org/rts/streetpolitics.htm (downloaded 9 April 2001; accessed 15 December 2001).

Ronson, J. (2001) *Them: Adventures with Extremists*, London, Picador.

Watney, S. (1994) 'Queer epistemology: activism, "outing", and the politics of sexual identities', *Critical Quarterly*, vol.36, no.1, pp.13–27.

Weeks, J. (1977) *Coming Out: Homosexual Politics in Britain, from the Nineteenth Century to the Present*, London, Quartet.

Zald, M.N. and McCarthy, J.D. (1987) *Social Movements in an Organizational Society*, New Brunswick, NJ, and London, Transaction Publishers.

Readings

5.1 Mario Diani, 'The concept of social movement' (1992)

A proposal for synthesis

The definitions introduced above emphasise at least four aspects of social movement dynamics: a) networks of informal interaction; b) shared beliefs and solidarity; c) collective action on conflictual issues; d) action which displays largely outside the institutional sphere and the routine procedures of social life.

Networks of informal interaction

The presence of informal interactions involving individuals, groups and organisations is widely acknowledged. ...

... Such networks promote the circulation of essential resources for action (information, expertise, material resources) as well as of broader systems of meaning. Thus, networks contribute both to creating the preconditions for mobilization ... and to providing the proper setting for the elaboration of specific world-views and life-styles ...

In spite of their different emphasis, these definitions agree in recognising the plurality of actors involved in social movements and the informality of the ties which link them to each other. A synthetic definition of this aspect of the concept of social movements therefore may run as follows:

> A social movement is a network of informal interactions between a plurality of individuals, groups and/or organisations.

Shared beliefs and solidarity

To be considered a social movement, an interacting collectivity requires a shared set of beliefs and a sense of belongingness. Respective authors refer to 'a set of opinions and beliefs' (McCarthy and Zald); 'solidarity' (Melucci); 'identity' (Touraine, Melucci, Tilly). ...

Collective identity is both a matter of self- and external definition. Actors must define themselves as part of a broader movement and, at the same time, be perceived as such, by those within the same movement, and by opponents and/or external observers.[1] In this sense, collective identity plays an essential role in defining the boundaries of a social movement. Only those actors, sharing the same beliefs and sense of belongingness, can be considered to be part of a social movement. However, 'collective identity' does not imply homogeneity of ideas and orientations within social movement networks. A wide spectrum of different conceptions may be present, and factional conflicts may arise at any time. Therefore, the construction and preservation of a movement's identity implies a continuous process of 'realignment' (Snow et al., 1986) and 'negotiation' (Melucci, 1989) between movement actors.

The presence of shared beliefs and solidarities allows both actors and observers to assign a common meaning to specific collective events which otherwise could not be identified as part of a common process (see also Oliver, 1989). ... The process of identity formation cannot be separated from the process of symbolic redefinition of what is both real and possible. Moreover, such collective identity may persist even when public activities, demonstrations and the like are not taking place, thus providing for some continuity to the movement over time (Melucci, 1989; Turner and Killian, 1987).

Taking these qualifications into account, we can define the second component of the concept of social movement as follows:

> The boundaries of a social movement network are defined by the specific collective identity shared by the actors involved in the interaction.

Collective action on conflictual issues

Some of the views reviewed here put a specific emphasis on conflict as a core component of the concept of social movement (Touraine, Melucci, Tilly). Others emphasise that social movements define themselves with respect to processes of social change (Turner and Killian, McCarthy and Zald). Even these latter, however, acknowledge that as promoters or opponents of social change, social movements become involved in conflictual relations with other actors (institutions, countermovements, etc.). …

…

Another presumed source of inconsistency consists in conceptions which focus on political movements and those emphasizing that social movements are also, and often mainly, involved in cultural conflicts. Several authors (among them Gusfield, 1981; Melucci, 1989) maintain that the true bulk of social movement experience has to be found in the cultural sphere: what is challenged is not only the uneven distribution of power and/or economic goods, but socially shared meanings as well, that is the ways of defining and interpreting reality. Social movements tend to focus more and more on self-transformation. Conflicts arise in areas previously considered typical of the private sphere, involving problems of self-definition and challenges to the dominant life-styles, for example. The difference with those who insist on the political side of movements like McCarthy and Zald and Tilly is undeniable. Yet, this is a difference in emphasis rather than one concerning incompatible notions of what a social movement is. …

The opportunity to include both cultural and political movements within the broader category of social movements bring us to the third component of the concept:

> Social movement actors are engaged in political and/or cultural conflicts, meant to promote or oppose social change either at the systemic or non-systemic level.

Action which primarily occurs outside the institutional sphere and the routine procedures of social life

Until the early 1970s debates on social movements were dominated by structural functionalists like Smelser (1962) who put a great emphasis on the non-institutionalized nature of their behaviour. Today, social movement scholars are more cautious on this point. …

If the relationship between non-institutional behaviour and social movements is not strong enough to identify the former as a fundamental component

of the latter, the same holds true for the idea that social movements may be distinguished from other political actors because of their adoption of 'unusual' patterns of political behaviour. …

Another widely shared assumption, at least in the more conventional version of the idea of social movements as 'unusual' phenomena, is that organizations involved in social movements are basically loosely structured. While informality and looseness are essential properties of the system of interaction, the same is not necessarily true for the single units of the system. Even though many loosely structured organizations are actually part, possibly the dominant one, of social movement networks, they are by no means their only component. …

This discussion suggests that features such as the extra-institutional nature of social movements, the prevalence of violent or disruptive political protest and the loose structure of social movement organisations cannot really be taken as fundamental characteristics of a social movement. These may however be extremely useful in differentiating between types of movements, or between different phases in the life of a specific movement. Thus, the following synthetic definition of the concept of social movement can be put forward:

> A social movement is a network of informal interactions between a plurality of individuals, groups and/or organisations, engaged in a political or cultural conflict, on the basis of a shared collective identity.

Social movement, organisations, political events

The different traditions of social movement analysis I have discussed so far show some degree of compatibility. To be fair, this 'immanent' consensus is sometimes only implicit in an author's formulation. In this reconstruction I have tried to emphasise the elements of continuity between different positions, rather than those of divergence – which are, by the way, the best known. The question is whether the effort to mediate between several distinct approaches is not detrimental to theoretical clarity. In this section I will discuss this point. I try in particular to show in what sense this particular definition of social movements helps to differentiate them from a) political and social organisations like parties, interest groups or religious sects; b) other informal networks of collective action such as political mobilization campaigns and political coalitions.[2]

Social movements vs. political or religious organisations

As we already noted in the previous section, social movements, political parties and interest groups are often compared under the assumption that they all embody different styles of political organisation (for instance, Wilson, 1973). At times, they are identified with religious sects and cults (for instance, Robbins, 1988). However, if our definition is correct, the difference between social movements and other political actors does not consist primarily of differences in organisational characteristics or patterns of behaviour, but on the fact that social movements are not organisations, not even of a peculiar kind (Tilly, 1988; Oliver, 1989). They are networks of interaction between different actors which may either include formal organisations or not, depending on shifting circumstances. As a consequence, a single organisation, whatever its dominant traits, is not a social movement. Of course it may be part of one, but the two are not identical, as the latter reflects a different, more structured organisational principle. Indeed, many influential scholars in the field keep using 'social movement' to mean both networks of interaction and specific organisations: citizens' rights groups like Common Cause, environmental organisations like the Sierra Club, or even religious sects like Nichiren Shoshu (McAdam *et al.*, 1988, p.695). Yet, this overlap is a source of analytical confusion, in so far as it fosters the application to social movement analysis of concepts borrowed from organizational theory, that only partially fit the looser structure of social movements.[3] Talking of Common Cause or the Sierra Club or Nichiren Shoshu as 'social movements' leads one to formulate concepts like 'professional social movement' (McCarthy and Zald, 1973) or 'single-organization movements' (Turner and Killian, 1987, pp.369–70) to emphasise differences between these cases and the nature of social movements as informal networks (which as we have seen they all agree upon). But qualifying Common Cause as a 'professional social movement' does not add very much to the understanding of it, that cannot be provided by concepts like 'public interest group' (see among others Etzioni, 1985). Similarly, a religious organisation like Nichiren Shoshu or Hare Krishna may be conveniently analysed as a 'sect'. This concept takes into account the greater organisational rigidity and the more hierarchical structure that these organisations display by comparison with social movement networks (see Robbins, 1988, pp.150–5). In contrast, what both 'public interest group' and 'sect'

do not really capture is the interaction processes through which actors with different identities and orientations come to elaborate a shared system of beliefs and a sense of belongingness, which exceeds by far the boundaries of any single group or organisation, while maintaining at the same time their specificity and distinctive traits.

If we accept that social movements are analytically different from SMOs we have also to redefine our notion of what is part and what is not part of a movement. Indeed, any organisation which fulfils the requirements I have pointed out (interactions with other actors, conflict and collective identity) may be considered part of a given movement. This may also hold for bureaucratic interest groups, and even political parties. The inclusion of political parties within social movements will surely raise many eyebrows and requires some qualification. By saying that political parties may be part of social movements I do not mean to suggest that 'social movements' is a broader theoretical category of which several types of organisations (interest groups, community groups, political parties and so forth) represent as many sub-types. Far from it. Rather, I suggest that the features of the processes I have described as a social movement do not exclude that under certain and specific conditions some political party may feel itself as part of a movement and be recognized as such both by other actors in the movement and by the general public. This is likely to be the exception rather than the rule, and to be largely restricted to parties originated by social movements, such as the Green Parties (Kitschelt, 1989; Rudig and Lowe, forthcoming).

...

Social movements, protest events, coalitions

If social movements do not coincide with SMOs, they do not coincide with other types of informal interaction either. In other words, they differ from both loosely structured protest events and political coalitions. Under what conditions may a protest against the construction of a motorway run by informal citizens' action groups, a 'wild-cat' strike for higher wages in a firm or a demonstration for better nursing facilities in a neighbourhood be considered part of a social movement? And when are they just simple isolated 'protest events'? Some have suggested looking at the scope, dimension and length of campaigns (see, for example, Marwell and Oliver, 1984; Turner and Killian, 1987) in making this distinction. In broad terms, this is consistent with the notion of collective identity, as long and sustained campaigns will be more likely to create new specific identities among participants than sudden and brief protest outbursts or riots. However, there is also empirical evidence which casts doubt on the strength of this relation. Actually, the emergence of collective identity appears to be dependent on a plurality of factors.

Even initiatives, which are apparently very specific, may thus be considered part of a social movement, provided they are interpreted in the light of a wider system of beliefs. This is possible if they develop in a context which is not only conducive to collective action in general terms, but where a realignment of frames (Snow *et al.*, 1986) can occur. As we have seen in the previous section, the essential condition is that the sense of belongingness exceeds the length of the public activities and campaigns. Collective identity may thus either become a precondition for the creation of new and different identities (and consequently, of new and different social movements); or provide a persistent, though latent, basis for a new upsurge of mobilization campaigns under the same heading. Social movements often persist even whey they are not active on the public stage, and are rather going through a 'latency' phase. Those countercultural movements which alternate sudden explosion of protest with long periods of latency may be analysed in this light, for example. In their case, collective identity provides the link between occasional outbursts which would be otherwise unexplainable (Melucci, 1984, 1989).

Notes

1   See among others Touraine, 1977; Turner, 1981; Melucci, 1989. The degree of inclusiveness or exclusiveness of such identifications is on the other hand subjected to shifting conditions (Zald and Ash, 1966).

2   I do not discuss on the other hand collective phenomena such as fashions, solidarity campaigns in favour of external constituencies (such as collective efforts to help starving African countries or the like), and crowd behaviour (for example, football hooliganism). This is partially due to limitations in space, partially to the fact that their differences to social movements have been long since emphasised (see among others Alberoni, 1984 and Melucci, 1989). Moreover, these differences are probably more obvious than those that I am going to consider in this paper. Suffice to say here, that differences between these phenomena and social movements consist basically in the absence/presence of conflict; for fashions and crowd behaviours, they also lie to a certain extent in the absence of collective identity.

3   Several protests were for instance promoted by nature protection associations in Italy during the 1960s and the 1970s. In absolute terms, they were probably more frequent than the protests against nuclear power which developed in a very restricted period in the late 1970s. Yet, the latter developed a specific collective identity and were perceived as a movement, while this was not so with the former, who have come to identify themselves as a part of the environmental movement only in the 1980s. The explanation may lie in the persistence, until the late 1970s, of attitudes of mistrust towards collective action within nature protection associations. These attitudes were not conducive to the formation of broader collective identities (Diani, 1990).

References

Alberoni, F. (1984) *Movement and Institution*, New York, Columbia University Press.

Diani, M. (1990) 'The Italian ecology movement: from radicalism to moderation' in Rudig, W. (ed.) *Green Politics 1*, Edinburgh, Edinburgh University Press.

Etzioni, A. (1985) 'Special interest groups versus constituency representation' in Kriesberg, L. (ed.) *Research in Social Movements, Conflict and Change*, vol.8, Greenwich, CT, JAI Press.

Gusfield, J. (1981) 'Social movements and social change: perspectives of linearity and fluidity' in Kriesberg, L. (ed.) *Research in Social Movements, Conflict and Change*, vol.4, Greenwich, CT, JAI Press.

Kitschelt, H. (1989) *The Logics of Party Formation: Ecological Politics in Belgium and West Germany*, Ithaca, NY, Cornell University Press.

McAdam, D., McCarthy, J.D. and Zald, M.N. (1988) 'Social movements' in Smelser, N.J. (ed.) *Handbook of Sociology*, Beverly Hills, CA/London, Sage.

McCarthy, J.D. and Zald, M.N. (1973) *The Trend of Social Movements in America: Professionalization and Resource Mobilization*, Morristown, NJ, General Learning Press.

McCarthy, J.D. and Zald, M.N. (1977) 'Resource mobilization and social movements: a partial theory', *American Journal of Sociology*, vol.82, pp.1212–41.

Marwell, G. and Oliver, P. (1984) 'Collective action theory and social movements research' in Kriesberg, L. (ed.) *Research in Social Movements, Conflict and Change*, vol.7, Greenwich, CT, JAI Press.

Melucci, A. (ed.) (1984) *Altri codici: Aree di Movimento nella Metropoli*, Bologna, Il Mulino.

Melucci, A. (1989) *Nomads of the Present*, London, Hutchinson Radius.

Neidhardt, F. and Rucht, D. (1990) 'The analysis of social movements: the state of the art and some perspectives for further research' in Rucht, D. (ed.) *Research in Social Movements: The State of the Art*, Frankfurt, Campus/Boulder, CO, Westview Press.

Oliver, P. (1989) 'Bringing the crowd back in: the nonorganizational elements of social movements' in Kriesberg, L. (ed.) *Research in Social Movements, Conflict and Change*, vol.11, Greenwich, CT, JAI Press.

Robbins, T. (1988) *Cults, Converts and Charisma: the Sociology of New Religious Movements*, London, Sage.

Rudig, W. and Lowe, P. (forthcoming) *The Green Wave: A Comparative Analysis of Ecological Parties*, Cambridge, Polity Press.

Smelser, N.J. (1962) *Theory of Collective Behaviour*, New York, The Free Press.

Snow, D.A., Burke Rochford, E., Worden, S.K. and Beford, R.D. (1986) 'Frame alignment processes, micromobilization and movement participation', *American Sociological Review*, vol.51, pp.464–81.

Tilly, C. (1988) 'Social movements, old and new' in Misztal, B. (ed.) *Research in Social Movements, Conflict and Change*, vol.10, Greenwich, CT, JAI Press.

Touraine, A. (1977) *The Self-Production of Society*, Chicago, IL, University of Chicago Press.

Turner, R. (1981) 'Collective behaviour and resource mobilization as approaches to social movements: issues and continuities' in Kriesberg, L. (ed.) *Research in Social Movements, Conflicts and Change*, vol.4, Greenwich, CT, JAI Press.

Turner, R. and Killian, L. (1987) *Collective Behaviour*, Englewood Cliffs, NJ, Prentice-Hall.

Wilson J.Q. (1973) *Political Organizations*, New York, Basic Books.

Zald, M.N. and Ash, R. (1966) 'Social movement organizations: growth, decay and change', *Social Forces*, vol.44, pp.327–41.

Source: Diani, 1992, pp.7–16

 ## 5.2 John D. McCarthy and Mayer N. Zald, 'Resource mobilization and social movements: a partial theory' (1977)

Resource mobilization

The resource mobilization perspective adopts as one of its underlying problems Olson's (1965) challenge: since social movements deliver collective goods, few individuals will 'on their own' bear the costs of working to obtain them. Explaining collective behaviour requires detailed attention to the selection of incentives, cost-reducing mechanisms or structures, and career benefits that lead to collective behaviour (see, especially, Oberschall, 1973).

...

Theoretical elements

...

A *social movement* is a set of opinions and beliefs in a population representing preferences for changing some elements of the social structure or reward distribution, or both, of a society.[1] A *countermovement* is a set of opinions and beliefs in a population opposed to a social movement. As is clear, we view social movements as nothing more than preference structures directed toward social change, very similar to what political sociologists would term *issue cleavages*. (Indeed, the process we are exploring resembles what

political scientists term *interest aggregation*, except that we are concerned with the margins of the political system rather than with existing party structures.)

The distribution of preference structures can be approached in several ways. Who holds the beliefs? How intensely are they held? In order to predict the likelihood of preferences being translated into collective action, the mobilization perspective focuses upon the preexisting organization and integration of those segments of a population that share preferences. Oberschall (1973) has presented an important synthesis of past work on the preexisting organization of preference structures, emphasizing the opportunities and costs for expression of preferences for movement leaders and followers. Social movements whose related populations are highly organized internally (either communally or associationally) are more likely than are others to spawn organized forms.

A *social movement organization* (SMO) is a complex, or formal, organization that identifies its goals with the preferences of a social movement or a countermovement and attempts to implement those goals.[2] If we think of the recent civil rights movement in these terms, the social movement contained a large portion of the population that held preferences for change aimed at 'justice for black Americans' and a number of SMOs such as the Student Non-Violent Coordinating Committee (SNCC), the Congress of Racial Equality (CORE), the National Association for the Advancement of Colored People (NAACP), and Southern Christian Leadership Conference (SCLC). These SMOs represented and shaped the broadly held preferences and diverse subpreferences of the social movement.

...

Let us now turn to the resource mobilization task of an SMO. Each SMO has a set of *target goals*, a set of preferred changes toward which it claims to be working. Such goals may be broad or narrow. ... The SMO must possess resources, however few and of whatever type, in order to work toward goal achievement. Individuals and other organizations control resources, which can include legitimacy, money facilities, and labor.

Although similar organizations vary tremendously in the efficiency with which they translate resources into action (see Katz, 1974), the amount of activity directed toward goal accomplishment is crudely a function of the resources controlled by an organization. Some organizations may depend heavily upon volunteer labor, while others may depend upon purchased labor. In any case, resources must be controlled or mobilized before action is possible.

From the point of view of an SMO the individuals and organizations that exist in a society may be categorized along a number of dimensions. For the appropriate SM there are adherents and nonadherents. *Adherents* are those individuals and organizations that believe in the goals of the movement. The *constituents* of an SMO are those providing the resources for it.

At one level the resource mobilization task is primarily that of converting adherents into constituents and maintaining constituent involvement. However, at another level the task may be seen as turning nonadherents into adherents. Ralph Turner (1970) uses the term *bystander public* to denote those nonadherents who are not opponents of the SM and its SMOs but who merely witness social movement activity. It is useful to distinguish constituents, adherents, bystander publics, and opponents along several other dimensions. One refers to the size of the resource pool controlled, and we shall use the terms *mass* and *elite* to describe crudely this dimension. Mass constituents, adherents, bystander publics, and opponents are those individuals and groups controlling very limited resource pools. The most limited resource pool individuals can control is their own time and labor. Elites are those who control larger resource pools.[3]

Each of these groups may also be distinguished by whether it will benefit directly from the accomplishment of SMO goals. Some bystander publics, for instance, may benefit directly from the accomplishment of organizational goals, even though they are not adherents of the appropriate SM. To mention a specific example, women who oppose the preferences of the women's liberation movement or have no relevant preferences might benefit from expanded job opportunities for women pursued by women's groups. Those who would benefit directly from SMO goal accomplishment we shall call *potential beneficiaries*.[4]

In approaching the task of mobilizing resources an SMO may focus its attention upon adherents who are potential beneficiaries and/or attempt to convert bystander publics who are potential beneficiaries into adherents. It may also expand its target goals in order to enlarge its potential beneficiary group. Many SMOs attempt to present their goal accomplishments in terms of broader potential benefits for ever-wider groupings of citizens through notions of a better society, and so on (secondary benefits). Finally, an SMO may attempt to mobilize as adherents those who are not potential beneficiaries. *Conscience adherents* are individuals and groups who are part of the appropriate SM but do not stand to benefit directly from SMO goal accomplishment. *Conscience constituents* are direct supporters of an SMO who do not stand to benefit directly from its success in goal accomplishment.[5]

William Gamson (1975) makes essentially the same distinction, calling groups with goals aimed at helping nonconstituents *universalistic* and those whose beneficiaries and constituents are identical, *nonuniversalistic*. Gamson concludes, however, that this distinction is not theoretically important, since SMOs with either type of constituents have identical problems in binding them to the organization. It is not more 'irrational', in Olson's sense, to seek change in someone else's behalf than in one's own, and in both cases commitment must be gained by other means than purposive incentives. The evidence presented by Gamson suggests that this dimension does not bear much relationship to SMO success in goal accomplishment or in the attainment of legitimacy. We argue below, however, that the distinction should be maintained: it summarizes important attachments and social characteristics of constituents. The problems of SMOs with regard to binding beneficiary and conscience constituents to the organization are different, not with regard to the stakes of individual involvement relative to goal accomplishment (the Olson problem) but with regard to the way constituents are linked to each other and to other SMOs, organizations, and social institutions (see also Wilson, 1973).

An SMO's potential for resource mobilization is also affected by authorities and the delegated agents of social control (e.g., the police). While authorities and agents of control groups do not typically become constituents of SMOs, their ability to frustrate (normally termed *social control*) or to enable resource mobilization are of crucial importance. Their action affects the readiness of bystanders, adherents and constituents to alter their own status and commitment. And they themselves may become adherents and constituents. Because they do not always act in concert, Marx (1974) makes a strong case that authorities and delegated agents of control need to be analysed separately.

The partitioning of groups into mass or elite and conscience or beneficiary bystander publics, adherents, constituents, and opponents allows us to describe more systematically the resource mobilization styles and dilemmas of specific SMOs. It may be, of course, to the advantage of an SMO to turn bystander publics into adherents. But since SMO resources are normally quite limited, decisions must be made concerning the allocation of these resources and converting bystander publics may not aid in the development of additional resources. Such choices have implications for the internal organization of an SMO and the potential size of the resource pool than can ultimately be mobilized. For instance, an SMO that has a mass beneficiary base and concentrates its resource mobilization efforts toward mass beneficiary adherents is likely to restrict severely the amount of resources it can raise. Elsewhere (McCarthy and Zald, 1973) we have termed an SMO focusing upon beneficiary adherents for resources a *classical SMO*. Organizations that direct resource appeals primarily toward conscience adherents tend to utilize few constituents for organizational labor, and we have termed such organizations *professional SMOs*.

Another pattern of resource mobilization and goal accomplishment can be identified from the writings of Lipsky (1968) and Bailis (1974). It depends upon the interactions among beneficiary constituency, conscience adherents, and authorities. Typical of this pattern is an SMO with a mass beneficiary constituency that would profit from goal accomplishment (for instance, the Massachusetts Welfare Rights Organization) but that has few resources. Protest strategies draw attention and resources from conscience adherents to the SMO fighting on behalf of such mass groups and may also lead conscience elites to legitimate the SMO to authorities. As a result of a similar pattern, migrant farmworkers benefited from the transformation of authorities into adherents (Jenkins and Perrow, 1977).

But an SMO does not have complete freedom of choice in making the sorts of decisions to which we have alluded. Such choices are constrained by a number of factors ... Also, of course, the ability of any SMO to garner resources is shaped by important events such as war, broad economic trends, and natural disasters.

Notes

1 There is by no means a clear consensus on the definition of the crucial term *social movement*. We employ an inclusive definition for two reasons. First, by doing so, we link our work to as much past work as possible. Second, there are important theoretical reasons that will be discussed below. Our definition of *social movement* allows the possibility that a social movement will not be represented by any organized groups but also allows for organizations that do not represent social movements at formation. Most earlier definitions have included other preferences and organizational factors. See Wilkinson (1971) for an extensive survey of definitions of *social movement*.

2 Making the distinction between a social movement (SM) and a social movement organization (SMO) raises the question of the relevance of the vast literature developed by political scientists on the subject of interest groups. Is an SMO an interest group? Interest group theorists often blur the distinction between the representative organization and the interest group (e.g. the AMA and doctors) (see Wootton [1970] for an extended discussion). Whereas political scientists usually focus upon interest groups' organizations and not the groups themselves, sociologists largely have focused upon social movements rather than upon social movement organizations. Though we are not fully satisfied with Lowi's (1971) distinction between the two terms, we will employ it for lack of a better one. Lowi maintains that an SMO that becomes highly institutionalized and routinizes stable ties with a governmental agency is an interest group. This way of approaching the problem, of course, flows from Lowi's distinctive view of the functioning of pluralistic politics.

3 Of course, the size of the resource pool controlled by an individual or an organization that might be allocated to an SMO is a dimension. We dichotomize the dimension only for the purposes of discussion, and the appropriate cutting point will vary from situation to situation.

4 A potential beneficiary group has normally been termed an interest group. The distinction between beneficiaries and adherents recognizes that interests and preferences may not coincide.

5 We have borrowed this term from Harrington (1968, p.291), who uses it to refer to middle-class liberals who have demonstrated strong sympathies for the interests of underdog groups. Our use broadens the meaning of the term.

References

Bailis, L. (1974) *Bread and Justice*, Springfield, MA, Heath-Lexington.

Gamson, W.A. (1975) *The Strategy of Social Protest*, Homewood, IL, Dorsey.

Harrington, M. (1968) *Toward a Democratic Left: A Radical Program for a New Majority*, New York, Macmillan.

Jenkins, C. and Perrow, C. (1977) 'Insurgency of the powerless: farm workers movements (1946–72)', *American Sociological Review*, vol.42, no.2, pp.249–67.

Katz, H. (1974) *Give! Who Gets Your Charity Dollar?*, Garden City, NJ, Doubleday.

Lipsky, M. (1968) 'Protest as a political resource', *American Political Science Review*, vol.62 (December), pp.1144–58.

Lowi, T.J. (1971) *The Politics of Disorder*, New York, Basic Books.

Marx, G.T. (1974) 'Thoughts on a neglected category of social movement participant: the agent provocateur and the informant', *American Journal of Sociology*, vol.80 (September), pp.404–42.

McCarthy, J.D and Zald, M.N. (1973) *The Trend of Social Movements in America: Professionalization and Resource Mobilization*, Morristown, NJ, General Learning Press.

Oberschall, A. (1973) *Social Conflict and Social Movements*, Englewood Cliffs, NJ, Prentice-Hall.

Olson, M., Jnr (1965) *The Logic of Collective Action*, Cambridge, MA, Harvard University Press.

Turner, R.H. (1970) 'Determinants of social movement strategies' in Shibutani, T. (ed.) *Human Nature and Collective Behaviour: Papers in Honor of Herbert Blumer*, Englewood Cliffs, NJ, Prentice-Hall, pp.145–64.

Wilkinson, P. (1971) *Social Movements*, New York, Praegar.

Wilson, J.Q. (1973) *Political Organizations*, New York, Basic Books.

Wootton, G. (1970) *Interest Groups*, Englewood Cliffs, NJ, Prentice-Hall.

Source: McCarthy and Zald, 1987, pp.20–25

5.3 Lisa Power, 'Power to the people' (1995)

Feeling the lack of a radical alternative to the 'straight gay' organizations, Bob Mellors agreed with Aubrey to hold a meeting to test the water. The London School of Economics (LSE) was known for its support of countercultural activities and there were a number of gay students there including Bob so, on Wednesday 13 October 1970 and with the minimum of publicity and fuss, the London Gay Liberation Front met for the first time in a basement classroom in the Clare Market building. Published estimates of the number present run from nine to nineteen, with the latter being the more likely according to survivors. Among those present were Aubrey Walter and Bob Mellors as the instigators, David Fernbach (Aubrey's partner), Richard Dipple (a friend of Aubrey and David who had been involved in the Albany Trust), Bill Halstead (like Richard, an LSE student) and one woman, Bev Jackson, a prominent student activist at LSE who later ran for college office under the arresting slogan 'Bev the Lez for Prez'. There was no chairing or formal organization because of the small size of the meeting, and most of what was discussed was the news from America and the possibilities of a London equivalent to GLF.

Almost everyone I spoke to who arrived over the course of the next two months assumed that what they attended was the second meeting or so, but in fact the big increase in attendance did not take place until early in November. Those who arrived before then were mainly other students and people such as new research graduate Jeffrey Weeks, sociologist Mary McIntosh and psychiatric social worker Elizabeth Wilson, who heard about it from other gay academics.. …

…

> I think Mary must have heard about it from Ken Plummer, she certainly heard about it from some sociologist mate, he's the most likely. It was in one of the small rooms in LSE, it hadn't got big then and it was in the same room that I'd had seminars with Donald Winnicott in when I was training to be a social worker there, so it was a very meaningful but strange coincidence because Winnicott, in the nicest and most genteel way, was very homophobic. I don't remember much about the meeting. There weren't very many women, there was all this buzz. David and Aubrey were making most of the running, they were Maoists. It was an exciting feeling and within a couple of weeks the meetings had grown absolutely huge.

(Elizabeth Wilson)

Elizabeth and Mary arrived at the third or fourth meeting in S101 upstairs. The leafleting was done in Earls Court just after that, and that's when most people started to arrive.

(Aubrey Walter) …

…

The leaflet stated that meetings were being held by now in Room 101 of the St Clement's Building at the London School of Economics, at 7.30 p.m. every Wednesday. The publisher's address was given as GLF, c/o 160 North Gower Street, London NW1. This was the address for Agitprop Bookshop, a popular revolutionary centre, and indicates that either or both of the gay workers there who were to become central figures in GLF, Andy Elsmore and Tony Reynolds, were already attending. Leaflets were pinned up there and at Compendium in Camden Town, where a gay Canadian hippie already heavily involved in politics, called Warren Haig, worked, and at Housmans in Kings Cross, where another gay man, David McLellan, worked. These brought in others, as did the Earls Court and scene leafleting:

I knew some other gays through cottaging. People I met this way would ask 'are you active or passive' and there were a lot of self-denigrating attitudes. I was very relieved when I finally found out that you didn't have to be one or the other. I saw a poster in Compendium for the first meeting and I thought that it was incredible, I wanted to go but I was afraid to walk into a room of openly gay people. It was Jeffrey [Weeks] who insisted I go to GLF, we were friends.

(Micky Burbidge)

I heard about the meetings at the LSE and went to about the third or fourth one. I was a dentist with a practice in St Johns Wood, a very straight law reform campaigner and had never thought of anything else. At GLF I saw lots of new, different people. I was exhilarated and shocked at the odd clothes, the hippies, hard left people, students, many different people. There was no chairman and the leading figures were mobile from week to week. I felt envious of it. Someone asked me early on if I was in the Communist Party and I was shocked. At the Balls, I envied their freedom and the way that people bounced around, it made me feel I was uptight. It was a nice sort of envy. After a couple of weeks, we talked about leafleting for more people.

I met others at Queensway tube and we did the Bayswater Road crowds on a Sunday, where the artists display their stuff on the railings. I wanted to do it but I was scared to be recognized as gay – I was shoving the leaflet into people's hands and running off. I didn't feel able to stop and talk to people the way that some of the others did. There were about four of us. I was hungry for action after three years of nothing and I found it exhilarating. It felt like a boiler, with the pressure building up and up for years and then suddenly released. I was angry, I was thrilled, we thought we could change the world, change the sexuality of everyone and not just homosexuals.

(Michael Brown)

The first known public action of London GLF certainly showed that they held a wider concern about sexism than a purely gay angle. *Time Out* reported in its last issue of October 1970 that the young organization had invaded the offices of *Sennet*, the London School of Economics student newspaper, in protests at an offensive article. The piece, supposedly on students and sex, was said to have denigrated 'queers', as it called them, but also women in general. The invaders sprayed slogans around the office and served notice to all the underground press, *IT, Oz* and *Friends* (later *Frendz*) that the same would happen to them if they persisted in operating on what was characterized as a 'tits and arse' basis. This willingness to stand up to the counterculture press, rather than slavishly courting them, seems to have done the GLF little harm.

The meetings soon began to need more organization as the numbers attending rose.

When we first met, we just organized it between us. Then when we went into the bigger room we had a rotating chair but they weren't elected as such. Then we got bigger, we had a steering committee that was elected and that happened for the first time at the New Theatre at the LSE. If it wasn't chaired, Warren tended to dominate it by making people feel stupid.

(Aubrey Walter)

But to be fair, Warren Haig was not the only person who flowered in the heady atmosphere of the early days at LSE. Even previously reticent people sometimes found their voice there and are remembered as making regular contributions to the debate. 'I think one reason GLF was important to me was because it did release something. I was terribly inhibited and never spoke at anything ever at all before that. It obviously unleashed something' (Elizabeth Wilson). And thanks to the leafleting, the people attending were soon not only greater in numbers but from a wider variety of backgrounds.

> I knew I was gay before GLF. I was adopted as a child into a very poor and dysfunctional family and went into the army at seventeen to get away from home. I bought myself out after four years because I was beginning to accept that I was gay, having realized I was 'queer' years before. This was in 1967 and I went to India and Morocco and became a hippie. I was very politically unaware and I hated myself. Warren Haig was the first man I kissed in public. I already knew a small group of gay people that I used to do acid with. Some of them ended up in GLF too, people like Mitch and Angus and Jeff Marsh who lived on Portobello Road. When I walked into the LSE, I saw lots of gay men and women who actually looked like me, not like the stereotype I had of mincing limp-wristed men. There was a real glow of being together, like I hadn't expected. I'd never even been into a gay bar by this stage. I remember Sue Winter being very forward. The most vocal people at those early meetings, the most memorable ones, were Warren, Aubrey, David Fernbach, Richard Dipple, Mary, Elizabeth and Sue Winter.
>
> (Paul Theobald)

> I was in GLF from the start because two friends were given a leaflet by a hippie in Oxford Street and they told me about it. I went and I was fascinated and I got very involved, which cost me my boyfriend because I got so into all the meetings. I was working at the time managing an employment agency in the City, which was pretty ironic. I was attracted to GLF by a general feeling of dissatisfaction with the world and the problems of being gay and people there were prepared to talk. There was only the cruising scene in the bars or private socializing – no gay debate whatsoever. It was Aubrey, Bob and co. that put gay sexuality into a political context and made sense of it in alliance with women and race.
>
> (Stuart Feather)

> I was mainly involved in GLF from 1970 to 1972. I identified as straight at the time, because you were only given two choices in those days. Now people understand that it's much more complicated. I came along to the second or third meeting. Paul Theobald's lover Trevor had brought Howard [Wakeling] home and I fell in love with him immediately, so I went along with them.
>
> (Sue Winter)

In the early days, there were very few women around. At that time there was so much pressure on all of us – people had been beaten up, aversion therapy, people in prison for being gay – Mick Belsten had spent time in prison. I know of several men who had had aversion therapy, and been beaten up in all sorts of places and the only place for lesbians to meet was the Gateways, only one place in all of London. Sometimes there were only a dozen (women), sometimes fifty – it grew fairly rapidly but there were very few at first. The belief that women would go off with men if offered that choice, that lesbians didn't exist – in the initial phase it was very important to identify as a lesbian or as gay, homosexual … It was really important. Now, twenty-five years on with thousands of people on Pride demonstrations what's important is choice for women. It's definitely a different kind of time now. I didn't know many women there. I was at the Gateways with Rosie, and Beverley handed us a leaflet, so we went together.

(Carla Toney)

Rumours about the growing crowds at the LSE attracted not only women from the bars and men from the streets, but also some experienced gay activists, curious to see what the fuss was about.

> They were the first really big gatherings of gays that I'd been to that weren't primarily a meat market. GLF meetings were very friendly. Since people didn't assume that you were trying to pick them up, they didn't feel the need to put you down or reject you. When GLF started I was not involved in much, so I went along as an individual but all sorts of things got read into it. Aubrey made odd comments. My emotional allegiance in a way was with GLF and that sort of thing rather than CHE, but I know that the political analysis is needed. It was unimaginable before it happened.
>
> (Antony Grey)

The arrival of what were seen by some of the founders as dangerously moderate traditional organizers was not the only subject of controversy. As Sue Winter soon noticed, the rhetoric about sexual freedom for all and the destruction of sexual categories foundered rapidly when power was at issue within the organization. This was not due to hypocrisy so much as the legacy from previous organizing, in which heterosexuals had often spoken for gay people or gay people themselves had posed as straight or at least sexually ambiguous on the assumption that this would be more palatable to the general public. So, while heterosexuals were welcome at GLF, they were not welcome to take positions of authority.

> Having straight people around was a very big issue at the start, over the elections to the Steering Committee. There were some straight women friends who came and a few hippies who wanted to be thought of as 'humansexuals', but there was a clear consensus amongst most people that gays needed to run GLF for themselves.
>
> (David Fernbach)

And that was not all. 'Cottaging was an issue very early on at the LSE. Andy Elsmore got up and spoke as someone who cottaged, which was felt to be quite radical and daring. There were a number of people who took the view that people who cottaged were in need of help' (David Fernbach).

But mostly the early days of the organization were taken up in planning the growth and activities of the new group and finding ways of bringing it to the attention of more gays and the general public. 'We used to pore over all the American publications – *Come Together* (the GLF paper) was based around *Come Out!*, which was the name of a New York paper put together by Steve Dansky, which only lasted a few months. Steve Dansky's piece "Hey Man" was reprinted in *Come Together 5* and was very influential over here' (David Fernbach).

Source: Power, 1995, pp.21–8

5.4 Alberto Melucci, 'The new social movements revisited: reflections on a sociological misunderstanding' (1995)

The metaphysics of the actor

One of the most resistant legacies of the nineteenth century is the tendency to attribute a kind of substantial unity to the observed actor. The essentialist and teleological idea of social movements as unified subjects acting on the stage of history, oriented towards luminous destinies or pledged to an inevitable collapse, is the last expression of a philosophy of history and metaphysical assumptions. That which one observes as unity, as a given reality, is actually the result of multiple processes, of different orientations, of a constructive dynamic which the actors bring about (or fail to bring about): in any case it is thanks to this dynamic that an action develops or fails to develop, evolves or is arrested, reaches its objectives or falls apart.

A collective actor is a composite, constructed reality, which nevertheless presents itself empirically as a unity. And it does so in a dual sense. On the one hand, the actors tend to give themselves a unified definition which reinforces, at least in terms of ideology, their capacity for action and their relationship to their opponents, allies and potential supporters. On the other hand observers tend to attribute this unity to an empirical collective phenomenon, simplifying it and transforming it in a homogeneous subject according to the logic of common sense. Thus the unity of collective action is currently seen as a given.

This unity, however, must be seen merely as an empirical starting point. There is no doubt that we can observe a group of individuals who, acting together, define themselves as 'we', and to whom we tend to attribute unity. But everyday common sense becomes naïve realism when it assumes the metaphysical existence of the actor. From the analytical point of view, it is precisely this datum which needs to be questioned. The unity is a result of exchanges, negotiations, decisions and conflicts that the actors continually bring about, but which are never in the foreground. Such processes are not immediately visible, as the actors tend to hide their fragmentation. But when unification is realized, this in itself is already a product. The commonsense understanding of social movements sees them as unified empirical actors, whose values, intentions and goals are taken for granted; so that the ideology of the leaders or the attributions made by the observers become the true reality of the movement. The task of sociological analysis should be to question the data in order to ascertain how it is produced, and to dissect the empirical unity to discover the plurality of analytical elements – orientations, meanings and relationships – which converge in the same phenomenon.

...

Collective action is not a unitary empirical phenomenon, and the unity, if it exists, should be considered as a result rather than a starting point, as a fact to be explained rather than as evidence. The events in which individuals act collectively combine different orientations, involve multiple actors, and implicate a system of opportunities and constraints that shape their relationships.

Is there anything new?

Information resources are at the centre of collective conflicts emerging in highly differential societies. Conflicts shift to the formal frameworks of knowledge: the codes. This shift is made possible by the increasing self-reflective capacity of information-based social systems.

Unlike their nineteenth-century counterparts, contemporary forms of collective action are not preoccupied with struggles over the production and distribution of material goods. They challenge the administrative rationality of systems based on information primarily on symbolic grounds: the ways in which an information-based society generates meaning and communication for its members.

The *self-reflective form of action* is another specific feature of the emerging collective phenomena. Action is a message sent to the rest of society, which speaks through its own forms and with a high degree of self-reflexivity. Organizational forms, patterns of interpersonal relationships and decision-making processes are themselves meaningful signs addressed to the society as a whole. But they are also a goal in themselves: actors consciously practise in the present the objective they pursue.

The *planetary dimension* of action is the expression of the global interdependence of our world. Even when the action is lodged at a specific and particularistic level, actors display a high degree of awareness of planetary interdependence. Movements acquire a transnational dimension.

They also rely on a *specific relation between latency and visibility.* Submerged networks in everyday life create and practise new meanings. The production of new codes challenges the dominant logic of technological rationality. These networks are the laboratories in which other views of reality are created. They emerge only on specific grounds to confront a public authority on a given issue. Submerged networks nourish and give meanings to public mobilizations by providing names and codes for issues raised. Cycles of mobilization feed the submerged networks with new members and new experiences.

The effectiveness of such forms of action should not be measured only at the political level. Movements produce both measurable and non-measurable effects. *Institutional change, new elites* and *cultural innovation* can be measured and are the most visible effects of collective action. But there are also less visible outcomes of collective action which can be detected only at the cultural level. The reversal of cultural codes is a challenge which addresses forms of power hidden in the allegedly neutral rationality of administrative apparatuses. The very existence of collective action is the message sent to the society: power becomes visible because it is challenged by the production of different meanings. Power hides behind the rationality of organizational and technological procedures and behind the construction of names and meanings. Making power visible is possible when other names, other meanings are offered to the society by the practice of collective action.

The ambivalence of representation processes

A necessary condition for the survival of such forms of action is the existence of public spaces (Keane, 1988) independent of the institutions of government, the party system and state structures. These spaces assume the form of an articulated system of decision-making, negotiation and representation, in which the signifying practices developed in everyday life can be expressed and heard independently of formal political institutions. Public spaces of this kind should include some guarantees that individual and collective identities can exist, soft institutionalized systems favouring the appropriation of knowledge and the production of symbolic resources, and open systems in which information can be circulated and controlled. Public spaces are highly fluid, and their size may increase or diminish according to the autonomy they are accorded: they are by definition a mobile system of instances kept open only by creative confrontation between collective actors and institutions.

Inasmuch as public spaces form an intermediate level between the levels of political power and decision-making and networks of everyday life, they are structurally ambivalent: they express the double meaning of the terms *representation* and *participation*. Representation means the possibility of presenting interests and demands; but it also means remaining different and never being heard entirely through the political channels that give voice to social demands. Participation also has a double meaning. It means both taking part, that is, acting so as to promote the interests and the needs of an actor, and also belonging to a system, identifying with the general interests of the community.

The ambivalence of public spaces is always part of the political game and it is regulated, to a certain extent, by the state, according to its more or less dominant role, its degree of centralization and the autonomy it allows representative institutions. The choice between freedom of expression and external regulation, as well as between particularism and general interests, is not made once and for all. On the contrary, substantial democracy in complex societies will increasingly be measured by the capacity of political systems to keep these polarities as open as possible. The transparency of the rules, the flexibility of the gatekeepers and agendas, and sensitivity to institutional change are all tentative ways of improving the quality of democratic life. Social movements can contribute to this game by their capacity to reveal the loci and language of power.

The main function of public spaces, then, is to make the questions raised by the movements visible and collective. They enable the movements to avoid being institutionalized as such and, conversely, ensure that society as a whole is able to assume responsibility for (that is, institutionally process) the issues, demands and conflicts concerning the goals and meaning of social action raised by the movements. In this sense, the consolidation of independent public spaces is a vital condition of retaining – without seeking to falsely resolve – the paradoxical dimension of post-industrial democracy. For when society assumes responsibility for its own issues, demands and conflicts, it subjects them openly to negotiation and to decisions, and transforms them into possibilities of change. It thereby makes possible a democracy of everyday life, without either annulling the specificity and the independence of the movements or concealing the use of power behind allegedly neutral decision-making procedures.

Some theoretical conclusions

Conflicts of a systematic nature, which used to be referred to as 'class conflicts', are therefore carried forward by temporary actors who bring to light the crucial dilemmas of the planetary society. The conflicts I describe here (which do not exhaust the range of social conflicts that can affect specific national societies or areas of the world system) concern the production and the appropriation of resources which are crucial for a global information-based society. These same processes generate both new forms of power and new forms of opposition: conflict emerges only in so far as actors fight for control and allocation of socially produced potential for action. This potential is no longer based exclusively on material resources or on forms of social organization, but to an increasing extent on the ability to produce information.

Conflicts do not chiefly express themselves through action designed to achieve outcomes in the political system. Rather, they raise the challenge which recasts the language and cultural codes that organize information. The ceaseless flow of messages acquires meaning only through the codes that order the flux and allow its meanings to be read. The forms of power now emerging in contemporary societies are grounded in an ability to inform (give form). Collective action occupies the same terrain and is in itself a message broadcast to society conveying symbolic forms and relational patterns which cast light on the dark side of the moon – a system of meanings which runs counter to the sense that the apparatuses seek to impose on individual and collective events. This type of action affects institutions because it selects new elites, modernizes organizational forms, and creates new goals and new languages. At the same time, however, it challenges the apparatuses that govern the production of information, and prevents the channels of representation and decision-making in pluralist societies from adopting instrumental rationality as the only logic with which to govern complexity. Such rationality applies solely to procedures and imposes the criterion of efficiency and effectiveness as the only measure of sense. The action of movements reveals that the neutral rationality of means masks interests and forms power; that it is impossible to confront the massive challenge of living together on a planet, by now become a global society, without openly discussing the ends and values that make such cohabitation possible. It highlights the insuperable dilemmas facing complex societies, and by doing so forces them openly to assume responsibility for their choices, their conflicts and their limitations.

By drawing on forms of action that relate to daily life and individual identity, some forms of contemporary collective action detach themselves from the traditional model of political organization and increasingly distance themselves from political systems. They move in to occupy an intermediate space of social life where individual needs and the pressures of political innovation come together. Because of the particular features of movements, social conflicts can only become effective through the mediation of political actors, even though they will never restrict themselves to politics. The innovative thrust of movements, therefore, does not exhaust itself in changes to the political system brought about by institutional actors. Nevertheless, the ability of collective demands to expand and to find expression depends on the way in which political actors are able to translate them into democratic guarantees.

Reference

Keane, J. (ed.) (1988) *Civil Society and the State*, London, Verso.
Source: Melucci, 1995, pp.113–17

5.5 Reclaim the Streets, 'The evolution of Reclaim the Streets' (1997)

The direct action group Reclaim the Streets (RTS) has developed widespread recognition over the last few years. From road blockades to street parties, from strikes on oil corporations to organising alongside striking workers, its actions and ideas are attracting more and more people and international attention. Yet the apparent sudden emergence of this group, its penetration of popular alternative culture and its underlying philosophy have rarely been discussed.

RTS was originally formed in London in Autumn 1991, around the dawn of the anti-roads movement. With the battle for Twyford Down rumbling along in the background, a small group of individuals got together to undertake direct action against the motor car. In their own words they were campaigning:

> FOR walking, cycling and cheap, or free, public transport, and AGAINST cars, roads and the system that pushes them.
> (Reclaim the Streets leaflet)

Their work was small-scale but effective and even back then it had elements of the cheeky, surprise tactics which have moulded RTS's more recent activities. There was the trashed car on Park Lane symbolising the arrival of Car-mageddon, DIY cycle lanes painted overnight on London streets, disruption of the 1993 Earls Court Motor Show and subvertising actions on car adverts around the city. However the onset of the No M11 Link Road Campaign presented the group with a specific local focus, and RTS was absorbed temporarily into the No M11 campaign in East London.

This period of the No M11 campaign was significant for a number of reasons. Whilst Twyford Down was predominantly an ecological campaign – defending a 'natural' area – the urban setting of the resistance to the M11 construction embodied wider social and political issues. Beyond the anti-road and ecological arguments, a whole urban community faced the destruction of its social environment with loss of homes, degradation to its quality of life and community fragmentation.

Beyond these political and social considerations, the M11 campaign developed the direct action skills of those involved. Phone trees were established, large numbers of people were involved in site invasions, crowds of activists had to be manoeuvred cunningly to outwit police. The protesters also gained experience of dealing with associated tasks such as publicity, the media and fund-raising.

Then in late 1994 a political hand-grenade was thrown into the arena of the M11 campaign: the Criminal Justice and Public Order Act. Overnight civil protesting became a criminal act, but what the government hadn't counted on was how this piece of legislation would unite and motivate the very groups it was aimed at repressing. The fight of the anti-road activists became synonymous with that of travellers, squatters and hunt saboteurs. In particular, the suddenly politicised rave scene became a communal social focus for many people.

The [No] M11 Link Road Campaign culminated in the symbolic and dramatic battle of Claremont Road. Eventually, and with the repetitive beats of The Prodigy in the background, police and security overpowered the barricades, lock-ons and the scaffold tower, but the war was only just beginning. The period of the M11 campaign had linked together new political and social alliances and in the midst of the campaign's frenzied activities strong friendships had been formed. When Claremont Road was lost, this collective looked for new sources of expression and Reclaim the Streets was reformed in February 1995.

The years that followed saw the momentum of RTS flourish. Street Parties I and II were held in rapid succession in the summer of 1995 and there were various actions against the likes of Shell, the Nigerian Embassy and the 1995 Motor Show. More recently, in July 1996 there was the massive success of the M41 Street Party, where for nine hours 8,000 people took control of the M41 motorway in West London and partied and enjoyed themselves, whilst some dug up the tarmac with jack-hammers and in its place planted trees that had been rescued from the construction path of the M11.

At a base level the focus of RTS has remained anti-car but this has been increasingly symbolic, not specific. RTS aimed initially to move debate beyond the anti-roads struggle, to highlight the social, as well as the ecological, costs of the car system:

> The cars that fill the streets have narrowed the pavements. [If] pedestrians ... want to look at each other, they see cars in the background, if they want to look at the building across the street they see cars in the foreground: there isn't a single angle of view from which cars will not be visible, from the back, in front, on both sides. Their omnipresent noise corrodes every moment of contemplation like acid.
> (Kundera, 1991, p.271)

Cars dominate our cities, polluting, congesting and dividing communities. They have isolated people from one another, and our streets have become mere conduits for motor vehicles to hurtle through, oblivious of the neighbourhoods they are disrupting. Cars have created social voids; allowing people to move further and further away from their homes, dispersing and fragmenting daily activities and lives and increasing social anonymity. RTS believe that ridding society of the car would allow us to re-create a safer, more attractive living environment, to return streets to the people that live on them and perhaps to rediscover a sense of 'social solidarity'.

But cars are just one piece of the jigsaw and RTS is also about raising the wider questions behind the transport issue – about the political and economic forces which drive 'car culture'. Governments claim that 'roads are good for the economy'. More goods travelling on longer journeys, more petrol being burnt, more customers at out-of-town supermarkets – it is all about increasing 'consumption', because that is an indicator of 'economic growth'. The greedy, short-term exploitation of dwindling resources regardless of the immediate or long-term costs. Therefore RTS's attack on cars cannot be detached from a wider attack on capitalism itself.

> Our streets are as full of capitalism as of cars and the pollution of capitalism is much more insidious.
>
> (Reclaim the Streets Agit Prop; distributed at the M41 Street Party on Saturday 13 July 1996)

More importantly, RTS is about encouraging more people to take part in direct action. Everyone knows the destruction which roads and cars are causing, yet the politicians still take no notice. Hardly surprising – they only care about staying in power and maintaining their 'authority' over the majority of people. Direct action is about destroying that power and authority, and people taking responsibility for themselves. Direct action is not just a tactic; it is an end in itself. It is about enabling people to unite as individuals with a common aim, to change things directly by their own actions.

Street Parties I, II and III were an ingenious manifestation of RTS's views. They embodied the above messages in an inspired formula: cunning direct action, crowd empowerment, fun, humour and raving. They have evolved into festivals open to all who feel exasperated by conventional society.

To some extent it is possible to trace the tactics behind the Street Parties in RTS's history. The mobilisation, assembly and movement of large crowds draws on skills from road protests. The use of sound systems draws on dominant popular culture whereas the initial inspiration for Street Parties

certainly reflects the parties of the Claremont Road days. However, RTS have retrospectively also realised that their roots lie deeper in history. The great revolutionary moments have all been enormous popular festivals – the storming of the Bastille, the Paris commune and the uprisings in 1968 to name a few. A carnival celebrates temporary liberation from the established order; it marks the suspension of all hierarchy, rank, privileges, norms and prohibitions. Crowds of people on the street seized by a sudden awareness of their power and unification through a celebration of their own ideas and creations. It follows then that carnivals and revolutions are not spectacles seen by other people, but the very opposite in that they involve the active participation of the crowd itself. Their very idea embraces all people, and the Street Party as an event has successfully harnessed this emotion.

The power which such activities embody inevitably challenges the state's authority, and hence the police and security services' attention has increasingly been drawn to RTS. The organisation of any form of direct action by the group is closely scrutinised. RTS has been made very aware of this problem. Vehicles carrying equipment have been broken into, followed and impounded en route to Street Parties, RTS's office has been raided, telephones have been bugged and activists from RTS have been followed, harassed and threatened with heavy conspiracy charges. On top of this a secret RTS action in December 1996 (an attempt to seize a BP tanker on the M25) was foiled by the unexpected presence of two hundred police at the activists' meeting point. How such information is obtained by the police is uncertain and can easily lead to paranoia in the group; fear of infiltration, anxiety and suspicion which can themselves be debilitating.

Yet RTS has not been deterred, they hold open meetings every week, they continue to expand and involve new people, and are also frequently approached by other direct action groups. Alliances have sprouted with other groups – the striking Liverpool Dockers and Tube Workers to name two – as recognition has grown of common ground between these struggles. Throughout the UK and Europe new local RTS groups have formed and late this summer [1997] there are likely to be Street Parties worldwide. These new groups have not been created by London RTS, they are fully autonomous. London RTS has merely acted as a catalyst; stimulating individuals to replicate ideas if they are suitable for others to use as well.

In many ways the evolution of RTS has been a logical progression which reflects its roots and experiences. Equally the forms of expression which RTS have adopted are merely modern interpretations of age-old protests: direct action is not a new invention. Like their historic revolutionary counterparts, they are a group fighting for a better society at a time when many people feel alienated from, and concerned about, the current system. Their success lies in their ingenuity for empowering people, their foresight to forge common ground between issues and their ability to inspire.

Reference

Kundera, M. (1991) *Immortality*, London, Faber & Faber.

Note: This article was published in *Do Or Die*, no.6, Summer 1997.

Source: http://www.rts.gn.apc.org/evol.htm (downloaded 9 April 2001; accessed 19 March 2002)

5.6 Reclaim the Streets, 'On disorganisation' (2000)

A statement from Reclaim the Streets (RTS) London

In relation to past and expected future press reports concerning trials of RTS 'leaders', Reclaim the Streets[1] London would like to emphasise that it is a non-hierarchical, leaderless, openly organised, public group. No individual 'plans' or 'masterminds' its actions and events. RTS activities are the result of voluntary, unpaid, co-operative efforts from numerous self-directed people attempting to work equally together.

The events of June 18th 1999[2] in London, just one among similar events in over 40 countries world-wide, were in fact organised by thousands of people throughout the UK; in part previously, in part spontaneously on the day itself. The event sought to both highlight and directly confront the present internationalised socio-economic system that causes massive environmental damage and is leading to increasing poverty and inequality for the majority of the world's people.

That the mass media and legal apparatus of the state lack the ability to comprehend – or purposefully seek to misunderstand all this – is unsurprising. Both are embedded in the system of centralised power and

control direct actionists oppose; a system that also produces a cult of personality – whether politician or celebrity. Still, we send this statement in the perhaps naïve hope that the mainstream media may be interested in reporting, occasionally, the facts.

RTS London is proud to be associated with the growing global anti-capitalist movement that raised its voice on the streets of The City of London, in Seattle, soon in Washington, again on Mayday 2000[3] and on many other occasions. In response to the ubiquitous 'who's in charge?' we reply in unison 'We all are!' and in response to the half-truths, distortions, and lies of the media and legal system, we will continue to reply in word and deed: 'Reclaim the Streets!'

Notes

1 Reclaim the Streets is a direct action network seeking the rediscovery and liberation of the city streets. For more details see www.reclaimthestreets.net

2 For full details see www.j18.org

3 For more details on Mayday events, see www.freespeech.org/mayday2k

Source: http://www.rts.gn.apc.org/disorg.htm (downloaded 9 April 2001; accessed 19 March 2002)

5.7 Reclaim the Streets, 'Street politics' (2000)

A response to the media mayday ...

Reclaim the Streets has again been caught up in a chorus of condemnation. May Days 'guerrilla gardening' action in Parliament Square, was the spark this time. *The Sun* used its language, 'scum', *The Times* its, 'terrorists', *The Guardian*, no different, 'incoherent vigilantes' according to George Monbiot, 'inchoate herbivores' according to Hugo Young. However, as ever, the media

failed to provide basic information about RTS or the May Day action to allow people to make up their own minds about RTS. I am involved with London RTS, and would like, within the thousand edited words I have been given, to provide some basic information.

When the media talk of 'Reclaim the Streets', they mean one of several different things. Sometimes RTS means 'London RTS', an open group that meets weekly to discuss, debate and plan events. Sometimes commentators mean the loose national network of non-hierarchical groups and individuals under the banner 'Earth First!', of which London RTS is a very visible part. At times the meaning is the wider radical environmental movement or direct action movement, including groups growing their own food, or building their own houses. Lately RTS has been used as shorthand for anything relating to the words 'anti-capitalist' or 'anarchist'. What they really mean is rarely stated. How can anyone have a sensible analysis when journalists have failed to take the time to define even the subject of their 'analysis'?

London RTS has existed in current form since 1995, born out of the fight against the building of the east London M11 link road. One stated purpose was to 'take back those things which have been enclosed within capitalist circulation, returning them to collective use as a commons'. Behind this elaborate language is a biting critique of the way in which public spaces have become increasingly privatised: choked with private cars, colonised by advertising; criminalised if used for enjoyment or protest, and stolen for 'development'.

The theft of time and space by capitalism, and resistance to it, along with a fusing of green (ecological), red (socialist) and black (anarchist) politics has always been central to London RTS. The links between occupying streets, targeting financial centres and celebrating May Day then become clear. Nobody should believe George Monbiot's critique that London RTS has somehow 'lost the plot', or mutated from some previous self.

London RTS uses direct action. This is not, as many commentators would suggest, a clever technique to gain media exposure at a time when competition for space is intense. Direct action is about perceiving reality, and taking concrete action to change it yourself. It is about working collectively to sort out our own problems, doing what we thoughtfully think is the right course of action, regardless of what various 'authorities' deem acceptable. It is about pushing back the boundaries of possibility, about inspiration, empowerment. It is about thinking and taking, not asking and begging. Nobody asked me if I wanted to work for 45 years as part of a low paid army to keep the rich rich, they just took. Why should I ask for my time back?

London RTS is leaderless. I write here as an individual. It purposefully lacks a party line, any official policy, any form of membership. People generate ideas, they are discussed and some are taken on, limited only by the time and energy people volunteer. Recent projects include producing thirty-two pages of articles by over a dozen writers in the form of 30,000 copies of a spoof *Evening Standard* newspaper called 'Evading Standards', and targeting the square mile in solidarity with the U'wa Indians of Colombia whose land and culture are being destroyed by the arrival of capitalism, specifically oil and finance companies. These and many of our other smaller actions are not mentioned by our critics – the media is interested in the spectacle of our large actions, not any issues.

Very occasionally a journalist forgets their day-to-day reality of producing a quick piece to keep the wages rolling in, increase the paper's share of the market, keep the editor happy, massage their ego, or whatever the real motivation is behind their piece, and thinks about the 'bigger picture'. As Hugo Young noted in his May Day 'analysis', no government, corporation or institution can deal with serious environmental problems such as climate change, biodiversity loss, or the endless expansion of the economy on a finite planet. Or social problems like colossal poverty, both nationally and globally, or the drudgery of working harder and harder every year.

If London RTS has no blueprint, are we only 'anti-politics'? No, RTS and the broader radical environmental movement, as individuals, groups and social movements are testing, exploring and refining methods of expressive, participatory and radically democratic forms of politics. This is inherent in the way we conduct our meetings, plan our events, how we participate in, create and maintain our national and international networks. We are not replicating existing structures, but developing new ones. We develop our solutions as we attack the forces that are destroying people and our planet.

Where next? I hope London RTS continues to be a catalyst for radical social and ecological change (remember June 18th was an inspiration for Seattle). I hope other ways of organising society shine through as we tear down the stock exchange brick-by-brick. I hope we make people laugh with our cheek and creativity. We are nothing more than a bunch of people radically remaking the world, inspiring others to do the same. We make mistakes, we learn, we try new things. But we are not content, like those in the media, to sit back and ride out capitalism until the fat lady sings. Are you?

Source: http://www.rts.gn.apc.org/streetpolitics.htm (downloaded 9 April 2001; accessed 19 March 2002)

6

Sociology unbound

Karim Murji

Contents

1 Introduction

**social
movements**

Is sociology a parasite? John Urry (1981, 2000) has written of it as such in two senses. First, Urry argues that it has been parasitic on **social movements** from which it has drawn its impetus and direction. He says:

> Most important developments in sociology have at least indirectly stemmed from social movements with 'emancipatory interests' that have fuelled a new or reconfigured social analysis. Examples of such mobilized groupings have at different historical moments included the working class, farmers, the professions, urban protest movements, student's movement, women's movement, immigrant groups, environmental NGOs, gay and lesbian movement, 'disabled' groups and so on.
>
> (Urry, 2000, p.210)

The concept of institutional racism provides an instance of this. The idea originated from within the radical Black Power social movement in the late 1960s. The years since then have witnessed an extended, and sometimes bitter, debate about the concept within sociology and beyond, most recently following the report of the inquiry into the murder of Stephen Lawrence (Macpherson, 1999). This inquiry and the subsequent discussion on it provided an important medium through which sociologists could contribute to public deliberations on institutional racism, and engage with public policy initiatives. These issues are the subject of section 2 of this chapter.

discourse

Second, Urry also argues that sociology's parasitic character is evident through its relationship with other academic disciplines, and we will look at an example of this in section 3. For Urry this is due to the organization of sociological **discourse** itself. In particular, he says sociology is characterized by openness, a relative lack of authority and control, and that it has no essence (Urry, 1981). These are important issues for this chapter so we should examine them in a little more detail. Urry writes that 'sociology's discursive formation has often demonstrated a relative lack of hierarchy, a somewhat unpoliced character, an inability to resist intellectual invasions' (Urry, 2000, p.3). Urry maintains that sociology is characterized by a lack of disciplinary closure – it is unable to 'police' its boundaries as successfully as some other disciplines. Because its boundaries are relatively fluid and permeable, it sometimes appropriates (and it can also develop and extend) social and intellectual currents that originate outside sociology. For example, in 1999 a 'state of the art' survey of teaching in race and ethnicity was published (Bulmer and Solomos, 1999). The contributions came from many disciplines including sociology, philosophy, history, cultural studies, anthropology, psychology, political science, English studies, geography and archaeology. This range of disciplines (and there are still others that could have been added – social policy, economics, literature, language studies, art history) indicates something of the breadth of contemporary work in the area of race and ethnicity. One notable feature of this collection is that, in spite of the diversity of the disciplines represented in it, there is some coming-together of themes and perspectives. In other words, there is some interdisciplinarity marking the study of race and ethnicity, crossing boundaries within and across the social sciences and humanities. These boundary crossings could also be extended to the natural sciences where questions about genetics, evolution, body-mapping and so on also figure in contemporary debates about race and ethnicity. Thus, the ideas that inform sociology – once regarded as 'the queen of the social sciences' – can come from many sources which it may parasitically absorb as well as contribute to.

For Urry, the open character of sociology flows from its lack of an essence. He believes that sociology's central concepts do not provide it with a discursive unity. For example, taking a central concept in sociology – the idea of '**society**' – Urry argues that sociology is made up of a multiplicity of perspectives that are not unified by a common idea of what society is. In section 3, we consider some implications of particular developments arising from other disciplines, especially historical, cultural and literary studies. We will show that these call into question the conventional histories of sociology's emergence, of the uses of sociology, and the idea of society. They suggest that the origins of sociology marked its role as a colonial discipline in which race and empire were central. This critique of sociological work has contemporary resonance with post-colonial perspectives and we will be looking at what the implications of this could be for sociology.

society

Sections 2 and 3 look at the nineteenth-century origins of sociology, its late twentieth-century impact and, perhaps, its twenty-first century future. They use examples concerned with race, ethnicity and racism to follow the two types of parasitism identified by Urry. It might be helpful to think of this as a process in which we are pulling on some 'threads' that 'unravel' as they are tugged. The underlying argument is that sociology's boundaries are fluid and can never be closed and that this is simultaneously a source of strength and weakness. Before moving on, I want to say a bit more about the theme of boundaries and its implication for this chapter.

We can introduce the discussion of boundaries by asking what the references to sociology and sociologists thus far cover? Is sociology equivalent to what is written by academic sociologists, that is those employed in sociology departments in universities and, if that were so, who or what might that exclude? Consider, for example, that at its inception in 1951 the British Sociological Association initially had a two-tier membership. This distinguished between those with qualifications (which could be academic, practical or publications, none of which necessarily had to be in sociology) and those who lacked any of these qualifications and just had an interest in sociology. This system was abandoned after only two years because, Barnes (1981) notes, of difficulties in distinguishing between these two levels of membership, particularly applications from people who seemed to be on the borderline between the two categories. Or, recall that in the Introduction to this book, it was pointed out that one in five of the 13,000 members of the American Sociological Association are not employed in universities and – apart from government departments – they presumably are based in think tanks, the media and voluntary associations. Sociologists may also be located in business, in industry and in commerce (an aspect that was considered in Chapter 4).

Sociologists working in think tanks conduct a good deal of sociological research into race and racial inequalities. Examples of such bodies in the UK include the Policy Studies Institute, the Institute for Public Policy Research, and the Runnymede Trust, among many others. The 'race-related' research produced by these bodies often aims to inform public debate and government policy, so its usefulness is often its key purpose. But, sometimes such work crosses the boundary from being engaged with such immediate governmental and policy concerns, to stand apart from that. Thus, even 'applied' social science research can reflect the boundary or division between sociologists as 'social administrators' (which was discussed in the Introduction, and in Chapter 7), against sociologists as 'social critics' (as Tony Bennett argued in Chapter 2). To pursue this distinction further let us look at why issues of race and ethnicity have become more central in sociology and other disciplines. Some reasons are:

power

- the role of race in contemporary social and political arrangements, including issues of **power** and inequality, citizenship, migration, and multiculturalism;

- the rise of new social movements, including both those pressing for greater racial equality, as well as neo-racist movements stressing ethnic purity and exclusionism;

post-structuralism

- shifts and developments in social theory away from grand or 'totalizing' narratives towards frameworks that can loosely be grouped under the heading **post-structuralism** which stresses the importance of language and textual analysis;

social problems

- criticisms of the construction of racialized minorities as **social problems** and of the ways these groups have been 'governed'.

(adapted from Bulmer and Solomos, 1999; Back and Solomos, 2000)

This is not intended as a comprehensive list but it does raise a division between 'external' (what's going on globally) and 'internal' (what's going on in academic disciplines) accounts. This can never be an absolute distinction and the question of the inter-relations between these two is what all of the chapters in this book have been considering – the changing relationship of sociology to the social world. However, do note that the last bullet point in the list seems to cut across the external/internal divide; indeed, it regards sociology – and the 'social administrative' tradition within it – as complicit in defining particular groups as social problems. This is an instance of the 'social critics' approach that we will be looking at further in section 3.

Sociology has always included both critics and administrators and, both historically as well as in current times, there is some overlap between the two. For example, as Ken Thompson points out in Chapter 7, some of the founders of sociology were critics of nineteenth-century individualism, and saw sociology as a vehicle for criticizing excessive individualism and capitalism. The first conference of the British Sociological Association in 1953 was on 'Social policy and the social sciences' and it included discussions on physical planning and the social services. At that time, the conception of sociology's role was closely tied with the growth of the welfare state (Platt, 2001). In this it had a clear lineage to the Sociological Society founded in 1903 and formed by urban planners, social statisticians, charity organizers and eugenicists. The eugenics movement and, more recently, sociobiology, appealed to ideas about 'race' and nation. But would this be 'scientific sociology' or 'political sociology', in terms of the

eugenics

categories that were identified in Chapter 1? **Eugenics** had a spurious scientific legitimation but its aims were explicitly 'political' – to control and limit the fertility of the 'degenerates' among the lower classes and 'others'. As this suggests, the boundaries between science and politics are often permeable and fluid. They often overlap rather than being separable into a neat dichotomy. Within sociology they reflect its relative openness and diversity, with its many strands, multiple perspectives and contested uses.

2 Sociology and institutional racism

The meaning, scope and applicability of the term 'institutional racism' have been debated extensively in recent years. Three examples provide a flavour of this controversy. In 1999, Minette Marrin felt that the term was being used as if it described an infectious epidemic in Britain, a condition that she saw as being close to 'mass hysteria' (Marrin, 1999). In 2000, the columnist Melanie Phillips argued that institutional racism had been 'used to damn the police to perdition' and that its use was based on 'utterly specious reasoning' (Phillips, 2000). And in 2001, Marion FitzGerald, a sociologist and former Home Office race relations adviser was noted as saying that institutional racism was a confusing, imprecise and 'empty phrase'; it 'offered no practical basis for action' (*BBC News*, 1 June 2001; *The Daily Telegraph*, 2 June 2001). The term has clearly been problematic, and by following some aspects of this discussion, we can indicate something about the impact of sociology and its role in public policy and media debates.

Why has the idea of institutional racism become a matter of – often – very heated argument in recent years? The immediate source is the report of the Macpherson inquiry into the death of the black teenager Stephen Lawrence who on 22 April 1993 was murdered by a group of white men in south London. Two days later the murder made the inside pages of the national press. There appeared to be little that made this event newsworthy for the media and it did not make the front pages. However, it went on to become one of the defining cases of the 1990s and its policy and symbolic ramifications are likely to continue for years to come. Following the failure to convict anyone of Stephen's murder, the Labour government that had been elected in 1997 announced the setting up of an inquiry into the case. Sir William Macpherson of Cluny, a retired judge, chaired the inquiry and its report was published in 1999. One of the most controversial aspects of the report was the view that the Metropolitan police's handling of the case had been marred by institutional racism.

The dispute about the term pre-dated the publication of the report. While the Macpherson inquiry was sitting there had been a continuing refusal from the hierarchy of the Metropolitan police and a significant, though un-quantifiable, number of police officers to accept that racism – whether institutionalized or otherwise – had anything to do with the failures of the investigation. The police argued that a finding of institutional racism condemned all police officers as acting with racist intentions. The distinction between *institutional* and *individual*

Figure 6.1 *The Stephen Lawrence memorial*

racism and the question of intentionality are important issues that flow from this and we will return to this in section 2.1.

As well as the police, Macpherson also recommended measures to tackle institutional racism in the public services. The Labour government accepted the report and pledged that it would implement the recommendations and monitor progress in an annual report (for an example, see Home Office, 2001). This represented an important acceptance of the idea of institutional racism. In terms of official policy, over the course of twenty years, British governments had gone from completely denying racism as a facet of British society to limited recognition and, most recently, official acknowledgement. For some sections of the media, it is this widening application of the term and the mirror that it appears to hold up to British society that are the basis of their rejection of it (for example, see Figure 6.2). It could be argued that a reason that the term and its connotations are disliked is because of its origins and association with the Black power group in the 1960s, which link the idea of institutional racism to left-wing and radical political movements. Yet, in the course of about 30 years, the term has become part of sociology and mainstream political discourse and been accepted by a British government.

Figure 6.2 *Cartoon from* The Independent *in the wake of the Macpherson report*

This movement from the margins into what seems to be the corridors of power is probably what makes it so unpalatable in some quarters. It certainly led to a backlash against Macpherson in the media. *The Daily Telegraph* and *The Sunday Telegraph*, for instance, condemned the report as incoherent and muddled. For these newspapers the finding of institutional racism was an unjustified slur on British society and on the police. Macpherson's acceptance and use of it led to him being called a 'useful idiot' for those pursuing political correctness, and of sounding 'like a lecturer in sociology from the Sixties … indulg[ing] in a series of sweeping generalizations' (McKinstry, 1999, p.30). These newspapers worried that there would be a government 'witch hunt' against anyone suspected of being a racist.

Let us turn to the source of the controversy. The main report of the Stephen Lawrence inquiry runs to over 300 pages but the nub of this debate flows from one chapter in the report.

READING 6.1

I would now like you to read the extract from the Macpherson report, which is Reading 6.1 at the end of the chapter.

As you read this, note the range of sources that the inquiry draws upon. Use these questions to focus your reading:

1   Why is the Scarman report regarded as significant and what parallels are drawn with it?

2   Why did the Commissioner of the Metropolitan police argue that the term institutional racism would be an unhelpful label?

3   What differences can you see between the Commissioner's view of institutional racism and the evidence (mostly in quotations) from others that are considered?

Several things struck me about this reading. First, note the many definitions presented. The inquiry apparently received 16 definitions of institutional racism in the evidence submitted to it and while it did not feel the need to consider each one, there is something laborious about its approach to the ones that are considered. It is easy to see why some have argued that establishing the meaning of institutional racism is essentially a form of 'sociological semantics'. This suggests that it is an academic exercise of interest only to sociologists, and that such a debate is far removed from the practical requirements of organizations and policy-makers. Second, there is a rather convoluted discussion using a wide range of sources. Significantly, among these it is notable that an official public inquiry considers the virtual manifesto of a militant social movement, namely Carmichael and Hamilton's *Black Power*. We will be looking further at this in section 2.1. Third, among the sources cited by the inquiry are several sociologists, and the inquiry says it found their contributions helpful in its deliberations – for instance, see paragraphs 6.31 and 6.33 of the extract. Let us look at this point further.

The sociologists who submitted evidence to the inquiry mostly did so in a personal capacity. There was no official response from the professional association for sociologists, or from similar bodies in related disciplines. What is significant about the sociologists whom the inquiry discusses (there were others who submitted evidence which is not mentioned) is that they have each played prominent roles in policing and race relations, maintaining a foot in both academic and policy work. As advisors to the Metropolitan police's Race Advisory Group, and as consultants working in police race-relations training, for example. In terms of influence and impact, it is noteworthy that sociologists should be at the centre of a major public inquiry and, particularly, in defining one of the key terms that inquiry considered. While none of them (or any of the other people who submitted evidence) are responsible for the inquiry's conclusions, or its own definition of institutional racism, it is obvious that Macpherson found their contributions useful. If one of the uses of sociology is to inform debate and discussion in the public sphere (as Jim McGuigan considers in Chapter 3) then here at least it seems to be a central player in a major public issue.

We can start to identify some of the key issues about institutional racism by referring back to Reading 6.1. In there, Macpherson can be seen as being in a dialogue with Lord Scarman's 1981 report. These are two key milestones in the public debate about institutional racism, though other reports and inquiries have also used the term. Both begin with issues of race (specifically, young blacks of African-Caribbean origins) and policing in the inner city. Scarman, a retired judge, inquired into the public disorders or riots that occurred in Brixton, south London, an area that had been characterized as suffering from high rates of criminality but also one with a long history of complaints about police misusing their stop-and-search powers to harass young black men. Scarman's inquiry examined both the immediate and longer-term causes of the 1981 riots. While he rejected the charge that police policies and actions in the area had been marked by institutional racism, Macpherson, in contrast, regards it as useful in accounting for the police's failures in the Stephen Lawrence case. However, beyond this 'headline' disagreement between them, there is something else going on that we need to look at more closely.

ACTIVITY 1

At this point, you may find it helpful to turn back to Reading 6.1 and to mark or highlight paragraphs 6.7, 6.15, 6.25, 6.28, 6.30, 6.33 and 6.34 as these are significant for the discussion that follows.

Macpherson cites Scarman's reasons for rejecting the term institutional racism (see paragraphs 6.7 and 6.15). In a nutshell, this is based on the absence of any explicit intent to discriminate or act in a racist manner. Furthermore, Scarman used the crucial phrase 'knowingly as a matter of policy' to dismiss the charge that the policies of the Metropolitan police were racist. However, Scarman did acknowledge 'unwitting discrimination', and for Macpherson *unintentional* or *unwitting* **discrimination** can lead to unequal and unfair outcomes and this is part of what constitutes institutional racism (see paragraph 6.15 and 6.34).

discrimination

The idea that people can be unwittingly or unintentionally racist is what sections of the press have most objected to in Macpherson's definition of institutional racism. For instance, this is the case made by Janet Daley in her column in *The Daily Telegraph*. She argues that rather than being seen as a personal attitude – that is, prejudice or dislike of black people – the Macpherson definition makes it seem that racism is everywhere. Because she regards racism as something that is individual, intentional and confined to a minority –

'benighted and vicious members of society' – as she puts it, she rejects the idea that racism can be institutional because it makes it intangible, amorphous and disconnects it from the intentions of individual people. As a result, she sees Macpherson's view as a form of 'thought crime' where people can be guilty simply because they refuse to admit to racism (Daley, 1999).

The words of the Metropolitan Police Commissioner (see paragraphs 6.25 and 6.46) and the views of some media commentators raise a shared objection to the term because they believe it is a broad-brush which contains the blanket accusation that all police officers are racist. They reject the 'we are all guilty' import that they believe the term carries. Indeed, some sociologists agree that this is a problem but regard other sociologists as culpable for such errors. For example, Simon Holdaway (who produced evidence for the inquiry on behalf of the Commission for Racial Equality, which is cited in Reading 6.1) states that the police's

> … refusal to accept the 'all officers are racists' version of institutional racism is reasonable. It is a version of the institutional racism thesis that has been implied by some sociologists who posit racialized inequalities at the societal and/or political levels and then, usually by implication, infer that all individuals are racists.
>
> (Holdaway, 1999a, paragraph 2.5).

Thus, the recurring theme of this debate is the unresolved individual/institutional dichotomy that pervades the question of whether institutional racism is witting (which, for Scarman, newspaper columnists such as Daley and others can only be applied to individuals) or unwitting (which, for Macpherson, includes thoughtlessness and ignorance).

ACTIVITY 2

Study this cartoon and make a brief note of what you think it indicates about an individual or institutional view of racism in an organization like the police. We will come back to this later.

Figure 6.3 *A blind spot?*

2.1 Sociology, social movements and politics

To gauge the extent to which the problems identified above are apparent in the origins of the term we can go back to its starting point. As noted earlier, the term institutional racism does not come from sociology. It was first used by Stokely Carmichael (who later changed his name to Kwame Ture) and Charles Hamilton in the USA in 1967. Carmichael was one of the leaders of the Black Panthers (a militant organization set up to combat racism) while Hamilton went on to become a professor of political science at Columbia University. Neither of them was, therefore, a sociologist, though the meaning and utility of the term they coined has continued to be debated in sociology and public life for over three decades since. Thus, to recall Urry's point, this is an instance of sociology acting parasitically on a social movement.

Carmichael and Hamilton's book *Black Power* is an explicit critique of the white establishment and a call for radical black political activity to oppose racism. Indeed, part of the preface of their book states that:

> *This book presents a political framework and ideology which represents the last reasonable opportunity for this society to work out its racial problems short of prolonged guerrilla warfare.*

ACTIVITY 3

The Macpherson Report cites a passage from *Black Power*. Please look briefly at paragraph 6.22 again in Reading 6.1 before moving on.

Carmichael and Hamilton (1992) argued that racism was pervasive and systemic in the USA. While they did not define institutional racism precisely, they used it to refer to three main things:

1   They treated individual and institutional racism as akin to the distinction between explicit and concealed – or overt and covert – forms of racism. While individual racism can be seen and heard, institutional racism is 'less overt, far more subtle, less identifiable in terms of *specific* individuals committing the acts. ... [it] originates in the operation of established and respected forces in the society' (p.4). Thus, they linked racism to powerful groups in society.

2   They saw institutional racism as based upon 'active and pervasive' (p.5) anti-black attitudes and practices and therefore suggested that racism was the outcome of normal and unquestioned bureaucratic procedures. White people benefited from these processes, even if they themselves did not wish to discriminate. Carmichael and Hamilton also maintained that whites believed themselves to be superior as a group to blacks and that this racist attitude operated on both individual and institutional levels, and overtly and covertly.

3   They regarded institutional racism as a form of internal colonialism in the USA, in that although blacks have the same citizenship status as whites, they stand in as colonial subjects in relation to white society.

In order to appreciate why their idea might have appealed to sociologists, we need to recall the political and academic context in which *Black Power* was published. Politically, in the USA in the 1960s there were a series of 'race riots' across that country; a burgeoning movement for civil rights (that eventually led to anti-discrimination legislation); and a prolonged debate about how to tackle and remedy the racial inequalities that were manifest in housing, employment, criminal justice and democratic representation (Williams, 1985). At the same time, this was a period of important changes within academic sociology. Jenny Williams notes how the dominance of **functionalism** within the discipline (a perspective concerned with social order and integration) was challenged by critical approaches such as interactionism, conflict and Marxist theories. Conflict and Marxist perspectives stressed the source of racial divisions as arising from the **social structure** and **political economy**. In doing so they questioned explanations of racial inequality and racism that were based on psychologically influenced accounts of prejudice and particular personality types (for example, '**the authoritarian personality**') or from anthropological models of a **culture of poverty** (Williams, 1985). In this way, sociologists moved beyond treating racism as a manifestation of prejudice (that is the view we saw from Daley, 1999), or of an individual attitude of hostility to others. Instead of prejudice, the term discrimination refers to the outcome of social processes – and the emphasis on process and outcomes can be seen in the definitions offered by sociologists to the Macpherson inquiry (for example, see paragraphs 6.30 and 6.33).

> **functionalism**

> **social structure, political economy, the authoritarian personality, culture of poverty**

The confluence of political and academic changes identified by Williams (1985) is significant because a number of sociologists took on the idea, with the aim of improving its utility for sociological analysis as well as for policy formulation and politics. While we can imagine why the idea was taken up by sociologists they also identified some problems with it. Carmichael and Hamilton's distinction between individual/overt and institutional/covert means that institutional racism can be regarded as something that may not be based on overt prejudicial attitudes, or even on any intention to discriminate. Although it may be difficult to detect, its manifestations are held to be observable in patterns of systematic inequality. But while they used it to refer to hidden and processual forms of racism not necessarily linked to prejudiced individuals, they also associated it with attitudes of group superiority. A difficulty with this is that it tends to treat racism as largely a case of white (institutional) power over blacks. However, this binary or 'Manichean' conception of whites and blacks as separate and opposed camps is not sensitive to variations in power within both groups. In addition, can we say that all racially skewed outcomes can be attributed to racism? To regard institutional racism as the root of such outcomes makes it impossible to isolate the specificity of racism from class and gender relations. For example, recruitment policies that rely on informal hiring practices may also be designed to exclude women and so cannot be treated as an instance of institutional racism (Miles, 1989).

For sociologists, the idea of institutional racism was useful as a way of accounting for systematic patterns of racial discrimination and disadvantage and stressing that these outcomes were not always based upon overt racist attitudes. Institutional racism was the process or mechanism that explained how racist outcomes were produced, even when individuals acted without racist intent. Thus, the term reinforced a conception of racism as a structural feature of society, rather than a psychological or cultural trait of individuals and groups. It was used to draw attention to the ways in which institutional practices can embody assumptions and values that are not explicitly biased but which nevertheless produce discriminatory outcomes. Macpherson's conception of unwitting racism reflects this, in part. It indicates that institutional racism can be unintentional and thoughtless, even unconscious (as the evidence of the Black Police Association (BPA) to Macpherson suggests – see paragraph 6.28 in Reading 6.1). Macpherson's definition (see paragraph 6.34) reflects an attempt to encapsulate both the idea of structural racism along with the cultural and organizational dynamics that the BPA's evidence brought out.

To the extent that sociology – parasitically? – linked up with the radical political and ideological movements of the 1960s and 1970s, it appealed to the 'social critics' who saw sociology's usefulness as a discipline and as a practice committed to egalitarian political and social aims, and which could probe and challenge existing relations of power and authority. Here we find an example of the somewhat porous nature of the boundary between sociological and political practices. Others, however, felt that this overlap between its sociological and political uses meant that institutional racism was being used largely as rhetoric – and that is why Scarman rejected it. For example, David Mason wrote that the term suffered from

> ... wide variation in uses ... [and] imprecision in many of the formulations of the concept ... [such] imprecise formulations, whose validity cannot be demonstrated, are a very poor basis indeed for the formation of policies or programmes of political action designed to combat racial disadvantage and oppression.
>
> (Mason, 1982, p.44)

Similarly, Williams writes that she wanted to improve the 'reform potential of anti-racist policies' (1985, p.323) and a barrier to this was that the uses of the term had become 'widespread and simplistic'. It had a 'catch-all' character, as if it explained all situations where racial inequalities could be observed (Williams, 1985).

These contributions were part of an extensive 1980s' post-Scarman discussion about the concept and meaning of institutional racism. Although sociologists tried to emphasize how it should be seen as a structural process (albeit with differences of emphasis about how it operated and was to be explained), sections of the media continued to insist that the idea of racism does not make sense unless it refers to the intentions of individuals. This either/ or approach is itself the problem (and it mirrors the **agency and structure** question in social theory), as it creates a dichotomy where racism has to mean one thing or the other. It can seem that the sociological position implies that no prejudiced or racist individuals are required to produce institutionally racist outcomes. Indeed, Miles (1989) notes this is seen as virtue of the term because intentionality is regarded as secondary to the consequences of actions. If the source or cause lies in the institution, individuals appear to be mere functionaries or 'dupes' who possess no choice or agency. As Philomena Essed points out, it is the individual/institutional dichotomy that is itself dubious because it places individuals outside of institutions, 'thereby severing rules, regulations and procedures from the people who make and enact them, as if it concerned qualitatively different racism rather than different positions and relations through which racism operates' (Essed, 1991, p.36).

In other words, it is the connections between institutional rules and procedures, and the people who frame and implement them that count, not

agency and structure

either one thing or the other. Indeed, following Scarman, Mason (1982) argued for theoretical approaches that could grasp both the interconnection of social structures and human action, as well as material and ideological forces. But what is unclear about some of those who are more sympathetic to the idea of institutional racism than the sections of the media we looked at earlier is whether they are employing the both or either/or conception. For example, during the Macpherson inquiry, one of the judge's advisers, Dr Richard Stone, urged the then Police Commissioner, Sir Paul Condon to 'just say yes' to the charge of institutional racism (we have seen in Reading 6.1 why he was disinclined to do so). While acceptance by the Commissioner would have been significant symbolically, the nature of this debate individualized the issue into one of personal rejection/acceptance. And looking back at Figure 6.3, we can see the same process at work. The implicit message is that 'if only' the Commissioner (personally, individually) overcame his blind spot and accepted the term the institutional recognition and remedy would follow. Thus, despite the attempts of sociologists, the individual/institutional and overt/covert dichotomies appear to remain as obstacles in public debates about racism. The next section considers some aspects of engagement and detachment in social research.

2.2 Social research and policy

Institutional racism turned out to be the key debating point stemming from the Macpherson inquiry and, as we have seen, sociologists undoubtedly had a significant impact on the inquiry's understanding and definition of it. Yet, in media discussions their impact seems much more muted. After the Macpherson inquiry, the only significant coverage given to sociological work on institutional racism was in September 2000 when most national newspapers covered the publication of two reports from a think tank, the Institute for the Study of Civil Society. One report was by the sociologist Norman Dennis and two colleagues (Dennis *et al.*, 2000). In it they reject the whole idea of institutional racism, saying that the term is incoherent, circular and that Macpherson is unable to demonstrate any instance or evidence of it by the police. The extent of the coverage this report received (for example, see Phillips, 2000) probably reflects the fact that it can be seen as a confirmation of views about Macpherson and about institutional racism already expressed in some newspapers.

But why did work by other sociologists not get covered? Sociology has sometimes been derided as a form of 'slow journalism', an accusation suggesting that the findings of sociological research, by the time they are produced, are banal and not particularly noteworthy. However, if this is even partially true, it also applies to Dennis *et al.* (2000). While their work is a detailed and almost line-by-line deconstruction of Macpherson, their conclusions are, in essence, no different from what columnists such as Daley (1999) and Marrin (1999) had already said about the Macpherson report.

Perhaps, as well as being regarded as too slow, sociologists are also seen as too disengaged and 'out of touch' with the pressing issues of the day. This is what Geoff Mulgan, the then head of the government's Performance and Innovation Unit, seems to suggest:

> I think government would benefit if every now and then think tanks and academics working together did do more quick and dirty research. So, for

example, when there are riots in Oldham or Burnley, when there is a fuel crisis, to me it is surprising that we don't get more people from universities and think tanks appearing in the media or offering to government empirically grounded analysis of how one should understand the phenomena and what some of the solutions might be. And this is another area where I think the time scales, the rhythms of academic life are, in many ways, just too slow for what government needs. There are some areas of work where you want that slowness, you want a real long-term, deep research to be done but equally there are some times when you need a quick illumination and I think too often we get neither one nor the other and too much in the middle ground.

(in Radio 4, *Analysis*, July 2001)

The events Mulgan refers to occurred during 2001 and were, at the time, urgent matters for the government. His remarks seem to question the speed, usefulness and quality of social research for government but, do not question whether, at least as far as universities are concerned, it is the business of academics to provide answers to the immediate questions that government faces – the government after all does employ its own researchers. In drawing this section to a close, I want to look at two issues about research that this raises: the first is where more engagement with policy from academic sociologists is sought and regarded as part of sociology's mission or purpose; the second suggests a need for some detachment between sociology and political agendas. The first aspect takes us back briefly to the coverage of research in the media.

In an article in a newsletter for sociologists, Holdaway discusses his contacts with the media around the time of the Stephen Lawrence inquiry and report. He reports how his own research on policing informed the evidence he submitted to the inquiry and he sees this work as standing on the boundaries between academic and policy work – seeking to influence both. He writes

The lesson I have learned about policy reform is to be resilient and dogged when pursuing one's ideas with government, the police, and whomever one tries to influence. I am now glad that, despite setbacks, I did not give up trying to influence the Home Office and other policy makers. I am glad that I have not tried to move my position as a sociologist away from the boundary between the police and the more detached academic world. The risk is to be viewed as a police sociologist by academic colleagues, as an idealistic academic by police officers. The point is to try and stay on the boundary, as uncomfortable as this might be.

(Holdaway, 1999b, p.11)

From this position he calls for more opportunities for sociologists to be involved in policy formulation and evaluation. Holdaway's view that sociologists should be involved in informing the policy questions that Macpherson raises is shared to some extent by John Solomos (1999). He agrees that existing research has not always been adequate for this purpose. However, with a focus not on policing issues, but on research on race, Solomos raises some cautionary remarks about the political tensions of sociological work on race issues, and stresses the stance of **John Rex** on this question in particular.

Rex, John

READING 6.2

Please turn to John Solomos, 'Social research and the Stephen Lawrence Inquiry' (Reading 6.2 at the end of this chapter).

Try to answer these questions as you read the extract:

1   What are the limitations of social research that Solomos identifies and what does he attribute these to?

2   What significance does he accord to the work of John Rex?

Solomos' view that social research on racism has been inadequate in addressing some of the key issues that Macpherson had to deal with is linked to the centres of race research in universities since the 1970s. These centres, he argues, employed a narrow and limited approach and the funds for research dedicated to them failed to engage with some important issues, in itself signalling an institutional failure of some sociology and social research. Solomos draws attention to the tensions between sociology and politics in race research by referring to Rex's work. Rex argued that sociologists should try to avoid the pitfalls of getting too drawn into immediate political and policy concerns, and instead focus on longer-term issues. Note that Rex does argue for political relevance and engagement but not necessarily in relation to the short-term and immediate questions of government.

In this way, we have come full circle to the issue of boundaries again. How closely should sociology be engaged with policy and political agendas? Will too close a connection with government mean it loses its integrity? Or, alternatively, will it be seen as too detached if it refuses to engage? The multiple boundaries between these proclaim different sorts of uses for sociology, where it can be close to the 'social administrative' tradition that seeks close involvement in progressive social policies, or, where it can also be part of the tradition that rejects these roles and sees sociology as a form of critical theory, as Merl Storr discussed in Chapter 5.

SUMMARY OF SECTION 2

This section has used institutional racism to explore several aspects of the uses of sociology. The main arguments have been that:

1   Sociology has been parasitic on a social movement.

2   Sociologists have had a significant impact on a major public inquiry and its discussion of institutional racism.

3   There is a gulf between the media and sociological discourse due to both the nature of media coverage and the limits of social research.

4   Sociology can be both engaged with and detached from policy and governmental concerns.

3 Sociology and post-colonialism

In section 3, our main reference point is the source and consequences of sociology's parasitic relations with other academic disciplines. We saw in section 1 that Urry argued that because sociology's boundaries are porous it is relatively open to developments and trends in other areas, and this may be one of the

post-colonialism

virtues of being a parasite (Urry, 1981). Sometimes, such developments are regarded as intellectual 'fashions' that come and go, and sociology (which is in any case very diverse) carries on regardless. The trend that we will be considering below is the impact and legacy of **post-colonialism**, which raises some fundamental questions about sociology's uses, concepts and methods. We will explore some of the consequences of postcolonial approaches (which originate from historical, cultural and literary studies) for sociology and society at the end of this section.

3.1 Sociology and empire

Does sociology have malign as well as benign uses? As Thompson argues in Chapter 7, some of the key founders of sociology thought that it could contribute usefully to progressive social change and a more ordered society. However, a straightforward notion of sociology as a useful way of analysing and ameliorating social concerns is questionable. In Chapter 2 Bennett argued that sociology plays an important role in technologies of government, and underlying this perspective is the key link between knowledge and power. Specifically, as Bennett says, from 'the perspective of governmentality, specific knowledges – like sociology – are examined to identify the role they play in making up certain kinds of power rather than to show how they legitimate power relations that have already been formed somewhere else' (Bennett, Chapter 2, p.65).

The discussion that follows also rests upon links between power and knowledge, in this case sociological knowledge itself and its relationship to government, empire and colonial domination. Following Bennett's point, what we should look for is sociology's role in 'making up' and legitimating power relations and we are going to consider two approaches that critically assess sociology's role in that. One comes from within sociology; the other does not. The latter follows from the work of Edward Said, a professor of comparative literature at Columbia University in the USA, especially his book *Orientalism* (1978) which is regarded as a founding text of post-colonial studies. The former draws upon an article by R.W. Connell, an Australian sociologist, in which he seeks to re-assess classical sociology by situating it in its social context. We begin with Said and to lead into this, we consider this statement from the editors of a book on Asian music cultures in Britain:

> We recognize interest in a sociology of South Asian culture in Britain, and especially youth cultures, as having close ideological connections with the disciplines of command that police inner-urban neighbourhoods, close down Black clubs, collude in migration control and so on.
>
> (Sharma *et al.*, 1996, p.2)

social control

Sharma *et al.* do not say what these disciplines of command are, but we can surmise that they see a close connection between sociology and various forms of **social control**. This is a rather vague term that, in this quotation, could encompass everything from urban planning to local licensing regulation, and beyond to policing and immigration control. The sociology they criticize is a form of social administration closely tied in with the welfare state and other forms of governance which they see as aiding the state and other agencies of control in containing and managing protest and dissatisfaction among young black and Asian people in Britain. They are particularly critical of the production of sociological knowledge derived from using ethnographic methods because they see it as a means by which cultural forms are 'imbued with an exoticized, othered status … [and this is] the Orientalist tradition of making knowable these cultural productions for an ever-eager academic audience and other agencies of control' (Sharma *et al.*, 1996, p.2). In their use of the term 'Orientalist' and the idea of 'making knowable' they invoke the tradition inaugurated by Said and to which we return in a moment.

Before that, it is useful to note that Sharma *et al.*'s critical perspective can be linked to other views of the **sociology of race**. Two examples illustrate this: first, following increased sociological interest in ethnicity in the 1980s, sociologists were accused of acting as 'cheerleaders' for a political strategy of divide and rule, which separated groups with common interests into competing and separatist 'ethnic enclaves' (Bourne, 1980). Bourne's approach, which draws upon a form of **Marxist sociology**, argues that an emphasis upon ethnic diversity militates against the common class interest of black and white groups. Second, other writers have criticized the sociology of race relations for being imbued with conservative and neo-colonial assumptions about ethnic and racial minorities. Assumptions about normal family structures, or appropriate forms of behaviour in public, for example, have been used as a yardstick against which some black cultures and behaviours have been regarded as deviant or in need of official intervention and correction through the agencies of the welfare state. In the early 1980s the authors of *The Empire Strikes Back* (CCCS, 1982) argued that a predominantly white sociology was one source producing such a 'black pathology'. Whatever the precise merits of both these arguments are, what they share, along with Sharma *et al.* (1996), is a view that sociological research and writing is a form of 'knowing' black cultures that is closely tied into relations of power, domination and subordination. These views therefore raise significant doubts about the uses of sociology and even suggest that it has malign purposes.

> **sociology of race**

> **Marxist sociology**

We now turn to explore Edward Said's approach. Said (1978) treats **Orientalism** as a systematic form of cultural discourse that creates and reproduces various inter-linked oriental stereotypes – ideas of 'the East' characterized by sexual exoticism, religious mysticism and corrupt despotism, for instance. These distinctive ways of conceptualizing the Orient as 'different' sets up a 'we–them' opposition or distinction to the 'West' through which the exoticism of the former is contrasted with the morality of the latter.

> **Orientalism**

It is important to underline that in Said's argument ideas about 'us' and 'them' are mutually constituted: they depend upon one another. They also establish the link between knowledge, power and government:

> The idea of the 'West' as white, Christian, rational, civilized, modern, sexually disciplined and indeed *masculine* was put into place in a protracted process in which the colonized Others were defined in opposition to these virtues. It was in constructing the 'natives' as black, pagan, irrational, uncivilized, pre-modern, libidinous, licentious, effeminate and child-like that the self-conception of the European as superior, and as not only *fit* to govern but as having the positive *duty* to govern and 'civilize' came into being.
>
> (Rattansi, 1997, p.482)

Said maintained that Orientalist discourse is to be found in the writings of academics as well as government officials. The academic category included historians, geographers, anthropologists and sociologists. Their writings dichotomize the East and the West and produced seemingly authoritative ways for Westerners to 'see' the Orient, its places and people. Orientalist discourse therefore shapes notions about civility, purity, cleanliness, and so on, which places – or rather 'centres' – the 'West' on one side and 'the rest' on the other, on the periphery (Clifford, 1988; Hall, 1992). Again, the imagined location of the 'West' depends upon, indeed it is constituted by, the notion of 'the other' as being on the margin. As Chandra Mohanty says: 'it is only insofar as … the East [is] defined as Other, or as peripheral that (Western) man/humanism can represent him/itself as the centre. It is not the centre that determines the periphery but the periphery that in its boundedness determines the centre' (Mohanty, 2000, p.317). For Said, the 'gaze' of sociological – as well as other disciplines – knowledge and expertise was instrumental in making and legitimating such distinctions.

ACTIVITY 4

Said's approach to the links between power, knowledge and government are related to the argument about this made in Chapter 2. You might find it helpful to look back at this now before reading on.

For another approach to the relations between sociology and empire, we turn to an article by R.W. Connell in which he sets out an argument about how classical sociology became classical, meaning how a particular period and group of writers became central to sociology's own sense of its origins. Sociology's origins and past are usually linked to its 'founding fathers' – Marx, **Durkheim**, **Weber**. Some or all of Simmel, Comte and Spencer are sometimes also added to the list. Connell calls this the conventional 'foundation story' of sociology, which:

Durkheim, Emile Weber, Max

> As a teaching discipline and as a discourse in the public arena was constructed at a particular time and place: the final two decades of the nineteenth century and the first decade of the twentieth century in the great cities and university towns of France, the United States, Britain, Germany and, a little later, Russia.
>
> (Connell, 1997, p.1515).

modernity

According to the foundation story, sociology emerged in these places because they were the centres of industrialization, urbanization and democratization, broadly the experience of **modernity**. Sociology came out of this experience because it was an approach that sought to account for the new kind of society that was being created. Connell's article, which we will ask you to turn to in a moment, questions the foundation story. Through a survey of the texts that sociologists were writing and referring to during this classical period: Connell maintains that most had little to say about modernization or the existing societies those sociologists were living in. A similar picture emerges from his review of sociological research as represented in 12 issues of *L'Annee sociologique* produced by Durkheim and others between 1898 and 1913: contemporary issues made up a minority of its contents. If this is correct, then the conventional story – that sociology came about as a way of making sense of the world around it – is dubious. Indeed, Connell says works on ancient societies, colonial or remote societies and global surveys of human history dominated sociology and that rather than studying the relatively recent experience of modernity, sociologists were examining a huge span of human history. Furthermore, he argues that their work was based on the key idea of a contrast between the metropolitan centre and the primitive periphery; this dichotomization creates a category of 'others' by which 'we' know our difference from 'them'. For Connell, in registering this as a key concern, sociology reflected its social location, in the time and place of empire. To follow this argument further I would like you to now read Connell's own words.

<hr>

READING 6.3

Please turn to Reading 6.3, R.W. Connell's 'Why is classical theory classical?' (1997).

Keep these questions in mind as you read:

1   How is the assumption of 'global difference' seen in ideas about evolution and progress in nineteenth century sociology?

2   Why does Connell stress the geopolitical context of nineteenth-century sociology?

3   Why and how does he see the topics of race and gender as integral to a social science based on evolution?

You may have found this a difficult reading because Connell surveys a wide range of sociologists and sociological history in it so it will be useful to review the questions above. Connell's argument is that the foundation story of sociology's origins in the urban, industrial and cultural centres of Europe and North America overlooks the fact that these were also the centres of modern **imperialism**. His examples of colonial expansionism locate some of the 'founding fathers' within this time-frame, and as providing them with some of their source materials. He contends that the time and place of sociology's origins are closely tied in with the social relations of empire. Because sociology was formed within this culture, it embodied the assumptions and values of empire in terms of its *content* and its *methods*. We now look at this point in more detail.

    With regard to its content, Connell maintains that ideas about evolution and progress constituted the cornerstones of sociology, especially in the work of Herbert Spencer, who in his lifetime was far more influential than Marx, Durkheim or Weber were in theirs. Sociology, in this sense, was the discipline that furnished the empirical basis for a linear conception of social change from the primitive to the modern, and from homogeneity to heterogeneity. Antonio Gramsci derided this version of **evolutionary theory** when he said that sociology was characterized by 'vulgar evolution' that predicted 'scientifically' that the oak tree would grow out of the acorn. For Connell, the evolutionary story in sociology relied upon (a) unquestioned disparity between the metropole and the colonial 'Other' and (b) the idea of linear development, and took these as the object of sociological research and theory. In other words, sociology took for granted that this 'difference' was real and set out to explain or account for it without questioning if it was true, or when and how it arose. In locating classical sociology within a geo-political perspective Connell highlights why 'global difference' was central to sociology. In an era of colonial expansion, sociology was, he suggests, a colonial science that gathered knowledge about the colonized world and used it in theories about the higher or superior status

imperialism

evolutionary theory

of European peoples. Furthermore, Connell states that ideas about racial (and gender) differentiation and superiority were integral to a social science based upon ideas of progress and evolution. This too reflected the concerns of empire. It was, he argues, evident in the texts produced in the metropole where ideas about racial hierarchy, degeneration and the consequences of miscegenation were propounded.

Finally, he links the content of sociology with a particular methodology: comparative sociology. Connell says that the form of comparative sociology employed at this time had one of two characteristics. It either relied upon a conception of the observer/sociologist as standing outside and above the society being studied or it aimed to survey and classify the whole world. Connell calls this unidirectional perspective the 'imperial gaze' and he says that such a gaze was evident in the works of both Durkheim and Weber, although this argument about the 'eurocentric' perspective of classical sociology could be extended to all of the other 'founding fathers' as well as other sociologies that followed in the twentieth century.

The arguments proposed by Said and Connell are not equivalent but they do overlap. They suggest that sociology, its content and methods are useful. At the very least, it contributes to, and perhaps 'makes up', or helps to constitute power and domination through which the 'West' saw others, and developed ideas about its own evolutionary superiority. Taken together, these arguments constitute a powerful challenge to a sociology that bases its sense of usefulness on the universalist claims to reason, prediction and progress. Inevitably, since these perspectives confront the core of some sociology's sense of its purpose and reason for existing, the positions that we have considered are not uncontested and we will turn briefly now to some criticisms of these views.

ACTIVITY 5

Before that, I would like you to reflect for a moment on what has been said so far. While our discussion has connected with the ideas about power and knowledge that Tony Bennett discussed in Chapter 2, it also raised some unfamiliar contexts in which these ideas are said to have operated. Has sociology been useful for the purposes that Said and Connell suggest (recall that in Chapter 1 Peter Hamilton questions the assumption that sociology is necessarily useful)? Are all the examples of sociological work that Connell discusses significant ones? For example, how many of them are names you might find in a sociology dictionary, or a contemporary textbook?

The aim here is not to try to provide a balance sheet weighing one set of arguments against the other, since that would be a diversion from the main theme. It is important though to indicate some difficulties identified with the positions that we have covered. Firstly, in referring to a contrast between the 'West' and the Orient, Said has been accused of regarding the 'West' as homogenous and of overlooking the fractures and fissures that have always existed within it (Rattansi, 1997). In other words, the 'West' possesses a degree of internal differentiation that is underplayed within his account. Secondly, the other kind of homogenization to be aware of is the assumption that colonialism and imperialism were the same everywhere. Different colonial projects involved diverse practices and, while they may overlap, they also need to be understood in their historical and cultural context. By extension this point would also mean that sociology and other disciplines were diverse rather than a consistent 'orientalizing' discourse. Thirdly, the form of textual analysis used by Said to critique 'colonial knowledge' could be regarded as overstating the power and influence of social scientists, and of ignoring differences between them (that is, of treating them as all the same). It is also sometimes argued that accounts based on textual analysis are unable to specify how the influence of these texts informs practices of government and domination, though detailed studies do make this link (Rattansi, 1997).

Turning to Connell, Randall Collins (1997) takes issue with much of what Connell says about the content and nature of early sociology. Collins argues that Connell glosses over differences between sociologists and, in particular, differences in the methods and theories of Anglo-American and European sociologists. Collins also insists that:

(a) Many sociologists of the time were concerned with contemporary matters and the transformation of their own societies.

(b) Some of the sociologists used to exemplify Connell's argument were minor figures who had little influence on sociology.

(c) Connell's account of the links between sociological ideas and colonialism is 'Anglocentric': it works best for Britain but does not necessarily fit other European countries.

(d) The connection between imperialism and sociology is overstated and does not explain why sociology did not develop under other, earlier, imperial powers – for example, Portugal and Spain.

Despite these (and there are others) criticisms, Said's analysis of orientalist discourses has been extremely influential, perhaps vital, in post-colonial studies, especially in the humanities. The extent to which this influence registers within sociology indicates its parasitic and porous qualities in picking up on developments elsewhere. It also marks an increasing interdisciplinarity on issues of race and ethnicity across the boundaries of the social sciences and humanities, as I suggested in section 1. Notwithstanding Collins' comments, Connell's questioning of the foundation story of sociology suggests to us a different approach to the uses sociology has and could have. What these are and some implications of postcoloniality for sociology will be easier to think about after we have looked at how the idea of society in sociology also illustrates connections between sociology, **nationalism** and empire.

nationalism

3.2 Sociology after society

This book is part of a series called 'Sociology and Society'. These words appear prominently on the cover and it might seem natural that they are coupled since sociology was once regarded as being the 'science of society', though this is a definition that few sociologists would now use. Bennett *et al.* (2002) consider some of the assumptions that a 'science of society' was based on and why each of those has been called into question. One of these assumptions is that society could be thought of as having an objective existence. As they say, developments in the history of sociology have undermined this assumption making 'it difficult to hold on to the view that society is, for sociologists, something which exists "out there" independently of sociological ways of thinking and doing' (*ibid.*, p.7).

To develop the point about the role of 'society' in sociology, let us recall that in his article Connell states that the origins of sociology can only be understood through the structure of world society. This suggests that he is invoking a tradition known as **world-system theory**, particularly associated with Imannuel Wallerstein. This is significant because, as we will see in the next reading, Wallerstein's theory criticizes the ways in which the idea of society is unthinkingly invoked in sociology. World-system theory has been challenged and probably overtaken by the idea of **globalization**, which also questions the validity, or usefulness, of the term society. Smart (1993) sums up some of these globalizing changes and their consequences for the idea of society:

> An acceleration of economic and technological change; associated transformations in the experience of space and time … the increasingly global scale of economic and cultural forms of life; and the (re)emergence of 'regional', 'ethnic' and traditional social divisions have rendered the idea of 'society' as a unity, equivalent to the geopolitical order of the nation state, problematic as the focus for contemporary sociology.
>
> (Smart, 1993, p.74).

The key argument here is that economic and cultural globalization signal the imminent demise of the **nation-state**; they make it increasingly difficult to identify the 'boundaries' of nations and of a society – indeed we could only think in terms of societies in the plural. What is 'inside' and what is 'outside' are unstable and not fixed. For example, is Britain one society or many societies? To regard it as one we would have to overlook the multiple social divisions as well as the regional and nationalist tensions of parts of Britain. If we add to this the ongoing debate about how far the European Union cuts into and across British national sovereignty, it becomes clear that to speak of 'British society' in the singular probably obscures more than it reveals. But even to speak of 'British societies' in the plural only leads to the question of what the connection between the two words is. As Smart (1993) suggests, the lack of clear boundaries leads to dissociation between 'society' and its equivalent identification with the nation state.

But how are these two associated in the first place? To look at this question we will now turn to an extract from Michael Billig's *Banal Nationalism*.

world-system theory

globalization

nation state

READING 6.4

Please turn to Michael Billig (1995) 'Banal nationalism' (Reading 6.4 at the end of this chapter). As you read, note his arguments about the centrality of society as well as some of the problems with it raised by particular sociologists. Then consider these questions:

1   What is the evidence that the idea of society equates with the nation state?

2   What are the difficulties with thinking of society/ies as self-contained units?

Billig (1995) suggests that the invocation of society has become an unexamined habit in sociology. It is embedded as part of sociological commonsense, as his discussion of some textbooks shows. However, a number of sociologists – he cites Wallerstein and Giddens as examples – have questioned its meaning and use.

Billig goes on to argue that references to society are an instance of what he calls 'banal nationalism'. That is, the image and idea implied in referring to 'our' society is an analogue of the nation-state. However, this association generally remains implicit, because 'nationalism' is regarded as something associated with 'hot spots' like the former Yugoslavia, or other places marked by inter-ethnic violence. While the image of society implied in sociology is related to the nation-state, Billig argues that allowing 'society' to stand in for 'nation' is an instance of banal nationalism. Such works, Billig argues, fail to consider societies in the plural and they obscure the link between society and nation. To illustrate how common or banal such nationalism is, take a brief look at the quote from the preface of Carmichael and Hamilton's *Black Power* on page 230. Note how, even in a radical and revolutionary text, the unexamined reference to 'this society' really means the nation state (the USA, for the context they were writing in).

Urry (2000) also argues the idea of society in all its guises in diverse sociological perspectives is not attuned to the connections between and beyond society, the nation and nation states. Like Smart and others, he argues that a globalizing world undermines the idea of society as a self-reproducing entity with clear and fixed boundaries. The conception of society he employs is one of it as 'a sovereign social entity and with a nation-state that organizes the rights and duties of each societal member or citizen. Most major sets of social relationships are seen as flowing within the territorial boundaries of the society' (Urry, 2000, p.8).

ACTIVITY 6

Before going on, I would like you to pause and reflect for a moment. Look at how Urry defines the conception of society again, particularly his reference to sovereignty and national citizenship. What societies or nations do you think this might apply to, or conversely, what does it exclude? In formulating your response, think back to Connell's description of the places and the period where sociology began.

The key objection that Urry raises is that the conception of 'sovereign' societies/ nation states,

> … only applied to the dozen or so societies of the north Atlantic rim (as well as Japan) [because] most of the rest of the world was subject to domination. It was the societies of the north Atlantic rim which were the colonial powers, having hugely significant economic, military, social and cultural relationships beyond their borders.

(Urry, 2000, p.11)

So, historically the social relations of empire and colonialism also framed what the idea of society meant. Society as a sovereign entity, equivalent to the borders of the nation-state and with powers over citizenship was, mostly, only applicable to Europe and North America. As colonial powers, however, they exercised power and influence that extended beyond any bounded conception of 'society', not least in terms of regulating citizenship. In other words, colonial powers were employed fluidly across borders, even while the idea of 'society' in sociology referred to a bounded and supposedly coherent entity. Urry's point underlines the partiality and unexamined assumptions of the idea of society, yet it is a term that sociology has commonly used without any acknowledgement of these problems.

So far, in this section we have seen that Said's and Connell's arguments raise questions about the uses of sociological knowledge. They suggest that its contents and methods have been useful, but for purposes quite different from the values of reason and progress. Rather, sociology – in its concepts and methods – has been a colonial science that has been closely involved in power–knowledge relations through which 'others' have been constructed, stereotyped and demeaned. Following that, we have also noted that Billig and Urry show how the conception of 'society' in sociology has, until recently, failed to acknowledge its use as a synonym for the nation-state. Historically, this has overlooked the very ones that sociology was founded in, and as Connell argued, these particular nation states were central in projects of empire and colonial domination during the formative or classical period of sociology.

While sociology has often had its purposes and uses questioned, the perspectives we have been considering disturb, disrupt and unsettle some of the boundaries and conceptions that sociology has usually worked with and within. They raise questions about its methods and concepts. They suggest that the boundaries between sociology and politics have been quite porous, and that while its political role is more diffuse it is also more far reaching – it helps to construct, inform and sustain the political culture of empire and of colonial domination. But is it possible to identify what elements of a post-colonial sociology would look like?

To draw the threads of these arguments together, it will be useful to begin by looking at Urry's (2000) idea of what a sociology that does not rely upon or invoke society could consist of. And to this we could add a sociology that is aware of its origins and social location. For Urry (2000), sociology requires a new and re-imagined agenda 'beyond societies' (as he puts it), and to do so it needs to be organized around ideas of networks, mobilities and horizontal fluidities across the globe. A key part of his argument refers to the corporeal and imaginative mobilities of people and to exemplify it, he invokes the idea of diaspora. This term refers to several examples of forced movement and migration of peoples to new territories. Thus it can be used in relation to Jewish people (the exodus) and the movement of Irish people in the eighteenth and nineteenth centuries. It is also used to denote a black diaspora, connected to exile and transportation due to slavery. But what is the significance of this for our purposes? Movement and mobility across borders and boundaries are central to the experience of diaspora and migration, in ways that must question what 'society' diasporic identities could be affiliated with. Consider, for example, the diaspora identities of the West Indian descendants of African slaves. Is Africa or the Caribbean the 'homeland'? For those whose parents and grandparents migrated to the UK, is Britain 'home'? These questions do not tend to clear or bounded answers – they indicate that diaspora identities are defined by shifting, rather than static, geographic locations. A sense of mixture and multiple locations signals hybridization and plurality rather than identification with society/the nation state. These transnational connections undermine the idea of a bounded society; they also suggest, as Clifford (1997) notes, that the nation-state is traversed and, perhaps, subverted, by diasporic attachments.

Put in this way, diaspora sounds like it is something to do with particular minorities. However, Avtar Brah (1996) makes a broader conceptual claim for the idea. Brah argues that diaspora spaces are where the boundaries of inclusion/

exclusion, of 'us' and 'them', are contested. In this space the identities and histories of those who 'move' as well as those who 'stay' are entangled and intertwined. Both 'inhabit' the diaspora space within which multiple identities and axes of differentiation (class, gender and race, for example) are inter-related, re-configured and cross over (Brah, 1996). In this overlapping schema, what is 'central' and what is 'peripheral' become indeterminate and fluid.

In addition to calling into question the boundaries of society and nation, diasporic identifications are significant in other ways. They can also challenge nationalist ideologies of space and time, as Bennett (**2002**) shows , and of linearity and teleology. The same point about space and time can be made in a different way. Connell (1997), as we saw, argues that sociology's ideas about progress and evolution were formed in the European colonial context. These employed a distinction between primitive/modern and assumed a linearity of development or progression from the former to the latter state. However, a post-colonial approach interrupts and re-orders the idea of progress and development so that:

> … societies that came into being through colonial encounters can no longer be discursively appropriated through a grid which reads them as re-runs of an oft-told narrative of the transition from one mode of production to another, whether in Marxist or Weberian vocabulary, and certainly not as an equally straightforward story of 'modernization' as functionalist, mostly American sociology would have it.
>
> (Rattansi, 1997, pp.482–3).

These points raise doubts about the concepts and categories of sociology and its foundations. They challenge and revise the hegemonic assumptions of 'western' cultures by creating a space for what Hesse (1999) calls a 'politics of interrogation'. This, he suggests, would entail calling into question the relation between the visible achievements of western humanism and culture (such as democracy and liberalism) and the invisible dehumanization and violence of western culture (such as slavery). Re-writing that history requires recognition that the latter is not an aberration of the former, but that they are closely and, perhaps necessarily, inter-linked. Such interrogation also challenges the attribution of a progressive, universal reason to a specific European cultural formation (Smart, 1993). It disrupts and displaces – or 'decentres' – western modernity through identifying alternative knowledges (sometimes called subaltern narratives) in order to recover hidden experiences of colonialism and resistances to it.

This is not a comprehensive list but it does signal some of the ways in which a post-colonial perspective could inform sociology. It would not entail simply trying to complete sociology by 'adding in' the rest of the world in a bid for 'totalizing' coherence. Rather, by interrupting and disturbing some or all of the established assumptions and methods of sociology it would re-configure the questions that sociology addresses and suggest that the answers are necessarily fragmentary.

SUMMARY OF SECTION 3

The main arguments of this section have been that:

1   Sociology's orientalist history and its location in the social relations of imperialism are disruptive of its foundation story.

2   Society is used as sociological commonsense in ways that obscure its connections with the nation-state and with nationalism.

3   Post-coloniality in sociology would invoke transnational conceptions of history, identity and space and time.

4 Conclusion

The two main parts of this chapter have followed Urry's conception of sociology as a parasite. In section 2 we saw that the idea of institutional racism initially came out of the Black Power movement and has been taken up and developed by sociology. In section 3 we touched on what some of the consequences for sociology of a post-colonial perspective – which has, to date, been more influential in some other disciplines – could be. While we can see that sociology has drawn upon, and can incorporate and adapt, both these sources, we should still ask if the general charge of parasitism is justified. If being a parasite implies a one-way relationship where sociology 'freeloads' on external sources then these two instances would suggest that it is not wholly accurate to describe sociology as parasitic. While sociology has drawn upon social movements, it has also contributed to them. In the example of institutional racism, it has refined its meaning and application conceptually and empirically. Sometimes, ideas from sociology move out into public debate and public inquiries (as in the case of the Macpherson inquiry). They may also be taken up in other disciplines, for example sociological work on institutional racism may also be used in criminology and social policy. As this implies, ideas from sociology may travel in diverse ways and sociological work on post-coloniality and diasporas may also inform what is going on elsewhere. These consequences mean that sociology does not simply absorb from the outside: it is not a one-sided parasite. Indeed, Urry (1981) argues that parasitism is a virtue, as well as a vice, of sociology because it provides a space where ideas from diverse sources can be debated and assessed.

The other theme of this chapter has been to stress the fluid and open nature of sociology's boundaries. We can conclude this theme by relating it to two sorts of worries within sociology about sociology and its boundaries. One is that sociologists could undermine the academic credibility and integrity of the discipline by becoming too closely involved and identified with political agendas and programmes. In section 2 we noted that sociology can influence major public issues in ways that connect with public policy. But it is a highly uneven, and perhaps unpredictable, impact with sociologists putting forward arguments for and against the concept of institutional racism, and some seeking a 'third-way' modification of the idea. We also saw that there is a gulf between sociology and media debate and, while this can partly be attributed to the media, it can also be linked to sociological research. There are sociologists who take differing views on the level of engagement/detachment that sociologists should have but in all of these cases, the boundaries between sociology and politics are porous and, sometimes, indistinct.

Scientific sociology can be seen as an approach that seeks the greatest distance between sociology and politics – for instance, association with radical social movements. But it is not the case that scientific sociology is apolitical (a point reinforced in the introduction, as well as in Chapters 1 and 7). Indeed, sociology has all kinds of associations with politics and policy, for example in its identification with the 'social administrative' tradition that Thompson discusses in Chapter 7. If sociology's key and original justification – what Smart calls its 'legitimating narrative' (Smart, 1993, p.69) – has been the development of the foundations for a more secure and ordered society through its contribution to the amelioration of social problems arising from modernity, there has always been a degree of cross-over between sociology and politics.

A second type of worry about sociology's boundaries is that forgetting or erasing its foundations and its history will undermine sociology. There are now many instances where the case for the centrality of classical sociology is stated. Such attempts to resurrect a sociological 'canon' – a list of the classics that define its core – could be understood as an attempt to draw a line or a boundary around its subject matter, to define what is 'in' and what is 'out'. This chapter has gone further than that by considering that sociology's 'core' can be revisited and revised to recall what may have been overlooked about the social location, as well as the concepts and methods, of sociology in the period that it was founded. What can also be revised are things that seemed to be central to sociology, such as the idea of society. But in noting how that term has become questionable, we can see that sociology develops and moves on through reviewing conflicting uses of a term and by questioning its own boundaries and purposes. In this way, sociology's flexibility, its unbounded and diverse character, is a strength rather than a weakness.

References

Abrams, P., Deem, R., Finch, J. and Rock, P. (eds) (1981) *Practice and Progress: British Sociology 1950–1980*, London, George Allen & Unwin.

Back, L. and Solomos, J. (eds) (2000) *Theories of Race and Racism: A Reader*, London, Routledge.

Barnes, J.A. (1981) 'Professionalism in British sociology' in Abrams, P. *et al.* (eds) *op. cit.*.

Bennett, T. (2002) 'Contesting time: conflicting histories in post-colonial contexts' in Jordan, T. and Pile, S. (eds) *Social Change*, Oxford, Blackwell/ The Open University. (Book 3 in this series.)

Bennett, T., Sherratt, N. and Thompson, K. (2002) *DD201 Course Guide*, Milton Keynes, The Open University.

Bennett, T. and Watson, D. (eds) (2002) *Understanding Everyday Life*, Oxford, Blackwell/The Open University. (Book 1 in this series.)

Billig, M. (1995) *Banal Nationalism*, London, Sage.

Bourne, J. (1980) 'Cheerleaders and ombudsmen: the sociology of race relations in Britain', *Race and Class*, vol.21, no.4, pp.331–52.

Brah, A. (1996) *Cartographies of Diaspora*, London, Routledge.

Bulmer, M. and Solomos, J. (eds) (1999) *Ethnic and Racial Studies Today*, London, Routledge.

Carmichael, S. (later known as Kwame Ture) and Hamilton, C. (1992) *Black Power: The Politics of Liberation*, New York, Vintage. First published in 1967.

CCCS (1982) *The Empire Strikes Back*, London, Routledge.

Clifford, J. (1988) *The Predicament of Culture*, Cambridge, MA, Harvard University Press.

Clifford, J. (1997) 'Diasporas' in Guibernau, M. and Rex, J. (eds) *The Ethnicity Reader*, Cambridge, Polity Press.

Collins, R. (1997) 'A sociological guilt trip: comment on Connell', *American Journal of Sociology*, vol.102, no.6, pp.1558–64.

Connell, R.W. (1997) 'Why is classical theory classical?', *American Journal of Sociology*, vol.102, no.6, pp.1511–57.

Daley, J. (1999) 'Coming soon: a new offence – institutional thought crime', *The Daily Telegraph*, 23 February.

Dennis, N., Erdos, G. and Al-Shahi, A. (2000) *Racist Murder and Pressure Group Politics: The Macpherson Report and the Police*, London, Institute for the Study of Civil Society.

Essed, P. (1991) *Understanding Everyday Racism*, London, Sage.

Hall, S. (1992) 'The west and the rest' in Hall, S. and Gieben, B. (eds) *Formations of Modernity*, Cambridge, Polity Press.

Hesse, B. (1999) 'It's your world: discrepant M/multiculturalisms' in Cohen, P. (ed.) *New Ethnicities, Old Racisms?*, London, Zed.

Holdaway, S. (1999a) 'Understanding the police investigation of the murder of Stephen Lawrence: A mundane sociological analysis', *Sociological Research Online*, vol.4, no.1, www.socresonline.org.uk.

Holdaway, S. (1999b) 'A sociologist's involvement with the Lawrence Inquiry', *Network*, no.74, October.

Home Office (2001) *Stephen Lawrence Inquiry: Home Secretary's Action Plan – Second Report on Progress*, London, Home Office.

McKinstry, L. (1999) 'Macpherson was just a useful idiot', *The Sunday Telegraph*, 28 February.

Macpherson, W. (1999) *The Stephen Lawrence Inquiry*, London, The Stationery Office.

Marrin, M. (1999) 'How racism fever gripped the nation', *The Sunday Telegraph*, 14 March.

Mason, D. (1982) 'After Scarman: a note on the concept of institutional racism', *New Community*, vol.x, no.1, pp.38–45.

Miles, R. (1989) *Racism*, London, Routledge.

Mohanty, C. (2000) 'Under Western eyes' in Back, L. and Solomos, J. (eds) *Theories of Race and Racism: A Reader*, London, Routledge.

Phillips, M. (2000) 'Now we know the truth: the police are not racist', *The Sunday Times*, 24 September.

Platt, J. (2001) 'History of the BSA', *Network*, no.78, January.

Rattansi, A. (1997) 'Postcolonialism and its discontents', *Economy and Society*, vol.26, no. 4, pp.480–500.

Said, E. (1978) *Orientalism*, London, Penguin.

Scarman, L. (1981) *The Brixton Disorders*, London, HMSO.

Sharma, S., Hutnyk, J. and Sharma, A. (1996) 'Introduction' in *DisOrienting Rhythms: The Politics of New Asian Dance Music*, London, Zed.

Smart, B. (1993) *Postmodernity*, London, Routledge.

Solomos, J. (1999) 'Social research and the Stephen Lawrence Inquiry', *Sociological Research Online*, vol.4, no.1, www.socresonline.org.uk.

Urry, J. (1981) 'Sociology as a parasite: some vices and virtues' in Abrams, P. e*t al.* (eds) *op. cit.*.

Urry, J. (2000) *Sociology Beyond Societies*, London, Routledge.

Williams, J. (1985) 'Redefining institutional racism', *Ethnic and Racial Studies*, vol.8, no.3, pp.323–48.

Readings

6.1 Sir William Macpherson of Cluny, 'The Stephen Lawrence Inquiry' (1999)

Racism

6.1 A central and vital issue which has permeated our Inquiry has been the issue of racism. The chilling condemnation, made by and on behalf of Mr and Mrs Lawrence … of the police and of the system of English justice, has sounded through all the months of our consideration of the evidence. Mr and Mrs Lawrence allege and fervently believe that their colour, culture and ethnic origin, and that of their murdered son, have throughout affected the way in which the case has been dealt with and pursued. …

…

6.3 **In this Inquiry we have not heard evidence of overt racism or discrimination, unless it can be said that the use of inappropriate expressions such as 'coloured' or 'negro' fall into that category. The use of such words, which are now well known to be offensive, displays at least insensitivity and lack of training. A number of officers used such terms, and some did not even during their evidence seem to understand that the terms were offensive and should not be used.**

6.4 **Racism in general terms consists of conduct or words or practices which disadvantage or advantage people because of their colour, culture, or ethnic origin. In its more subtle form it is as damaging as in its overt form.**

6.5 We have been concerned with the more subtle and much discussed concept of racism referred to as institutional racism which (in the words of Dr Robin Oakley) can influence police service delivery *'not solely through the deliberate actions of a small number of bigoted individuals, but through a more systematic tendency that could unconsciously influence police performance generally.*

6.6 **The phrase 'institutional racism' has been the subject of much debate. We accept that there are dangers in allowing the phrase to be used in order to try to express some overall criticism of the police, or any other organisation, without addressing its meaning. Books and articles on the subject proliferate. We must do our best to express what we mean by those words, although we stress that we will not produce a definition cast in stone, or a final answer to the question. What we hope to do is to set out our standpoint, so that at least our application of the term to the present case can be understood by those who are criticised.**

6.7 In 1981 Lord Scarman's Report into The Brixton Disorders was presented to Parliament. In that seminal report Lord Scarman responded to the suggestion that '*Britain is an institutionally racist society,*' in this way:

If by [institutionally racist] *it is meant that it* [Britain] *is a society which knowingly, as a matter of policy, discriminates against black people, I reject the allegation. If, however, the suggestion being made is that practices may be adopted by public bodies as well as private individuals which are unwittingly discriminatory against black people, then this is an allegation which deserves serious consideration, and, where proved, swift remedy.*

(Scarman Report, Para 2.22, p.11)

6.8 In policing terms Lord Scarman also rejected the allegation that the MPS was a racist force. He said:

The direction and policies of the Metropolitan Police are not racist. I totally and unequivocally reject the attack made upon the integrity and impartiality of the senior direction of the force. The criticisms lie elsewhere – in errors of judgment, in a lack of imagination and flexibility, but not in deliberate bias or prejudice.

(Paragraph 4.62, p.64)

...

6.13 ... **Lord Scarman accepted the existence of what he termed *'unwitting'* or *'unconscious'* racism. To those adjectives can be added a third, namely *'unintentional'*. All three words are familiar in the context of any discussion in this field. ...**

...

6.14 Dr Oakley indicates (in his first submission to the Inquiry, Paragraph 2) that in spite of Lord Scarman's use of the words '*hidden and unconscious*' and '*unwitting*' the concept of 'racist conduct' that became established following his Report

> *... was one of overt acts of discrimination or hostility by individuals who were acting out their personal prejudices. Racism was therefore a problem specifically of individual officers, of 'rotten apples' within the service who 'let the side down'. ... This conception of racism appears still to be the normal understanding in police circles. ...*

6.15 When Lord Scarman asserted his final conclusion that '*institutional racism does not exist in Britain: but racial disadvantage and its nasty associate racial discrimination have not yet been eliminated*' (Paragraph 9.1, p.135), many took this statement as the classic defence against all allegations that '*institutional racism*' exists in British society. His earlier words '***knowingly***, *as a matter of policy, discriminates*' and '*practices may be adopted ... which are **unwittingly** discriminatory*' were not separated and given equal weight. Whilst we must never lose sight of the importance of explicit racism and direct discrimination, in policing terms if the phrase 'institutional racism' had been used to describe not only explicit manifestations of racism at direction and policy level, but also unwitting discrimination at the organisational level, then the reality of indirect racism in its more subtle, hidden and potentially more pervasive nature would have been addressed.

...

6.17 **Unwitting racism can arise because of lack of understanding, ignorance or mistaken beliefs. It can arise from well intentioned but patronising words or actions. It can arise from unfamiliarity with the behaviour or cultural traditions of people or families from minority ethnic communities. It can arise from racist stereotyping of black people as potential criminals or troublemakers. Often this arises out of uncritical self-understanding born out of an inflexible police ethos of the 'traditional' way of doing things. Furthermore such attitudes can thrive in a tightly knit community, so that there can be a collective failure to detect and to outlaw this breed of racism. The police canteen can too easily be its breeding ground.**

...

6.21 **The failure of the first investigating team to recognise and accept racism and race relations as a central feature of their investigation of the murder of Stephen Lawrence played a part in the deficiencies in policing which we identify in this Report. For example, a substantial number of officers of junior rank would not accept that the murder of Stephen Lawrence was simply and solely 'racially motivated'. The relevance of the ethnicity and cultural status of the victims, including Duwayne Brooks, and Mr and Mrs Lawrence, was not properly recognised. Immediately after the murder Mr Brooks was side-lined, and his vital information was inadequately considered. None of these shortcomings was corrected or overcome.**

6.22 What may be termed collective organisational failure of this kind has come to be labelled by academics and others as institutional racism. This is by no means a new term or concept. In 1967 two black activists, Stokely Carmichael and Charles V. Hamilton stated that institutional racism

> *... originates in the operation of established and respected forces in the society. It relies on the active and pervasive operation of anti-black attitudes and practices. A sense of superior group position prevails: whites are 'better' than blacks and therefore blacks should be*

subordinated to whites. This is a racist attitude and it permeates society on both the individual and institutional level, covertly or overtly.

(pp.20–1)

6.23 Reference to a concept described in a different national and social context over 30 years ago has its dangers; but that concept has been continuously debated and revised since 1968. History shows that 'covert' insidious racism is more difficult to detect. Institutions such as Police Services can operate in a racist way without at once recognising their racism.

6.24 **It is vital to stress that neither academic debate nor the evidence presented to us leads us to say or to conclude that an accusation that institutional racism exists in the MPS implies that the policies of the MPS are racist. No such evidence is before us. Indeed the contrary is true. It is in the implementation of policies and in the words and actions of officers acting together that racism may become apparent. Furthermore we say with emphasis that such an accusation does not mean or imply that every police officer is guilty of racism. No such sweeping suggestion can be or should be made. The Commissioner's fears are in this respect wholly unfounded.**

6.25 Sir Paul Condon himself said this in his letter to the Inquiry dated 2 October 1998:

I recognise that individual officers can be, and are, overtly racist. I acknowledge that officers stereotype, and differential outcomes occur for Londoners. Racism in the police is much more than 'bad apples'. Racism, as you have pointed out, can occur through a lack of care and lack of understanding. The debate about defining this evil, promoted by the Inquiry, is cathartic in leading us to recognize that it can occur almost unknowingly, as a matter of neglect, in an institution. I acknowledge the danger of institutionalisation of racism. However, labels can cause more problems than they solve.

Sir Paul will go thus far, but he did not accept that there is institutional racism within his force.

6.26 We understand Sir Paul's anxiety about labels. But the fact is that the concept of institutional racism exists and is generally accepted, even if a long trawl through the work of academics and activists produces varied words and phrases in pursuit of a definition. We repeat that we do not pretend to produce a definition which will carry all argument before it. We approach the question by setting out some helpful quotations from evidence put before us, and we then set out our current standpoint. We began our Inquiry without presuppositions in this field. All the evidence and submissions that we have heard have driven us to the conclusions set out in this Report.

. . .

6.28 The oral evidence of the three representatives of the MPS Black Police Association was illuminating. It should be read in full, but we highlight ... from Inspector Paul Wilson's evidence:

The term institutional racism should be understood to refer to the way the institution or the organisation may systematically or repeatedly treat, or tend to treat, people differently because of their race. So, in effect, we are not talking about the individuals within the service who may be unconscious as to the nature of what they are doing, but it is the net effect of what they do.

(Part 2, Day 2, p.209)

. . .

6.30 The Commission for Racial Equality (CRE) in their submission stated:

Institutional racism has been defined as those established laws, customs, and practices which systematically reflect and produce racial inequalities in society. If racist consequences accrue to institutional laws, customs or practices, the institution is racist whether or not the individuals maintaining those practices have racial intentions.

(Para 2)

... organisational structures, policies, processes and practices which result in ethnic minorities being treated unfairly and less equally, often without intention or knowledge.

(Para 3)

6.31 Dr Robin Oakley has submitted two helpful Notes to our Inquiry. ... In Dr Oakley's view ...

> ... *There is great danger that focusing on overt acts of personal racism by individual officers may deflect attention from the much greater institutional challenge ... of addressing the more subtle and concealed form that organisational-level racism may take. Its most important challenging feature is its predominantly hidden character and its inbuilt pervasiveness within the occupational culture.*

He goes on:-

> **It could be said that institutional racism in this sense is in fact pervasive throughout the culture and institutions of the whole of British society, and is in no way specific to the police service. However, because of the nature of the police role, its impact on society if not addressed in the police organisation may be particularly severe. In the police service, despite the extensive activity designed to address racial and ethnic issues in recent years, the concept of 'institutional racism' has not received the attention it deserves.**

> (Institutional Racism and Police Service Delivery, Dr Robin Oakley's submission to this Inquiry, parts of paras 6,7,8, and 11)

6.32 ...

> **The term institutional racism should be understood to refer to the way institutions may systematically treat or tend to treat people differently in respect of race. The addition of the word 'institutional' therefore identifies the source of the differential treatment; this lies in some sense within the organisation rather than simply with the individuals who represent it. The production of differential treatment is 'institutionalised' in the way the organisation operates.**

> (Para 2.2)

...

6.33 We are also grateful for the contribution to our Inquiry made by Dr Benjamin Bowling. Again it must be said that summaries of such work can be unhelpful. But we hope that he will forgive us for quoting here simply one important passage:-

> *Institutional racism is the **process** by which people from ethnic minorities are systematically discriminated against by a range of public and private bodies. If the result or **outcome** of established laws, customs or practices is racially discriminatory, the institutional racism can be said to have occurred. Although racism is rooted in widely shared attitudes, values and beliefs, discrimination can occur irrespective of the intent of the individuals who carry out the activities of the institution. Thus policing can be discriminatory without this being acknowledged or recognised, and in the face of official policies geared to removal of discrimination. However, some discrimination practices are the product of **uncritical** rather than unconscious racism. That is, practices with a racist outcome are not engaged in without the actor's knowledge; rather, the actor has failed to consider the consequences of his or her actions for people from ethnic minorities. Institutional racism affects the routine ways in which ethnic minorities are treated in their capacity as employees, witnesses, victims, suspects and members of the general public.*

> (Violent Racism: Victimization, Policing and Social Context, July 1998, paras 21–2, pp.3–4)

6.34 Taking all that we have heard and read into account we grapple with the problem. For the purposes of our Inquiry the concept of institutional racism which we apply consists of:

> **The collective failure of an organisation to provide an appropriate and professional service to people because of their colour, culture, or ethnic origin. It can be seen or detected in processes, attitudes and behaviour which amount to discrimination through unwitting prejudice, ignorance, thoughtlessness and racist stereotyping which disadvantage minority ethnic people.**

It persists because of the failure of the organisation openly and adequately to recognise and address its existence and causes by policy, example and leadership. Without recognition and action to eliminate such racism it can prevail as part of the ethos or culture of the organisation. It is a corrosive disease.

...

6.39 **Given the central nature of the issue we feel that it is important at once to state our conclusion that institutional racism, within the terms of its description set out in Paragraph 6.34 above, exists both in the Metropolitan Police Service and in other Police Services and other institutions countrywide. ...**

...

6.46 In reaching our conclusions we do not accept the contention of the Commissioner of the Metropolitan Police Service that

... if this Inquiry labels my Service as institutionally racist the average police officer, the average member of the public will assume the normal meaning of those words. They will assume a finding of conscious, wilful or deliberate action or inaction to the detriment of ethnic minority Londoners. They will assume the majority of good men and women who come into policing ... go about their daily lives with racism in their minds and in their endeavour. I actually think that use of those two words in a way that take on a new meaning to most people in society would actually undermine many of the

endeavours to identify and respond to the issues of racism which challenge all institutions and particularly the police because of their privileged and powerful position.

(Part 2, Day 3, pp.290–1)

We hope and believe that the average police officer and average member of the public will accept that we do not suggest that all police officers are racist and will both understand and accept the distinction we draw between overt individual racism and the pernicious and persistent institutional racism which we have described.

...

6.54 **Racism, institutional or otherwise, is not the prerogative of the Police Service. It is clear that other agencies including for example those dealing with housing and education also suffer from the disease. If racism is to be eradicated there must be specific and co-ordinated action both within the agencies themselves and by society at large, particularly through the educational system, from pre-primary school upwards and onwards.**

Reference

Carmichael, S. and Hamilton, C.V. (1967) *Black Power: the Politics of Liberation in America*, Penguin Books.

Source: Macpherson of Cluny, 1999, pp.20–30, 33

6.2 John Solomos, 'Social research and the Stephen Lawrence Inquiry' (1999)

Changing research agendas and the Lawrence report

4.1 ... I now want to move on somewhat to a wider question that social scientists working in this field should be discussing, namely our own role in the current situation and the limitations of our research agendas. I was made to think about this point as a result of looking at *Appendix 18 of Volume II* of the report, which lists the publications seen by the Inquiry.

4.2 This is in many ways a very partial list, and one that ignored some important studies that have helped to shape the field of race and ethnic studies in recent years, and it could be argued that at least part of the reason for the relative absence of rigorous and informed research insights into the analysis to be found in the Macpherson Report can be put down to the ways in which the report has been cobbled together on the basis of submissions by various bodies and individuals rather than influenced by sustained research. While this is undoubtedly true, it must also be acknowledged that the research that has been produced over the past three decades and more has been at best very limited in the manner it has explored important facets of racism in British society. On a whole range of important aspects of contemporary racism social researchers have had little to say. We can take, for example, areas such as political institutions, the police, the criminal justice system, racial violence, social class and exclusion, white racism, racist movements. All of these areas are central to the concerns of the Macpherson Report, and yet it is clear that there has been a paucity of substantial research on them. No doubt there are examples of individual pieces of research that have somehow not been looked at by the Inquiry. But in general terms it seems beyond doubt that part of the problem we face is that core issues of concern have featured at best as a low priority on the social research agenda.

4.3   Why has this situation arisen? Part of the problem is seems to me can be found in the rather limited agenda that has guided the work of the main research centre in this field over the past three decades, namely the Research Unit on Ethnic Relations at the University of Bristol in 1970. The Unit continued its research in another form at the University of Aston from 1978 to 1994 and from 1984 as the Centre for Research in Ethnic Relations at the Warwick University. Although ESRC core funding of the Centre ceased in 1998, there is little doubt that for three decades it consumed the bulk of social science funding in this field. Despite the large amount of money that the ESRC invested in the Unit/Centre over the years there are notable gaps in the range of research questions that it covered.

4.4   Another important facet of research in this field is that in practice researchers have been pulled in a variety of directions, by both political and academic pressures. Given the politicised nature of this field of sociological work this is not surprising, but the consequences for research

and scholarship have been negative. This is an argument that others working in the field have recognised for some time. Take for example John Rex, who in 1978 became Director of the ESRC Research Unit on Ethnic Relations. Writing in 1979, and drawing on his long experience of research in this field, he argued perceptively that anyone embarking on research in this field of race relations was pulled in a number of alternative directions:

- First, there was the demand that research should be put to the service of policy, as though there was a consensus about ends, and the only questions which need to be researched were about means;

- Second, there was the pull for a retreat into academic theorising, in which the research questions asked are not seen as necessarily related to the issues that made race relations a public issue;

- Third, there was the option of rejecting academic research in this field as a whole, in favour of political activism or action oriented work.

4.5   Rex himself rejected all of these options, and called for an approach to race relations research that was both theoretically informed and politically relevant, but essentially concerned with a longer term structural view of race relations. This is what Rex called 'a perspective on race relations based on a serious political sociology' (Rex, 1979, p.17).

4.6   With hindsight, Rex's typology of different approaches to research in this field captured some of the recurrent problems that social researchers working in this field have had to come to terms with. It helps to make clear why researchers working in this field have found it hard to (i) establish a rounded research agenda that included all facets of race and racism in British society and (ii) have been pulled in different directions by contrasting political and academic pressures.

4.7   In the years after Rex published his typology, there have been tremendous changes in both the theoretical and the empirical focus of much of the literature on race and racism. There has been a pronounced broadening of research paradigms and a plethora of theoretical perspectives have come to the fore, particularly from a range of radical schools of thought. ...

Whatever the merits of some of the recent theoretical debates, there have been few sustained attempts to link them to research on institutions and processes of social change. In this environment there has been, if anything, a retreat by researchers into abstracted theoretical debates and discourses.

References

Macpherson of Cluny, Sir W. (1999) *The Stephen Lawrence Inquiry: Report of an Inquiry by Sir William Macpherson of Cluny*, London, The Stationery Office, http://www.official-documents.co.uk/document/cm42/4262/4262.htm.

Rex, J. (1979) 'Race relations research in an academic setting: a personal note', *Home Office Research Bulletin*, vol.8, pp.29–30.

Source: Solomos, 1999, pp.4–7

 ## 6.3 R.W. Connell, 'Why is classical theory classical?'[1] (1997)

...

Foundation stories

In any recent introductory sociology textbook, whether written in the United States (Calhoun *et al.*, 1994) or on the other side of the world (Waters and Crook, 1993), there will almost certainly be, in the first few pages, a discussion of founding fathers, focused on Karl Marx, Émile Durkheim, and Max Weber. The introductory chapter will probably, though not certainly, also mention Auguste Comte, Herbert Spencer, and Georg Simmel. It will sometimes mention members of a second team: Ferdinand Tönnies, Friedrich Engels, Vilfredo Pareto, William Graham Sumner, Charles H. Cooley and G.H. Mead.

In the view normally presented to undergraduates, these founding fathers created sociology in response to dramatic changes in European society: the industrial revolution, class conflict, secularization, alienation, and the modern state. 'It was above all *a science of the new industrial society*' (Bottomore [1962] 1987, p.7). This view is repeated in more sophisticated form in advanced training. American graduate programs in sociology normally have courses (often required courses) in which students are introduced to 'classical theory' and make a close study of certain texts written by Marx, Durkheim and Weber.

This curriculum, in turn, is backed by a disciplinary history in which sociologists account for their origins in virtually the same terms. For instance Swingewood's *Short History of Sociological Thought* (1991), a reliable and well-regarded British text, presents a three-part narrative: 'Foundations' (leading up to Comte and Marx), 'Classical Sociology' (centering on Durkheim, Weber, and Marx), and 'Modern Sociology'. Similarly, according to Münch (1994, p.ix) in Germany, the 'classical period ... was the time when the founding fathers set the framework of sociological theory.'

...

... [However] sociologists in the 'classical period' themselves did not believe this origin story. When Franklin H. Giddings (1896), the first professor of sociology at Columbia University, published *The Principles of Sociology*, he named as the founding father – Adam Smith. Victor Branford (1904), expounding 'the founders of sociology' to a meeting in London, treated as the central figure – Condorcet. Durkheim's and Weber's academic contemporaries did not see them as giants and often disregarded Marx.

Turn-of-the-century sociology had no list of classics in the modern sense. Writers expounding the new science would commonly refer to Comte as the inventor of the term, to Charles Darwin as the key figure in the theory of evolution, and then to any of a wide range of figures in the intellectual landscape of evolutionary speculation.

...

To understand ... what the classical canon means for modern sociology, it is not sufficient to deconstruct the canon and show its artifactual character. Nor is it sufficient to trace the waxing and waning 'influence' of particular theorists, though these are useful steps along the way. The question concerns the structure of sociological thought as a whole. Accordingly we must examine the history of sociology as a collective product – the shared concerns, assumptions, and practices making up the discipline at various times –

and the shape given to that history by the changing social forces that constructed the discipline.

Sociology, global difference, and empire

…

… most general treatises or textbooks of sociology, up to the First World War, did not have a great deal to say about the modernization or the contemporary structure of the society authors lived in. Their main interest was elsewhere. Giddings's *Readings in Descriptive and Historical Sociology* (1906), typical in this respect, ranged from polyandry in Ceylon via matrilineal survivals among the Tartars to the mining camps of California. It was so little focused on modernity that it took as its reading on 'sovereignty' a medieval rendering of the legend of King Arthur.

The evidence of college textbooks needs not correspond to the research focus of sociology, but on this topic too, we have abundant evidence, collected by no less a figure than Durkheim. Between 1898 and 1913, Durkheim and his hardworking collaborators produced 12 issues of *L'Année sociologique*, an extraordinarily detailed international survey of each year's publications in or relevant to sociology. In these issues, nearly 2,400 reviews were published.[2] Modern industrial society was certainly included. … But works focused on the recent or contemporary societies of Europe and North America made up only a minority of the content of *L'Année sociologique* – about 28 per cent of the reviews. Even fewer were focused on 'the new industrial society,' since the reviews on Europe included treatises on peasant folktales, witchcraft in Scotland, crime in Asturias, and the measurement of skulls.

The bulk of the research material of sociology, as Durkheim and his colleagues documented it, did not concern modernity. Twice as many of the reviews concerned ancient and medieval societies, colonial or remote societies, or global surveys of human history. Studies of holy war in ancient Israel, Malay magic, Buddhist India, technical points of Roman law, medieval vengeance, Aboriginal kinship in central Australia, and the legal systems of primitive societies were more characteristic of 'sociology' as seen in *L'Année sociologique* than studies of new technology or bureaucracy. …

The enormous spectrum of human history that the sociologists took as their domain was organized by a central idea: difference between the civilization of the metropole and an Other whose main feature was its primitiveness. I will call this the idea of 'global difference'. Presented in many different forms, this contrast pervades the sociology of the late nineteenth and early twentieth centuries. Together with the idea of 'progress' from the primitive to the advanced …, it is both the key assumption of sociological research and the major object of sociological theory.

The idea of global difference was often conveyed by a discussion of 'origins'. In this genre of writing, sociologists would posit an original state of society (or some aspect of society, such as law, morality, or marriage), then speculate on the process of evolution that must have led forward from there. The bulk of the three volumes of Spencer's *Principles of Sociology* ([1874–77] 1893–96), was spent in telling such a story for every type of institution that Spencer could identify: domestic institutions, political institutions, ecclesiastical institutions, and so forth. Spencer proceeded as if the proof of social evolution was not complete without an evolutionary narrative, from origins to the contemporary form, for each and every case. (This was a much more important feature of his theorizing than the 'society as organism' analogy for which he is now mostly remembered.)

The formula of development from a primitive origin to an advanced form was widespread in Victorian biological and social thought (Burrow, 1966). Sociologists simply applied a logic that their audience would take for granted. The same architecture is found in works as well known as Durkheim's *Division of Labor in Society* ([1893] 1964) and as obscure as Fairbanks's *Introduction to Sociology* ([1896] 1901).

In none of these works was the idea of an 'origin' taken as a concrete historical question. It could have been. Knowledge of early societies was growing dramatically in these decades. Troy, Mycenae, and Knossos were excavated, Flinders Petrie systematized the archaeology of Egypt, the first evidence of Sumerian culture was uncovered at Lagash and Nippur (Stiebing, 1993). But sociology was not interested in where and when a particular originating event occurred. This insouciance was not confined to origins. Treatise after treatise offered surveys of social evolution or contrasts of primitive and advanced institutions, with only the slightest reference to when the major changes actually happened. Time functioned in sociological thought mainly as a sign of global difference. What was early could be taken to be Other.

Durkheim did not have to find a precise time in the past for 'segmentary societies'; they existed in his own day. In a move characteristic of sociology at the time, Durkheim used the example of the Kabyle of Algeria as well as the ancient Hebrews and made no conceptual distinction between the cases. He knew about the Hebrews because the ancient texts were in his library. How did he know about Kabylia? Because the French had conquered Algeria earlier in the century and, at the time Durkheim wrote, the French colonists were engaged in evicting the local population from the best land (Bennoune, 1988). Given the recent history of violent conquest, peasant rebellion, and debate over colonization, no French intellectual could fail to know something about the Kabyle. For the curious, the social life of France's North African subjects was being documented in great detail by a series of private and official inquiries (Burke, 1980).

This was far from being the only French adventure into the world of the primitive Other. In the dozen years before *Division of Labor* was published, the armies of the French republic had moved out from Algeria to conquer Tunisia, had fought a war in Indochina, conquered Annam and Tonkin (modern Vietnam), and seized control of Laos and Cambodia, and had established a protectorate over Madagascar. Under the Berlin Treaty of 1885, French trading posts in central and western Africa became the basis of a whole new empire. As Durkheim was writing and publishing the *Division of Labor* and *The Rules of Sociological Method*, French colonial armies were engaged in a spectacular series of campaigns against the Muslim regimes of inland north and west Africa, which produced vast conquests from the Atlantic almost to the Nile.

Impressive as this growth was, it was only part of a larger process. The British Empire, also a maritime empire with a preindustrial history, similarly gained a new dynamism and grew to a vast size in the nineteenth century (Cain and Hopkins, 1993). Imperial expansion went overland as well as overseas. The 13-colony United States became one of the most dynamic imperial powers throughout the nineteenth century, with about 80 years of overland conquest and settlement (the 'westward expansion'), followed by a shorter period of overseas conquest. The tsarist overland conquests, begun in earlier centuries, were extended in the Far East and Central Asia. In the later part of the nineteenth century, they were consolidated by Russian settlement. Prussia's expansion as an imperial power began with conquest within Europe – in the process, setting up a relationship between dominant and conquered races in the East that became the subject of the young Weber's first sociological research (Weber, [1894] 1989).

In this light, the time and place where the discipline of sociology was created take a new significance. The locales were the urban and cultural centres of the major imperial powers at the high tide of modern imperialism. They were the 'metropole', in the useful French term, to the larger colonial world. The intellectuals who created sociology were very much aware of this. One of the major tasks of sociological research – and of *L'Année sociologique* as a record of sociological knowledge – was to gather up the information yielded by the colonizing powers' encounter with the colonized world. The idea of global difference was not invented by European and North American intellectuals. It was given to them by the process of economic and colonial expansion, inscribed in the social structure of the empires that the North Atlantic powers constructed.

The birth of sociology cannot be understood by internalist models, then, because it crucially involves the structure of *world society*. It can only be understood in geopolitical terms.

Since Kiernan's ([1969] 1986) remarkable survey, *The Lords of Human Kind*, historians have begun to grasp the immense impact that the global expansion of North Atlantic power had on popular culture (MacDonald, 1994) and intellectual life (Asad, 1973; Said, 1993) in the metropole, as well as in the colonies. It would be astonishing if the new science of society had escaped the impact of the greatest social change in the world at the time. In fact, the relationship was intimate. Sociology was formed within the culture of imperialism and embodied a cultural response to the colonized world. This fact is crucial in understanding the content and method of sociology as well as the discipline's cultural significance.

The content and method of sociology

The concept of progress

As … Todd (1918, p.vii) remarked … 'From Comte onward sociologists have pretty generally agreed that the only justification for a Science of Society is its contributions to a workable theory of progress.'… As Comte had argued, sociology itself embodied intellectual progress, its place 'definitely fixed' (Ward, 1907) at the summit of the hierarchy of sciences.

John Stuart Mill ([1843] 1989, p.596) … had cautioned against equating historical change with improvement. Few of the sociologists took heed. Spencer's first social theory, in *Social Statics* ([1850] 1954), made moral improvement the touchstone of analysis of 'the social state'. Both the teaching enterprise of sociology departments (as documented in text-books such as Giddings's *Principles* (1896) or

Fairbanks's *Introduction* ([1896]/1901), and the popular expositions of the new science (such as Spencer's *Study of Sociology* ([1873] 1887) or Benjamin Kidd's *Social Evolution* (1898), centered on the moral, intellectual, and material improvement of society. Discovering and expounding laws of progress was the core of what sociology *meant* to those two generations.

There was, however, a shift of meaning within the concept of progress. In Comte's writings, the idea of progress, while extremely generalized, mostly had to do with the ancient–medieval–modern sequence within Western culture. … Sociological critiques of Comte in the next generation rejected the arbitrariness of his system and demanded an empirical base for the concept of progress.

This was the common ground between Spencer and Letourneau, and it is a fact of the greatest significance that both turned to the ethnographical dividend of empire as their main source of sociological data. Spencer's *Principles of Sociology* documented its evolutionary stories from the writings of European travelers, missionaries, settlers, and colonial officials, as well as historians. … Letourneau's *Sociology, Based upon Ethnography*, while setting the facts out in a finer grid, was very similar in its sources. For instance, discussing the condition of women, Letourneau (1881, pp.182–3), in two pages, cites social facts from China, Cochin China (Vietnam), Burma, India, Afghanistan, Africa, ancient Rome, and Arabia – apart from the last two, a roll call of British and French colonial expansion in the nineteenth century.

By the time sociology was being institutionalized in the final decade of the nineteenth century, the central proof of progress, and therefore the main intellectual ground on which the discipline rested, was the contrast of metropole and colonial Other. Sociologists did not debate the reality of this contrast; they debated how it should be interpreted – whether through physical evolution from lower to higher human types or through an evolution of mind and social forms and whether competition or cooperation was the motor of progress. In this context, Durkheim's *Division of Labor* was no founding text. It was a late intervention in a long-running debate. Durkheim quarrelled with Comte and Spencer about how to explain the evolution of society, and he drastically reformulated the relation between social change and morality. Yet he did so by offering new 'laws' within the same problematic, not by establishing a new framework.

The concern with progress was not a 'value' separable from the science; it was constitutive of sociological knowledge. The arguments of Ward, Du Bois, L.T. Hobhouse, Durkheim, Spencer and Comte himself are absurd if one does not presuppose the *reality* of progress. It was as an account of progress that 'sociology' spread to colonized peoples and others beyond the metropole.

Race and gender

The topics addressed by the new discipline also reveal its underlying connection with empire. Internalist accounts of classical sociology emphasize class, alienation, and industrialization and pay little attention to such topics as race, gender and sexuality. 'Race', for instance, was not one of the 'unit-ideas of sociology' recognized by Nisbet (1967) and does not even appear in the index of Swingewood's *Short History* or Münch's *Sociological Theory*. But a social science based on the social relations of empire must deal with race, and a social science concerned with evolutionary progress and hierarchies of populations must deal with gender and sexuality.

It is, then, an important fact that race, gender, and sexuality *were* core issues in sociology. When Du Bois ([1950] 1978, p.281) proposed in 1901 that the color line was 'the problem of the twentieth century', he was saying nothing unusual for the time. The first 'sociology' published in the United States in the 1850s, was a defense of slave society in the South (Ross, 1991, p.32). After slavery was abolished, the wider colonial world remained as the object of sociological knowledge and was persistently interpreted in terms of race. Letourneau's (1881, pp.5–6) 'ethnography' meant a science of racial differences, and his *Sociology* opened with an enumeration of the human races: the black man, 'whose brain is small', the yellow man, whose brain 'is better shaped', and the white man, who has 'ascended a few degrees higher in the organic hierarchy' and whose 'brain is developed'.

Spencer did not go so far but still displayed a genial contempt for the 'primitive' races. Ward (1897) was confident that global race conflict reflected the superiority of the European races and that universal progress was dependent on their universal triumph. The extermination of other races was possible; at best, they could join the march of progress on the Europeans' terms. The Canadian author of *Sociology Applied to Practical Politics* (Crozier, 1911) was blunter. To him, sociology proved that race mixing was a 'crime' that would lead to the degeneracy of the white races' culture. The solution was political: form a party of evolution and prevent miscegenation.

Here sociology reflected, in the most direct way, the social relations of imperialism. Racial hierarchies were the characteristic outcome of North Atlantic world power, the rule over indigenous peoples, and the creation of plantation economies and colonies of settlement. This is not to say that all sociologists were racists, though some certainly were. Others, Du Bois and Durkheim among them, suffered from racism. The point is, rather, that racial hierarchy on a world scale was a perception built into the concept of 'progress' and a central part of what sociology was thought to be about: 'It is evidence that, despite the greater consideration now shown for the rights of the lower races, there can be no question as to the absolute ascendancy in the world today of the Western peoples and of Western civilization' (Kidd, 1898, p.316).

...

In the imperial context, racial and sexual issues were not separate. The interplay between them was most powerful in the colonies, and its vehemence is hard to grasp for those unfamiliar with the history of empire. In the later nineteenth century, the expansion of the North Atlantic powers was accompanied by a growing fear of miscegenation, a hardening color line, contempt of the colonizers for the sexuality or masculinity of the colonized (Sinha, 1995), and fears of racial swamping that gave rise to panics about the 'yellow peril', pogroms against the Chinese in the United States and Australia, and racist immigration policies. Echoes are heard even in the most abstract texts from the metropole. Giddings (1896, p.xiii), expounding his theme of 'consciousness of kind', remarked that 'living creatures do not commonly mate with individuals of other than their own species', and his first example was 'white men do not usually marry black women'.

These concerns underlie the discipline's interest in eugenics. This pseudoscience of controlled evolution by selective breeding of humans was then regarded as a reputable and even important part of sociology. Francis Galton, the leading advocate of eugenics, was carefully evaluated by Durkheim in *The Division of Labor*. Galton's (1904) work was published in the *American Journal of Sociology*, noticed in *L'Année sociologique*, and, in due course, reprinted in Park and Burgess's ([1921] 1924) famous text-book.

Method: the imperial gaze and grand ethnography

The most striking feature of sociological method was its bold abstraction. Comte offered cultural 'laws' of vast scope, and the inaugural meeting of the American Sociological Society, 60 years later, was still celebrating tremendous 'laws' of social evolution. ...

Durkheim ([1895] 1964, p.139) argued convincingly that this approach was the basis of the whole enterprise: 'Comparative sociology is not a particular branch of sociology; it is sociology itself, insofar as it ceases to be purely descriptive and aspires to account for facts.' The comparative method meant assembling examples of the particular social 'species' under study and examining their variations. For all Durkheim's criticisms of Spencer, that was exactly what Spencer's *Principles of Sociology* had done.

Comparative method rested on a one-way flow of information, a capacity to examine a range of societies from the outside, and an ability to move freely from one society to another – features that all map the relation of colonial domination. Letourneau (1881, p.15) expressed the sociological point of view in a striking image:

> Let us imagine an observer placed somewhere high up in the air above our terrestrial equator, far enough from the globe on which we live to take in a whole hemisphere at one glance, and yet close enough to distinguish with the aid, if need be, of a magnifying glass, the continents and the seas, the great ranges of mountains, the white frozen tops of the polar regions, etc. etc.

Sociology had limited interest in 'ethnography' in the modern sense, the detailed description of a whole way of life. ... Rather, it was the structure of empire *as a whole* that provided the basis of sociological knowledge. Sociology's comparative method embodied the imperial gaze on the world.

This is seen most fully in surveys such as Spencer's *Descriptive Sociology* and the collective project of the *Année sociologique*. Perhaps the most striking was Hobhouse *et al.*'s *Material Culture and Social Institutions of the Simpler Peoples* (1915), an attempt to overcome the unsystematic use of data in theories of social evolution by providing a statistical base for comparative sociology. Hobhouse and his colleagues surveyed the whole world, collecting information on more than 500 societies. They classified societies by grade of economic development and tried to establish correlations of development with institutional patterns of law, government, family, war, and social hierarchy.

These surveys are virtually forgotten now, but the imperial gaze can also be found in more familiar texts. Sumner's *Folkways*, published in 1906, is his last major work and perhaps the most influential book written by an American in the 'classical' period. It sought to 'put together all that we have learned from anthropology and ethnography about primitive men and primitive society' (Sumner, 1934, p.2). The whole world and the whole of history was the field of Sumner's gaze. Take an entirely typical passage:

> In Molembo a pestilence broke out soon after a Portuguese had died there. After that the natives took all possible measures not to allow any white man to die in their country. On the Nicobar islands some natives who had just begun to make pottery died. The art was given up and never again attempted. White men gave to one Bushman in a kraal a stick ornamented with buttons as a symbol of authority. The recipient died leaving the stick to his son. The son soon died. Then the Bushman brought back the stick lest all should die. Until recently no building of incombustible materials could be built in any big town of the central province of Madagascar, on account of some ancient prejudice. A party of Eskimos met with no game.
>
> (Sumner, 1934, p.25)

Few cases delayed the author for more than two sentences. As this passage shows, for Sumner, the force of the argument did not lie in the depth of his ethnographic understanding. It was provided by the assemblage itself, the synoptic view of human affairs from a great height.

Durkheim's (1964, pp.174–7) own use of the comparative method, for instance, in his analysis of transition from the horde to segmental societies, has been mentioned above. The imperial gaze can also be observed in Weber, in those late works where he was deliberately setting out to write sociology. In the manuscripts collected after his death and published as *Economy and Society*, Weber ([1922] 1978) had sometimes used the method of 'ideal-types' with which the canon associates him. But more often he used the same procedure as Durkheim and Sumner, comparing actual social forms. … part 1 set up the categories of theory in such a way as to require transhistorical content. In the studies of part 2, Weber swept across continents and civilizations in vast comparative analyses of economic forms, authority, religious groups, states, music, cities, and so forth. …

Notes

1   Work for this article was supported by research funds from the University of California, Santa Cruz, and the University of Sydney. I am grateful for research assistance from John Fisher and advice from Pam Benton, Craig Calhoun, Wally Goldfrank, Barbara Laslett, James O'Connor, Jennifer Platt, Daniel Schulman, Andy Szasz, Barrie Thorne, students in my 'classical theory' classes, and *AJS* reviewers. Direct correspondence to R.W. Connell, Faculty of Education, A35, University of Sydney, Sydney NSW 2006, Australia.

2   I have counted only reviews in large type, whatever their length, not the brief notices in small type in the early issues nor the listings of titles without reviews. The reviews concerning Western/Northern Europe and modern North America increase with time: they average 24 per cent of all reviews in the first six issues, 28 per cent in the next five issues, and 32 per cent in the bumper issue in the year before the war.

References

Asad, T. (ed.) (1973) *Anthropology and the Colonial Encounter*, New York, Humanities Press.

Bennoune, M. (1988) *The Making of Contemporary Algeria, 1830–1987*, Cambridge, Cambridge University Press.

Bottomore, T. (1962/1987) *Sociology: A Guide to Problems and Literature*, 3rd edn, London, Allen & Unwin.

Branford, V. (1904) 'The founders of sociology', *American Journal of Sociology*, vol.10, no.1, pp.94–126.

Burke, E. III (1980) 'The French tradition of the sociology of Islam' in Kerr, M. (eds) *Islamic Studies: A Tradition and Its Transformation*, Malcolm Kerr (ed.), Santa Monica, CA, Undena University Press.

Burrow, J.W. (1966) *Evolution and Society: A Study in Victorian Social Theory*, Cambridge, Cambridge University Press.

Cain, P.J. and Hopkins, A.G. (1993) *British Imperialism: Innovation and Expansion 1688–1914*, New York, Longman.

Calhoun, C., Light, D. and Keller, S. (1994) *Sociology*, 6th edn, New York, McGraw-Hill.

Crozier, J.B. (1911) *Sociology Applied to Practical Politics*, London, Longmans Green.

Du Bois, W.E.B. ([1950] 1978) 'The problem of the twentieth century is the problem of the color line', *On Sociology and the Black Community*, Chicago, IL, University of Chicago Press.

Durkheim, E. ([1893] 1964) *The Division of Labour in Society* (trans. G. Simpson), New York, Free Press.

Durkheim, E. ([1895] 1964) *The Rules of Sociological Method* (trans. A. Solovay and J.H. Mueller), Glencoe, IL, Free Press.

Fairbanks, A. ([1896] 1901) *Introduction to Sociology*, 7th edn, New York, Scribner.

Galton, F. (1904) 'Eugenics: its definition, scope, and aims', *American Journal of Sociology*, vol.10, no.1, pp.1–25.

Giddings, F.H. (1896) *The Principles of Sociology*, New York, Macmillan.

Kidd, B. (1898) *Social Evolution*, 3rd edn, London, Macmillan.

Kiernan, V.G. ([1969] 1986) *The Lords of Human Kind: Black Man, Yellow Man, and White Man in an Age of Empire*, New York, Columbia University Press.

Letourneau, C. (1881) *Sociology, Based upon Ethnography*, London, Chapman & Hall.

MacDonald, R.H. (1994) *The Language of Empire: Myths and Metaphors of Popular Imperialism, 1800–1918*, Manchester, Manchester University Press.

Mill, J.S. ([1843] 1989) *A System of Logic, Ratiocinative and Inductive*, people's edition, London, Longmans, Green.

Münch, R. (1994) *Sociological Theory, Volume 1, From the 1850s to the 1920s*, Chicago, Nelson-Hill.

Nisbet, R.A. (1967) *The Sociological Tradition*, London, Heinemann.

Park, R.E. and Burgess, E.W. ([1921] 1924) *Introduction to the Science of Sociology*, Chicago, IL, University of Chicago Press.

Ross, D. (1991) *The Origins of American Social Science*, Cambridge, Cambridge University Press.

Said, E.W. (1993) *Culture and Imperialism*, New York, Vintage.

Sinha, M. (1995) *Colonial Masculinity*, Manchester, Manchester University Press.

Spencer, H. (1954) *Social Statics*, New York, Robert Schalkenbach Foundation. First published in 1850.

Spencer, H. (1887) *The Study of Sociology*, 13th edn, London, Kegan Paul, Trench. First published in 1873.

Spencer, H. ([1874–77] 1893–96) *The Principles of Sociology*, 3 vols, New York, Appleton.

Stiebing, W.H. (1993) *Uncovering the Past: A History of Archaeology*, Buffalo, NY, Prometheus Books.

Sumner, W.G. ([1906] 1934) *Folkways: A Study of the Sociological Importance of Usages, Manners, Customs, Mores, and Morals*, Boston, MA, Ginn.

Swingewood, A. (1991) *A Short History of Sociological Thought*, 2nd edn, New York, St Martin's Press.

Todd, A.J. (1918) *Theories of Social Progress: A Critical Study of the Attempts to Formulate the Conditions of Human Advance*, New York, Macmillan.

Ward, L.F. (1897) *Dynamic Sociology*, 2nd edn, New York, Appleton.

Ward, L.F. (1907) 'The establishment of sociology', *American Journal of Sociology*, vol.12, no.5, pp.581–7.

Waters, M. and Crook, R. (1993) *Sociology One: Principles of Sociological Analysis for Australians*, 3rd edn, Melbourne, Longman Cheshire.

Weber, M. (1989) 'Developmental tendencies in the situation of East Elbian rural labourers' in Tribe, K. (ed.) *Reading Weber*, London, Routledge. First published in 1894.

Weber, M. (1978) *Economy and Society* in Roth, G. and Wittich, C. (eds) Berkeley, CA, University of California Press. First published in 1922.

Source: Connell, 1997, pp.1151–547

6.4 Michael Billig, 'Banal nationalism' (1995)

Nationalism and sociological common sense

…

A quick glance at the subject indexes of standard textbooks in sociology would reveal that nationalism is not a major, disciplinary preoccupation. … Britain's most widely read textbook, Haralambos and Holborn's *Sociology* (1991), has no index entry for nationalism. Similar absences can also be found in important academic texts. …

Sociology, from the classic works of Durkheim and Weber onwards, has been presented by sociologists as the study of 'society'. Sociologists routinely define their discipline in these terms. Edward Shils, writing on 'Sociology' in *The Social Science Encyclopaedia*, describes sociology as 'at present an unsystematic body of knowledge gained through the study of the whole and parts of society' (1985, p.799). According to Kornblum, 'Sociology is the scientific study of human societies and human behaviour in the many groups that make up a society' (1988, p.4). Macionis begins his textbook by defining sociology as 'the scientific study of society and the social activity of human beings' (1989, p.2). Haralambos and Holborn define a sociological theory as 'a set of ideas which claim to explain how society or aspects of society work' (1991, p.8). All these definitions assume that there is such a thing as 'a society' which exists in an unproblematic way.

A number of critics of orthodox sociology have drawn attention to the way that sociologists take the existence of 'society' for granted. According to Giddens, it is a term which is 'largely unexamined' in sociological discourse (1987, p.25). Immanuel Wallerstein claims that 'no concept is more pervasive in modern social science than society, and no concept is used more automatically and unreflectively than society' (1987, p.315). Mann (1986), in making a similar point, announces that, if he were able, he 'would abolish the concept of "society" altogether' (p.2; see also Turner, 1990; Bauman, 1992a, 1992b; Mann, 1992; McCrone, 1992). The problem is not that sociologists, whether in textbooks or works of theory, leave 'society' undefined. It lies in the assumption that 'we' readers will know more or less what a 'society' is: 'we' have common-sense ways of understanding 'society' (Bowers and Iwi, 1993).

It often turns out that the 'society' which lies at the heart of sociology's own self-definition is created in the image of the nation-state. Indeed, in the case of Max Weber there is evidence that his support for German political nationalism directly influenced his conception of 'society' (Anderson, 1992). The connection is continued in today's textbooks. Macionis (1989), having defined sociology as the scientific study of 'society', unusually goes on to give a definition of 'society': it is 'a people who interact with one another within a limited territory and who share a culture' (p.9). This is, of course, precisely how 'nations' are typically viewed both by themselves and by theorists: as peoples with a culture, a limited territory and distinguished by bonds of interaction. For sociologists it is a banal cliché to define their discipline as the 'science of society'; and it is just as banal a habit of thought to imagine 'society' as a bounded independent entity. A number of years ago Norbert Elias put the issue well: 'Many twentieth century sociologists, when speaking of "society", no longer have in mind (as did their predecessors) a "bourgeois society", or a "human society" beyond the state, but increasingly the somewhat diluted ideal image of a nation-state' (1978, p.241).

Far from leading to nationhood's being in the forefront of sociological inquiry, the emphasis on 'society' and the implicit modelling of 'society' on

nation, has both reified and concealed nationhood. 'Society' is conceived as a universal entity. All human social life is presumed to take place within the orbit of 'society'; 'societies' are to be found wherever humans live socially. The problematic for orthodox sociology, particularly Parsonian sociology, has been to study how members of a 'society' become socialized into adopting the 'values', 'norms' and 'culture' of their 'society'. Haralambos and Holborn (1991), in the opening chapter of their textbook, specifically introduce readers to these concepts. These are all universal terms: it is presumed that all 'societies' have 'norms' and 'values'. Thus, 'our' society is not unique, but is an instance of something which is universal.

The image of 'our' society, however, is a nation-state. Kornblum (1988), in his textbook, asserts that the nation-state is 'the social entity that, for most people in the world today, represents "society" itself' (p.72). If the nation is merely a variant of something universal (a 'society'), then the processes by which it is reproduced need not be identified by special words. Its particularities can be subsumed under general terms such as 'norm', 'value', 'socialization' etc. 'Nationalism' in this context need not make an appearance. Yet, it can return as a special subject to demarcate those who are striving to have their own 'society', or those who might be threatening the integrity of 'ours', or those who are proposing an extreme, fascistic politics of nationality. If the repressed continues its dramatic return in Eastern Europe and elsewhere, then the textbooks of sociology, in their future editions, are likely to add sub-sections or even whole chapters on nationalism. If they do, nationalism will still be seen as something surplus, even contingent. It will be a special subject. 'Society', modelled on the image of 'our' nation, will continue to be treated as necessarily universal. In this way, 'our' nationalism need not return textually.

This sort of sociological common sense can leave its mark on investigations of individual nations. For example, American sociologists, examining the state of American 'society', often overlook the national dimension of their topic, as they transform the particular into universal categories (Woodiwiss, 1993). For example, Bellah *et al.*'s *Habits of the Heart* is a superbly executed study, investigating the effects of individualism in contemporary American culture. … The authors utter a message of warning, as they argue that individualism is undermining a sense of community. According to Bellah *et al.*, 'we live in a society that encourages us to cut free from the past … no tradition and no community in the United States is above criticism' (1986, p.154).

The phrasing of the argument is significant. The sense of community, which is being lost, refers to feelings of township or locality. There is still a presumed locus in which the sense of community and tradition is evaporating. As the authors state, 'we live in a society': the 'society', of course, is the United States. And the 'we', whom the authors are invoking, are Americans. Whatever the decline of 'community', the national society continues to exist. The authors' analysis seems to overlook their respondents' sense of being American; this sense is shared by the authors, as their text flags its own national identity. In this way, the authors take the framework of their own nation ('our society') for granted.

References

Anderson, P. (1992) 'Science, politics, enchantment' in Hall, J.A. and Jarvie, I.C. (eds) *op. cit.*.

Bauman, Z. (1992a) *Intimations of Postmodernity*, London, Routledge.

Bauman, Z. (1992b) 'Soil, blood and identity', *Sociological Review*, vol.40, pp.675–701.

Bellah, R.N., Madsen, R., Sullivan, W.M., Swidler, A. and Tipton, S.M. (1986) *Habits of the Heart*, New York, Harper and Row.

Bowers, J. and Iwi, K. (1993) 'The discursive construction of society', *Discourse and Society*, no.4, pp.357–93.

Elias, N. (1978) *This History of Manners*, Oxford, Basil Blackwell.

Hall, J.A. and Jarvie, I.C. (eds) (1992) *Transition to Modernity*, Cambridge, Cambridge University Press

Haralambos, M. and Holborn, M. (1991) *Sociology: Themes and Perspectives*, 3rd edn, London, Collins.

Kornblum, W. (1988) *Sociology in a Changing World*, New York, Holt, Rinehart & Winston.

Macionis, J.J. (1989) *Sociology*, Englewood Cliffs, NJ, Prentice Hall.

Mann, M. (1986) *The Sources of Social Power, Volume 1*, Cambridge, Cambridge University Press.

Mann, M. (1992) 'The emergence of modern European nationalism' in Hall, J.A. and Jarvie, J.C. (eds) *op. cit.*.

McCrone, D. (1992) *Understanding Scotland: the Sociology of a Stateless Nation*, London, Routledge.

Shils, E. (1985) 'Sociology' in Kuper, A. and Kuper, J. (eds) *The Social Science Encyclopaedia*, London, Routledge.

Turner, B.S. (1990) 'The two faces of sociology: global or national', *Theory, Culture and Society*, vol.7, pp.343–58.

Wallerstein, I. (1987) 'World-systems analysis' in Turner, J.H. and Giddens, A. (eds) *Social Theory Today*, Cambridge, Polity Press.

Woodiwiss, A. (1993) *Postmodernity USA*, London, Sage.

Source: Billig, 1995, pp.51–5

Understanding the past and predicting the future: sociologists as prophets

Kenneth Thompson

Contents

1 Introduction

This is the last chapter in a journey of exploration during which we have attempted to map out some of the main contours of sociology. Earlier books in the series covered topics under the broad headings of *Understanding Everyday Life* (**Bennett and Watson, 2002**), *Social Differences and Divisions* (**Braham and Janes, 2002**) and *Social Change* (**Jordan and Pile, 2002**). In this book we have looked at some of the topical uses of sociological analysis and at how sociologists have been engaged in various ways with their subject matter. Having covered so much, the reader might be tempted to ask: what more is there left to say?

There is more, but it is more of a reflection on certain aspects of what has gone before and a look at possible ways forward. We can make a start by thinking of two characteristics that are commonly attributed to prophets: forecasting the future and engaging in social criticism. In the nineteenth century, along with claiming to be creating *the* science of society, the social thinkers who became recognized as the founders of sociology were also confident that they could forecast the future and criticize present social failings. Today, sociologists tend to be more modest and prophets are out of fashion, although there are exceptions.

In an untypical burst of attempted prophecy, brought on by the Millennium, the official journal of the British Sociological Association (*Sociology*) devoted its first issue of the year 2000 to the topic: 'Society and Sociology: Britain in 2025'. In his Editor's Introduction, David Mason stated:

> A criticism persistently levelled at social science in general, and sociology in particular, is that it is unable to make predictions. Whatever the truth of this claim, and there is not space here to review the various arguments, it is undoubtedly true that sociologists themselves have characteristically eschewed the role of soothsayers, although there are a number of celebrated exceptions to this general pattern. Whether for reasons of expediency (a fear of being exposed as wrong) or principle, there has been a tendency for the discipline to focus its efforts on *post hoc* empirical or theoretical analysis. In this context, we may note that many of those initially approached felt unable to assay the task of speculation while, even among those who accepted, there remained some unease about assuming the role, as one contributor put it, of Mystic Meg. In the light of this, it is interesting to note that there is a remarkable degree of convergence in the analyses offered by authors who have approached different topics from divergent theoretical and methodological starting points …
>
> (Mason, 2000, p.1)

David Mason then went on to summarize four main points of agreement, which echo some of the key points made in the books in this series, *Sociology and Society*, and which we will consider again in this chapter. The first point is that knowledge of the past and present is the prerequisite for forecasting future trends:

> First, there is a more or less implicit view, in all the contributions, that the analysis of present and past patterns is a necessary starting point for informed speculation about the future. This suggests that, despite its historic unwillingness to grasp the predictive nettle, sociology has not, in fact, operated either theoretically or methodologically in a manner that, in principle, ruled this out.

Indeed, … a clear understanding of present trends, and the notes of caution this sounds, is a precondition for resisting some of the more apocalyptic predictions of popular futurology.

(*ibid.*, p.2)

The next point Mason makes relates to a general trend concerning global and local spatial relationships (a topic underlying several of the chapters in **Jordan and Pile, 2002**):

Secondly, while none of the authors represented here embraces the perspectives embodied in the more extreme versions of the globalisation thesis, there is a clear recognition in a number of papers that the character and place of the nation state is likely to continue to change as we enter the twenty-first century.

(*ibid.*)

The third point made by Mason concerns trends towards increasing diversity, especially with regard to ethnicity and religion in a more multicultural society, and gender and sexuality:

In line with theoretical developments in the discipline in the wake of post-structuralist and postmodernist critiques, a key element in a number of contributions is the theme of increasing diversity.

(*ibid.*)

The final issue highlighted by Mason is one that has long been central to sociology, although its focus may have changed or broadened, and that is inequality (which is the central theme of **Braham and Janes, 2002**):

Given its historic centrality to post-war British sociology, the theme of inequality features, in various ways, in several papers. In several, there is an implicit challenge to the optimistic strand in some postmodernist writing. This can be found in the emphasis on the continuing significance of the structural determination of opportunity and the potential for continued conflicts between groups (dare one say classes?) which are the product of those structural conditions.

(*ibid.*)

We have chosen to quote these summary points because they provide a useful guide to key issues and even a degree of consensus in contemporary sociology (and in *Sociology and Society*) as it cautiously ventures forth towards the future. It is not a very daring image of sociology in its prophetic mode, which contrasts with earlier times, as we shall see. Nor is it very optimistic. As Mason concludes:

It was once the case that economics was branded the 'dismal science'. In recent years some of us have come increasingly to the view the sociology may well have made that mantle its own. Indeed, in early discussions about this special issue, one of our potential contributors suggested that the subtext of a proposed paper would be: 'It's all awful and it's going to get worse'. Given this, it is interesting to note that the papers here do not in any simple way, represent an outpouring of *fin de siècle* gloom. While they eschew uncritical acceptance of the wilder optimism of much popular futurology, all identify opportunities as well as challenges for Britain in the early years of the twenty-first century. These are also challenges and opportunities for our discipline.

(*ibid.*, p.3)

In the following sections we will attempt to provide a similar balanced account of sociology's efforts to be both prophetic and useful. We shall focus especially on the role of values in theory and research, and we hope to be able to conclude that, whilst being challenging, sociology need not be dismal.

ACTIVITY I

Now might be a good time to reflect on the parallels that we have drawn between the points of consensus that Mason found among his contributors and other writings on social trends (including relevant chapters in the *Sociology and Society* series).

A few written notes made at this stage would be a useful revision and help you achieve the aims of the discussions that are to follow.

AIMS

The main aims of this chapter are:

1   To show how sociology, from its beginnings, has sought to characterize the present age by comparing it with the past and by making predictions about the future. In other words, it has presented historical models and theories of social development. Where appropriate, the intention will be to show how implicit values have given the predictions an imperative prophetic character.

2   To explain some of the main models of historical development.

3   To examine the question of values in theory and research.

4   To review some sociological predictions about the future.

2 The sociologist's vocation – traditions and values

From the time when it was first given a name by Auguste Comte in his *Cours de philiosophie positive* (published in parts between 1830 and 1842), until quite recently, sociology has been seen by many of its practitioners as a science that seeks to understand the present age by comparing it with the past and then making predictions about the future. The quest was to discover universal scientific laws that would explain connections, causes and developments. As Comte expressed it: 'From science comes prevision; from prevision comes action' ('*Savoir pour prevoir et prevoir pour pouvoir*') (Comte, 1896, in Thompson, 1975, p.51).

However, as we have noted in Chapter 1, this scientific vision – sometimes referred to as **positivism** – is only one of the intellectual or stylistic ingredients that can be found in sociology. Another approach has been more like that of the Humanities, where the emphasis is on interpreting the meanings of human actions, often by creating new narratives (stories) about the accounts and performances given by social actors. The aim is to present insightful interpretations of events, viewed from different perspectives. For example, the

positivism

sociologist Erving Goffman developed his 'dramaturgical' perspective, in which social actors are viewed as if they are playing roles and presenting themselves in ways analogous to theatre performances. Goffman's ethnographic methodology, and the theorizing that went with it, had some of the characteristics of Shakespeare's observation that 'all the world's a stage' (Goffman, 1959). A different kind of dramaturgical interpretation can be discerned in some historical narratives – even where the author's first consideration is to develop a scientific approach, as when Marx interrupts his account of class struggles in the history of France with the comment: 'Hegel remarks somewhere that all great, world-historical facts and personages occur, as it were, twice. He has forgotten to add: the first time as tragedy, the second time as farce' (Marx, 1852/1954, p.10).

Sometimes the interpretative perspectives offered are politically engaged and deliberately critical of more conventional or 'scientifically detached' views, as in the case of the contemporary feminist, Donna Haraway:

> Feminism loves another science: the science and politics of interpretation, translation, stuttering, and the partly understood. Feminism is about the sciences of the multiple subject with (at least) double vision. Feminism is about a critical vision consequent upon a critical positioning in inhomogeneous gendered social space.
>
> (Haraway, 1991, p.195)

Despite the differences between the various styles of theorizing, sociologists frequently present narratives of historical events – social actions that occur in time and space. The different styles may involve different methods of collecting, ordering and interpreting data, but there is always a story ('*narrative*' or '*account*') being told. Of course, the events may be very local or 'micro-social' and so seem to have little connection to the bigger picture or the 'macro-social' level. However, it is one of the aims of sociology to make connections between the micro- and macro-social levels, and to seek to place events in a larger historical context. Consequently, some of the most famous and influential sociological theories are those that attempt to provide a comprehensive and coherent narrative – usually involving statements about historical trends and often with an implicit judgement on the trends. As the American sociologist Jeffrey Alexander puts it:

> Despite the fact that we have no idea what our historical possibilities will be, every theory of social change must theorise not only the past but the present and future as well. We can do so only in a non-rational way, in relation not only to what we know but to what we believe, hope and fear. Every historical period needs a narrative that defines its past in terms of the present, and suggests a future that is fundamentally different, and typically 'even better' than contemporary time.
>
> (Alexander, 1995, pp.9–10)

One of the major debates in sociology at the end of the twentieth century was about whether such 'grand narratives' were now played out. With the apparent triumph of capitalism and the ideology of liberal-democracy, it was suggested that we had seen the end of competing grand narratives – the 'end of history', as the US presidential adviser Francis Fukuyama put it (Fukuyama, 1989). Another interpretation was that this was the end of the epoch of modernity and of the Enlightenment project of progress through science. We were said to be entering a new epoch of 'post-modernity', in which there could be no convincing grand narrative, but only diverse and partial perspectives. To quote the famous definition by the French philosopher, Jean-Francois Lyotard: 'I define post-modern as incredulity toward metanarratives' (Lyotard, 1984, p.xxiii).

The main aims of this chapter do not include settling the question of whether we are entering a new post-modern epoch. However, we are interested in looking at some of the different partial perspectives, or listening to voices from different positions, that illustrate the variety and richness of contemporary sociology's attempts to tell convincing stories about past, present and future social developments. They range from the founding 'classical' social thinkers of the nineteenth century – Comte, Spencer, Marx, Weber and Durkheim, to more recent feminist and post-colonial theorists.

The claim that sociology could predict future developments was criticized by some outsiders, and even some sociologists, because it made its practitioners sound like prophets, rather than social scientists. However, this would be to mistake what is involved – both for sociologists and, perhaps, for prophets. In predicting the future, sociologists cannot have 'prevision' of specific future events. What they can seek to do, however, is estimate the probabilities of future developments on the basis of past and present trends. But there is also another possible prophetic role for sociologists and that is to present a critique of these trends on the basis of the professed values and goals of those they are studying. Just as the ancient prophets were often notorious for telling their society where its actions were at odds with proclaimed values, so too sociologists can put forward uncomfortable findings. Sometimes, social actions can be shown to have unintended consequences that are at odds with professed goals and values; at other times, the problem may be traced to contradictory goals and values. In both cases, as we will see, sociology is likely to exercise its critical function.

Finally, it has to be admitted that sociologists frequently bring their own values to bear in their analyses and this raises controversies. In 1972, students taking the first Open University sociology course (*The Sociological Perspective*) were asked to read and consider the view of the emergence of sociology presented by the conservative American sociologist, Robert Nisbet, in his book *The Sociological Tradition* (Nisbet, 1967).

His view, which he also presented in one of the course's radio programmes, was that the central ideas of sociology arose from an artistic frame of thought and had a strong moral basis (his examples included Marx's idea of **alienation**, Weber's theme of **rationalization** and Durkheim's concept of **anomie**). However, Nisbet also admitted that sociology had developed as a result of certain inherent creative paradoxes. In his view, one of the paradoxes was that, although sociology fell, in its objectives and in the political and scientific values of its principal figures, into the mainstream of modernism, its essential concepts and its implicit perspectives placed it closer to philosophical conservatism. Hence, he claimed, its preoccupation with the effect of social change on community, authority, tradition, the sacred, and its concern with the spread of alienation and bureaucracy (Nisbet, 1967, pp.17–18).

The criticisms subsequently levelled against Nisbet were that he over-emphasized the conservative side of the modernism versus conservatism paradox, and also the artistic element in the scientific versus artistic paradox. It was argued by such critics that, in the processes of emphasizing the distinctive character of sociology among the social sciences, Nisbet neglected those aspects

alienation, rationalization, anomie

Figure 7.1 *Front cover of D283, Book 1, James Gillray's reflections on the French Revolution in 1973, Open University Press, 1971*

of sociological thinking that were shared with the other social sciences and which they all inherited from prior developments in the natural sciences and philosophy. As regards the moral standpoint of those nineteenth-century thinkers whose ideas contributed to the development of sociology, at least two of them, **Karl Marx** and **Herbert Spencer**, had very little respect for the qualities of pre-industrial society. Marx spoke disparagingly about the 'idiocy' of rural life in such a society. In the case of Spencer (the most widely read sociologist in the nineteenth century), his social evolutionary theories and grasp of contemporary science neatly fitted the *laissez faire* atmosphere of mid-Victorian Britain. And so, in the case of the scientific vs. artistic paradox in the work of the early contributors to sociology, the scientific spirit was clearly predominant in Comte and Spencer, and in the later works of Marx. If anything, Nisbet's account of the preoccupations and values of early sociology applies more to the second

generation of sociologists (**Durkheim**, **Weber** and **Simmel**, for example). They were subjected to the full brunt of the *fin de siècle* anxieties about 'the world we have lost' (so-called 'traditional society') as the price to be paid for modern progress, and so struggled most acutely with the paradox of modernity vs. tradition.

The debate in the 1970s over Nisbet's account of the sociological tradition and its dilemmas over intellectual styles and values took place within a social context where there was still a relative consensus in the UK over the welfare state and its values. There had been radical stirrings in the universities in 1968 and even talk of a 'cultural revolution', but it was not until the period of economic retrenchment in the later 1970s and the rise of the neo-liberal New Right (Thatcherism in Britain and Reaganism in the US) that sociology itself came under attack. In the 1980s, some sociologists at The Open University, and others elsewhere, were accused of 'Marxist bias' and felt themselves to be under political pressure. (It was said that the Secretary of State for Education had himself telephoned The OU and asked a secretary about the initials of an organization, referred to in a course book, which he wrongly suspected of being marxist).

The changed economic and political climate was not the only source giving rise to criticism of sociology's implicit values. Since the 1960s, new social movements were also developing their critiques. Feminists complained about sociology being dominated from the beginning by patriarchal perspectives. Why, they asked, was the history of sociology always about 'Founding Fathers' and the sociological perspective based on male interests and experience? The gay and lesbian movement accused sociological discourses on deviance and 'the family' of normalizing heterosexuality and the nuclear family, thus marginalizing or even pathologizing other non-'normative' forms. Movements representing non-Western peoples have objected to the predominance of Western world-views in sociology and demand recognition of post-colonial and indigenous perspectives. From Marx to Weber and even against contemporary sociologists,

the charge is levelled of constructing **Orientalism**, drawing a contrast between the presumed superior West (modern and rational) and the inferior, subordinate East (traditional and irrational).

In the light of this experience, we cannot escape confronting directly the question of values implicit in sociology. Should sociologists aim for scientific detachment or are they inevitably going to be guided by their own values in their studies, allowing those values to enter into their conclusions as well as when selecting how and what to study?

Before reading further, you might find it useful to consider your own impressions of sociology:

1   Do you associate sociology with a particular set of values?

2   Do you think sociologists should strive for **value neutrality** when studying a topic?

3   Or, should sociologists simply state what their own values are?

value neutrality

There is no one correct answer to these questions about the values of the theorist or researcher. As you may have inferred, sociologists differ not only with regard to the values they hold, but also about the extent to which it is possible to exercise value neutrality or **value freedom** (see the discussion by Hamilton in Chapter 1). This is a topic Weber discussed at length, recommending that sociologists should avoid making value judgements, but suggesting they could make value interpretations in terms of the **value relevance** of people's actions (establishing the values towards which an activity is directed). A generally accepted rule might be that sociologists should exercise reflexivity. This means that they should reflect on their own value orientations and how these might affect their study, whilst also attempting to gain an imaginative empathetic understanding of the values of those they are studying. At the very least, they should not seek to impose their values either by skewing their findings or by misrepresenting them. In the next section we will examine the role of values in sociology, and this will also have relevance to considerations of ethical issues that arise in sociological work.

value freedom

value relevance

3   The heritage of classical sociology

3.1   Laying the foundations – the values of science and progress

There is no doubt that early contributors to the development of sociology had some of the characteristics of the prophets, even if shorn of religion. The accounts of the genesis of the subject and its 'Founding Fathers' (as they are often called) can sound almost biblical. In the beginning was the word and the word was *sociology*. If the act of naming an intellectual discipline entitles its author to the title of Founder, then **Auguste Comte** merits that designation. He was even named 'founder-in-chief' by a leading American sociologist in an article commemorating the centenary of Comte's invention of the term (Hankins, 1939, p.16). But not only did Comte consider he was founding a science of society, he also wanted that science to be the basis for reconstructing society and generating a new devotion to the social good; in effect, sociology was to be a moral cause or a secular 'religion of humanity', with sociologists as its priests.

Comte, Auguste

The necessary intellectual climate for the emergence of sociology had been provided by the achievements of the eighteenth century philosophical movement described as the **Enlightenment**, which had removed the study of social phenomena from the realm of the supernatural and viewed them as elements

Enlightenment

Figure 7.2 *Portrait of Auguste Comte, 'founder of sociology?'*

of the world of nature. In place of one that had tended to view the existing social order as immutable and God-given, the Enlightenment promoted a way of thinking based upon ideas of human freedom and the relative nature of social arrangements. This movement itself had been facilitated by social forces – the powerful anti-traditional forces of nationalism and capitalism. However, by the end of the eighteenth century, and throughout the nineteenth, the new forces of industrialization and democratization created problems that could not be solved on the basis of the existing economic and political theories of the Enlightenment:

> [E]ighteenth century political science was too preoccupied with deriving all social forms from rational agreement (social contract) to permit the study of the full panoply of social forms. Eighteenth-century economics was too determined to explain economic behaviour on the basis of rational self-interest to contemplate the full possibilities of the sociology of motivation.
>
> (Martindale, 1961, p.41)

Comte, like the other great systematic social thinker, Karl Marx, was insistent that the political and economic spheres could not be understood in a scientific way (as opposed to a merely philosophical or speculative way) without taking account of interrelationships with other spheres and their place in the total social system. To ignore those interrelationships and divide up human life into abstract and fragmented categories tended to mean that political economy ignored contemporary social problems. This was the charged levelled by both Comte and Marx in their day, and it is one that found echoes among sociologists when faced with a revival of neo-liberal economic doctrines under Thatcherism in the 1980s. (We will consider this more recent period and sociological discussions of the values of the 'enterprise culture', and the resurgence of the model of society as a market, in section 4.) For all its technical brilliance, economics tended to develop a partial and misleading model of society. As Marx put it:

> Political economy conceives of the social life of men [*sic*], their active human life, their many-sided growth towards a communal and genuinely human life, under the form of exchange and trade. ... According to Adam Smith, society is a commercial enterprise. Every one of its members is a salesman. It is evident how political economy establishes an alienated form of social intercourse, as the true and original form, and that which corresponds to human nature.
>
> (quoted in Bottomore and Rubel, 1963, p.179)

The development of the sociological perspective was premised on the critique of the values of nineteenth century **laissez-faire** individualism and **utilitarianism**, whose model of social action was of individuals pursuing their own self-interest; its conception of society (in so far as 'society' featured at all) was that of an aggregation of atomized individuals who entered into contracts to further those self-interests. Significantly, the most influential figure in the establishment of sociology as an academic subject – Emile Durkheim – made these doctrines his main target of criticism (Thompson, 1982, pp.73–5). In his major work on the subject, *The Division of Labour in Society* (1893/1933), he had more than forty references (mostly of rebuttal) to the writings of **Herbert Spencer**, who had sought to promote a sociological theory combining utilitarianism with social evolutionism. One of Durkheim's key arguments was that individuals could not enter into contracts unless there was a prior social order with a culture containing moral values that supported these contracts. While Durkheim accepted that modernization required changes in the forms of the **division of labour** (specialized roles and functions) and a greater emphasis on the freedoms and rights of the individual, he criticized contemporary capitalism for imposing contracts on workers that amounted to a 'forced division of labour' (Thompson, 1982, pp.86–8). Marx would have agreed with some of this, but differed in believing that such exploitation was intrinsic to capitalism. Sociologists on the Left of the political spectrum have remained divided over this issue – some following Durkheim's line in favour of reforming capitalism and reducing inequalities (such as Anthony Giddens' **third way politics**, discussed in Chapter 2), and others accepting the more radical view of Marx. In so far as the utilitarian individualist approach has any continuing existence within sociology, it is to be found mainly in the American sociological schools of **exchange theory** and **rational choice theory**.

The other major contributor to classical sociology, Durkheim's German contemporary, Max Weber, is often described as having been in a dialogue with the ghost of Marx. This refers to two aspects of his sociology. The first is that, unlike Marx (and Comte), he denied the possibility of social science discovering laws of social development analogous to those in the natural sciences. Nevertheless, he presented the process of rationalization as the master trend of western capitalist society, which would result in social life being turned into a meaningless 'iron cage' (the spread of bureaucracy was his prime example). Secondly, he argued that Marx placed too much emphasis on economic factors as determinants of social change, and Weber's **Protestant ethic** thesis stressed the role of religious beliefs in the rise of capitalism (Weber, 1930). However, there is often a tendency to exaggerate the difference between Weber and Marx

laissez-faire
utilitarianism

Spencer, Herbert

division of labour

third way politics

exchange theory, rational choice theory

Protestant ethic

on these analytical issues. Where they did differ considerably was in their political values and judgements. Weber believed that socialism would only increase rationalization and bureaucratization, and so present an even greater threat to freedom than capitalism.

It will not have escaped your attention that all these Founding *Fathers* of sociology are indeed men, and European men at that. One explanation might be that social circumstances limited women's opportunities to attain prominent intellectual positions and that men had a vested interest in maintaining a patriarchal society. But even allowing for that, it still seems surprising that these men, who claimed to be devoted to developing a science of society in order to bring about social progress and human emancipation, still failed to give a central place to female inequality. A partial explanation might lie in the very prestige that they attributed to science and its findings. A good example is to be found in the correspondence between Comte and John Stuart Mill (Thompson, 1976, pp.181–210). Mill said he had been firmly in the Utilitarian camp, but had been persuaded to break away under the influence of Comte's sociological ideas. However, their correspondence discloses how, what they originally spoke of as a difference over a 'secondary matter' – the reasons for the inequality of the sexes – had wider ramifications. Comte believed that each new science had to build on its predecessors, and the immediate predecessor to sociology in his classification of the sciences was biology. Within biology, Comte included phrenology (or craniometry), which claimed to have established that women's brains were smaller and so less equipped for intellectual endeavour than men's. Mill was less respectful of these scientific claims and maintained that the social scientist should not settle for explaining differences by reference to essentialist innate characteristics until every social explanation had failed. (Comte himself had taught that each science had its own proper sphere and should not allow reductionism to the level of a prior science.) The political implications of the disagreement were important: if inequality was the result of conditions in which women had lived for generations, then it might still be altered by changing conditions. Mill went on to write a powerful essay proposing the elimination of social practices that maintained women's inequality – *The Subjection of Women* (1869/1911). Comte's conviction of the differences between men's and women's natures took him in the opposite direction, and he devoted much of his multi-volumed final work, *System of Positive Polity*, to celebrating women's superior caring and loving nature, even forecasting that this would become the defining characteristic of a future, more civilized, society (Comte, 1848–54/1877).

An interesting footnote to this dispute between Comte and Mill over scientific methodology in relation to the inequality of the sexes is that a similar kind of dispute has occurred between contemporary feminist sociologists, some of whom maintain that quantitative 'scientific' methods are an instrument of masculine domination, while qualitative 'interpretative' methods (such as ethnography) are claimed to be more in tune with female characteristics. One of the opponents of this second view, Anne Oakley, pointed out that feminists in the past used quantitative methods to good effect and that, from the nineteenth century, 'There was a feminist tradition of defending women from the "science" of craniometry', and other justifications for inequality, which could only be done by using statistics to disprove it (Oakley, 1998, p.722).

Now might be a good time to take stock of the various elements that we have described as contributing to the making of the sociological tradition or perspective, including the contributions of the Founding Fathers, and their different values, key concepts, intellectual models and styles. An obvious place to start would be with the sociology dictionary entries for the names and concepts that have been highlighted above.

The questions to ask yourself are:

1   Is there a single sociological tradition (as Nisbet claimed) and, if so, what are its characteristics?

2   What similarities and differences are there between the values and intellectual styles or models of the sociologists discussed so far?

3   What were the values that may have led them to focus on certain issues and not others?

Clearly, Nisbet's account of a single sociological tradition represents a particular viewpoint. He was keen to stress what, from his conservative value orientation, was a paradox: that these heirs of the Enlightenment project to achieve social progress through the construction of a modern social science were also conscious that the particular form modernity was taking brought with it repeated social crises. However, in the course of wrestling with these dilemmas, these thinkers did develop some useful conceptual tools and methodologies for sociology. Having looked at some of the key concepts, we need to say a brief word about their methods.

3.2 Methodology

The other point common to these founding figures in sociology, in addition to their effort to produce a comprehensive model of society that focused not just on one institution but on the relation of parts to the whole, was their concern to develop scientific methods for the study of social development. This entailed some elements of what we would regard as historical research, but it was more a case of 'systematic history'. By that, we mean constructing historical models or, in Weber's case 'ideal types', in order to explain the course of social developments, especially changes from one form to another. Some examples of changes are: Comte's model of stages of intellectual development (from theological to metaphysical and then the positive/scientific); Marx's account of changes in modes of production (slavery, feudalism, capitalism); Durkheim's explanation of changes in the forms of the division of labour (from mechanical to organic); Weber's typology of forms of authority (traditional, charismatic, rational-legal). At the same time that these general models of social development were being constructed, more systematic methods for collecting and analysing data were being developed, particularly by government agencies. (The development of statistical data for governmental purposes was discussed in more detail in Chapter 2.)

The use of quantitative data by the classical sociologists was very patchy. Comte, who in fact was a mathematician by training, made very little use of such data and contented himself with broad generalizations about stages of historical development. This contrasted with the quite sensible things he had to say about the methods appropriate to sociology, which he listed as: observation, experiment, comparison, and history (Thompson, 1976, pp.21–2). Marx, in *Capital* (1867/1970), made extensive use of secondary statistics, such as those gathered by factory inspectors and other agencies of government. Weber resembled professional contemporary historians in his mastery of statistical data, as shown in his analysis of the development of modern capitalism in *General Economic History* (Weber, 1927/1961). While Durkheim's *Suicide* (1897/1951), meanwhile, developed the comparative analysis of suicide statistics for different groups in testing his hypotheses about the effects of social factors on this seemingly most individual of acts.

These historical and statistical methods were the mainstay of classical sociology. They suited the values of the early sociologists who, as we have seen, were concerned to develop a social science that would comprehend the broad sweep of historical change, from traditional agrarian society to modern industrial society. In constructing their narratives, they drew on the discourses that were to hand: scientific, medical, statistical, philosophical and historical. What was not in evidence, as a method, was any detailed ethnographic observation of everyday life, particularly from a woman's angle (such as the contemporary ethnographies featured in **Bennett and Watson, 2002**). This has prompted some sociologists, especially feminists, to raise the question: Are certain methods more in tune with feminist values?

READING 7.1

Now read the extract from Anne Oakley (1998), 'Gender, methodology and people's ways of knowing', which is Reading 7.1 at the end of this chapter.

As you read, please consider the following questions:

1   What are the arguments presented by some feminists against quantitative methods and in favour of qualitative methods?

2   What is your own judgement, in the light of what you have read here and in other chapters?

Oakley is clearly not convinced by the arguments of feminists who believe that qualitative methods are intrinsically more in tune with women's experience and feminist values and that the reverse is the case for quantitative methods. However, your own reading and experience may have brought you to a different conclusion to that reached by Oakley. Sometimes, how we judge something depends on the purpose at hand, which may cause us to find one study more insightful and useful than another. Many women academics (but perhaps also men) may find ethnographic studies help them to see their own experience in a new light and they also feel more ethically comfortable with its procedures (provided the observer does not employ subterfuge). Others, engaged in a struggle against inequalities, may find quantitative methods suit their purpose.

The Canadian feminist sociologist Dorothy Smith, who favours ethnographic studies, also emphasizes the important difference in perspective that is produced if you start from one standpoint rather than another (Smith, 1987; and discussed in **Hemmings *et al.*, 2002**). On one level this relates to the everyday life situation of the observer. A middle-class, European man may have very different experiences to those of a relatively poor, black woman in Africa; just as the latter will probably have a difference of viewpoint to that of a middle-class, American woman, whilst having something in common. On another level, their differences of perspective may derive from a set of values articulated in more general theories or ideologies, as illustrated by the differences between liberal, socialist and radical feminisms (discussed by **Janes, 2002**).

The legacy of the first generation of practitioners of sociology continues to reflect their standpoint: 'Its object of knowledge was social progress, conceived on the grandest possible scale' (Connell, 2000, p.291). Although, even then, there were differences within that position:

> This project allowed social critique. It even encouraged criticisms of institutions or practices that stood in the way of progress – criticism made, naturally, in the name of science. But evolutionary sociology did not yield a consistent political standpoint, since the same warrant of science could be claimed for Spencer's defence of free-market capitalism, Durkheim's mild socialism, and tough-minded economistic Marxism.
>
> (*ibid.*)

The grand narrative of progress has waned, but the other standpoints remain, although varying in their fortunes. Marxism was weakened by the failures of socialist and communist regimes; sociology became more closely linked to the sort of mild socialism associated with the welfare state and to the professions dealing with 'social problems'. There was an increasing tendency to collect and analyse statistical data that was useful for governmental and administrative purposes (as Tony Bennett discussed in Chapter 2). There is still scope for critique, but it is limited to documenting inequalities of class, race and gender (as discussed in **Braham and Janes, 2002**) or to questioning the one-sided and partial view of the social whole that results from the increasing spread of market ideas and mechanisms.

What is left of the legacy from the nineteenth and twentieth centuries, and are there any other futures for sociology in the twenty-first century, other than those generated by these standpoints? Previous chapters in this book have begun to suggest that there might be (for example, Merl Storr in Chapter 5). We should now consider the prospects for other possibilities.

4 Values and uses for twenty-first century sociology

In a special symposium, 'Charting Futures for Sociology', published at the beginning of the new millennium, the official review journal of the American Sociological Association, *Contemporary Sociology*, invited the Australian sociologist R.W. Connell to write the opening article. He begins by noting that it was not pre-ordained that sociology should come into existence in the way that it did, and goes on to point out that it is not guaranteed that sociology will continue to exist unless it draws on new sources of experience and discovers new standpoints. The question he poses is whether there is a future for sociology if it is confined to being a 'reformist science' (providing useful expertise in carrying out surveys and making field observations in the form of small-scale ethnographies), or might there be more challenging futures? Your first reaction might be to think that there is nothing wrong with being reformist and useful. Which is fair enough. However, Connell is being true to the more prophetic aspects of the sociological tradition in the ways in which he poses and answers the question, so it is worthy of our attention.

READING 7.2

Now read the article by Connell, 'Sociology and world market society' (Reading 7.2 at the end of this chapter).

As you read, consider the following questions:

1   What does Connell have to say about the ways in which changing political and economic conditions have affected the standing and role of sociology?

2   What kind of functions does he see sociology performing in the past and at the present time?

3   What possible alternatives does he foresee for sociology in the future?

First of all, it is relevant to observe that the social position and character of those who practise sociology has changed from the nineteenth century. The early practitioners had a large and ambitious perspective that embraced the whole of history, often translated into a broadly evolutionary view of social development. Europe was viewed as being at the highest point of human development and as showing the only way forward to its colonies and former colonies. The composition of the ranks of those contributing to sociology was a coalition of middle-class men, whose relatively comfortable conditions of existence as residents of the imperial powers were sometimes in tension with their liberal principles. The broadly evolutionary view in sociology began to wane in the twentieth century, partly because of catastrophic events such as the First World War, which not only dented the evolutionary optimism but also decimated the ranks of sociology and even brought some personal tragedies. Durkheim's son, a talented sociologist, was killed in the war, and Durkheim wrote a war-time pamphlet denouncing German nationalist ideology. On the other side, Weber supported German imperial interests, but hated the incompetence of the nation's leadership, which he foresaw would lose the war and ruin German's world chances for ever (Coser, 1971, p.256). Another reason for the weakening of the evolutionary view was that it had begun to be taken in very illiberal directions, **eugenics**   as in the **eugenics** movement, which towards the end of the nineteenth century gained the support of some British sociologists for a policy of selective breeding to weed out the less intelligent and less fit. The eugenicists' views were soon expunged from sociology and their only legacy was in the statistical techniques that they bequeathed (MacKenzie, 1999).

It should be noted that social evolutionary views did not disappear entirely from twentieth-century sociology. In the US, which was less affected by the First World War, a generally optimistic set of values about social progress remained in place. There, the leading sociologist of the mid-twentieth century **Parsons, Talcott**   was **Talcott Parsons**. Parsons developed a version of social evolutionary theory that described progressive changes in society resulting from increasing **differentiation**   **differentiation** (a broader application of the concept of the division of labour).

Of British sociology during the first half of the twentieth century, it has been said that the profession was divided between those carrying out 'administrative and intelligence functions for government' (Abrams, 1968, pp.4–5) and a few theorists who maintained evolutionary progressivist views (most prominently, the two successive occupiers of the only chair of sociology in England during the first half of the twentieth century – L.T. Hobhouse and Morris Ginsberg at the London School of Economics) (Kumar, 2001, p.45). It was only from the 1960s onwards that sociology departments and chairs of sociology became widely established in British universities, as distinct from departments of social administration (Oxford University did not have a chair of sociology until 1999, although the sociologist A.H. Halsey was given a chair in social and administrative studies in the 1970s). However, this does not mean that sociology has played no critical role. According to one recent commentator (Kumar, 2001) there has been an 'implicit' or 'concealed' sociology that has worked its way into historical and cultural studies in Britain. It is to these that we will return later for further suggestions about values and uses of sociology in the future (sociological issues concerning culture and the public sphere were raised by McGuigan in Chapter 3; some key contributors to cultural studies of everyday life were mentioned in the Introduction to **Bennett and Watson, 2002**, and in **Hemmings _et al._, 2002**).

Figure 7.3 _The main entrance of the London School of Economics_

Since the 1970s and into the opening years of the twenty-first century, market ideas and forces have become dominant throughout the world. In these circumstances, it is suggested, sociology may be left with few functions. One is that of performing a kind of 'salvage ethnography' of marginalized life-styles – what Connell refers to disparagingly as similar to the old ethnographies of 'nuts, sluts, and perverts'. Another possible function, according to Connell, for those who still want to affect the world, is for market-society sociology to be a science of the 'losers' – people who are poor, chronically sick, disturbed, violent; linguistic minorities, illiterate (including the computer illiterate) and unemployed people. None of these functions, however valuable in itself, seems to meet the challenge of working out a future for sociology that matches the comprehensive scope and critical edge of the earlier sociological tradition (although some professional sociologists may disagree and regard this, realistically and modestly, as no bad thing). To escape marginalization and slow decline, Connell argues, sociology must be 'reconstituted as a democratic science', which entails stepping outside the confines of the western academic world and entering into partnerships with new participants.

Where are the new partnerships to be found? Among those mentioned as possible candidates are activists in various spheres of society – union organizers, teachers, broadcasters, community activists, and even some bureaucrats. Connell's more general point is that, in a knowledge-based society, knowledge is an important tool of social control, and so it is crucial to spread access to that tool, especially to those who are disadvantaged. Sometimes it is simply a case of revealing the salient facts about inequalities; in other cases it may involve giving a community group the tools to reveal the processes that have been obscured by ideology, for example with regard to the social construction of distinctions between normal and deviant sexualities, or exposing the sources of land pollution. Finally, sociology needs to broaden its perspectives to encompass non-western intellectual resources. The latter presents, perhaps, the most difficult challenge, as it can come directly into conflict with deeply ingrained aspects of western thought and values that can seem to be an inextricable part of the sociological heritage – notions of rationality and science or progress and modernity, for instance. What is being called for is a sociology that 'deconstructs' the binary opposites that have structured western discourses, including some of sociology's own assumptions: Occidental/Oriental; modern/traditional; rational/emotional; active/passive.

Figure 7.4 *Portrait of a cyborg: the replicant Rachel in* Blade Runner

This call, for deconstructive strategies to display the artifice involved in the construction of binaries in western discourses and cultural identities, has also been applied to other oppositions, such as: male/female; heterosexual/homosexual. Sociologists have been challenged by feminist and gay–lesbian movements to engage with questions of sexuality and sexual difference in ways that destabilize and de-essentialize such categories as 'woman' and question the simple binaries of sex/gender and public/private (Butler, 1990). It is to these latter issues and the challenge they present for sociology to imagine new, even 'utopian', standpoints, that we turn in our final reading, by Donna Haraway.

READING 7.3

Now turn to Reading 7.3, 'A cyborg manifesto: science, technology, and socialist-feminism in the late twentieth century', which is an extract from Donna Haraway's, *Simians, Cyborgs, and Women: The Reinvention of Nature*. This is an imaginative, futuristic piece of writing, which draws on science fiction to challenge our conceptions of gender and sexuality. You might want to consider your initial reaction to such a piece of writing and you might find it useful to read it more than once as the style of writing is very difficult.

1   What do you think of it being set as essential reading in a serious book about sociology?

2   Is your initial reaction one of impatience or do you find it intriguing?

3   If you find her imaginings persuasive, how might they change our conceptions about such statuses and identities as 'man or woman, human, artefact, member of a race, individual entity, or body'?

We have already seen that sociological narratives, including that of the sociological tradition as described by Nisbet in section 2, draw on imaginative constructions and reconstructions of history and its possible futures. The solemn nature of those narratives may seem to contrast with the ironic and playful imaginings of Haraway. However, as she points out, irony is about humour and serious play, of 'holding incompatible things together'. Such a rhetorical strategy has been described as 'postmodernist', which is often characterized by a playful pastiche of discrepant elements, including nostalgic 'retro' elements alongside modern forms (as in the retro styling of some pubs). But Haraway's use of the cyborg myth about identities and boundaries has the same intention that Nisbet said gave the sociological tradition its creative power – that of holding incompatible elements together in fruitful tension.

It is not only contemporary science fiction that is full of cyborgs – creatures simultaneously animal and machine – the world is increasingly populated by such hybrid beings. At the simplest level, we can accept that our bodies are often reconstructed or extended by manufactured devices ranging from spectacles and dentures to artificial limbs and heart pace-makers. But a similar conjunction is also found at the place of work (which increasingly is also the home), as we become dependent on computers and electronic communication devices. On a deeper level, that of sex and gender identities, there is also increasing crossing of the boundaries, the most apparently drastic one being that of sex change operations. In many other, less drastic ways, both in everyday life as well as in feminist science fiction, the boundaries between once seemingly fixed and essential identities are rendered permeable and unstable.

Haraway's conclusion is that her cyborg imagery helps to express two important arguments, which are relevant to sociology for the future.

The first is that the attempt to produce the kind of universal, totalizing theory characteristic of early sociology is a mistake because it misses much of reality (a point made by advocates of multiplicity of standpoints rather than a totalizing approach, as discussed by **Jordan, 2002**). The second is that we still have to take responsibility for developments, such as those in science and technology, and not succumb to reactionary ideologies, so this entails embracing the skilful task of reconstructing the boundaries of daily life in partnership with others (as suggested by Connell).

Another argument, relevant to sociology for the future, is about the need to examine more closely the ways in which we, as humans (or cyborgs) are embodied. A sociology of the body is not something that classical sociology considered to be within its sphere of the intellectual division of labour (sometimes with disastrous results, in the case of Comte who simply accepted psuedo-scientific statements about the differences between men and women's brains). This is now changing (there is even a professional sociological journal devoted to the topic!).

5 Beyond the sociology of modernity

The grand narrative about modernity and progress that characterized the classical tradition in sociology no longer seems as adequate or compelling as it once did. A universal social science that could discover laws of social development to match those of the natural sciences is not on the agenda for most sociologists, although there are many who would hold that there is scope for a more modest and useful view of scientific practice. The sociologist, Zygmunt Bauman, suggests that sociologists should now see their activity as more like that of 'interpreters' than 'legislators' (Bauman, 1987). Whereas earlier sociologists saw themselves as developing a science that would hand down judgements of what is true, based on laws, Bauman believes their successors today may have to be content with seeking to interpret the different varieties of discourse that exist in the **post-modernity** pluralized and fragmented cultures of **post-modernity**, as he describes it.

Debates about whether we are leaving modernity and entering post-modernity are still ongoing and the terms of the debates are not always clear; consequently, it is difficult to know what would count as evidence for or against their propositions. What we can say is that some of the cultural and social realities emphasized by the classical sociologists of modernity have been transformed significantly. These transformations have stimulated sociologists to develop new theoretical analyses, often in interdisciplinary partnerships, such as in the interdisciplinary area of cultural studies. Among the questions that are hotly debated, including some that have been discussed in this book (and other books in the *Sociology and Society* series) are:

1 Post-industrialism

In the advanced economies of the world, manufactured goods have declined as a proportion of gross domestic product (GDP), as has the workforce devoted to producing them. Economic activity devoted to services has increased. The question then arises: Does this mean that such societies merit the sociological designation of '**post-industrial society**', or would such a description be misleading? (See the discussion of post-industrial society and Information Society by **Hamilton, 2002**). Does it ignore the fact that they are inextricably part of a global industrial system and that the production of services is sometimes organized in ways that resemble factories, for example, large telephone call centres?

post-industrial society

2 De-rationalization

Despite the advances made by science, it is argued, there is now less confidence that science provides all the answers, or that its effects are benign. There are also resurgences of non-scientific modes of thought, including religious fundamentalism, ethnic nationalism and 'racism', traditional healing practices, and New Age spiritual practices and beliefs. Does this undermine the classical sociological theory of modernity, with its belief in science and progress? Or are these simply isolated or temporary reactions to the onward march of science?

3 New social movements

Since the second half of the twentieth century, there has been a proliferation of new, consciousness-raising, social movements (as Merl Storr discussed in Chapter 5). The most visible and successful has been the women's movement, but others have become prominent, such as the gay/lesbian movement, anti-racist groups, and ecological movements. These movements are not simply political pressure groups in the public sphere, seeking to influence government policies, they are also concerned with lifestyles and identities. In this respect, they erode the boundaries between the private and public spheres (as you will have explored in Jim McGuigan's Chapter 3). We are reminded of the slogan – 'The personal is political'. But, once again, there is room for argument about whether this is really something new. Cultural historians can point to social movements in the nineteenth century that were also concerned with lifestyle and consciousness-raising – the Temperance Movement is one example. It can even be argued that in some cases, these movements were related to the development of 'governmentality' in modern, liberal society (you will recall Tony Bennett's discussion of Foucault's concept of governmentality in Chapter 2). Some of the new social movements, as Merl Storr showed in the case of Reclaim the Streets, are also not so different from earlier social movements in their opposition to the workings of capitalism, even if their methods are different.

4 Multiculturalism and difference

As with new social movements, it can be argued that there has been a change of focus from the classical sociological problem of social integration. An earlier view of the object of citizenship would have been to regard it as homogenizing – producing a colour-blind unity (see the discussion by **Turner, 2002**). In multicultural society there is more recognition and celebration of diversity and difference (see the account of changes in racial governmentality by Karim **Murji, 2002**). Groups strive for public recognition and respect for their lifestyle or culture, and are concerned to maintain their distinctiveness.

5 Consumption and consumerism

It sometimes seems that, in the relatively affluent economies, the majority of people are now increasingly preoccupied with shopping for non-essential goods and making consumer choices that define their lifestyle identities. It is argued that consuming has taken on much of the significance in forming a person's identity that was once taken by their functions in the production process. However, some sociologists point out that there is still a close correspondence between divisions based on occupation and income, on the one hand, and place of residence and lifestyle, on the other hand (see **Janes and Mooney, 2002**). It is also argued that the importance of consumption and advertising in the nineteenth century has been underestimated by sociologists, who focused exclusively on production and neglected the productive activity of consumption (as you explored in Chapter 4).

6 Sexuality and the life-cycle

Classical sociology has been described as 'male-stream' sociology; that is to say, it was written by men from a male angle and excluded women's standpoints and concerns. The impact of feminist thought within sociology has gone some way towards changing that situation, as has the impact of research and writing from the standpoint of gay men and lesbians. Issues concerning gender and sexuality might now be regarded as part of mainstream sociology (see Linda **Janes**' discussion of the relative importance of gender and class, **2002**; also **Woodward, 2002**), except that, as we have hinted in this chapter, post-modern sociology is characterized by a suspicion of totalizing theories or grand narratives such as those that characterized the classical sociological tradition, although some sociologists still attempt to characterize the contemporary society with terms that are totalizing (see **Jordan, 2002**).

7 Globalization

The implicit framework of society, in the narrative of the sociology of modernity, was that of the nation-state (as shown by Murji in Chapter 5). Recently, sociological debate has arisen over the thesis of globalization, which maintains that nation-state boundaries are becoming irrelevant in the face of an increasing global interconnectedness, due to economic and technological developments. There has even been talk of information technologies turning the world into a 'global village' (see the criticisms of these claims by **Hamilton, 2002** and **Mackay, 2002**). Some critics claim that there is a tendency to exaggerate the extent to which international connections represent a weakening of nation-state boundaries. These claims and counter-claims may be settled by collecting more detailed empirical evidence relating to specific trends. The challenge to sociology is to join with geographers and other social scientists to develop concepts and data that pay sufficient attention to variations in the spatial and temporal aspects of various social changes (a theme stressed in **Jordan and Pile, 2002**).

8 Mediatization

In contrast to the period of modern society in which the founding figures of sociology lived, cultural life is now pervaded by mass media that provide a constant kaleidoscope of representations of events and lifestyles. They have been likened to a hall of mirrors, in which there are only simulations of 'reality', undermining the sense of certainty about knowledge that earlier sociologists believed possible. (This notion that post-modern society is like a hall of mirrors, or simulations, is developed by Baudrillard, whose work was described in Chapter 1 by Peter Hamilton.) Whether this applies equally to all aspects of social life is doubtful. For example, most of us still have some first-hand knowledge of social divisions based on material wealth or deprivation (as described in **Braham and Janes, 2002**). However, it is an issue that is very relevant to questions concerning the possibility of sociologists and informed citizens being able to participate in rational debates in a democratic public sphere (you will recall the discussion of the public sphere by Jim McGuigan in Chapter 3, or Karim Murji's account of the role of sociology in relation to media controversies in Chapter 6).

Some of these developments and issues are of longer standing than others and may have already begun to engage the attention of earlier sociologists. Furthermore, there is plenty of disagreement about each of them. However, as we have seen, they are symptomatic of the kinds of topics with which contemporary sociologists are having to engage, irrespective of whether or not this constitutes a break with the classical sociological tradition. The usefulness of sociology continues to rest on its capacity to discern the most significant social trends and to increase people's understanding of them, so that they might be better able to choose how to respond. Sometimes this has led sociology to being accused of 'trendiness', but it can also be seen as an imaginative willingness to adapt thinking to meet new challenges.

6 Conclusion

The earliest sociologists, emboldened by the success of the natural sciences, believed that they could develop a science of society – sociology – that would uncover the laws of social life and enable them to predict and guide future developments. Their values were those of science, progress and reason. Of course, they varied in their political inclinations and involvements, ranging from the close involvement of Marx in radical politics to the rather aloof posture of Comte, who contented himself with writing letters of advice (or requests for money) to royalty and other notables. The methods of the early sociologists were mainly those of philosophical and historical studies, on the basis of which they felt able to make wide-ranging generalizations about social developments.

Subsequently, sociology has become much more cautious in its claims and more rigorous and precise in its methods. It has also become more reflexive. An important part of sociological consciousness has to be an awareness by the researcher of his or her own standpoint, which includes his or her own values, as well as an attempt to understand the position of those being studied – their values, meanings, and needs. And because the subjects studied by sociologists are themselves conscious beings, they are often able to take account of and react to sociology. The researcher carrying out ethnographic research on a radical social movement is likely to have to take account of this kind of awareness, but so too is the government-employed sociological forecaster of future social trends.

In this book we have attempted to examine the different ways in which sociologists have engaged with their subject matter. At one level it has been a matter of describing different styles or approaches, such as the scientific, the political, and the expressive. On another, it is possible to view the chapters as accounts of sociologists in action in various fields – government, the media, social movements, and economic activity – taking on roles such as social-policy advisors, media commentators, activists, and consultants. More generally, and perhaps more importantly, this book (and the *Sociology and Society* series), has been concerned with describing the development and character of a sociological reflexiveness that is now an essential ingredient of modern consciousness. One way or another, we all draw on a stock of sociological knowledge to understand the actions of other individuals and organizations, and this knowledge guides our own actions. The more we can refine that knowledge, the more hope we can have that our actions will be effective.

References

Abrams, P. (1968) *The Origins of British Sociology: 1834–1914*, Chicago, ILL, University of Chicago Press.

Alexander, J.C. (1995) 'Modern, anti, post and neo – how intellectuals have coded, narrated and explained the "New World of Our Time"' in *Fin de Siècle Social Theory*, London, Verso, pp.6–64.

Bauman, Z. (1987) *Legislators and Interpreters*, Oxford, Polity Press.

Bennett, T. and Watson, D. (eds) (2002) *Understanding Everyday Life*, Oxford, Blackwell/The Open University. (Book 1 in this series.)

Bottomore, T. B. and Rubel, M. (eds) (1963) *Karl Marx: Selected Writings in Sociology and Social Philosophy*, Harmondsworth, Penguin Books.

Braham, P.H. and Janes, L.P. (eds) (2002) *Social Differences and Divisions*, Oxford, Blackwell/The Open University. (Book 2 in this series.)

Butler, J. (1990) *Gender Troubles: Feminism and the Subversion of Identity*, London, Routledge.

Comte, A. (1896/1975) *The Positive Philosophy* (3 vols, trans. and condensed by H. Martineau, London, G. Bell (from the French original in 6 volumes published 1830–42)), edited extracts in Thompson, K. (ed.) (1975) *Auguste Comte: The Foundation of Sociology*, London, Thomas Nelson/New York, Wiley.

Comte, A. (1848–54/1877) *System of Positive Polity*, 4 volumes (various translators from the French), London, Longmans Green.

Connell, R.W. (2000) 'Charting futures for sociology: sociology and world market society', *Contemporary Sociology*, vol.29, no.2, pp.291–6.

Coser, L. (1971) *Masters of Sociological Thought*, New York, Harcourt, Brace Jovanovich.

Durkheim, E. (1893/1933) *The Division of Labour in Society* (trans. G. Simpson), New York, Macmillan. Originally published in French in1893.

Durkheim, E. (1897/1951) *Suicide* (trans. J. Spaulding and G. Simpson) , Glencoe, NY, The Free Press. Originally published in French, in1897.

Fukuyama, F. (1989) 'The end of history?', *The National Interest*, no.16, pp.21–8.

Goffman, E. (1959) *The Presentation of Self in Everyday Life*, Garden City, NY, Doubleday.

Hamilton, P. (2002) 'From industrial to information society' in Jordan, T. and Pile, S. (eds) *op. cit.*.

Haraway, D. (1991) *Simians, Cyborgs, and Women: The Reinvention of Women*, London, Free Association Books.

Hemmings, S.M., Silva, E.B. and Thompson, K. (2002) 'Accounting for the everyday' in Bennett, T. and Watson, D. (eds) *op. cit.*.

Hankins, F. (1939) 'A Comtean centenary: invention of the term "sociology"', *American Sociological Review*, vol.4, no.16.

Janes, L. (2002) 'Understanding gender divisions: feminist perspectives' in Braham, P. and Janes. L. (eds) *op. cit.*.

Janes, L. and Mooney, G. (2002) 'Place, lifestyle and social divisions' in Braham, P. and Janes, L. (eds) *op. cit.*.

Jordan, T. (2002) 'Totalities and multiplicities: transformations in sociological thinking' in Jordan, T. and Pile, S. (eds) *op. cit.*.

Jordan, T. and Pile, S. (eds) (2002) *Social Change*, Oxford, Blackwell/The Open University. (Book 3 in this series.)

Kumar, K. (2001) 'Sociology and the Englishness of English social theory', *Sociological Theory*, vol.19, no.1, pp.41–64.

Lyotard, J.-F. (1984) *The Postmodern Condition: A Report on Knowledge*, Manchester, Manchester University Press.

MacKenzie, D. (1999) 'Eugenics and the rise of mathematical statistics in Britain' in Dorling, D. and Simpson, S. (eds) *Statistics in Society*, London, Arnold, pp.55–61.

Mackay, H. (2002) 'New media and time-space reconfiguration' in Jordan, T. and Pile, S. (eds) *op. cit.*.

Martindale, D. (1961) *The Nature and Types of Sociological Theory*, London, Routledge and Kegan Paul.

Marx, K. (1954) *The Eighteenth Brumaire of Louis Bonaparte*, Moscow, Progress Publishers. First published in 1852.

Marx, K. (1970) *Capital* , London, Lawrence and Wishart. First published in 1867.

Mason, D. (2000) 'Editor's introduction to society and sociology in Britain in 2025', S*ociology*, vol.34, no.1, pp.1–3.

Mill, J.S. (1869/1911) *The Subjection of Women*, London, Longmans Green Popular Editions.

Murji, K. (2002) 'Race, power and knowledge' in Braham, P. and Janes. L. (eds) *op. cit.*.

Nisbet, R. (1967) *The Sociological Tradition*, New York, Basic Books.

Oakley, A. (1998) 'Gender, methodology and people's ways of knowing: some problems with feminism and the paradigm debate in social science', *Sociology*, vol.32, no.4, pp.707–31.

Smith, D. (1987) *The Everyday World as Problematic*, Milton Keynes, Open University Press.

Thompson, K. (ed.) (1976) *Auguste Comte: The Foundation of Sociology*, London, Thomas Nelson, New York, Wiley.

Thompson, K. (1982) *Emile Durkheim*, London, Routledge.

Turner, B.S. (2002) in Braham, P. and Janes, L. (eds) *op. cit.*.

Weber, M. (1930) *The Protestant Ethic and the Spirit of Capitalism* (trans. T. Parsons), London, Allen and Unwin.

Weber, M. (1961) *General Economic History*, New York, Collier. First published in 1927.

Woodward, K. (2002) 'Intimacy and the public sphere?' in Jordan, T. and Pile, S. (eds) *op. cit.*.

Readings

7.1 Ann Oakley, 'Gender, methodology and people's ways of knowing' (1998)

Since the 1960s, feminist social scientists have had a great deal to say about methodology. The case that has been mounted against mainstream/'malestream' social research has been an important part of the project of women's studies; and within this, the dualism of 'quantitative' and 'qualitative' methods has played a central role. The use of 'qualitative' research methods has been aligned with a feminist perspective, while 'quantitative' methods have been seen as implicitly or explicitly defensive of the (masculinist) status quo. The feminist critique has joined other modern approaches to knowledge which dispute the appropriateness of a 'natural science model' to the social sciences (Bryman, 1988; Hammersley, 1989; Phillips, 1992).

This paper takes a critical look at what has been called a 'paradigm dialog' (Guba, 1990) – although the character of the discussion is often more oppositional than this phrase would suggest. The paper argues that the debate about research methods is more than a dialogue/argument concerning the best research technique to use in which circumstances; it offers a narrative which is about the relations between the social and scientific division of labour, the cultural production of masculinities and femininities, and the processes used to establish an understanding of the social and material world. Seen from this viewpoint, *methodology is itself gendered*; and one of the chief functions of the quantitative/qualitative dichotomy is as an *ideological representation*. The paper suggests that, in order to understand the relationship between methodology and gender, we need to consider the intellectual and social origins of both social and natural science, and the history of the relationship between them. This history indicates that the 'feminist methodological case' has been made largely in ignorance of the way in which different approaches to knowledge have historically been sited within social and natural science and have been used by social reformers, including feminists. One explanation of the feminist dispute with the value of quantitative methods and the claim to own qualitative ones is that

this methodological position contributes an important part of the 'professionalisation project' of feminist social science. The paper ends by suggesting that maintaining the division between 'quantitative' and 'qualitative' methods and the feminist case against quantification is ultimately unhelpful to the goal of an emancipatory social science.

...

Hearing the silent

When academia was first challenged by feminism in the late 1960s and early 1970s, and the biases of 'masculine' knowledge and women's invisibility were revealed, the argument quickly developed that 'positivist, quantitative research methodology' (Mies, 1983, p.120) cannot be used uncritically to further the political goals of academic women's studies, because the voices of women as an oppressed social group are unlikely to be heard using such an approach. Accordingly, the early feminist methodology texts all celebrated qualitative methods as best suited to the project of hearing women's accounts of their experiences (see, for example, Bowles and Duelli Klein, 1983; Roberts, 1981; Stanley and Wise, 1983).

'Qualitative' methods include participant observation, unstructured/semi-structured interviewing, (some) life history methods and focus groups. These came to be seen as epistemologically distinct from the 'quantitative' methods of surveys, experiments, statistical records, structured observations and content analysis, although, in practice, the feminist critique mainly equated qualitative methods with indepth face-to-face interviews (Stanley and Wise, 1993, p.3), and quantitative methods with enumeration in some form or other, and with the epistemological/philosophical position underlying the use of statistical techniques (Mies, 1991, p.67). As Bryman (1988) has noted of the methodological literature generally, quantitative and qualitative methods tend to be portrayed as mutually antagonistic ideal types, and even as representing two different 'paradigms' of social science itself. The contemporary opposition dates from the 1960s, when Glaser and Strauss's *The Discovery of Grounded Theory* (1967) was followed by a spate of books on qualitative methods (see, for example, Fletcher, 1974; Lofland, 1971; Schatzman and Strauss, 1973).

While the 'paradigm argument' pre-dated the feminist critique of methodology, the arrival of feminist scholarship introduced new themes. It became clear that the dualism of quantitative and qualitative is paralleled by others: hard/soft; masculine/feminine; public/private; rational/intuitive; intellect/feeling; scientific/artistic; social/natural; control/understanding; experiment/observation; objective/subjective; separation/fusion; repression/ expression; autonomy/dependence; voice/silence (Belenky *et al.*, 1986; Gilligan, 1982; Millman and Kanter, 1987; Reinharz, 1984). The dualism of 'quantitative' and 'qualitative' methods became inextricably bound up with the central contentions of women's studies – that traditional social science ignores or marginalises women, that all the major social theories explain the public world of labour but not the private world of work and the home (Elshtain, 1981; Stacey, 1981), and that the areas of social life which have particularly concerned women – caring, bodies, emotions (Rose, 1994; Martin, 1987; Williams and Bendelow, 1996) – have hardly been part of the sociological landscape at all.

The feminist critique contests quantitative research on a number of grounds: that the choice of topics often implicitly supports sexist values; female subjects are excluded or marginalised; relations between researcher and researched are intrinsically exploitative; the resulting data are superficial and over generalised; and quantitative research is generally not used to overcome social problems (Jayaratne and Stewart, 1991, p.86; Jayaratne, 1983, pp.145–6). Significantly, such criticisms of quantitative research overlap with general feminist critiques of mainstream/ 'malestream' social research (see, for example, Eichler, 1988). 'Normal' social science research has been equated by feminist critics with 'rape': 'Research is frequently conducted on rape model: the researchers take, hit and run' (Reinharz, 1984, p.95).

The three Ps

Underlying the various arguments in the feminist case against quantitative methods are three fundamental objections: the case against *positivism*; the case against *power*, and the case against *p values*, or against the use of statistical techniques as a means of establishing the validity of research findings.

(a) The reality of positivism

Positivism is an approach to knowledge which sees material and social worlds as equivalent, and which limits knowledge to 'facts' knowable through human experience (Kolakowski, 1972; see Bryant, 1985). A positivist social science is primarily a search for social 'facts' and for social laws which will predict behaviour. The adequacy of a scientific theory within positivism is guaranteed by its 'objectivity' or lack of bias; following rules of valid inference means that knowledge claims should be verifiable by anyone. Removal from the research process of researchers' own values and experiences is essential to this requirement of verifiability (Jagger, 1983). A basic precept is the 'subject/object' dichotomy: what is studied is an 'object', which the knower/researcher can look at in a value-free and neutral way. All these constructions are problematic within feminist and other modern critiques of knowledge. For this reason, positivism has effectively become a 'term of abuse' (Giddens, 1978, p.237). In the most extreme versions of feminist anti-positivism, the difference between 'fact' and 'fiction' disappears completely, and 'truth' and 'objectivity' are regarded as synonymous with 'lies' and 'subjectivity' (Stanley and Wise, 1993, p.171). 'Objectivity' is reframed as 'male subjectivity' (Caplan, 1988).

Supporting the rationale for the rejection of positivism is the association between it and 'the scientific method' which is condemned on political grounds. Science props up 'the fantasy of a calculable universe where everything operates according to quantifiable laws', a fantasy which is 'central to the calculating project of bourgeois democracy and the strategies of global domination' (Walkerdine, 1989, p.208).

(b) The power of knowing

When social science imitates natural science, the resulting delusion is that the barriers between researcher and researched keep researchers 'safe from involvement or risk' (Reinharz, 1984, p.368). The idea of a social world to be known about implies a knower; the knower is the expert, and the known are the objects of someone else's knowledge, not, most importantly, of their own. But feminist knowers must reject 'any mode of explanation which requires or sanctions the imposition upon the female subject of the theorist's own views as to who she is, what she wants, and what she should have'. This is because, 'One cannot survey the human race from a great and learned distance, proclaiming loudly that one has found the truth for the good of all the nameless, faceless abstractions one has never really bothered to take seriously' (Elshtain, 1981, p.303). The hierarchical situation – the position of the researcher as expert knower – invalidates any data that come out of the research process (Mies, 1983, p.123). Just as hierarchy produces data that are by definition *invalid*, so it is contended that where non-hierarchical relationships between researcher and researched exist, the resulting data are intrinsically *more valid* (Acker *et al.*, 1991, p.146).

There may be practical reasons why hierarchical research methods do not work, for example because research participants treated in this way respond to their objectification by not trusting researchers, and therefore by lying to them (Edwards, 1990). But this is not the essential objection. The essential objection is that the unequal power relationship between the knower and the known conflicts with the *moral obligation* at the heart of feminism to treat other women as you would yourself wish to be treated, and in this sense is seen to be at odds with feminism's emancipatory ideal. The notion of 'objectivity' calls up the ideological screen of 'objectification' and the adjective 'objectionable'. It has been argued that objectivity in research methodology is nothing more or less than an excuse for the same sort of obscene power relationship which leads women to be sexually assaulted and murdered (Stanley and Wise, 1983, p.169).

(c) The sin of number-crunching: p values and all that

The tendency of positivism towards enumeration and the use of statistical techniques has not helped its credibility to the feminist cause, or, to the whole postmodern project of conceiving knowledge in essentially relativist terms. As Silverman says in his *Qualitative Methodology and Sociology*, 'Since the 1960s, a story has got about that no good sociologist should dirty his [sic] hands with numbers' (Silverman, 1985, p.138). While the feminist literature accepts that some numbers can be used in qualitative studies for 'directional orientation', it is argued that statistical formulae and techniques can only serve to obscure qualitative meaning, and therefore are not part of the practices of a feminist social science (Leininger, 1994, p.103). Here we have the famous dispute between 'number-crunchers' and 'navel-gazers' (Swanson and Chapman, 1994, p.89). Feminist qualitative researchers argue that the ps they are interested in do not concern the probabilistic logic of statistical p values, but the value of *people*, and this can only be deduced by constructing a qualitative knowledge about them (Sidell, 1993, p.107).

The use of numbers is seen by many feminists as a 'machismo' element closely tied to the habit of manipulating variables and thus creating artificially 'controlled' realities (Bernard, 1973) in an 'unpleasantly exaggerated masculine style of control' (Millman and Kanter, 1987, p.35). 'Patriarchal' measurements are 'artificial' and 'abstract' (Griffin, 1980, p.107); the urge to predict and control as the underlying drive of the quantitative method is ideologically linked with men's desire to dominate, to exert power over people as well as nature, in other words it is a veritable 'exercise in masculinity' McCormack, 1981, p.3).

…

The 'qualitative' solution

In so far as there are distinctly feminist answers to the problems of 'quantitative' methods, these lie mainly in the direction of acknowledging the authenticity of multiple viewpoints, the role of values, and the subjectivities of both researcher and researched (Du Bois, 1983). This position produces feminist research as research advocating 'an integrative, trans-disciplinary approach to knowledge which grounds theory contextually in the concrete reality of women's everyday lives' (Stacey, 1988, p.212). The resulting solutions include such devices as the theory of *passionate scholarship* – a heretical challenge to the objectification of experience (Du Bois, 1983); and the postulate of *conscious partiality* as a substitute for the rule of value-neutral research (Mies, 1983). More sustained versions of this argument develop a case for using sociology in an emancipatory way, to further the political goals of feminism. The best-known statement of the difference between a sociology 'of' and a sociology 'for' women is that of the Canadian sociologist Dorothy Smith. Smith suggests the notion of a feminist 'standpoint' as a place outside the dominant frame of organized social science knowledge from which it is possible to construct a sociology respectful of women's subjectivity. Everything begins with everyday life; all concrete experience, and all abstract knowledge. In the case of women, situated as they are in a nexus of domestic labour and emotional work for others, the resultant 'thinking from caring, produces different versions of both social and natural science from the ones that have dominated most intellectual discourse and knowledge-production (Rose, 1994). Smith recommends something she calls 'institutional ethnography' as the core of a feminist methodology. Such an ethnography means a commitment to investigating and explaining 'actual practices and relations' (Smith, 1988, p.160). The use of research methods based on 'indepth' interviewing with selected samples of women, a meticulous, iterative attention to the details of what women say, and forms of analysis dedicated to reproducing all of this as 'faithfully' as possible, construct an alternative feminist scholarship in which the enemy of 'the scientific method' appears to lack even a foot in the door.

However, feminists' use of qualitative methods reveals problems in relation both to the validity of truth-claims and conflict with feminist values. For example, the use of women-only samples can give us exactly the same problem as men-only samples, raising questions about, for example, claims to have established authentically female ways of knowing (Belenky *et al.*, 1986; see Crawford, 1989) or thinking about moral choice (Gilligan, 1982), and ignoring the tendency for sex differences to disappear when direct comparisons are made between samples of men and women (Walker, 1984); methods such as interviewing do not necessarily rid the research situation of hierarchy (Ribbens, 1989; Finch, 1984; Wise, 1987; Edwards, 1990; Graham, 1984; McKee and O'Brian, 1983); appeal to such devices as sharing book royalties with informants (Wolf, 1996, p.25) and discussing data analysis with them (Stacey, 1988) may lead researchers away from 'truth-seeking' as a legitimate goal of inquiry. Many of these issues are shared with qualitative research more generally. The 'qualitative' researcher asked to explain the methods used to derive findings from data has been compared to a centipede which is paralysed when asked to think about how it moves all its legs (Sandelowski, 1994). Validity and 'bias' are general problems. Although the aims of qualitative research theoretically exclude generalisability, the insights gained are likely to reflect the social world of research participants, so that bias in qualitative research is just as possible as in the quantitative sort, and possibly more so, given the smaller sample sizes (Jayaratne and Stewart, 1991), the emphasis on the need for homogeneous samples (Cannon *et al.*, 1991), and the absence of 'visible research standards' (Sprague and Zimmerman, 1989, p.73). There are particular problems which can lead to false inferences being made with the lower participation rates in much qualitative research of people from working-class and ethnic minority backgrounds (Cannon *et al.*, 1991).

While quantification is a strategy which emphasises explicitness in each stage of research (measurement techniques, data, evaluation processes), there is no accepted model for 'good' qualitative research with agreed criteria for evaluating its truth content (Griffin and Ragin, 1994; Jayaratne and Stewart, 1991). Many qualitative researchers do not provide adequate and clear justifications for their methods, findings or conclusions (Howe and Eisenhart, 1990); indeed, the 'almost mystical advocacy of the virtues of qualitative ethnology' (Shadish *et al.*, 1991, p.397) leads sometimes to missing information about how research was *actually* done.

Some researchers argue that establishing the validity of truth claims made for qualitative data is an activity so different from the parallel exercise with quantitative data that it is unreasonable to think of using the same criteria (Leininger, 1994; Muecke, 1994). There is very little systematic training in how to *do* qualitative research (Richardson, 1996). Those who claim that qualitative techniques protect from research bias ignore the selection process inherent in the collection and reporting of qualitative data which by no means saves it from 'the intrusion of the researchers' values' (Sprague and Zimmerman, 1989, p.74). As Marsh has pointed out, problems of valid data and valid inferences from data run through all social research and 'you do not escape the difficulties by pretending that you can extract unproblematic information yourself in a pub over a pint of beer' (Marsh, 1984, p.96). Reactivity – the influence of researchers on their data – is a problem to be faced in all types of research (Bryman, 1988). Even when quoted material is allowed 'to speak for itself', it is not clear that the unmediated views of research participants provide the best way to understand the social world. A preference for 'multi-level multi-method' studies using triangulated evidence from a variety of sources 'which would be sufficiently convincing for a jury to commit themselves to action' can be a good deal more complicated than it sounds. Triangulating data means mixing interpretations and these may be at odds with one another. Moyra Sidell (1993) gives an example of this in a study of the health status of older women. She used three levels of data ranging from 'very hard' (national statistics on mortality and morbidity) through 'medium' (two large sample surveys) to 'very soft' (biographical interviews with thirty older women). The result was 'a mass of paradox and downright contradictory evidence' (Siddell, 1993, pp.111–12). It is not simply a question of checking one dataset against another; different 'types' of data may yield very different conclusions.

The feminist critique puts a new emphasis on the extent to which different methodologies imply different forms of power relations, but much of what is argued is otherwise not decisively new. Similar issues have occupied a central place in many 'isms' and 'ologies', for example poststructuralism, ethnomethodology,   phenomenology, postmodernism and hermeneutics (Hammersley, 1995). All of these, like feminism, criticise the idea of an objective social science as ignoring the constitution of the social world by agents whose meanings and intentions are essential to our understanding of it. In Britain, sociologists showed more interest in qualitative research from the late 1960s on; the Chicago school was more advanced in this regard in its practices, if not in its theories, during the 1920s and 1930s. Cicourel talked about 'quantofrenia' in 1964 (Desrosières, 1991). Glaser and Strauss's critique of verification theory (1967) is very like the later feminist case. Foucault, Habermas and Heidegger all comment on the dissolution of the subject/object distinction, and the need for a more reflexive, socially-located approach to knowledge.

The problem of dichotomy: weakness or strength

Many of the supposed differences between qualitative and quantitative ways of knowing are not a matter of a hard-and-fast distinction, but of a continuum, with points on it where one would find it difficult to say which method was in the ascendant. For example, either 'quantitative' or 'qualitative' research may include the development and progressive (or unprogressive) testing of theory, or it may not. Analysing data as numerical values – seen as an aspect of quantitative research – often requires qualitative judgements about data and the construction of categories for statistical testing. In just the same way, there is a false synonymity between being systematic and being quantitative; one may be an unsystematic quantitative researcher, or a systematic qualitative one, or vice versa, in each case (Jayaratne and Stewart, 1991). 'Qualitative' data can be analysed systematically or formally (Griffin and Ragin, 1994). In practice, few such analyses proceed without relying on the occurrence of a theme to derive an interpretation of meaning, and the analysis of open-ended interviews by counting the number of times particular themes occur 'can hardly be called qualitative, especially if the themes are assigned a significance based on the frequency of occurrence (Dreher, 1994, p.284). As Bryman has argued: 'a good deal of qualitative research shares an empiricist streak with quantitative research; much quantitative research shares a concern for subjects' interpretations, which is supposedly the province of the qualitative researcher' (Bryman, 1988, pp.172–3). Many research studies collect both 'objective' and 'subjective' data, and the transformation of such issues into 'dichotomous choices is unnecessary, inaccurate and

ultimately counter-productive' (LeCompte and Goetz, 1982, p.54).

Although there are some signs of a new recognition within feminist social science of the usefulness of non-qualitative methods (see, for example, Gorelick, 1991; Kelly *et al.*, 1992; Oakley, 1992), both feminist methodology and feminist epistemology remain strongly founded on qualitative methods. Applying Kuhn's arguments about cultures of 'normal science', it could be suggested that feminism holds onto qualitative methodology because this has become part of its normal intellectual repertoire. To be a feminist social scientist one must have a certain allegiance to the qualitative paradigm, and a willingness to go along with the habit of dualist either/or thinking (even if this is, at the same time, the enemy of both an emancipatory social science and an emancipatory social order). Thus, feminists who use quantitative methods may be expected to apologise for so doing (Graham and Rawlings, quoted in Reinharz, 1992, p.87). Drawing on the sociology of professions and professionalisation literature, it can also be argued that the claims of feminist social science preferentially to own the qualitative method are part of its own professionalising agenda (Freidson, 1970; Witz, 1992). Feminism needed a research method, a distinct methodology, in order to occupy a distinctive place in the academy and acquire social status and moral legitimacy. Opposition to 'traditional' research methods as much as innovation of alternative ones thus provided an organising platform for feminist scholarship. This opposition, and the whole contention of positivism and realism as inherently anti-feminist, were reinforced when postmodernism entered the feminist critique in the 1980s. As Wolf (1996, p.6) has commented, it is probably no accident that the 'often inaccessible, abstract and hyper-theoretical language' of postmodernism gained ascendancy at the same time as women increased their representation within academia.

...

The dangers of simple histories

We can say, then, that the history of methodology in science, including social science, is more complex than the paradigm argument within, and outside, feminism would suggest. Continued adherence to the idea of opposed methodological paradigms depends on an oversimplified view of the positivism implied by quantitative methods; but the truth about positivism, as the above brief history indicates, is 'less straightforward than the fantasy' (Phillips, 1992, p.96). Sociology did not mistakenly imitate the positivism of the natural sciences, and then discover its mistake, a mistake which is particularly acute with respect to the representation in what counts as knowledge of the experiences of oppressed social groups. As Jordanova (1989, p.162) has put it, 'It is all too easy to see the tangles around gender, science and medicine as simply evidence of sexism ... such a judgement is both simplistic and facile'. The origins of positivism lay in the abandonment of metaphysics as a way of establishing knowledge about the world, and an alternative insistence on the importance of knowing through experience (Kolakowski, 1972). The dismissal of the role of values was similarly intended to emphasize the importance of separating out valid from invalid knowledge (Giddens, 1978). While at each point in their history, ways of knowing have been anchored in the social context and political concerns of the time, we cannot abstract from this a straightforward picture of two communities of scientists – the social and the natural – developing methods of study which bear no relation to one another. Nor is it clearly the case that 'quantitative' methods have served no relevant feminist goal. Historical innovations in empiricist methodology such as the social survey were made primarily by people, including women, who sought policy-relevant knowledge as ammunition for social reform. Reformers such as Jane Addams, Harriet Martineau, Florence Nightingale and Beatrice Webb carried out social investigations which served the reformist cause by revealing the extent of poverty and inequality (McDonald, 1993). Feminist social reformers advocated the need for statistics to demonstrate the conditions of women's lives. For example, the astronomer Maria Mitchell in 1875 urged the collection of statistics to describe the situation of women scientists in the United States. In the campaign against women's exclusion from higher education, statistics were used to disprove the masculinist medical notion that education damaged women's health (Reinharz, 1992). There was a feminist tradition of defending women from the 'science' of craniometry, the first biological theory to be 'supported' by quantitative data. Craniometrists found that women generally had smaller brains than men, and contended that in this regard they belonged to the same category as Negroes, apes and children. Those who advocated and practised craniometry regarded themselves as 'servants of their numbers, apostles of objectivity' (Mastroianni *et al.*, 1994, p.112). The painstaking gathering of statistics was even seen as a uniquely feminine capacity (Reinharz, 1992). Significantly, the work of feminist social reformers often combined the numerical approach of the social survey with other ways of knowing; for example, Beatrice Webb became a participant observer by getting a job in tailoring to help her find out how the industry functioned (McDonald, 1993, p.277); Charles Booth, Webb's cousin, lived in working-class lodgings in the East End of London to collect data for his poverty survey, widely hailed as the first example of such an investigation, and carried out to win an argument with a friend of Marx's that the extent of poverty was not as great as the socialists claimed it was.

...

Quantification for women?

Today, most feminist critics of quantitative methodology do ultimately concede that there *is* a social reality which has an objective existence beyond people's competing interpretations of it (Stanley and Wise, 1993, p.9). We cannot end up with a phenomenological morass, either as feminists or as social scientists. The danger of rooting knowledge in the description of individual experiences is that one never moves beyond them. The grounding of research questions and findings in women's experiences of everyday life is a laudatory feminist aim; and an essential aid to a comprehensive understanding of the social world. But the subjectivity of the researcher remains, as in all science, a potential influence on the knowledge-claims that are made.

Feminism's interest in an emancipatory social science suggests a need for a range of methods within which 'quantitative' methods would have an accepted and respected place. The extensive socio-demographic mapping of women's position that underscored second-wave feminism would not have been possible without large-scale quantitative surveys. Women's oppression could neither have been demonstrated nor understood without an opportunity to examine their relative positions *vis-à-vis* men in the labour market, the education, health and welfare systems, political organisations and government, and the private world of the home and domestic relations. The underlying gendering of structural inequalities that occurs in most societies could not be discerned using qualitative methods on their own. Statistics derived from official records or from large-scale surveys continue to demonstrate the ways in which gender, class and ethnicity intersect as axes of discrimination (see, for example, Arber and Ginn, 1991; Bagilhole, 1994; Department of Health, 1995; Dex, 1987; Humphries and Rubery, 1995). A recent example of the use of survey data on women's position as a feminist consciousness-raising strategy is the development and work of the 'Support

Stockings' in Sweden. The Support Stockings are a network of women engaged in supporting women in politics. The network was formed in 1991, when the percentage of women in the Swedish parliament fell for the first time since 1919, and a number of political and social developments suggested a move away from a gender-equal society. One of the Support Stockings' strategic tools was the use of gender-based statistics as a way of disseminating information about women's position (Stark, 1997). Such examples are fuel for the rehabilitation of 'quantitative' methods within feminist social science research techniques, and for a development of these in the direction of a 'quantification for women', to borrow Dorothy Smith's (1988) phrase. Similarly, there is a strong case (which is not considered here) for developing experimental research methods so as to reflect feminist values and the goals of an emancipatory social science. In both cases what is likely to be required is adaptation of the 'malestream' models to suit feminist values; there is much work to be done collecting and integrating examples of 'good practice' and providing guidelines for future research.

The call for feminist models of quantitative and experimental work to be developed clearly recognises that 'the baby need not be thrown out with the bathwater', and that procedures used in 'malestream' research which are inconsistent with feminist values can be altered without abandoning the basic methodological techniques themselves. The critical question remains the appropriateness of the method to the research question.

...

References

Acker, J., Barry, K. and Esseveld, J. (1991) 'Objectivity and truth: problems in doing feminist research' in Fonow, M.M. and Cook, J.A. (eds) *op. cit.*, pp.33–153.

Arber, S. and Ginn, J. (1991) *Gender and Later Life*, London, Sage.

Bagilhole, B. (1994) *Women, Work and Equal Opportunity*, Aldershot, Avebury.

Belenky, M.F., Clinchy, B.M., Goldberger, N.R. and Tarule, J.M. (1986) *Women's Ways of Knowing*, New York, Basic Books.

Bernard, J. (1973) 'My four revolutions: an autobiographical history of the American Sociological Association', *American Journal of Sociology*, vol.78, pp.773–91.

Bowles, G. and Duelli Klein, R. (eds) (1983) *Theories of Women's Studies*, London, Routledge.

Bryant, C.G.A. (1985) *Positivism in Social Theory and Research*, London, Macmillan.

Bryman, A. (1988) *Quantity and Quality in Social Research*, London, Unwin Hyman.

Cannon, L.W., Higginbotham, E. and Leung, M.L.A. (1991) 'Race and class bias in qualitative research on women' in Fonow, M.M. and Cook, J.A. (eds) *op. cit.*, pp.107–18.

Caplan, P. (1988) 'Engendering knowledge: the politics of ethnography: Part I', *Anthropology Today*, vol.4, no.5, pp.8–17.

Crawford, M. (1989) 'Agreeing to differ: feminist epistemologies and women's ways of knowing' in Crawford, M. and Gentry, M., *Gender and Thought*, New York, Springer Verlag.

Department of Health (1995) *Variations in Health: What Can the Department of Health and the NHS Do?*, London, HMSO.

Desrosières, A. (1991) 'How to make things which hold together: social science, statistics and the state' in Wagner, P., Wittrock, B. and Whitley, R. (eds) (1991) *Discourses in Sociology: The Shaping of the Social Science Disciplines*, Dordrecht, Kluwer Academic Publishers, pp.195–218.

Dex, S. (1987) *Women's Occupational Mobility*, Basingstoke, Macmillan.

Dreher, M. (1994) 'Qualitative research methods from the reviewer's perspective' in Morse, J.M. (ed.) *op. cit.*, pp.281–97.

Du Bois, B. (1983) 'Passionate scholarship: notes on values, knowing and method in feminist social science' in Bowles, G. and Duelli Klein, R. (eds) *op. cit.*, pp.105–16.

Edwards, R. (1990) 'Connecting method and epistemology: a white woman interviewing black women', *Women's Studies International Forum*, no.13, pp.477–90.

Eichler, M. (1988) *Nonsexist Research Methods*, Boston, MA, Allen and Unwin.

Elshtain, J.B. (1981) *Public Man, Private Woman*, Oxford, Martin Robertson.

Finch, J. (1984) '"It's great to have someone to talk to": the ethics and politics of interviewing women' in Bell, C. and Roberts, H. (eds) *op. cit.*, pp.70–87.

Fletcher, C. (1974) *Beneath the Surface*, London, Routledge & Kegan Paul.

Freidson, E. (1970) *The Profession of Medicine*, New York, Dodd, Mead & Co.

Giddens, A. (1978) 'Positivism and its critics' in Bottomore, T. and Nisbet, R. (eds) *A History of Sociological Analysis*, London, Heinemann.

Gilligan, C. (1982) *In a Different Voice*, Cambridge, MA, Harvard University Press.

Glaser, B.G. and Strauss, A. L. (1967) *The Discovery of Grounded Theory*, Chicago, IL, Aldine.

Gorelick, S. (1991) 'Contradictions of feminist methodology', *Gender and Society*, vol.5, pp.459–77.

Graham, H. (1984) 'Surveying through stories' in Bell, C. and Roberts, H. (eds) *op. cit.*, pp.104–24.

Griffin, L. and Ragin, C.C. (1994) 'Some observations on formal methods of qualitative analysis', *Sociological Methods and Research*, vol.23, pp.4–21.

Griffin, S. (1980) *Women and Nature: The Roaring Inside Her*, New York, Harper Colophon.

Guba, E.G. (1990) *The Paradigm Dialog*, Newbury Park, CA, Sage.

Hammersley, M. (1989) *The Dilemma of Qualitative Method: Herbert Blumer and the Chicago Tradition*, London, Routledge.

Hammersley, M. (1995) *The Politics of Social Research*, London, Sage.

Howe, K. and Eisenhart, M. (1990) 'Standards for qualitative (and quantitative) research: a prolegomenon', *Educational Researcher*, May, pp.2–9.

Humphries, J. and Rubery, J. (eds) (1995) *The Economics of Equal Opportunities*, Manchester, Equal Opportunities Commission.

Jagger, A. M. (1983) *Feminist Politics and Human Nature*, Brighton, Harvester Press.

Jayaratne, T.E. (1983) 'The value of quantitative methodology for feminist research' in Bowles, G. and Duelli Klein, R. (eds) *op. cit.*, pp.140–61.

Jayaratne, T.E. and Stewart, A.J. (1991) 'Quantitative and qualitative methods in the social sciences: current feminist issues and practical strategies' in Fonow, M.M. and Cook, J.A. (eds) *op. cit.*, pp.85–107.

Jordanova, L. (1989) *Sexual Visions*, Hemel Hempstead, Harvester Wheatsheaf.

Kelly, L., Regan, L. and Burton, S. (1992) 'Defending the indefensible? Quantitative methods and feminist research' in Hinds, H., Phoenix, A. and Stacey, J. (eds) *Working Out: New Directions for Women's Studies*, London, Falmer Press, pp.149–60.

Kolakowski, L. (1972) *Positivist Philosophy: From Hume to the Vienna Circle*, Harmondsworth, Penguin Books.

LeCompte, M.D. and Goetz, J.P. (1982) 'Problems of reliability and validity in ethnographic research', *Review of Educational Research*, vol.52, pp.31–60.

Leininger, M. (1994) 'Evaluation criteria and critique of qualitative research studies' in Morse, J.M. (ed.) *op. cit.*, pp.95–115.

Lofland, J. (1971) *Analyzing Social Settings: A Guide to Qualitative Observation and Analysis*, Belmont, CA, Wadsworth.

Marsh, C. (1984) 'Problems with surveys: methods or epistemology?' in Bulmer, M. (ed.), *Sociological Research Methods: An Introduction*, London, Macmillan, pp.82–102.

Martin, E. (1987) *The Woman in the Body*, Boston, MA, Beacon Press.

Mastroianni, A.C., Faden, R. and Federman, D. (1994) *Women and Health Research*, Volume I, Washington, DC, National Academy Press.

McCormack, T. (1981) 'Good theory or just theory? Toward a feminist philosophy of social science', *Women's Studies International Quarterly*, vol.4, pp.1–12.

McDonald, L. (1993) *The Early Origins of the Social Sciences*, Montreal, McGill-Queen's University Press.

McKee, L. and O'Brian, M. (1983) 'Interviewing men: taking gender seriously' in Gamarnikow, E., Morgan, S., Purvis, J. and Taylorson, D. (eds) (1983) *The Public and the Private*, London, Heinemann, pp.147–76.

Mies, M. (1983) 'Towards a methodology for feminist research' in Bowles, G. and Duelli Klein, R. (eds) *op. cit.*, pp.117–39.

Mies, M. (1991) 'Women's research or feminist research? The debate surrounding feminist science and methodology' in Fonow, M.M. and Cook, J.A. (eds) *op. cit.*, pp.60–84.

Millman, M. and Kanter, R.M. (1987) 'Introduction to *Another Voice: Feminist Perspectives on Social Life and Social Science*' in Harding, S. (ed.) *Feminism and Methodology*, Bloomington, IN, Indiana University Press, pp.29–36.

Muecke, M.A. (1994) 'On the evaluation of ethnographies' in Morse, J.M. (ed.) *op. cit.*, pp.187–209.

Oakley, A. (1992) *Social Support and Motherhood: The Natural History of a Research Project*, Oxford, Basil Blackwell.

Phillips, D.C. (1992) *The Social Scientist's Bestiary*, Oxford, Pergamon Press.

Reinharz, S. (1984) *On Becoming a Social Scientist*, New Brunswick, NJ, Transaction Books.

Reinharz, S. (1992) *Feminist Methods in Social Research*, New York, Oxford University Press.

Ribbens, J. (1989) 'Interviewing – an "unnatural" situation?', *Women's Studies International Forum*, vol.12, pp.579–92.

Richardson, J.T.E. (1996) 'Introduction' in Richardson, J.T.E. (ed.) *Handbook of Qualitative Research Methods*, London, BPS Books.

Roberts, H. (1981) *Doing Feminist Research*, London, Routledge.

Rose, H. (1994) *Love, Power and Knowledge*, Cambridge, Polity Press.

Sandelowski, M. (1994) 'The proof is in the pottery: toward a poetic for qualitative inquiry' in Morse, J.M. (ed.) *op. cit.*, pp.46–63.

Schatzman, L. and Strauss, A.L. (1973) *Field Research: Strategies for a Natural Sociology*, Englewood Cliffs, NJ, Prentice-Hall.

Shadish, W.R., Cook, T.D. and Leviton, L.C. (1991) *Foundations of Program Evaluation*, Newbury Park, CA, Sage.

Sidell, M. (1993) 'Interpreting', pp.119–30 in Shakespeare, P., Atkinson, D. and French, S. (eds) *Reflecting on Research Practices*, Buckingham, Open University Press.

Silverman, D. (1985) *Qualitative Methodology and Sociology*, Aldershot, Gower Press.

Smith, D.E. (1988) *The Everyday World as Problematic*, Milton Keynes, Open University Press.

Sprague, J. and Zimmerman, M. K. (1989) 'Quality and quantity: reconstructing feminist methodology', *The American Sociologist*, Spring, pp.71–86.

Stacey, J. (1988) 'Can there be a feminist ethnography?', *Women's Studies International Forum,* vol.11, pp.21–7.

Stacey, M. (1981) 'The division of labour revisited or overcoming the two Adams' in Abrams, P.O., Deem, R., Finch, J. and Rock, P. (eds) *Practice and Progress: British Sociology 1950–1980*, pp.173–204.

Stanley, L. and Wise, S. (1983) *Breaking Out: Feminist Consciousness and Feminist Research*, London, Routledge.

Stanley, L. and Wise, S. (1993) *Breaking Out Again: Feminist Ontology and Epistemology*, London, Routledge.

Stark, A. (1997) 'Combating the backlash: how Swedish women won the war' in Oakley, A. and Mitchell, J. (eds) *Who's Afraid of Feminism?*, London, Hamish Hamilton, pp.224–44.

Swanson, J.M. and Chapman, L. (1994) 'Inside the black box: theoretical and methodological isues in conducting evaluation research using a qualitative approach' in Morse, J.M. (ed.) *op. cit.*, pp.66–93.

Walker, L. (1984) 'Sex differences in the development of moral reasoning: a critical review', *Child Development,* vol.55, pp.667–91.

Walkerdine, V. (1989) *Counting Girls Out.* London, Virago.

Williams, S. J. and Bendelow, G.A. (1996) 'The "emotional" body', *Body and Society,* vol.2, pp.125–39.

Wise, S. (1987) 'A framework for discussing ethical issues in feminist research: a review of the literature' in Griffiths, V. *et al., Writing Feminist Biography 2: Using Life Histories*, Manchester, University of Manchester.

Witz, A. (1992) *Professions and Patriarchy,* London, Routledge.

Wolf, D.L. (1996) 'Situating feminist dilemmas in fieldwork' in Wolf, D.L. (ed.) (1996) *Feminist Dilemmas in Fieldwork*, Boulder, CO, Westview Press, pp.1–55.

Source: Oakley, 1998, pp.707–11,713–16,721–4

7.2 R.W. Connell, 'Charting futures for sociology' (2000)

Sociology and world market society

It was not pre-ordained that sociology should come into existence; and it is by no means guaranteed that sociology will continue to exist. In this essay I reflect on sociology's conditions of existence as a global project in the past, and on its possible conditions of existence in the future.

Sociology, as an intellectual project and an academic practice, was created in the late nineteenth and early twentieth centuries as a specific formation within the growing domain of 'social science'. To many of its first-generation practitioners, sociology *was* 'the social science', or the universal social science. Sociology was the integration of all scientific attempts to understand social facts and social problems. Its object of knowledge was social progress, conceived on the grandest possible scale.

This project allowed social critique. It even encouraged criticism of institutions or practices that stood in the way of progress – criticism made, naturally, in the name of science. But evolutionary sociology did not yield a consistent political standpoint, since the same warrant of 'science' could be claimed for Spencer's defence of free-market capitalism, Durkheim's mild ethical socialism, and tough-minded economistic Marxism.

The loose implications of evolutionary sociology had much to do with the character of the group who created it – a loose coalition of liberal intellectuals, ranging from journalists and clergymen to academics, officials and independent men of letters. Most were men; almost all were residents of the imperial powers at the high tide of imperialism, and beneficiaries of bourgeois class advantage as well. The lives of sociology's creators were beset with contradictions between liberal thought and their actual conditions of existence – contradictions that both fuelled the creation of 'sociology' and gave it characteristic problems and limits.

During the twentieth century, the enterprise of sociology fell into the hands of the academics. Evolutionary sociology collapsed for a variety of reasons, not least the undermining of the liberal intelligentsia by militarism and war in the metropole (a war which the metropole with characteristic arrogance called the 'First World War', ignoring the recently concluded global war of conquest over other societies).

In its new conditions of existence within academia, sociology was transformed into a speciality, one of a patchwork quilt of territories within the continent of 'social science'. It laid claim (as all academic specialities must do) to special expertise on a particular set of topics and methods. Its object of knowledge, increasingly, was social differentiation within the metropole.

In the English-speaking world, sociology became more closely linked to the developing welfare state and to the professions that dealt with 'social problems' – such as social work, social administration, education, and public health. Sociology became useful for its expertise in surveys and field observation. This still allowed critique, though of a more limited sort. Sociologists became noted for their documentation of inequalities within metropolitan society (hence the trio class/race/gender).

But this critique circulated mostly within a professional community. As an academic speciality, sociology increasingly adopted the techniques of closure – qualifications, professional membership, publication in technical journals – that were becoming dominant features of academic life in general through the twentieth century. By the mid-twentieth century, professional sociology had recovered enough self-confidence to adopt ambitious generalizing theories about 'society' once more. But this was now on a systems model that took the metropole as a self-sufficient unit and, if it spoke about the colonized world at all, usually regarded it as under-developed.

The huge growth in student numbers after the 1950s, along with the expansion of professionalized sociology across the world in the growing international university system of the later twentieth century, expanded sociology's academic base and

diversity. The radical movements of the 1960s and 1970s injected socialist, feminist, and anticolonial thought, without doing much to change sociology's institutional structure. It is not surprising to see a gradual taming of these impulses, even as their influence has spread.

But the external conditions under which professional sociology formed and flourished have now changed. The welfare state, which both defined many of the problems for sociology to investigate and employed many of sociology's graduates, is in decline across the metropolitan world.

This decline is, of course, connected with the rise of a form of politics which in Australia is called 'economic rationalism', in Latin America 'neoliberalism', and in Britain simple 'Thatcherism'. Attempts at collective will-formation and rational policy debate have been drowned steadily by a mighty celebration of the competitive market as the only social decision maker. In this political framework the role of government progressively is reduced to securing the unfettered operation of private capital. Initially an agenda of hard-line conservatives, in the 1980s and 1990s the 'market agenda' also came to dominate the thinking of labour, social-democratic, and reformist parties. The current convergence among Clinton, Blair, and Schroeder perfectly reflects this shift.

The almost complete ascendancy of the market agenda in mass media and mass politics worldwide – secured by the collapse of the USSR and the restoration of capitalism in China – poses sharp problems for a discipline so closely connected to the welfare state as sociology. A quite probable future for sociology is gentle decline into an atmosphere of nostalgia. As the realm of 'the market' expands, the realm of 'the social' shrinks.

In a world dominated by the market agenda, sociology will still have some functions. One is to perform a kind of salvage ethnography on modern society. As the market overwhelms all nonmarket relations, sociology can perform a valuable role documenting ways of life now doomed to pass away: bureaucracies, neighborhoods, ethnic communities, sexual subcultures, public schools, and the like. Since market society numbs the intellect as well as the conscience, this may even be a lucrative role for sociology, providing bored utility-maximizers with social-scientific entertainment, as the old ethnographies of 'nuts, sluts, and perverts' once did.

For those sociologists who still want to affect the world, market society has many residual problems that the market does not solve, or does not solve quickly: the poor, the chronically sick, the disturbed, the violent; linguistic minorities; people who can't read, hold a job, or manage the Internet. There are many practical problems of adjustment for people who can't engage in market competition, or who lose out in the race to be 'winners'. Market-society sociology, then, could be the science of the 'losers', explaining why they lose and working out what to do with them.

Of course there is not much money in this. By definition, the losers are not in a position to buy the services of sociologists on the market, in the way corporations can buy the research they need. But there will still be a residual role for government in holding the ring for capital. This involves not just enforcing property rights through courts or police, but also preventing disruptions to the market from those on its margins. Sociology, therefore, could eke out a living by writing reports for market-agenda governments on how to manage problems for which the market hasn't yet produced an answer. Some of us are doing that already.

The market agenda has gained much of its stranglehold on politics because it has come with a panic factor: globalization. In Australia, for instance – an early example of the virtually complete takeover of a Labor Party by free-market ideologues – a policy of deregulation and privatization was driven through in the 1980s on the argument that this was the *only* way to prevent the country from going under in global competition. The nature of the 'global competition' was specified only vaguely (as is characteristic of alien threats of all kinds), but the effect on the overall mood of public debate was very strong, as it has been elsewhere.

Globalization is a current buzzword in business, where it loosely signifies both the existence of worldwide arenas – global commodity markets, global capital markets, global stock exchange, global telecommunications – and their growing importance vis-à-vis local arenas for business. Much hype and loose talk has created some strikingly false impressions:

- that globalization is something radically new;

- that globalization has already integrated local economics into a monster world economy;

- that the state, and local, national, and regional social forces are necessarily overwhelmed by the pressures of the international economy;

- that in global markets all are equal, and in 'global culture' all local cultures mix and match on equal terms.

Hence the familiar media images of the world citizen. We come to believe a typical world citizen is the businesswoman in Kuala Lumpur in a Chanel suit giving orders on a cellular phone to her stockbroker in New York to sell Japanese shares to a Brazilian rubber baron. Yet the construction of world society is not a myth, but a real social process, infinitely more complex and problematic than the pretty picture of globalization. It began with the growth of overseas power by Portugal and Spain in the fifteenth century, followed by the creation of other permanent overseas empires by Holland, France, and England, and by the overland expansion of Russia and the United States. This was a process both violent and destructive, on an immense scale. Along with millions of deaths, epidemic disease, large-scale slavery, and other forms of forced labor and migration went the disruption of local gender orders and political systems, and assault on indigenous religions and cultures.

But imperialism was not only destructive, it was also creative – producing new social orders both in the colonized world and in the metropole. It reshaped not only economies but also cultures. Imperialism indeed had become the condition of existence of Western society by the time the new social sciences began to take society as an object of knowledge and offer generalizations about it.

This connection was quite plain to the sociologists of the late nineteenth century and, in however distorted a form, became the central theme of the sociology of progress (Connell, 1997). But twentieth-century sociology, rightly rejecting the muddy concept of 'social evolution', also rejected the sense of connection with the colonized world that underpinned it. Twentieth-century social science, treating the society of the metropole as if it existed on a separate planet, thus formed itself on a gigantic lie: that modernity formed itself within North Atlantic society independent of the rest of the world. That lie can be undone, not by fables about the merging of cultures, but by recognizing the constitution of modernity *within* the history of imperialism. Contemporary world society is not an extension of the North Atlantic 'modern' across the globe, but a transformation within an already-global system of social relations.

In the transformation of the last 60 years, the political structures of earlier imperialism have been dismantled – with one important exception, the United States. The United States has never decolonized its nineteenth-century conquests, but instead has integrated them more and more tightly into a gigantic nation-state, thereby succeeding at a task at which the French and the Russians failed. Apart from the United States, in place of politically integrated empires we have a set of economic institutions, most importantly global capital markets and multinational corporations, which now frame the policies of individual governments.

The global structures that have developed in the postcolonial era are massively unequal and strikingly undemocratic. While universal suffrage in national legislatures is now widespread, and ideologies of capitalism tell us of the global triumph of liberal democracy, the most important decisions are made by the top officials of private bureaucracies, over which there is no democratic control at all. The self-selected elite of global business – mainly American, European, and Japanese, with an admixture of oil wealth from the Middle East – are highly unrepresentative in social character. Almost all are men, from a limited set of ethnic groups, mostly drawn from the privileged classes of the most privileged countries. It is not surprising that they operate with only occasional reference to the well-being of the rest of humanity.

Under the aegis of this new global elite, a new cultural order is being created. In market society, the leading science is the science of markets – that is to say, economics: not political economy, not even 'economics' in its sense of public housekeeping. Rather, it is the stripped-down economics that is interior to market society – that concerns itself only with the internal dynamics of markets, and not with their conditions of existence, with what is outside the markets.

But that is only the leading science. The cultural impact of the new global capitalism is much wider. For the ascendancy of the market places a premium, quite literally, on what succeeds in markets. This applies to cultural production as much as to other forms of production. What is encouraged, in all areas of cultural production, is not what is true, or beautiful, or profound, or necessary, but exclusively what sells.

So we get global systems of mass communication dominated by commercial fantasy – Hollywood, TV soaps, consumer advertising, celebrity gossip, the major content of mass culture. And we get political discourse whose leading feature is the dominance of spin, where political leaders never talk honestly about their problems or the public's problems, but always talk in ways calculated for personal, party, or national advantage. We now live in a world where the normal content of mass communication is lies, distortions, and calculated fantasies. I don't think it is any wonder that the last 20 years have seen a steady decline in political party membership, a deepening public disillusion with politicians, and a collapse of citizenship. These are all too reasonable responses to the global commercialization of public spaces.

More than ever before, we are in need of critical sciences of society – intellectual projects that concern themselves with what lies beneath, beside, and beyond the market. Indeed, we may now say that this intellectual project is even more important the more the market itself gains a grip on intellectual culture. And anyone who works in contemporary universities knows how that grip is tightening – in forms ranging from 'enterprise culture' in neoliberal Britain, through the power of commercialized sports in US universities, to the new business-oriented managerial elite of Australian universities.

This sounds apocalyptic. Am I proposing that the cultural future of humanity depends on a tiny band of gimlet-eyed sociologists standing shoulder to shoulder with iron determination against the tides of commercialization? Well, yes. But they cannot stand alone. For the most determined sociologists have only a tiny impact unless they are part of a larger movement, in which sociology is itself transformed. A democratic project cannot be carried by a small elite. If we have learned anything else from the history of twentieth-century socialism, we must have learned that.

The future of sociology, if it is to escape marginalization and slow decline, is to be reconstituted as a democratic science – as the self-knowledge of global society. This necessarily means new media, new forms of research, and above all, new participants. The greatest obstacle to the advancement of sociology is sociology's own professionalism. Every organizational move that limits participation in sociological work, that constitutes sociology as a closed unit or a self-contained culture, is against sociology's long-term interests.

A democratic science is defined less by its intentions or its rhetoric than by its place in a process of democratization. In a knowledge-based economy, knowledge is a crucially important resource, and distortions of knowledge are a crucially important tool of social control. A democratic sociology, then, will be the enterprise of producing and circulating knowledge relevant to the democratization of social institutions – knowledge that serves the goals of broad participation in decision making, mutual respect among social groups, and social equality.

Sociologists already know how to do this, in principle. Studies of power structures, ideologies, systems of domination, and the production of privilege and exclusion are familiar in the discipline. What must be developed – and what would make a qualitative shift if strongly developed – are ways of making these genres of research and analysis more useful to the dominated and excluded than they currently are.

I believe that such an agenda will lead to forms of knowledge that are more dispersed or decentralized than an academic discipline is accustomed to be. Sometimes what will be needed is simply a group of facts, which reveal the state of play in a given sphere – for instance, inequalities of educational provision in a particular region. Sometimes what will be needed is a technique, an approach to producing knowledge that a community group can use for itself – as advocated in Yoland Wadsworth's *Do It Yourself Social Research* (1983). Sometimes what will be needed is an explanation of processes that had been obscured, neglected, or distorted by ideology – as in Gary Dowsett's dissection of sexuality in *Practicing Desire* (1996). Sometimes what will be needed is new insights or themes that show connections that had not been seen before – as in Valerie Kuletz's study of nuclear landscapes, *The Tainted Desert* (1999).

Such work will often involve 'doing sociology' in settings outside academia, with partners who have no background in the discipline, and with agendas and deadlines that are hard to reconcile with the rhythms of universities. It may involve cooperative work with union organizers, with teachers, with broadcasters, with community activists, with bureaucrats. This will certainly produce difficulties for university-based sociology, given the way university finances and career structures work. The 'body of knowledge' produced will not look much like the bodies academics are familiar with, the anatomy we see in *Social Science Citation Index* or even *Contemporary Sociology*. But it will depend on empirical truth, it will be open to rigorous testing, and it will be capable of development. That is to say, it will be *science*, even if it does not wear a lab coat of traditional cut.

Yet to argue that sociology should develop in a democratic direction is not to suggest evacuating the university, or abandoning the idea of a discipline or even the project of systematic theory. The university system is too strategic a social institution to abandon. But the historical moment in which we find ourselves gives a specific character to what a democratic social science in the university context must be.

The central point here, I would argue, is the global triumph of the market and the motivated self-ignorance of market society. Crucial intellectual tasks for sociology are defined by this: to re-invigorate the study of the market as a social form, and of the cultural and social processes that underpin its dominance. As argued above, there is desperate need for a critical analysis of the culture that the dominance of the market is producing, the beliefs and forms of knowledge that flourish in market contexts, and the

human consequences of their dominance. The particular form that these projects must now take is defined by the world scale of contemporary market society – which distinguishes them from the 'critical theory' or 'critical sociology' of earlier generations. It is now a question of analyzing a market society whose formation includes the whole history of imperialism, and whose structure now includes world-embracing systems of power, communication, and exploitation. These issues now pose formidable intellectual challenges to older areas of sociology. For example, in deviance: How can we now study drug abuse or violence without understanding the world drug trade and the world arms trade? Or organization theory: How can we ignore the global grip of neoliberalism and the creation of transnational organizations? And the challenges extend to newer areas as well. For example, gender: Feminism is global, but gender theory is still focused on the metropole. Or cultural studies, where a certain recognition of globalization is now common.

These issues, however, are not just intellectual; they are also practical issues in the struggle for democratization, which must, increasingly, operate globally. So the points made above about the connection of sociological knowledge and methods with the practical search for participation, respect, and equality must also be rethought on a world scale. A sociology developing as a critical science of world society must connect at a practical level with the democratization of world society.

Again, there are ironies aplenty. The largest issue about inequality in world society is the huge disparity in income and wealth between the populations of rich and poor countries. Sociology was created in the metropole – the countries that were becoming rich through the contributions of others – and today mainly exists, as a recognizable set of practices, institutions, and people, in the rich countries. The intellectual techniques on which sociology is based, and which one must master to become a good practitioner of sociology, were developed by Western intelligentsias and passed on within Western university systems. This intellectual culture is now dominant internationally, but its dominance over other cultural systems is precisely part of the problem in global culture, part of what a critical science of world society must problematize.

In the long run, I believe, Western sociology must be transformed by interaction with the intellectual techniques and cultural resources that have been generated in other parts of the world – not as a gesture of intercultural understanding, but because it will be forced into those encounters by the demands of the project of democratization. This will be a slow process. Most Western sociologists don't at present know there are significant intellectual resources, for instance, in Islamic critiques of modernity, or in Chinese analyses of the complex encounter with Western imperialism. No one can predict the outcome of sociology's encounter with these traditions of thought; but we can at least recognize that they must happen, and try to make them as inclusive and productive as we can.

All of this reinforces the importance of open intellectual boundaries for sociology, and an inclusive approach to participants and practitioners. As an academic profession, sociology can exist in market society only in the place assigned to it by the science of markets. It would be a special science of market failures, explaining the poor, the deviants, the

unsuccessful, and the odd. As a democratic science, sociology has the potential to become a strategic starting point for the creation of a new world culture.

References

Connell, R.W. (1997) 'Why is classical theory classical?', *American Journal of Sociology*, vol.102, pp.1511–57.

Dowsett, G.W. (1996) *Practicing Desire: Homosexual Sex in the Era of AIDS*, Stanford, CA, Stanford University Press.

Kuletz, V. (1999) *The Tainted Desert: Environmental and Social Ruin in the American West*, New York, Routledge.

Wadsworth, Y. (1983) *Do It Yourself Social Research*, Melbourne, VCOSS and Allen Unwin.

Source: Connell, 2000, pp.291–6

Donna J. Haraway, 'A cyborg manifesto: science, technology, and socialist-feminism in the late twentieth century (1991)

An ironic dream of a common language for women in the integrated circuit

This chapter is an effort to build an ironic political myth faithful to feminism, socialism, and materialism. Perhaps more faithful as blasphemy is faithful, than as reverent worship and identification. Blasphemy has always seemed to require taking things very seriously. I know no better stance to adopt from within the secular-religious, evangelical traditions of United States politics, including the politics of socialist feminism. Blasphemy protects one from the moral majority within, while still insisting on the need for community. Blasphemy is not apostasy. Irony is about contradictions that do not resolve into larger wholes, even dialectically; about the tension of holding incompatible things together because both or all are necessary and true. Irony is about humour and serious play. It is also a rhetorical strategy and a political method, one I would like to see more honoured within socialist-feminism. At the centre of my ironic faith, my blasphemy, is the image of the cyborg.

A cyborg is a cybernetic organism, a hybrid of machine and organism, a creature of social reality as well as a creature of fiction. Social reality is lived social relations, our most important political construction, a world-changing fiction. The international women's

movements have constructed 'women's experience', as well as uncovered or discovered this crucial collective object. This experience is a fiction and fact of the most crucial, political kind. Liberation rests on the construction of the consciousness, the imaginative apprehension, of oppression, and so of possibility. The cyborg is a matter of fiction and lived experience that changes what counts as women's experience in the late twentieth century. This is a struggle over life and death, but the boundary between science fiction and social reality is an optical illusion.

Contemporary science fiction is full of cyborgs – creatures simultaneously animal and machine, who populate worlds ambiguously natural and crafted. Modern medicine is also full of cyborgs, of couplings between organism and machine, each conceived as coded devices, in an intimacy and with a power that was not generated in the history of sexuality. Cyborg 'sex' restores some of the lovely replicative baroque of ferns and invertebrates (such nice organic prophylactics against heterosexism). Cyborg replication is uncoupled from organic reproduction. Modern production seems like a dream of cyborg colonization work, a dream that makes the nightmare of Taylorism seem idyllic. And modern war is a cyborg orgy, coded by C^3I, command-control-communication-intelligence, an $84 billion item in 1984's US defence budget. I am making an argument for the cyborg as a fiction mapping our social and bodily reality and as an imaginative resource suggesting some very fruitful couplings. Michael Foucault's biopolitics is a flaccid premonition of cyborg politics, a very open field.

By the late twentieth century, our time, a mythic time, we are all chimeras, theorized and fabricated hybrids of machine and organism; in short, we are cyborgs. The cyborg is our ontology; it gives us our politics. The cyborg is a condensed image of both imagination and material reality, the two joined centres structuring any possibility of historical transformation. In the traditions of 'Western' science and politics – the tradition of racist, male-dominant capitalism; the tradition of progress; the tradition of the appropriation of nature as resource for the productions of culture; the tradition of reproduction of the self from the reflections of the other – the relation between organism and machine has been a border war. The stakes in the border war have been the territories of production, reproduction, and imagination. This chapter is an argument for *pleasure* in the confusion of boundaries and for *responsibility* in their construction. It is also an effort to contribute to socialist-feminist culture and theory in a postmodernist, non-naturalist mode and in the utopian tradition of imagining a world without gender, which is perhaps a world without genesis, but maybe also a world without end. …

The cyborg is a creature in a post-gender world; it has no truck with bisexuality, pre-oedipal symbiosis, unalienated labour, or other seductions to organic wholeness through a final appropriation of all the powers of the parts into a higher unity. In a sense, the cyborg has no origin story in the Western sense – a 'final' irony since the cyborg is also the awful apocalyptic *telos* of the 'West's' escalating dominations of abstract individuation, an ultimate self untied at last from all dependency, a man in space. An origin story in the 'Western', humanist sense depends on the myth of original unity, fullness, bliss and terror, represented by the phallic mother from whom all humans must separate, the task of individual development and of history, the twin potent myths inscribed most powerfully for us in psychoanalysis and Marxism. Hilary Klein has argued that both Marxism and psychoanalysis, in their concepts of labour and of individuation and gender formation, depend on the plot of original unity out of which difference must be produced and enlisted in a drama of escalating domination of woman/nature. The cyborg skips the step of original unity, of identification with nature in the Western sense. This is its illegitimate promise that might lead to subversion of its teleology as star wars.

The cyborg is resolutely committed to partiality, irony, intimacy, and perversity. It is oppositional, utopian, and completely without innocence. No longer structured by the polarity of public and private, the cyborg defines a technological polis based partly on a revolution of social relations in the *oikos*, the household. Nature and culture are reworked; the one can no longer be the resource for appropriation or incorporation by the other. The relationships for forming wholes from parts, including those of polarity and hierarchical domination, are at issue in the cyborg world. Unlike the hopes of Frankenstein's monster, the cyborg does not expect its father to save it through a restoration of the garden; that is, through the fabrication of a heterosexual mate, through its completion in a finished whole, a city and cosmos. The cyborg does not dream of community on the model of the organic family, this time without the oedipal project. The cyborg would not recognize the Garden of Eden; it is not made of mud and cannot dream of returning to dust. Perhaps that is why I want to see if cyborgs can subvert the apocalypse of returning to nuclear dust in the manic compulsion to name the Enemy. Cyborgs are not reverent; they do not re-member the cosmos. They are wary of holism, but needy for connection – they seem to have a natural feel for united front politics, but without the vanguard party. The main trouble with cyborgs, of course, is that they are the illegitimate offspring of militarism and patriarchal capitalism, not to mention state socialism. But illegitimate offspring are often exceedingly unfaithful to their origins. Their fathers, after all, are inessential.

I will return to the science fiction of cyborgs at the end of this chapter, but now I want to signal three crucial boundary breakdowns that make the following political-fictional (political-scientific) analysis possible. By the late twentieth century in United States scientific culture, the boundary between human and animal is thoroughly breached. The last beachheads of uniqueness have been polluted if not turned into amusement parks – language, tool use, social behaviour, mental events, nothing really convincingly settles the separation of human and animal. And many people no longer feel the need for such a separation; indeed, many branches of feminist culture affirm the pleasure of connection of human and other living creatures. Movements for animal rights are not irrational denials of human uniqueness; they are a clear-sighted recognition of connection across the discredited breach of nature and culture. Biology and evolutionary theory over the last two centuries have simultaneously produced modern organisms as objects of knowledge and reduced the line between humans and animals to a faint trace re-etched in ideological struggle or professional disputes between life and social science. With this framework, teaching modern Christian creationism should be fought as a form of child abuse.

Biological-determinist ideology is only one position opened up in scientific culture for arguing the meanings of human animality. There is much room for radical political people to contest the meanings of the breached boundary. The cyborg appears in myth precisely where the boundary between human and animal is transgressed. Far from signalling a walling off of people from other living beings, cyborgs signal disturbingly and pleasurably tight coupling. Bestiality has a new status in this cycle of marriage exchange.

The second leaky distinction is between animal–human (organism) and machine. Pre-cybernetic machines could be haunted; there was always the spectre of the ghost in the machine. This dualism structured the dialogue between materialism and idealism that was settled by a dialectical progeny, called spirit or history, according to taste. But basically machines were not self-moving, self-designing, autonomous. They could not achieve man's dream, only mock it. They were not man, an author to himself, but only a caricature of that masculinist reproductive dream. To think they were otherwise was paranoid. Now we are not so sure. Late twentieth-century machines have made thoroughly ambiguous the difference between natural and artificial, mind and body, self-developing and externally designed, and many other distinctions that used to apply to organisms and machines. Our machines are disturbingly lively, and we ourselves frighteningly inert.

Technological determination is only one ideological space opened up by the reconceptions of machine and organism as coded texts through which we engage in the play of writing and reading the world. 'Textualization' of everything in poststructuralist, postmodernist theory has been damned by Marxists and socialist feminists for its utopian disregard for the lived relations of domination that ground the 'play' of arbitrary reading. It is certainly true that postmodernist strategies, like my cyborg myth, subvert myriad organic wholes (for example, the poem, the primitive culture, the biological organism). In short, the certainty of what counts as nature – a source of insight and promise of innocence – is undermined, probably fatally. The transcendent authorization of interpretation is lost, and with it the ontology grounding 'Western' epistemology. But the alternative is not cynicism or faithlessness, that is,

some version of abstract existence, like the accounts of technological determinism destroying 'man' by the 'machine' or 'meaningful political action' by the 'text'. Who cyborgs will be is a radical question; the answers are a matter of survival. Both chimpanzees and artefacts have politics, so why shouldn't we (de Waal, 1982; Winner, 1980)?

The third distinction is a subset of the second: the boundary between physical and non-physical is very imprecise for us. Pop physics books on the consequences of quantum theory and the indeterminacy principle are a kind of popular scientific equivalent to Harlequin romances[1] as a marker of radical change in American white heterosexuality: they get it wrong, but they are on the right subject. Modern machines are quintessentially microelectronic devices: they are everywhere and they are invisible. Modern machinery is an irreverent upstart god, mocking the Father's ubiquity and spirituality. The silicon chip is a surface for writing; it is etched in molecular scales disturbed only by atomic noise, the ultimate interference for nuclear scores. Writing, power, and technology are old partners in Western stories of the origin of civilization, but miniaturization has changed our experience of mechanism. Miniaturization has turned out to be about power; small is not so much beautiful as pre-eminently dangerous, as in cruise missiles. Contrast the TV sets of the 1950s or the news cameras of the 1970s with the TV wrist bands or hand-sized video cameras now advertised. Our best machines are made of sunshine; they are all light and clean because they are nothing but signals, electromagnetic waves, a section of a spectrum, and these machines are eminently portable, mobile – a matter of immense human pain in Detroit and Singapore. People are nowhere near so fluid, being both material and opaque. Cyborgs are ether, quintessence.

The ubiquity and invisibility of cyborgs is precisely why these sunshine-belt machines are so deadly. They are as hard to see politically as materially. They are about consciousness – or its simulation. They are floating signifiers moving in pickup trucks across Europe, blocked more effectively by the witch-weavings of the displaced and so unnatural Greenham women, who read the cyborg webs of power so very well, than by the militant labour of older masculinist politics, whose natural constituency needs defence jobs. Ultimately the 'hardest' science is about the realm of greatest boundary confusion, the realm of pure number, pure spirit, C^3I, cryptography, and the preservation of potent secrets. The new machines are so clean and light. Their engineers are sun-worshippers mediating a new scientific revolution associated with the night dream of post-industrial society. The diseases evoked by these clean machines are 'no more' than the miniscule coding changes of an antigen in the immune system, 'no more' than the experience of stress. The nimble fingers of 'Oriental' women, the old fascination of little Anglo-Saxon Victorian girls with doll's houses, women's enforced attention to the small take on quite new dimensions in this world. There might be a cyborg Alice taking account of these new dimensions. Ironically, it might be the unnatural cyborg women making chips in Asia and spiral dancing in Santa Rita jail[2] whose constructed unities will guide effective oppositional strategies.

So my cyborg myth is about transgressed boundaries, potent fusions, and dangerous possibilities which progressive people might explore as one part of needed political work. One of my premises is that most American socialists and feminists see deepened dualisms of mind and body, animal and machine, idealism and materialism in the social practices, symbolic formulations, and physical artefacts associated with 'high technology' and scientific culture. From *One-Dimensional Man* (Marcuse, 1964), to *The Death of Nature* (Merchant, 1980), the analytic resources developed by progressives have insisted on the necessary domination of technics and recalled us to an imagined organic body to integrate our resistance. Another of my premises is that the need for unity of people trying to resist world-wide intensification of domination has never been more acute. But a slightly perverse shift of perspective might better enable us to contest for meanings, as well as for other forms of power and pleasure in technologically mediated societies.

From one perspective, a cyborg world is about the final imposition of a grid of control on the planet, about the final abstraction embodied in a Star Wars apocalypse waged in the name of defence, about the final appropriation of women's bodies in a masculinist orgy of war (Sofia, 1984). From another perspective, a cyborg world might be about lived social and bodily realities in which people are not afraid of their joint kinship with animals and machines, not afraid of permanently partial identities and contradictory standpoints. The political struggle is to see from both perspectives at once because each reveals both dominations and possibilities unimaginable from the other vantage point. Single vision produces worse illusions than double vision or many-headed monsters. Cyborg unities are monstrous and illegitimate; in our present political circumstances, we could hardly hope for more potent myths for resistance and recoupling. ...

...

To recapitulate, certain dualisms have been persistent in Western traditions; they have all been systemic to the logics and practices of domination of women, people of colour, nature, workers, animals – in short, domination of all constituted as others, whose task is to mirror the self. Chief among these troubling dualisms are self/other, mind/body, culture/nature, male/female, civilized/primitive, reality/appearance, whole/part, agent/resource, maker/made, active/passive, right/wrong, truth/illusion, total/partial, God/man. The self is the One who is not dominated, who knows that by the service of the other, the other is the one who holds the future, who knows that by the experience of domination, which gives the lie to the autonomy of the self. To be One is to be autonomous, to be powerful, to be God; but to be One is to be an illusion, and so to be involved in a dialectic of apocalypse with the other. Yet to be other is to be multiple, without clear boundary, frayed, insubstantial. One is too few, but two are too many.

High-tech culture challenges these dualisms in intriguing ways. It is not clear who makes and who is made in the relation between human and machine. It is not clear what is mind and what body in machines that resolve into coding practices. In so far as we know ourselves in both formal discourse (for example, biology) and in daily practice (for example, the homework economy in the integrated circuit), we find ourselves to be cyborgs, hybrids, mosaics, chimeras. Biological organisms have become biotic systems, communications devices like others. There is no fundamental, ontological separation in our formal knowledge of machine and organism, of technical and organic. The replicant Rachel in the Ridley Scott film *Blade Runner* stands as the image of a cyborg culture's fear, love, and confusion.

One consequence is that our sense of connection to our tools is heightened. The trance state experienced by many computer users has become a staple of science-fiction film and cultural jokes. Perhaps paraplegics and other severely handicapped people can (and sometimes do) have the most intense experiences of complex hybridization with other communication devices. Anne McCaffrey's pre-feminist *The Ship Who Sang* (1969) explored the consciousness of a cyborg, hybrid of girl's brain and complex machinery, formed after the birth of a severely handicapped child. Gender, sexuality, embodiment, skill: all were reconstituted in the story. Why should our bodies end at the skin, or include at best other beings encapsulated by skin? ...

...

There are several consequences to taking seriously the imagery of cyborgs as other than our enemies. Our bodies, ourselves; bodies are maps of power and identity. Cyborgs are no exception. A cyborg body is not innocent; it was not born in a garden; it does not seek unitary identity and so generate antagonistic dualism without end (or until the world ends); it takes irony for granted. One is too few, and two is only one possibility. Intense pleasure in skill, machine skill, ceases to be a sin, but an aspect of embodiment. The machine is not an *it* to be animated, worshipped, and dominated. The machine is us, our processes, an aspect of our embodiment. We can be responsible for machines; *they* do not dominate or threaten us. We are responsible for boundaries; we are they. Up till now (once upon a time), female embodiment seemed to be given, organic, necessary; and female embodiment seemed to mean skill in mothering and its metaphoric extensions. Only by being out of place could we take intense pleasure in machines, and then with excuses that this was organic activity after all, appropriate to females. Cyborgs might consider more seriously the partial, fluid, sometimes aspect of sex and sexual embodiment. Gender might not be global identity after all, even if it has profound historical breadth and depth.

The ideologically charged question of what counts as daily activity, as experience, can be approached by exploiting the cyborg image. Feminists have recently claimed that women are given to dailiness, that women more than men somehow sustain daily life, and so have a privileged epistemological position potentially. There is a compelling aspect to this claim, one that makes visible unvalued female activity and names it as the ground of life. But *the* ground of life? What about all the ignorance of women, all the exclusions and failures of knowledge and skill? What about men's access to daily competence, to knowing how to build things, to take them apart, to play? What about other embodiments? Cyborg gender is a local possibility taking a global vengeance. Race, gender, and capital require a cyborg theory of wholes and parts. There is no drive in cyborgs to produce total theory, but there is an intimate experience of boundaries, their construction and deconstruction. There is a myth system waiting to become a political language to ground one way of looking at science and technology and challenging the informatics of domination – in order to act potently.

One last image: organisms and organismic, holistic politics depend on metaphors of rebirth and invariably call on the resources of reproductive sex. I would suggest that cyborgs have more to do with regeneration and are suspicious of the reproductive matrix and of most birthing. For salamanders, regeneration after injury, such as the loss of a limb, involves regrowth of structure and restoration of function with the constant possibility of twinning or other odd topographical productions at the site of former injury. The regrown limb can be monstrous, duplicated, potent. We have all been injured, profoundly. We require regeneration, not rebirth, and the possibilities for our reconstitution include the utopian dream of the hope for a monstrous world without gender.

Cyborg imagery can help express two crucial arguments in this essay: first, the production of universal, totalizing theory is a major mistake that misses most of the reality, probably always, but certainly now; and second, taking responsibility for the social relations of science and technology means refusing an anti-science metaphysics, a demonology of technology, and so means embracing the skilful task of reconstructing the boundaries of daily life, in partial connection with others, in communication with all of our parts. It is not just that science and technology are possible means of great human satisfaction, as well as a matrix of complex dominations. Cyborg imagery can suggest a way out of the maze of dualisms in which we have explained our bodies and our tools to ourselves. This is a dream not of a common language, but of a powerful infidel heteroglossia. It is an imagination of a feminist speaking in tongues to strike fear into the circuits of the supersavers of the new right. It means both building and destroying machines, identities, categories, relationships, space stories. Though both are bound in the spiral dance, I would rather be a cyborg than a goddess.

Notes

1 The US equivalent of Mills & Boon.

2 A practice at once both spiritual and political that linked guards and arrested anti-nuclear demonstrators in the Alameda County jail in California in the early 1980s.

References

De Waal, F. (1982) *Chimpanzee Politics: Power and Sex Among the Apes*, New York, Harper & Row.

Marcuse, H. (1964) *One-Dimensional Man: Studies in the Ideology of Advanced Industrial Society*, Boston, MA, Beacon.

McCaffrey, A. (1969) *The Ship Who Sang*, New York, Walker.

Merchant, C. (1980) *The Death of Nature: Women, Ecology, and the Scientific Revolution*, New York, Harper & Row.

Sofia, Z. (also Sofoulis) (1984) 'Exterminating fetuses: abortion, disarmament, and the sexo-semiotics of extra-terrestrialism', *Diacritics*, vol.14, no.2, pp.47–59.

Winner, L. (1980) 'Do artifacts have politics?', *Daedalus*, no.109(I), pp.121–36.

Source: Haraway, 1991, pp.149–54,177–8,180–81

Readings on the uses of sociology

Contents

Auguste Comte:
'The positive philosophy' (1853)

The need for sociology and its relation to other disciplines[1]

The Positive Philosophy offers the only solid basis for that Social Reorganization which must succeed the critical condition in which the most civilized nations are now living.

It cannot be necessary to prove to anybody who reads this work that Ideas govern the world, or throw it into chaos: in other words, that all social mechanism rests upon Opinions. The great political and moral crisis that societies are now undergoing is shown by a rigid analysis to arise out of intellectual anarchy. While stability in fundamental maxims is the first condition of genuine social order, we are suffering under an utter disagreement which may be called universal. Till a certain number of general ideas can be acknowledged as a rallying-point of social doctrine, the nations will remain in a revolutionary state, whatever palliatives may be devised; and their institutions can be only provisional. But whenever the necessary agreement on first principles can be obtained, appropriate institutions will issue from them, without shock or resistance; for the causes of disorder will have been arrested by the mere fact of the agreement. It is in this direction that those must look who desire a natural and regular, a normal state of society.

Now, the existing disorder is abundantly accounted for by the existence, all at once, of three incompatible philosophies, the theological, the metaphysical and the positive. Any one of these might alone secure some sort of social order; but while the three coexist, it is impossible for us to understand one another upon any essential point whatever.

[…] In all Social phenomena we perceive the working of the physiological laws of the individual; and moreover something which modifies their effects, and which belongs to the influence of individuals over each other – singularly complicated in the case of the human race by the influence of generations on their successors. Thus it is clear that our social science must issue from that which relates to the life of the individual. On the other hand, there is no occasion to suppose, as some eminent physiologists have done, that Social Physics is only an appendage to physiology. The phenomena of the two are not identical, though they are homogeneous; and it is of high importance to hold the two sciences separate. As social conditions modify the operation of physiological laws, Social Physics must have a set of observations of its own. […]

Thus we have before us Five fundamental Sciences in successive dependence, Astronomy, Physics, Chemistry, Physiology and finally Social

Physics. The first considers the most general, simple, abstract and remote phenomena known to us, and those which affect all others without being affected by them. The last considers the most particular, compound, concrete phenomena, and those which are the most interesting to Man. Between these two, the degrees of speciality, of complexity and individuality are in regular proportion to the place of the respective sciences in the scale exhibited. [...]

The only really universal point of view is the human, or, speaking more exactly, the social. This is the only one which recurs and is perpetually renewed, in every department of thought; in regard to the external world as well as to Man. Thus, if we want to conceive of the rights of the sociological spirit to supremacy, we have only to regard all our conceptions, as I have explained before, as so many necessary results of a series of determinate phases, proper to our mental evolution, personal and collective, taking place according to invariable laws, statical and dynamical, which rational observation is competent to disclose. Since philosophers have begun to meditate deeply on intellectual phenomena, they have always been more or less convinced, in spite of all prepossession, of the inevitable reality of these fundamental laws; for their existence is always supposed in every study, in which any conclusion whatever would be impossible if the formation and variation of our opinions were not subject to a regular order, independent of our will, and the pathological change of which is known to be in no way arbitrary. But, besides the extreme difficulty of the subject and its vicious management hitherto, human reason being capable of growth only in social circumstances, it is clear that no decisive discovery could be made in this way till society should have attained a generality of view which was not possible till our day. Imperfect as sociological study may yet be, it furnishes us with a principle which justifies and guides its intervention, scientific and logical, in all the essential parts of the speculative system, which can thus alone be brought into unity. [...]

Note

1   Vol. 1, pp.14–15, 27–8, 503–4; Vol. 2, pp.63–73.

Note that deletions shown in square brackets are as in the 1971 edition.

Source: Excerpts from Auguste Comte, *The Positive Philosphy* (freely translated and condensed by H. Martineau and J. Chapman, 1853, 2 vols) taken from Thompson, K. and Tunstall, J. (eds) *Sociological Perspectives*, Harmondsworth, Penguin Books, 1971, pp.21–3.

Robert A. Nisbet:
'Sociology as an art form' (1962)

I admit readily that both by temperament and academic background I have always been more interested in the non-uses of our discipline than the uses. I admit further to believing that theories should be tested as much by their reach as their grasp, their importance as their validity, and their elegance as their congruence with such facts as may be at hand. It is my major contention that the science of sociology makes its most significant intellectual advances under the spur of stimuli and through processes that it largely shares with art; that whatever the differences between science and art, it is what they have in common that matters most in discovery and creativeness.

Nothing I say is intended to imply that sociology is not a science. I am quite willing, for the present purposes, to put sociology on the same line with physics and biology, applying to each of these the essence of what I say about sociology. Each is indeed a science, but each is a form of art, and if we forget this we run the risk of losing the science, finding ourselves with a sandheap empiricism or methodological narcissism, each as far from science as art is from billboard advertisements.

My interest in sociology as an art form was stimulated recently by some reflections on ideas that are by common assent among the most distinctive that sociology has contributed to modern thought. Let me mention these: *mass society, alienation, anomie, rationalization, community, disorganization.* I will have more to say about these ideas and their contexts a little later. Here it suffices to note that all of them have had lasting effect upon both the theoretical and empirical character of sociology. And all have exerted notable influence on other fields of thought, scientific and humanistic.

It occurred to me that not one of these ideas is historically the result of the application of what we are today pleased to call scientific method. If there is evidence that any one of these ideas as first set forth in the writings of such men as Tocqueville, Weber, Simmel and Durkheim, is the result of problem-solving thought, proceeding rigorously and self-consciously from question to hypothesis to verified conclusion, I have been unable to discover it. On the contrary, each of these profound and seminal ideas would appear to be the consequence of intellectual processes bearing much more relation to the artist than the scientist, as the latter tends to be conceived by most of us. Apart from processes of intuition, impressionism, iconic imagination (the phrase is Sir Herbert Read's), and even objectification, it seems unlikely that any one of these ideas would have come into being to influence generations of subsequent thought and teaching. [...]

It is time to return to the ideas in sociology I referred to at the outset of my paper. Let me describe them briefly again, for they are indubitably the most distinctive and illuminating contributions of sociology to the study of culture and society. There is, first, the view of human association as containing endemic processes of disorganization, dysfunction, call them what we will. Second, there is the view of the individual as alienated and anomic. Third, there is the perspective of community – in contrast to rationalistic and contractual forms of relationship – involving the key concepts of hierarchy and status. Fourth, we have the great theme of rationalization as a process in history and in the whole structure of modern society.

We know where these ideas came from: from the writings of four or five remarkable minds in the late nineteenth century: Tocqueville, Weber, Simmel, Tönnies and Durkheim. I need not enlarge upon their formulations of the ideas. I am more interested in the processes by which the ideas came into being: that is, the contexts in which the ideas were uttered, the traditions they came out of, and, if it were possible, the mental states behind the ideas. Obviously, we are limited in what we can say positively, but I believe certain points are clear.

There is, first, the manifest discontinuity of these ideas in the history of modern social thought. Not one of them could have been deduced from the propositions of rationalism on human behavior that flourished in the Enlightenment. The true heritage of the Enlightenment is to be found, not in sociology, but in classical economics, individual psychology and utilitarian political science. What we find in sociology – that is, in its distinctive currents – is a revolt against the rationalist view of man and society.

The second point is this. Not only are the key ideas of sociology unrelated to prior 'scientific' ideas; they have their closest affinity with an art movement, Romanticism. In the same way that the Renaissance image of man proceeded from prior currents in art, so, I argue, the sociological image arises in the first instance from visions which had their earliest and most far reaching appeal in Romantic art.

Weber has somewhere likened his own concept of rationalization to the poet Schiller's earlier view of the 'disenchantment of the world'. He was candid and accurate. Tocqueville, Simmel and Durkheim might well have done likewise. From the first burst of the Romantic spirit in the late eighteenth century – rising to do battle with the classicist-rationalist view – we find luminously revealed two central visions:

1   The estrangement of the individual from a growingly impersonal and disorganized society (and the consequent spiritual inaccessibility of modern institutions – city, factory, mass society).

2   A celebration of status and community – whether rural, religious or moral – in contrast to the individualistic and contractural society of the *philosophes*.

Third, and most important, even if most elusive, are the psychological affinities between the Romantic artists and the sociologists. It is impossible, as I have already suggested, to entertain seriously the thought that these major ideas were arrived at in a manner comparable to what we think of as scientific methodology. Can you imagine what would have happened had any one of them been subjected, at the moment following its inception, to a rigorous design analysis? Can anyone believe that Weber's vision of rationalization in history, Simmel's vision of metropolis or Durkheim's vision of *anomie*, came from logico-empirical analysis as this is understood today? Merely to ask the question is to know the answer. Plainly, these men were not working with finite and ordered problems in front of them. They were not problem-solving at all. Each was, with deep intuition, with profound imaginative grasp, reacting to the world around him, even as does the artist, and, also like the artist, objectifying internal, and only partly conscious, states of mind.

Consider one example: the view of society and man that underlies Durkheim's great study of suicide. Basically, it is the view of the artist as much as that of the scientist. Background, detail and characterization blend into something that is iconic in its grasp of an entire social order. How did Durkheim get his controlling idea? We may be sure of one thing: he did not get it, as the stork story of science might have it, from a preliminary examination of the vital registers of Europe, any more than Darwin got the idea of natural selection from his observations during the voyage of the *Beagle*. The idea, the plot and the conclusion of *Suicide* were well in his mind before he examined the registers. Where, then, did he get the idea? We can only speculate. He might have got it from reading Tocqueville who could certainly have got it from Lamennais who could have got it from Bonald or Chateaubriand. Or, it could have come from personal experience – from a remembered fragment of the Talmud, from an intuition born of personal loneliness and marginality, a scrap of experience in Paris. Who can be sure? But one thing is certain. The creative blend of ideas behind *Suicide* – a blend from which we still draw in our scientific labors – was reached in ways more akin to those of the artist than to those of the data processor, the logician, or the technologist.

It is not different with the ideas and perspectives of Simmel – in many ways the most imaginative and intuitive of all the great sociologists. His treatment of fear, love, conventionality, power and friendship show the mind of the artist-essayist, and it is no distortion of values to place him with such masters as Montaigne and Bacon. Remove the artist's vision from the treatments of the stranger, the dyad and the role of secrecy, and you have removed all that gives life. In Simmel there is that wonderful tension between the esthetically concrete and the philosophically general that always lies in greatness. It is the esthetic element in Simmel's work that makes impossible the full absorption of his sociological substance by anonymous, systematic theory. One must go back to Simmel himself for the real insight. As with Darwin and Freud, it will always be possible to derive something of importance from the man directly that cannot be gleaned from impersonal statements in social theory.

This leads to another important fact. Our dependence upon these ideas and their makers is akin to the artist's dependence upon the artists who precede him. In the same way that the novelist will always be able to learn from a study and re-study of Dostoyevsky or James – to learn a sense of development and form, as well as to draw inspiration from the creative source – so the sociologist can forever learn from a re-reading of such men as Weber and Simmel.

It is this element that separates sociology from some of the physical sciences. There is, after all, a limit to what the young physicist can learn from even a Newton. Having once grasped the fundamental points of the *Principia*, he is not likely to draw very much as a physicist from re-readings (though he could as a historian of science). How different is the relation of the sociologist to a Simmel or Durkheim. Always there will be something to be gained from a direct reading; something that is informative, enlarging and creative. This is precisely like the contemporary artist's return to the study of medieval architecture, the Elizabethan sonnet or the paintings of Matisse. This is the essence of the history of art, and why the history of sociology is so different from the history of science.

That such men as Weber, Durkheim and Simmel fall in the scientific tradition is unquestioned. Their works, for all the deep artistic sensitivity and intuition, no more belong in the history of art than the works of Balzac or Dickens do in the history of social science. The conclusion we draw is not that science and art are without differences. There are real differences, as there are among the arts and among the sciences.[1] No one asks a Picasso to verify one of his visions by repeating the process; and, conversely, we properly give short shrift to ideas in science that no one but the author can find supported by experience. The ideas of Durkheim may, as I have suggested, be dependent upon thought-processes like those of the artist, but none of them would have survived in sociology or become fruitful for others were it not for criteria and modes of communication that differ from those in art.

The conclusion, then, is not that science and art are, or should be, alike. It is the simpler but more fundamental conclusion that in both art and science the same type of creative imagination works. And everything that impedes or frustrates this imagination strikes at the source of the discipline itself.

Note

1   Charles Morris, the philosopher, has suggested that the major difference is this: although both science and art communicate by the use of ideas and representations not completely describable in terms of sense experience, science typically seeks to make its communications capable of identification or verification by the largest number of individuals, whereas art tends to insist that each individual translate the original vision into something peculiarly his own creation.

Note that deletions shown in square brackets are as in the 1971 edition.

Source: Excerpts from Robert A. Nisbet, *Tradition and Revolt*, Random House, 1968, pp.143–62. First published in the *Pacific Sociological Review,* 1962. Taken from Thompson, K. and Tunstall, J. (eds) *Sociological Perspectives*, Harmondsworth, Penguin Books, 1971, pp.477–81.

C. Wright Mills:
'The sociological imagination' (1959)

Nowadays men often feel that their private lives are a series of traps. They sense that within their everyday worlds, they cannot overcome their troubles, and in this feeling they are often quite correct: what ordinary men are directly aware of and what they try to do are bounded by the private orbits in which they live; their visions and their powers are limited to the close-up scenes of job, family, neighbourhood; in other milieux, they move vicariously and remain spectators. And the more aware they become, however vaguely, of ambitions and of threats which transcend their immediate locales, the more trapped they seem to feel.

Underlying this sense of being trapped are seemingly impersonal changes in the very structure of continent-wide societies. The facts of contemporary history are also facts about the success and the failure of individual men and women. When a society is industrialized, a peasant becomes a worker; a feudal lord is liquidated or becomes a businessman. When classes rise or fall, a man is employed or unemployed; when the rate of investment goes up or down, a man takes new heart or goes broke. When wars happen, an insurance salesman becomes a rocket launcher; a store clerk, a radar man; a wife lives alone; a child grows up without a father. Neither the life of an individual nor the history of a society can be understood without understanding both.

Yet men do not usually define the troubles they endure in terms of historical change and institutional contradiction. The well-being they enjoy they do not usually impute to the big ups and downs of the societies in which they live. Seldom aware of the intricate connection between the patterns of their own lives and the course of world history, ordinary men do not usually know what this connection means for the kinds of men they are becoming and for the kinds of history making in which they might take part. They do not possess the quality of mind essential to grasp the interplay of man and society, of biography and history, of self and world. They cannot cope with their personal troubles in such ways as to control the structural transformations that usually lie behind them.

Surely it is no wonder. In what period have so many men been so totally exposed at so fast a pace to such earthquakes of change? That Americans have not known such catastrophic changes as have the men and women of other societies is due to historical facts that are now quickly becoming 'merely history'. The history that now affects every man is world history. Within this scene and this period, in the course of a single generation, one-sixth of mankind is transformed from all that is feudal and backward into all that is modern, advanced and fearful. Political colonies are freed; new and less visible forms of imperialism installed. Revolutions occur; men feel the intimate grip of new kinds of authority.

Totalitarian societies rise and are smashed to bits – or succeed fabulously. After two centuries of ascendancy, capitalism is shown up as only one way to make society into an industrial apparatus. After two centuries of hope, even formal democracy is restricted to a quite small portion of mankind. Everywhere in the underdeveloped world, ancient ways of life are broken up and vague expectations become urgent demands. Everywhere in the over-developed world, the means of authority and of violence becomes total in scope and bureaucratic in form. Humanity itself now lies before us, the super-nation at either pole concentrating its more coordinated and massive efforts upon the preparation of the Third World War.

The very shaping of history now outpaces the ability of men to orient themselves in accordance with cherished values. And which values? Even when they do not panic, men often sense that older ways of feeling and thinking have collapsed and that newer beginnings are ambiguous to the point of moral stasis. Is it any wonder that ordinary men feel they cannot cope with the larger worlds with which they are so suddenly confronted? That they cannot understand the meaning of their epoch for their own lives? That – in defence of selfhood – they become morally insensible, trying to remain altogether private men? Is it any wonder that they come to be possessed by a sense of the trap?

It is not only information that they need – in this Age of Fact, information often dominates their attention and overwhelms their capacities to assimilate it. It is not only the skills of reason that they need – although their struggles to acquire these often exhaust their limited moral energy.

What they need, and what they feel they need, is a quality of mind that will help them to use information and to develop reason in order to achieve lucid summations of what is going on in the world and of what may be happening within themselves. It is this quality, I contend, that journalists and scholars, artists and publics, scientists and editors are coming to expect from what may be called the sociological imagination.

The sociological imagination enables its possessor to understand the larger historical scene in terms of its meaning for the inner life and the external career of a variety of individuals. It enables him to take into account how individuals, in the welter of their daily experience, often become falsely conscious of their social positions. Within that welter the framework of modern society is sought, and within that framework the psychologies of a variety of men and women are formulated. By such means the personal uneasiness of individuals is focused upon explicit troubles and the indifference of publics is transformed into involvement with public issues.

The first fruit of this imagination – and the first lesson of the social science that embodies it – is the idea that the individual can understand his own experience and gauge his own fate only by locating himself within his period, that he can know his own chances in life only by becoming aware of those of all individuals in his circumstances. In many ways it is a terrible lesson; in many ways a magnificent one. We do not know the limits of man's capacities for supreme effort or willing degradation, for agony or glee, for pleasurable brutality or the sweetness of reason. But in our time we have come to know that the limits of 'human nature' are frighteningly broad. We have come to know that every individual lives, from one generation to the next, in some society; that he lives out a biography, and that he lives it out within some historical sequence. By the fact of his living he contributes, however minutely, to the shaping of this society and to the course of its history, even as he is made by society and by its historical push and shove.

The sociological imagination enables us to grasp history and biography and the relations between the two within society. That is its task and its promise. To recognize this task and this promise is the mark of the classic social analyst. […]

No social study that does not come back to the problems of biography, of history and of their intersections within a society has completed its intellectual journey. Whatever the specific problems of the classic social analysts, however limited or however broad the features of social reality they have examined, those who have been imaginatively aware of the promise of their work have consistently asked three sorts of questions:

1   What is the structure of this particular society as a whole? What are its essential components and how are they related to one another? How does it differ from other varieties of social order? Within it, what is the meaning of any particular feature for its continuance and for its change?

2   Where does this society stand in human history? What are the mechanics by which it is changing? What is its place within and its meaning for the development of humanity as a whole? How does any particular feature we are examining affect, and how is it affected by, the historical period in which it moves? And this period – what are its essential features? How does it differ from other periods? What are its characteristic ways of history making?

3   What varieties of men and women now prevail in this society and in this period? And what varieties are coming to prevail? In what ways are they selected and formed, liberated and repressed, made sensitive and blunted? What kinds of 'human nature' are revealed in the conduct and character we observe in this society in this period? And what is the meaning of 'human nature' for each and every feature of the society we are examining?

Whether the point of interest is a great power state or a minor literary mood, a family, a prison, a creed – these are the kinds of questions the best social analysts have asked. They are the intellectual pivots of classic studies of man in society – and they are the questions inevitably raised by any mind possessing the sociological imagination. For that imagination is the capacity to shift from one perspective to another – from the political to the psychological; from examination of a single family to comparative assessment of the national budgets of the world; from the theological school to the military establishment, from considerations of an oil industry to studies of contemporary poetry. It is the capacity to range from the most impersonal and remote transformations to the most intimate features of the human self – and to see the relations between the two. Back of its use there is always the urge to know the social and historical meaning of the individual in the society and in the period in which he has his quality and his being.

That, in brief, is why it is by means of the sociological imagination that men now hope to grasp what is going on in the world, and to understand what is happening in themselves as minute points of the intersections of biography and history within society. In large part, contemporary man's self-conscious view of himself as at least an outsider, if not a permanent stranger, rests upon an absorbed realization of social relativity and of the transformative power of history.

The sociological imagination is the most fruitful of this self-consciousness. By its use men whose mentalities have swept only a series of limited orbits often come to feel as if suddenly awakened in a house with which they had only supposed themselves to be familiar. Correctly or incorrectly, they often come to feel that they can now provide themselves with adequate summations, cohesive assessments, comprehensive orientations. Older decisions that once appeared sound, now seem to them products of a mind unaccountably dense. Their capacity for astonishment is made lively again. They acquire a new way of thinking, they experience a transvaluation of values: in a word, by their reflection and by their sensibility, they realize the cultural meaning of the social sciences.

Perhaps the most fruitful distinction with which the sociological imagination works is between 'the personal troubles of milieu' and 'the public issues of social structure'. This distinction is an essential tool of the sociological imagination and a feature of all classic work in social science.

Troubles occur within the character of the individual and within the range of his immediate relations with others; they have to do with his self and with those limited areas of social life of which he is directly and personally aware. Accordingly, the statement and the resolution of troubles properly lie within the individual as a biographical entity and within the scope of his immediate milieu – the social setting that is directly open to his personal experience and to some extent his wilful activity. A trouble is a private matter: values cherished by an individual are felt by him to be threatened.

Issues have to do with matters that transcend these local environments of the individual and the range of his inner life. They have to do with the organization of many such milieux into the institutions of a historical society as a whole, with the ways in which various milieux overlap and interpenetrate to form the larger structure of social and historical life. An issue is a public matter: some value cherished by publics is felt to be threatened. Often there is a debate about what the value really is and about what it is that really threatens it. This debate is often without focus if only because it is the very nature of an issue unlike even widespread trouble, that it cannot very well be defined in terms of the immediate and everyday environments of ordinary men. An issue, in fact, often involves a crisis in institutional arrangements, and often too it involves what Marxists call 'contradictions' or 'antagonisms'. [...]

In so far as an economy is so arranged that slumps occur, the problem of unemployment becomes incapable of personal solution. In so far as war is inherent in the nation-state system and in the uneven industrialization of the world, the ordinary individual in his restricted milieu will be powerless – with or without psychiatric aid – to solve the troubles this system or lack of system imposes upon him. In so far as the family as an institution turns women into darling little slaves and men into their chief providers and unweaned dependants, the problem of a satisfactory marriage remains incapable of purely private solution. In so far as the overdeveloped megalopolis and the overdeveloped automobile are built-in features of the over-developed society, the issues of urban living will not be solved by personal ingenuity and private wealth.

What we experience in various and specific milieux, I have noted, is often caused by structural changes. Accordingly, to understand the changes of many personal milieux we are required to look beyond them. And the number and variety of such structural changes increase as the institutions within which we live become more embracing and more intricately connected with one another.

To be aware of the idea of social structure and to use it with sensibility is to be capable of tracing such linkages among a great variety of milieux. To be able to do that is to possess the sociological imagination.

Note: deletions shown in square brackets are as in the 1971 edition.

Source: Excerpt from C.Wright Mills, *The Sociological Imagination*, Oxford University Press, Inc., 1959, pp.3–11; taken from Worsley, P. (ed.) *The New Modern Sociology Readings*, Harmondsworth, Penguin Books, 1991, pp.13–18.

Zygmunt Bauman:
'Legislators and interpreters' (1987)

Intellectuals: from modern legislators to post-modern interpreters

The typically post-modern view of the world is, in principle, one of an unlimited number of models of order, each one generated by a relatively autonomous set of practices. Order does not precede practices and hence cannot serve as an outside measure of their validity. Each of the many models of order makes sense solely in terms of the practices which validate it. In each case, validation brings in criteria which are developed within a particular tradition; they are upheld by the habits and beliefs of a 'community of meanings' and admit of no other tests of legitimacy. Criteria described above as 'typically modern' are no exception to this general rule; they are ultimately validated by one of the many possible 'local traditions', and their historical fate depends on the fortunes of the tradition in which they reside. There are no criteria for evaluating local practices which are situated outside traditions, outside 'localities'. Systems of knowledge may only be evaluated from 'inside' their respective traditions. If, from the modern point of view, relativism of knowledge was a problem to be struggled against and eventually overcome in theory and in practice, from the post-modern point of view relativity of knowledge (that is, its 'embeddedness' in its own communally supported tradition) is a lasting feature of the world.

The typically modern strategy of intellectual work is one best characterized by the metaphor of the 'legislator' role. It consists of making authoritative statements which arbitrate in controversies of opinions and which select those opinions which, having been selected, become correct and binding. The authority to arbitrate is in this case legitimized by superior (objective) knowledge to which intellectuals have a better access than the non-intellectual part of society. Access to such knowledge is better thanks to procedural rules which assure the attainment of truth, the arrival at valid moral judgement, and the selection of proper artistic taste. Such procedural rules have a universal validity, as do the products of their application. The employment of such procedural rules makes the intellectual professions (scientists, moral philosophers, aesthetes) collective owners of knowledge of direct and crucial relevance to the maintenance and perfection of the social order. The condition of this being so is the work of the 'intellectuals proper' – meta-professionals, so to speak – to be responsible for the formulation of procedural rules and to control their correct application. Like the knowledge they produce, intellectuals are not bound by localized, communal traditions. They are, together with their knowledge, extra-territorial. This gives them the right and the duty to validate (or invalidate) beliefs which may be held in various sections of society. Indeed, as Popper observed, falsifying poorly founded, or unfounded, views is what the procedural rules are best at.

The typically post-modern strategy of intellectual work is one best characterized by the metaphor of the 'interpreter' role. It consists of translating statements, made within one communally based tradition, so that they can be understood within the system of knowledge based on another tradition. Instead of being orientated towards selecting the best social order, this strategy is aimed at facilitating communication between autonomous (sovereign) participants. It is concerned with preventing the distortion of meaning in the process of communication. For this purpose, it promotes the need to penetrate deeply the alien system of knowledge from which the translation is to be made (for example, Geertz's 'thick description'), and the need to maintain the delicate balance between the two conversing traditions necessary for the message to be both undistorted (regarding the meaning invested by the sender) and understood (by the recipient). It is vitally important to note that the post-modern strategy does not imply the elimination of the modern one; on the contrary, it cannot be conceived without the continuation of the latter. While the post-modern strategy entails the abandonment of the universalistic ambitions of the intellectuals' own tradition, it does not abandon the universalistic ambitions of the intellectuals towards their own tradition; here, they retain their meta-professional authority, legislating about the procedural rules which allow them to arbitrate controversies of opinion and make statements intending as binding. The novel difficulty, however, is how to draw the boundaries of such community as may serve as the territory for legislative practices.

Source: Zygmunt Bauman, *Legislators and interpreters: On Modernity, Post-modernity and Intellectuals*, Cambridge, Polity Press in association with Basil Blackwell, 1987, pp.4–5.

Michel Foucault:
'Governmentality' (1978)

In what way did the problem of population make possible the derestriction of the art of government? The perspective of population, the reality accorded to specific phenomena of population, render possible the final elimination of the model of the family and the recentring of the notion of economy. Whereas statistics had previously worked within the administrative frame and thus in terms of the functioning of sovereignty, it now gradually reveals that population has its own regularities, its own rate of deaths and diseases, its cycles of scarcity, etc.; statistics shows also that the domain of population involves a range of intrinsic, aggregate effects, phenomena that are irreducible to those of the family, such as epidemics, endemic levels of mortality, ascending spirals of labour and wealth; lastly it shows that, through its shifts, customs, activities, etc., population has specific economic effects: statistics, by making it possible to quantify these specific phenomena of population, also shows that this specificity is irreducible to the dimension of the family. The latter now disappears as the model of government, except for a certain number of residual themes of a religious or moral nature. What, on the other hand, now emerges into prominence is the family considered as an element internal to population, and as a fundamental instrument in its government.

In other words, prior to the emergence of population, it was impossible to conceive the art of government except on the model of the family, in terms of economy conceived as the management of a family; from the moment when, on the contrary, population appears absolutely irreducible to the family, the latter becomes of secondary importance compared to population, as an element internal to population: no longer, that is to say, a model, but a segment. Nevertheless it remains a privileged segment, because whenever information is required concerning the population (sexual behaviour, demography, consumption, etc.), it has to be obtained through the family. But the family becomes an instrument rather than a model: the privileged instrument for the government of the population and not the chimerical model of good government. This shift from the level of the model to that of an instrument is, I believe, absolutely fundamental, and it is from the middle of the eighteenth century that the family appears in this dimension of instrumentality relative to the population, with the institution of campaigns to reduce mortality, and to promote marriages, vaccinations, etc. Thus, what makes it possible for the theme of population to unblock the field of the art of government is this elimination of the family as model.

In the second place, population comes to appear above all else as the ultimate end of government. In contrast to sovereignty, government has as its purpose not the act of government itself, but the welfare of the population, the improvement of its condition, the increase of its wealth, longevity, health, etc.; and the means that the government uses to attain these ends are themselves all in some sense immanent to the population; it is the population itself on which government will act either directly through large-scale campaigns, or indirectly through techniques that will make possible, without the full awareness of the people, the stimulation of birth rates, the directing of the flow of population into certain regions or activities, etc. The population now represents more the end of government than the power of the sovereign; the population is the subject of needs, of aspirations, but it is also the object in the hands of the government, aware, *vis-à-vis* the government, of what it wants, but ignorant of what is being done to it. Interest at the level of the consciousness of each individual who goes to make up the population, and interest considered as the interest of the population regardless of what the particular interests and aspirations may be of the individuals who compose it, this is the new target and the fundamental instrument of the government of population: the birth of a new art, or at any rate of a range of absolutely new tactics and techniques.

Lastly, population is the point around which is organized what in sixteenth-century texts came to be called the patience of the sovereign, in the sense that the population is the object that government must take into account in all its observations and *savoir*, in order to be able to govern effectively in a rational and conscious manner. The constitution of a *savoir* of government is absolutely inseparable from that of a knowledge of all the processes related to population in its larger sense: that is to say, what we now call the economy. I said in my last lecture that the constitution of political economy depended upon the emergence from among all the various elements of wealth of a new subject: population. The new science called political economy arises out of the perception of new networks of continuous and multiple relations between population, territory and wealth; and this is accompanied by the formation of a type of intervention characteristic of government, namely intervention in the field of economy and population. In other words, the transition which takes place in the eighteenth century from an art of government to a political science, from a regime dominated by structures of sovereignty to one ruled by techniques of government, turns on the theme of population and hence also on the birth of political economy.

This is not to say that sovereignty ceases to play a role from the moment when the art of government begins to become a political science; I would say that, on the contrary, the problem of sovereignty was never posed with greater force than at this time, because it no longer involved, as it did in the sixteenth and seventeenth centuries, an attempt to derive an art of government from a theory of sovereignty, but instead, given that such an art now existed and was spreading, involved an attempt to see what juridical and institutional form, what foundation in the law, could be given to the sovereignty that characterizes a state. It suffices to read in chronological succession two different texts by Rousseau. In his *Encyclopaedia* article on 'Political economy', we can see the way in which Rousseau sets up the problem of the art of government by pointing out (and the text is very characteristic from this point of view) that the word 'oeconomy' essentially signifies the management of family property by the father, but that this model can no longer be accepted, even if it had been valid in the past; today we know, says Rousseau, that political economy is not the economy of the family, and even without making explicit reference to the Physiocrats, to statistics or to the general problem of the population, he sees quite clearly this turning point consisting in the fact that the economy of 'political economy' has a totally new sense which cannot be reduced to the old model of the family. He undertakes in this article the task of giving a new definition of the art of government. Later he writes *The Social Contract*, where he poses the problem of how it is possible, using concepts like nature, contract and general will, to provide a general principle of government which allows room both for a juridical principle of sovereignty and for the elements through which an art of government can be defined and characterized. Consequently, sovereignty is far from being eliminated by the emergence of a new art of government, even by one which has passed the threshold of political science; on the contrary, the problem of sovereignty is made more acute than ever.

As for discipline, this is not eliminated either; clearly its modes of organization, all the institutions within which it had developed in the seventeenth and eighteenth centuries – schools, manufactories, armies, etc. – all this can only be understood on the basis of the development of the great administrative monarchies, but nevertheless, discipline was never more important or more valorized than at the moment when it became important to manage a population; the managing of a population not only concerns the collective mass of phenomena, the level of its depths and its details. The notion of a government of population renders all the more acute the problem of the foundation of sovereignty (consider Rousseau) and all the more acute equally the necessity for the development of discipline (consider all the history of the disciplines, which I have attempted to analyze elsewhere).

Accordingly, we need to see things not in terms of the replacement of a society of sovereignty by a disciplinary society and the subsequent replacement of a disciplinary society by a society of government; in reality one has a triangle, sovereignty–discipline–government, which has as its primary target the population and as its essential mechanism the apparatuses of security. In any case, I wanted to demonstrate the deep historical link between the movement that overturns the constants of sovereignty in consequence of the problem of choices of government, the movement that brings about the emergence of population as a datum, as a field of intervention and as an objective of governmental techniques, and the process which isolates the economy as a specific sector of reality, and political economy as the science and the technique of intervention of the government in that field of reality. Three movements: government, population, political economy, which constitute from the eighteenth century onwards a solid series, one which even today has assuredly not been dissolved.

In conclusion I would like to say that on second thoughts the more exact title I would like to have given to the course of lectures which I have begun this year is not the one I originally chose, 'Security, territory and population': what I would like to undertake is something which I would term a history of 'governmentality'. By this word I mean three things:

1 The ensemble formed by the institutions, procedures, analyses and reflections, the calculations and tactics that allow the exercise of this very specific albeit complex form of power, which has as its target population, as its principal form of knowledge political economy, and as its essential technical means apparatuses of security.

2   The tendency which, over a long period and throughout the West, has steadily led towards the pre-eminence over all other forms (sovereignty, discipline, etc.) of this type of power which may be termed government, resulting, on the one hand, in the formation of a whole series of specific governmental apparatuses, and, on the other, in the development of a whole complex of *savoirs*.

3   The process, or rather the result of the process, through which the state of justice of the Middle Ages, transformed into the administrative state during the fifteenth and sixteenth centuries, gradually becomes 'governmentalized'.

We all know the fascination which the love, or horror, of the state exercises today; we know how much attention is paid to the genesis of the state, its history, its advance, its power and abuses, etc. The excessive value attributed to the problem of the state is expressed, basically, in two ways: the one form, immediate, affective and tragic, is the lyricism of the *monstre froid* we see confronting us; but there is a second way of overvaluing the problem of the state, one which is paradoxical because apparently reductionist: it is the form of analysis that consists in reducing the state to a certain number of functions, such as the development of productive forces and the reproduction of the relations of production, and yet this reductionist vision of the relative importance of the state's role nevertheless invariably renders it absolutely essential as a target needing to be attacked and a privileged position needing to be occupied. But the state, no more probably today than at any other time in its history, does not have this unity, this individuality, this rigorous functionality, nor, to speak frankly, this importance; maybe, after all, the state is no more than a composite reality and a mythicized abstraction, whose importance is a lot more limited than many of us think. Maybe what is really important for our modernity – that is, for our present – is not so much the *étatisation* of society, as the 'governmentalization' of the state.

We live in the era of a 'governmentality' first discovered in the eighteenth century. This governmentalization of the state is a singularly paradoxical phenomenon, since if in fact the problems of governmentality and the techniques of government have become the only political issue, the only real space for political struggle and contestation, this is because the governmentalization of the state is at the same time what has permitted the state to survive, and it is possible to suppose that if the state is what it is today, this is so precisely thanks to this governmentality, which is at once internal and external to the state, since it is the tactics of government which make possible the continual definition and redefinition of what is within the competence of the state and what is not, the public versus the private, and so on; thus the state can only be understood in its survival and its limits on the basis of the general tactics of governmentality.

Source: This is an extract from a lecture given in 1978 and first published in English in *I&C*, no.6, Autumn 1979 (trans. Rosi Braidotti). This version revised by Colin Gordon and taken from Michel Foucault, 'Governmentality' in Burchell, G., Gordon, C. and Miller, P. (eds) *The Foucault Effect: Studies in Governmentality*, London, Harvester Wheatsheaf, 1991, pp.99–103.

Anne Witz:
'The feminist challenge' (1997)

Women entering sociology in the 1970s experienced a problem: they saw the actions and experiences of men reflected in sociological writings, but not that of women. Traditionally sociology has been both gender-blind and gender-biased: gender-blind because its practitioners have not regarded gender difference and gendered power relations as a significant element in the constitution of the social; gender-biased because most sociologist have been men, have looked predominantly at men in their research, and have seen men as the active, thinking subjects inhabiting the social terrain. In short, men's lives have been the stuff of which sociology is made. Since the 1970s feminists working within sociology have been correcting this partial image and the main impact of their work has been to gender our understanding of the social, so that the gender of people is always made explicit in sociological analysis, and men can no longer be taken to represent humanity as a whole.

Any assessment of feminism's impact on sociology needs to consider a number of different, though interrelated, aspects of its critique of sociology. First, feminists have argued that the epistemological basis of traditional sociological knowledge (i.e. the basis on which evidence and ideas are regarded as valid and/or significant) bears the fingerprints of its male producers: sociological theory has been written from the particular standpoint of men, whilst masquerading as an objective and disinterested account of the social. This spurious claim to universality must be challenged. Second, gender relations are not simply the expression of benign 'differences' between men and women but are constituted by a system of gendered power relations. All sociological research (not just that explicitly 'concerned with women') must build on a recognition of this. Third, the characteristic research methods of existing sociology which distance themselves from the subjects of research in order to make 'objective' claims about the social world, are symptomatic of a particularly male way of thinking that feminists find unacceptable. Together these arguments pose a severe challenge to sociology's traditional view of society as existing independently of the researcher and capable of being known in an objective, disinterested way. We shall consider each argument in turn.

Feminists have worked both within and against the existing body of sociological knowledge and interpretation. Some do both simultaneously – asking feminist questions (such as how we can document, understand and improve women's lives) but drawing upon the sociological heritage of concepts, theories and methods to explore women's lives and gender relations. Others believe that feminism works with a distinctive epistemology and so aim to produce sociology from a 'feminist standpoint' using methods that tap into women's subjectivity and experiences. The priority for them is to understand the social world as women know and experience it – producing a 'feminist sociology' that is different from the masculinist version in form, content and intent (for feminists hope their research will change women's lives for the better). At the risk of some simplification we could follow Harding (1987) in calling the first approach 'feminist empiricism' and the second 'feminist standpointism'.

Feminism and sociological paradigms

One way of carving out a distinctive feminist perspective is through the critical re-evaluation of existing sociological theories and paradigms – a paradigm being a framework of assumptions and questions on the basis of which the social world is interpreted. Sometimes feminists criticize these paradigms 'from a distance', seeking to debunk the paradigm as a whole and showing how it precludes the asking of feminist questions. At other times feminists work critically within a particular paradigm, seeking to develop it as a way of exploring the specifically gendered nature of society.

To begin with feminists have examined the historical legacy of sociology's 'founding fathers', exposing the fact that the key actors which they placed at the centre of the stage of modernity were male rational actors: in the new social class relations of production (as in Marx), in civil society and civic associations (Durkheim), or in new bureaucratic organizational forms (Weber). In contrast what little the founding fathers had to say about women was heavily coloured by the 'naturalistic' assumption that women are less social beings than men – that is closer to biologically determined nature.

This was especially true of the once dominant paradigm in Western sociology: 'structural-functionalism'. Feminists were particularly critical of its implicit biological reductionism when accounting for distinctive gender roles in modern society. Functionalist research into 'sex roles', looking at ways in which men and women are socialized into different behaviours, attitudes and social orientations, generally concluded that women display 'expressive orientations' through their family roles and men 'instrumental' ones through their work roles. Feminists argued that the 'role' concept was unsatisfactory since it de-politicized experience by stripping it from its historical and political context, neglecting issues of power and conflict (Stacey and Thorne, 1985). Feminists began to distinguish between 'sex' as a relatively fixed biological property and 'gender' as socially and culturally more variable (Oakley, 1974). The idea that gender relations are neither natural nor immutable marked the emergence of a specifically feminist sociological paradigm. Moreover the distinction between 'sex' and 'gender' opened up the way for a third term to enter feminist sociology: 'sexuality' referring more explicitly to forms of power centering around desire and identity, and also seen as socially constructed.

Many feminists concerned to debunk the dominant structural-functionalist paradigm, and desiring a theoretical home for the new analyses of women's oppression, became increasingly engaged with Marxism in the 1970s. Working both within and against the existing Marxist paradigm feminists have used the concept of gender ideology to explain how women's oppression is secured within capitalist societies, and that of 'social reproduction' to pinpoint the specifically gendered ways in which the daily and generational reproduction of class society is ensured (through, for example, women's domestic work) (Barrett, 1988). Other feminists, whilst continuing to conduct their analyses at the broad level of structural and systemic social relations, have adopted a more critical stance towards Marxism, focussing on patriarchy rather than capitalism as the system in which men dominate women (Hartmann, 1979; Walby, 1990; Delphy, 1984).

All these paradigms, and the feminist responses to them, operate at the structural or macro level – delineating commonalities and differences between women, explaining why these social patterns exist and change and, most significantly, locating them within a systematically ordered set of power relations between men and women. But other feminists have preferred to explore the micro-processes of social life, grounding their feminist sociology in the everyday negotiation of the social world and the on-going production of social meanings by its participants. This work, which is informed by traditions such as symbolic interactionism, phenomenology and ethnomethodology, focuses less on structures of gender and power, and more on the everyday accomplishments of gender. It relies heavily on detailed empirical documentation to reveal how we 'do gender' or 'do difference' as we engage in social interaction (West and Zimmerman, 1987).

What impact has feminism had on traditional sociological paradigms? Regrettably it has been pretty minimal. To take but one important example, the 'stratification agenda', which revolves around the theory and analysis of social class, has proved highly resistant to feminist accusations of 'intellectual sexism' on the grounds that the class position of wives (and children) was derived from the husband's occupation. Instead of seeing major shifts in traditional paradigms, we have seen rather the development of a new feminist paradigm of gender, sexuality and power. In the above case, for example, feminists have responded to the sexism of class analysis by going their separate ways, concentrating instead on how gender inequalities and divisions are generated, sustained or changed (Walby, 1990).

Indeed some feminists regard any kind of abstract theorizing as a peculiarly male-centred way of doing sociology. They have argued that only particular ways of doing sociology provide the means of developing a specifically feminist sociology and have adopted a 'feminist standpoint' position (Smith, 1988; Stanley and Wise, 1993). Smith advocates 'a sociology for women' rather than a sociology of or about women, urging that the everyday social world as women experience and know it should form the subject matter of feminist sociology, and that in working from the standpoint of women it is important not to erase the subjectivities of those women who are the subject of feminist sociology. This view is based on a critique of white male sociology as a patriarchal discourse located in the 'relations of ruling', and is underpinned by a notion that since women experience the world in ways that are fundamentally different from men, so their knowledge of the social world will be different. It is men who enter the abstract disembodied, conceptual mode precisely because women attend to the concrete, embodied, material everyday world. Sociological conventions are man-made, and therefore consist of objectifying practices which subdue local positions, perspectives and experiences (Smith, 1988). The task of feminist sociology is to work outside these objectifying practices, in the everyday world where women live out their lives, understanding and interpreting the world in gender-specific ways.

Feminism and substantive sociology

Many feminists work within a particular substantive field and focus specifically on women's lives or on gendered social relations. This approach has generated a vast amount of empirically based knowledge by asking feminist questions, and then proceeding to investigate them using the inherited methodological and conceptual tools of the sociological trade, i.e. 'doing sociology as usual'. This is perhaps the route by which feminist sociology has made the greatest impact on sociology generally, an impact that has been felt in several different ways.

First, feminists have 'gendered' our understanding of many substantive areas of social life such as education, work, the family or crime .... . These subfields have felt the full force of feminist arguments because they demonstrate, quite simply, that gender matters in these areas, and show convincingly that a gender-inflected sociological analysis contributes to a better understanding of what is going on. The feminist focus on the gendering of jobs and hierarchies shows, for example, how male careers are carved out at the expense of women's. Feminist analysis of male violence against women has led to an explicit recognition of the links between masculinity and crime.

Second, feminists have established the sociological significance of areas of experience previously overlooked by sociologists or dismissed by them as trivial. These new areas include motherhood, pregnancy and childbirth; resource distribution in families and households; housework and forms of caring work in the family and community; sexuality, romantic love and friendship; violence (sexual harassment, domestic violence, rape) in both the public and private spheres; and new reproductive technologies. This means that the sweep of topics regarded as the legitimate subject matter of sociology has been considerably expanded by feminist work. Of particular importance is the way feminists have opened gendered activities in the private sphere to sociological scrutiny, and have used sociological concepts to analyse these activities – for example, treating housework as work, and showing that it is distinguished not by the tasks involved but by the social relations of marriage within which it is performed; examining gendered power relations and decision-making processes in relation to household finances; looking at how parenting work is gendered, and so on. In opening up the whole topic of domestic violence against women, feminist sociologists have taken C. Wright Mills' notion of turning 'personal troubles' into 'public issues' ... considerably further than before. They have shown that domestic violence is not to be understood in terms of the aberrant behaviour of a few men, and that it is not a 'private matter' between husband and wife. It is rather a means by which men exert power over women within patriarchal household relations, and is therefore a public issue amenable to sociological analysis.

Third, feminists working empirically have felt compelled to re-work many of the conceptual tools of sociology. Concepts may be seen as intellectual tools for 'naming' aspects of the social world which we wish to think about sociologically, and to explain. Feminist empiricism poses challenging issues when studies of women's lives reveal that existing concepts do not provide the means to analyse typical forms of female sociality. 'Work', for example, has long been a core sociological concern, but when feminists came to investigate the nature of women's work they began to fill the concepts of 'work', 'labour' and 'the worker' with gendered, sexualized and embodied content that had hitherto been unacknowledged. The masculinist connotations of the previously existing concepts were brought to the surface and exploded. Sociology, and particularly Marxism, had operated with concepts which assumed a disembodied, abstract social actor living out a life of labour in the public sphere of employment, where the only real worker was one able to contract freely with an employer and 'go out to work'. Thus the concept of 'worker' had become virtually synonymous with a 'male worker' (Acker, 1990). This became most evident when sociologists fleshed out the disembodied abstract worker in research studies – it was working men (coalminers, car assembly workers, managers and bureaucrats) who manned the pages of sociological texts.

One response, as mentioned above, was to name housework as 'domestic labour'. This represented an attempt by Marxist-feminists to de-naturalize housework (i.e. to challenge the assumption that it was essentially the same in all times and places and was 'naturally' women's work) and to analyse its relation to capitalism in the same way as waged labour. But, even more radically, the analysis of women's work led to the development of new concepts to 'name' the gendered and sexualized content of work: for example,

- 'emotion work' to analyse the management and control of emotions, disposition and demeanour of airline stwardesses (Hochschild, 1983 …)

- 'caring work' to name gender-specific forms of unpaid work in the family and community, and paid work in occupations such as nursing (Finch and Groves, 1983)

- 'sexual work' to describe how women in many service occupations are required to 'sell' their sexuality, constantly presenting themselves in ways defined as attractive to men, responding to sexualized demands for women to smile, flirt, etc. (Adkins, 1995).

Feminism and sociological research methodology

Feminist sociologists have also been critical of received ways of researching the social. The critique of 'objectivity' in sociology led to a rejection of quantitative in favour of qualitative methods. Feminists argue for reflexivity in the research process, meaning that women sociologists should not adopt the 'hit and run' techniques encouraged by standard textbooks, but should think about the relationship between the researcher and the women who are the subjects of the research, both in terms of the interview itself and the ownership of data gathered during the course of research. Feminist sociologists are, after all, attempting to produce knowledge-from-below, as well as ensuring that this knowledge will be of benefit to women. The attitude of feminist researchers is 'involved' rather than 'detached' (Fonow and Cook, 1992). Feminists have pioneered new kinds of reflexivity in research, reflecting on the research itself as a social process, and advocating practices that empower rather than disempower women subjects of research.

Qualitative rather than quantitative methods have been advocated as a means of tapping into women's experiences and emotions on their own terms rather than replicating masculinist attempts to order and objectify the world in measurable categories. However, some feminists have begun to re-think this position recognizing that, for all their problems, quantitative methods may be appropriate for some purposes. Certainly these have been extremely important in demonstrating what factors influence women's health; the extent to which women, as single mothers or pensioners, are particularly vulnerable to poverty; and patterns of gendered occupational segregation in labour markets.

Unsettling sociology/unsettling feminism

Any assessment of the impact feminism has had on sociology has to take into account the different ways in which feminists have worked. Feminist standpointism advocates an autonomous path of constructing a 'sociology for women' through accounts of women's lives that are epistemologically and methodologically quite different from male-stream sociological practices and accounts. Other feminists look to a paradigm shift in sociology, pressing it to acknowledge that social processes are gendered to the very core (Acker, 1989).

Certainly a vast amount of feminist sociology remains ignored or resisted by the male-stream. But at the same time, in specific subfields of sociology, the innovative work done by feminists has reverberated throughout the area, not only forcing a recognition that gender is important but also identifying new kinds of questions and developing new kinds of conceptual tools. In addition the role played by feminist sociologists in pioneering more reflexive modes of research has been considerable.

But we end on a note of reflexive uncertainty. Concerned to establish its different voice, feminist sociology often failed to recognize the 'difference within', i.e. it worked with universal and ethnocentric categorizations of 'woman'. Most importantly, in claiming its own distinctive voice within sociology, feminist sociology did not hear itself speak solely of gendered whiteness, and thus created the conditions for its own critique by Black feminists, and the emergence of a distinctive Black feminist standpoint (Hill Collins, 1990). Ironically the feminist critique of sociology has generated the grounds for its own unravelling. The argument that social knowledges are situated has opened the way for a cacophony of different voices all claiming a hearing. Many claim an intellectual affinity between feminism and post-modernism and the challenges they pose to the nature of sociological explanation and theory.

Thus feminism has unsettled sociology and, in so doing, has unsettled itself. Nonetheless, as I have tried to show, it has in the process not only challenged received ways of thinking and doing sociology, but also enriched sociology. It has critically and reflexively taken up the tarnished tools of the sociological trade – methodological, conceptual and theoretical – polished them up, and added new tools of its own.

References

Acker, J. (1989) 'Making gender visible' in Wallace, R.A. (ed.) *Feminism and Sociological Theory*, London, Sage.

Acker, J. (1990) 'Hierarchies, jobs and bodies: a theory of gendered organisations', *Gender and Society*, vol.4, no.2, pp.139–58.

Adkins, L. (1995) *Gendered Work*, Milton Keynes, Open University Press.

Barrett, M. (1988) *Women's Oppression Today*, London, Verso.

Delphy, C. (1984) *Close to Home*, London, Hutchinson.

Finch, J. and Groves, D. (1983) *A Labour of Love*, London, Routledge & Kegan Paul.

Fonow, M. M. and Cook, J. A. (eds) 1992: *Beyond Methodology: Feminist Scholarship as Lived Research*, Bloomington, IN, Indiana University Press.

Harding, S. (1987) 'Introduction' in Harding, S. (ed.) *Feminism and Methodology*, Milton Keynes, Open University Press.

Hartmann, H. (1979) 'Capitalism, patriarchy and job segregation by sex' in Eisenstein, Z.R. (ed.) *Capitalist Patriarchy and the Case for Socialist Feminism*, New York, Monthly Review Press.

Hill Collins, P. (1990) *Black Feminist Thought*, London, Routledge.

Hochschild, A.R. (1983) *The Managed Heart*, Berkeley, CA, University of California Press.

Oakley, A. (1974) *Sex, Gender and Society*, London, Temple Smith.

Smith, D. (1988) *The Everyday World as Problematic*, Milton Keynes, Open University Press.

Stacey, J. and Thorne, B. (1985) 'The missing feminist revolution in sociology', *Social Problems*, vol.32, no.4, pp.301–16.

Stanley, L. and Wise, S. (1983) *Breaking Out Again: Feminist Ontology and Epistemology*, London, Routledge.

Walby, S. (1990) *Theorizing Patriarchy*, Oxford, Blackwell.

West, C. and Zimmerman, D.H. (1987) 'Doing gender', *Gender and Society*, vol.1, pp.125–51.

Source: Anne Witz, 'The feminist challenge' in Ballard, C., Gubbay, J. and Middleton, C. (eds) *The Student's Companion to Sociology*, Oxford, Blackwell, 1997, pp.114–20.

John Urry:
'Sociology as a parasite: some vices and virtues' (1981)

Introduction

I think that Giddens is wrong in suggesting that there are only four myths in the history of sociology – there is a further myth, namely, that there is an essence to sociology, that it has some essential characteristics that give it and its practitioners a unity, coherence and common tradition (Giddens, 1977). Giddens of course is well aware of the ambiguous nature of sociology as a subject – but he leaves its character merely as uncertain through the employment of terms like 'social thought' rather than 'sociology'. In this chapter I want to consider the status of the subject in more detail: just what kind of academic discourse is it? It is only by carrying out such an investigation that we can see exactly what we are defending when, for example, we argue against cuts in sociological teaching and research. In particular, I want to make sense of an interesting contradiction which first led me to this problem. On the one hand, it is commonly argued in public debate that there is no such subject as sociology, that you can make it up since there is not a rigorous structure of learning, research and content, that since everyone knows about society there is no need for a specific subject to study it. On the other hand, sociologists generally perceive that their subject is both important and difficult, that most people are sociologically ignorant, that a long period of training is involved and that it is more complex and worthwhile than most of the other social sciences. Sociologists generally get round this contradiction by rejecting or even ridiculing the first view, that of public opinion, and by adopting the latter. However, I think there is something mistaken about this – there is more to the public opinion view than we are normally willing to acknowledge. What this exactly is I shall try to indicate below.

In particular, I want to consider one aspect, namely, that sociology is a parasite subject since it has no essence, no essential unity. In a sense it feeds off developments in neighbouring disciplines to an extraordinary degree. To illustrate this, consider three BSA [British Sociological Association] conferences on the state, culture and ideology, and law (see Littlejohn *et al.*, 1978, and Barrett *et al.*, 1979, on the 1977 and 1978 conferences). How much of the content of these conferences could be described as 'sociology' – indeed, how many 'sociologists' attended, how many gave papers or made substantial oral contributions, how much sociological material was referred to in these papers? In each case the answer is 'relatively few' or 'relatively little'. The developments in these three topics have been appropriated *within* sociology, but sociology *per se* has not contributed much to such developments, except in a rather special sense … I shall … consider in the following section some important implications of this for the social and intellectual organization of sociology. In particular, it will be seen first that sociology develops in part through *appropriating* theoretical and empirical work conducted in neighbouring disciplines and related social movements; second, that it can never be understood in terms of the idea of a paradigm, or even of a scientific community, or communities (Kuhn, 1970); and third, that its intellectual strength predominantly lies in its parasitism, its openness and relative lack of authority and control. It is perhaps the only scientific community to resemble Popper's ideal precisely because it is not organised like other natural or social scientific subjects (see Popper, 1970). This might suggest of course that it does contain some essence which produces these distinctive characteristics. But this is only so in one sense, that it has a particular organisation as *an academic discourse* and this is because its central concepts neither generate a distinctive unity nor demarcate it in a strong sense from neighbouring subjects which may well employ similar concepts (but not necessarily the same terms). I shall conclude the chapter with some more general comments on the virtues of sociology's parasitic character.

Three provisos should be made before I proceed. First, although some of my argument rests on implicit comparisons with other social sciences, I am not claiming that sociology is unique among such sciences. It may well be that certain social sciences are also in part parasitic – 'politics' is the most obvious example. However, I would still want to argue for the greater parasitism of sociology, and hence, as we shall see, for its greater virtue. Second, most of my discussion is related to recent developments in British sociology. Yet there is little doubt that in Britain sociology has generally enjoyed a more marginal academic status than in the United States or Western Europe, and this has increased it tendency here to feed off and incorporate the more established (and 'respectable') social sciences. This is, however, only a question of degree. Indeed, for reasons that I shall discuss, this parasitism is particularly important in a period of advance within sociology and British sociology since the mid-1960s has been advancing. It is thus worth exploring for this particular reason. Third, the term 'sociological discourse' refers to the set of social practices characteristic of the members of such a discourse – such practices being structured in terms of common concepts, beliefs, theories, traditions, institutions, methods, techniques, exemplars and so on. In most cases those individuals who happen to bear the official label 'sociologist' are agents who are part of, and contributors to, this on-going set of reproducible social practices known as 'sociological discourse'. However, this is not always the case, in part precisely because of sociology's parasitic and hence rapidly changing nature. There is thus an important disjuncture between 'sociological discourse'/practitioners of 'sociology' – the latter may not be agents of the former.

        …

The organisation of sociological discourse

The parasitic character of sociology can not only be seen in the analysis of the state. Consider, for example, how the sociology of the family has recently been transformed not because of the debate between sociologists on the relationship between industrialisation and the extended family, but because of the incorporation of arguments, insights and research material produced within both the anti-psychiatry and the women's movements (see Morgan, 1975, for very helpful discussion). Likewise, the sociology of development was greatly changed through the incorporation of work produced outside sociology, namely, certain texts of Frank on the manner in which development produces underdevelopment (see Frank, 1969, for example). Similarly, if we consider BSA conferences, the debates on culture and ideology in 1978 very largely reflected the theoretical and empirical insights of semiology, psychoanalysis and neo-Gramscian Marxism (Barrett *et al.*, 1979). Also the sociology of law, as in the 1979 conference, has been transformed through critical confrontation with Pashukanis' by now historic attempt to relate the legal subject to the commodity form (Pashukanis, 1978; and see, for example Fine *et al.*, 1979). Even if we consider Bottomore and Nisbet's massive and authoritative *A History of Sociological Analysis*, many of the texts which are referred to were produced within philosophy, economics, politics and so on (Bottomore and Nisbet, 1979). What is the explanation of sociology's parasitic character? I will try to answer this by considering Bottomore and Nisbet's 'Introduction' to this collection, which I will take as an authoritative statement about the history of sociology.

They argue that there is 'now a single discipline, a realm of scientific discourse outside of which sociological analysis cannot properly be pursued at all', and this 'constitutes a relatively autonomous sphere' (Bottomore and Nisbet, 1979, pp.xiv–xv). What, though, provides the basis of this unity, around what central concepts or principles is this discourse organised? They say that this unity is provided by the 'more precise conception of society as an object of study', this being a concept separate from both the state and politics, and from vaguer notions of civilisation or mankind (Bottomore and Nisbet, 1979, p.viii). The concept of 'society' has constituted sociology as a scientific discipline. This has then developed in a fairly normal manner, first, through the continued elaboration of alternative paradigms and theoretical controversy among adherents, second, through the accumulation of an ordered body of knowledge 'directed' by one or other paradigm, and third, through the 'specialisation of research' (Bottomore and Nisbet, 1979, pp.viii–ix). However, they also say that there have been three unsatisfactory features in sociological development: that there has been a multiplicity of paradigms such that no particular theory ever dies and no new theory ever becomes dominant; that sociological knowledge is too close to everyday common-sense knowledge; and that there has been a failure to progress in important areas.

What are the deficiencies of Bottomore and Nisbet's interpretation? First, they imply that sociology is like any other science in being characterised by alternative paradigms and theoretical controversy. Since they quote Kuhn they must be employing the term 'paradigm' in his sense (Kuhn, 1970; Masterman, 1970). Yet for Kuhn it is the crucial fact of science that there are *not* alternative paradigms except in the limited periods of scientific revolution. If a particular discourse is, during normal periods, characterised by interparadigmatic competition, then it is not, as yet, a fully fledged science. But what Bottomore and Nisbet have done is to construct a spurious teleology, to view all kinds of earlier social thought as somehow contributing to the end-state – the present organisation of sociology oriented around particularly the concept of 'society'. Yet it is clear that this structuring of history is largely a fiction – the history has no such unity, purpose or direction. This is implied by them when they refer to the three unsatisfactory characteristics of sociology – but they cannot have it both ways. If these three characteristics are important then sociology is not a conventional science comprehensible through even a minimally accumulationist model of its development. I will now try to show that these features are both correct and so important that they undermine Bottomore and Nisbet's attempt to suggest that we have already achieved a systematic, unified, sociological discourse. In particular, I shall argue that the term 'society' does not provide the sought-for unity, that sociology cannot be demarcated adequately from the common-sense, and that there is little in the way of sociological progress, except in a highly paradoxical sense.

First, then, let me consider the concept 'society' in relationship to the main perspectives incorporated within sociology. There are eight such perspectives, not necessarily similar in organisation, structure or intellectual coherence. They are: critical theory, ethnomethodology, functionalism, interactionism, Marxism, positivism, structuralism and Weberianism (see Urry, 1980, for more details). There is no common external object 'society' which brings together these disparate perspectives into a unified discourse. This can be seen from the following where I set out the central notion of society specific to each of these various perspectives:

critical theory: society as a form of alienated consciousness judged by the criterion of reason

ethnomethodology: society as the fragile order displayed by the common-sense methods members use in practical reasoning

functionalism: society as the social system in which all the parts are functionally integrated with each other

interactionism: society as social order negotiated and renegotiated between actors

Marxism: society as the structure of relations between the economic base and the political ideological superstructures

positivism: society as the structure of relations between observable (generally measurable) social phenomena

structuralism: society as the system of signs generated from fundamental structures in the human mind

Weberianism: society as the relations between different social orders and of the social groupings present within each order.

Obviously particular writers may disagree with these formulations – but in general this list indicates the diverse concepts of 'society' which are employed within perspectives generally taken to be part of sociological discourse.

Second, it has been plausibly argued by Bachelard that the objective of science is to create something which is in a radical discontinuity with the world of common sense (see the discussion in Lecourt, 1975). There has to be a discontinuity between the two and this provides one of the guarantees of scientific progress. Even it this is broadly true of natural science, it is clear that sociology is organised differently. Sociology is thoroughly contaminated with common-sense terms, concepts and understandings and most of the attempts to create and sustain a separate, purely academic, discourse have been unsuccessful. One reason for this has been the manner in which contemporary political and social movements affect sociology more than most of the other social sciences, let alone the natural sciences. In recent years, the students', black, and women's movements have all become, in a sense, part of sociological discourse, juxtaposed and assessed within that discourse. I have already mentioned how the previously dormant sociology of the family has been revitalised through incorporating the common-sense understandings and theoretical reflections of women seeking to develop alternative forms of social relations between the sexes.

Third, there is little that can be described as sociological progress in the sense understood by that notion within science. Bottomore and Nisbet point out that specific theories are rarely worked through sufficiently to establish whether a particular research programme is progressive (see Lakatos, 1970, on this notion of science). There is considerable emphasis placed upon novelty – on making sociological reputations through developing and employing a new theory. Progress is thus generally achieved and indicated not primarily by working through existing theory, not by puzzle-solving practices of normal science – it rather follows from the generation of new theories and of the critical discussions engendered through these. This is not, incidentally, to be arguing for that well-worn cliché in sociology, for theory rather than empirical research. It is rather that in sociology 'progress' seems to take the form of theoretical innovations – and these may derive from many sources which include empirical research, philosophical speculation or the incorporation of, or juxtaposition of, contributions made from outside sociological discourse. This emphasis upon the making of theoretical innovations means that there is a tendency for the cyclical repetition of theories, rather than for one wholly to replace that already in existence. This is not entirely the case – Parkin suggests, for example, that Lloyd Warner is unlikely ever to make a come-back (1979, p.603). But there is nevertheless a tendency for new theories to bear strong similarities with those once discarded. He also points out that most of what counts as important and interesting in the field of class and stratification analysis is almost entirely derived from the competing theoretical perspectives of Marx/Engels, Weber and Pareto/Mosca (Parkin, 1979, p.599).

I will conclude this section by relating the discussion of sociology to Kuhn's account of how a scientific discourse is organised (Kuhn, 1970; Lakatos and Musgrave, 1970). Kuhn presumes at least during normal science that there is a unity of the discourse which results from the role of the paradigm as exemplar. Sociology is obviously not organised in this manner, since sociological change and development does not result from the working through of the paradigm until anomalies arise. I am not presuming that Kuhn's account of change and revolution is philosophically correct – in particular he requires sociological categories to do too much epistemological work. But sociologically there are great differences between his account of the discourse of a natural scientific community and my account of the discursive organisation of sociology. This means that attempts to employ Kuhn as providing philosophical protocols for developments in sociology are unjustified – whether these involve the non-radical advocacy of positivism of sociology's normal science or the radical advocacy of sociological revolutions and the founding of a plethora of new paradigms (see my discussion of this in Urry, 1973).

The virtues of being a parasite

I have so far argued that sociological discourse is organised as follows:

1 there is a multiplicity of perspectives with no common concept of 'society' which unifies them;

2 sociological concepts and propositions cannot be clearly demarcated from common-sense concepts and propositions;

3 it is difficult to establish that there is sociological progress – it mainly follows *theoretical* innovations;

4 one major form of such innovation results from the parasitic nature of sociology, from the fact that innovations originate in discourses outside sociology itself.

I shall now consider certain aspects of the fourth point in more detail. What, we might ask, are the circumstances that permit the parasitism to occur? Within sociology's neighbouring disciplines there is a simultaneous process of both presupposing and rejecting what I will loosely call the 'social', by which I mean the general social relations which link together individuals and groups. In these disciplines, which include economics, geography, history, Marxism, psychology and politics, these social relations are presumed to be of importance, and yet are in part ignored. The social is thus both present and absent simultaneously. Instead, in these disciplines some particular dimension or aspect of social life is abstracted for study, such as people's behaviour as agents in the market, or their distribution within space, or their behaviour in the past. But this means that each of these disciplines is discursively unstable. On occasions, certain texts will break through the limitations implied by that discourse. New understandings emerge which will involve more systematic comprehension of the general form of these social relations which will not obscure or neglect the realm of the social. How, though, does such a development in a neighbouring discipline relate to sociology? First, these other disciplines are to varying degrees discursively unified – which will mean that blocks will be placed upon the new, more 'social', interpretation. Yet, second, because there is no essence to sociological discourse, apart from a broad commitment to this idea of the interdependence of individuals and social groups, sociology may attract this new 'social' interpretation. So simultaneously we encounter two likely developments; a process of at least partial repulsion from the originating discourse and attraction into sociological discourse. There are a number of examples of where both developments have occurred. I will mention one for each of the social sciences recently listed: in economics, Frank and the development of the underdevelopment thesis; in geography, analysis of the growth of multinational corporations and changes in the spatial division of labour; in history, the nature of class relations in nineteenth century Britain; in Marxism, the theorisation of the state and ideology; in psychology, the critique of the family in the anti-psychiatry movement; and in politics, the class structuring of local power structures.

Thus far I have claimed that in many social sciences there is a simultaneous presupposing and rejecting of the social. Where social relations in a sense break through, the innovation may get elaborated in part outside the originating discourse and within sociology instead. So sociology is important in permitting analysis and elaboration of aspects of the social world which are generally neglected by the other social sciences. It can thus be defined negatively – as a discourse with minimal organisation, structure or unity into which many contending developments from other social sciences get incorporated. So although it is parasitic it enjoys two crucially important features: first, to provide a site within which further elaboration of the original innovation may occur; and second, to provide the context in which a wide variety of contending social theories can be placed in juxtaposition with each other. This has the function of promoting interdiscursive debate and confrontation. I am not claiming that this is sufficient to permit a necessarily rational evaluation of such social theories – but there are nevertheless some very important positive effects of these processes which may then react back on the originating discourse.

1   *Positive overlap* In some cases it becomes clear through the juxtaposition of perspectives that there are certain shared concepts and related propositions. There can be very positive effects which follow from this juxtaposing of related perspectives in terms of producing new bases of empirical work or novel theoretical insights. A good example is the collective work which resulted in *Capitalism and the Rule of Law* (Fine *et al.*, 1979) – a book which developed from the positive overlap between the 'left interactionism and conflict theory' of the National Deviancy Conference and the fairly fundamentalist Marxism of the CSE (Conference of Socialist Economists) Law and State Group.

2   *Improved rigour and precision* Because of the critical confrontation between two or more perspectives the original theory is made more specific, its referents are clarified and the logical consistency of the propositional structure is improved. This is what has happened in development studies where the original Frankian thesis that 'development produces underdevelopment' has been taken up and greatly clarified within sociological discourse, first in Laclau's critique, and then in many other texts, including some of those in the Oxaal collection (Oxaal, 1975; Laclau, 1979).

3   *Mutual weaknesses expose* Through the critical confrontation of perspectives the relative deficiencies of each are brought more clearly into view. An example would be the recent debate as to the relationship between Marxism and psychoanalysis. The effort by Coward and Ellis (1977) to synthesise Althusserian Marxism with Lacanian psychoanalysis has demonstrated both that this cannot be satisfactorily achieved and that each perspective is theoretically partly in ways highlighted by the other.

4   *Further empirical research* The challenge of perspectives produces increased specification of the research implications of one or both theories which then get taken up and elaborated. The theoretical debates between Marxist and neo-Weberian theories of class and stratification have produced more detailed empirical support for both: good examples, if very different, would be Nichols and Beynon (1977) and Goldthorpe (1980).

5   *Synthesis* In rare circumstances different perspectives can get incorporated into a single work and elements fused. A good example of this is Newby (1977) in which there is an effective synthesis of a number of different

theoretical traditions, in particular of political economy, political sociology, labour history and industrial sociology.

These points 1–5 are not intended to be exhaustive, only illustrative of the kinds of benefits that follow from sociology's parasitic character and of how a variety of perspectives may be brought into beneficial critical confrontation. One interesting effect takes us back to the Introduction, namely that sociology is one of the most difficult social sciences because competent practitioners have to acquire familiarity with this successive range of incorporated perspectives. Recent examples of this would include the way in which Lacan, Foucault and Derrida have become part of contemporary sociological discourse. In Britain Giddens has been particularly important in providing a means by which this parasitism has been achieved (see Giddens, 1976, 1977, 1979). He has interpreted the latest foreign import for sensitive Anglo-American readers and has located it within a sociological context. Sociology in such a golden age changes very rapidly and it may be difficult for the old guard to police effectively. Indeed, although Kuhn showed that generational differences are important in natural science, this is even more marked in sociology where new tendencies have been taken up and incorporated every four or five years. It is interesting to see how this produces difficulties for established sociologists who have to run hard just to keep up with the latest fashionable foreign import.

Finally, it might be wondered what the political implications are of my position. It is obviously the case that sociology involves a large degree of political struggle over exactly which aspects of which discipline can be incorporated within it. And this struggle is likely to be more complicated and involve more diverse interests than in the neighbouring social sciences. In the latter the lines of struggle are more clearly drawn; in economics, for example, between the orthodoxy, once Keynesian, now part-Keynesian/part-monetarist, and the Marxists, as represented in the Conference of Socialist Economists. In the site of sociology many new developments enter, and the radicals of one generation may, five years later, be the conservatives of the new generation. Thus, it is not the case that sociological discourse needs to be dominated by the left – indeed my argument would suggest that domination is difficult for any perspective. Indeed, given the present move to the right, nationally and internationally, it would be possible to expect that the next discourse on which sociology will be parasitic will be the conservative New Philosophy of the failed Parisian left. However, an even worse prospect would be that what has been a relatively golden age for sociology, especially in Britain, is coming to a close. One very important reason for this is the rapid decline in the number of young staff and graduate students in the early 1980s. It is an implication of my argument that graduates have been particularly important in effecting this parasitism. Yet with the current decline in the number of such students this will not occur to anything like the same degree, and of course this will be even more the case if most graduates are turned into deskilled research trainees. So my final claim would be that if the parasitic nature of sociology is in fact correct, and if the current main social grouping which has effected this is being decimated, then we have to consider very carefully just what kind of alternative social/intellectual structures can be devised. What are the means by which we can defend a space for sociology? What are the social preconditions for sustaining this particular discursive structure?

Incidentally, it may be wondered whether to view sociology as a virtuous parasite is the same as seeing it as the Queen of Sciences. I think that depends on whether one regards monarchs not only as parasitic but also as virtuous. For me sociology, unlike a monarch, is both parasitic and virtuous. Whether this will continue to be the case is another and equally controversial question.

References

Altvater, E. (1973a) 'Some problems of state interventionism I', *Kapitalistate*, I, pp.96–116.

Altvater, E. (1973b) 'Some problems of state interventionism II', *Kapitalistate*, II, pp.76–83.

Barrett, M. *et al.* (eds) (1979) *Ideology and Cultural Production*, London, Croom Helm for the British Sociological Association.

Bottomore, T.B. and Nisbet, R.A. (eds) (1979) *A History of Sociological Analysis*, London, Heinemann.

Coward, R. and Ellis, J. (1977) *Language and Materialism*, London, Routledge & Kegan Paul.

Fine, B., Kinsey, R., Lea, J., Picciotto, S. and Young, J. (eds) (1979) *Capitalism and the Rule of Law*, London, Hutchinson.

Frank, A. (1969) *Latin America: Underdevelopment or Revolution*, New York, Monthly Review Press.

Giddens, A. (1976) *New Rules of Sociological Method: A Positive Critique of Interpretative Sociologies*, London, Hutchinson.

Giddens, A. (1977) *Studies in Social and Political Theory*, London, Hutchinson.

Giddens, A. (1979) *Central Problems in Social Theory*, London, Macmillan.

Goldthorpe, J.H. (1980) *Social Mobility and Class Structure*, London, Oxford University Press.

Kuhn, T.S. (1970) *The Structure of Scientific Revolutions*, Chicago, IL, University of Chicago Press.

Laclau, E. (1979) *Politics and Ideology in Marxist Theory*, London, Verso.

Lakatos, I. (1970) 'Falsification and the methodology of scientific research programmes' in Lakatos, I. and Musgrave, A. (eds) *op. cit.*.

Lakatos, I. and Musgrave, A. (eds) (1970) *Criticism and the Growth of Knowledge*, Cambridge, Cambridge University Press.

Lecourt, D. (1975) *Marxism and Epistemology*, London, New Left Books.

Littlejohn, G., Smart, B., Wakeford, J. and Yuval-Davis, N. (eds) (1978) *Power and the State*, London, Croom Helm.

Masterman, M. (1970) 'The nature of a paradigm' in Lakatos, I. and Musgrave, A. (eds) *op. cit.*.

Morgan, D.H.J. (1975) *Social Theory and the Family*, London, Routledge & Kegan Paul.

Newby, H. (1977) *The Deferential Worker*, London, Allen Lane.

Nichols, T. and Beynon, H. (1977) *Living with Capitalism: Class Relations and the Modern Factory*, London, Routledge & Kegan Paul.

Oxaal, I. (ed.) (1975) *Beyond the Sociology of Development*, London, Routledge & Kegan Paul.

Parkin, F. (1979) 'Social stratification' in Bottomore, T.B. and Nisbet, R.A. (eds.) *op. cit.*.

Pashukanis, E. (1978) *Law and Marxism: A General Theory*, London, Ink Links.

Popper, K. (1970) 'Normal science and its dangers' in Lakatos, I. and Musgrave, A. (eds.) *op. cit.*.

Urry, J. (1973) 'Thomas S. Kuhn as sociologist of knowledge', *British Journal of Sociology*, vol.24, pp.462–73.

Urry, J. (1980) 'Sociology: a brief survey of recent developments' in Dufour, B. (ed.) *New Perspectives in the Humanities and Social Sciences*, London, Temple Smith.

Source: This article first appeared in Abrams, P., Deem, R., Finch, J. and Rock, P. (eds) (1981) *Practice and Progress*, London, Allen & Unwin. This version partly amended, and with the original footnotes removed, taken from John Urry, *Consuming Places*, London, Routledge, 1995, pp.33–45.

Acknowledgements

Grateful acknowledgement is made to the following sources for permission to reproduce material in this book:

Text

Reading 1.1: From Max Weber: Essays in Sociology by Max Weber, edited by H.H. Gerth & C. Wright Mills, translated by H.H. Gerth & C. Wright Mills, copyright 1946, 1958 by H.H. Gerth and C. Wright Mills. Used by permission of Oxford University Press, Inc.; *Reading 1.2:* Reprinted by permission from Gouldner, A. W. (1961) 'Anti-minotaur: the myth of a value-free sociology', *Social Problems*, vol.9, no.3, Winter 1962. Copyright © 1962 by The Society for the Study of Social Problems; *Reading 1.3:* Lovell, T. (1996) 'Feminist social theory: situated knowledges?', *The Blackwell Companion to Social Theory*, ed. Bryan S. Turner, Blackwell Publishers Ltd. Copyright © Blackwell Publishers Ltd, 1996; *Reading 1.4:* Smart, B. (1996) 'Post-modern social theory', *The Blackwell Companion to Social Theory*, ed. Bryan S. Turner, Blackwell Publishers Ltd. Copyright © Blackwell Publishers Ltd, 1996; *Reading 2.1:* Giddens, A. (2000) *The Third Way and its Critics,* Polity Press; *Readings 2.2 and 2.3:* Giddens, A. (1998) *The Third Way: The Renewal of Social Democracy,* Polity Press; *Reading 2.4:* Hacking, I. (1991) 'How should we do the history of statistics?' in Burchell, G., Gordon, C. and Miller P. (eds.) (1991) *The Foucault Effect: Studies in Governmentality,* Harvester Wheatsheaf; *Reading 2.5:* O'Malley, P. (1996) 'Risk and responsibility' in Barry, A., Osborne, T. and Rose, N. (eds.) (1996) *Foucault and Political Reason: Liberalism, Neo-liberalism and Rationalities of Government,* UCL Press; *Reading 2.6:* Rose, N. (1999) *Powers of Freedom: Reframing Political Thought,* Cambridge University Press; *Reading 3.1*: Habermas, J. (1974) 'The public sphere: an encyclopedia article', translated by Sara Lennox and Frank Lennox, *New German Critique*, vol.1, no.3, 1974, Telos Press Ltd; *Reading 3.2:* Reprinted by permission of Sage Publications Ltd from Livingstone, S. (1994) 'Watching talk: gender and engagement in the viewing of audience discussion programmes', *Media, Culture and Society*, vol.16, no.3, July 1994. Copyright © 1994 Media, Culture and Society; *Reading 3.3:* Klein, N. (2000) 'The tyranny of the brands', *New Statesman*, 24 January 2000, Guardian Newspapers Limited. Copyright © 2000 Naomi Klein; *Box 4.1:* Beard, M. (2001) 'Sacked M&S European staff bring protest to London', *The Independent*, 17 May 2001, Independent Newspapers Limited; *Box 4.2:* Copyright © Happy Computers; *Reading 4.1:* Roberts, Y. (2001) 'Happy days', *The Guardian*, 16 January 2001. Copyright © The Guardian; *Reading 4.2:* Miller, D. (1998) 'Taking Marx to Sainsbury's', Copyright © 1998 Professor Daniel Miller, University College of London; *Reading 4.3:* Reprinted by permission of Sage Publications Ltd from du Gay, P. and Negus, K. (1994) 'The changing sites of sound: music retailing and the composition of consumers',

Media, Culture and Society, vol.16, no.3, July 1994. Copyright © 1994 Media, Culture and Society; *Reading 4.4:* Reprinted by permission of Sage Publications Ltd from Miller, P. and Rose, N. (1997) 'Mobilizing the consumer', *Theory, Culture and Society*, vol.14, 1997. Copyright © 1997 Theory, Culture and Society; *Reading 5.1:* Diani, M. (1992) 'The concept of social movement', *The Sociological Review*, vol.40, no.1, February 1992. Copyright © The Editorial Board of Sociological Review; *Reading 5.2:* McCarthy, J.D. and Zald, M.N. (1977) 'Resource mobilization and social movements: a partial theory', *American Journal of Sociology*, vol.82, no.6, May 1977, The University of Chicago Press. Copyright © 1977 The University of Chicago Press; *Reading 5.3:* Power, L. (1995) 'Power to the people', *No Bath But Plenty of Bubbles: An Oral History of the Gay Liberation Front 1970–73*, Cassell plc. Copyright © Lisa Power 1995; *Reading 5.4:* Reprinted by permission of Sage Publishing Ltd from Melucci, A. (1995) 'The new social movements revisited: reflections on a sociological misunderstanding' in Maheu, L. (ed.) *Social Movements and Social Classes: The Future of Collective Action.* Copyright © International Sociological Associations/ISA 1995; *Readings 5.5, 5.6 and 5.7:* 'The evolution of Reclaim the Streets', 1997; 'On disorganisation', A Statement from Reclaim the Streets (RTS) London, 2000; and 'Street politics', A Response to the Media Mayday ...', 2000. Copyright © London Reclaim the Streets, c/o London Action Resources Centre, 62 Fieldgate Street, London, E1 1ES, Tel: 020 7281 4621, www.reclaimthestreets.net; *Reading 6.1:* Sir William Macpherson of Cluny (1999) *The Stephen Lawrence Inquiry*, CM 4262-1, The Stationery Office. Crown copyright material is reproduced under Class Licence Number C01W0000065 with the permission of the Controller of HMSO and the Queen's Printer for Scotland; *Reading 6.2:* Solomos, J. (1999) 'Social research and the Stephen Lawrence inquiry', *Sociological Research Online*, vol.4, no.1, March 1999. Copyright © Sociological Research Online, 1999; *Reading 6.3:* Connell, R.W. (1997) 'Why is classical theory classical?', *American Journal of Sociology*, vol.102, no.6, May 1997. The University of Chicago Press. Copyright © 1997 by The University of Chicago. All rights reserved; *Reading 6.4:* Reprinted by permission of Sage Publishing Ltd from Billig, M. (1995) *Banal Nationalism.* Copyright © Michael Billig 1995; *Reading 7.1:* Oakley, A. (1998) 'Gender, methodology and people's ways of knowing: some problems with feminism and the paradigm debate in social science', *Sociology*, vol.32, no. 4, November 1998. Copyright © B.S.A. Publications Limited, published by Cambridge University Press; *Reading 7.2:* Connell, R.W. (2000) 'Charting futures for sociology', *Contemporary Sociology*, vol.29, no.1, January 2000. Copyright © 2000 American Sociological Association; *Reading 7.3:* Copyright © 1991. From *Simians, Cyborgs and Women: The Reinvention of Nature*, by Donna J. Harraway. Reproduced by permission of Routledge, Inc., part of The Taylor & Francis Group; *Reading B:* Nisbet, R. A. (1962) *Sociology as an Art Form*, Random House, Inc. Used by permission of Random House, Inc.; *Reading C:* From *The Sociological Imagination* by C. Wright Mills, copyright © 2000 by Oxford University Press, Inc. Used by permission of Oxford University Press, Inc.; *Reading D:* Bauman, Z. (1987) *Legislators and Interpreters: On modernity, Post-modernity and Intellectuals*, Polity Press. Copyright © Zygmunt Bauman, 1987. Reprinted by permission of Blackwell Publishers Limited; *Reading E:* Burchell, G., Gordon, C. and Miller, P. (eds) (1991) *The Foucault Effect: Studies in Governmentality*, Harvester Wheatsheaf/The University of Chicago Press; *Reading F:* Witz, A. (1997) 'The feminist challenge', in Ballard, C., Gubbay, J. and Middleton, C. (eds) *The Student's Companion to Sociology*, Blackwell

Publishers. Copyright © Blackwell Publishers Ltd 1997; *Reading G:* Urry, J. (1981) 'Sociology as a parasite: some vices and virtues', *Consuming Places*, Routledge. Copyright © 1995 John Urry.

Figures

Figure 1.1: Office for National Statistics, *Population Trends*, no.101, 2001. Crown copyright material is reproduced under Class Licence Number C01W0000065 with the permission of the Controller of HMSO and the Queen's Printer for Scotland; *Figure 1.2:* Copyright © British Centre for Durkheimian Studies, Oxford; *Figure 1.3:* Copyright © University College London; *Figure 1.4:* Copyright © University College London; *Figure 1.5:* Copyright © Steve Pyke; *Figure 1.6:* Copyright © Josef Koudelka/Magnum London; *Figure 1.7:* Copyright © Peter Hamilton; *Figure 1.8:* Copyright © Steve Pyke; *Figure 2.1: Marxism Today,* July 1990; *Figure 2.2:* Steve Bell; *Figure 3.1:* Copyright © Jim McGuigan; *Figure 3.2:* Caricature of Jürgen Habermas from Prospect Magazine, March 2001, p. 45. Copyright © Stephen Lee; *Figure 3.3:* Copyright © Mary Evans Picture Library; *Figure 3.4:* Copyright © Gaetan Cotton; *Figure 3.5:* Copyright © Tony Kyiacou/Rex Features; *Figure 3.6:* Copyright © Claudio Cruz/Associated Press; *Figure 3.7:* Copyright © David Simonds; *Figure 3.8:* Front page from *The Mirror,* 2 May 2000. Copyright © Syndication International; *Figure 3.9:* Image courtesy of www.adbusters.org; *Box 4.1 photograph:* John Voos, Independent Newspapers Limited; *Box 4.2 image:* Copyright © Happy Computers; *Box 4.3 image:* Wernick, A. (1996) 'Resort to nostalgia: mountains, memories and myths of time', in Nava, M. *et al.* (eds) *Buy This Book: Studies in Advertising and Consumption*, Routledge; *p.160:* Peperami animal Copyright © Unilever Bestfoods UK; *Figure 5.1:* from Power, L. (1995) *No Bath But Plenty of Bubbles*, Cassell, unknown photographer; *Figures 5.2 and 5.3:* K. and Heath, E. (1984) *Men in Frocks*, Gay Men's Press, photographer unknown; *Figure 5.4 (a):* Poster for the first London 'Reclaim the Streets' party, 14 May 1995. Courtesy of Mark Brown; *Figure 5.4(b):* Copyright © Andrew Testa; *Figure 5.5:* Copyright © Mike Slocombe; *Figure 6.1:* Stefano Cagnoni/Report Digital; *Figure 6.2:* First published in *The Independent*, 25 February 1999. Copyright © Dave Brown/The Independent; *Figure 6.3:* First published in *The Independent*, 23 February 1999. Copyright © Dave Brown/The Independent; *Figure 7.1:* Copyright © The British Museum; *Figure 7.3:* Courtesy of LSE Archives; *Figure 7.4:* Courtesy of Ladd/ Warner Brothers/Ronald Grant Archive.

Cover photographs

Gay Mardi Gras, anti-hunt protestors and Tony Blair: © Kiran Ridley/UNP; Duwayne Brooks with protestors outside London County Court: © Guardian Newspapers, PD 601665; office: © copyright 1998 PhotoDisc, Inc.; WTO protestors, Seattle, 30 November 1999: © Beth. A. Kaiser/Associated Press; Zapatista National Liberation Army (EZLN)'s Subcommandante Marcos at a news conference, Mexico City 19 March 2001: © Eduardo Verdugo/ Associated Press.

Every effort has been made to trace all copyright owners, but if any has been inadvertently overlooked, the publishers will be pleased to make the necessary arrangements at the first opportunity.

Index